THE
GLADSTONE
DIARIES

Gladstone in Oxford, 25 October 1892, photographed by Miss Sarah Acland

THE
GLADSTONE
DIARIES

WITH
CABINET MINUTES
AND
PRIME-MINISTERIAL
CORRESPONDENCE

VOLUME XIII
1892–1896

Edited by

H. C. G. MATTHEW

CLARENDON PRESS · OXFORD
1994

Oxford University Press, Walton Street, Oxford OX2 6DP
Oxford New York Toronto
Delhi Bombay Calcutta Madras Karachi
Kuala Lumpur Singapore Hong Kong Tokyo
Nairobi Dar es Salaam Cape Town
Melbourne Auckland Madrid
and associated companies in
Berlin Ibadan

Oxford is a trade mark of Oxford University Press

Published in the United States
by Oxford University Press Inc. New York

© Oxford University Press 1994
Introduction © H. C. G. Matthew

British Library Cataloguing in Publication Data
Data available
ISBN 0–19–820464–7

Library of Congress Cataloging in Publication Data
Data applied for

1 3 5 7 9 10 8 6 4 2

Set by Joshua Associates Limited, Oxford
Printed in Great Britain
on acid-free paper by
Biddles Ltd., Guildford and King's Lynn

CONTENTS

LIST OF ILLUSTRATIONS

NOTE ON ABBREVIATIONS &c.

Lists of abbreviations used in this volume and an introduction covering its
years will be found at the start of Volume XII.

Friday Jan. One. 1892. Circumcision. [Biarritz]

Ch. 11 AM. Excellent sermon from Mr Broade. Read Marbot—Ly G. Stock's 'Wasted Life'—Butcher on Greek Genius (finished). Conversation with Morley. God prosper 1892.

2. Sat.

Wrote to Rev. N. Hall—King of the Belgians—Press Assn & Central News[1]—J.A. Robertson—F. Schnadhorst—Messrs Brown—Ld Howth. Read Marbot—Ly G. Stocks 'Wasted Life'. Drove to the bar of the Adour to see the grand sea and struggles of the ships. Dined with the Tollemaches & much conversation. Saw Mr Lawrence.

3. 2 S. Xm.

Ch. 11 A.M. with H.C. and 3½ P.M. Read Lady G. Stock—Smith on Isaiah[2]—Moberly Bampton Lectures—and the [blank.] Conversation with Morley. Sea abated but grand.

4. M.

Wrote to Herbert J.G.—Mad. Bashkirtseff—Mr H. Bowen. Read Marbot Vol. III—Lady G. Stock. Began article for Mr Stuart's new Rural paper.[3] Drive with C. & Helen. Tea at Mr Chapman's—(why?)

5. Tu.

Wrote to Scotts—Lady G. Stock[4]—J. Gleeson—Jas H. Wells—C. Cheston. Finished MS of Article. Conversation with West. Long conversation & walk with Rev. Wentworth Webster,[5] a remarkable man half invalided in this country. Finished Lady G. Stock. Read Marbot—Pironneau, Discours de Rentree (Irlande).[6]

6. Wed. Epiph.

Dearest C.s birthday. God prosper her noble soul. Ch. & H.C. 11 A.M.
Wrote to Enrique Coll [sic]—Sec. Lib. Assocn B.P.—Principal S. Edm. Hall.

---

[1] Letter of thanks for birthday and Christmas greetings; *D.N.*, 5 January 1892, 5d.

[2] Sir G. A. Smith, *The Book of Isaiah*, 2v. (1889–90).

[3] 'The English labourer' published in *The Weekly Star*, 5 February 1892, a new liberal publication. See also *T.T.*, 5 February 1892, 3e. Gladstone was paid £20; Add MS 44514, f. 25.

[4] Lady Gertrude Georgina, 1842–93; da. of 7th marquis of Queensberry; m. 1882 T. H. Stock; for her novel, see 25 Dec. 91 and Add MS 44514, f. 23.

[5] Wentworth Webster; Lincoln College, Oxford; chaplain at St. Jean de Luz 1869–82; lived at Sare, Basse Pyrenées. Gladstone formed a high opinion of him, arranged a pension of £150 p.a. in 1894 and contributed to his son's school fees from the Secret Service money; Add MS 44518, ff. 14, 120.

[6] A. Pironneau, *Discours de rentrée . . . L'Irlande et son legislateur M. Gladstone* (1886).

Saw M. Leon Say. Read Marbot—McKail's Gk Epigrams[1]—Broade on the Holy Coat [*sic*].[2] Backgammon with Mr A[rmitstead]. Conversation at breakf. on [blank] & on Rosebery.

7. *Th.*

Wrote to Mr Stuart BP.—Reperused article. Read Marbot—Mackail, Greek Epigrams—and [blank.] The grand sunset gave us an admirable view of the Spanish mountains. Backgammon with Mr A. Saw Mr Broade +

8. *Fr.*

Wrote to M. Pironneau[3]—Lady Phillimore B.P.—Mr Tollemache—Dr Hertyka. To Bayonne with J. Morley to see the Library incl. Basque books. Finished Marbot—Read Mackail—and [blank.]

9. *Sat.* [*Pau*]

Ch. 10 A.M. for a *Vale*. Off to Pau[4] arr. 5½. Saw Consul at B.—M. Leon Say (at Pau)—The Mayor of Pau. +—Lord St . . . .—Rev. Mr Acland Troyte.[5] Dined with the Herschels. Read M. Müller Anthropological religion[6]—Innocencia.[7] Wrote to Mr L. Hunter—and [blank.]

10. *First S. Epiph.*

St Andrew's Ch [Pau] mg.—Ch.Ch.[8] aft. Went to the great Ch. near Gassion for Prône at 3 PM but it did not come off. Read M. Muller—Wilson's Analogies[9]—Maclaughlin's book received from M. Stuart.[10] Wrote to Count Povoleri—Mary Stuart (a meditated letter). An evil night—I believe from eating (like my friends) fish insufficiently dressed. Relief came both ways.

11. *M.*

Kept my bed all day: but the enemy had quitted the field after the shortest battle I recollect. Poor C.s night was ruined. Read Max Müller—a rather wild compound. Read through Innocencia. Conversation with J. Morley—Mr Armitstead (Hawarden Deed)—and in evg with Ld H[erschell]'s guests whom I joined in the drawing room.

---

[1] Perhaps J. W. Mackail, *Thermopylae* (1881).
[2] Untraced work by G. E. Broade, priest at Biarritz; see 20 Dec. 91.
[3] Armand Pironneau, apparently a lawyer in Limoges; see 5 Jan. 92.
[4] Start of a tour E. across the foothills of the Pyrenees.
[5] Reginald Henry Acland-Troyte, chaplain of St. Andrew's Anglican church, Pau.
[6] F. Max Müller, *Anthropological religion* (1892); Gifford lectures.
[7] Perhaps M. O. Oliphant, *Innocenta; a tale of modern life* (1892).
[8] Christ Church, another Anglican church in Pau.
[9] Probably J. Wilson, *Letters on the truth and certainty of natural and revealed religion . . . an introduction to Bishop Butler's 'Analogy'* (1810).
[10] Perhaps J. MacLaughlin, *Les voyageurs, historiens et économistes anglais* (1892).

12. Tu. [*Toulouse*]

Wrote to M.G.—H.N.G.—Mr J.W. Wells. Saw M. Leon Say and his friends (15 to 20) at the Hotel. Conversation on education—St Martin—The Mayor & others bid us farewell at the Station. Saw Dr Greene—Ld Herschell. Most lovely drive along N. of the Pyrenees. Lourdes[1] hardly inferior to Istel.[2] At Toulouse we were met by a sympathetic crowd & by the Prefect, Mayor, and other authorities. Salutations followed & in evg I sent a note of thanks. Walked out to see the shops.

13. Wed. [*Nîmes*]

At Carcassonne we were again met by a crowd and by authorities. Bridge of Louis XI interesting. Fortifications a matchless monument. Ch of St Nazaire only second to them. Saw the Bishop. Arr. at Nimes in evg. At Toulouse in mg we drove largely about the city: & saw the very remarkable Church of St Sernon;[3] rich in relics. In evg sent telegram on the illness of Card. Manning.[4] Read Gleig[5]—H. Heyne.[6]

14. Th.

Wrote to Gertrude G.—J. Macveagh—Dr Carpenter—and at night to the Prince of Wales on the grievous news which had just reached us of the death of the Duke of Clarence at Sandringham this morning. Helen went off: a great loss to our party. Saw the Amphitheatre & the Maison Carrée,[7] the latter even surpassing the first. Drove up to the tower. Saw Churches. Read Gleig's Subaltern. We had also the news of Manning's death: in his ripeness. Saw the Prefect of the Dept.

15. Fr. [*Valescure, St. Raphael*]

Walk & bookbuying: *I* think the restorations of the Amphith. deplorable. The Prefect bade us farewell. 11¼ AM-10 P.M. To Villa Magabi, St Raphael: we were made most welcome.[8] Finished Gleig. Began Bourget, or rather Larcher's Amour Physiologique.[9]

---

[1] Lourdes was by 1892 a well-known place of pilgrimage.

[2] Word smudged.

[3] *sc.* St. Sernin, one of the finest of Romanesque churches.

[4] 'I received, with surprise as well as pain, at Nîmes, a telegram from Sir A. Clark, which intimated the crisis and suggested I should send a message. I did this the same evening, but addressed it to Sir A. Clark, as I did not know whether the suggestion was his own, and felt a scruple about a spontaneous invasion of the death chamber'; *T.T.*, 9 February 1892, 9f.

[5] G. R. Gleig, *The subaltern* (1825).

[6] *sic*; see 16 Dec. 91.

[7] The amphitheatre was restored in 1858 and used for bullfights (see next day); the Maison Carrée is one of the best preserved Roman temples.

[8] The Gladstones stayed with the Rendels at the Villa Magabi in Valescure, 2 miles N.W. of St. Raphael and much frequented by the British as a winter resort. For this visit, see *Rendel*, 81 ff.

[9] *Physiologie de l'amour moderne. Fragments posthumes d'un ouvrage de Claude Larchier*, ed. P. Bourget (1891).

16. Sat.

Beautiful drive, and walk. Read Larcher—Nos Désastres[1]—and [blank.] Wrote to Mr Madden[2]—Mr Schnadhorst—Rev. Dr. Lunn[3]—Mr G. Cadbury[4]—Mr V. Davis—Mr Bunting Tel. Saw Mr Rendell (*re* V. II). Backgammon with Mr R.

17. 2 S. Epiph.

Ch mg & room prayers aft. Wrote to Sir R. Morier—Sir P. Currie—Mr Scharf—Baroness Reizenstein.[5] Walk with Mr Rendell. Conversation with Mrs R. Read J. Wesley Vie et Oeuvr.[6]—Séché Jansenistes III[7]—Religions of the world.[8]

18. M.

Wrote to Reeves & Turner—W. Downing—M. Malhet—M. Leon Séché. Beautiful drive in the Esterelles scenery.[9] Read Léon Séché Vol. III—Le Chatillon, Seule Aimée[10]—Amour Moderne.[11] Conversation with Mr Waldron—Mr Bryce MP.—Mr Crawford MP.[12]

19. Tu.

Read Léon Séché—Amour Moderne—Chastillon, Seule Aimée. Games with Mr R. and with Daphne. Small dinner party.

20. Wed.

Read Seule Aimée—Amour Moderne—Nos Désastres (began)[13]—Filon on Parnell.[14] Drive to the Aqueduct, and walk. Saw Mr Lyell (Geology and crofters).[15]

21. Th.

Wrote a little on St D[einiol']s: but my brain is very lazy. Read Kennans Siberia[16]—Seule Aimée finished—Filon on J. Morley: fine[17]—Amour Moderne: sick of it. Saw Childers—Hibbert. Backgammon with Mr R.

---

[1] Duchâtel, *Nos désastres et leur origine* (full citation untraced) on the 1870 war, bought in the Nîmes station bookstall; see Rendel, 99.

[2] J. H. Maden, liberal candidate at Rossendale; see 24 Jan. 92. Letter in *T.T.*, 20 January 1892, 6e.

[3] John Robert Lunn, fellow of St. John's, Cambridge.

[4] George Cadbury, 1839–1922; chairman of Cadbury's and founder of Bournville model village.

[5] Baroness Franziska Reitzenstein; draft copy in Add MS 44514, f. 52. See also 2 Feb. 92.

[6] M. Lelièvre, *John Wesley, Sa vie et son oeuvre* (1891).

[7] L. Séché, *Les derniers Jansénistes 1710–1870*, 3v. (1891); see Rendel, 89 and 6 Jan. 91n.

[8] G. M. Grant, *Religions of the world in relation to Christianity* (n.d.).

[9] Mountains inland from St. Raphael and Fréjus.

[10] Untraced.   [11] See 15 Jan. 92.

[12] Donald Crawford, 1837–1919; Scottish lawyer and legal officer; liberal M.P. 1885–95. Divorced his wife Virginia 1886, citing Dilke as co-respondent.

[13] But see 16 Jan. 92.

[14] Probably an article by A. Filon, whose *Profils anglais* (1893) included Parnell, Morley, Churchill and Chamberlain.

[15] Leonard Lyell, 1850–1926; nephew of the geologist; professor of natural science; liberal M.P. Orkney and Shetland 1885–1900; cr. bart. 1894.

[16] G. Kennan, *Siberia and the exile system*, 2v. (1891).   [17] See 20 Jan. 92.

22. Fr.

Wrote to S.F. Pells—A.F. Lightfoot—J. Burgess. Fine drive into the Esterelles, and walk. Read Nos Desastres—the romance of calamity!—Kennan on Siberia—The Swiss smuggler.[1]

23. Sat.

Wrote to A. Morley—Parl. Circular (2 forms)—M. Journot. A still finer drive: & walk. Family reserve arrived. Finished Nos Desastres—Read Kennan—Finished Swiss Smuggler.

24. 3 S. Epiph.

Ch mg & aft. Read Wesley Vie et Oeuvr.—Moberly Bampton L.[2] Conversation with Mrs R. Examined remains from the Tuileries. An instructive conversation or discourse from Mr R. on Navy construction.

Trying to get back the text of Cinque Maggio through Goëthe's Tr.[3] Splendid report from Rossendale.[4]

25. M.

Wrote to Mr Hulton—Mr Wilfrid Meynell. Hill drive. Read Rogers's Recollections[5]—and Kennan's book which is heart-rending, & of great importance.

26. Tu.

Drive to Malpey.[6] Walks & luncheon there 11–3¾. Read Kennan—Rogers—David Grieve (Mrs H. Ward).[7] Made a beginning: unpropitious. Received the Mayor & his company 5 P.M. Conversation with Mrs R[endel] (Future retribution). Backgammon with Mr A.

27. Wed.

C. & a party went off (she to Cannes; *they* to Nice). Wrote to M. Leon Séché—Rev. Nothrop—W.F. Newman—J. Berthier—Dr Wendt. Read David Grieve: better, but singular as a novel. Read Kennan—Contemp. R. on Stundists—and on Broad Ch (Snow).[8]

28. Th.

Wrote to A. Morley. 9½–5½. To Hyères by special train: a beautiful and interesting drive. Conversation with the Mayor: curious *horse*-information. Backgammon in evg. Read David Grieve.—Hulton's Rixae Oxon.[9]

[1] T. Combe, *Jonquille; or, the Swiss smuggler*, tr. B. L. Tollemache (1891).
[2] See 25 Dec. 91.   [3] See 8 Feb. 88.
[4] By-election on Hartington's succession to the dukedom of Devonshire: the liberals won the seat with a majority of 1225.
[5] See 13 Mar. 88.
[6] Where the road through Valescure joins the Fréjus–Cannes road.
[7] Mrs. Humphry Ward, *The history of David Grieve*, 3v. (1892).
[8] *C.R.*, lxi, 1, 106 (January 1892).   [9] S. F. Hulton, *Rixae Oxonienses* (1892).

29. Fr.

Wrote to M. Malvezin—Ld Latham—Sir A. Gordon—Ld Acton—M. Notovich[1]—
M. Drew. Drive & walk with Mr R. Backgammon in evg. Read Dav. Grieve—Mr
Kennan's remarkable book—and [blank.]

30. Sat.

Wrote to A. Morley—Mons. B. d'Agen[2]—Mr Stuart MP. 10¾–5. Beautiful drive to
Bagnolles: yet more lovely walk over part of the old road back. Read Herbert G.
on Labour and Liberals.[3] Capital. Read D. Grieve—Young—Mr Kennan Vol. II.
Backgammon Mr A.

31. 4 S. Epiph.

Service mg and aft. Wrote to T.P. O'Connor. Read (through) Mr Webster on
Romanism[4]—Vol. on Religions—Lecky on Burials W. Abbey.[5]

Mond. Feb. One 1892.

Wrote to Mr Wemyss Reid—A. Morley—Rev. Webster—E.C. Davey—Mr Spur-
geon—D.D. Cairne. Full conversation with Herbert on his excellent paper.[6]
Read Young's France[7]—Life of Raleigh[8]—David Grieve. Much conversation Mr
R.—and Mr A.

2. Tu.

Wrote to J. Morley—Sir F. Knollys—W. Bethell—Sir W. Harcourt[9]—M.Q. Holyoake.[10] Drive v. Pesque Brune. Read Life of Raleigh—Young—David Grieve—
Madame Reizenstein. Backgammon in evg. C. in the hands of our intelligent
little Dr., Buss.

3. Wed.

Read Raleigh (largely)—Reizenstein—Grieve. Drive to Lampey—& walk back:
2 h: 6 m: my longest for a long time. Saw Mr Bryce—Backgammon in evg.

[1] Nicolai Notovich, Russian religious author living in Rue Daru, Paris, wrote on current affairs;
Hawn P.
[2] Auguste Jean Boyer d'Agen; had sent his book; see 7 Feb. 92.
[3] H. J. Gladstone, 'The liberal party and the labour question', *The Albemarle Review*, i. 52 (February 1892).
[4] Untraced pamphlet by Wentworth Webster (see 5 Jan. 92).
[5] Untraced article.
[6] See previous day.
[7] A. Young, *Travels in France 1787–89* (1889 ed.).
[8] See 22 Dec. 91.
[9] Gladstone advised Harcourt, MS Harcourt dep. 12, f. 1: 'I do not well see that much is to be
gained by pressing Dissolution at this moment, while a taunt for not dissolving may be fair enough. I
have long thought we should be justified in a positive step if we had a brilliant series of bye elections
like Rossendale. We have however had brilliant bye elections but not a series.'
[10] Malthus Questall Holyoake had sent his *Memories of Charles Dickens* (no copy found); Hawn P.

4. Th.

Expedition by Malpey beyond Ardrets [de l'Esterel] in sight of Cannes. Very beautiful. C. unable to venture. Read as yesterday. Backgammon in evg. Wrote to Miss Beal—Mr Wallace—Rev. S.E.G.—Mr Westell.

5. Fr.

Read Raleigh (finished)—D. Grieve—Kampf der Gesch.[1] Backgammon in evg. Saw Dr Buss. C. has had I think a *touch* of influenza.

6. Sat.

Wrote to Baronne Reizenstein—Ld Acton. Walk with Mr R. and expl. to him as Father about David Grieve.[2] Read D. Grieve—Papers on the Llangollen Ladies[3]—Kampf der Geschlechter—Rixae Oxon (finished). Backgammon in evg.

7. 5 S. Epiph.

Ch. mg with H.C. and aftn. Wrote to Sir W. Harcourt[4]—M. Boyer d'Agen—A. Morley. Read Kampf der Geschl.—Wallace, Analogies[5]—B. d'Agen, Clergé Francais[6]—Moberly, B. Lectures.

8. M.

Wrote to Mrs Vyner—Mme Bashkirtseff—Mr Westell BP.—Mr Stead. Drive & walk with Mr R. Read Stead Art. on Dilke[7]—Kampf der Geschlechter—The Grenville Book Catal.

Tu. 9. Feb. [Nice]

Off by train 9.30. At Cannes saw the Lakes—Mrs Vyner—The Duke of Cambridge. Reached Nice 3¼. Saw the Mayor—Mad. Bashkirtseff and a Tea party including the Prefect & Contesse de Tholouse. Saw Mr Agnew. Read Kampf. &c.—David Grieve. Wrote to M. Ballart—Mr Agnew.

10. Wed.

Wrote to Mr Tollemache—Mr M'Vickars—Mr Stephenson. Drive to Beaulieu. Examined shops. Saw Princess Troubetskoi.[8] Read D. Grieve. Largely.

---

[1] A. Lennius, *Der Kampf der Geschlechter und der Volkspartei zu Athen* (1829).
[2] Rendel noted: Gladstone 'consulted me most gravely, after a solemn discussion with his wife, as to whether my daughters should read it, and gave me the incriminated portion to read'; Rendel, 99.
[3] J. Hicklin, *The Ladies of Llangollen, as sketched by many hands* (1847).
[4] On the death of the Duke of Clarence; *T.T.*, 11 February 1892, 11f.
[5] C. J. Wallace, *The analogy of existence and Christianity* (1892).
[6] A. J. Boyer d'Agen, *Le Clergé de France devant la République* (1892).
[7] W. T. Stead, 'Deliverance or doom? The choice of Sir Charles Dilke' (1892); reprinted from the *P.M.G.*
[8] Princess Elizaveta Esperovna Troubetskoi; correspondence in Add MS 44514.

11. Th.

Wrote to Mr Knowles—Mlle Schayer—W.A. Gibb. Fine drive to Mont Falicon &
by Pont de Magnau. C. thrives here. Finished D. Grieve. Read part of Zola's
astonishing Bete humaine.[1] Dinner party. Saw Ld & Ly Marr.[2] Wrote draft as a
basis for C. to write to Pembroke on the Russian famine.[3]

12. Fr.

9-6½. Made the journey by St Jeannet, Vence, St Michel, Le Bar, to Grasse:
wonderful in beauty and interest.[4] Much conversation with M. Martin. Visited
the Grasse parfumery, all but empty: but Mons. S.(?) makes near 80 m per ann.
Back by rail. Read McAdam on Hungary[5]—Zola's Bête Humaine: what a picture.

13. Sat.

Wrote to A. Morley—Sir R. Morier—E. Menkel—Me. Bashkirtseff—M. Amaldi.
We took the New Fort Drive. Read Bête Humaine (the last half). I think it
shows what would be a world without Christ. Read Laveleye on Italy—Parkes
on Labour [in Australia] (Cont. R.).[6]

14. Septa S.

American Ch morning. English Church afternoon. Saw Mr Cornell. Read
Contemp. R. (Symposium) on Card. M.—Driver's Reply to Cave[7]—Thomas a
Kempis IV—Reply to Robertson Smith[8]—Montecarlo Intime.[9]

15. M.

Wrote to Ld Brougham—Mr Hayman—Mr Gell—Madame Zenyoske—Mr
Stockwell. Saw Mr Gambart (+)—Mr Agnew. 10½-1. To Villa Magali. Mr A.
prudently saw the Doctor and went to bed. Walk with Mr R. Read Montecarlo
Intime—F. Morris on Manning[10] & Trashy art. on Homer—19th Cent. on
Panama Canal.[11] Backgammon with Mr R.

Parliaments	Elections	Contested[12]
1832–5	1	1
1835–7	1	. . . . . .
1837–41	1	. . . . .
1841–7	1 . 1	1

---

[1] E. Zola, *La bête humaine* (1890).
[2] *sc.* Mar; see 14 Apr. 79.   [3] Untraced.
[4] Spectacular train journey W. from Nice to Grasse, the centre of the perfume industry.
[5] Untraced.   [6] *C.R.*, lxi. 153, 197 (February 1892).
[7] *C.R.*, lxi. 172, 262.   [8] Many pamphlets on this famous 'heresy' case.
[9] P. Monfalcone, *Monte-Carlo intime* (1891).
[10] Untraced article.   [11] *N.C.*, xxxi. 293 (February 1892).
[12] Holograph, initialled and dated 15 February 1892; Add MS 44774, f. 191.

1847–52	1	1
1852–7	1 . 1	1 . 1 .
1857–9	1 . 1 .	
1859–65	1 . 1	1[+] . 1
1865–8	1 . 1	1 . 1[+] .
1868–74	1 . 1 . 1	1 . 1 .
1874–80	1	1 . . . .
1880–5	1 . 1 . 1 .	1 . 1 .
1885–6	1 . 1	1
1886–92	1	. . . . . .
Totals 14	*24*	*15*

+ Defeats Oxford 1865
        S. Lancashire 1868[1]

16. *Tu.*

Wrote to J. Morley—M. Benoist. Read Symposium on Manning[2]—Wilberforce on Card. Manning[3]—Kampf der Geschlechter[4]—Jephson's 'Platform'.[5] Conversation with Ld Reay—Mrs R. on Providence & Bp Butler. Backgammon Mr R.

17. *Wed.*

Wrote to Mr Wemyss Reid. Backgammon in evg Mr R. Morleys' tel. for 1. to Geo. Russell requires thought.[6] Read The Platform—Kampf der Geschl.—and Taine, Origines.[7]

18. *Th.*

Read Platform—Kampf der Geschl. (finished)—Taine, Origines. $10\frac{3}{4}$–$4\frac{1}{2}$. Drive to the Malinfuna: of the most original beauty, narrow pass of pr. 3 m long, red needle rocks on both sides. Backgammon Mr R.

19. *Fr.*

Wrote to Mr H. Jephson[8]—Lord Bute—Mad. . . . .—Dr Bus. Rain. Walk with Mr R. Backgammon Mr A. Read Taine—The Platform—Ly Malmesbury on Marriage.[9]

---

[1] Gladstone omits his defeat at Manchester in 1837, where he was run by local tories without his permission; see Morley, i. 141.
[2] See 14 Feb. 92.
[3] In *N.C.*, xxxi. 280 (February 1892).
[4] See 5 Feb. 92.
[5] H. Jephson, *The Platform, its rise and progress*, 2v. (1892); for Gladstone's review, see 19 Mar. 92.
[6] See 26 Feb. 92.
[7] Further volume in Taine's history; see 10 Apr. 84.
[8] Henry Jephson, civil servant in the Irish Office; had presumably sent his book, see 16 Feb. 92.
[9] *F.R.*, lxvii. 272 (February 1892).

20. Sat.

Wrote to A. Morley—Sir W. Harcourt—Geo. Russell—Miss Wilson. Park Calvey
drive & walk. Read The Platform—Taine Origines—and [blank.]

21. Sexa S.

Ch mg & aft. Wrote to J. Morley—Mr Wemyss Reid. Visited the graveyard. Read
Taine (Napoleon)—Moberly B.L. finished.[1] Worked on Cinque Maggio.[2] Saw
Mrs Lyell (relig.)[3]

22. M.

Read Taine—The Platform (largely). Worked on 'Cinque Maggio'. Backgammon Mr R. Steady rain. Saw Sir E. Watkin.

23. Tu.

Saw Mrs Bishop—The Bp of Frejus: also his Chapel, &c. Drive, walk with Mr R.
Backgammon with Mr A. Read the Platform (largely)—Coup de Foudre.[4]

24. Wed.

Saw the Bp: return visit, paid in a good private carriage. Drive to Lemey: walk
to Chapell des Œufs: notable *kluft* or *graft*. Made Notes. Tried again the
[Cinque Maggio] Ode: I have recovered 103 lines but five are obstinate and will
not come. Read The Platform: and Monte Carlo Intime.

25. Th. [On train]

Wrote to .... Finished The Platform—also Montecarlo Intime. Packed
books &c. & bid a reluctant farewell to the hospitable & charming mansion. Off
by 4.11. train: travelled all night.

26. Fr. [Paris]

Wrote to Mr A. Morley—Sir W. Harcourt—Mr Geo. Russell in reply to very
interesting letters.[5] Reached Hotel Bristol at 10.30. Saw M. Jusserand—Mrs
Talbot. Visited Notre Dame—La Sainte Chapelle—but Paris is greater than anything in Paris. Shopwork. Read Monte Carlo Intime (finished). Eight at dinner:
including Léon Say & the Mayor. Much conversation.

---

[1] See 25 Dec. 91.
[2] See 6 Feb. 88, 24 Jan. 92.
[3] Mary, wife of L. Lyell (see 20 Jan. 92).
[4] Untraced.
[5] Row involving *The Speaker* and Wemyss Reid, who had defended Gladstone against *The Times'*
charge that he had treated Hartington with ingratitude over the formation of the govt. in 1880. See
Gardiner, ii. 162 and Gladstone's memorandum, 'The Speaker, *The Times*, and the Duke of Devonshire', MS Harcourt dep. 12, f. 9.

27. Sat.

Wrote to J. B. Latham—Rev. Mr Washington—and [blank.] Saw M. Jusserand who took us to the Louvre—and the Victory.[1] Luncheon with Mrs Talbot: M. Taine, Prince Borghese, M. Jusserand. Saw Count Münster—long & interesting conversation chiefly on French matters. Read Roman d'une Croyante[2]—Maisons de Tolérance.[3]

28. Quinqua S.

Rue d'Ag. Ch. 11 AM 3½ P.M. Visited the great & very peculiar Church on Montmartre.[4] A disappointment as to the fabric. Wrote to President of the Rep.[5]—Prefet of Basses Pyrenees—Sir W. Harcourt—Mr Morley—Mrs Ingram. Saw Count Münster—Mayor of St Raphael. Read Le Christ et son oeuvre[6]—and [blank.]

M. Feb. 29. [London]

9½–6. To London. 6–7. H. of C. saw many friends. Began work on my chaos.[7] Read Maisons de Tolerance—Roman d'une Croyante.

Tues. March One 1892.

Wrote to Dean of Maritzburg—Sec. S.P.G.—J.B. Lamb—Sir F. Knollys—Dr Hayman—Lord E. Fitzmaurice. H. of C. 3½–6½.[8] Eight to dinner. Saw Mr Murray—Mr Marjoribanks & Mr A.M.—Mr Campbell Bannerman. Tea at the Speaker's. Read Maisons de Tolérance.

2. Ash Wed.

St James Ch. 11 A.M. Wrote to Messrs Grevel—Rev. Dr. Wace—Mrs Guild—W. Downing—J. Lewis—E.H. Lewes—Prof. Romanes. H. of C. 4¼–5¾.[9] Saw A. Lyttelton & his bride[10]—The Miss Peels—A. Morley & E. Marjoribanks—Mr Whitbread—Ly Cobham & Duchess of W[estminster]. Visited Winter Exhibn Pict. Read Lugard's Report[11]—Maisons de Tolerance.

---

[1] The 'Winged Victory' statue in the Louvre.
[2] J. de la Brète, Le roman d'une croyante (1892).
[3] Untraced.
[4] The church of the 'Sacré Coeur', then nearing completion.
[5] i.e. President Carnot.
[6] Untraced tract.
[7] The Gladstones stayed at 1 Carlton Gardens, placed at their disposal by Stuart Rendel.
[8] Misc. business; 4H 1. 1581.
[9] Evicted Tenants Bill; 4H 1. 1665.
[10] Alfred Lyttelton m. secondly Edith, da. of Archibald Balfour.
[11] Lugard's report on the East Africa railway and the value of Uganda to the East Africa Company; the report was prepared for the Company; copies of it were 'in the hands of Gentlemen on this [liberal] side of the House' (Labouchere, 3 March 1892, 4H 1. 1882). Following demands next day from Gladstone and Labouchere, the Report was published as PP 1892 lvi. 599; C. 6555.

3. Th.

Wrote to Sir E. Watkin—Messrs Osgood[1]—Mr Lumley—Rev. S.E.G.—Mr Wemyss Reid—Mr A. Hutton—Rev. Dr Kinns. H. of C. $3\frac{1}{2}$–$7\frac{1}{2}$, 9–12. Spoke on Mombasa Railway.[2] Saw Sir A. West—Mr Geo. Russell—Mr A. Morley—do *cum* Mr Marjoribanks—Mr E. Wickham—Mr Morley. Read Macmillan's France[3]— Maisons. Worked on Lugard.

4. Fr.

Wrote to Mr Cowan—Mr Wemyss Reid—A. Sutton—Mr G. Russell—Sec. SPCK—Rev. Dr. Lowe—W. Downing—Mrs Valentine. H. of C. $3\frac{1}{4}$–7.[4] Saw Mrs Guild[5]—Mr A. Morley—Ld Kimberley—Mr M'Carthy—Herbert J.G. Read Maisons—'At Sundry Times' &c.[6]

5. Sat.

Wrote to Mrs Th.—Sir W. Gurdon—A. Morley—Ld E. Fitzmaurice—J.S. Vickers—Mr Atherley Jones[7]—P. Millet—D. Nutt—G.H. Pownall—J.W. Harrald[8]—J.B. Hobson—H.M.B. Ruth—W. Canton. Read Maisons—A woman unsexed.[9] Mrs Guild came 10–$11\frac{1}{2}$. Saw Geo. Russell l.l.—A. Morley—Sir A. West[10]—J. Morley. Six to dinner. Tea at Duchess of Marlborough's (Dowager).

6. 1 S. Lent.

Ch 11 AM with H.C. (St James)–7 PM. Wrote to Mr Hankey. Long conversation with the Farquhars. Sir A. Clark dined with us. Read Life of Brett[11]—[blank] on Russia.

7. M.

Wrote to Sir R. Morier—The Phillimores—W. Downing—Mr Pascoe Glyn—Dr Lowe—A.R. Gladstone—Mrs Th.—Rev. Burnside. H. of C. before dinner.[12] Saw Mrs Guild—Sir J. Carm[ichae]l—Mr Massingham—F. Leveson—A. Morley *cum* Schnadhorst—A. Hutton—Mr Morley—Messrs M'Carthy, Dillon, Sexton, on

[1] Agents for Harper's, the publishers.
[2] And on business of the House; he made a powerful attack on the govt.'s handling of East Africa; 4 *H* 1. 1804, 1868.
[3] H. Macmillan, *The Riviera* (1892 ed.).
[4] Argued with Goschen about East Africa; 4 *H* 2. 87.
[5] Emma Marie Cadwalader-Guild, 1843–1911, sculptress with studio in Fulham; Gladstone gave her several sittings, including a 'quasi-sitting', see 24 Mar. 92. She exhibited various busts of prominent persons at the R.A., but that of Gladstone has not been traced.
[6] See 29 Nov. 91.
[7] Llewellyn Archer Atherley-Jones, 1851–1929; radical lawyer; liberal M.P. N.W. Durham 1885–1914.
[8] C. H. Spurgeon's secretary; on Spurgeon memorial publications; *T.T.*, 9 March 1892, 12b.
[9] H. H. Chilton, *Woman unsexed. A novel* (1892).
[10] West resigned from the Inland Revenue and acted, at first informally, as Gladstone's secretary.
[11] T. W. Belcher, *Robert Brett of Stoke Newington* (1889).
[12] Condition and costs of the army; 4 *H* 2. 184.

Home Rule—Mr Marjoribanks—A. Morley—Sir J.C. Dined at Ld Aberdeen's. Read Les Maisons.

8.

Wrote to Mr A. Carnegie—Mr Armitstead—Jas Arnot—Rev. Macdonald—H.C. Bennett—Miss Lambert—Rev. Dr. Wace—Mr R. Anderson—Mr Dalziel—P. of Wales—Ld Rosebery—Mrs Guild, forenoon. Saw Prince of Wales (an hour)—Sir F. Knollys—Ld Ripon—Mary Drew—Sir J.C.—Ld Cobham—Alf. Lyttelton. Read Les Maisons. Tea at Ld Strafford's.

9. Wed.

Wrote to Mr Ingram—Dean of Winchester—Lady Salisbury—Prof. Romanes— Mr Montagu MP.—J.G. Moore—Mr Pascoe Glyn—G. Hutchinson—& minutes. Saw Sir J.C.—Mr Morley—Mr A. Morley—Mr Woodall—Mr Lefevre. Dined with the Speaker. Tea with Lady Salisbury. Read Fanny Bora[1]—Robin Jacquemyn on Armenia[2]—Woman unsexed.

10. Th.

Wrote to Bull & Auvache—M. Jusserand—Mr Stead—Miss Bright—Mr J.G. Cook—Edinb. Chamb. of Commerce—and minutes. Saw Miss Guild (final)—A. Morley—Sir J.C.—M. Florian & Attaché—J. Morley—W. Peel. H. of C. $3\frac{3}{4}$–7.[3] Tea at the Speaker's. Read Confessions d'un Jeune Anglais[4]—Armenian Question.

11. Frid.

Wrote to C.S. Palmer—G.H. Gladstone[5]—J.M. Burt—Miss A.A. Smith—T. Kennard—Rev. F. Meyrick—A. Alston. H. of C. $2\frac{1}{2}$–5. Spoke on disallowance of votes.[6] Saw Sir J.C.—A. Morley—HNG on the Penrhyn Corresp.[7]—Prof. Romanes—Dowager Lady Stanley—Mrs Grandt [sic].

12. Sat.

Wrote to Mary Drew—Mad. Novikoff—Miss Dow—Dr. Wace—Mr Lloyd Bryce—A.S. Smith—C.G.[8] Read [blank]. Saw Mr Pascoe Glyn—Fr. Lawley—A. Morley—Sir A. Clark—Mr Armitstead—Mr Stead[9]—Ld Cobham. Dined at Ld Cobhams: & explained the strange Penrhyn correspondence.

---

[1] Untraced as either author or title.   [2] Untraced article.
[3] Eastbourne Improvement Act; questions; 4H 2. 475.
[4] Untraced.   [5] See 10 Sept. 88.
[6] Successfully supporting motion to disallow votes on 4 March of M.P.s who were directors of the East Africa Company; 4H 2. 651.   [7] See 11 Aug. 91 ff.
[8] To Mrs. Gladstone: '... Clark on examining at once hit the nail on the head and said it was *exema* in the eye. I recollected that it had risen and gone down with the exema in the hands. He gave me prudent directions and ... provided me with coloured spectacles'; Hawn P.
[9] Interview arranged by Stead in preparation for his 'Character sketch of Mr. Gladstone' to be published at the time of the election; Stead followed up the interview by questions about Gladstone's statement to Wilberforce in 1865 that there would be a third Gladstonian 'transmigration of spirit'; Gladstone's reply untraced; Add MS 44303, ff. 466 f.

13. 2 S. Lent.

St Jamess mg, Wells St aft: both with Harry. Wrote to C.G. Read Fairley Epitaphium[1]—Volorieff La Russie[2]—Dr Reilly, Ch. & State.[3]

14. M.

Wrote to C.G.—Prof. Romanes—M. Drew—Rev. Mr Tims—Ld Reay—Rev. Elkington—H. Brand. Kept the house for my exemous eyelid. Saw Madam Novikoff—Sir A. West—A. Morley—Mr Armitstead—J. Morley. Six to dinner. Read Murray's Greek Art[4]—Introd. to Melmoth[5]—Le Naturalisme.[6]

15. Tu.

Wrote to Mr Kennard—Mad. Novikoff—W.T. Stead—Dr Rentoul—J. Maude—Mr Anderson. Visited Christie Sale. H. of C. $2\frac{1}{2}$–$3\frac{1}{2}$.[7] Saw Sir A. West—A. Morley—J. Morley—Sir W. Harcourt. Dined with Ly Lyttelton. Conversation with Sarah—Lavinia Talbot—Mrs Leigh—Mr Asquith—Mr Farrell. Read [blank] on Poland—Melmoth.

16. Wed.

Wrote to C.G.—Mr Harding—F. Bellis—E.M. Powell—P.M. Hill—Messrs Beatley[8]—T. Prothero—W. Digby—C.G. H. of C. $12\frac{1}{4}$–$2\frac{3}{4}$. Spoke on Welsh Land Tenure: and $4\frac{3}{4}$–6.[9] Dined at Ld Sandhurst's. Saw Sir A. West—E. Marjoribanks—Sir Jas Paget—Mr A. Cecil.[10] Read Murray, Greek Art—Melmoth.

17. Th.

Wrote to Miss Colenso—Dowager Ly Lothian—Capt. Ramsay—Messrs Watson—Messrs Virtue—Ln & County Bank. Dined, Mr Marjoribanks's. Saw Sir A. West—Sir W. Harcourt—Mr Sotheby—E. Hamilton—Lady Londonderry—Dowager Dss Marlborough. Consulted Sir W.H., J.M., Sir H. James on the case of my 23 letters in the Farr papers.[11] Read Melmoth finished I—True Cause of Chinese Riots[12]—Flower on the Horse.[13]

---

[1] W. Fairley, *Epitaphiana: or, the curiosities of churchyard literature* (1873).
[2] Possibly S. Nossoff, *La Russie comique* (1891).
[3] E. J. O'Reilly, *Relations of the church to society* (1892).
[4] A. S. Murray, *Greek archaeology . . . mural paintings* (1892).
[5] W. Melmoth, *père, The great importance of a religious life considered* (1812).
[6] Untraced.   [7] Questions; supply; 4*H* 2. 877.
[8] Thomas Gage Beatley, steamship owners; business untraced.
[9] Supporting an inquiry into land tenure in Wales, as unable to vote for T. Ellis's bill: 'the question . . . is not ripe for a definitive solution such as is proposed by the Bill'; 4*H* 2. 982.
[10] Possibly Algernon Cecil, 1879–1935; later a writer on foreign policy.
[11] Sotheby's planned the sale of the papers of W. W. Farr (see 4 Feb. 26), an Eton friend, including Gladstone's letters to Farr; 'Messrs. Sotheby were instructed to hold back these letters if I should deem their publication objectionable. I read a sufficient portion of them and expressed a desire that they should be withdrawn from the sale, as piecemeal biography, and otherwise . . .'; *Autobiographica*, i. 34 and App. I.
[12] Perhaps *The anti-foreign riots in China in 1891* (1892).
[13] W. H. Flower, *The horse; a study in natural history* (1891).

18. Fr.

Wrote to J. Westell—Rev. Dr. Jessop—Jas Young—Hon. A. Lyttelton—A. Clarke—Wms & Norgate—Rev. Mr Hole. Dined at J. Morley's. Mr Prothero worked here. Saw Sir A.W.—A. Morley—Ld Justice Bowen. Read Vicar's Wife[1]—Naturalisme.

19 Sat.

Wrote to Mr Stedman—Mr Robinson MP.—Mr Everett—Ashley Cooper—A. Tate. Walk & drive with C. Dined at Mrs Dugdale's: saw Ly E. Fitzmaurice—Miss Booth—Sir A.W.—A. Murray. Worked on MS 'Platform'.[2] Read Vicar's Wife—Le Naturalism.

20. 3 S. Lent.

St James mg—Chapel Royal aft. We visited Mrs Th's Lodge[3] & saw Miss Ponsonby. Read Vicar's Wife—Brett's Memoirs[4]—and [blank.]

21. M.

Wrote to E. H. Hare—Mrs Bolton—Mr Godley—Messrs Sotheby—Ld Rosebery—Mr Knowles—Laicus [sic]—H. Martin—A.R. Gladstone. Saw Sir A.W.—A. Morley. H. of C. 4–6.[5] Read Hadfield 8 hour Bill[6]—Savan, Naturalisme—Major, Hist.[7]—Dict. Biogr. Finished MS on 'Platform'.

22. Tu.

Wrote to Sir C. Russell—Mr Squibb S.P.G.[8]—Sig. de Gubernatis—Sec Chester Lib. Club. Memorial service for Ld Hampden St Marg. at $12\frac{3}{4}$. Saw Sir A. W[est]—A. Morley—Ld Spencer. H. of C. $9-12\frac{19}{2}$[9] Read 'The Horse'—Maitresses de Lord Byron.[10]

23. Wed.

Wrote to N. Geary—Sir C. Russell—E. Hamilton—Spottiswoode's—Mr Gullich. Saw Sir A.W.—Mr James MP.—Mr A. Morley—Mr Morley—Mr Waddington—Mr Hare—Lady Ponsonby. Visited Mrs Guild's studio: much struck. She got a quasi-sitting.[11] Read The Horse—Maitresses de Lord Byron. H. of C. $12\frac{1}{4}-2$.[12] Dined at Mr Gardner's.

[1] E. Dickinson, *A vicar's wife* (1892).
[2] 'The platform, its rise and progress', *N.C.*, xxxi. 686 (April 1892); review of Jephson; see 16 Feb. 92.
[3] i.e. her cottage in Hampstead.   [4] See 6 Mar. 92.
[5] Spoke on expulsion of G. W. Hastings; 4*H* 2. 1341.
[6] Untraced article.
[7] J. Major, *A history of Great Britain, as well England as Scotland* (1892 tr. and ed.).
[8] Probably George Meyer Squibb, rector of Totteridge and formerly chaplain in East Africa.
[9] Law of Conspiracy; 4*H* 2. 1496.
[10] F. Rabbe, *Les Maîtresses authentiques de Lord Byron* (1890).
[11] The sculptress (see 4 Mar. 92n.); this bust untraced.
[12] Eight Hours Bill; 4*H* 2. 1557.

24. Th.

Wrote to the Speaker—Messrs A. Brown—Isbisters—Mr Mitchell—Miss Southam—Gilbert & Fowler. Saw Sir A.W.—A. Morley—Ld Rosebery—Mr Samuelson[1]—Mr Haldane MP. H of C. 4–7½. Spoke on Small Holdings.[2] Read Maitresses de Lord Byron. Finished The Horse. Eight to dinner. Saw dear Gerty and her children on their way.

25. Fr.

Wrote to Ld Northbourne—J.M. Milner—A.R. Harrard—J.A. Cooper—Mr Pitney—A.M. Beale—Mr Williamson MP—Mr Robinson MP[3]—R.A. Everett. Read Byron Maitresses—Memoires de Roche Chouart.[4] Saw Mr Gullich—Rev. Mitchell—Sir A.W.—Mr A. Morley—Mr Murray. Dined with Lucy.

26. Sat.

Wrote to Mr D. Nutt—Sir F. Sanderson—Sir F. Milbank—Lady Milbank—Dr. Leffingwell—Q. Hogg[5]—C.R. Low—A.S. Cobb[6]—Mr Gilbey. Saw Sir A.W.—Mr Wigram—Mr A. Morley—Miss Phillimore. Read Roche Chouart—Lefevre on Rosebery (challenge)[7]—C. Lloyd on Ireland[8]—Cobb on Currency. Dined at Mr Hankey's.

27. 4 S.L.

Chapel Royal mg—St James's aft. Long tea at Lady Brownlow's. Saw Mr Tree—Dowager Lady L.—Sir A. West. Read Smith on Isaiah—Miss Benson's Tale[9]—Memoirs of R. Brett—Hist. of Marriage.[10]

28. M.

Wrote to Mr Cartbery—Mr Bennett (B.P.)—G. Harding—Mr Bryce MP. H. of C. 4½–7¾ and 10¼. Spoke on Indian Councils.[11] Saw Sir A.W.—S. Lyttelton—Mr Stuart MP—Mr Lewis MP.—Sir U. Shuttleworth. Wrote for 'Rock' 2d Edn.[12] Read Byron et ses Maitresses—Roche Chouart.

---

[1] Godfrey Blundell Samuelson, 1863–1941; liberal M.P. Forest of Dean 1887–92; Mundella's secretary.

[2] 4H 2. 1709.

[3] Thomas Robinson, 1827–97; Gloucester merchant and liberal M.P. there 1880 (unseated), 1885–95; kt. 1894.

[4] L. V. L. de Rochechoart, *Souvenirs sur la Révolution, l'Empire et la Restauration* (1889).

[5] Quintin Hogg, 1845–1903; educationalist. Business untraced.

[6] Had sent his 'Metallic reserves' (1892).

[7] Untraced.

[8] Clifford D. C. Lloyd, *Ireland under the Land League* (1892).

[9] See 4 Mar. 92.

[10] Perhaps L. Baldwin, *The story of a marriage*, 3v. (1892).

[11] 4H 3. 78.

[12] Revised and enlarged ed. (1892) of *The impregnable rock of holy scripture* (see 6 Jan. 90, 10 Nov. 91).

29. *Tu.*

Wrote to Abp of Canterb.—Dr Ginsburg—Mr Claydon—Rev. Petrie. Saw S.L.—
Mr Rendell—A. Morley. Wrote again for 'Rock'. Dined with Rosebery: long but
retrospective conversation. Read Byron et ses M.—Illegitimacy.[1]

30. *Wed.*

B. Museum in the forenoon to work on 'Rock' with Dr Ginsburg. Also I read
books on Univ. Paris. Dined at the French Embassy. Saw Ld Reay—Mad.
Konigsmark[2]—Lady Rayleigh. Read 19th Cent. on Keats[3]—Byron Maitresses—
De Windt.[4]

31. *Th.*

Wrote to Rev. Mr Urwick—Mr Trumbull—A. Nichol—The O'Clery.[5] Saw S.L.—
A. Morley—Mr Haldane MP—Mr Lidderdale—Mr Chaplain—& others. Read De
Windt's Siberia—Finished Byron et ses Maitresses. H. of C. 5–6¾.[6] Dined with E.
Hamilton. Sat 2 hours to Mr Adams Acton.[7]

Frid. Ap. One 1892.

Wrote to Sir John Cowell—Rev. Dr. Caldecott—A.S. Cobb—Lady Lindsay—W.
Canton—H.G. Taylor—Mrs Bolton. Saw S.L.—A.M.—Mr Rendell—Mad. Konigs-
mark—Mr Cecil. Conversation with C. on plans for the year. She went off to St
L.[8] H. of C. 3–5.[9] Worked on 2d Edn Rock. Read De Windt—The O'Clery on
Italy. He is a Codino.[10] Dined at Sir G. Hayter's.[11]

2. *Sat.*

Wrote to Watsons—J.W. Buckley—A. Nield—Jas Irvine—Mr Turnbull. Worked
on 'Rock' 2d Ed. Saw S.L.—A. Godley—Lady Holker—Mr Hutton *cum* Mr
Cohen. Dined at Mr Arbuthnot's. Read De Windt—Roche Chouart.

---

[1] A. Leffingwell, *Illegitimacy and the influence of seasons* (1892).
[2] A fortuneteller; see 1 Apr. 92n.
[3] *N.C.*, xxxi. 586 (April 1892).
[4] H. De Windt, *Siberia as it is . . . with an introduction by Olga Novikoff* (1892).
[5] Patrick Keyes O'Clery, known as The O'Clery; historian of Italy, see next day.
[6] Scottish education and taxation; 4*H* 3. 373.
[7] Further sitting to the sculptor; see 7 Nov. 64, 22 Sept. 91.
[8] To St. Leonard's-on-sea.
[9] Spoke on the register and the timing of dissolutions; 4*H* 3. 508.
[10] 'a little tail'; P. K. O'Clery, *The making of Italy* (1892).
[11] Gladstone told his wife, 3 April 1892, Hawn P: '. . . The Hayter party was very pleasant. But
Madame K. not quite wise in fortune-telling from cards after dinner without asking leave. She was
most bountiful to me, promising three Ms:
1. A majority as large as I desire (my desire is for three figures)
2. Money! to come here: no specification of how when or what
3. Marriage, a satisfactory one, in the family. So she pitched upon Helen: rather hard on her.'

3. 5 S.L.

Ch. Royal mg with H.C.—St Andrew's aft. Wrote to Mr Murray jun.—Mr
Knowles—C.G. Read 'At Sundry Times'[1]—Contemp. on Eastern Religion—Nonconformists[2]—&c.—Life of R. Brett.

4. M.

Wrote to C. Marseilles [*sic*]—Mr Canton.[3] Eight to dinner. H. of C. 5–7¾ and
10½–12¼.[4] Sent 2d Ed. to press. Read De Rochechouart—Moulton on Pensions.[5]
Saw A. Morley—S.L.—Ld Herschell—Mr Bryce.

5. Tu.

Wrote to J.F. Moulton—Ld Reay—Rev. G. John—A. Grove—Rev. J. Cullen—S.A.
Walker—W. Downing. Saw S.L.—A. Morley—Sir C. Russell—Mr Peel—Mrs
Guild—Mr Maclaggan and deputation.[6] H. of C. 2½–7.[7] Read De Windt—Roche
Chouart.

6. Wed.

Wrote to Mr Cowan—Ld Kimberley—Provost of North Berwick. Dined at Mr P.
Stanhope's. Saw S.L.—Mr A. Morley—Dr Ginsburg. Visited Christie's. Funeral
service (Mr Murray)[8] at St James's. Read Rochechouart—De Windt.

7. Thurs.

Wrote to Mr Canton—Dean of ChCh—J.W. Buckley—Rev. R. Jenkins—H.S.
Keith—Lady Londonderry. Saw S.L.—A. Morley—Mr Rendel. Read De Windt—
Rochechouart—Jenkins Recollections of Manning.[9] H. of C. 5–8½. Spoke on
Privilege.[10]

8. Fr.

Wrote to Lady Aberdeen—Sec. Home Dept—Mr Weir. H. of C. 2½–7. Spoke I
fear near one hour on compulsion.[11] Never in my life more dependent: never
more helped. I never rose with less knowledge or idea of what I should say; and
it seemed to bubble up. Saw S.L.—A. Morley—Herbert J.G.—Sir W. Harcourt—

---

[1] See 29 Nov. 91, 4 Mar. 92.   [2] *C.R.*, lxi. 498, 512 (April 1892).
[3] Of Isbister's, publishers of *The Impregnable Rock*; in correspondence on the 2d. edition; Hawn P.
[4] Spoke on Smallholdings Bill; 4*H* 3. 664.
[5] J. F. Moulton, 'Old age pensions', *F.R.*, lvii. 465 (April 1892).
[6] P. McLagan, liberal M.P., led a depn. from the Scottish Permissive Bill Association to present a
memorial on the Scottish Direct Veto Bill; *T.T.*, 6 April 1892, 6a.
[7] Smallholdings Bill; 4*H* 3. 701.
[8] John Murray, who published many of Gladstone's books. See 16 Apr. 91 for Gladstone's review
of his biography
[9] Untraced; probably an article.   [10] Case of railway servants; 4*H* 3. 910.
[11] He followed Chamberlain, appealing to him to recall the liberal sentiments of his youth and
middle age; the liberal amndt. inserted the word 'compulsorily' into the Smallholdings Bill; 4*H* 3.
1016.

and others. Dined at Lady Farnborough's. House again afterwards. Read De Windt—Rochechouart.

9. Sat.

Wrote to Rev. S.E.G.—J.A. Bailey—W. Downing—Lady Holker—Mr Irvine—Sec. R. Acad.—J. Grant—Tel to Mr A. Carnegie—Euston Stationmaster—and a long letter to Mr S. Smith M.P. on the Woman's Suffrage Bill.[1] Saw S.L.—Mr A. Morley—Mr Stuart MP. Dined at Sir G. Trevelyan's. Saw the Abp—Mrs Benson—Mrs Humphry Ward. Finished De Windt—finished Roche Chouart.

10. 6 S. Lent.

Chapel Royal mg—St James's evg. Saw Miss Murrays—the Wests. Wrote to Rev. Dr Belcher—Miss Ritso. Wrote to A. Morley & placed the Smith letter in his hands. Read Brett (finished)—Tondini, Ch. of Russia[2]—Xtn Rulers in U.S.[3]

11. M.

Wrote to Mr Knowles—Rev. Dr Stokes—Mr C.S. Palmer—Keeper of P[rinted] B[ooks], B. Museum—Rev. Mr Halcombe—Rev. J. Forbes—W.C. Wagstaff—Mr Stockwell—Mrs J.A. Clark—Sir A. Clark—Mr Murray. H. of C. 5–8. Short speech on Budget.[4] Six to dinner. Saw S.L.—Mr A. Morley—Mr S. Rendel. Read 'Nell Horn'.[5] Worked on books & papers in preparation for departure.

12. Tu. [Hawarden]

10–3½ C.G. to Hawarden. Accident on the way to Euston. Wrote to Veuve Meissonier—Messrs Isbister—Mr Blackie—Sir E. Watkin—Mrs Th.—and . . . . Read Rabbe's Shelley[6]—Champfleury on the Cat[7]—Palmer on Revelation.[8] Found dear Mary still suffering from her eye: Dorothy in immense force: the Stepneys welcome guests: Rectory all well. Church at 7. Passion Lecture with transparencies to 9.30 very striking.

13. Wed.

Ch. 8½ A.M. Wrote to Mr Realf (U.S.)[9] Tel.—Miss Millard—J. Wilson—Mrs Whitehead—Mrs Ingram—Mrs A.M. Moore—W. Woodings—Messrs Osgood—

[1] Hoping the Commons will reject the bill of 23 April: the bill, applying only to unmarried women, is too narrowly drawn; given the 'immaturity' of the public mind on the subject, more discussion is necessary; released to the press (see next day) and printed in Samuel Smith, *My life-work* (1902), app. xi and as a pamphlet published by Murray on 21 April (see *D.N.*, 20 April 1892, 5d); draft in Add MS 44774, f. 7.
[2] C. Tondini, *The future of the Russian church* (1876).
[3] Perhaps F. C. Morehouse, *Some American churchmen* (1892).
[4] Immediately following Goschen's financial statement; 4*H* 3. 1170.
[5] J. H. Rosny, *Nell Horn de l'Armée du Salut. Roman de moeurs londoniennes* (1886).
[6] F. Rabbe, *Shelley, sa vie et ses oeuvres* (1887).
[7] 'Champfleury' [i.e. J. F. F. Husson], *The cat past and present* (tr. 1885).
[8] E. R. Palmer, *The development of revelation* (1892).
[9] Not further identified.

Sec. of French Academy—Rev. E. Griffiths—Mr Stuart Glennie. Read Palmer on Revelation—Champfleury on the Cat—Rabbe's Shelley. Backgammon with S.— Wrote on O[lympian] R[eligion].

14. *Th. Dies Natalis Eucharistiae.*

Mg prayer and H.C., 8½ A.M. Vespers 7. P.M. Wrote to Ed. Illustrated News[1]— Messrs Griffith—A.B. Burchall—Thos Gough—T.G. Gullick—Rev. J.G. Deed[2]— Robn & Nichn—Rev. W.C. Ingram—H.N.G.—Mr J. Marshall—J.S. Shaw—Mr D. Lowe—Jas Yates. Read Rabbe—Palmer—Atkinson's Moorland Parish.[3] Worked on my Bibliography—B. Museum Papers.

15. *Good Friday.*

Ch 10½ A.M. & 12¼–3½ for the 3 hours service. Wrote to Miss Linette—A. Morley—S.A.K. Strahan—B.H. Davis—Canon Barker—H.W. Green—Messrs Hine— J. Salmon—D. Whiteley. Read Palmer Development of Revelation—Strahan Marriage & Disease[4]—Fuller on Jerusm Bpric[5]—Gall, Imme. Salvation.[6]

16. *Easter Eve.*

Ch. 8½ AM and 7 P.M. Wrote to Mr S. Hazzopulo—J. Davidson—Miss Hardy— Rev. G.B. Roberts—W.H. Denny—Rev. D. M'Gregor—Gay & Bird—D. Talleman—Ld Halifax. Saw Mr Taylor Innes. Worked on Dante Rivers.[7] Read Palmer—finished Champfleury. 12 deg. of frost last night!

17. *E. Sunday.*

Holy C. at 8 A.M. Mg service 11 AM. Excellent sermon. Evg 7 P.M. The scenes of services were pleasant to witness. Wrote dft letter for C. to Lady Carlisle.[8] Wrote to M. Léon Séché—W.T. Stead—Lady West—Jas Old—C. Mijatovich—Mr Maclaren MP.—Miss Martin—Mr C.S. Palmer—Mr Murray. Read Palmer (finished)—Ingram & Wesleyan Preachers.[9]

[1] Not published.
[2] John George Deed, secretary of the Additional Curates Society.
[3] J. C. Atkinson, *Forty years in a moorland parish* (1891).
[4] Samuel Alexander Kenny Strahan, barrister and physician, had sent his *Marriage and disease. A study of heredity* (1892).
[5] Untraced article, probably by John Mee Fuller.
[6] J. Gall, *Immediate salvation for the chief of sinners* (1864); an abbreviation of his chief work (see 26 June 70).
[7] 'Did Dante study at Oxford?', *N.C.*, xxxi. 1032 (June 1892). The article places especial weight on Dante's references to rivers as a means of transport, concluding that he probably visited Oxford *via* the Thames.
[8] Mrs. Gladstone was President of the Women's Liberal Federation, whose Council, encouraged by Lady Carlisle, voted to promote the Parliamentary enfranchisement of women; it was expected she would resign, but she did not do so until 1893; see E. A. Pratt, *Catherine Gladstone* (1898), 252 ff. and Gardiner, ii. 172.
[9] Untraced.

18. *Easter M.*

Ch 8¼ & H.C. Wrote to Mrs Bartlett—Rev. Trollope[1]—C.S. Woodruff—Mr Stuart (B.P.)—Miss Stuart—Tel. for C. to Lady Carlisle. Saw the Fry party. Worked on Dante Rivers. Backgammon with S. Read Matthew Tindale[2]—Mijatovich's Constantine Palaeologus.[3]

19. *E. Tu.*

Ch. 8½ A.M. Wrote dft 2° for C. to Lady Carlisle. Wrote to Miss Ponsonby BP.— Mrs Morrell—T.H. Furlsham—W.T. Morgan—A.M. Linkham—Sir J. Lacaita—Mr Montagu MP.—Saw the Dean of St Asaph (Educn). Visited St John's [Pentrobin] with S. in order to judge about the organ. Mr Stack was with us. Read Mijantovich Pal.—Matthew Tyndall—Montagu on Money.[4] Backgammon with S[tephen].

20. *Wed.*

Ch. 8½ A.M. Wrote to D. Grant—Messrs Clowes—Mr Blackie. Backgammon with S. Read Denifle, Universitaten des Mittelalters[5]—Constantine (finished)— Matthew Tyndale. Worked on Dante Rivers. Worked at St Deiniol's.

21. *Th.*

Ch. 8¼ A.M. Wrote to Mr Edwin Johnson—C. Child—Mr A.H. Hutton— C. Higham—Mr W.H. Lever—Sotherans—Prof. Romanes—J. Hamer—Mr J.G. Talbot—Sir J. Evans—M.G. Spielmann—T.J. Claveley—Rev. Dr Hayman—S. Holden—Mr S.H. Lough—H. Golding—Lady West—J. Ingles—Mr Jos. Pallessy. Also dft to Lady C. for C.

The Carnegies came at 12.30. Took them to the new Library, & about. Dined with them at the Castle. The Carnegies came. I took him to the Library. After dinner we went to the African singers: I closed with a short speech. Long conversation on Election monies.[6] Read Hutton's Manning—Matthew Tyndale.

22. *Frid.*

Ch. 8½ A.M. Further & very friendly conversation with the giant millionaire. Wrote to Abp of Canterbury—A. Morley MP. l.l.—J.C. Humphreys—A. Galton— Rev. J. Hastings—F. Bucher—Mr C.S. Palmer—H. Aitken—H. Macpherson. Pursued long my Dante research. Read Hutton's Manning—Matth. Tyndale.

---

[1] Probably John Joseph Trollope, vicar of Lydney.
[2] E. Curll, *Memoirs of the life and writings of Matthew Tindall* (1733).
[3] C. Mijatovíc, *Constantine, the last Emperor of the Greeks* (1892).
[4] S. Montagu, 'Dangers of modern finance', *F.R.*, lvii. 322 (March 1892).
[5] H. F. Denifle, *Die Universitäten des Mittelalters bis 1400* (1885); much used in Gladstone's article on Dante (see 16 Apr. 82).
[6] A meeting arranged some time before; Carnegie had again encouraged Gladstone to write his autobiography, and had raised the question of payment of members, so as to increase working-class representation: 'I should like to give ten thousand pounds for a bill paying members three hundred pounds per annum'; *Carnegie*, i. 418. It is unclear whether Carnegie gave a further donation to the Liberals' election fund.

23. Sat.

Ch. 8½ A.M. Missed Mrs Allen's funeral[1] by a mistake. Wrote to Mr. Guinness Rogers—Rev. Dr. Kinns—S.J. Reid[2]—A. Macdonald—A. Atkins—Sec. Academy of France—T.H. Stockwell.[3] Worked on Dante. Rad Matth. Tyndale—Dante Books—Tennyson's Foresters.[4]

24. 1 S.E.

Holy Commn 8 A.M. mg & evg service 11 & 6½. Worked on Dante. Read Manning: much: finished Mr Hutton's Volume—S.E.G. Toxteth Sermon—Halcombe on the Gospels[5]—and [blank.]

25. M. St Mark.

Ch. 8½ A.M. Wrote to Duke of Argyll—Mr R. Neville MP[6]—Mr Stead—Rev. Mr Halcombe—Ly F. Dixie—Lady C. Swamey[7]—Miss Clarke—Mr Moscow[?]—Messrs Evans—C.S. Palmer—Eyre & Spottiswoode—Chester Station Master. Finished MS on Dante & Oxford.[8] Saw Mr Holmes (U.S.). Order work at the Castle. Ten to dinner. Read Matthew Tyndale.

26. Tu.

Ch. 8½ A.M. Saw S.E.G. on St Deiniol's & Toxteth—Mr Douglas on Rood Screen—M. Drew on St Deiniol's. Wrote to Robn & Nichn—Rev. Mr King—J. Stanley Little—A.W. Hutton—Miss C. Millard—Mr F. Green—Rev. Dr Cox—A. Morley MP.—E.S. Purcell—Sotherans—Rev. J. Stephenson—Jas Wilson—Sampson Low—Mr Vickers—Rev. Mr Stone—C. Geddes—Jas Jack. Corrected Speech proofs. Worked on sorting & settling. Finished Matthew Tyndale. Finished Tennyson's Foresters. Began Ring in the True.[9] Backgammon with S.

27. Wed. [London]

Ch. 8½ A.M. At 10.50 we bid farewell to these dear houses and people. Reached H. of C. at 4: & voted against the Woman Suffrage Bill in an uncomfortably small majority of 23.[10] Conclave on poor C.s embarrassing question about her President's Wife [sic].[11] Saw Mr S. Rendell—Mr Bright M.P.—J. Morley—Mr Armitstead. Dined at Mr Armitstead's. Wrote to ..... Rev. Mr. ....
.... Read Ring in the True—Pareto on Italian Protectionism.[12]

---

[1] Jane Allen, aged 49, wife of the curate of Sealand.
[2] I. Stuart Johnson Reid, author.
[3] Thomas Henry Stockwell, editor of the *Baptist*.
[4] A. Tennyson, *The Foresters: Robin Hood and Maid Marian* (1892).
[5] J.J. Halcombe, *The fourfold gospel* (1890).
[6] Ralph Neville, 1848–1918; barrister and strong home-ruler; liberal M.P. Liverpool Exchange 1887–95.
[7] The widow, *née* Beeby, of Sir M. Coomara Swamy (d. 1879).
[8] See 16 Apr. 92.   [9] E. Stone, *Ring in the true* (1892).
[10] His letter to Smith was extensively discussed; 4 *H* 3. 1453.   [11] See 17 Apr. 92.
[12] V. F. Pareto, *Il protezionismo in Italia e i suoi effeti* (1891?); see 30 Apr. 92n.

28. Th.

Wrote to J. Westell—Rev. J. Strong—Mr W. Snow—Mr Stedman. Worked hard on proofs of 'Rock'.[1] Saw Gerty & her children—also Edward [Wickham] on his going to School. Saw A. Morley—J. Morley—Harcourt & Fowler on Finance. H. of C. 3¾–8. Spoke on Clergy Discipline Bill.[2]

29. Fr. [Dollis Hill]

Wrote to Isbisters—Mr Balfour—Mr Shipton[3]—Dr Ginsburg—Mr Lane—Ed. Methodist Times.[4] Worked hard on proofs. Visited R.A. Exhibition. [Read] Le Tellier & St Simon—Ring in the True. Down to Dollis at 6 PM.

30. Sat.

Wrote to Mr Knowles—Hon S. Coleridge—Mrs Ingram—Rev. J.J. Chambers—C. Higham—Sig. V. Pareto[5]—Mrs Th. Worked much on proofs of Rock 2d Ed. And revised MS. of Dante at Oxford.[6] Drive with C. to Hendon. Finished Ring in the True. Read Le Tellier & St Simon—Tess of the D'Urbervilles.[7]

2 S. Easter. 1 May 1892.

Willesden Ch. & H.C. 11 A.M. Prayers read at home aft. Sir C. & Lady Tennant came. H.J.G. to dinner. Wrote to Edw. Wickham jun.—Rev. S.E.G.—Memm for

[1] See 10 Nov. 91.
[2] 4H 3. 1601.
[3] George Shipton, secretary of the London Trades Council, campaigning for the Eight Hours Day, had written to Salisbury, Balfour and Gladstone. Gladstone's reply promised careful consideration, but declined to express a view until the subject had been more fully discussed by 'the multitude of classes affected by it'. An 'animated discussion took place after the reading of the letters, and very strong epithets were used. One of the delegates moved that the letters be consigned to the waste-paper basket, but this was ruled out of order'; *T.T.*, 3 May 1892, 12d. See also Add MS 44514, f. 219.
[4] Sending, not for publication, 'a note of my recollections of the C[ontagious] D[iseases] Acts, of course not infallible but very different indeed from yours'; the note sent in ignorance that the editor was Hugh Price Hughes, 1847–1902, methodist minister, propagandist and radical imperialist. See *The life of Hugh Price Hughes by his Daughter* (1905), 375.
[5] Vilfredo Federico Pareto, 1848–1923; economist. Pareto had sent Gladstone a copy of his book (see 27 Apr. 92). Gladstone's letter was by arrangement published in *Fanulla*, 11–12 May 1892; it reads: 'Ho letto con molto interesse l'opuscolo che mi avete mandato. Esse pone in chiara luce i gravissimi pericoli che all'estero sono considerati e deplorati da coloro che amarono e compatriono l'Italia nei giorni in cui soggiaceva a stranieri e a dispotici governi, e quando i suoi pericoli ed e suoi mali non per opera di lei sorgevano, ma da altri le erano imposti; mentre ora appare che da essa stessa procedano, per mezzo del suo governo parlamentare. Il protezionismo e il militarismo sono congiunti in un infausto valido matrimonio, e credo fermamente che sono egualmente nemici della libertà'; see V. F. Pareto, *Lettere a Maffeo Pantaleoni*, 3v. (1962), 210–14 and Hawn P.
[6] See 16 Apr. 92.
[7] By Thomas Hardy, 3v. (1891); in an undated letter to Mary Drew, Gladstone noted: 'About Tess I said while reading it that it was a plum pudding stone full of faults and merits, but on finishing and surveying it as a whole, while still feeling its talent and even value in certain respects, I am provoked and disgusted. All the moral elements of the book are at war; nothing is sound and harmonious . . . I cannot make out the author's aim, unless it is to throw over both morality and belief. I sometimes hope it is ironical and misread by me . . .'; *The Gladstone Papers* (1930), 45. See 8 May 92.

C.G. on this unending resignation business.[1] Read Le Tellier—Rabbe, Joan of
Arc[2]—Thomas a Kempis.

2. M. [London]

Wrote to J. Rutherford—Abp. of Canterbury. Read Tess—Joan of Arc. Off to
London at 4¾. Tea at Mrs Th.s. H. of C. 6–7.[3] Dined at Ld Reay's. Saw D. of
Connaught—Mr Morley *cum* Mr A. Morley—Mr Bryce—Mr Fowler—Dutch
Premier. Worked on Mr Palmer's book.[4]

3. Tu. [Dollis Hill]

Wrote to Mr Irving—Rev. Price Hughes—T. Bonnar—Ld Just. Bowen—Mr Bal-
four—Mr P. Campbell—Mrs Th.—Mr L. Morris[5]—R.F. Wood—Rev. Mr Baron—
A. Hutton—Rev. Mr. Jenkins—Mrs Goring—Mr Longrigg—D. Met . . . [*sic*].
Dined with Sir R. Welby. Saw Abp. of Cant.—Sir J. Millais—Agnews—F.
Leveson—A Morley—Mr S. Kendall—H.N.G.—S.L. Worked on proofs. Read
Tess—Plumptre on Dante[6]—and [blank.] Back to Dollis 11.30 PM.

4. Wed.

Wrote to S.E.G.—Mr Stead—Mr J.J. Hatch—Mr Hebblethwaite—Dr Ginsburg—
A. Morley. Wrote Mema on a plaguy speech of Sir C. Dilke.[7] Saw Mr Armitstead. Worked on Palmer. Read Tess—La Terreur[8]—Delbos Les Deux Rivales.[9]

5. Th.

Wrote to J. Hitchman—Miss Roberts—Mr S. Lucas—Fisher Unwin—C.H.
Palmer—Mr Ridgway—Ex Exp. T. [*sic*] Worked on Rock Proofs with Dr
Ginsburg. Attended the Levee. Read H.J.G.s excellent paper.[10] H. of C. 4–6¾.[11]
Saw A.M. l.l.—J.M.—Harcourt—Mr Fowler—Dollis at 7¾. Read Tess—and Talley-
rand.[12]

[1] Intended resignation as President of the Women's Liberal Federation; see 17 Apr. 92n.
[2] F. Rabbe, *Jeanne d'Arc en Angleterre* (1891).   [3] Scottish education; 4*H* 3. 1784.
[4] Further revisions for the never-completed 2nd ed. of Palmer's *Treatise on the Church of Christ*.
[5] See 22 Feb. 77.
[6] E. H. Plumptre, *The Commedia and Canzoniere of Dante . . . a new translation* (1886).
[7] A speech by Dilke reported in *Forest of Dean Mercury*, 29 April 1892; Gladstone objected to
Dilke's implication that Gladstone supported his candidature; the mem. was originally a letter to
Cyril Flower, but his name is deleted in the extant version dated 12 May 1892; Add MS 44514, f.
261. On 30 May 1892, Gladstone wrote to Stead (Add MS 44303, f. 495): 'I must apologise for not
having answered your first question, which I did not associate with that respecting Sir Charles Dilke.
My impressions on the great subject of conjugal life are as sombre as they were at the time when we
conversed together: but I have never yet seen my way to an improvement by means of penalty or
disqualification. You are right in supposing that my lately published letter is meant to show my
entire and absolute disconnection from all matters associated with the Candidature of Sir Charles
Dilke.'
[8] Untraced.
[9] L. Delbos, *Les deux rivales. L'Angleterre et la France* (1890).
[10] H. J. Gladstone, 'Ireland blocks the way', published in *N.C.*, xxxi. 899 (June 1892).
[11] Question on Smallholdings Bill; 4*H* 4. 191.
[12] C. M. de Talleyrand-Perigord, ed. G. Pallain, *Correspondance diplomatique* (1891).

6. *Fr.*

Wrote to Cyril Flower—A. Morley—Mr Dibdin—Mr Menken—Mr Taylor Innes—G. Ensor—Beaumont Tel. Long sederunt with F. Leveson Gower on the Granville affairs[1]—Also walk with him. Worked on Palmer. Read Daughters of Men[2]—Lombard, l'Agonie.[3]

7. *Sat.*

Wrote to (missed).[4] Worked on Dante, corr. and additions. Read Tess— L'Agonie. Tea with Mrs Turner at Harlesden. Saw Mr H. Turner. Saw Flower. Wrote dft on Dilke.[5] Saw Archdn Atlay.[6]

8. *3 S.E.*

Willesden Ch. mg and aft. prayers at home. Wrote to A. Morley. Read Warring on Genesis[7]—Tess: finished: a deplorable anticipation of a world without a Gospel. Walk with Helen.

9. *M.*

Wrote to Spottiswoodes—Rev. J.S. White—Mrs Th.—Dr Ginsburg. To London at 3. P.M. Back at 11. H. of C. 5–7¼.[8] Finished Dante proofs. Dined at Grillion's. Read Warring—L'Agonie. Satis? Saw S.L.—A.M.—J.M.—Harcourt—Cyril Flower.

10. *Tu.*

Wrote to R.L. Johnson—Rev. Dr. Ginsburg—Isbisters—Dr Warring—Mr Yates. Worked on Pref. to Rock. Finished Warring's remarkable book. Read Lust for gold[9]—Goncourt Journal[10]—Mort d'Ivan le Terrible.[11]

11. *Wed.*

Wrote to D. Grant—Prof. Romanes—E. Menken—J. Hitchman—A. Morley— E.H. Simmons—R.F. Wood—Rev. D. Greig—S. Ramsden. Off to London at 1. Saw Scotts—Dr Ginsburg—Mr Douglas—Mr Palmer—Mr A. Morley—Mr Budge—cum J. Morley—S.L.—Mr Irving & Miss Terry. We saw Henry VIII. Even on the stage I heard but ill. Read Ivan le Terrible—Les Deux Rivales.[12]

---

[1] Memorandum on its affairs, dated 12 May 1892, at Add MS 44774, f. 547.

[2] H. Lynch, *Daughters of men* (1892).

[3] J. Lombard, *L'Agonie* (1891).

[4] Word added in pencil.

[5] See 4 May 92.

[6] Brownlow Thomas Atlay, 1832–1912; archdeacon of Calcutta 1883–8; vicar of Willesden 1888–1902.

[7] See 11 Dec. 75.

[8] Spoke on Smallholdings Bill; 4 *H* 4. 390.

[9] A. Watson, *Lust for gold: a romance* (1892).

[10] E. L. A. and J. A. de Goncourt, *Journal. Mémoires de la vie littéraire*, 9v. (1887–96).

[11] A. K. Tolstoi, *La mort d'Ivan le Terrible: drame* (1879), one of three blank verse plays published in Russia (1866–70) and tr. into French (1879).

[12] See 4 May 92.

12. Th.

Wrote to Mr R.D. Holl—Ld Herschell—M. Hirsch[1]—Lt. Danacott—E. Roe—Mrs Stanford—Mary Drew—Mr Cyril Flower. H. of C. $3\frac{1}{4}$–$6\frac{1}{2}$.[2] Saw S.L.—A. Morley—Abp's Chaplain—Mr D. Grant—J. Morley. Read Paley Evidences[3]—Henry VIII—La Terreur. Eight to dinner. Nearly all the evening on Granville affairs.

13. Fr.

Wrote to Rev. D. Mitchell—Mr Canton—Prof. Romanes—Mr Bryce MP—Miss Browne—L. Appleton—M. Hirsch. Dined with the Jameses. Drive with C. Saw S.L.—A. Morley—Mr Godley—Mr Scharf—Mr Rendel (Granville aff.)—Lucy Cavendish—H.N.G. Read Henry VIII—Kennan Tent Life in Siberia.[4]

14. Sat.

Wrote to Mr Talbot—Spottiswoodes BP—Mrs Talbot—Mad. Novikoff—Bp of Dover—A. Maclachlan—Rev. O. Newnham[5]—Mrs Brown—Rev. A. Turner—Rev. Travers—Rev. Dr. Hutton—Rev. Atkinson—Adm. Alexander. Called on D. of Devonshire:[6] out. Mr Cohen with proofs 11–12. Worked $2h\frac{1}{2}$ on Dante Revises. Saw S.L.—H.J.G. Read Henry VIII finished—Tent Life in Siberia—Tolstoi, Zycor Feodor.[7]

15. 4 S.E.

Willesden Ch 11 AM & HC.—aft. prayers at home. Wrote to Ld Tennyson—Mr J. Tennant—J. Westell—C. Acland MP. Read Fellowes What is Truth[8]—Hayman & others in 'Churchman'[9]—and divers Tracts.

16. M.

Wrote to S. Hallifax—Mr Heinemann—J. Massie—F.A. Russell—A. Fellowes—Pursebearer Holyrood—Alderman Fowler. Sat 50 m. to Adams Acton. Back to town $12\frac{3}{4}$. Read Tolstoi 'Fedor'. Nine to dinner. S.E.G.s came. H. of C. $3\frac{1}{2}$–$7\frac{1}{2}$.[10] Saw Sir J.C.—A.M.—J.M.—H.N.G. (Gr[anville] affairs).

17. Tu.

Wrote to Mr Shirwin—Mr Bailey—Miss Browne—Dr Wright—A.Q. Review. Wrote MS. on modes of future Irish rep[resentatio]n at Westmr.[11] Difficult

[1] Rev. Maurice Hirsch of the Librairie Parisienne in Coventry Street, London; on prosecution for selling 'improper French books'; see Add MS 44522, f. 65.
[2] Question on the budget; $4H$ 4. 729.
[3] See 30 Sept. 27.
[4] G. Kennan, *Tent life in Siberia* (1870).
[5] Obadiah Samuel Newnham, rector of St. Stephen, New Brunswick.
[6] i.e. the 8th duke, formerly his colleague Lord Hartington.
[7] See 10 May 92.
[8] Arthur Fellowes had sent his *What is the truth?* (1892).
[9] *The Churchman*, vi. 354 (April 1892).
[10] Budget debate; $4H$ 4. 985.
[11] Not found. See 24 May 87.

enough. Dined with the Miss Monks. Saw Abp of Canterbury—The French Ambassador—Lady Reay—Sir J.C.—A. Morley—Lady Derby—Ld Derby (NB)—Sir R. Morier. Saw Agnew Pictures. Read Stuart's Reply to W.E.G.—Tolstoi's Fedor—Kennan's Tent Life.

18. Wed.

Wrote to Dr Martin—Ld Herschell—Mr Galton—Isbisters—Dr V. Smith. H. of C. 4–6¼.[1] Corrected the last proofs for Rock. Revised MS. of yesterday: gave it to J.M. for perusal. Dined at Mr Mundella's. Saw S.L.—A.M.—J.M.—Mr F. Harrison. Finished Kennan—Read Tolstoi.

19. Th.

Wrote to Mr Galton—Rev. E. Edminson—Rev. Dr. Wright—Spottiswoodes. Revised Dante revises. Comm. on Clergy Bill & H. of C. 12–7½.[2] Conferred with Mr Fowler—J. Morley—Att. Gen.—Campbell Bannerman—The Speaker—Sir W.H. Attended Fool's Paradise[3] at the Garrick. Saw S.L.

20. Fr.

Wrote to Hon G. Curzon—Mr Wilkes—H. Brown—Mrs Henniker. H. of C. 2¼–4½.[4] Saw S.L.—A. Morley—Mr Sexton—Mr Guinness Rogers—Sir H.J.—Sir G. Trevelyan—Mr Colman—Mr Foljambe—J. Morley—Sir C. Russell. Twelve to dinner. Read Tolstoi's Boris (finished)—St Michael's Eve.[5] Drive with C.

21. Sat.

Wrote to Mr Wilkins—Rev. Ballachay[6]—J.T. Page—and minutes. Saw S.L.—Mr A. Galton—Messrs Hutton & Martin (Scotch Disestabl.)—Mr Dillon MP.—Mr B. Currie—Mr A.M. cum Mr Labouchere.[7] Worked much on Irish Local Govt Bill. Twelve to dinner. Drove to Dollis afterwards. Read St Michael's Eve—and [blank.]

22. 5 S.E.

Ch. mg. Aft. prayers at Dollis Hill. Callers in aftn. Read Vickers on the True Jesus[8]—Vance Smith, Bible & Theol.[9]—Armenische Kirche.[10] Saw Sir A. Clark: who reported well of me.

---

[1] Plural voting bill; 4 *H* 4. 1220.
[2] Questions; intervened on Irish local government; 4 *H* 4. 1343.
[3] With John Hare.
[4] Irish local government; 4 *H* 4. 1469.
[5] W. H. de Winton, *St Michael's eve*, 2v. (1892).
[6] Probably Arthur Watts Ballachey, curate in Lincoln.
[7] Gladstone lectured Labouchere on the unconstitutionality of various governmental manoeuvres; see E. Alexander, *Lord Chilston, Chief Whip* (1961), 233.
[8] J. Vickers, *The real Jesus . . . from a Jewish standpoint* (1891).
[9] G. V. Smith, *The Bible and its theology* (1892).
[10] A. Der-Mikelian, *Die Armenische Kirche* (1892).

23. M. [London]

Off at ten. Wrote to Mr (Surgeon) Parke.[1] Sat near 6 hours on Clergy Immorality Committee[2]—then H. of C. to $7\frac{1}{2}$.[3] Saw S.L.—A.M.—J.M. Dined at Mr C.
Bannerman's. Read Sappho & Phaon—and [blank.]

24. Tu.

Wrote to Mr J. Gray—Messrs Macmillan—Mr Archer—Mr Taylor Innes—&
minutes. Saw S.L.—A.M.—J.M.—Ld V. Cavendish[4]—Duchess of Abercorn—Mr
Rendel—Ld Lathom—The Speaker. H. of C. $2\frac{3}{4}$–$7\frac{1}{4}$ and 11–$12\frac{1}{4}$. Spoke a long
hour on Irish Govt Bill.[5] Read Hoskens's Dramas[6]—Williams Autobiogr.[7]

25. Wed.

Wrote to J. Ellaby—Lady Aberdeen—Rev. Page—Mr W.H. Rideing—Miss Little-
johns. Revised proof on S.G. Thomas.[8] Read Brodrick[9]—Williams. Saw S.L.—
A.M.—J.M.—F.L. Gower. Visited Canon [T. J.] Rowsell,[10] who is deeply afflicted,
all the light hidden from him. Dined at Ld Compton's. Conversation with Lady
C.—Miss Montgomery—Mr Bret Harte. H. of C. $4\frac{3}{4}$–$6\frac{1}{4}$.[11]

26. Ascension.

Chapel Royal. A noble sermon from the Bp—and H.C. H. of C. $3\frac{1}{2}$–$7\frac{1}{4}$.[12] Dined at
Mr B. Currie's. Saw S.L.—Sir W. Harcourt 1 1 1—Sir C. Russell—Sir A. Lyall.
Wrote to Tupper—Durton—Harris. Read Newman[13]—Fitzgerald.[14]

27. Frid.

Wrote to E.D. Morgan—J.A. Pickworth—C.S. Cooper—Mad. Novikoff—Mr A.
Balfour[15]—Rev. E.R. Palmer—A.W. Hutton. Saw Lady Waterford's works at Ld
Brownlow's. They are wonderful. Saw S.L.—A. Morley—Ld Belmore—Count

[1] Thomas Heazle Parke, 1857–93; African explorer (with Stanley) and surgeon-major.
[2] Meeting of unprecedented length of the Commons' Standing Cttee. on Law to discuss the
Clergy Discipline (Immorality) Bill; *D.N.*, 24 May 1892, 3f.
[3] Irish local government; $4H$ 4. 1537.
[4] Victor Christian William Cavendish, 1868–1938; heir presumptive to the dukedom 1891;
liberal unionist M.P. W. Derbyshire 1891–1908; 9th duke of Devonshire 1908.
[5] Attacking aspects of the bill and commenting on the 1886 proposals; $4H$ 4. 1691.
[6] J. D. Hosken, *Phaon and Sappho*; a play (1891).
[7] *The autobiography of Isaac Williams*, ed. Sir G. Prevost (1892).
[8] Resumption of his review of the biography of the steel-process inventor (see 17 Apr., 5 May
91); the review appears not to have been published.
[9] Perhaps G. C. Brodrick, *Memorials of Merton* (1885).
[10] See 3 May 50.
[11] Registration bill; $4H$ 4. 1840.
[12] Questions; misc. business; $4H$ 4. 1892.
[13] J. H. Newman, *The idea of a University* (1873).
[14] P. H. Fitzgerald, *The entertainer* (1892?).
[15] Balfour wrote the previous day reporting his conversation with Harcourt in which he
announced the Dissolution; for Gladstone's acknowledgement and comments on parliamentary
arrangements, see Add MS 44514, ff. 303.

Münster—Dowager Duchess of Marlb.—Lady Harcourt. Read Byzance[1]—Newman on Univv. Dined at A. Morley's.

28. Sat. [Hatchlands, Guildford]

Wrote to . . . . and Professor Dougherty. Off at 9: Hatchlands 10.45.[2] Drive in evg. Read Darwin & after D.[3]—A la cour de Napoleon III[4]—Art[icle]s on Manning—Freeman[5]—and [blank.] Backgammon with Mr R[endel].

29. S. aft Asc.

Ockham Ch mg (capital choir: saw S. Neville)[6] Crandon in evg. Read I. Williams (finished)—D'Alvilla Origin of Religion.[7]

30. M. [London]

Wrote to Mons. Tchirny—Jas Westell—Miss Dawe—W.T. Stead[8]—Hugh Dellow. Back to London at 11.45. Saw S.L.—A. Morley—Mr Rendell (Scott's Bank)—do (Ld Granville's estate)—Chancr of Exchr on his Bank Scheme. Read A la cour de Nap. III—and [blank.]

31. Tu.

Wrote to . . . . . and . . . . . . Worked on books & papers. Worked on questions for speech. Spoke $1\frac{1}{4}$ hour Meml Hall.[9] H. of C. 3–5$\frac{1}{4}$.[10] Read Oxford (Boase)[11] and do Rex Rudyard.[12]

Wed. Jun. 1. 1892.

Wrote to Mr Fairweather—B.J. Field—Rev. Briggs[13]—C. Hodges—Rev. E.S. Ffoulkes—Mr Bridge—Rev. Dr Moore. Worked much on books & papers. Saw S.L.—Rev. Mr Palmer—A. Morley—Mr Leveson Gower—J. Morley—Jas Westell—A.W. Hutton—Ld Herschell—Abp. of Canterbury—Mrs Benson—Ld Spencer. Fourteen to dinner: small evening party. Read Castle Desolation[14]—Moeurs Irlandaises.[15]

[1] J. Lombard, *Byzance* (1890).
[2] Rendel's country house.
[3] G. J. Romanes, *Darwin and after Darwin* (1892).
[4] I. de Taisey-Chatenoy, *A la cour de Napoléon III* (1891).
[5] Perhaps the last volume of E. A. Freeman, *Historical essays*, 4v. (1871–92).
[6] Seymour Neville, rector of Ockham.
[7] Count d'Avila, *Lectures on the origin and growth of the conception of God* (1892).
[8] See 4 May 92n.
[9] Addressing the London Liberal and Radical Union; *T.T.*, 1 June 1892, 7c.
[10] Misc. business; 4*H* 5. 382.
[11] C. W. Boase, *Oxford* (1887).
[12] Untraced.
[13] Perhaps Cornelius Briggs, vicar of St. Thomas, Bradford.
[14] W.C. Dawe, *Mount Desolation. An Australian romance* (1892).
[15] Untraced.

2. *Th.* [*Hawarden*]

Wrote to Canon Luccock—Prof. Romanes BP—Mr Cowan—Sir J. Lacaita BP—J.
Harris—Mr P. Campbell—Isbisters—Sir C. Dalrymple[1]—A.W. Hutton—Mr
Channing MP—Dr Ginsburg—Sig. Castelar—J. Otham—Ld Rosebery—M.
Menpes[2]—Ld Acton. Wrote Preface to Speeches.[3] Saw S.L.—Mr Stuart MP—Mr
A. Morley. 3¾-9¼. To Hn. Rectory. Read Moeurs Irlandaises—Jusserand, 'A
French Ambassador' &c.[4] Backgammon with the Rector.

3. *Frid.*

Ch. 8½ A.M. Wrote to Mr A.G. Fullerton—Mr G. Russell—Bp of Bedford—Mr
H.W. West[5]—J.L. Clarke—Central News (Tel.) Worked on Oriental Congr.
Addr.[6] Read Moeurs Irlandaises—Clarke on Deluge (G. Words)[7]—Colquhoun &
Wassa on Pelasgi[8]—K. Blind on Schliemann.[9] Backgammon with S.

4. *Sat.*

Ch. 8½ A.M. Wrote to T.J. Canadien—Mr Mather MP—J.P. Lewis—A. Morley
MP.—W.T. Stead—Rev. H.P. Hughes—Mr Rideing—Mr Fairweather. Worked a
little on O[lympian] R[eligion]: also on O.C. Address. Met the Volunteers at Mr
Hurlburt's. Finished Moeurs Irlandaises—read Mather on Labour q.[10]—Jusserand's Ambassador.

5. *Whits.*

Ch mg with H.C. & evg. Excellent sermons from S. Read D'Alvilla Hibbert L.—
Book of Deuteronomy—Morrison on Crime in N.C.[11]—The Disintegrator.[12]
Walk with S., H. and H. Tea at C. Dorothy[13] delightful: and Mary's eye we trust
really mending.

[1] Sir Charles Dalrymple, 1839–1916, tory M.P. Bute 1868–85; beaten by Gladstone in Midlothian
1885 (see 28 Nov. 85); M.P. for Ipswich 1886–1906.
[2] Mortimer Menpes, artist with 'a very slight acquaintance' sent a portrait etching of Manning;
Add MS 44515, f. 1.
[3] Preface dated 'June 1892' to vol. x of the edition of his speeches by A. W. Hutton and H. J.
Cohen; see 26 Apr. 90.
[4] J. A. A. J. Jusserand, *A French ambassador at the Court of Charles II* (1892).
[5] Henry Wyndham West, Q.C. and M.P., dealing with potential bankruptcy of Granville's estates
(£60,000 loan being needed to save them); Add MS 44515, f. 7. A plan for settlement 'generously
initiated by the duke of Devonshire' was vetoed by Bertram Currie; Add MS 44516, f. 66.
[6] See 5 Sept. 92.
[7] *Good Words* (June 1892), 411.
[8] Authors' names scrawled; work untraced.
[9] K. Blind, 'Life and labours of Schliemann', *National Review*, xvi. 734 (February 1891).
[10] Perhaps an early draft of W. Mather, 'Labour and the hours of labour', *C.R.*, lxii. 609 (November 1892).
[11] W. D. Morrison, 'The increase of crime', *N.C.*, xxxi. 950 (June 1892).
[12] A. Morgan and C. Brown, *Disintegrator. A romance* (1892).
[13] Dorothy Drew, his grand-daughter.

6. M.

Ch. 8½ A.M. Wrote to W.H.G. Flood[1]—E. Menken—J.C. Humphreys—H.J. Cohen—Rev. Dr. Moore—A. Galton. Saw L. Cavendish on St Thomas Toxt. Worked a little on O.R. & O.C. Addr. Read Mount Desolation—Jusserand—Disintegrator. Worked at St Deiniol's. Backgammon with S.

7. Tu.

Ch 8½ AM & H.C. Wrote to Ld Mayor L. (Tel.)—C. Waddie—D. Macgregor—H.N.G.—F.G. Edwards—W.T. Stead—J. Romans [sic]. Worked at St Deiniol's. Met Warwickshire party at Castle—a few sentences.[2] Worked on OR & OC addr. Read Jusserand (finished)—Mount Desolation.

8. Wed.

Ch. 8½ AM. Wrote to Sir H. Verney—T.J. Mason—H.N.G. Wrote Mem. on Granville's affairs.[3] A sad business. Worked 'some' on O.R. Worked at St Deiniol's. Drive & conversation with C. Read Jessop & Rees in NC[4]—Persian Tales[5]—Lyte & Hallam on Oxford and Paris[6]—Persian Tales—The greatest possibility.[7] Backgammon with S.

9. Th.

Ch. 8¼ A.M.—Much examination with reference to proposed rood loft & gates. Wrote to Hon. Secs Dublin—M. Jusserand—S. Buxton MP.—Mr Maddison—R.T. Reed MP.[8]—Mr Matheson (Oxf.)—Rev. Mr Blogg[9]—T.J. Gullick—Miss V. Smith—Author of Life's greatest Possibil[it]y. Worked on Books at the Castle. Read Life's Greatest &c. (finished)—Esther Van Homrigh[10]—Persian Tales—Klein's Address.[11] 11–12½. Meeting of River Dee Trustees. Worked on books & papers. Backgammon with S. Saw Lucy [Cavendish] on St Thomas Toxteth.

10. Fr.

Ch. 8½ A.M. Wrote to Mr W.W. Henry (U.S.)[12]—Mr A. Holborow—S.V. Klein—Mr W.A. Colmige—J. Wilson—A. Morley MP—J.T. Calton—Mr Mundella—

[1] William Henry Gratton Flood of Stoke on Trent, unreliable historian of Irish folkmusic; on voluntary schools; Hawn P.

[2] T.T., 8 June 1892, 8b.

[3] Add MS 44774, f. 27; see 3 June 92n.

[4] N.C., xxxi. 964, 950 (June 1892).

[5] J. H. McCarthy, ed., The thousand and one days. Persian tales, 2v. (1892).

[6] H. C. M. Lyte, A history of the University of Oxford (1886).

[7] Life's greatest possibility. An essay in spiritual realism (1892).

[8] Robert Threshie Reid, 1846–1923; liberal M.P. Hereford 1880–5, Dumfries 1886–1905; solicitor general 1894, attorney general 1894–5; lord chancellor 1905–12; cr. Baron Loreburn 1906.

[9] Henry Birdwood Blogg, vicar of Frodsham, Cheshire.

[10] M. L. Woods, Esther Vanhomrigh, 3v. (1891–2).

[11] Untraced.

[12] William Wirt Henry, 1831–1900; President of the American Historical Association; had sent his Life, correspondence and speeches of Patrick Henry, 3v. (1891); Hawn P.

J. Hilton—C.R. Brown. Worked on books at St D[einiol's] and Castle. Conclave (with Mr Douglas) on Memorial to dearest W.[1] Read E. Van Homrigh—Ulster Volunteers of 1783[2]—and [blank.] Backgammon with S.

11. Sat.

Ch. 8½ A.M. Wrote to Chester Stationmaster—Mr Bryce—Sir E. Saunders—Mr Budge—Miss Swanwick—Ld Acton—Sir E. Watkin—Mrs Sands—Mr Trumbell, U.S., Tel.—Mr Summers MP.[3]—Rev. Hughes—W. Gardiner—H. Pierce—Mr J.J. Bisgood—Rev. Mr Harshaw—A. Brownfield—Rev. Bainton. Saw Baron Halkett[4]—Conclave with Mr Douglas—11-12 Mr Cohen with proofs of Speeches.[5] Read Esther Vanhomrigh—Jacobite Hist. War 1689[6]—and other books. Backgammon with S.

12. Trin. S.

H.C. 8½—Ch. 11 A.M. and [blank] P.M. Wrote to Rev. R.R. Bromage[7]—A. Morley MP.—H.S. Newman—Mr Ch. Waddie—Mr Sikes[8]—Mr Cameron. Read Fry on the Social Quest.[9]—Mother of all Churches[10]—Romanes's Darwin[11]—Lyons on Infallibility(!)[12]—Bray & Essay on RCm in Engl.[13]—Mason on Dogmatic Faith.[14]

13. M. [London]

Ch. 8½ A.M. A reluctant farewell to S. and his wife, both so kind. Wrote to Miss Phillimore—Mr Gullick—J.T. Jackson—M. Friesenhaben. Reached H. of C. at 4 (4-6¼).[15] Saw A. Morley—Sir W.H.—J.M.—C. Parker—Mr [H.J.] Roby—Ly Rothschild—Mr Armitstead—H.N.G. Read The Venetians[16]—Clayden Hist Coalition[17]—Six Years of Tory Government.[18]

---

[1] John Douglas, of Douglas and Fordham, architects in Chester, designed the alabaster and mosaic tablet memorial to W. H. Gladstone in the Gladstone Memorial Chapel in Hawarden Church; it was 'placed by his father and mother'.
[2] C. Lennox, duke of Richmond, *Letter from the Committee of Ulster Volunteers to the Duke of Richmond; the Duke of Richmond's answer; together with his Bill for Parliamentary Reform* (1783).
[3] William Summers, 1853–93; liberal M.P. Stalybridge 1880–5, Huddersfield 1886–93.
[4] Apparently staying, but not in the Visitor's Book; see 25 June 92n.
[5] See 26 Apr. 90, 2 May 92.
[6] *A Jacobite narrative of the war in Ireland, 1688–1691*, edited by J. T. Gilbert (1892).
[7] Richard Raikes Bromage, vicar of Frome; temperance reformer.
[8] Francis Henry Sikes, 1862–1943, headmaster of Hawarden Grammar School 1891–3; photographer and natural historian; sent a photograph and a song; Hawn P.
[9] Article reprinted in T. C. Fry, *A social policy for the church* (1893).
[10] Untraced.
[11] See 28 May 92.
[12] D. Lyons, *Christianity and infallibility, both or neither* (1891).
[13] Possibly *Roman Catholicism: being an historical and legal review* (1851).
[14] A. J. Mason, *Faith of the gospel* (1892).
[15] Misc. business; 4*H* 5. 922.
[16] M. E. Braddon, *The Venetians. A novel*, 3v. (1892).
[17] P. W. Clayden, *England under the Coalition* (1892).
[18] Perhaps Clayden's 'Five years of liberal and six years of conservative government' (1880?).

14. Tu.

Wrote to Mr Billson[1]—Circular l. for P.A. & C.N.[2]—Mayor of Darlington—Rev. Mr Rogers—R. Johnston—C.G. Hodgkinson. Saw H.N.G. (Hn Inst)—S.L.—E. Wickham—M. Jusserand—A. Morley—Mr Redington: long conversation on Irish difficulties. Dined at Lucy's. Tea at Argyll Lodge & much conversation with the Duke. Read Esther Vanhomrigh—Report on Railway Labour.

15. Wed.

Wrote to T.J. Gullick—Mr Rendel (& dft)—J. Auld—Lady Russell—J.J. Hitchings. Read E. Vanhomrigh. [3]Dined with Mr Sands. Two women accosted me [R]. H. of C. 4–5½.[4] Saw S.L.—E. Hamilton—A. Morley—Mr Agnew—Dr Leitner—Mr Mundella—Mr Illingworth *cum* A. Morley—Mr Marjoribanks (Midlothian)—Mr Astor—Mrs Astor[5]—Sir W.H.

16. Th.

Wrote to G. Russell—Sir E. Jenkinson—Rev. S.E.G.—Archdn Denison. 2–4. Deputation on the Eight Hours Bill. Stiff![6] Saw S.L.—A. Morley—Mr Lefevre—Sir L. Playfair—Sir W. Harcourt—Mr Fowler—Ld Spencer. Finished Esther Van Homrigh—*a book*. Read La Cité Antique[7]—And other books. Dined at Ld Spencer's. Evg. party. H. of C. early.

17. Fr.

Wrote to Mr Roby MP—Isbisters—and [blank.] Long conversation with Harcourt on the future. H. of C. 3½–5½.[8] Saw S.L.—A.M.—J.M.—Bp of Rochester—Prof. Pelham—Ld Acton—and others. Dined at Mr Bryce's. Accosted [R]. Read Confessions d'un Jeune Anglais[9]—& diversa.

Sir W. H[arcourt] June 17. 92.[10]

1. As to his own position.
2. As to numbers in Cabinet.
3. As to men.
   agt. Stansfield [*sic*]
   wishes Vernon U. Secship.
       Spencer Admty but admits spending depts. shd. be in H. of C.

---

[1] See 10 Dec. 67.
[2] Regret at being unable to reply to all the requests from liberals for visits, speeches and letters; *T.T.*, 15 June 1892, 7e.
[3] This and next phrase added at bottom of page.
[4] Irish education; 4*H* 5. 1193.
[5] William Waldorf Astor, 1848–1919 (lawyer, diplomat and novelist) and his wife Mary (d. 1894).
[6] Deputation, arranged by G. Shipton, from the London Trades Council. Gladstone in the course of close questioning remarked: 'I am not the instrument by which your purpose can take effect for I should disgrace myself if I abandoned the great question to which I have devoted weeks and months in endeavouring to stimulate the country'; *T.T.*, 17 June 1892, 10c.
[7] N. D. Fustel de Coulange, *La Cité antique*, tr. (1871) as *Aryan civilization*.
[8] Questioned Balfour on date of the dissolution and its parliamentary arrangements; 4*H* 5. 1470.
[9] Untraced.   [10] Holograph; Add MS 44774, f. 29.

on (2) thinks I must work by minor combinations.
A. Morley for Cabinet
doubts Ripon for Indian Secship.

Same day.
J. Morley: *fast* to Irish Secship.
will consider further as to Ab[erdee]n.

18. Sat.

Wrote to Mr McColl—Ld Northbrook. Saw S.L.—Ld Herschell—A. Morley—do cum Mr Byles: tough morsels. Worked on Ulster debate & materials. $2\frac{1}{4}$–$5\frac{1}{2}$. To Clapham: at Rev. Mr [Guinness] Rogers's spoke 1 h. on Ulster branch of Irish question.[1] Much enthusiasm. Read Lola Montes[2]—Grey Friars in Oxford[3]—Periodicals. 13 *vice* 14 to dinner. Saw Mr Budge—Ld Acton—Ld J. Bowen.

19. 1 S. Trin.

Chapel Royal at noon. St James's evg. Sermons excellent. Read Ld Kelvin on Energy[4]—France & the Jews[5]—Price Hughes on Wesley[6]—Two voices of children[7]—Grey Friars in Oxford.

20. M.

Wrote to Mrs Frethey—Ly Breadalbane—Mrs Th.—Bp of St Asaph—Mr Thos Gee[8]—Ld E. Fitzmaurice—Ld Rosebery—Mr Fred. Howard—Mr Dugdale—Mr Schnadhorst—Mr W. Taylor—and minutes. Saw Sir J. Lacaita—S.L.—Lucy—Mr Rendel—A. Morley—do *cum* Sir W.H. Children's party H. House. Tea with Lady Stanley. Interesting conversation. Dined at Mr Stewart Gladstone's.[9] Saw Mrs Garrivon (U.S.) & Sir Walter Riddell (near 82).[10] Read Greyfriars in Oxford—Anarchie Francaise.[11]

21. Tu.

Wrote to Jas Knowles—R. Cameron—J. Murray—Mr Menken—S.E.G.—Rev. Mr Gough—J. Dobbie. Ld Acton & Lacaita came to breakfast. Saw J. Murray (to

---

[1] *T.T.*, 20 June 1892, 12a.
[2] *Autobiography and lectures of Lola Montez*, ed. C. C. Burr (1858).
[3] A. G. Little, *The Grey Friars in Oxford* (1892).
[4] Lord Kelvin, 'On the dissipation of energy', *F.R.*, lvii. 313 (March 1892).
[5] Untraced.
[6] H. P. Hughes, 'John Wesley', *N.C.*, xxix. 477 (March 1891).
[7] Untraced.
[8] Thomas Gee, 1815–98; Welsh nationalist publisher, disestablishmentarian and Methodist minister.
[9] Samuel Steuart Gladstone of Capenoch, 1837–1909; s. of T. S. Gladstone (see 30 Apr. 27); or, perhaps more likely (given the presence of Riddell), Robert Steuart Gladstone, 1839–1909, of Tenterden, s. of W. Gladstone (see 31 July 32).
[10] Sir Walter Buchanan Riddell, 1810–August 1892; recorder of Tenterden, later a judge; 10th bart.
[11] *L'Anarchie Française* (1892).

republish Irish tracts).[1] 12 to 1½. Long & interesting conversation with Messrs McCarthy, Sexton & Dillon. Saw S.L.—A.M.—Sir A. Clark. Saw the Dudley Pictures. Gaikwar of Baroda[2] came; pleased me much. Dined at Mr Foljambe's. Saw S.L.—A. Morley—Adm. Egerton:—F. Leveson. Read Le Secret de Benoit.[3]

22. Wed.

Wrote to Ld Acton—Herbert J.G.—W. Downing—Rob. Gladstone—G. Green-lees—N. Maclennan—H. Roberts—Mr Summers MP.—W. Budden—Rev. Dr Ginsburg—S. Erskine—Mr Knowles—W.H. Rideing—Mr Murray. Saw S.L.—A. Morley—Mrs Morton—Lady Camoys—Sir C. Russell. Worked hard 3-7½ (a short drive in the midst) to write my Election Address.[4] Dined at Viscount Stair's.[5]

23. Th.

Wrote to Mr Murray—Mr Illingworth—Mr Henry—Mr Campbell WS—R. Mowatt—H. Macpherson[6]—R.W. Perks—Rev. J. Algar—Canon M'Coll—Mr MacCulloch—Mr Clowes Tel. Saw S.L.—H.N.G.—Mr Adams Acton—Lady Brownlow—Mr A. Morley l.l.—Canon M'Coll. Revised & dispatched Address. Dined at Lady Sydney's. Conversation with Ly Colebrook, Miss Wemyss, Mr Marshall, Ld Acton. Waterford pictures. Read Macpherson on W.E.G.—Prohibition (U.S.) and [blank.]

24. Fr.

Wrote to E. Johnson PP—Mrs Correa BP—Rev. Harwood—Mrs Bromley—Author of Psychothen.[7] Saw Ld Acton—S.L.—A. Morley—Canon M'Coll—Sir A. West—Mr Henri—Mr E. Hamilton—Mr Erskine[8]—Lady Lansdowne. Read Memorials of Johnson—Dumfriess Families[9]—and [blank.] Worked on letters papers & books. Opera in evg with the Brasseys. Mme. Calvy[10] very considerable indeed.

---

[1] *Special aspects of the Irish question. A series of reflections in and since 1886. Collected and reprinted* (1892); published by Murray.
[2] The Maharajah Gaekwar of Baroda was on a visit to England, dining with the Queen etc.; he was installed 1875 following his father's trial for poisoning the English resident.
[3] Untraced.
[4] In *T.T.*, 24 June 1892, 7a.
[5] See 12 May 70.
[6] Hector Carsewell Macpherson had sent his *The Rt. Hon. W. E. Gladstone: political career* (1892); no copy traced. See H. Macpherson, *Hector Macpherson* (1925), 11: 'Naturally Gladstone made a strong appeal to him, and the great statesman was the subject of his first pamphlet'.
[7] *Psycothen, or Reflections in verse on some of the graver aspects of human life. By Laicus* (1892); the anon. and unknown author had doubtless sent a copy.
[8] R. J. Erskine, s. of 5th Baron Erskine; an 'ardent liberal' who had had 'flirtations with the new Jacobite movement, but he is repentant & reformed'; letter of introduction from T. G. Law, Add MS 44515, f. 65.
[9] C. L. Johnstone, *Historical families of Dumfries-shire* (1889).
[10] Mme. Calvé in 'Cavalleria Rusticana', at Covent Garden.

25. Sat. [Hawarden][1]

11¾–4¼. To Chester. Drove through crowded streets to the Liberal Club. Fifty yards from the door I was attracted by seeing a middle aged bony woman fling something with great force and skill about two yards off me. The next moment I felt a heavy blow sideways on my left & only serviceable eye. After a few minutes of rest & assurance from two casual doctors I went on & made my speech, short of an hour, only reading when needful with the utmost difficulty.[2] Afterwards Dr Grainger[3] the chosen oculist found the surface grazed & bound up the eye to heal. The hardbaked little gingerbread say 1½ inch across glanced off against the nose & cut the skin. I remained much in bed & in the dark till Tues. evg. I thank God for a great escape. Wrote to Dr Marsham.[4] Read Prohibition (U.S.)—Memorials of Johnson (U.S.). . . . Saw many in Chester.

26. 2 S. Trin.

See above. Litany by repetition. Helen & Mama read me services. Great opportunity to confirm the life by faith not by sight. Wrote by dictation to Mr Lough[5]—Beale—Schnadhorst—Tel. to C. News & Press Assocn. Composed inscription for the dear stone in Ch.[6] Saw Gerty—S.—Mr A[rmitstead]—HJG— Helen—Dr Grainger—children.

27. M.

As yesterday. Tell to C.N. and P.A. Rose at luncheon. Backgammon with Mr Armitstead. Groped [sic] some things into a sort of order. Wrote to Mr Black.

28.

As yesterday. Half blind sorting of papers for journey. Dr Gr[anger] again much pleased, healing complete. HNG came: the Commr in Chief. Helen read us Guinevere:[7] how great it is.

[1] Entries until *ca.* 30 June written up late.
[2] 'During Mr. Gladstone's progress through the streets there was a most regrettable occurrence. Baron Halkett, who was in the carriage with Mr Gladstone, states that he saw a woman raise her hand and throw something with great violence at Mr. Gladstone. It struck him in the corner of his left eye and inflicted a slight wound, and caused bleeding of the nose. Mr. Gladstone immediately put his hand over his eye and fell back into his carriage, and said to Baron Halkett, "It was a cruel thing to do. I hope some notice will be taken of it". The substance thrown fell to the knees of Mr James Tomkinson, and turned out to be a hard gingerbread nut . . . Dr Grainger found that the missile had gone across the left eye, inflicting a wound on the corner a little to the inner side of the pupil, and it then struck upon the bridge of the nose, inflicting a slight wound, which bled a little. Mr. Gladstone remarked to the doctor that he had never seen a woman throw with such spite and energy . . .'; *T.T.*, 27 June 1892, 12a. The woman was reported to have disappeared into the crowd.
[3] Farington Marsden Granger (sometimes Grainger), eye surgeon at Chester General Infirmary. He advised Gladstone several times on his deteriorating eyesight, especially in 1894.
[4] Robert Marsham, on origins of the tag 'Vox Populi Vox Dei'; Add MS 44515, f. 70.
[5] On West Islington election; *T.T.*, 28 June 1892, 10d.
[6] i.e. the memorial in Hawarden Church to W. H. Gladstone.
[7] By Tennyson in *Idylls of the King*; see 17 June 59.

29. *Wed.* [*Dalmeny House*][1]

9.20–7 P.M. journey in dark spectacles. Small speeches all the way.[2] Very large numbers in Edinburgh. Hospitable Dalmeny once more. Saw Mr Campbell.[3]

30. *Th.*

Worked much on papers: eye again in use. To Edinb. at 4.30. Spoke 1 h. 25 m. in Music Hall.[4] Great enthusiasm outdoors and in. Saw Acton—Rosebery—Mr H. Ivory—and others. Read Miller on the Heavens.[5]

Dalmeny.
Frid. Jul 1. 1892.

Wrote to Sir J. Carmichael—Mr Broadhurst[6]—Mr Baxter—Sir H. Davey. Tel.— Mr Bayley Potter Tel.—Mr Percy Bunting—& minutes. Worked on Election papers. Read Miller on the Heavens—England on morals of the Ancients.[7] Conversations: Acton—West[8]—Rosebery—and others. Though the rule is against company we came to dine fourteen.

2. *Sat.*

Wrote to Mr P. Bunting. Worked up materials for Glasgow. Read Denver Irish in Britain.[9] 1¼–7. By train from Dalmeny station to Glasgow. Vast & enthusiastic masses in our two street processions. Spoke in the Theatre 1 h. 20 m. Audience 3000 or more.[10] Conversation with Morley Acton & others. After my speech, of which the physical effort was very considerable, I thought small thin flat scales were descending upon me: & afterwards observed with some discomfort that there was a fluffy object floating in the fluid of my serviceable eye. It incommoded reading without preventing it; but if this first indication should lead to others it might be grossly inconvenient. I determined to forswear for the time continuous reading and limit my eyework on papers & material for speeches to '*le strict necessaire*'. This also is well, in the hands of God.

3. *3 S. Trin.*

Went to Church at Queensferry (Ex-Convent of Carmelites) and to Holy C. Walk with Acton: and with Rosebery. Conversations also with Donaldson[11] and

---

[1] Rosebery's house by Queensferry, W. of Edinburgh.
[2] In *T.T.*, 30 June 1892, 10a.
[3] P. W. Campbell, the Midlothian liberal agent; see 17 Feb. 79.
[4] *T.T.*, 1 July 1892, 12a.
[5] See 9 Dec. 83.
[6] Supporting Broadhurst for Nottingham, where he was opposed by an Eight Hours candidate; *T.T.*, 4 July 1892, 6d; broadsheet version in Add MS 44515, f. 86.
[7] G. England, *An enquiry into the morals of the ancients* (1735).
[8] Sir A. West, now acting as his secretary.
[9] J. Denvir, *The Irish in Britain, from the earliest times to the fall and death of Parnell* (1892).
[10] *T.T.*, 4 July 1892, 4b.
[11] Sir J. Donaldson; see 4 July 79.

West.[1] Some secular, some not. Much conversation with Morley. I reluctantly put reading aside.

Discuss with J. Morley. July 2–3. 92.[2]

✓ Ridgway
✓ Sir R. Hamilton
✓ Aberdeen
✓ Acton
✓ Rosebery
✓ Spencer
✓ Harcourt
  Labouchere. Office. 'Truth'.

4. M.

Wrote to Mr Richardson—Mr Pearson (Dante).[3] My letters are now much managed by directions to H[arry] & H[elen] both excellent. Conversation with Rosebery. The contingencies before us now become the obtrusive subject.[4] Worked on materials for speeches. $1\frac{3}{4}$–$7\frac{1}{2}$. Tour to Stow—meeting & speech of 10 minutes—then to Gore Bridge, saw deputation of miners and at meeting spoke 50 minutes on Labour.[5] In the evening the telegrams of the first day's contests came in. At first they were even too rosy: afterwards toned down but the general result satisfactory, pointing to a gain in G. Britain of 80 seats. This may be exceeded.

5. Tu.

Wrote to M. Josse Tel.—Mr Pease (flag of distress, minor[it]y). Dipped a little: *only* dipped. Election returns unsatisfactory. Wrote up journal. Saw A. West. Worked on materials. By rail first, & then a carriage progress in E. Midlothian of 25 miles, ending with speech of an hour at Dalkeith tea &c and return $1\frac{1}{4}$ to $8\frac{1}{2}$.[6] C.G. suffering.

6. Wed.

Wrote to Mr Strahan—Mr L. Morris—Mr Byles—Mr Blackie. Worked on materials. Dipped into Michel (France & Scotland).[7] Read Blackie on 1707.[8] Conversation with Mr T.G. Law—Principal Rainy—Ld Rosebery. The returns of

[1] West pressed Marjoribanks as chief whip and Spencer for the Admiralty; West, *P.D.*, 35.
[2] Holograph; Add MS 44774, f. 34.
[3] Edward Pearson of Wilmslow; Add MS 44515, f. 80.
[4] The Gladstones' stay at Dalmeny was unhappy, each of them being ill, and Rosebery in a black mood. Rosebery had decided not to take office and evaded Gladstone's various attempts to raise questions of policies and offices; James, *Rosebery*, 236 ff.
[5] *T.T.*, 5 July 1892, 12a.
[6] Speech on Scottish home rule and questions addressed to him on it by G. Romanes; *T.T.*, 6 July 1892, 11a.
[7] See 17 July 62.
[8] J. S. Blackie, *The union of 1707 and its results; a plea for Scottish Home Rule* (1892).

tonight were a little improved: but the burden on me personally is serious: a small Liberal majority being the heaviest weight I can well be called to bear. But all is with God. His blessed will be done. Work with Harry. $6\frac{1}{2}$-$8\frac{3}{4}$. To Corstorphine. Speech of 40 m., & heckling of a trumpery character.[1]

7. Th.

Wrote to Mrs Matheson—P.H. Brown—Mr Caine. Prudentially read little. Worked upon materials. Work with Harry (as usual) who is admirable. So is Helen. Interesting conversation with Ld Rosebery. Saw Mr Law—Mr Ivory—Dr Casenove. $3\frac{1}{4}$-$7\frac{1}{4}$. To West Calder. Excellent hall, & meeting. Spoke $1\frac{1}{4}$ hour.[2]

8. Fr.

Wrote a very strong letter, to & for Mr Jacks!! So revolves the wheel of Fortune.[3] Wrote to Mr Caine (Tel.)—J. Murray (NB)—J. Wallop—Canon Wilberforce—C. News—Press Assn. Drive with Rosebery. Saw Ld R. *cum* Mr Ivory—Dr Casenove. Read a little of Coleridge's Letters to Stuart.[4] Being almost shut out from reading in order to give my eye a fair chance, I turn to writing which works it much less, and I made today an actual beginning of that quasi Autobiography which Acton has so strongly urged upon me.[5] Also wrote notes respecting St Deiniol's.

9. Sat.

Wrote to Mr Bryce—Schnadhorst Tel.—Mr Clough—Mr Thomson. Letter business with Helen. Pursued my Autobiogr. Notes: also sketched a provisional plan of policy for the future.[6] The Elections still bear a lingering character. The pressure has been great. My hope that the struggle if sharp would be short, has melted away. But an actual minority, while a personal relief to me would have been worse in a public view. It has been a week of many searchings of heart. $3\frac{3}{4}$ hours of drive through the County for exhibition. Saw Sir J.C. Gibson—Ld Acton—Mr Ivory—Mr Campbell—Mr M. Fergusson. Read a very little of Sharman Crawford's noteworthy pamphlet of 1833.[7]

[1] Speech on minor points, e.g. marriages in Malta; heckled on the 'Plan of Campaign'; *T.T.*, 7 July 1892, 10a.

[2] On protection, and the eight hours day; *T.T.*, 8 July 1892, 5c.

[3] Letter successfully supporting W. Jacks (see 21 June 86n.) as liberal candidate for Stirlingshire. In 1886 Jacks had voted against the Home Rule Bill and Gladstone had successfully stood against him in Leith; see to Marjoribanks, 10, 13 July 86.

[4] S. T. Coleridge, *Letters... to Daniel Stuart* (1889).

[5] He began with 'some recollections of my infancy and earliest childhood'; *Autobiographica*, i. 13 and Add MS 44790, f. 5. Subsequent notes are also printed in that volume, mostly arranged in the chronology of Gladstone's life, not in the order written.

[6] See 20 July 92.

[7] Probably the reprinted pamphlet sent by Sharman Crawford's daughter (see 26 July 92n.); in 1833 W. Sharman Crawford published two pamphlets, 'A review of circumstances connected with the past and present state of the protestant and catholic interests in Ireland' and 'Trade of Ireland and repeal of the Union'. No copy of a reprint of either found, but probably the first. See B. A. Kennedy, 'Sharman Crawford's federal scheme for Ireland', in H. A. Cronne *et al.*, *Essays in British and Irish history* (1949).

10. *4 S. Trin.*

Queensferry Church at 11.30. Aftn service read at home. Wrote to Gerty G.—
Mr Morley—Mr S. Walker. Walk with the party among the splendid views of
New England so called. Saw E. Marjoribanks[1] & gave him full explanations—Ld
Acton—Mr Ivory—Mr Wallace. Dipped a little into Bp Morgan's Life.[2]

11. *M.*

Business with Harry. Wrote to Mr Cunningham—Rev. Mr Knowles—Rev.
S.E.G.—Jas Wooller—Sir A. West—Mr Harvey Morgan. $3\frac{1}{4}$–$8\frac{3}{4}$. To Penicuick,
speech over an hour, 30 m. by rail eighteen of village progress by road.[3] Thank
God all this is over. Worked on papers. Wrote Autob. Notes. Saw the Ld
Provost-Bailie Wallace[4]—and others in evg.

12. *Tu.*

Wrote to Mr Evans—Mr H.G. Reid MP.[5] Mr Armitstead came & our journey to
Deeside was settled. Wrote Autob. Notes: much. Conversations: with Ld Acton,
most anxious,[6] chiefly on Ld R. who is certainly a man not on the common
lines—with Ld R. himself glancing at the leadership—with J. Morley on the
future policy: most satisfactory—with Mr Ivory—Ld Young. Read a few pages
Coleridge.

13. *Wed.* [*Aberdeen*]

Wrote to Mr Stilly—Ld Spencer—Mr Crawford—A. Morley—Electors of Mid-
lothian. The 'Church' has pulled down my majority much beyond expectation.[7]
But this is a small matter. General prospects improve. Wrote Autob. Notes. Saw
A. Morley—Ld Rosebery—Mr Cowan—Mr Campbell. Off at 4.45. Aberdeen at
nine. Imperial hotel excellent. The reception by the crowd enthusiastic. Saw N.
News writer.

To LORD SPENCER, 13 July 1892.   Althorp MSS K8.
'Secret'.[8]

   I was indeed angry with myself for not having obtained an opportunity of full conversation with you before you left London. But as matters have thus far turned out the loss is
not so great, since the conversation would on my part have been conducted under
anticipations which have not been verified.

---

   [1] Marjoribanks was about to become chief whip, succeeding A. Morley.
   [2] W. Hughes, *The life... of Bishop William Morgan* (1891).
   [3] *T.T.*, 12 July 1892, 10a.
   [4] Reading uncertain.
   [5] Presumably Hugh Gilzean Reid, 1836–1911; liberal M.P. Aston 1885–6; defeated candidate
1892; owned newspapers in central Scotland.
   [6] Acton was already lobbying on his own behalf; West, *P.D.*, 36.
   [7] The Edinburghshire result was: Gladstone, 5845, Col. A. G. Wauchope, 5155. 'When the first
announcement was made that the majority was only 673 there was profound amazement'; *T.T.*, 14
July 1892, 7b.
   [8] Partly printed in *Spencer*, ii. 211.

The argument from the by-elections and the computations of our skilled and sober-minded friends at headquarters appeared to justify the expectation of a minimum majority of 80 or 90, probably rising into three figures. With such a majority we should have been very strong, and could have carried Home Rule into the House of Lords with a voice and impetus somewhat imperative. Our majority is now placed by Marjoribanks at 30, and though I do not abandon the hope of its coming near 40, yet it is not homogeneous throughout and much reduces the scale of our immediate powers, as compared with our hopes ten days ago.

I have meditated much on the proper line of policy to adopt, in the event of our coming in, which I suppose the party hardly can avoid.

One consideration to be borne in mind which I think is true, and if true I am sure is vital, is this, that if we had thrown British questions into the shade we should have had no majority at all. And supposing now we were on coming in so to arrange matters as to *appuyer*[1] on Home Rule alone for the Session, we should run a most serious risk with the constituencies which might I think amount to a great deal of temporary sacrifice if they saw us conducting a Parliamentary movement for Home Rule so strong as to have a chance of over-awing the House of Lords, but who if they saw immediate Home Rule to be out of the question would feel with some justice that we ought not to postpone all their wants with no hope of an equivalent.

All this looks like some degree of shifting of our polarity and the whole Irish department of our case will require anxious consideration. Postponements of the whole subject of Home Rule over the next Session does not seem to be possible. But if we are not strong enough to carry it at once we shall have to consider our subject mainly under two subjects.

1. What we can do for Ireland, in a situation which forbids simple postponement of the main Irish issue, and also forbids carrying it.

2. What satisfaction we can give to other wants, English, Welsh and Scotch.

In this view I think we should study the husbanding of our strength for a decisive movement: and I do not despair of its being so husbanded if we address ourselves to those subjects of Liberal legislation which would be both *concise* and telling, in the various divisions of Great Britain.

In Ireland we might repeal Coercion: we might (this is Morley's) make some provision in favour of the evicted tenants: but a main portion of our plan must we both suppose evidently be to *Drummondise*[2] (so to speak) the administration of Ireland. The operation of this method under the Melbourne government was wonderful. I dare say you remember a declaration of Hartington's when he was propounding alternatives, and before he had hardened into practical Toryism, to the effect that "Dublin Castle" must be fundamentally recast. This would require a strong hand. One of the principal subjects of thought in the coming weeks or months is how far it can be done; and, when the time comes, no one can speak on it with such authority as you.

I will not now attempt to set before you further food for meditation. Today we move northwards and I may probably be from Friday to Monday at (Castleton of) Braemar. This is done not from free-will but as a matter of prudence.

My greatest personal difficulty is the gradual closing of the doors of sense. It would become serious, were they to show a disposition to close more quickly. I am not yet certain whether I have thrown off the whole effect of the blow administered to my eye at Chester. I am advised to try the effect of the most stimulating climate that I know, that of

---

[1] To lean.

[2] Thomas Drummond, 1797–1840; as Irish undersecretary 1835–40 reformed Irish government and introduced police and stipendiary magistrates.

Deeside. For the present I hardly read at all: but I can write tolerably, & thank God am very well.

[P.S.] I am so glad you are satisfied with the result of your trip to Hamburg.[1]

14. Th. [*Fife Arms Hotel, Braemar*]

Wrote to Sir W. Harcourt—Mr Pulley. The Aberdeens came. Saw the Lord Provost—Lady A. Off at 12.20. Ballater luncheon Braemar[2] before six. Drive lost nothing by repetition. Read a few Odes & meditated a little on translating.[3] Walk up the Spital[4] Road. Returns still improving.

To Sir W. V. HARCOURT, 14 July 1892.   MS Harcourt dep. 12, f. 19.
'*Secret*'.

I hope you, and yours, have got well through this trying and anxious time so far as it has yet passed. I congratulate you on your large majority, but could have wished and hoped it even larger. I heard well of you through Morley and feel the value of your great labours.

Two thousand voters seem to have gone over from me in a mass. It is simply due to the question of Scotch Disestablishment. In Kincardineshire the election was fought between two Liberals on that question only, and the Disestablisher won hollow. My election seems to show that *a* majority of the electors of Midlothian are for Disestablishment. I am very much more vexed about the Poll at Newcastle on Tyne and [*sic*] which was a sore disappointment. Sadder still was the wanton giving away of seats both here and in Ireland. We were able however to strike a blow at this senseless proceeding in Stirlingshire.

As to the future I am as you know deeply bound to Ireland my only public pledge and tie in honour to public life when I am prosecuting it against nature. Nevertheless I see these things: had we not put English Scotch & Welsh questions well forward we should probably have had no majority at all. Ireland herself has by her incidents a good deal damaged herself and us. Our majority while small will not be quite homogeneous. The centre of gravity is somewhat shifted.

In 1835 the Melbourne Government came in with a British minority, swelled into a majority hardly touching thirty by the O'Connell contingent of forty. And they staid for $6\frac{1}{2}$ years, the longest lived Government since Lord Liverpool's. But the Irish were under the command of a master: and Ireland scarcely beginning her political life had to be content with small mercies. Lastly that Government was rather slack, and on this ground perhaps could not well be taken as a pattern.

These are my crude initial thoughts on the future. But I have been inwardly hammering or trying to hammer some things out. I have a hankering after legislation which shall be at once concise and decisive, to help[5] the *British* part of the bill of fare. West told me he *thought* you were inclined more or less to entertain his scheme of the Death Duties. This I think for the present purpose could be made to fulfil the two conditions. There is

---

[1] Spencer replied, 14 July, Add MS 44314, f. 35, that Gladstone's letter 'set me thinking on points which had not occurred to me', not immediately answerable, and better discussed verbally.

[2] The Gladstones occupied 'the suite or apartments on the first floor of the hotel in which the late German Emperor lodged in 1887'; *T.T.*, 15 July 1892, 4d.

[3] Start of preparation of *The Odes of Horace translated into English by the Rt. Hon. W. E. Gladstone* (1894), printed by Horace Hart, printer to Oxford University, published by John Murray. The title on the binding reads *The Odes of Horace and the Carmen Saeculare*.

[4] The Spital of Glenshee, south of Braemar.

[5] Remainder of letter missing from MS Harcourt; taken from copy, Add MS 44202, f. 158.

also the question of taxing ground rents. Enfranchising leaseholds would I suppose be more complex.

I hope your son is well & a bird in the air whispered to me that he *might* come among us, whereat I should greatly rejoice.[1]

P.S. I have some things to say about myself but they will keep. This trip, under advice, has reference to my eye.

15. Fr.

Wrote to Duke of Fife—Sir Alg. Borthwick. Business with Helen (Harry went last evg). Wrote much of Autob. Notes. Drove & walked to Invercauld. Back by the Lion's face. Mr Fogge the factor gave us an interesting account of the young Laird.[2] The situation is indeed noble: far away at the head, so far as I know. Conversation with Acton. Mr A. though our junior is paternally kind as ever.

Frankly: from the condition (*now*) of my senses, I am no longer fit for public life: yet bidden to walk in it. "Lead Thou me on".[3]

16. Sat.

Ch. 8½ A.M. Wrote to Mr Walter Leaf[4]—Mr Crombie MP.[5]—Rev. Mr Petty—Ld Provost of Aberdeen—Lady Ashburnham—Rev. J.P. Carrick. Drove to the Linn [of Dee], & walk. Wrote Autob. Notes. A little work on the Odes. Rev. Mr Currie dined.

17. 5 S. Trin.

Ch mg & evg. Wrote to Sir W. Harcourt—Mr Shelley[6]—Mr A. Morley. Wrote some Autob. Notes. Worked on the Psalms. Read a few pages of Dr Langen Röm. Kirche III.[7] Walk in afternoon.

18. M.

Ch. 8½ A.M. Wrote to Mr J.B. Balfour—Sir W. Harcourt. Worked on the [Horacian] Odes. The rendering is most difficult. Drove to the Colonel's Bed &c.— Back by Corriemulzi.[8] Conversation Lord A. & Mr A. on Scots Disestabl. Wrote Autob. Notes.

To Sir W. V. HARCOURT, 18 July 1892.   MS Harcourt dep. 12, f. 21.
'*Secret*'

Many thanks for your letter.[9] It strengthens my hope that as our path becomes more thickly beset with difficulties we shall all hold the more closely together in proportion, for is not difficulty the nurse of manhood.

[1] Harcourt replied next day, with a further bulletin on 16 July, Add MS 44202, f. 159, remarking on the need for British measures.
[2] Obscure.
[3] The refrain from Newman's verses, 'Lead, kindly light'.
[4] Walter Leaf, 1852–1927; banker, alpinist and classical scholar, had sent his *Companion to the Iliad* (1892); Add MS 44515, f. 107.
[5] See 29 Oct. 86.   [6] Reading uncertain.
[7] See 16 Oct. 81.   [8] Both on the Dee west of Braemar.
[9] See 14 July 92n.

The election, with its narrow or moderate majority, at once brings the 'other parts of the constitution', i.e. the House of Lords, upon the field. If we come in, as it will be late in August, with the Supply voted, we shall not want our legislative programme for production: unless in the single point, if it be thought wise not to lose a moment in the simple repeal of the Coercion Act. But I feel that we ought to have the substance of it *in petto*. And I have exercised myself much in thought upon these two questions.

1. How to give for 1893 a just satisfaction to Ireland without spending the Session on Home Rule.
2. And to make a good though of course incomplete bill of fare for England Scotland Wales (with some aid from Executive Acts) by means of those subjects which will allow of very concise legislation, such as will be most likely to defy obstination.

I am of opinion that there is much which may be done: but I reserve details.

My reason for going mentally so far into the matter is that there have often been governments and even longlived governments with small majorities. But they have been easy going governments without such sharp issues as we have probably to confront. I therefore incline to believe that we must prepare a series of measures which will be challenges to the Lords and which will give a stronger position with (London and) the country, than Ireland could if alone.

I am due at Hawarden late on Thursday, and I think of coming up to town on such day of next week as shall seem needful.

All this seems to be written on the assumption that I am doomed to be the head. But before going into what would follow I shall hope to talk to you freely and familiarly on the smallness of the resources I have to place at the command of the new Government, while undoubtedly the "country" will ascribe to me a considerable share.

[P.S.] My two points of finance were only meant as those parts of a policy which might specially fall to your consideration.

I hope to hear well of your boy when you write.

To J. B. BALFOUR, M.P., 18 July 1892.   Add MS 44515, f. 110.
'*Secret*'

I congratulate you on your being so splendidly returned & this as one of a majority.

One thing is clear to me, that we ought to make a decided effort to get Disestablishment in Scotland out of the political arena before the *next* General Election.

I have asked myself whether this might not be done by cutting off the public stipends, i.e. the Parliamentary and the Teind stipends. Are there any other *public* stipends, as distinguished from the voluntary, & from private endowments? If there are not the way seems pretty clear. If there are, by what definition can they be got at?

If it be practicable to deal thus with the stipends in *a bill of a few lines*, it seems to me that the Scotch Disestablishers ought to be tolerably satisfied?

This would leave unsettled

1. The future title of the (now) Established Church.
2. The question of Kirks, manses, & glebes might be settled between the Kirk & the heritors at some convenient time.
3. The private endowments would remain where they are: as they would have to do in any more complete measure.
4. The Teind stipends would be reserved for the future decision of Parliament. In the meantime, they might be paid to the National Debt Office to accumulate for the fund, with a view to their application eventually for the benefit of the parishes from which they accrue. The future appropriation of Church Funds was reserved by the Irish Church Act of 1869.
5. It may be a question whether this could and should be done by a private member's Bill.

I mentioned an idea of this kind to Mr. Holmes Ivory, with liberty to name it to you only. He did not seem to be aware of any fatal preliminary bar. You may know of such a bar. If you do not, and if you are in vacation, & would think the matter worth discussing, Mr. Armitstead our host begs you to be one of his party to dinner at Pitlochrie on Wednesday (Fisher's Hotel), it being we hope not above some two hours from Edinburgh. I should be very glad of the conversation.

Please reply to Pitlochrie.[1]

19. Tu.

Ch. 8½ A.M. Wrote to Rev. R. Wilson—Ld Rosebery—Rev. Dr. Walker—Mr M. Sasse[2]—A. Graham—and Mr Labbi MP.[3] Transacted correspondence with Helen. Finished rendering Hor. Od. II.4. Worked on the Psalms. Read 3 or 4 Odes.

To LORD ROSEBERY, 19 July 1892.   N.L.S. 10024, f. 70.

Tomorrow we turn southwards. I therefore feel that we are leaving Scotland, for this, no common, occasion: and I cannot quit it without sending you a word of thanks for all your hospitality, so gracious, & be assured all the more valued, because of what under the circumstances it must have cost you in effort. It was indeed time for you to be relieved.

I inclose to you a letter which contains some reference to you, simply on account of such [?] reference. I have answered it in the dilatory sense without noticing any particulars, but I thought you would like to know.

You may be amused by the inclosed telegram[4] from six Italian deputies of the democratic party. I do not expect much from them. I think however that their politics are Italian and not at bottom anti-French or anti-German. That is the base of my Italian ideas. Italy had no strength to sustain the pranks which she has played since the days of Cavour, Ricasoli, and Minghetti, and this with the Pope, necessarily arch-enemy, at the door. It will be of profound interest to watch the course of the Italian elections.

I do not know if you ever saw an article written by me in the Edinburgh Review of October 1870[5] on the Franco German question. In any case I should be very glad if you would undergo the bore of looking at it again. I really believe it was impartial: and I also believe that my thoughts have always run in precisely the same channel. You probably have not the Review—who has? But I can send it you at a moment's notice from Hawarden where we hope to arrive from Pitlochrie late on Thursday night with Mr Armitstead. At Pitlochrie tomorrow I have a vague hope of seeing Campbell Bannerman, Balfour, or both.

Deeside in no way disappoints my former recollections.

Do not think of replying except it be to *order* the article.[6]

[1] Balfour replied next day, Add MS 44515, f. 112, that he would go to Pitlochry; he included some details about Teinds.
[2] Maurice Sasse, manager of the International Telegraphic and Correspondence Bureau and London representative of the German Liberal Party; on the Triple Alliance; see N.L.S. 10024, f. 72.
[3] i.e. Labouchere, who hoped for a place in the Cabinet; see Thorold, 373.
[4] N.L.S. 10024, f. 68.
[5] See 1 Sept. 70.
[6] For Rosebery's reply, written in various drafts and eventually sent on 3 Aug. 92, see N.L.S. 10024, f. 74 and 4 Aug. 92n.

20. *Wed.* [*Pitlochry*]

Wrote to A. Morley—W. Lamont. 10–6 P.M. Pleasant journey to Pitlochrie.
Walk there. Luncheon at Spital. Received addresses at Kirkmichael, and made a
speech of 15 or more minutes. Read a few Odes. Long conversation with Mr
[J. B.] Balfour as to my scheme for the Scotch Establishment.[1] Conversation
with Ld Acton whom to our great regret we lose tomorrow. Ch. 8½ A.M. A nice
congregation about 30.

The accompanying sketch is intended to present a *first* view of the possibilities of 1893.
   It aims at obtaining a judgment upon the great Irish question without spending the
bulk of the Session upon its particulars (viewing the unlikelihood as far as can now be
seen of their at once passing into law): and obtaining a good or fair Sessional result for the
various portions of the country by the three-fold method
1. Of Government Bills (marked +)
2. Of Executive Acts.
3. Of Bills in charge of private members countenanced or aided by the Government.
                                                        WEG Jul 20. 92.[2]

Great Britain.[3]

+ 1. Registration.
+ 2. One man one vote.
+ 3. C. Councils Amending Bill.
       (a) to controul police
       (b) to have compulsory powers of Land-purchase
       (c) to controul Licensing
       (d) to make provisions respecting placing on the rates necessary election charges &
            pay[men]t of members if they think fit.
       (e) as to Parish C[ouncils]
+ 4. Eight hours Miners' Bill by local option.
   5. Local option? See A [below]
   6. Abolish University representation [by M.P.]
   7. Parish Councils under Small Holdings Act. Temporary Bill. Q[uer]y through C.C.
       Conspiracy
       C.C. to have power to take land
       Election Expenses out of rates

Scotland.

All stipends from public services to cease on vacancy. Teinds reserved for parishes
whence accruing.[4]
[Q[uer]y by M.P. assisted]

Wales.

   1. Land Commission
   2. Welsh Disestablishment [by M.P. similarly assisted]

---

[1] See next day.
[2] Holograph; Add MS 44774, f. 36.
[3] Initialled and dated 19 July 1891; Add MS 44774, f. 37; phrases in [ ] are Gladstone's.
[4] See J. B. Balfour's mem. of 27 July 1892 on details of this; Add MS 44515, f. 123.

London

+ 1. General powers for County Council.

Finance.

+ Budget { 1. Tax ground-rents.
2. Abolition of Death Duty Acts from a distant day: impose uniform duty.

Ireland.

+ 1. Abolition of coercion Act.
2. Provision to re-admit evicted tenants [By M.P. assisted]
3. Cabinet Minute on Home Rule and Resolution thereupon.
4. Fill Irish Judgeships on alternate vacancies.
5. Arrest recruiting in Constabulary.
6. Bill to remove the remaining religious disabilities [In H. of L? By independent Peer & assisted M.P.?]

A. Local Option.

Qy 1. Insert among Bill, by M.P.s assisted by Govt. (NB. 1874)
2. Areas to be regulated.
3. Vote of extinction by a majority of $\frac{2}{3}$ or $\frac{3}{4}$.
4. After a term of [three?] years
5. Or sooner with an allowance based on rateable value.
6. Separate provision for Hotels and eating houses

21. *Th.* [*Hawarden*]

Pitlochrie: capital Inn: lovely place. Wrote to Mr Campbell—Mr Cowan (Circular). Drive thro' Faskali[1] & up to Killiecrankie stone: of loveliness unsurpassed. Read a little in Odes. Saw Mr Barry's pictures. Tried to express to Mr A. our thanks: *some* of them. Drew out my plan for the Scotch Established Church. 2½–1 A.M. To Hawarden: an easy & rapid journey. Conversation with Herbert on the Elections till 2 A.M.

22. *Fr.*

Ch. 7 P.M. Rose late by agreement.

Much conversation with H. on payment of members & other matters.[2] Conversation with S.E.G. Worked upon a gaol delivery of accumulated clothes. Eight to dinner. Backgammon with S. Dr Grainger came: examined the eyes: a good report: more tone wanted. The *fluff* I think smaller. Wrote to Sir W. Harcourt l.l.—Sir Edw. Watkin—Mr Balfour (Edinb.). Read a little 'Abbot'.[3]

---

[1] Faskally, north of Pitlochry, on the way to the 'Soldier's Leap' rock at Killicrankie on the Garry (site of the battle in 1689).

[2] He wrote out the heads of a bill headed 'Secret. Scottish Established Church' to come into force on 1 January 1894, abolishing the office of the Lord High Commissioner of the General Assembly and ending ministers' stipends paid from the Consolidated Fund or from any Scottish public source as the offices became vacant through death or removal; Add MS 44774, f. 46.

[3] By Scott (1820); see 18 Aug. 52.

Payment of members of Parliament in block.[1]

1. Will the Cabinet propose it?
2. If so, in 1893?
3. Our List seems too full for it.

———————

Could not actively support
Could silently acquiesce, rather than positively dissent.
Aware however that this wd. cause some difficulties in passing the measure.
  My opinions are
1. That members who require it should draw a Salary or allowance.
2. That this might be done without creating any invidious distinction: they need not apply: their names shd. only appear in conjunction with all MP recipients of public money.
    The wider measure is open to the following objections
    1. It subjects the country to a charge absolutely unnecessary.
    2. It is a question bad to fight in the constituencies against an opposing & renouncing candidate.
    3. It tends towards a general breaking up of our system of unpaid service, which is a good system.
    4. It seems violent to hold that because $\frac{1}{10}$ or $\frac{1}{20}$ of an Assembly need pecuniary aid in the discharge of public duty, the other $\frac{9}{10}$ or $\frac{19}{20}$ who do not need it or desire it are nevertheless to have it.
    5. The argument in favour is the 'point of honour' for the Labour members. But these members are already returned to Parliament mainly I believe by the subscriptions of the Liberal party.
    6. The difficulty in the constituencies would not end with the passing of the measure: local popularity would attend the man who renounced or who gave the money to the constituency.

To Sir W. V. HARCOURT, 22 July 1892.   MS Harcourt dep. 12, ff. 31–3.
'*Secret.*'

[Letter 1:] I have employed myself very much upon an anticipatory review of the situation, and I am in hope that the length of my own Parliamentary retrospect may now for once be of some use to my friends.

In detail you present to me formidable difficulties especially with regard to the payment of members, on which it is not necessary to enter now.[2] Suffice it to say that I shall not knowingly get upon my high horse without cause, and I am sure we shall all act in the same spirit.

It is more important to observe that your ideas and mine as to the general form of action seem to be much the same.

I consider that we have

1. To cast the balance fairly between Irish and British claims.
2. To anticipate mischief as most probable in the House of Lords.
3. To open on that House as many good *bouches a feu* as possible.
4. To frame our proposals with a view particularly to passing them through the Commons.

———————

[1] Undated holograph which may refer to this day's conversation; Add MS 44774, f. 166.
[2] Harcourt letter, 19 July, Add MS 44202, f. 168: 'I find that what the labour Party most care for is the Payment of M.Ps.—indeed without it I doubt if I should have had a majority.'

5. To study particularly with this view those subjects which can be very concisely handled in Bills.

I also like your view about the amendment: but I should like to see the full terms, & also to see the amendment of Aug. 19(?) 1841 both of which I expect to get from Arnold Morley.

I see the not-unlikelihood of another Dissolution before Session 1894: but after that event [*sic*] in my *most* sanguine moods I can only regard myself as a possible *amicus curiae*.

What do you think of Asquith and Sir E. Grey to move & second amendment? Should there be an Irishman? Blake? could *he* or *they* accept.[1]

[Letter 2:] '*Private.*' Forgive my taking a great liberty. Since my incident at Chester I have often thought sympathetically of you because I had heard that you were in some way menaced as to vision. Now though mine is a slight affair to all appearance and may be altogether temporary I have at once of course under advice taken rigorous care: have renounced reading newspapers and almost all letters, and have reduced my dearly beloved reading of books virtually to zero. But I am under the impression that you work your sight relentlessly: and I also recollect or seem to recollect your doctrines about medical advisers, and I cannot help feeling some misgiving lest you should be running unnecessary or aggravating necessary risks, and doing yourself less than justice.

I may in all this be as visionary as I am intrusive, but I know you will forgive it. The singular depth and force, with which you always feel for others, cannot but a little incline others a little to feel about you, and may have the incidental disadvantage of their manifesting a right sentiment in a wrong way.

I find writing much less injurious than reading and I do it a good deal in spectacles somewhat darkened. I hope it will cause some reform in my hand-writing and thereby benefit my friends.

Again I ask your forgiveness.[2]

23. Sat

Ch. 7 P.M. Wrote to Dr. Furnival—A. Morley Tel.—Ld Spencer—Ld Ripon—Mr Melville—Rev. Fowler. Made out my version of Hor. Od. III. 30. Not very good. Some other work on Odes. Read a little Abbot—Life of Burleigh.[3] More work on clothes. Backgammon with S. Curious game.

To LORD SPENCER, 23 July 1892. '*Secret*'. Althorp MSS K8.

In my last letter to you,[4] which was seen by Morley before I sent it, I expressed the innermost of all that was in my mind when I wrote it: and the sympathetic character of your reply left no occasion for asking you to take a journey especially to the far North.

I am here for a few days with the visits and orders of my oculist for a chief care but I hope to be in London on Wednesday. If you move southward by that time I should be very glad to see you without loss of time.

[1] Harcourt replied, 25 July, Add MS 44202, f. 178, thanking Gladstone for his letter: 'I entirely concur in the views you express in it'; but uncertain 'that Asquith and E. Grey are the best men for the purpose. . . . We don't particularly want good speaking but straight voting'; he suggested Whitbread and Burt.
[2] In Gardiner, ii. 186. Harcourt wrote a letter of heartfelt thanks; 25 July, Add MS 44202, f. 184.
[3] R. C[ourteville], *Memoirs of the life and administration of William Cecil Baron Burleigh* (1738).
[4] See 13 July 92.

I could see you at five or at six on Wednesday and in any case should hope for your presence at eleven on Thursday when I hope to get Harcourt and Morley for a full talk.

Meantime I send you a Memorandum seen by no other eye as yet, and intended to work out the best method of fixing a most difficult question, namely the just relation between Irish and British claims. Please to let me know whether it strikes you favourably.[1]

24. 6 S. Trin.

Ch 11 A.M. and 6½ P.M. Wrote to Maharajah Holkar—J. Morley—A. Morley— Rev. Harshaw—Ld Acton—Messrs Humphreys. Worked on the Psalms. Wrote out Eucharistica.[2] Helen read aloud to me 9–10.

25. St James.

Ch. 8½ A.M. and H.C. on this our 53d marriage anniversary. Read Transl. Brethren of the Cross,[3] a little: also Anson on the Constitution.[4] Worked on Psalms. A little on Homer. Much on papers in preparation for storing them. Also conversation with S. & search respecting the man 'after God's own heart'. Wrote to Mr Maule—Miss Lewis. Helen read me the Abbot for an hour.

26. Tu.

Ch. 8½ A.M. We both manage the morning up hill on foot by going slowly. Wrote to Sir W. Harcourt—Ld Ripon—Mr Gourley MP.—Miss Sharman Crawford[5]—Rev. Mr M'Karness[6]—Mr Richardson—Mrs Penny. Worked on Odes.

To Sir W. V. HARCOURT, 26 July 1892.					MS Harcourt dep. 12, f. 42.

Writing for our early post I must be very brief but there is little difficulty as in substance I have nothing to do but agree and thank. Your letter to Balfour is I think admirable. I think however your argument and the precedents go the full length of requiring a declaration of policy, as do the precedents of 1835, 1841, 1859. To your precedent of 1855 I would add that of 1847. The statement you have made leaves no more to be said. You are one of the few men alive who seem to be aware that we have a constitution.

I should like to see you immediately on my arrival tomorrow, so leaving a margin for any lateness of train I propose that you should come at *five* o'clock.

Will you also dine quietly on Thursday.

---

[1] Spencer replied, 25 July, Add MS 44314, f. 38 and *Spencer*, ii. 211; 'I am rather doubtful as to dealing with the Irish question next Session by Resolution. . . . I fear we shall be considered as faint hearted, if we did not bring in a Bill, & send it up to the H. of Lords. . . . Next Session must necessarily be a long one, you ought to be able to carry a Home Rule Bill through Committee of the House, and if the House of Lords rejects it & other British measures, you will be able to present them again to Parliament in the Session of 1894 with great effect.'

[2] See Lathbury, ii. 421.

[3] A translated tract published by the Society of the Holy Cross.

[4] Anson's second volume, whose writing Gladstone had discussed with the author; see 3 Feb. 90.

[5] Mabel, da. of J. Sharman Crawford, sent a pamphlet republishing her father's views on home rule; Hawn P. See 9 July 92.

[6] Charles Coleridge MacKarness, vicar of St. Martin's, Scarborough, and biblical scholar. Had sent his biography, see 7 Aug. 92.

About Asquith and Grey[1] I followed precedents: but I am quite open to consideration. Of course you shall have your letter back again: I hope you will *conserve* it.

Plainly the natural course is that the Government shall do some act & that we shall object & amend by our motion.

The whole debate will be simple iteration.

Jul. 27. Wed. [*London*][2]

Ch. 8½ A.M. Wrote to Rev. Mr Knowles. 10¾–4. To 1. Carlton Gardens.[3] Saw Sir W. Harcourt 1¾ hour. Formidable especially at my age. Saw J. Morley—Ld Acton—Sir A. West—Dr Granger[4] who repeated his favourable report. Stiff conversation in evening on the Irish reports with Spencer & J. Morley. Saw A. Morley. In Railway Carriage, worked on Odes. Wrote a little anti Argyll for NAR.[5] Bed after a heavy day.

July 27
Points discussed with Sir W. Harcourt[6]

1. New whip. Marjoribanks—Acland.
2. Ld Lieut. of Ireland. H. named Houghton, Conington, Brassey. I named Bessborough, Aberdeen
3. Form of our motion.
4- Mover and Seconder—Both rather inclined to Asquith & Birt—others discussed
5. Begun with much private & personal explanation.
6. Possible appointment or rejection of Labouchere
7. Ponsonby's conv[ersation] with H[arcourt]s
8. Knollys d[itt]o.

28. Th.

Wrote to Ld Kimberley—Mr Schnadhorst. Settled correspondence with S. Lyttelton. Saw Spencer & Morley on the course to be pursued as to Home Rule in forenoon. Meeting in aftn 2½–4¼. Same subject more largely discussed.[7] Saw

[1] See 22 July 92.
[2] This and next three entries written on a separate sheet tipped into the volume.
[3] Staying with Stuart Rendel.   [4] The oculist; see 25 June 92.
[5] 'A vindication of Home Rule. A reply to the Duke of Argyll', *N.A.R.* (October 1892); a reply to Argyll's article in the August number.
[6] Holograph; Add MS 44774, f. 54. 'P[apa] was with Mr. G. for more than two hours. He also found him very averse to Acland & wanting Marjoribanks for [Chief] Whip. P. strongly opposed this and said he did not think he could be responsible for the work of the H. of C. without Acland. I think this is putting the thing too high . . . P. was much shocked at the physical & mental change for the worse in Mr. G. since he left the H. of C. in June. He thinks him confused & feeble . . . P. spoke to him very seriously about the way he (Mr. G.) was & has been treating Rosebery . . . Mr. G. promised to write within 48 hours . . .'; L. V. Harcourt's diary this day; MS Harcourt dep. 383. Marjoribanks was persuaded to serve.
[7] 'I went to see Mrs Gladstone at tea time—Mrs Drew and Miss Helen Gladstone there—they told me that Mr. G.'s voice was hoarse with arguing with people and that though J. Morley had seen him for a short time this afternoon he was shut up now and not allowed to see anyone. However when Mrs G. took his tea in to him she told him I was there & he insisted on coming out into the hall & saying a few words to me and giving me a copy of a collection of his articles on the Irish Question. . . . He soon went off again saying that if he stayed he should talk which he was forbidden to do . . .'; L. V. Harcourt's diary this day, MS Harcourt dep. 383.

A. Morley—Sir A. West—Mr Stuart Rendel. Drive with C. Worked on the antiArgyll paper. In the evening there was an inkling of a cold perceived by C.

29. *Frid.*

Wrote to Mr Riding—Ld Rosebery. Saw A. Morley l.l.l.—S. Lyttelton—J. Morley —Sir J. Lacaita—L. Harcourt.[1] Worked pretty hard on the reply to Argyll & finished it. In the evening the signs of bronchial cold obliged me to go to bed and plunge myself in a perspiration bath.

30. *Sat.*

Sent off the Reply to Argyll for the N.A. Review. C. read me all the Psalms: how wonderful they are. Worked on Odes & made some translation. But practically the use of my eyes is much impeded. I pass perforce into the region of meditation, & the next great step is brought before me. With my sins mountain high, the mercies of God seem piled up higher yet. Helen read to me from the Abbot in the evening. Sir A. Clark came thrice. Saw A. West—A. Morley.

31. *7 S. Trin.*

Litany for myself. C. gave me the Lessons—& all the Psalms. Wrote to Sir W. Harcourt—and minute of a joint reply to Balfour. All by Helen's efficient aid. Sir A. Clark came twice. Saw Mr Armitstead—J. Morley.

Now is the time for the thoughts that wander through eternity. When I look at the task apparently before me, and at the equipment of spirit and sense with which I am furnished I cast up my eyes to heaven abashed and dismayed. A reply came from thence. My grace is sufficient for thee. O thou of little faith wherefore didst thou doubt. Either it must be a life of and by faith, or no life at all. The Almighty & not any counsel of mine has brought it about: surely He will provide for it.

To Sir W. V. HARCOURT, 31 July 1892.   MS Harcourt dep. 12, f. 67.[2]

I return the inclosed[3] from Mr Balfour of which I keep a copy.[4]

It is such a curious specimen of Tory authorship.

My inclosure shows in substance the length to which I think you may safely go towards giving Balfour his assurance. I should not like to go farther without full consideration.

[1] 'I drove to Carlton Gdns. with P[apa] at 2.30. He is determined to be very self restrained & to let the others talk but will resist the idea of 1893 being wholly given up to Ireland & will press for English measures too.... P[apa] returned to Brook St. at about 4.45. They had talked nothing but "policy" and not "persons" at Mr. G's this afternoon'; L. V. Harcourt's diary this day, MS Harcourt dep. 383.

[2] Letter written by secretary, signed by Gladstone.

[3] Sent by Harcourt, Add MS 44202, f. 188, with the comment 'It is obvious what they are afraid of is a sort of Jesse Collings amendment [see 26 Jan. 86] on some Labour question or other matter which would make the votes of their own people difficult.'

[4] Not found. Balfour's copy in Add MS 49696, f. 202, referring to 'the tactics of Feb. 1886' and requesting Harcourt to follow the precedent.

I have put in the *if* simply because one cannot yet absolutely speak for the intentions of the Irish contingent of the present majority.
[P.S.] Clear hopes I may be in the House on Thursday

Suggested

I have referred to Mr. Gladstone & we are both of opinion that it would not be right for us to enter on any negotiations of terms for the delivery of a Queen's Speech, neither have we any authority for such a purpose resembling that of a Cabinet which you represent. We cannot therefore surrender our liberty of action.

At the same time we think it plain from the known circumstances of the case, that if there is to be a movement of the Liberal party at this juncture against the existing Government, the question of confidence ought to be directly raised.[1]

Mond. Aug. One. 92.

Sir A. Clark came early made much examination & bid me rise to luncheon. To keep the house still for two or three days. Saw Ld Acton—A. Morley—J. Morley l.l.—Mr Childers. Wrote sketch of Sessional work for 1893. Et alia. Helen read to me from the Abbot.

Secret. Provisional outline of Work for the Session of 1893[2]
I. Bills to be worked by the Govt. in the House.
II. Bills to be worked through Grand Committees
III Bills of private members to be supported by the Govt.
IV. Executive Acts.

I.

1. Bill for the Government of Ireland.
2. County Councils Bill
3. Budget.
4. One man one vote.
5. Transfer of Election charges to rates
6. Miners Eight hours by Local option?
7. Repeal of Coercion Act.

II.

2. Employers' liability.
1. Registration.
3. Law of Conspiracy Amendment

III.

1. Welsh Church Suspensory Bill.
2. Scotch Church Bill to provide for the cessation of all Stipends from public sources when present incumbencies shall terminate: and for other purposes.
3. Bill to put an end to the Representation of Universities in Parliament.
4. Readmission of evicted Tenants

[1] Harcourt forwarded Gladstone's draft to Balfour; see Add MS 44202, f. 195.
[2] Holograph initialled and dated 1 August 1892; Add MS 44774, f. 41. See also 20 July 92.

IV

1. Wales. Land Commission
2. England. Poor Law Commission
3.   Labour Department.
4. Ireland. Gradual reduction of Constabulary?
   Of Judgeships
   And reform of Administration generally

County Councils Bill.
main provisions.

1. Controul of police
2. Controul of licensing
3. Compulsory powers to take land for *small* holdings.
4. London C.C. Enlargement of powers.
5. Parish Councils for the purposes of small Holdings.

WEG   Aug. 1.   1892

2. Tu.

Wrote to Mr Asquith[1]—Sir W. Harcourt—Mr Burt—Ld Spencer—L. Harcourt.
Down to luncheon. Saw Sir E. Saunders l.l.[2]—Sir A. West—Mr Morley—L. Harcourt—A. Morley—Ld Spencer. Some long. Sir J. Gladstone. An indifferent night
was followed by a good day. Read 20 p. 'The Wrecker'.[3] Helen read me 'Abbot'.

To Sir W. V. HARCOURT, 2 August 1892.   MS Harcourt dep. 12, f. 71.[4]

   I have been thinking that there might be much advantage in giving to our amendment
as far as possible the character of matter of fact rather than matter of opinion, & I have
drawn the enclosed sketch with that view. If you and J. Morley would kindly take it in
hand, I should be perfectly satisfied with whatever form you may adopt.
   Of course the speech might require something to be added, but I hope not. I have written preliminary letters to Asquith & Burt.

Honourably to represent
The recent elections as a whole have placed it beyond doubt that Your Majesty's present
advisers do not enjoy the confidence of the constituencies (country) and accordingly they
cannot possess the confidence of Your Majesty's faithful Commons.[5]

3. Wed.

Wrote to Dr Ginsburg—Sir E. Saunders—minutes settled with S.L. 12–1½. Conversation with the Irish chiefs. See note.[6] Meeting of chief Liberals at 3 to
make known the upshot. All went well. Saw Ld Spencer—Sir W. Harcourt. Both
rebut Rosebery & Labouchere: very diverse. Mr Rendel here. Backgammon.

[1] Asking him to move the amndt. to the Address; Add MS 44515, f. 129.
[2] His dentist.
[3] R. L. Stevenson and L. Osbourne, *The Wrecker* (1892).
[4] Written by secretary, signed by Gladstone.
[5] Harcourt thought this—especially 'elections as a whole'—too openhanded, preferring a formula
based on 1841 and 1859 (when moved by the young Hartington); Add MS 44202, f. 200.
[6] Untraced.

Read 'The Wrecker'—a little. Helen read Abbot aloud. Drive: but in brougham. Saw Sir A. Clark.

4. Th. [*Hatchlands*]

Wrote to J. Murray—Miss Murray. Attended the House & seconded Mr Peel's nomination.[1] Conclave on Rosebery's letter of refusal. Dictated, discussed, & then wrote out my letter in reply which J. Morley most gallantly carries down. Saw Sir A. West—A. Morley—J. Morley—Mr Peel—Mr Whitbread—& others. $3\frac{1}{2}$–$4\frac{3}{4}$ to Hatchlands:[2] now a delightful residence. Read the Wrecker. Helen read me the Abbot. Backgammon with Mr R.

To LORD ROSEBERY, 4 August 1892.[3]   N.L.S. 10024, f. 79.

My first duty is to thank you most cordially for the personal kindness, indeed I must say tenderness, of your letter.[4] But the letter is an event, with which you will I am sure desire me to deal frankly according to my sense of the facts.

There are three points to which I must refer.

The first is your conviction of your own unfitness for public life. I distinguish between this conviction, and your desire to escape from public life, for I am quite sure that, under the circumstances of the case, you would regard that devise as no more than dust in the balance.

With respect to the conviction I have only to say that I have never known a case where such a conviction on the part of the person concerned was allowed by him to prevail against the clear, unhesitating, unanimous judgment of friends, and the no less unequivocal judgment of the world.

Your most touching reference to me leads me to say a word upon this isolated aspect of the case; to repeat, in fact, to you what I have more than once during the last six years urged upon others, sometimes with success. It is the undeniable truth, that in contemplating what may happen next week, and what has to follow the probable event, I am simply waging a daily and hourly battle against Nature, with no sort of personal assurance as to my capacity to sustain it. On the contrary, full of apprehension and misgiving; but yet irresistibly forced on by the knowledge or belief that the demand is one made upon me by the crisis, and that that demand is morally irresistible, I have not the same command over the actions of others as over my own. But my convictions about them may be as clear, or even clearer. And in this case I feel that the very same appeal, which the facts make to me, they also make to you; and that the appeal entails the very same obligations.

I will not now dwell on what happened at Dalmeny, further than to say that, when I left in your hands provisional statements connecting your name with the Foreign Office, when I discussed with you, and leant to its association with, the Leadership in the Lords, and when I also spoke of the representation of the Department in the Commons, without receiving from you an adverse sign (any more than one positively favourable), my impressions were such that I am now taken by surprise.

---

[1] As Speaker; 4 *H* 7. 8.

[2] Rendel's house near Guildford.

[3] Various drafts of this letter are in Add MS 44289, f. 163 ff. The final version was taken to Rosebery at Dalmeny by Morley.

[4] Rosebery's letter, 31 July, Add MS 44289, f. 157, which had been 'deferred as long as possible— perhaps too long', reiterated his reluctance to take office, mentioning that 'Kimberley would make an admirable Foreign Secretary'; Rosebery declared himself 'the best judge of my unfitness for public life'.

But I go back, as you do, from that period to our conversation at Mentmore in the winter; when you made the same plea, and when I found myself compelled to offer the same reply. It is my fixed assurance, founded on all I know of public life, of Great Britain, and of its people, that what I then said was right; that you had no open choice before you; that your acceptance was predetermined by previous acts; and that the nation would not tolerate your refusal.

What I then stated was, I think, absolute; and did not need, and scarcely admitted, strengthening. Nevertheless much corroboration has been supplied to it by the varied and admirable services which you have since rendered to the public cause.

I am aware that we, your friends and colleagues, are deprived of all semblance of a title to urge this plea with respect to your public speeches in the interval. But the main element of the whole case, in my mind, is the solid, permanent judgment of the nation. And as regards that judgment, and the grounds which the nation will think it has for forming it, the force of the facts is I think stubborn, and not to be denied.

I am sure I may rely upon your kindness not to send an unfavourable decision in this important matter without seeing me.[1]

5. Fr.

Progress continued. Wrote to A. Morley l.l. Drive with C. & Mr R[endel]. Worked on Odes. Conversation with Mr Goodhart. With Sir A. West. Backgammon with Mr R. Read The Wrecker (50 pages my extreme).

6. Sat.

Wrote to J. Morley—Lady Sherbrook. Worked on Odes. Read The Wrecker. Worked on MS. & materials for coming speech, an important one as to consequences. Delightful drive: saw anew the curious yews.

7. S. 8 Trin.

Ockham Ch mg with H.C.—Ch. again 6 PM. Saw Mr Paulet Mildmay. Worked on Psalms. Read Hutton on position of Catholics[2]—Life of Bp Mackarness.[3] Still rather languid.

8. M. [London]

Back to London. Completely nauseated & without appetite. H. of C. 4–7$\frac{1}{2}$.[4] Saw Sir A. Clark & off to bed. Helen read me 'Abbot'. Saw J. Morley—A. Morley—Sir A. West—Sir W. Harcourt—Ld Kimberley—Major . . . . . Conclave at 1 PM to hear the Queen's Speech: *ridiculus mus*.[5]

---

[1] Rosebery replied, 5 August, Add MS 44289, f. 171, that he 'shall remove myself tonight to a less morbid atmosphere [than Dalmeny], and come and see you early next week'.

[2] A. W. Hutton, *Our position as Catholics in the Church of England* (1872); Hutton was the editor of Gladstone's *Speeches*.

[3] C. C. Mackarness, *Memorials of the Episcopate of J. F. Mackarness* (1892).

[4] Asquith moved an amndt. to the Address on the Speech, that the govt. did not have the confidence of the House; 4 *H* 7. 93.

[5] 'Parturiunt montes, nascetur ridiculus mus': the mountains are in labour: a ridiculous mouse will be born; Horace, *Ars Poetica*, 139. The Speech was brief and unspecific; 4 *H* 7. 21.

9. Tu. [Hatchlands]

Wrote to E. Hamilton—and Ld Coleridge. Saw Sir A. West on correspondence—J. Morley—A. Morley—Mr Wood MP. Saw Sir A. Clark 9½. I improved under good treatment. H. of C. 3–5¼. Felt weak but spoke 70 m.[1] Then off to Hatchlands. Backgammon with Mr R. Worked further on Notes. Read on the Skinners in the Burns Book II.[2]

This has been a period of inner education, and disclosure of special wants: the spirit of faith: the spirit of prayer: the spirit of dependence: the spirit of manhood: the spirit of love. The weight on me is great & presses at many points: but how trifling when compared with the trials of great Christians.

10. Wed.

Wrote to H.J.G. Saw him in evg. Walk with Mr Rendel. Also Backgammon in evg. Worked on Odes: but how slow the turning into versions rhymed. Worked on Autob. Notes. Read The Wrecker.

11. Th. [London]

Wrote to Mrs Th.—Sir H. Ponsonby—and l. for consn to Mr Bertram Currie: difficult.[3] Got quit of my physic just in time and reached No 1 C[arlton] G[ardens][4] at 2 PM. Read Forbes in N.C. (on Empress Eugenie) &c.[5]—and The Wrecker. Saw Rosebery at 2 PM: it was very trying & rather sad.[6] Sir H. Ponsonby 3–4.[7] Conclave at H. of C. on the L. case.[8] H. of C. 4–7¼ and 10–12½. Divided in 350:310. An astonishing muster.[9] Saw Sir A. West—Mr Arch—Mr Burns—Mr Rendel—and others.

12. Fr.

Wrote to Mr Allen MP—Sir H. Ponsonby—Mr Campbell. A day of hard work on the initial tasks.[10] Saw Mr Rendel—Sir A. West—E. Hamilton—Mr A. Morley

[1] On Asquith's amndt.; Gladstone compared Disraeli's 'sound and manly judgment' in resigning in 1868 with Salisbury's waiting to be voted down in the Commons; 4 H 7. 195.
[2] Rev. John Skinner of Aberdeenshire wrote two letters and a poetic epistle to Burns; for these, with Burns' replies, see The works of Robert Burns, ed. C. Annandale (1888), iv. 74 ff.
[3] Currie was acting as intermediary with Labouchere; see later this day and West, P.D., 46.
[4] Rendel's house.   [5] N.C., xxxii. 285 (August 1892).
[6] Rosebery declined office; James, Rosebery, 246.
[7] Holograph note reads: 'Queen's wishes through Sir H. P[onsonby] Aug 11. 92. Rosebery F.O.; Kimberley Indian O.; Bannerman War'; Add MS 44774, f. 65.
[8] i.e. on Labouchere, a candidate for the Cabinet to whom the Queen objected; see West, P.D., 46 ff. and Thorold, ch. 15.
The Queen noted: '[Ponsonby] found Mr. Gladstone eager and excited, talking a great deal about Home rule, and then discussed Mr. Labouchere, whom I am very anxious not to see in office, on account of his personal character. He would not hear of any objections being brought forward on Mr. Labouchere's moral conduct, but upon his paper [Truth]'; L.Q.V., 3rd series, ii. 138 (with Ponsonby's mem. of the interview, which shows the Queen again encouraged Gladstone to go to the Lords). See 13 Aug. 92n.   [9] 4 H 7. 434.
[10] Salisbury went to Osborne at 4.45 p.m. to resign; the Queen then wrote to Gladstone to ask, Salisbury's resignation being accepted 'with much regret', whether Gladstone was prepared to try to form a government; Gladstone accepted in next day's letter; L.Q.V., 3rd series, ii. 141 ff. See next day.

l.l.–J. Morley 1 1–Ld Herschell. Saw Scotts & did some private business: also made a short sitting to Mr Adams Acton. Dined at Mr Armitstead's. Read The Wrecker.

13. Sat.

Wrote to Mr B. Currie[1]–Mr Stansfeld–Sir L. Playfair–Mr Pickersgill. $11\frac{1}{2}$–$1\frac{1}{2}$ Conclave on heavy business. Saw Sir A. West 1 1 1–A. Morley 1 1–J. Morley–Mr Schnadhorst–Mr Fowler–Mr C. Bannerman–Sir H. Ponsonby, from the Queen[2]–Mr Rendel–Ld Aberdeen–Lady Aberdeen. Dined at Dollis Hill. Read The Englishman in Paris.[3]

14. 9 S. Trin.

St James's Ch. 11 AM. and 7 P.M. Wrote to Mr Mundella–Sir G. Trevelyan–Mr Asquith–Lord Houghton–Lord Ripon–Mr A. Acland. Saw A. Morley–Ld Spencer *cum* Ld Kimberley–Mr A.M. *cum* Mr Marjoribanks.

Conclave 3–5. A storm. I am sorry to record that Harcourt has used me in such a way since my return to town that the addition of another Harcourt would have gone far to make my task impossible. All however is *well*: it comes ἄνωθεν.[4]

Read Hutton 'Catholics'–A Liberal to Liberals[5]–Pusey on responsibility of Intellect.[6]

[7]1. Kimberley–Ripon–Spencer
 2. Presidentship of the Council—*in commendam*.
 3. Asquith–Acland.
 4. Mundella–Educn
    Trevelyan–B. of Works
    Bryce. Scottish Dept
    Lefevre–Duchy
 5. H of Lords.
    minimum of appointments.
    (can the political officers be increased) NB *Ld Sandhurst*)
    5 Cabinet   10 Minor Household
    1 Ld Lieut I[reland]
    3 Great Household
    –
    9

[1] Two letters (one to be shown to Labouchere), giving his editorship of *Truth* ('a Journal rather of comment and animadversion than of record') as reason for lack of offer of office; docketed by the secretary 'Mr. Gladstone to Mr. Labouchere. Not delivered'; Add MS 44515, ff. 141, 167.
[2] Ponsonby brought the Queen's letter; see 12 Aug. 92.
[3] [A. D. Vandam], *An Englishman in Paris*, 2v. (1892).
[4] 'from above'. Long lists of possible Cabinets at Add MS 44774, f. 58.
[5] Perhaps J. H. Hawkes, 'A liberal's appeal for the toleration of the Christian morality' (1892).
[6] E. B. Pusey, 'The responsibility of intellect in matters of faith. A sermon' (1873).
[7] Holograph dated 14 August 1892; Add MS 44774, f. 76.

To LORD RIPON, 14 August 1892. 'Secret'.   Add MS 43515, f. 71.

I propose if it be agreeable to you to submit your name to the Queen for the charge of the Colonial Department. And this will be a special pleasure, if it be true as I have heard in some way not authoritative, that the assignment would meet your personal inclinations.[1]

15. M. [Osborne House]

Wrote to Ld Rosebery—Sir C. Russell—Mr Rigby—Ld Herschell—Mr Bryce l & tel.—The Queen—C.G.—Electors of Midlothian—Mr Campbell. 11.40-4. To Osborne. Saw Sir H.P. first. P. of Wales before & after dinner. The Princess, who was delightful as usual & very sympathetic without direct committals. At the main interview, the Queen was cautiously polite.[2] In nothing helpful. Not however captious. Perfect in temper. Not one sympathetic word on any question however detached. After dinner a little unfrozen. Read Englishman in Paris. West as usual invaluable.

To J. BRYCE, 15 August 1892.   MS Bryce 10, f. 117.

I accepted on Saturday the task of forming an Administration, and, although the office you formerly held was one of great interest and importance, it did not confer on you the character of a Minister[3] which I hope that even in the present pressure (for the weather partakes of *sturm und drang*) you will bear. My powers are more limited than I could wish: but I can ask you to take your choice between the Department of Works and the Chancellorship of the Duchy of Lancaster. If you take the latter you will have time on your hands for general business. I am inclined to hope you will choose the Works. Plunkett *seems* to have filled that department with ⟨jud⟩ success and I hope with judgment. It is a department which opens up many weak idiosyncracies. Of these as far as I know you have none; and it would be quite safe in your hands.

If you were able at once to reply by wire it *might* reach me here before 9.45 when I turn my face northwards. L or W with the appropriate monosyllable would suffice.[4]

To Mrs. GLADSTONE, 15 August 1892. 'Secret'.   Hawarden MS 780, f. 209.
My own C.

The world moves rapidly and on arriving here I found I had been outstripped by a telegram which, after all our mountain high difficulties, brought Rosebery's final acceptance.

So I have prepared a list of nearly the whole Cabinet, which will go forward.

I had an audience of the Queen very shortly after my arrival. She looked well but did not move in my presence. I imagine she does it with difficulty. I sat a little nearer to her than usual on account of deafness. She inquired for you with evident sincerity, and perhaps a touch of warmth. In all other respects the interview was carefully polite and nothing else.

[1] Gladstone was determined to ensure the liberal front bench in the Lords held senior Cabinet positions; see his recollections at 3 Mar. 94.
[2] The start of Gladstone's fourth administration (none of the sources mentions that he kissed hands).
[3] Bryce was puzzled as to whether either post carried a seat in Cabinet; A. Morley explained next day that this phrase was intended to convey an offer of the Cabinet; MS Bryce 10, f. 119.
[4] Bryce next day accepted as Chancellor of the Duchy, also asking for departmental work; MS Bryce 12, f. 65. There is a curious absence of his letters for 1892-4 in the Gladstone Papers (unusually, some of them seemed to have been returned to him, perhaps by Morley, for those in the Bryce MSS are the originals, with Gladstone's dockets).

There is a great change since 1886; another lurch in the direction opposed to ours. I am to see the Prince of Wales tonight when as I expect the case will be different. More when we meet. I have actually eaten a rather good five o'clock tea—which is giving an excellent account of myself. West is beyond anything kind. I am struck again with Ponsonby's looking *aged*. Ever Your affte. W.E. Gladstone
Due at Waterloo tomorrow 1.35 P.M.

To LORD ROSEBERY, 15 August 1892.   N.L.S. 10024, f. 84.

I received the Queen's Commission on Saturday; and I am now going off to Osborne. So early however as last Thursday, the Queen made known to me her anxiety that you should take the Foreign Office. I have not yet heard from you, but, viewing the flight of time, and all the circumstances, I propose to submit your name to her today in conformity with her wish, and I trust you will allow the matter to terminate in this way for the advantage and happiness of all parties as well as for the public good.[1]

16. Tu. [*London*]

Wrote to Mr J.B. Balfour—Sir U. Shuttleworth l.l.—Ld Breadalbane—Sir H. Ponsonby—Mr Asher—Mr Hibbert—Mr O. Morgan—The Queen. Left Osborne 9.45. I am dispensed with on Thursday. Saw Ld Rosebery—Sir H. Ponsonby—Major Bigge—Sir A. West—A. Morley l l l l l—J. Morley l.l.—Sir C. Reid—Mr Canston *cum* Mr Ellis[2]—Sir C. Russell—Ld Herschell—E. Marjoribanks—Sir W. Harcourt—G. Leveson. Attended the Leveson–Morrison marriage (Kensn Ch.).[3] Conclave 3½-5½: peaceful & progressive. Eight to dinner. Read Engln in Paris. Helen read me 'Abbot'.

17. Wed.

Wrote to Sir E. Reed—Mr Seale Hayne—Mr Story—Mr O. Morgan—The Queen l.l.—Mr Asquith[4]—Mr [R. W.] Duff—Sir Walter Foster MP.—Mr G. Leveson MP. Conclave 3–5: & progress. (NB. Kimb. Harc. re Vernon).[5] Saw Sir A. West—Ld Oxenbridge—Ld Spencer—Ld Rosebery—Mr M'Arthur—Mr A. Morley *cum* Mr Marjoribanks—Mr M. finally after 10 PM. Drive with C. Read Englishman in Paris.

18. Th.

Wrote to Sir E. Reed—Sir G. Trevelyan—Sir E. Grey—Mr Sydney Buxton—Geo. Russell—Ld Brassey—Ld Rosebery—The Queen l l—Mr Rendel Tel.—Herbert J.G. Saw Sir A. West l l l—n.

[1] Rosebery replied from London by telegram, at 1.57 p.m. this day to Gladstone at Osborne, 'So be it. Mentmore'; Add MS 44289, f. 174.
[2] Thomas Edward Ellis, 1859–99; liberal M.P. Merionethshire from 1886; the 'Welsh Parnell'; minor office 1892-5.
[3] Lady Sophia Leveson-Gower, Granville's younger da., m. Hugh Morrison.
[4] 'My son Herbert would like to be your U. Sec. I think you would find it a good arrangement: & if it meets your approval I propose that it should go forward'; Asquith agreed; Add MS 44515, f. 181.
[5] Successful offer to Vernon of Captaincy of Gentlemen at Arms; see L. V. Harcourt's diary, 17 August 1892, MS Harcourt dep. 385.

Mr Murray ⎱   on the Private
Mr Shand ⎰   Secretariat[1]
Mr A. Morley—Mr Duff—Mr Marjoribanks—Ld Acton—Sir R. Welby—Ld Brassey—Herbert. Read Englishman in Paris. Drive with C. Worked on books & papers for departure.

To LORD ROSEBERY, foreign secretary, 18 August 1892.   N.L.S. 10024, f. 86.
'*Secret*'.

Exercising the discretion you gave me I consulted with your Peer colleagues and they are all of the opinion which I expressed at Dalmeny, that the Leadership in the Lords will be best in your hands.

It may be well to mention one or two matters incidental to it.

You will probably communicate with Oxenbridge, the outgoing whip, as to a successor.

It is I think understood that if Elgin accepts a captaincy he also undertakes to speak for Scotch business

that if Brassey comes in he shall have the option of speaking for the Board of Trade

and that *some* Department shall be entrusted in the same way to Vernon.

19. Fr.

Wrote to Mrs Ingram—Scotts—Mr Robertson MP.—J. Westell—The Queen l.l.l.—Mr Broad MP[2]—Lord Elgin—Mr Herbert Gardner. An actual initiatory Cabinet 12–1. Well placed for a deaf chief: and nothing could be better in conduct. Saw Sir A.W.—Mr Morley—Mr A. Morley *cum* Mr Marj.—Ld Kimberley *cum* Ld Rosebery—Ld Carrington—Mr Marj.—Mr Bryce—Ld Houghton (Viceroy of I.)[3]—Ld Acton. Dined with H.N.G. by order at Mr Armitstead's. Drive with C. Read Engln in Paris.

Cabinet. 1 C[arlton] Gardens. Noon. Aug. 19.92.[4]
The whole Cabinet attended. Not seated with portfolios &c. round the table but in looser order & in two ranks.

Explained general situation.

Dissuaded from holding appointments of emolument & care[?] along with political or civil offices.[5]

Considered question of preliminary correspondence with a view to the case of the Crofters in Scotland and to the possible creation of Parish Councils in Great Britain.[6]

W.E.G. had conferences with Ld Kimberley & Ld Rosebery; Ld Spencer; Mr Bryce.

W.E.G. In Cabinet Aug. 19. 92.[7]
1. Liberal Ministries with majority under 40.
2. Twin purpose of the session.

[1] Hans George Leslie Shand, secretary to Gladstone as Lord Privy Seal; see 23 Dec. 92n.
[2] Harrington Evans Broad, 1844–1927; accountant; liberal M.P. Derbyshire South 1892-5.
[3] Gladstone was unable to secure his first choice, Aberdeen; see to Ripon 21 Aug. 92.
[4] Add MS 44648, f. 1.
[5] i.e. decision that members of the government should not hold company directorships.
[6] i.e. the Bill of 1894 whose amendments in the Lords were the subject of Gladstone's last speech in the Commons; see 1 Mar. 94n.   [7] Add MS 44648, f. 2.

3. Prospect of much work.
4. Fourfold method of action.
5. To contemplate by preference (except Home Rule) subjects capable of the most concise treatment.

Cabinet. 1 Carlton Gardens. Aug. 19. 92.[1]
1. W.E.G. adverted to the late debate & policy as laid down in his speech for a Liberal Govt.
2. Ld Rosebery raised a question as to the holding of lucrative Directorships & the like by official persons. He was much averse. Feeling of Cabinet in same sense.
WEG S. 29. 92.[2]

20. Sat. [Hawarden]

Wrote to The Queen—Ld Sandhurst—Mr Milner[3]—Mr de Coverley—The Speaker—Mr Adams Acton—Mr Woodall—Ld Ribblesdale—Sir H. Ponsonby: & from Hn Priv. Secretary Tel.—Ld Rosebery Tel. Saw Sir A.W.—Mr A. Morley—Mr Marj.—and the two *cum* Mr Campbell Bannerman—Mr S. Rendel.
1-6¾. To Hawarden. Renounced reading on the journey. Finished Engln in Paris II—Helen read to me from the Abbot. We were very warmly received on the way and on reaching home.

21. 10 S. Trin.

Ch. 11 AM and 6½ P.M. Wrote to The Queen l.l.l.—Ld Breadalbane l. and tel.—Ld Ripon—Mr Foote Tel.—Ld Oxenbridge—Sir R. Welby. Read David by Rev. Stone[4]—Vox Clamantis[5]—H. Jones on Browning.[6]

To LORD RIPON, colonial secretary, 21 August 1892.   Add MS 43515, f. 73.
'*Secret*'.
In connection with your important office I ought to tell you, and ought to have told you sooner, that very early indeed in the confabulations on the formation of a Government Irish arrangements were on the carpet. Aberdeen had certain presumptive elements of claim to the Viceroyalty [of Ireland] but I soon found the difficulties were grave, and finally they proved insurmountable: and I certainly think we have now the promise of a stronger hand [i.e. Houghton] in Irish government, where every thing is or may become vital. Under these circumstances, without anything like a covenant, and under the strictest confidence (nothing for example having been said to the Queen) intimations have been made to him as to Canada which gave him great consolation & pleasure. Ireland had such precedence that it was not possible to wait, and I am sure your candid mind will feel that the circumstances were urgent, although he, being one of the best fellows upon earth never would have taken offence had we given him less than his due.[7]

---

[1] Add MS 44648, f. 3.   [2] Presumably a record written later.
[3] Alfred Milner, asking him, with Welby and Hamilton, to make an examination of the financial relations of Britain and Ireland; Milner agreed; Add MS 44515, f. 267.
[4] H. E. Stone, *David; the man after God's own heart* (1888).
[5] Perhaps *Vox Clamantis; or, a cry to Protestant Dissenters* (1683).
[6] H. Jones, *Browning as a philosophical and religious teacher* (1891).
[7] Ripon replied next day, Add MS 43515, f. 75, that he regretted Aberdeen's disappointment and agreed with earmarking Canada for him, though Stanley would not ordinarily retire until June 1894.

22.

Wrote to Mr Murray tel. l.l.l.—Mr Morley—Mr Stuart MP.—The Queen—Mr Labouchere—Sir H. Ponsonby—& minutes. Breakfast in bed. Worked on Odes. Read the Venetians.[1] Worked on 'from Chaos to kosmos'.[2] Drive with C. Backgammon with Mr Armitstead. Worked on Phoenicia.[3]

To H. LABOUCHERE, M.P., 22 August 1892.[4]   Add MS 44515, f. 256.

My attention has been called to a letter addressed by you to Mr. Tonsley, and printed in the *Times* of to-day, and I have to assure you that the understanding which has been conveyed to you is not correct.

I am alone responsible for recommendations submitted to her Majesty respecting the tenure of political office, or for the absence of such recommendation in any given instance. I was aware of the high position you have created for yourself in the House of Commons, and of the presumption, which would naturally arise, that your name could not fail to be considered on an occasion when a Government had to be formed. I gave accordingly my best consideration to the subject, and I arrived at the conclusion that there were incidents in your case which, while they testified to your energy and influence, were in no degree disparaging to your honour, but which appeared to me to render it unfit that I should ask your leave to submit your name to her Majesty for a political office, which would involve your becoming a servant of the Crown.

23. Tu.

Ch. 8½ A.M. Wrote to Sir H. Ponsonby l.l.l.—Ld Northbrook—Mr C. Flower—Ld Rosebery l.l.—Ld Brassey—Sig. Schilizzi—Mr Murray Tel.—Ld Chesterfield—& minutes. Read The Venetians—Alsace-Lorraine.[5] 16 to dinner: I sat at the end like a desert island. Backgammon with Mr A. 10000 in house grounds and park. Made a short flowershow address.[6] Everything topsyturvy: but the organisation did Herbert much credit.

To Sir H. F. PONSONBY, the Queen's Secretary, 23 August 1892.   RA C39/130.

As regards the Mistress of the Robes I am sorry the Queen should have had trouble. The Duke of Roxburghe I think has ceased to be in any sense a Liberal. Not so the Duke of Bedford and in this case I should have [*sic*] perfectly ready to leave the question of voting in the Duke's hands. When there was something like a balance of parties in the Lords, it may have been rational to stickle for this or that vote. To us it matters little at what figure between 30 and 40 our professed adherents are to stand. I only wish they were the least of the inconveniences likely to follow the recent turn of affairs in the House of Lords, inconveniences of which I, for one, take a most serious view.

[1] See 13 June 92.
[2] Further work on 'The Olympian Religion'.
[3] For his address to the Oriental Congress; see 7 Sept. 92n.
[4] Published in *Truth*, 1 September 1892, with Labouchere's reply of 23 August stating that he had never 'directly or indirectly' asked for any post, and admiring Gladstone's 'chivalry in covering the Royal action by assuming the constitutional responsibility of a proceeding'. Labouchere prefaced the letter: 'I publish (by permission) . . .'; Gladstone put an ink 'X' on his copy against 'by permission'; Add MS 44515, f. 304. See also 25 Aug. 92.
[5] J. Heimweh, *Questions du temps présent. Triple Alliance et Alsace Lorraine* (1892).
[6] On small holdings; *T.T.*, 24 August 1892, 6a.

Unless H.M. is disposed to recommend further communications on the ground of what I have said, I have only to acquiesce readily in the suggestion you have conveyed: it would I conceive take the form of allowing the question of appointment to stand over, and having the attendances performed under a temporary understanding as the Queen might please.

To LORD ROSEBERY, foreign secretary, 23 August 1892.   N.L.S. 10024, f. 90.

Will it not be well for me to offer the Lord High Commissionership[1] to Lord Aberdeen?

The interval before actual expiry in Canada is long: June 1894. His resignation at an earlier date seems to be not unlikely.

I telegraphed to Acton through Downing St that I wished to recommend him for a Captaincy (£1200): and I am (1½ P.M.) rather anxiously awaiting his answer.[2]

24. Wed. St Bartholomew.[3]

Ch 8½ A.M. with H.C. Wrote to Mr J. Cowan tel.—S. Lyttelton tel. l.l.—Sir A. West—Sir H. Ponsonby 1 & Tel.—Ld Breadalbane—The Queen l.l.—Ld Rosebery—Ld Acton—Princess Cassano[4]—Ld Kensington. Went over the tents. Also among the crowd: & made a very short address of welcome: some 12 m.[5] Drive with Mr A & backgammon. Could not rally for my Phoenician paper. Hope better tomorrow.

To LORD ACTON, 24 August 1892.   Cambridge University Library.

I learn your acceptance[6] with much selfish pleasure: it does us honour.

With regard to your closing paragraph,[7] you may remember that both Granville and Spencer began with household appointments. But an anecdote received from Granville's own mouth, will be more to purpose than any explanation I could offer.

When he received the office of the Buckhounds he had a fear that he might lie stranded in the Household. He consulted his old friend Lord Lansdowne (after whose descendants he subsequently looked with grateful care). Lord Lansdowne said to him 'Did you ever hear, or find, that a man was less likely to get a given office, because he had some other office to surrender'? He accepted.

I dare say I shall hear of you again before long. I shrewdly suspect you will have a humdrum interval to dispose of before your duties begin.

P.S. You will hear before this reaches you what I have replied to the overture for making you a Lord-in waiting. If you agree, it is a costly compliment but it *is* a compliment from

---

[1] Of the Church of Scotland in 1893.

[2] Rosebery thought Aberdeen would decline, and reported he had urged Acton to accept; Add MS 44289, f. 177.

[3] He was this day re-elected for Midlothian, his 26th and last election.

[4] Princess de Cassano; on Father Lockhart; see Add MS 44549, f. 2.

[5] *T.T.*, 25 August 1892, 5c.

[6] Offer of the Captaincy of the Yeomen of the Guard; Acton stated that 'I shall accept it, cheerfully and gratefully. Rosebery assures me that you would prefer it, and there is no other opening to employment at present. My difficulty is ... that it is incongruous, and scarcely compatible with any position I may aspire to in a more obscure walk of life' (23 August 1892, Add MS 44094, f. 205). In fact Gladstone's p.s. showed the way, and Acton was appointed to a lordship-in-waiting, worth less than the Captaincy.

[7] Acton's recollection of Gladstone's remark that 'if one of the Five Peers had been out of the way, you would have regarded me as standing next to the Five ... [i.e. as a candidate for the Cabinet]; ibid. For Acton's hopes and manoeuvres for a Cabinet place, see Chadwick, *Acton and Gladstone*, 38 ff.

the Queen herself. You would then no doubt have a turn at Windsor (a month?) and I think would not dislike it: time not very much invaded, exit on the Terrace, & a good *Library*.

To LORD ROSEBERY, foreign secretary, 24 August 1892.   N.L.S. 10024, f. 94.

I think you are making excellent beginnings: but I have suggested a small change in the draft to the Turk for fear he should misinterpret 'considerable'.

In 1884 or 5 Hobart Pasha told me the Sultan looked on me as his greatest enemy. There was then[?] no other foundation [for] it than that I had perhaps spoken the most plainly, but I think he may have inflicted on himself injury through that erroneous belief.

In what you say of me, you are safely within the mark. Desiring to be just to him I have thought he seemed to behave well in the Bulgarian business since the Union: and my Egyptian views lie in the same directions as his, unless he seeks, as he may, to encroach on Egyptian privileges.

I *am* afraid that both the Sultanate and the Popedom have in so far become stark from their old age that even the advent of a really great man could perhaps do no effectual good.

25. *Th.*

Ch. 8½ A.M. Wrote to Ld Kimberley—A.E. West—Sir H. Ponsonby l.l.l.—Mr Labouchere—Ld Ribblesdale—Lady Aberdeen—& minutes. Walk with H. talk on mines. Read Venetians—Heimweh, Alsace-Lorraine. Worked on paper for the Oriental Congress: (Phoenikes). Party began to melt: 25000 have been here!

To H. LABOUCHERE, M.P., 25 August 1892.[1]   Add MS 44515, f. 291.

I cannot hesitate to answer to your appeal. At no time and in no form have I had from you any signification of a desire for office.

You do me personally more than justice. My note to you is nothing more or less than a true while succinct statement of the facts as well as of the constitutional doctrine which applies to them.

I quite agree with you that men in political office are servants of the country, as well as of the Crown. There are incidents attaching to them in each aspect, and I mentioned the capacity which alone touched the case before me.

26. *Fr.*

Ch. 8¼ A.M. Wrote to Ld Chesterfield—J. Morley—Rev. Dr Ginsburg—Sir A. West—Mr Bertram Currie—Ld Rosebery—& minutes. Helen read from The Abbot. Read Venetians—and Heimweh. Worked on MS for Congress. Worked on Chaos.

[1] Published in *Truth*, 1 September 1892 with Labouchere's reply of 26 August recognising that Gladstone did not ask his permission to submit his name to the Queen. His editorial following the letters (see also 22 Aug. 92) stated: 'I now say, in the most unqualified manner, that I know that she did interfere.'

To J. MORLEY, Irish secretary, 26 August, 1892.   Add MS 44549, f. 2.

Three million cheers, & one million more![1] You really have done it right well & manfully. We have three strands of good in one rope. 1. You are returned. 2. Newcastle has saved herself from black disgrace. 3. The creature Ralli is defeated. I call him by this term because I conceive that he being a Greek can be a so called Unionist only through sheer flunkeyism: to which I hear that he is much given socially.

A minor compliment to your accurate recollection is inclosed:[+] not without humble confession of error.

[+] Pamphlet entitled "Why Irishmen in Ireland have so little respect for the law."[2]

To LORD ROSEBERY, foreign secretary, 26 August 1892.   N.L.S. 10024, f. 97.

I have read with interest Lord Vivian's No 162 but I am totally unable to appreciate the value of Signor Brisi's apprehensions because

1. I am wholly uninformed as to Salisbury's policy concerning the balance of power in the Mediterranean; except that negatively I understand he had entered into no covenant.[3]

2. I am wholly uninformed as to any agreements or engagements under which Italy has come anew with some hesitation (p. 2) and which may have a direct bearing on Mediterranean equilibrium.

3. I am also wholly uninformed what is the British policy in Egypt to which the Italian Government has recently given its loyal and cordial support.

This is an important subject. But I believe a political crisis is awaiting solution in Italy through a general Election. If this be so, and in the absence of any immediate cause for uneasiness, I suppose we need not make haste, and it is possible that the Election might clear the path.

27. Sat.

Ch. 8½ A.M. Wrote to Mr Herbert Gardner—Sir A. West—Ld Chancellor—Mr Giffen—Priv. Sec. (Tel.). Read Heimweh (finished)—The Venetians—Poems of Eta[4]—Blackwood on Ministry.[5] Worked on MS as yesterday. Tea at Mr Toller's.

To LORD HERSCHELL, lord chancellor, 27 August 1892.   Add MS 44549, f. 3.

It occurs to me to remind you that Bryce might be a person most convenient for you to refer to about the question of restriction on Irish legislative power as to Contracts from his rich & accurate knowledge of the American constitution.

28. 10 S. Trin.

Ch 11 AM and 6½ PM. God bless dear Helen. Wrote to J. Morley—Princess Troubetzkoi—Ld R. Gore—Sir A. West. Read The Semitic Philosophy[6]—Life of

[1] Morley held Newcastle, at the by-election on taking office, against P. Ralli, standing as a liberal unionist. Gladstone was in fact quite well acquainted with Ralli (see 8 May 71).

[2] Secretary's original note.

[3] Rosebery replied, 27 August, Add MS 44289, f. 181 that Salisbury stated 'he promised the Italians no material assistance', but that the truth of this was as yet not investigated. He also reported on Russian advances in Paris.

[4] 'Eta' [W. Cunningham], *Virgil's first pastoral . . . preceded by a MS. poem* (1884).

[5] *Blackwood's*, clii. 293 (August 1892).

[6] P. C. Friese, *Semitic philosophy; showing the ultimate social and scientific outcome of original Christianity in its conflict with surviving ancient Heathenism* (1890).

St Columba[1]—W.H.S. on Current Literature[2]—Vox Clamantis—Memoir of Mrs Drummond.[3]

29. M.

Ch. 8½ A.M. Wrote to Lady Aberdeen—W. Ridler—Sir W. Harcourt—Mr [R.] Morris Lewis—and minutes. Finished MS for Congress. Worked on Chaos & books. Read Local Option in Norway[4]—The Venetians.[5]

Drive with C. Then walked & came unawares in the quietest corner of the park on a dangerous cow which knocked me down and might have done serious damage.[6] I walked home with little difficulty & have to thank the Almighty. Early to bed.

To Sir W. V. HARCOURT, chancellor of the exchequer,   MS Harcourt dep. 12, f. 86b. 29 August 1892. '*Private.*'

Your letter[7] gives me an opportunity of expressing partly congratulation on the egregious failure of that crack-brained opponent, but, very much more, vexation at your having been subjected to annoyance and expense from such a source.

I go with you strongly about bimetallism & am rather indignant with Goschen whose particularity when he was a Liberal was the stiffness & purism with which he stood upon his personal opinions but who now shows no difficulty in making compromises which are all on one side.

I am a little afraid that if you appoint Rivers Wilson official, and Farrer non-official, the cry will go forth that the Commission is wanting in independence.

I mentioned an independent gentleman Sir F. Forbes Adam[8] who has sufficiently high qualifications to be worth inquiring about. He is or has been connected with India but is I understand firm and sound.

Lubbock I presume is sound, and if so would have some advantages. It is desirable to have a sane man on the Commission who is not of our politics.

Again, is it known what are Courtney's opinions? If he is sound, might he not be very valuable.

[1] E. A. Cooke, *Life and work of St. Columba* (1888).
[2] Untraced.
[3] C. K. Paul, *Maria Drummond: a sketch* (1891).
[4] T. M. Wilson, *Local option in Norway* (1891).
[5] See 13 June 92.
[6] He was knocked down by a wild heifer which had escaped into the park; pretending to be dead, he waited until he could escape behind a tree (Magnus, 402). The heifer was shot, its head now being displayed in the Glynne Arms, Hawarden.
[7] Of 28 August, Add MS 44202, f. 213 (dictated to E. W. Hamilton) on bimetallism and a talk with Goschen before he left the Treasury: 'it is quite plain that he [Goschen] found himself between the devil and the deep sea, with Salisbury, Balfour & Chaplin as bi-metallists on the one side and his own mono-metallic convictions on the other'; Britain now committed to attend the Conference. Harcourt added: 'I am very pleased to know . . . that you approve of strengthening our Delegation by sound mono-metallists.'
[8] Note by Murray in MS Harcourt dep. 12: Forbes Adams is 'a Bombay merchant with mono-metallic opinions'; Courtney is practically a mono-metallist but leans to bimetallism 'in its theoretical aspects'; Lubbock is 'probably the best man you could find for your purposes', but would have to be the senior delegate, as would B. W. Currie.

30. Tu.

Rose at eleven. Wrote to Sir H. Ponsonby—Sir A. West—Rev. Dr. Ginsburg—Ld Rosebery—Ld R. Gower—and minutes. Examining & arranging papers in the forenoon. Drive with C. Read Venetians (finished)—Contemp. Rev.[1]—Homère et Socrate.[2] Helen finished the Abbot aloud.

To LORD ROSEBERY, foreign secretary, 30 August 1892.   N.L.S. 10024, f. 100.

1. I am glad to hear that Salisbury disclaims having promised material aid:[3] when the time comes I should ask can this be Brisi's belief? A clever writer in Blackwood for August sets out the whole argument, quite in the opposite sense & holds Italy would have been mad to enter the T.A. [Triple Alliance] without a promise of this kind.

2. About Pamir I am utterly in the dark: the name as new to me as the merits.

I do not know why we have not a resident in Afghanistan. As I recollect we used to have one an Asiatic Mahomedan? and then that most guilty war was made upon the 'earthen pot'. Cannot something be done to put us into a better position for getting information than that which you so feelingly describe?

I wish heartily, with you, that the Staal and Giers proposition could be revived.

The Ameer himself ought to supply information if he is afraid.

The telegram from Berlin is disagreeable but if Berlin had meant Bismarck we should have to remember that there would be a disposition there to set us by the ears with Russia.[4]

[P.S.] The arrangements about answering for departments used to be made by Granville with the Departments, & without reference to me.

31. Wed.

Ch. 8½ A.M. Wrote to Warden of All Souls—Priv. Sec. Tel.—Sir W. Harcourt—Sir A. Gordon—Sir H. Ponsonby Tel.—and minutes. Made a beginning for my possible Romanes Lecture at Oxford.[5] Read Nineteenth Century[6]—Mansfield's Don Juan[7]—Biographies. Worked on books. Walk with Helen.

To Sir W. V. HARCOURT, chancellor of the exchequer,   MS Harcourt dep. 12, f. 86h.
31 August 1892.[8]

I am almost sorry you suggested The Hague, as they will probably plead this in applying: but I shall not be at all sorry if they fail in getting any central seat & are nonplussed altogether.

I agree that the weight of the Rothschild name recorded for orthodoxy would be great.

But one of the difficulties into which this foolish scheme plunges us seems to be this;

[1] C.R., lxii. 1 (August 1892).

[2] Untraced.

[3] Rosebery replied, 31 August, Add MS 44289, f. 183, that he would send 'a secret memorandum' (not found) on Salisbury and Italy.

[4] Rosebery commented on 2 September, ibid., f. 185: 'I hear you want to see the Triple Alliance. So do we all, but we have never succeeded.'

[5] 'The Romanes Lecture, 1892. An Academic Sketch' (1892); see 24 Oct. 92.

[6] N.C., xxxii. 177 (August 1892); series on 'Why I voted for Mr. Gladstone'.

[7] R. Mansfield, Don Juan. A play in four acts (1891).

[8] Undated on the letter, probably that written this day; docketed by Harcourt '2 Sept. 92' (i.e. received that day).

who will *conduct the case* for monometallism? Important men will hardly consent to dance attendance at The Hague or elsewhere abroad.

I am glad you are to have a breath abroad.

There was a rule about getting the Queen's consent to leave the country. It applied to the Prime Minister—I know not whether to others. If it does Salisbury must have worked it pretty well.

Thurs. Sept 1. 1892.

Ch. 8½ A.M. Wrote to Mr Hayes (Labby)—The Queen l.l.—Mr Westell—Priv. Sec. Tel.—Mr D. Nutt—and minutes. Worked on books. Read Ride across Norway—Don Juan (finished). Helen began Waverley[1] for me.

To T. J. HAYES,[2] 1 September 1892.   Add MS 44549, f. 5.

Whatever be the correct opinion on the subject of your letter I am desirous to relieve you from any misapprehension as to the material facts.

Mr. Labouchere's Vote on the recent Royal Grant was no ban to a proposal that he should become a member of the present administration, for there are various gentlemen forming part of it who gave a similar vote.

It is not true that H.M. declined to appoint Mr. Labouchere to office, for no one can decline that which has not been proposed. In the present case there was no such proposal. For the absence of it, I am the person responsible. I did not make it because of incidents connected with Mr. Labouchere's position & occupation, which were in no degree disparaging to his honour but which appeared to bear upon the propriety of his holding office under the Crown.

To Sir H. F. PONSONBY, the Queen's secretary, 1 September 1892. Add MS 44549, f. 5.

On the 26th you spoke of some delay in appointing two of the Lords in Waiting; I have not however heard the names of the five about whom there is no difficulty.

Since 1868 there has prevailed, at least in the Governments with which I have been concerned, a practice begun by Ld. Granville of arranging with Household Peers for their taking charge severally of departmental business in the Lords when there is no Peer charged by his office with the care of it. It is desirable not to leave these arrangements in doubt and hardly possible to make them until the appointment of Lords in Waiting is either completed or well advanced.

[P.S.] I am sorry for the fate of Lord Hamilton whom I had always found agreeable and taken to be popular; but I cannot press him against H.M.'s adverse leaning.

2. Fr.

Ch. 8½ A.M. Wrote to Ld Kimberley—Dr Talmage Tel.—Mr Morley—Sir J. Lacaita—Rev. S.E.G.—Hon. S. Lyttelton—and minutes. Worked on Romanes paper. Grosvenor party from Saighton in afternoon.[3] Short visit to St Deiniol's.

---

[1] By Scott; see 14 Aug. 26.

[2] Liberal in South Lancashire (see the letter's subscription to 'old friends and supporters in South Lancashire'). Though recorded *sic*, this is probably Thomas Travers Hayes, of Fairfield, Leigh, Lancashire, member of the National Liberal Club.

[3] Including Wilfrid Blunt; good description of the visit in *My Diaries being a personal narrative of events 1888–1914*, i. 73 (1921).

Read Denifle (Univv.)[1]—Ride across Iceland (finished)[2]—Lorne's Palmerston—bad.[3]

To Sir J. P. LACAITA, 2 September 1892.[4]   Add MS 44234, f. 210.

Will you kindly tell me, for you are sure to know, whether I am right in believing that the Government of Italy, at some date since the union of the country, abolished the theological faculty in the Universities? following in substance the example, I fear the bad example, of France.

I know not when this note may catch you—but you would be very welcome here if you would make your appearance between the 8th and the 12th instant, or again about the 20th—your appearance not in Downing Street but at Hawarden.[5]

To LORD KIMBERLEY, lord president and Indian secretary,   Kimberley MSS.
2 September 1892.

Harcourt is I believe going abroad but I hope the rule will not be made general that on that account his work is to come to me.[6]

But I do not in the least grudge any time given to the subject which though his properly and primarily cannot be exclusively his.

I have not sufficient knowledge to see my way to any conclusion in this difficult and complex business but there are several points on which I have put down my opinion on the sheet enclosed.

There cannot be a better introduction to it than your letter.

[P.S.] I approve of your proposal about a Committee. But I think we might get ourselves embarrassed by it unless we place at the head of it some responsible member of the Government who would follow its proceedings and represent generally our view. You are perhaps too much occupied for this. But if you think the proposition sound, we might think of some one. *Bryce* laments the smallness of his work: Lefevre has not a heavy department.

[Memorandum on an Indian Gold Standard]

Without attempting to dive into the great question of the Indian Standard, I note my opinion on one or two points.

1. It appears to me that we ought not to postpone considering the application of the Indian Government until the proceedings of the proposed Commission have run their course. The application is urgent. The Commission may spin out its work: and its issue in [*sc.* is?] involved in uncertainty.

---

[1] H.S. Denifle's book (in fact already begun, see 20 Apr. 92); sent by Lord Brassey (see 3 Sept. 92).
[2] *sc.* Norway.   [3] J. D. S. Campbell, Lord Lorne, *Viscount Palmerston* (1892).
[4] Holograph; some of Gladstone's letters were returned in 1931.
[5] Lacaita replied, 5 September, Add MS 44234, f. 212, that 'the Theological Faculty was abolished in all the Italian Universities!'; he hoped to come on 9 September.
[6] On 31 August, Add MS 44229, f. 34, Kimberley sent a despatch from the Indian government on bimetallism, which argued that if 'we do not adopt bimetallism, they should be allowed to take immediate steps for the introduction of a gold standard into India'; Kimberley commented: 'Now I apprehend there is no chance of our adopting bimetallism, (I should be very sorry if I thought there were any)', consequently the Cabinet would have to consider the proposal for a gold standard for India after the Bimetallic Conference (which he assumed would be 'without any result'). He sent a résumé of Treasury opinions since the 1870s, with his own view: 'I confess my predisposition is against tampering with the silver currency . . .'.

2. It seems also plain that the question should be considered on Indian grounds, and with reference to the special wants and capacities of India rather than as part of the general question.

3. The proposal of the Indian Government appears to be motivé [*sic*] largely by the consideration that we may be indisposed to proceed in the direction of bimetallism. But be this as it may, and be the difficulties surmountable or insurmountable, the movement towards a gold standard, which is so manifestly the best, seems to be a movement in the right direction, and one to which we ought to accord as good a preliminary reception as we can.

4. I am under the impression that in the great mass of small every day & popular transactions the rupee still does its work without sensible dislocation. If this be so, does it deserve consideration whether in the event of a change to gold as the standard, silver might still be left, permanently or for a time, as legal tender in discharge of obligations up to a point higher than with us, e.g. £5, or even £10.

5. Would it not be well to proceed promptly in the preparation of illustrative tables and particulars, and to include in these a practical account of the actual steps taken in Germany, France & any other important countries, upon proceeding to the change or modification of their respective standards.

6. I agree with Lord Kimberley that this subject may properly be referred to a Committee but I think that we should take care to have such a Committee as would remain in touch with the Government. This might be considered in its composition.

7. I am given to understand that the Dutch have quite recently performed in Java the operation, or something very near it, which is now brought upon the carpet for India. If this be so their example would be much to the purpose, though the scale is much smaller. I do not know whether that Government is now as close and mysterious as it was half a century ago about its proceedings in Java: but it seems most desirable if possible to obtain an explicit narrative of the measures their [*sic*] taken, which I am told produced some temporary shock but have been effectual in their result.

8. What I have written has reference to the proposal of the Indian Government to introduce a gold Standard into India (p. 2 paragraphs, 3, 4, 5) and not to the minute of Sir D. Barbour.

3. Sat.

Ch. 8½ AM. Wrote to Mr Stuart Rendel—Ld Rosebery—Lord Brassey—Sir A. West—Mr Birkbeck—Mr Nield—& minutes. Saw HNG on E.T. Standard.[1] Read Lorne's Palmerston—Saintsbury's Lord Derby[2]—Q.R. on Freeman.[3] Helen read Waverley for me. Almost a blank on the Romanes business.

To LORD BRASSEY, 3 September 1892.   Add MS 44549, f. 6.

I have read your inclosure[4] with great interest & with no dissent unless upon points purely collateral & incidental.

It was to me matter of much regret that the effort to connect you with the Government could not take effect & the subject has remained upon my mind. I do not know whether you are aware, but it is the fact that owing to the limited number of our friends in the Lords we were obliged to cut off from that House all political appointments outside the Cabinet except the u. sec. ship which we could not help and the Viceroyalty of Ireland.

[1] Presumably a newspaper; but no details found.
[2] G. E. B. Saintsbury, *The* [*fourteenth*] *Earl of Derby* (1892).
[3] *Q.R.*, clxxv. 1 July (1892).
[4] The letter is docketed: 'Dennifer book' (i.e. Denifle); see 1 Sept. 92.

To S. RENDEL, M.P., 3 September, 1892.   Add MS 44549, f. 7.

I think the representations made to you by Mr Ellis[1] were more suited for conversation than for letter & I hope that you will soon give me an opportunity of speaking to you here about them, if as I trust I may assume your trying anxieties about Mrs. Goodhart are now effectually relieved.

We expect John Morley & others from (say) 8th to 12th & Alfred Lyttelton about 20th—I mention these as it is humane to give you indications of times when you would not find Hawarden quite a desert. I had though Mr E. an intelligent man but this account puzzles me. Does he think Welsh Disestablishment can be carried at the same time with a Home Rule Bill & other claims? or does he recommend making promises through the Queen's Speech with a moral certainty that they cannot be fulfilled. Or would he like us to tell the Irish Members that they are to be kept at Westminster till all the claims of all the interests have been satisfied?

4. 12 S. Trin.

Ch 11 A.M. with H.C.—6½ P.M. Read [blank] (mahometan) on Islam[2]—Atkinson, Forty years[3]—Westcott, Rel. Thought in the West.[4] Wrote to Sir H. Ponsonby . . . . and minutes.

5. M.

Ch. 8½ A.M. Wrote to Ld Rosebery l. & tel.—Dr Ginsburg—Mr Fowler—Rev. Mr Trotter—Mr Stanford—Messrs Macmillan—and minutes. Read Archd. Howell's Address[5]—Rolle, Culte to Bacchus[6]—Naulahlea.[7]

6. Tu.

Ch. 8½ AM. Wrote to (all forgotten).[8] Worked on MS Romanes Lecture. J. Morley came: long conversation. Read Denifle—Naulahlea. Saw Cunliffes and Buxtons—who came over for tea.

To E. MARJORIBANKS, chief whip, 6 September, 1892.   Add MS 44332, f. 234.

1. L[abouchere] is a very clever fellow but probably often outwits himself in handling his own case through Truth.[9] In handling the retention of Irish Members he is extremely acute. It doubles the difficulties of the question.

2. Hunter[10] sore. In none of my previous Cabinet making has there been anything like

---

[1] For T. E. Ellis's efforts to promote Welsh issues from his position as junior whip, see Morgan, *Wales in British Politics*, 121 ff.

[2] D. C. Hannigan, 'A Mohammedan on Mohammedanism', *Westminster Review*, cxxxviii. 8 (July 1892).   [3] See 14 Apr. 92.

[4] B. F. Westcott, *Essays in the history of religious thought in the West* (1891).

[5] D. Howell, 'Welsh nationality. An address' (1892).

[6] P. N. Rolle, *Recherches sur le Culte de Baccus*, 3v. (1824).

[7] R. Kipling and W. Balestier, *The Naulahlea: a tale of West and East* (1892).

[8] Phrase added in pencil.

[9] Letter from Labouchere to Marjoribanks forwarded to Gladstone: 'it suggests that L. himself is not altogether satisfied with the results of the ferment he has endeavoured to raise over his exclusion from office'; Add MS 44332, ff. 227, 232.

[10] William Alexander Hunter, 1844–98; professor of law at London University; liberal M.P. N. Aberdeen 1885–96. No office 1892–5.

the development of personal ambitions that this occasion has produced (Stuart almost heart broken). Your communication to him was I think a little early. But no doubt you made it a secret? & he can keep one? I am always terribly afraid of too early disclosures of any Government plan. This is a very delicate one.

But it is not a Suspensory Bill. It is a Bill for putting an end to all public ecclesiastical stipends in Scotland & settles 9/10 of Disestablishment. There are two preliminary questions which it would be beneficial to test if it can be done without any sort of committal. a. How would the Disestablished take it? b. (less vital) Would the established be at all mollified? A little later on perhaps Hunter might see [J. B.] Balfour who is so sensible.

3. Hunter's plan for Scotch Bills[1] is bold, perhaps might be modified, should not be peremptorily cast aside.

4. My notes are gone on to Trevelyan.

5. I am indeed sorry about Winterbotham.[2] It will give a bad *start* if we do not retain the seat & the very greatest care should be taken in the choice of the candidate. [P.S.] Many thanks for excellent grouse.

7. *Wed.*[3]

Ch. 8½ A.M. Wrote to The Queen Tel.—Ld Rosebery—Mrs Th.—Mr Rendel— and minutes. Read Denifle—Budinszky[4]—Collier's Hist.[5]—Naulahlea. Drive & walk with J. Morley—who went at night, after doing me the favour of reading my MS (partial) when he encouraged me to proceed. He left late.

To LORD ROSEBERY, foreign secretary,   N.L.S. 10024, f. 123.
7 September 1892.

1. I agree with you about Greek finance.[6] I have no doubt the Greeks might learn much from us in financial machinery but this would be best done by sending a Greek here. The object seems to be to 'make capital' out of our report & so mend the situation: this is slippery work for us. I think we could not advise without a guarantee that our advice would be taken, & this guarantee would hardly be compatible with the independence of the Greek Government.

2. Pamirs. I quite agree that Afgan = Indian for your purpose. I should like the neutrality.

3. Very glad you are going to Balmoral. Perhaps you will be able gently to help on the Lords in Waiting, who appear to be waiting Lords indeed. If there is a hitch you may find out where it lies.

There is also a question of mistress of the Robes. Lady Granville would be our best. But I am loath to ask the Q. to lower the rank hitherto uniformly maintained.

[1] Proposal to refer all Scottish bills for 2nd reading, cttee. and report, to Scottish members sitting as a Grand Committee; Add MS 44332, f. 228.

[2] A. B. Winterbotham, liberal M.P. Cirencester, d. 8 September 1892. The result of the subsequent by-election was a tie (after a petition); on a rerun H. L. W. Lawson, 1862–1933, just held the seat for the liberals. See to Schnadhorst, 6 Oct. 92.

[3] Max Müller this day read out Gladstone's paper, 'The Phoenician elements in the Homeric Poems', to the International Oriental Congress meeting in London; *T.T.*, 8 September 1892, 6b.

[4] See 19 Sept. 92.

[5] Probably W. Collier, *The central figures of Irish history* (1891).

[6] Untraced paper sent on 5 September; Add MS 44289, f. 187. Rosebery qualified his view following a telegram from Egerton; he concluded: 'French influence is now paramount in Greece and it would be pleasant if we could reestablish British influence by a friendly act or two.'

4. I hope you will like Balmoral—I always thought it the pleasantest part of my Court experience.

P.S. I do not quite see *how* you are to help the Chinaman in getting his frontier.

8. Th.

Ch. 8½ A.M. Wrote to Lady Chesterfield—Ld Rosebery—Sir A. West—Ld Ripon—The Queen—Reeves & Turner—Ld Kimberley—& minutes. Read Naulahlea—Mullinger Hist. Cambridge.[1] H. read me Waverley. Walk with her.

To LORD KIMBERLEY, lord president and Indian secretary,   Kimberley MSS.
8 September 1892.

I am glad to have seen the Indian currency papers.[2] Probably we shall all hear enough about it.

My encounter with the cow might have·been serious and was not at the time agreeable but I have no inconvenience worth naming, only a stiffness of muscles not yet quite gone, which a *little* restricts respiration, only I believe for the immediate present. Many thanks. [P.S.] I think you are quite right in *devolving* the enquiry.

9. Fr.

Ch. 8½ A.M. Wrote to Persian Minister—Grand Vizir of Persia[3]—Sir H. Ponsonby—C. Lowe—Prof. Romanes—E. Menken—Mr S. Rendel. Read The Naulahlea—Zart Einfluss des Engl. Th. I.[4] Worked on Romanes Lecture. Backgammon with Mr A.

To G. J. ROMANES, 9 September 1892.   Add MS 44549, f. 8.

As the recent political crisis may cause you, or rather may have caused you, some uncertainty, I write this note to say that, after reflection & consultation, & feeling my ground, I hope to fulfil my engagement for the delivery of the Inaugural Lecture on your foundation. It stands I think for the 17th of Oct. Should there be any disposition to postpone it to the last days of that month or the first days of November, such a change would entirely fall in with my occasions, indeed would be rather advantageous than otherwise.[5]

10. Sat.

Ch. 8½ AM. Wrote to Sir W. Harcourt—Mrs Vyner—and minutes. Worked on Romanes MS. Read (largely) Hume[6]—La Devote[7]—Cheshire Conv.[8] aloud, evg. Walk with party. Conversation with A. Gordon—Lady Aberdeen.

---

[1] J. B. Mullinger, *A history of the University of Cambridge* (1888).
[2] See 2 Sept. 92. Kimberley, 6 September, Add MS 44229, sent a sympathetic note on the heifer incident.
[3] Thanks for a letter of congratulation; Add MS 44549, f. 8.
[4] G. Zart, *Einfluss der Englischen Philosophen* (1881).
[5] See 24 Oct. 92. Romanes replied on 24 September (delayed in Germany), Add MS 44516, f. 64, welcoming Gladstone's continued intention to lecture, and pointing out that 24 October was the date Gladstone earlier suggested, which the Vice-Chancellor had accepted.
[6] Presumably Hume's *History*; see 15 Dec. 26.
[7] L. Gagneur, *Une dévote fin de siècle* (1891).
[8] See 6 Feb. 86?

To Sir W. V. HARCOURT, chancellor of the exchequer,   MS Harcourt dep. 12, f. 91.
10 September 1892.

I received with extreme pleasure your highly favourable report from Weisbaden[1] &
hope there may be nothing to interfere with service for many long years to come.

Your account of Labouchere[2] and his interlocution is curious and suggests various
thoughts one would rather be without. Of its accuracy I am sorry to say I have a strong confirmation in this. He wrote it all to Wemyss Reid who read it out to my informant! with a disagreeable specification of the supposed motive of the desire to be on good terms.

I think that, as you have sounded Alfred Rothschild, Rivers Wilson will probably do
very well to fill up the remaining place. But who is to work the case in the [Currency]
Commission? We cannot expect R. to do it or Bertram Currie. The Commission not
being able to sit in London, I would that it should now here find a local habitation.

Meantime the subject comes up in another & more pressing form from India whether
[sic] they are meditating a gold standard without being very clear in their explanations.

I hear from my son Harry, and Kimberley confirms it, that in Java—no doubt on a much
more limited stage—the Dutch Government have discarded the silver standard and introduced a gold one with success. But if they establish a ratio of gold to silver lower than the
true, i.e. require people to give for silver more than it is worth, their gold will soon be
carried off.

I am very glad Rosebery is at Balmoral. J. Morley went to Ireland in excellent heart.

To LORD HERSCHELL, lord chancellor, 10 September 1892.   Add MS 44549, f. 8.

With some regret I feel that the position of the Liberal minority of Clergy is now so dis-
advantageous,[3] that *some* regard ought in justice to be had to politics in the disposal of
Crown preferment: though it is a consideration which in former Governments I have
very much avoided. *In case* you should share this feeling I inclose to you a Home Rule
address where most of the names appear, as you might like to keep a copy of it.[4] Of
course I do not mean that at most it should be more than auxiliary.

11. 13 S. Trin.

Ch 11 AM & 6½ P.M. Wrote to Bishop of Lincoln—The Queen—Sig. Schilizzi—
Mayor of St Raphael[5]—Ld Rosebery—Mr Morley—and minutes. Read La
Devote—A Penitent Soul[6]—Records Dunblane Synod.[7] Saw Sir A. Gordon: on
divers matters, including my court relations, & their cause. Also saw Lady
Aberdeen. And worked on the Romanes MS.

To LORD ROSEBERY, foreign secretary, 11 September 1892.   N.L.S. 10024, f. 132.

I think you will be quite safe in employing any one who is already in your service at
Athens to report upon the Greek Finance. I should not in your place go beyond that
without considering precedents—Cave is indeed a warning.[8]

[1] Report from Harcourt's oculist, 7 September, Add MS 44202, f. 221.
[2] Ibid.; 'Is it possible to conceive a greater want of prudence, self respect and dignity!' than
Labouchere's.
[3] For Gladstone's earlier views, see above, x. clxix.
[4] Not found. No reply from Herschell found.
[5] Had sent the town's congratulations; Add MS 44549, f. 9.
[6] *The story of a penitent soul* (1892).
[7] *Register of the diocesan Synod of Dunblane 1662-1688* (1877).
[8] A pun (Latin *cave*: beware).

2. I shall write to Schilizzi to find a little fault with him.

3. I think that at the F.O. you have the excellent practice of keeping up *Precis* of principal questions. Will you kindly send me whatever you have of this kind about Egypt, for I am sadly in the dark as to the particulars of what has passed while we have been in opposition.

4. I am a good deal surprised to learn that F.O. does not know the conditions of the Triple Alliance[1] and I think it implies not a little *brass* on the forehead of the Italian Minister of Foreign Affairs to talk to us about supporting Italy *rebus sic stantibus*.

[P.S.] We are going to wander a little, but address D. St.

Poor Stuart was heartbroken at not getting office.

12. M. [*Beddgelert, Snowdon*]

Wrote to Mr Trotter—Ld Kimberley—S. Lyttelton—& minutes. Ch. 8½ A.M. Off at 10.45. Reached the Chalet[2] about 4. Two speeches at Carnarvon on the way! by which I was cheated of the Castle.[3] Read A Penitent Soul. Most kind reception. Nine to dinner.[4]

To LORD KIMBERLEY, lord president and Indian secretary,   Add MS 44549, f. 9.
12 September 1892.

Not only am I sensible of the practical difficulty created by the necessity of applying to Parliament,[5] but I also admit with reference to my suggestion, that I am not fully *equipped* with knowledge of the facts as Godley is, and what I do know, or have known, has been fragmentary and occasional only. Standing mainly on the ground of general assumption, I am not at all in a condition to insist. I admit also that there are cases, such as the administration of County Rate by the Magistrates, where irresponsible bodies have been economical (as I believe). These however have lived in the atmosphere, in the neighbourhood so to speak, of responsibility. I cannot say much more than this: that, if the Indian Council here, and much more if the Indian Council of the Governor General, administer finance and apply principles of economy in the spirit of the British Treasury, it is nothing less than a *moral marvel*. And I remain a little sceptical on the subject: but I fully admit that my scepticism does not constitute a reason for finding any body of men guilty in any particular.

There is however another class of questions, rising to a higher scale and level than those of economy in detail, and at this time assuming a vast importance, and as to which I do not know whether Godley would feel so well satisfied, as he is upon the matter of the economical administration. I mean the enormous amount of home payments and the difficulty & loss which they entail. I presume that these home payments run largely under three great heads: debts contracted in England, stores & commodities bought in England, and payments in England on account of covenants with public servants. As to the third of

[1] See 30 Aug. 92n.
[2] Sir E. W. Watkin's chalet on the slopes of Snowdon. The visit to the Carnarvon district was organised by T. Ellis through H. J. Gladstone.
[3] The Gladstones drove through Carnarvon in a carriage with Lloyd George, who called for silence in Welsh before Gladstone's speech; *T.T.*, 13 September 1892, 4a.
[4] Including Lloyd George; for his description, see B. B. Gilbert, *David Lloyd George* (1987), i. 105 and D. Lloyd George, *War memoirs*, 2v. (1938), i. 2–3.
[5] Kimberley, 10 September, Add MS 44229, f. 41, forwarded a note by Godley on the proposal 'to add some one from the Treasury to the Indian Council. I think the necessity [argued by Godley] for an Act of Parliament is a fatal objection.'

them, I do not know that there is any thing to say. But with reference to the two first, [are] we certain that there is no room for beneficial change. I only suggest this matter as one which might in particular cases deserve consideration, and on which I should think instincts & habits corresponding with those of the Treasury might be useful in case of need.

13. Tu.

Wrote to Ld Rosebery—Sir D. Wolff—Ld Ripon—Duca di San Donato[1]—Mrs Eldersheet—& minutes. Drive to the pass of Glaslyn: of wonderful beauty. In afternoon to a point on the ascent, where I had to address 2000 *malgré moi*:[2] but I heard *noble* music: and again in the evening at the Chalet. Read A Penitent Soul, finished—Michael on Dollinger[3]—and Ld Cromer on Egypt.[4]

To LORD RIPON, colonial secretary, 13 September 1892.   Add MS 43515, f. 66.

I quite agree that you will do well to refer to Lord Stanley about the Macdonald suggestion, and I have no doubt you will do it sympathetically.

You named to me the date when Lord Stanley's commission would die a natural death: there came however through some channels intimations of his return home at an earlier date.[5]

To LORD ROSEBERY, foreign secretary, 13 September 1892.   Add MS 44549, f. 9.

On the back of my request for a Precis or narrative (all I still hope for)[6] has come the Cromer Memorandum.[7] I have read it here on Snowdon and with lively interest. It is extremely clever, extremely frank, & full of most important matter. It is painful to add that it leads up to embarrassing & disheartening conclusions. There is no hope, except in the training of Egyptians, & this only 'to some extent' pp. 14, 18. On the other side come our engagements & promises with our interests [?] to boot which however are less ⟨important⟩ imperative. Ld. Cromer has rendered such service that he may naturally look for ⟨achievement⟩ advancement: but what an inheritance he will bequeath. Somebody will have to look these difficulties in the face. There is however not a line of this long Memm. without force in it.
2. Sir H. Ponsonby promised me the return of my paper about Lords in Waiting: but it has not yet come.

14. Wed.

Wrote to Mrs Th.—S.L.—The Atty General—H.N.G.—Mr Villiers Stuart—C. Lowe—Mr M. Müller—Priv. Sec. Tel.—& minutes. Read M. Müller's Address[8]—

[1] Thanks for congratulations; Add MS 44549, f. 9.
[2] Gladstone opened Watkin's new roadway to the summit of Snowdon in a speech to a large crowd which sang hymns in Welsh before and after it; 'the platform had been erected upon a huge boulder [later known as "Gladstone's Rock"] standing in the centre of a grand mountainous amphitheatre'; *T.T.*, 14 September 1982, 4b.
[3] E. Michael, *Ignaz von Döllinger* (1892).
[4] i.e. Cromer's memorandum; see to Rosebery this day.
[5] See 21 Aug. 92n.
[6] Rosebery next day promised it: Add MS 44289, f. 191.
[7] Cromer's memorandum, 'The present situation in Egypt'; CAB 37/31/19.
[8] Perhaps F. Max Müller, 'Goethe and Carlyle. An inaugural address' (1886).

Michael's Dollinger—Mackale Oberon.[1] Four hours on Snowdon mounted about ⅔: say 1000 f. on foot. Fine day & views. This is really a very pleasing domestic interior.

To Sir C. RUSSELL, attorney general, 14 September 1892.   Add MS 44549, f. 10.

I will not fail to make a note of the case of Mr Buss.[2] I ought perhaps to say that the Liberal minority of Clergy, tho' not numerically large, contains, relatively, many distinguished names. Lichfield is not yet vacant. Norwich Canonries are in the gift of the Lord Chancellor.

I must not close without saying how glad I am that your high spirit surmounted the difficulties which seemed to bar the way to the office which you adorn, while wholly independent yourself of any distinction it confers. To some extent it may be said that for Webster's & Clarke's pranks you pay the piper.[3]

We write to Mr Buss.[4]

15. Th. [*Marine Hotel, Barmouth*]

Wrote to Sir H. Ponsonby—M. Jusserand—& minutes. Off at 10. Lovely drive to Port Madoc. Special rail to Barmouth: there seized for a speech, say 20 m. Also Welsh music. Read Bad company:[5] argument with Mary.

16. Fr.

Wrote to Mr Morley—Sir G. Trevelyan—Mr M. Müller—Mr P.W. Campbell—C. Herbert—and minutes. Drive up the beautiful estuary. Read The General's Daughter[6]—and . . . . .

To J. MORLEY, Irish secretary, 16 September 1892.   Add MS 44549, f. 10.

1. The question of the evicted tenants is one on which I should like to have some idea of the prospective difficulties. For, if they are great, it might be proper to have a meeting of the Cabinet for the purpose of considering it. I say nothing against the appointment of a Commission which I dare say be the proper measure. But have we any idea what the Commission *will* recommend, or ought to recommend? Hesitation at the public expense, even if an economical proceeding, would be one so grave that I think all the facts & considerations bearing upon it ought to be set out before a decision is come to. And in the first place we ought to know pretty exactly what is the actual state of the evicted farmers. I have been writing on the supposition that you speak of a Royal & not a Departmental Commission. This latter would I presume be primarily & mainly a Commission to collect the facts, & would involve I think no grave political responsibility, not [*sic*] would it greatly commit the Cabinet. But a Royal Commission would in a great degree involve action, & we ought to see our way.

[1] Possibly G. Macfarren, *Oberon; or the charmed horn* (1826).
[2] Septimus Buss, vicar of Shoreditch from 1881; he was not preferred by this government.
[3] Russell defended Parnell before the Commission, with Clarke appearing for O'Shea and Webster, as attorney general, for the Unionist government.
[4] No reply from Russell found.
[5] Perhaps *Bad company, or the Magpye* (1796); verses.
[6] *The General's daughter. By the author of 'A Russian Priest'* (1892).

2. The charges of a Commission are a matter between you & the Treasury with Harcourt as its ordinary Departmental head.

3. I entirely agree that you should fill the vacancy in the Land Commission if the business requires it. And if there is anything to be said for the apparently monstrous Salary of £3000 it shd. be listened to. But I should like the appointment to be made with the reservation, as in the Chancellor's case, to deal with the Salary should it be thought expedient.

17. Sat.

Wrote to Sir A. West—Ld Rosebery l.l.—Ly Herbert—Dean of Ch.Ch.—Dr N. Hall—Priv. Sec. Tel.—Rev. J.M. Jones[1]—& minutes. Lovely drive to Dolgelly & tea there. Conversation at the school. Backgammon with Mr A. Read Acland on Boyle[2]—The General's Daughter finished.

To Rev. J. MORGAN JONES, 17 September 1892.   Add MS 44549, f. 10.

I thank you very much for your letter[3] & for the accompanying work which I welcome as a marked sign of the increased ability & life of the Church in Wales. I shall read with much interest the portion to which you direct my attention. I certainly agree more as to some important facts of Church History with some of my political opponents than with my (own friends?).[4] In reply to your inquiry, I do not know how to exclude disendowment from disestablishment in the Welsh case. It was included in the case of Ireland. At Carnarvon my reference was to Archdeacon Howell's Address in Liverpool, Dec. 1. 1891.

To LORD ROSEBERY, foreign secretary, 17 September 1892.   N.L.S. 10024, f. 144.
'*Private.*'

1. I have read Sir P. Anderson's paper[5] with care. I thought it was a pleading from a missionary society or from the Company, or should have thought so but for the date from the F.O. What makes the F.O. Précis and memoranda so valuable is that they are (I think) usually addressed to the simple facts or that they state both sides of the case if either.

2. You have not expressed any opinion, but you point out most justly the pressing character of the Uganda business, as it stands, in Sir P.A.s memorandum. I take it for granted—though it is not mentioned!—that the late Government were parties to the decision and order to withdraw. They seem to have thought that they had gone far enough: we in the House of Commons thought they had already gone too far—I am very partially informed but as at present advised I cannot see any new facts to warrant or recommend the reopening of the question decided by the late Govt. I write this in consequence of the pressure of time: hoping as a general rule to follow upon your initiative.

3. It is rather a sad spectacle on the whole—there are few things to my mind more hazardous and objectionable than missionary operations dependent upon military support from their Govt. A case not mended, when the missionaries are in two rival sets with two Governments at their back.[6]

---

[1] John Morgan Jones, probably the vicar of Abererch, Bangor; had sent his history of the Bangor diocese (see next day); no copy traced.
[2] Sir H. W. Acland, 'The inaugural Robert Boyle Lecture' (1892).
[3] Not found.
[4] Secretary's brackets.
[5] Mem. of 10 September 1892, PRO CP 6249.
[6] Anglican missionaries had British, and Catholic White Fathers French, support.

4. It seems to me that these two Governments cannot too soon have a frank and full interchange of ideas: nor does it seem to me very difficult to conjecture what some at least of those ideas might reasonably be.

[P.S.] I do not know who Sir G. Portal[1] is but his second paragraph of Sept 15 is indeed astounding. We are asked to go in, as I understand, to prevent the respective converts from massacring one another.

18. 15 S. Trin.

Barmouth Ch. mg: the curious old parish Ch. aft. Wrote to Lady Aberdeen— Helen G.—Dr Ginsburg—and minutes. Read N. Hall Xtn Brotherhood[2]—Rev. J.M. Jones Hist. Bangor Diocese—Acland's Boyle finished—Woodward's Folkestone Ch.[3]

To H. H. ASQUITH, home secretary, 18 September 1892.   MS Asquith 9, f. 21.

Once when Palmerston had been put out I commended in speaking to Graham his conduct in Opposition as being moderate, when Graham replied to me "His bones are sore . ." My bones are still sore, since the Queen laid me on my back for my birthday list of Knights and made me cut out a fair percentage. I think however with you that the case is good, but I should wish to reserve it for three or perhaps four weeks when there would I think still be time for accomplishing the business before the expiry of the year.

19. M.

Wrote to Priv. Sec. Tel.—Ld Monkswell—Ld Acton—Ld Kimberley—Ld Camoys—Ld Hamilton—Mr Morley—Ld Wolverton—Prof. Evans—Mr A. Carnegie—Mr Agnew—Mr H. Fowler—and minutes. Drove to tea at Mr Holland's aet. 90:[4] deaf and speechless, nearly. He pressed our hands. A lovely spot. Walk on beach. Read Horace's Odes—The herb of love.[5]

To LORD ACTON, lord-in-waiting, 19 September 1892.[6]   Add MS 44094, f. 206.

The strange miscarriage and loss of an official box has delayed the formal appointment of Lords in Waiting, but they will now go forward.[7] I cannot but think yours will bring you to England before the year is out.

My lecture at Oxford, planned several months ago, is to come off in October.[8] Now that it is on paper I could much have wished for the advantage of perusal by you. But it is not yet *verbally* quite complete: and I should not like to trust it to the post.

---

[1] Sir Gerald Herbert Portal, 1858–94; East African diplomat and explorer; led mission to Uganda 1892–3.

[2] C. Newman Hall, 'Divine brotherhood' (1892).

[3] M. Woodward, *The past and present of the parish church of Folkestone* (1892).

[4] Samuel Holland of Dolgelly (in fact 89); quarry owner and liberal M.P. Merionethshire 1870–85.

[5] Untraced.

[6] Holograph; in Figgis and Laurence, *Acton*, i. 227.

[7] For the negotiations which led to Acton taking this office, see Chadwick, *Acton and Gladstone*, 42 ff.

[8] See 24 Oct. 92.

One or two points of literary conscience I may submit to you.

1. I have got together tolerably the great Oxford men of the middle age. I have difficulty in doing the like for Paris: though Budinszky's book[1] gives the foreigners who repaired thither to teach or learn. I do not know if you can tell me any names—besides Wm. of Champeaux, Abelard, Stephen Langton.

2. I have given Cambridge the credit of a trio unapproachable by Oxford for the 17th century—in Milton, Bacon and Newton. Will European opinion justify placing Bacon by the side of the other two? Evidently Locke had much greater influence: but I could not *pit* him against Bacon. I should think that as philosopher Boyle came nearer Bacon.

3. I have been reading Zart.[2] He does not even mention Butler. I think you believe that Kant does. He is honourably mentioned by Lotze[3] but I think only as an apologist.

We are due at Hawarden on Wednesday. I have got Michael's book on Döllinger.[4] So far as I have got he makes no ground against his subject.[5]

To A. CARNEGIE, 19 September 1892.[6]   Add MS 44516, f. 41.

My wife has long ago offered my thanks with her own for your most kind, & *joint*, congratulations. But I do not forget that you have been suffering yourself from anxieties, & have been exposed to imputations in connection with your gallant efforts to direct rich men into a course of action more enlightened than that which they usually follow. I wish I could relieve you from these imputations of journalists, too often rash conceited or censorious, sometimes ill-natured.[7] I wish to do the little, the very little, that is in my power, which is simply to say how sure I am that no one who knows you will be prompted by the unfortunate occurrences across the water (of which manifestly we cannot know the exact merits) to qualify in the slightest degree either his confidence in your generous views or his admiration of the good and great works you have already done.

Wealth is at present like a monster threatening to swallow up the moral life of man: you by precept and by example have been teaching him to disgorge.

I for one thank you.

20. Tu.

Wrote to Ld Rosebery l.l.—Lady Aberdeen—Dr. Ginsburg—Helen G.—and minutes. Drove to Harlech: a noble relic. Wrote Mem. on Uganda. Began Mem. for H.M. a serious business.[8] Backgammon with Mr A.

---

[1] A. Budinszky, *Die Universität Paris und die Fremden an derselben im Mittelalter* (1876).
[2] See 9 Sept. 92.
[3] H. Lotze, *Geschichte der Deutschen Philosophie seit Kant* (1882).
[4] See 13 Sept. 92.
[5] Acton replied, 23 September, Add MS 44094, f. 208: 'If I rightly grasp your question about Paris, my answer would be that almost all the great divines were there, as students, or teachers, or both . . .'; he then criticized 'the other [i.e. Francis] Bacon: 'no metaphysician; still less a divine; and he was the worst of politicians. He did not understand the science of his time'; Butler 'is little remembered, or read, in Germany, because of Kant. They do not know it, but Kant is the macrocosm of Butler. He is Butler writ very large. . . .'
[6] Partly printed in *Carnegie*, i. 410, with Carnegie's grateful reply, explaining that his conciliatory letter on the Homestead strike arrived too late (he was at Rannoch Lodge in Perthshire).
[7] Strong attacks in the British press; see *Carnegie*, i. 403.
[8] See 28 Oct. 92.

To LORD ROSEBERY, foreign secretary, 20 September 1892.   N.L.S. 10024, f. 156.

1. My telegram to you will I hope by this time have conveyed my great desire to have the information about Uganda which seems necessary for touching even the threshold of the question. The Memorandum inclosed herewith exhibits some of the difficulties I feel. In these matters without doubt every foreign Minister informs himself in his Department: but his colleagues are famished until they are supplied with information from thence.

I had hoped some progress from our conversation if we could have had one: but you will derive much greater advantage from being in town, as you will probably be able to see those of our colleagues who took part in the Commons debate upon Uganda. I remember that Harcourt got up the case with a great deal of pains.[1]

2. I have sent you a paper from Zebir Pacha.[2] I forgot to say how sorry I am to see something about Marriot as trying to get his finger into that pie. If he finds he can fleece Zebir as he fleeced the Khedive, he is a very likely man to take up Zebir's case in Parliament: and I should like to feel sure that the ground is solid under our feet.

We go to Hawarden on Thursday. I shall after Sunday be in readiness to come up should Uganda require it.

[Memorandum on Uganda]

1. Debate on Uganda 1892. My recollection is that the Railway was regarded on both sides as a probably essential part of any plan for the retention of Uganda: but that the debate on our side had for its basis objection to any interference or responsibility of Govt. in either.

I recommend reference to Sir Wm. Harcourt and to Mr Bryce whose memories are more trustworthy than mine.

2. In illustration of my telegram of today, I plead that I am totally in the dark as to the most important facts of the Uganda case. So far as I can gather (I admit it is like gathering a history from broken Assyrian tablets) the Company has changed its mind thrice on the vital question of evacuation. But when?

And (in each case) why?

3. I have not as yet found any explanation of the part if any taken by the late Administration as to each of these changes, or of the reasons for taking or not taking it.

4. If it be a question of the responsibility for the lives of Missionaries, who have gone there with noble motives at their own risk, what strikes me first is that the French R.C. Missions being 'vastly' more considerable, the French Govt. is largely pressed with this responsibility

5. It appears that this was a Mahometan country, & I presume a slave-trading one. This might be a strong reason for the religious enterprise. Is it a reason why the British Govt. should go into a "hornets nest", the scene of 'anarchy for six years' past (p. 6), to make war upon all and sundry? Possibly for there is some appearance of this, to secure by the strong hand the dominance of the Protestants though a very small minority?

6. In one place I am told Bp Tucker and his brave band will remain till the death: in another that on the evacuation the whole of the Christians will fly. In one place the Mahommedans are to massacre the Christians: in another that is not the question

---

[1] Rosebery this day sent a mem. on Uganda, which crossed with Gladstone's, commenting, 'It is a ticklish business and a pressing business. The Company are bankrupt, they must evacuate the country, and the consequences of evacuation will, I fear, be most grave'; Add MS 44289, f. 195.

[2] The Sudanese slaver; see above, x. lxxxi.

(p. 7.[)] but that the Christians are to massacre one another: in another that the Mahommedans *in April* sent a message for peace upon (apparently) very moderate terms.

7. I am doubtful whether the determination to 'do something' ought to precede a careful inquiry what can rationally be done, within what bounds, with what prospect of maintaining them: but I am fully sensible that there is a preliminary question whether any proof has been shown that there is an obligation for the Government to make itself a party at all.

                                                            WEG S 19.92.[1]

The time from Mombasa to Uganda, which I had seen stated at 90 days is put by Smith at 70, 60, and less than 60. But I am not for running it out, if we have all needful information.

To Sir C. RIVERS WILSON, comptroller-general of the National   Add MS 44549, f. 13.
Debt Office, 20 September 1892.

The National Debt office is in such immediate connection with the C. of E. that I cannot do more in answer to your letter than state my first impressions, especially as I have not yet seen the report. I should at once give way to any opinion which Sir W. Harcourt may form in examining the case. In the absence of any real or definite reason for an advance (*sic*),[2] I am not aware that there is any general ground for changing the scope of the information heretofore supplied periodically to Parlt.

There is no parallel here with the reports of our Revenue Departments. Yours is a vast banking business: & I am for giving results rather than details, because so very few of those under whose eyes they would come are in any way capable of understanding them. The whole affair of Annuities, now so important, is still I think a mystery to the outer world. I remember very well that before trying to extend that system I fortified myself by getting the opinion of John Mill. But if the question be about a Report in the nature of an historical essay which would aim at giving a true idea of the general character of your very valuable & vitally important office, and a summary record of its proceedings, that I think would be an excellent contribution to political education: as would be a corresponding history of the Public Works Loan Board. Such a report might be either once for all or might be a foundation for supplements or repetitions at rather long intervals.

Perhaps I ought to add that I never much liked the present weekly or frequent publication of even the Revenue accounts: which are quite as likely to mislead as to inform. The Quarterly or yearly sheets inform & do not mislead. There was no reference to me before the adoption of this change by (I think) Ld. Sherbrooke.[3]

21. *Wed.*

Wrote to S.L. (Tel.)—Ld Rosebery l.l.l.—The Qu.—Sir W. Harcourt—H.N.G.—Mr Douglas—& minutes. Worked on Mem. for H.M. Saw Mr Hughes. Visited the damaged Ch. fabric. Shameful! Received Deputation with Album of Photographs. Last drive up the lovely valley. Backgammon with Mr A. Read Uganda papers—Heritage of the Kurts[4]—Life of A. Kauffmann.[5]

[1] Holograph memorandum; N.L.S. 10024, f. 158.
[2] Copyist's interpolation.
[3] No reply found.
[4] B. Bjornson, *Heritage of the Kurts* (1892).
[5] G. G. de Rossi, *Angelica Kauffmann* (1866).

To Sir W. V. HARCOURT, chancellor of the exchequer,   MS Harcourt dep. 12, f. 93.
21 September 1892.

I have not liked to write to you about Uganda, which has much troubled me, till you had given an independent expression of your views.[1]

I have asked Rosebery for an account of the recent transactions in correspondence between the Govt. & the Co. It appears to me that the late Govt. cannot escape responsibility for the evacuation, *or rather* for silence on it: in which evacuation, or inaction, on the facts so far as now before me, I have every disposition to concur. Having now seen your mem. I have no scruple in saying this.

[P.S.] Due at Hn. tomorrow evg.

The inclosed is from my son Harry. He writes simply as Calcutta merchant (& on the side rather opposed to a merchant's temptations). But I imagine your Commission may be full. B. Currie comes to Hn on Friday: in case you like me to ask him any thing.

Your revenue to an outside eye does not look brilliant.

To LORD ROSEBERY, foreign secretary, 21 September 1892.   Add MS 44549, f. 13.

[Letter 1:]   I am sorry to have given you so much trouble but I misapprehended your sketch of your movements. I send the inclosed Scrap Memm. only because one or two of the points raised are of interest. No. 3. I always think it is sound policy to hold such a declaration if clear to be of binding authority. No. 4. Much for my own information. (I have not the map *here*) 5. 'Spheres of influence' a phrase recognised I see by Giers. But I think it may be worth your while to have some reference made to Clarendon's correspondence with Russia in his short secretariate 1869–70. We were then enamoured of a 'central zone': but could not manage it. 6. I do not know if you feel quite sure about this contrast: but the subject is too large to enter on. 7. I think you will find on reference that as to some region (Badakshan??) the Emperor adopted our contention on the ground that we had better geographical knowledge than he had. This requires no notice.

Dft. to Sir R. Morier. S/5[2]

1. "Explained away"
2. "Of course"
3. Value of assurances like that of M. Giers
4. "Their territories". A portion of *British* frontier is there in question?
5. "Spheres of influence"[.] Qu[ery] refer to Clarendon's correspondence on neutral sphere[?] in 1869–70
6. 'The contrast so disastrous in the East'
7. The perfect[?] knowledge before 1872.

WEG S. 17. 92

[Letter 2: '*Private*']   We go to Hawarden tomorrow evening.

I do not wonder at your being startled at Harcourt's trenchant tone in his all but illegible [dispatch] Memorandum, which has cost me some eyesight. You would I think be less startled at it, and more at the case itself, had you gone through like Harcourt and some of us, the terrible and instructive experience of the Gordon Mission, in which we adopted a ruinous decision under the most seductive appearances.

[1] At length on 20 September, Add MS 44202, f. 229 and Gardiner, ii. 191.
[2] N.L.S. 10024, f. 164.

I am very anxious for the F.O. Memorandum of the facts. What I want is the sequence of events, which I now can only pick out with difficulty and *uncertainty*.

As I understand the Co. changed its course thrice.
1. Aug 10. 91
2. Nov. 3. 1891
3. May 17. 1892

Is it then the fact that these three vitally important events were communicated to the Govt. without any statement of reasons, and were received with bare acknowledgments?

And this although between 2d & 3d event the Govt. railway guarantee for the Railway had been debated in the H. of Commons and no division taken by us.

I do not think we can allow them to urge that they were *in articulo mortis* on May 17. They were in full charge & responsibility: & they knew that according to their plans there could be no new Govt for 3 months—with 2 or 3 months more required between Mombasa and Uganda. Besides, what had they done on the *first* decision to evacuate?

I do not like to say any thing positive without seeing in due form the facts asked for in my Telegram (I do not at all care to see the originals which would seem like distrust). Upon so much as is now before me I am bound to say that I should in the main agree with Harcourt. There is Bryce however and perhaps others who may have a word to say. I think I ought to add that perceiving your attitude not to be quite the same as mine, I have rigidly abstained from communicating with them until they should have spoken for themselves: as Harcourt has now done.

Of course there should be a Cabinet if and when you wish it; but I think you would find it worth while to communicate *préablement* with those who took part in the debate of March 3.[1]

[P.S.] You may be sure that Bryce will give you his views whatever they may be with strict measure [of] circumspection.

22. Th. [*Hawarden*]

Wrote to Mr Murphy BP.—and minutes. Backgammon with Mr A. Worked hard on Mem. for H.M. 3.20-6.20. To Hawarden. Seven to dinner. Read Life of Angelica Kauffman.

To LORD ROSEBERY, foreign secretary, 22 September 1892.   N.L.S. 10024, f. 178.

I hope Uganda will not long continue to be part of your daily bill of fare: but the inclosed letter of Kimberley's is I think well worth your reading. I agreed closely with it. The others are Episcopal and from the Missionary point of view.

23. Fr.

Wrote to S.L. Tel.—Ld Rosebery l.l.l. & Tel. l.l.l.—J. Morley L.l.l. & Tel. l.—Sir W. Harcourt—Ld Kimberley—Mr Asquith MP.—and minutes. Ch. 8½ A.M. Walk with Mr A. and Backgammon in evg. Conversation with Mr B. Currie on Indian

---

[1] Rosebery replied, 22 September, Add MS 44289, f. 203: 'There is an agreeable incongruence about your suggestion that I should consult our colleagues in town, for I am the only minister in London'; he warned against hasty decisions, arguing for waiting until Lugard, 'the principal witness and authority', reached London in a month's time.

Currency. A hard day: chiefly Uganda. Read A. Kauffmann—Heritage of the Kurts.

To H. H. ASQUITH, home secretary, 23 September 1892.   Add MS 44549, f. 14.

I entirely concur in the spirit of your letter:[1] & indeed in its terms, except that, as I conceive, *our* making temporary provision against the emergency foretold[?] would involve the acknowledgement that the matter belongs to *us* for decision: whereas the Company, who are the parties mainly responsible, & the late Government, who had some responsibility as having given a Charter to the Company, accepted without resistance or remonstrance (as I understood the decision of the Co. [)]. The 'massacre' if any, as I understand it, is likely to be the mutual slaughter of two Christian parties. Some ten years ago we sent Gordon on a mission which he & we alike declared to be essentially one of peace; but to a country some hundreds of miles off, not under our controul. The difference now is that we should *begin* with military measures.
[P.S.] Manifestly no step can be taken unless it be agreed by the Cabinet.

To Sir W. V. HARCOURT, chancellor of the exchequer,   MS Harcourt dep. 12. f. 99.
23 September 1892. '*Secret*'.

You have been "exercised" about Uganda—and so have I. It has occupied eyes & hand for some hours almost every day for the last week, and *mind* outside of them.
I inclose copy of the last of three letters which I have written to Rosebery today, besides two telegrams—and I am not yet at luncheon time.
There has been a delay, which I do not quite understand, in my getting the papers on which the inclosed letter is founded.
In my opinion, after reading these papers, there is no Uganda question, properly speaking, before us for decision. It has been settled by the Co. and the late Govt. Of course the Foreign Minister is ⟨of course⟩ fully entitled to reopen it, or any other question.
I agree with you in objecting to any ambiguous measure. I think *the Co.* ought to spend a little money for a peaceful agent to use his moral influence *after the evacuation*. *Any* sort of interference with it would be like a new Gordon mission; perhaps worse. If the Co. were to say they approved of Ld Salisbury's suggestion of Aug. 25 (£1000 a year) but had not a brass farthing, would you object to paying them *ex post facto* if their proceedings had been prudent? I have said this to no one except yourself. If you approve, it might mollify F.O.

To LORD ROSEBERY, foreign secretary,   N.L.S. 10024, ff. 196–202.
23 September 1892.

[Letter 1:] It appears clear to me that any interposition on our part to interfere with the evacuation would saddle us with the entire responsibility of the case which now belongs to the Company, with *some* share for the late Government. The best *modus vivendi* that I can conceive possible, lies in another quarter. As yet I know nothing whatever of the views of the French Government. I should have thought that the two Governments should in concert warn their respective Missionary bodies and their friends

---

[1] Of 22 September, Add MS 44516, f. 53, on need for discussion of Rosebery's mem. on Uganda: 'for myself, as at present advised, I should strongly oppose the assumption of any responsibility either with a view to our securing for ourselves, or with a view to prevent other Powers from securing, control of the headwaters of the Nile. Nor can I see any sufficient reason for our undertaking the duty of policing Uganda against the possible depredation of the slave-raiders. . . . On the other hand there may be a case for making temporary provision against the emergency of a massacre of Englishmen. . . .'

against violence and this in the very strongest manner. Here from the papers seems to lie the main danger. As regards the Mahomedans, the latest account that I read was that they desired peace and the *restoration of a portion of their lands*. It seems to me however that the Company might, perhaps positively ought, to keep an agent on the ground who on their behalf should use his influence to *shame* the Christians out of their apparent enmities, and to induce the Mahometans to act as Lugard reported their willingness to act. Still this is their question: but considering the Railway Guarantee I cannot understand how the Company could convey the Resolution of May 17 without some form of explanation to the late Ministers.

[Letter 2:] I separate this from my other Uganda letter, because a sentence of yours involves a general question. I believe it to be the fixed and constitutional tradition of our form of government that for any and every affair of state transacted in any Department of the Government, and not least in the Foreign Department, the Prime Minister, if he has been consulted on it in its various stages, is not less responsible than the Minister of the Department himself. And I am quite sure that any attempt of a Prime Minister to abate his responsibility in such cases would be received with universal condemnation. I speak not only of my own case with Granville & Clarendon at the F.O. but with Hartington as War Minister, with Chancellors of the Exchequer and others, but of a general law.

The *doctrine* indeed goes further and may be said to embrace the whole Cabinet when consulted: but this doctrine is not so surely applied.

On other points I add two words. This is your first case of encountering the alarming prophecies of agents, who are either irresponsible, or, naturally enough, inclined to shift their responsibility to others. But I have had many of them: and I see that Governments are often led into their worst errors in this way.[1]

I admit Lugard to be a witness. I hardly attach much value to his authority. But *if you do*, and you think you cannot[2] be responsible for a decision until he comes, I am not certain that you mean things to remain as they are in the interval?[3]

[Letter 3:][4] Since writing my two letters founded on your private letter of yesterday, I have read the important correspondence between the Co. and the late Govt.

In my opinion, subject of course to correction, they prove that the decision of the Co. to withdraw to Dagoreti was fully accepted by the late Ministry. Lord Salisbury's letter of *May 26* in answer to one of *May 17* is, both from its date and its matter, a well considered document, and leaves the question a *settled question*.

1. It seeks to amend the resolution of the Company by altering a purely incidental point.
2. It makes no reservation of the question of policy.
3. It does not even renew the regret which had been expressed on Aug. 25.
4. All this is the more remarkable, because in the last paragraph but two of the final instructions to Lugard, responsibility for consequences is by a very clear insinuation charged upon the Government.
5. The correspondence leaves the late Ministers perfectly free to oppose a vote for Uganda. But in Salisbury's letter of Aug. 25 there is a recommendation to secure Mwanga's[5] good conduct by offering a small money allowance. It seems to me this was a

[1] Rosebery replied, 25 September, Add MS 44289, f. 225, that when the First and the department minister differed, the latter 'cannot disengage himself of responsibility'.
[2] Illegible overwritten phrase omitted.
[3] See 21 Sept. 92.
[4] Docketed by Gladstone: 'No. 3. Had better be read first'. For Salisbury's correspondence, see *PP* 1893–4 lxii. 335 ff.
[5] Mwanga, Kabaka of Buganda 1884, deposed 1897.

good suggestion, and may apply to the actual head of the Mohammedan party on the spot, whoever he be. I do not comprehend why no notice of it has been taken by the Company.

[P.S.] I return the dictated Memorandum. This note will show where I diverge.

24. Sat.

Ch. 8½ A.M. Wrote to Sir W. Harcourt l & Tel.—Ld Rosebery L.l.l. & tel l.l.—Mr A Reader—and minutes. Read A. Kauffmann's Life. Walk with Mr Currie. Saw F. Leveson on the sad state of the Granville affairs. Twelve to dinner. Backgammon with Mrs Arthur.

Confidential   *Memorandum on Uganda.*[1]

When Lord Salisbury received the first announcement from the East Africa Company of withdrawal from Uganda (then termed 'temporary'), he expressed (26th August, 1891) his regret for the *causes* of his decision.

He did not, however, express any intention of taking any measure, nor did he reserve any question, on behalf of the Government.

On the contrary, he excluded everything of the kind by pointing out to the Company what *they* ought to do after evacuating, namely, to have a paid agent in the country to induce the Mahommedan King Mwanga to keep the peace.

I find no answer from the Company to this apparently reasonable suggestion, probably because the decision then taken was soon after reversed, so far as date was concerned; that is to say, the occupation was prolonged for a year.

I am not informed what communications, after this suspension, passed between the Church Missionary Society and the Government; but, whatever they were, it is plain from the sequel that they did not then induce the Government either to oppose the evacuation by the Company, or to enable the Company further to suspend the measure, or (the extremest step) in any manner or degree to substitute the Government for the Company. The Government accepted the evacuation as a to-be-accomplished fact.

On the 17th May, 1892, the Company made known their final decision to evacuate without any discretion to their agent even as to time (Foreign Office Paper, p. 2, paragraph 5). They made no request to the Government for aid or intervention; perhaps because they had reason to know it would not be accepted. For this was clearly shown by Lord Salisbury's letter of the 26th August, 1891.

In answering the letter of the 17th May, Lord Salisbury held firmly by his text. If he had any reserves on the subject of evacuation, it was his absolute duty to inform the Company, to whom such knowledge would have been highly important. He not only accepted the decision in silence, but gave this acceptance the highest force by proposing to amend the instruction on an incidental point.

Thus, then—

1. The occupying agency has withdrawn.

2. The Government of the day accepted the withdrawal.

3. There is, therefore, no question handed over to us for decision, though of course a *res judicata* may be reopened.

If I now consider it as thus reopened, then my opinion is that it is inadmissible—

1. To substitute the Government for the Company in action of any kind.

2. Either to sanction or adopt any military measure whatever.

---

[1] Memorandum printed for the Cabinet on 28 September 1892; CAB 37/31/29.

But I know no reason why—

1. Lord Salisbury's suggestion to the Company of the 26th August, 1891, may not still be applicable in principle, whether Mwanga is or is not still the head of the Mahommedan inhabitants of the country.

2. Nor why the British and French Governments should not in concert enjoin their respective missionaries, as subjects, to keep the peace, and in all ways promote the keeping of it.

3. All the better if they were to add that no infraction of religious liberty in Uganda on whatever pretext would, under any circumstances, receive any countenance from them.

W. E. G.

Hawarden, September 24, 1892.

P.S.—The absolute acceptance of the main decision by Lord Salisbury is all the more conclusively shown, because the Company, in its orders to Captain Lugard, throws on the Government a portion of the responsibility for the original occupation. (Foreign Office Paper, p. 2, paragraph 4.)

September 26.—See also Mr. Balfour's answer to Sir W. Barttelot in the House of Commons on the 16th June, 1892:—

"I believe the Company have sent instructions to their agents to retire from Uganda at the end of the year. The Government have not, as I understand the matter, any power to compel them to stay. But it must be borne in mind that the withdrawal of the Company's officers by no means implies the abandonment of the country. I can give no opinion on the question[1] put to me in the last paragraph until we obtain information as to Captain Lugard's actual position and prospects. But I may remind my right honourable and gallant friend that, in our opinion, the proper way to maintain our position in Uganda is to construct a railway to the eastern shore of Lake Victoria Nyanza; that the surveys are being rapidly proceeded with, and would so far seem to show that the project presents no engineering difficulties."

To Sir W. V. HARCOURT, chancellor of the exchequer,   MS Harcourt dep. 12, f. 102.
24 September 1892.

Yours of yesterday[2] received. I am not sure of having made out every word. But I at once telegraph to you the essential.[3] The truth is your letter, in its substance expresses better than I could have done it myself what I think and feel: and I admire the penetration with which you detect and expose the true motive of the Jingoes for an Equatorial Empire.

Rosebery however he may have been misguided by the Jingoes is absolutely loyal and never dreams of passing by the Cabinet. It is I rather than he who has not been forward to call one, that I might exhaust every chance of inducing him to recede from his untenable and most dangerous position.

This naturally enough Lefevre & Asquith do not understand. What I have felt is a great anxiety to save Rosebery from the position in which he would find himself (as I think) when the Cabinet met. But he has pressed on so fast and far that I have (reluctantly) suggested to him a Cabinet for Friday 30th.
[P.S.] B. Currie is here and as you would suppose most sound and satisfactory on his subject [i.e. bi-metallism].

---

[1] Note added by Gladstone: 'Whether any attempt is to be made to sustain Captain Lugard and his men in the position which they have occupied up to the present time.'
[2] Add MS 44202, f. 234 and Gardiner, ii. 193; of great length on Uganda and the need for a speedy evacuation to avoid a 'British Nile'.
[3] 'Yours of yesterday received[.] I agree[.] Gladstone'; MS Harcourt dep. 12, f. 101.

To LORD ROSEBERY, foreign secretary, 24 September 1892.   N.L.S. 10024, f. 222.
'*Secret*'.

[Letter 1:]   Undoubtedly you have a full title to circulate whatever you think fit. But you will already have found from letters of mine which have crossed your Memorandum that I have in view a course of proceeding varying from yours. I think the proper course of action is that taken by Salisbury on the *first* intimation of withdrawal: viz. to suggest to *them* to use *moral* influence for peace in Uganda after evacuation. Would it not be awkward to have these two plans circulated in apparent conflict? If the Co. say they have no money even for moral influence I cannot but think that point might be met.[1]

In making this proposal I seek to go as far as I can towards meeting your idea.
[P.S.] I retain your Mem. only for the present
Would you like a Cabinet next week? if so, on Friday?

[Letter 2:]   I wrote to you by the early post on account of Sunday closure in London.
Inclosed is my Memorandum from which you will see on what points we differ.

My view about the position of the late Government, formed upon the papers, is very clear and strong.

The views of some of our scattered colleagues, unsought, have become known to me. They are all against moving to occupy.

I needed no assurance, believe me, as to the manner in which you were certain to deal with the Church Missionary Society.
[P.S.] F. Leveson has announced himself suddenly as a visitor. I wish it were more difficult to divine the cause.

25. 15 S. Trin.

Ch 11 A.M. (Mr Trotter, *excellent*)[2] & 6½ PM. Wrote to Duke of Devonshire[3]—Ld Rosebery—F. Leveson—Sir W. Harcourt—Priv. Sec. Tel.—Prof. Romanes—and minutes. 12 to dinner. Mr Currie showed himself very agreeable to all. Read The One Book[4]—Deverell's Pilgrims[5]—Lewin on Father Gilpin[6]—E. Parry Ch. Hist.[7]—Jones on Browning.[8]

To Sir W. V. HARCOURT, chancellor of the exchequer,   MS Harcourt dep. 12, f. 108.
25 September 1892. '*Private.*'

I agree with the suggestion you have made about the Garter.[9] But I think that a tender of it from me to him at a moment of such tension might almost compel him to decline. At any rate that I cannot wisely act at once.

---

[1] Rosebery, 25 September, Add MS 44289, f. 227, replied: '3. I think, with great deference, that your view that the late Government were parties to the policy of evacuation is arguable but not correct. The Mombasa railroad blocks the way. Had they accepted evacuation definitely they would never have dreamed of the railroad . . .'; he sent further details next day; ibid., f. 229.

[2] Henry Edward Trotter, 1856–1910; curate of Hawarden 1882–92; rector of Althorpe 1892–1910.

[3] On the state of the Granville estate; Add MS 44549, f. 14.

[4] J. H. Games, *The one book: the unique character of the Bible* (1892).

[5] W. T. Deverell, *The Pilgrims and the Anglican Church* (1887).

[6] G. H. R. Lewin, *Father Gilpin* (1891).

[7] E. W. Parry, *An epitome of Anglican Church history* (1879).

[8] See 21 Aug. 92.

[9] For Rosebery.

[P.S. I am puzzled by your date from D. St. while I am told from London you are at Mal-wood.

Cabinet 29th at noon. You would find me at 21 Carlton Gardens 28th about 4 P.M.

To LORD ROSEBERY, foreign secretary, 25 September 1892.   N.L.S. 10024, f. 232.
'*Secret*'.

In consequence of your telegram I altered the date [of the Cabinet] to Thursday at noon. Considering the season of the year and the wide dispersion, you would perhaps agree with me that we could not further hasten the day.

It is with pain, though with no hesitation, that I meet your wish in summoning this Cabinet. I could not until the last abandon my hope that you might forbear to press the suggestion. You are in no way responsible for my reluctance to part company with that hope. It was my weakness.

It is the *first* time, during a Cabinet experience of 22 or 23 years, that I have known the Foreign Minister & the Prime Minister to go before a Cabinet on a present question with diverging views. It is the union of these two authorities by which Foreign Policy is ordinarily worked in a Cabinet: not that I have the smallest fear that this incidental miscarriage of ours will occur again.

26. M.

Ch. 8½ A.M. Wrote to Ld Rosebery L.l.l. & tel. l.—Sir W. Harcourt L. & tel l.l.—Sir E. Watkin—Ld Acton—Ld Spencer—Mr Morley—Priv. Sec. Tel. l.l.—and minutes. Saw F. Leveson—C. saw Duke of W[estminster] who was disappoint-ing.[1] Lady Herbert came. Finished Life of Angelica Kauffmann. Ten to dinner. Backgammon with Lady H.

To LORD ACTON, lord-in-waiting, 26 September 1892.   Add MS 44549, f. 15.

Let me thank you for your even more than usually interesting letter. I answer in haste but I must answer. 1. I mean to hold forth at Oxford on Monday 24th. My host is the Dean. 2. I have failed to make my point clear about Oxford. I speak of rearing only. As to men who, apart from rearing, studied & taught, the position of Paris is overwhelming. 3. Barrow was indeed a great man. He died under 50 & had not the chance given to Hockheads like me. The world knows little of him. Cambridge had also a strong fifth in Bentley, summus ille Benthius as he is I think classically called by German scholars. 4. In dealing with Butler, you are not dealing with his sermons? only? To me he seems a great moral discoverer as you say Martineau makes him. Bravo Martineau. I want to know when did Time produce a greater—perhaps so great—a teacher on the laws of moral action as between God & Man? And all action (not 75%, as M. Arnold says) is moral. 5. If you are in England soon enough will you be benevolent & as a victim look at my sheets? 6. I send by post a copy of my address to the Oriental congress; tho' it was nearly ludicrous that I sd. venture on it. 7. Our 'Lords' are not yet complete. I wish we could get one man at least who could be in some degree competitor as well as colleague: but we can't. The royal fisherwoman angled well & caught a big fish such as was never before landed from those waters. 8. The Jingoes are endeavouring to persecute the Foreign Minister & Cabinet into mad acts about Uganda. But I hope in vain.
[P.S.] I make a plea for Hawarden during your visit.

---

[1] About helping with Granville's debts.

To Sir W. V. HARCOURT, chancellor of the exchequer,　　MS Harcourt dep. 12, f. 110.
26 September 1892.

[*Telegram*:]
26 September 1892—
I presume you will have the correspondence today but refer also to answer given in
Commons June 16 which absolutely confirms my view of the correspondence Hope to
see you Wednesday Gladstone

[*Letter*:] '*Secret*'
1. Telegraph to you this forenoon.
2. To avoid the scandal and mischief of patent differences between Foreign Sec. and
Prime Minister, I have *not* circulated the inclosed paper, though it was drawn with much
reserve.[1]

　In this painful matter—only relieved by Rosebery's excellent personal tone—I have had
a tempest of hard words in my mind but have put none on paper. I am aware however
that you have taken greater pains & know more than any of us, and I am anxious that you
should see this paper before we meet (as I trust) on Wednesday.
3. I proceed on this double basis
(a) I am not willing at this moment sharply to close every door lest we drive our friends to
despair.
(b) I am satisfied—and I think you will say so when you have seen the papers—that for the
present the *hinge* of the whole matter is, *not to interfere with the evacuation on Jan 1*. And this
I think my memorandum secures. It is in effect simple adhesion to the ground taken by
the late Govt. *so far as this evacuation is concerned*. Let any body propose (or oppose) a railway or any thing *else*. About that there will be no hurry: and probably no tension. The last
ten days have been simply horrible.
[P.S.] I will explain to you about the Mwanga money.

To J. MORLEY, Irish secretary, 26 September 1892.　　　　　Add MS 44257, f. 1.
'*Secret*'[2]
　1. Your letters are a great refreshment amidst my incessant & astounding correspondence on the Uganda business. I send on the M. Guardian to R.
2. The letter respecting L[abouchere] is a marvel. I think he would *do* diplomacy well
enough: but he would be a loss in the House of Commons, on questions of war & intervention. Who would take his place? Unhappily, Storey has mismanaged, & has hardly got
a position.
3. I should have been quite clear with the Romanes ⟨address⟩ MS & also with the paper I
named to you which I fly as a kite, into a high quarter but for Uganda—*la Maledetta*.
4. I inclose *copy* of one of my scores of letters to R. which gives some idea of the ground I
take. The grand point is to have the question of *evacuation* substantially as it is & in no
consn. to step into the shoes of the Co. which even the late Govt would not do.
5. Forgive my sending the inclosed—not for notice.

To LORD ROSEBERY, foreign secretary, 26 September 1892.　　N.L.S. 10024, f. 249.
　[Letter 1:] '*No 1. Balfour's reply*'
　One of my very private Secretaries yesterday made known to me what in my opinion
(with much beside) Sir P. Anderson ought to have informed us of.
　On the 16th of June Balfour gave an answer to Barttelot which I hope you will refer to.

---

[1] i.e. the mem. of 24 September, circulated on 28 September.
[2] Secretary's copy.

It completely establishes my construction of the conduct of the late Government so far as the evacuation on Dec. 31 is concerned.

It also establishes yours as to the intention still to keep alive the idea of a railway which it says is the true policy.

Now pray remember that my contention has been and is simply this that there should be nothing done to touch the essence of the coming evacuation by the Company.

If the question be only on the railway which in a rather abstract way Balfour certainly adhered to, that would have to begin 800 miles or 700 from Uganda—could be maturely considered in the Autumn. Personally I am not favourable to it.

But Balfour's answer of June 16 in Commons based on both the evacuation and the railway completely shifts the ground of the question and removes the tension.

You will now I think see that your proposals are absolutely beyond and outside the intentions of the late Government and this revives the hope of which I spoke in my letter of yesterday. Part of this (in inverted commas) I cipher to you today.[1]

[Letter 2:] '*No. 2*. Circulation of papers'   N.L.S. 10024, f. 252.
1. I have been looking over the Uganda papers which have accumulated so rapidly since you first glanced at the subject on Sept. 14. I thank you for not circulating your last Memm. of proposals (of which I have no copy). Your Memm. of S. 16 however remains in circulation: and I am afraid that not being accompanied with any indication from me, some of the Cabinet may suppose that I have offered no impediment. Nevertheless, so strong is my sense of the mischief of ostensible and resolute divergence between us that I hold back my memorandum of Saturday, though not *in professo* in opposition to you.
2. Will you let me say now what Sir P. Anderson if he is worth his salt, ought long ago to have pointed out to you that the *first duty* of his Department, when it becomes a question of papers for the Cabinet, is to supply an impartial narrative of fact; and this, as far as my memory serves, is the old tradition of the F.O. His excuse may be this that under the last Govt. a new situation had been created, and the function of the Cabinet may have become purely formal.[2]
3. When I named Friday I was quite unaware of any letter from Mackinnon.
4. It appears to me as if Co. & C.M.S.,[3] repulsed by the late Govt., effaced all traces, & then organised a virgin assault on me.

To LORD SPENCER, first lord of the admiralty,   Althorp MSS K8
26 September 1892. '*Secret*'.

I ought to have answered your kind letter long ago. But I have of late had a really terrible time. Rosebery has I think been carried quite off his legs by the Jingoes of the Foreign Office and its agents & correspondents here & elsewhere & wants us to interfere with the coming *evacuation* which even the late Govt. had accepted, though they had not abandoned ulterior views about a railway. His tone has been excellent throughout and this is the only consolation in what otherwise I reckon as one of the very strangest occurrences of my life of 60 years [in the Commons].
2. On the other I am so glad to find Morley proceeding in close communication & in

---

[1] Rosebery, next day, Add MS 44289, f. 233, apologised for Anderson's omission, but disputed in detail Gladstone's interpretation of Balfour's answer on 16 June, and pointed out that Portal was already Commissioner for an area including Uganda. Sir Henry Percy Anderson, 1831–96; foreign office clerk; negotiated Anglo-German treaty 1890; assistant secretary, foreign office, 1894.
[2] For Anderson's mem. of 10 September 1892, see PRO CP 6249.
[3] i.e. the East Africa Company and the Church Missionary Society.

harmony with you from the *penetralia* of Dublin Castle. You have I daresay notice[d] the 14 days hard labour awarded as it is said for cheers given to Home Rule: Morley is most properly inquiring into the matter.

3. I have had F. Leveson Gower here about the Granville Estate. The Duke (ex Hartington) has behaved right ducally. With all that, the figure is large & the affair grave.

4. I expect to sleep at 21 Carlton H[ouse] Terrace & am due there on Wednesday soon after four.

To Sir E. W. WATKIN, M.P., 26 September 1892.   Add MS 44549, f. 15.

I thank you much for your inclosures:[1] & *re*thank you and Ly W. for your gracious hospitality. My vote for the Jews[+] was my second step into Liberalism,[2] Free Trade the first. I paid for it by a sharp contest. You will much oblige me if you will apply the inclosed check to the Self-aiding Societies whatever they may be of the employees of the Manchester & Sheffield, which has earned such a title to honourable recollection [in] our little Wales. I hope we may shortly meet at a sort of function for the Wirral.[3] But I trust that getting at the [Channel] Tunnel will not be long delayed.

[+] On consideration I see my vote must refer to Maynooth[4] [Gladstone's note].

27. Tu.

Ch. 8½ A.M. Wrote to Sir W. Harcourt Tel.—Priv. Sec. Tel. l.l.—Ld Rosebery—J. Morley Tel.—Prof. Romanes—J. Grant—and minutes. Worked on Romanes paper & consulting authorities. Walk with Mrs Arthur. Read A.L. on population.[5] Backgammon with Lady H.

To LORD ROSEBERY, foreign secretary, 27 September 1892.   N.L.S. 10025, f. 7.
'*Secret*'.

1. I am compelled to write if only to thank you for your exceeding kind tone.
2. My view of the position of the late Govt. is this
a. I saw clearly that they accepted the evacuation.
b. I did not know whether or not they adhered to the railroad
c. Balfour's answer showed that they did.
and this was what seemed to me the natural position for you to take, from your point of view.
3. When I spoke of dissidence between F.O. and P.M., I included not my own only but all I have ever known—beginning in 1843.
4. I have sent directions to print my Mem.
5. I come up tomorrow afternoon.[6]

[1] Not found; nor a reply.
[2] See 16 Dec. 47.
[3] See 21 Oct. 92.
[4] i.e. in 1845.
[5] Untraced.
[6] On 29 September, Add MS 44289, f. 236, Rosebery wrote before the Cabinet to emphasise that 'the pressing point before the Government is not now the expediency of an East African Empire', or various other factors, 'But whether, in view of the fact that a company has been allowed so to interfere, with a royal charter granted by the Executive for that purpose, we are content to face the consequences of leaving the territory, the inhabitants, and the missionaries, to a fate which we cannot doubt'; Portal 'declares that the certain result will be a general massacre' (Gladstone underlined the last two words twice).

28. Wed. [London]

Wrote to Lord Rosebery—Miss Stanley—Prof. Romanes—C.G.—Mr Stanford—
and minutes. 10½-4½. Hawarden to London. Saw H.J.G.—Sir A. West—Sir R.
Welby—Mr Godley—Sir W. Harcourt—Mr Morley—Mr F. Leveson[1]—Ld Rosebery. Read Maury: Croyances de l'antiquité.[2] An uneasy night. Dined with West
at Brooks's.

29. Th.

Wrote to The Queen—Ld Rosebery—Wms & N.—C.G.—and minutes. Cabinet
11-12½. We found a way out of the present difficulty. Saw S.L.—Sir A. West—Ld
Rosebery—Mr Morley—Sir W. Harcourt—Mr A. Morley—Mr Fowler—Mr
Bryce—Sir J. Lacaita. Tea with Mrs Th. Read Maury—Estourmel, Souvenirs.[3]

Cabinet. Thurs. Sept. 29. 92. Noon. In W.E.G's room exceptionably.[4]
1. Uganda. W.E.G.'s view a) as to money to promote a pacific transition, b) France &
   England to enjoin peace on their resp. subjects, c) Time thus given for friends of a railway policy to consider it.
   The Portal telegram scrutinised[?] & considered to have weight.
2. Morley—recited his acts.
3. Preparation of Bills. Jenkyns.[5]
4. Attorney General reports & consideration of salary.
   Memorandum to be circulated.[6]
There is a disposition to postponement. What if Rosebery, Herschell, & Harcourt consider this afternoon proper terms for a postponement & Cabinet meet at 11 tomorrow to
consider it? Agreed to.[7]

1. Have we to devise a policy, or is there one in possession, which we are asked to
   reverse.
2. Evacuation ⟨being⟩ at hand; it must entail great cost on the Co. which would be
   avoided if their establishment were simply taken over. If there had been any intention
   of replacing them, the Govt. *must have informed them.*
3. Neither in Aug. 91 nor in May 92 on receiving the notices of evacuation from the
   Company did we give *the smallest hint of such intention.*

[1] On Granville's estate. Following a report from Edwin Waterhouse, accountant, the following
were asked to give up to £10,000 each so that the estate could be wound up: Westminster, Spencer,
Lansdowne, Rothschild, Brassey, Northbrook, Sefton, Derby, Burton; Add MS 44516, f. 78 ff. Gladstone later also sent the circular to B. Currie, Aberdeen, Rosebery and Northbourne; ibid., f. 112.
Gladstone's view, supported by Currie, was that the appeal would fail unless Granville's relatives
also subscribed. F. Leveson-Gower felt that none could; all, including the duke of Sutherland(!)
being in 'more or less straitened circumstances'; ibid., f. 119. Despite Gladstone's efforts, Westminster declined; ibid., f. 173. List of subscribers and amounts (Westminster absent) totalling
£18,500, at Add MS 44517, f. 21. Gladstone then (25 January 1893) subscribed £300 which with
others covered the deficit of £1,300; ibid., f. 26.
[2] See 28 June 63.
[3] Count J. d'Estourmel, *Souvenirs de France et d'Italie dans les années 1830–1832* (1848).
[4] Add MS 44648, f. 4. Held in 1 Carlton Gardens.
[5] Sir Henry Jenkyns, parliamentary draftsman; see 15 Mar. 86.
[6] Restrictions on the private practice of the law officers; CAB 37/31/26.
[7] Undated holograph note; Add MS 44648, f. 6.

4. On the *second occasion*, Lord S. noticing a clause in the Instruction to Lugard expressed a desire should be left out [*sic*]: but not one affecting evacuation.
5. On the *first occasion* he suggested that the Company's agents should pay money to Mwanga for good behaviour at the time of transition.
   Thus *accepting evacuation*.
6. Questioned in both Houses the Govt. announced not an evacuation policy but a railway policy. They think *a railway the proper* road to holding the country: & meant to ask *the new Parlt. to make one* (800 miles).
7. This was a policy: right or wrong: but in itself incomplete.
8. This policy we are now asked to alter—by interfering with the evacuation.[1]

To Mrs. GLADSTONE, 29 September 1892.   Hawarden MS 780, f. 213.
   My own C.
   How stupid of me to address you last night at Hawarden! But the excuse is, not a justification, that I was in such an anxious and absorbed state of mind, as to be totally unfit to carry any memory or recollection.
   Today we have had a Cabinet, and, though I cannot say the difficulty is at an end, we are likely to adopt a measure which removes the immediate pressure and which we hope will injure nobody. This looks like a relief. The Cabinet meets again at 11 tomorrow. I hope to get down by an afternoon train: perhaps not a very early one.
   If you hear nothing to the contrary, let carriages meet me at Sandycroft 6.16 PM.
   Rosebery has shown an immense tenacity, worthy of a better cause.
   The Queen we are told is strong in his sense. I have little doubt she would if she [rest of letter cut out]

30. *Fr.* [*Hawarden*]

Wrote to Mr Bryce—W.H. James[2]—Ld Rosebery—The King of the Belgians— The Queen l.l.l. Cabinet 11–12. Saw Sir Alg. West—J. Morley—Ld Rosebery—Ld Spencer—Sir W. Harcourt. 1¾–7. To Hawarden. Read Estourmel, Souvenirs—A Modern Romance.[3]

Cabinet. Sept. 30. 92. 11 AM.[4]
1. Uganda Minute recd. by me[?] last night read & accepted with slight amendments.
2. Letter of K. of the King of the Belgians [*sic*][5]—WEG will write a dilatory reply to the Foreign Office.
3. Capt Macdonald to follow Ld Salisbury's commission if circumstances allow him to do it.[6]

---

[1] Undated holograph; Add MS 44648, f. 7.
[2] William Hill James, b. 1834; soldier, on church matters, see Add MS 44549, f. 16.
[3] L. Bliss, *A modern romance* (1892).
[4] Add MS 44648, f. 9.
[5] 'It appeared to glance at some plan for the administration of Uganda and Unyore by the King subject to Your Majesty's authority'; Gladstone to the Queen this day; CAB 41/22/12.
[6] (Sir) James Ronald Leslie Macdonald, 1862–1927; in India 1885–91; engineer in charge of Uganda railway survey 1891; acting-commissioner Uganda protectorate 1893. Salisbury had commissioned Macdonald to report on Lugard's supposed atrocities and mishandling of affairs in Uganda; Rosebery's telegram this day confirmed the commission; FO 84/2235 and M. Perham, *Lugard* (1956), i. 335. Frederick Dealtry Lugard, 1858–1945; commanded expedition for East Africa Chartered Company to Uganda 1889–92 as its administrator. See 20 July 93.

4. Kimberley. Roberts Mission. No *addition* to be made to the assurances already given to the Ameer. Roberts cannot be changed.

5. Ld Rosebery reported his having suggested a Commission of delimitation.

The Chr. of the Exchr. & I agree with Ld Rosebery that Capt. Macdonald ought to be recalled, but that, without receiving any new commission, he should proceed to fulfil[1]

Uganda. Minute embodying the decision of the Cabinet.[2]

The Co. having finally determined to evacuate Uganda on the 31st December, as notified to the late Govt. and accepted by them in May 1892, and its being evident that the resources of the Co. are unequal to their continued occupation of Uganda, which has likewise been declared by Ld. Salisbury to be arduous if not impossible in the present state of communication, the Govt. adhere to the acceptance of their predecessors of the principle of that evacuation.

It having been however pressed upon them by various communications, especially in a recent telegram of Sir G. Portal, that danger may arise from immediate evacuation at the appointed time, which might be obviated by some further delay which would give time for preparation calculated to facilitate evacuation with greater safety, the Govt. are prepared to assist the Co. by pecuniary contribution towards the cost of prolongation of the occupation for 3 months up to March 31, on a scale not exceeding that of the present expenditure. It must however be distinctly understood that this measure is taken solely with a view to facilitate the safe evacuation by the Co., owing to their pecuniary difficulties; that the responsibility for the measures to be taken in carrying out the evacuation will rest with the Co. alone; that the Govt. do not intend by this step to take upon themselves any of the liabilities incurred by the Co. or their agents in respect of Uganda or the surrounding territories; and that the Govt. reserve to themselves absolute freedom of action in regard to any future measures consequent upon the evacuation.

It must be further understood that if in the opinion of the Co.'s officials no additional security is obtained by delay the evacuation is to take place as originally proposed.

To LEOPOLD II, King of the Belgians, 30 September 1892.   Add MS 44549, f. 16.

I have the honour to thank Your Majesty in the first place for the kind personal words contained in the letter which Your Majesty has been so good as to address to me.[3]

With regard to Uganda, the date of the approaching evacuation by the Company for East Africa is still in question, it having been suggested to the Government that a prolongation of the term would under the circumstances be favourable to life and property in connection with the question of removals. This matter being in course of settlement, the Cabinet are not in a condition even to entertain any other, and I do not even make any enquiry in order to learn exactly the character of the idea which Your Majesty has been graciously pleased to place before me.

To LORD RIPON, colonial secretary, 30 September 1892.   Add MS 43515, f. 78.

I have one word to say on what is a contingency only, but an important contingency, should it arise.

If the Irish Government find it necessary to unship Ridgway, the claim to find a place for him in your Department and perhaps the Indian, will be really a claim not of a Dept. but of the entire Govt. This requires no answer but perhaps you will speak to J. Morley.

[1] Undated and incomplete draft; Add MS 44648, f. 10.
[2] CAB 41/22/13; final version in Asquith's hand.
[3] On 29 September; Add MS 44516, f. 98; personal greetings and 'une demande de concession' for Belgium in Uganda should the British government decide 'de maintenir le drapeau'.

Sat. Oct. One. 1892.

Wrote to Lady Aberdeen—Atty General—Ld Ripon—Mr C. Bannerman—Mr Bryce—Spencer L[yttelto]n—Sir E. Watkin—Dean of Winchr—A. Morley. Read Estourmel—A. Crepaz on Frauen Emancipation[1]—Redmond Home Rule Stat.[2] Saw Dear Gerty. Ch. 8½ A.M. Saw HNG on residence.

To J. BRYCE, chancellor of the duchy, 1 October 1892.   MS Bryce 10, f. 123.
'*Most Private*'.

In considering the question of the formation of Chambers, and especially of a second Chamber or Order for Ireland please to bear in mind a point which is not on the surface but yet I think important.

The Irish Peers are deservedly unpopular. They are anti-national. They are an inferior set of men. But it is desirable if we can to bring them back to nationality, to love of country, to popularity; for they are the natural heads of Irish Society, and in the 18 Cent. they were true Irishmen and were of a higher intellectual level than now.

I have a yearning to recognise them in some way, to favour their moral repatriation, which they need so much.

The Nationalities have no favourable leanings to them, and this cannot be wondered at.

I seek no reply but please to ponder this.[3]

To H. CAMPBELL BANNERMAN, war secretary, 1 October 1892. Add MS 41215, f. 41.

One line to say that when in your Department you want a man good, sound, able, & of enlightened ideas, you may find him in my nephew Col. [N. G.] Lyttelton, made ready to your hand. He was private Secretary to Childers and I believe left a very favourable recollection of himself in the Department. This I assure you is no job.[4]

[P.S.] I was struck by what you said yesterday of Capt. Macdonald. I suppose it his [*sc.* is] his survey of the Railway line [to Uganda] on which we have to depend.

To Sir E. W. WATKIN, M.P., 1 October 1892.   Add MS 44549, f. 17.

If you will kindly supply me with any proposals to which you think the Cabinet ought to accede about the Channel Tunnel, I will gladly bring it before them for consideration when they meet again before the end of this month.[5]

I do not understand why my poor draft cannot be received. But I hope to persuade you on this point when we meet.

2. *16 S. Trin.*

Ch. 11 AM with H.C. & 6½ PM. Wrote to Priv. Sec. (Tel)—The Queen (Ashburnham)—Mr D. Nutt—& minutes. Read 'Oracles of God'[6]—Lewin on Continuity [7]—Crepaz—and [blank.] Worked a little on Oxf L[ecture].

---

[1] Adèle Crepaz, *Die Gefahren der Frauen-Emancipation. Ein Beitrag zur Frauenfrage* (Leipzig 1892); the English tr. (1893) included Gladstone's letter (see 3 Oct. 92). She opposed equal social and political rights for women, arguing '*the happiest marriages in America are those conducted between American men and German women*'.

[2] See to Morley, 5 Oct. 92.   [3] No reply found.

[4] Bannerman replied, 6 October, Add MS 44117, f. 97, that he knew Lyttelton and had 'a strong personal friendship for him', and would keep him in mind for a position.

[5] None found, though clearly sent (see to Watkin, 26 Oct. 92).

[6] W. Sanday, *Oracles of God: lectures on biblical inspiration* (1891).   [7] See 5 June 81.

3. *M.*

Ch. 8½ A.M. Wrote to Mad. A. Crepaz[1]—Lady Stepney—Ld Rosebery l.l.—Sir A. West Tel.—Ld Spencer—Lady Eastlake—Rev. Trotter—Lady Derby—& minutes. Read A Modern Romance finished—Mad. Crepaz finished—Piozzi's Love Letters[2]—Sir W. Stanley's Garland.[3] Helen read Waverley. Worked on books &c.

To Adèle CREPAZ, 3 October 1892.[4]   Add MS 44549, f. 17.

I recently found that I had had the honour to receive, possibly from yourself, your tract on the *Frauen-Emancipation*. The German type is somewhat trying to my failing eyesight, but I could not resist at once reading it; and having read it I cannot resist offering you more than a merely formal acknowledgment. And this is not merely because my mind inclines strongly to agree in your foundation-arguments: but because, apart from mere concurrence in this or that special remark, it seems to me by far the most comprehensive, luminous, and penetrating work on this question that I have yet met with. My great grief is this, speaking for my own country only: that, while the subject is alike vast and profound, it is commonly treated in the slightest and most superficial, as well as sometimes in the most passionate manner. In such a region it is far better, as between opposite risks, to postpone a right measure than to commit ourselves to a wrong one. To save us from this danger what we want is *thorough* treatment; and you have given it the most thorough treatment that I have yet seen applied to it. You have opened up many new thoughts in my own mind, but I cannot follow them out. I only wish the treatise had been open to my countrymen & countrywomen in their own tongue.
[P.S.] For this as well as other subjects, I deeply regret the death of J. S. Mill; he had perhaps the most *open* mind of his generation.[5]

To LORD ROSEBERY, foreign secretary, 3 October 1892.   Add MS 44549, f. 17.

[Letter 1:]   It is too soon for me to go before the Queen about the unhappy Duke's bunch of honours: and I shall delay it for a little: but I do not think it too soon to ask you to let me propose you to her for the Garter. You will I hope fall into my view.[6]
Speaking generally, but not for the moment, this question of honours upon vacancies may open out a difficulty on wh. I may have to consult the Cabinet, once for all.
I have had the most extraordinary letter from Lady Hothfield but I need not trouble you with it.
Lady Ashburnham has sent me what I think a perfect answer about her son. I fear and indeed feel sure that the Queen is much victimised through her having too much zeal & too much limitation in her channels of information.

[Letter 2:]   In answer to your ciphered tel., I think the subject is a little fishy, Capt. L[ugard] being to a considerable degree, as I gather, at loggerheads with his Co., and they probably much afraid of him.

[1] Adèle Crepaz, b. 1849; wrote conservatively on motherhood and the position of women; see 1 Oct. 92.
[2] *Love letters of Mrs. Piozzi, written when she was eighty, to W. A. Conway* (1843).
[3] W. Stanley, Lord Derby, *Sir William Stanley's Garland* (1800?).
[4] Published as a foreword to the English translation, A. Crepaz, *The emancipation of women* (1893).
[5] No reply found.
[6] Rosebery replied, 6 October, Add MS 44290, f. 3: 'My first impulse is, I confess, to ask you to excuse me'; see Crewe, *Rosebery*, ii. 411. He eventually accepted.

But were I in your place, I would see him on his request, not otherwise or what Virgil called *ultro*.[1] Floods of rain.

To LADY STEPNEY, 3 October 1892.					Add MS 44549, f. 18.

I believe you are favourable to the Frauen-Emancipation, which my frame of mind, not absolutely and finally settled on this *vast* question, has opened me to much censure from both sides—With this knowledge I am very desirous that you should read the enclosed remarkable pamphlet, and tell me what you think of it. I have just been writing to the Authoress, and have told her how I wish it were open to British readers in their own tongue—I do not follow her on one point, but I lean strongly to the foundation argument. I am not against all changes; but I dread a Verallgemeinerung[2] by legislation in its effects on the great offices of wife and mother. In 1838 I consulted an eminent Dr Farr[3] about my eyes, and after he had advised me, and went on politics [*sic*], & said "It is not the whigs that will save England, or the Tories that will save England; it is the mothers of England that will save England"—I then & always agreed with him; and I think it not without a deep meaning, apart from all abuses, that three fourths of Christiandom have placed the Blessed Virgin at the top of humanity. I wonder if you will think with me that this treatise tries to go to the foundations, & stands therefore in refreshing contrast with the treatment one commonly sees, so slight & superficial, & sometimes so passionate too.[4]

4. *Tu.*

Ch. 8½ A.M. Wrote to Ld Northbourne—Ld Rosebery—Mr F. Leveson—Ld Aberdeen—S. Lyttelton—Mr B. Currie—Sir E. Reed MP—Sir H. Ponsonby—The Queen—Lady Hothfield—Sir A. West—Mr Hartwell—Mr Silas—Hon. F. Lawley —& minutes. Read Capron[5]—Ld G. Bentinck, Racing Life.[6] Helen read me Waverley. Backgammon with Mr S. Saw Mr Deedes. Worked at St Deiniol's.

To Sir E. J. REED, M.P., 4 October 1892.					Add MS 44549, f. 18.

There is no likelihood of my applying to H.M. for honours at present, but I have a high opinion of Mr. Tenniel and I think your suggestion well deserves to be carefully weighed.[7]

5. *Wed.*

Ch. 8½ A.M. Wrote to Ld Rosebery Tel.—Sir G. Trevelyan Tel.—Lady Derby—Sir A. West—Lady Aberdeen—Ld Reay—Ld Chancellor—Ld Acton—Mr Hallam Tennyson—Mr Mundella—J. Grant—also Mr Morley l.l.—and minutes. Worked on Univ. Books. Worked at St Deiniol's. Saw G.G. (tea). Read Ld G. Bentinck—

---

[1] According to Perham, Lugard was 'in constant touch with Rosebery' at this time, but left no record of their conversations. Rosebery did not report these meetings to Gladstone; Perham, *Lugard*, i. 416.

[2] 'Generalisation'.

[3] J. R. Farre; for this visit, see 23 Nov. 37.

[4] See 18 Oct. 92. Letter of thanks, 5 October, Add MS 44516, f. 115, and a promise of her views (not found), though her German poor.

[5] F. H. Capron, *The antiquity of man from the point of view of religion* (1892).

[6] Frank Lawley, once Gladstone's secretary (see 10 Jan. 47), had sent his *The racing life of Lord George Cavendish Bentinck*, written with John Kent, the trainer (1892); Add MS 44516, f. 99. Lawley drew attention to Bentinck's 'generous & sympathetic views about Ireland expressed . . . nearly 50 years ago . . .'.

[7] Tenniel was knighted in 1893. Reed's letter untraced.

F. Harrison on Huxley¹—Lady Jeune in N.A.R.²—Montagu on Bimetallism.³
Helen read me Waverley. Ah dear Scott.

To LORD ACTON, lord-in-waiting, 5 October 1892.   Cambridge University Library.

I regret to say there are & I fear will be no *proofs* of my Lecture.⁴ I may continue to bore
you with a question or two—as with this—is there any serious reason for doubting that
Occam was at Oxford?⁵ Budinszky does not mention it. Biogr. Universelle gives it. Could
you when at the Athenaeum look at Greyfriars in Oxford. Merton is given as his College.
I am reading De Menorval on Paris but I find him [to] clash a little with Denifle.

To J. MORLEY, Irish secretary, 5 October 1892.   Add MS 44257, f. 7.

1. I think you ought to see the enclosed letter from the Queen, as the last moiety bears
directly upon your proceedings. I am afraid I must notice it: briefly, respectfully, but intel-
ligibly.
2. I have read Redmond's article in the N.C.⁶ Is it not cool, & even impudent, in him to
speak for Ireland with his perpetual "we", while *we* know that he cannot even speak with
or to Ireland, i.e. with or to her constitutional representatives. His argument for the
special guarantee is naught: had the representation at Westminster been sought by and
for Ireland, there would have been something in it. It will be made a plea in Parliament
for varying the Bill after a fashion the very opposite to Redmond's; and in *this* view of
neutralising what is wrong on the other side, his contention may be of use.
3. I forgot to speak about the strange account of L[abouchere] conveyed by Mr Wemyss
Reid.⁷ Have you said anything about it to R. in connection with possible vacancies at
diplomatic posts? Pauncefoot is or was just now here on leave. On many questions L.
would be a real loss. His claim seems not a bad one.
4. I send you herewith a Memorandum I have written tentatively about Egypt.⁸ Unless it
more or less smiles to you I think it may perhaps drop still-born. But it is a subject which
gives me trouble.

6. *Th.*⁹

Ch. 8¼ A.M. 7½ P.M. Wrote to Mayor of Lpool—Mr B. Currie—Mr A. Hutton
—Ld Rosebery—Ly Hothfield—Sir A. West—Mr B. Holt—Mr Godley—Sir G.

¹ F. Harrison, 'Mr Huxley's controversies', *F.R.*, lviii. 417 (October 1892).
² Lady Jeune, 'London society', *N.A.R.*, cliv. 603 (May 1892).
³ S. Montagu, 'Silver and Indian finance', *F.R.*, lviii. 545 (October 1892).
⁴ Acton wrote asking to see the proofs, 3 October 1892, Add MS 44094, f. 210.
⁵ Acton replied that he did not think that there was 'any evidence that Occam was at Oxford';
6 October 1892, ibid., f. 221.
⁶ J. E. Redmond, 'Readjustment of the Union: a nationalist plan', *N.C.*, xxxii. 509 (October 1892);
see to Morley 17 Oct. 92 and 1 Oct. 92.
⁷ Request for the Washington embassy; see to Morley, 15 Oct. 92.
⁸ Morley replied, 9 October, Add MS 44257, f. 11, that he approved the Egyptian memo. but
doubted the wisdom of 'excluding the case of a native revolt from the sources of danger which
would justify re-entry'.
⁹ Tennyson died this day; some of his last words were '"Have I not been walking with Gladstone
in the garden, and showing him my trees?" I [Hallam Tennyson] answered, "No". He replied, "Are
you sure?"' (*Life of Tennyson*, ii. 426). Once the Romanes lecture was delivered, Gladstone began
reading the poems of possible successors to the laureateship, but he never recommended one. For
his abortive search, see following letters and Alan Bell, 'Gladstone looks for a Poet Laureate', *T.L.S.*,
21 July 1972, p. 847.

Trevelyan—Sir H. Verney—Rev. H. Rashdall[1]—E. Marjorib.—Mr Schnadhorst—and minutes. Worked on Oxf. paper. Helen read to me. Read Estourmel—and [blank.] Walk with Helen.

To R. D. HOLT, mayor of Liverpool, 6 October 1892.   Add MS 44549, f. 20.

I have to acknowledge alike with pleasure and with gratitude, both the personal tone of the letter you have been good enough to address to me, and the announcement of the public honour which the Municipal Council of the City of Liverpool has been pleased unanimously to tender to me.

I cannot hesitate to accept at once so gratifying an offer; with all the desires for the welfare and greatness of Liverpool, which can be entertained even by the youngest & the most attached of those who already count among her citizens.[2]

To A. W. HUTTON, 6 October 1892.   Add MS 44549, f. 20.

I received the book[3] & that thankfully from Westell, and I believe (but my bill is un-receipted) settled with him in the course of business.

Your article appeared to me most able, and in important points unanswerable (forgive me for adding) by you or anybody else.

And this I ought to have said to you long ago. Possibly your trip abroad delayed my reply.

With respect to revision,[4] I fear the chances of my being able to give time, always in-different, are now wofully attenuated. In the case of the Scotch speeches, Mr. Parker's case [care?], after lasting without a flaw over all these years, was quite recently found to have failed in a Report relating to Disestablishment.

The persons most likely to know whether a given thing was or was not likely to have been said by me are Mr. Godley (India Office) Mr Hamilton (Treasury) and Sir A. E. West (now retired) who is permanently helping me and would perhaps be best to refer to.

To LORD ROSEBERY, foreign secretary, 6 October 1892.   N.L.S. 10025, f. 52.

Dufferin's letters are delightful but his ink is vile and will soon place them wholly beyond the cognisance of my old eyes.

I have *never* been within the doors of the sublime temple of Secret Service.

But as an outsider I think the appearance of a large figure in the annual votes tends to generate rumours both silly & mischievous.

[P.S.] I have written to B. Currie on the Granville matter.

To F. SCHNADHORST, secretary of the National Liberal   Add MS 44549, f. 19
Federation, 6 October 1892.

I think that during the last six or seven years I never refused a request for a letter to a candidate in the field when backed by you or Mr. A. Morley.

But the proposal that I should write one in the case of Stroud[5] is I think altogether

---

[1] Hastings Rashdall, 1858–1924; theologian and historian of universities; supplied Gladstone with information, especially about Paris, for his lecture; see 8 Oct. 92 and Add MSS 44516, ff. 107, 123 and 44549, f. 22.

[2] Freedom of Liverpool. See 3 Dec. 92.

[3] See 7 Aug. 92.

[4] i.e. Hutton and Cohen's edition of Gladstone's *Speeches*.

[5] In fact Cirencester (see secretary's docket), where H. L. W. Lawson just held the seat in February 1893; see to Marjoribanks, 6 Sept. 92n. Schnadhorst's request untraced.

novel, so far as my practice when Prime Minister is concerned—(Did not Disraeli do it, when in office, at Bath with very bad effect?) Apart from this I think the rule has been that I commonly wrote these letters when the chance was believed to be a good one. But no such assurance has been given me in this case.

My present feeling is that were I to comply with the suggestion, 1. it would be a precedent and as such would entail embarrassment in future cases.

2. that in case of defeat it would very seriously aggravate the blow to the Government.

3. that, if defeat be the probable alternative, the chance offered of converting it into success by a letter is infinitely remote, and that the risk (2) ought not to be run.

To Sir G. O. TREVELYAN, Scottish secretary, 6 October 1892.   Add MS 44549, f. 20.

Many thanks for your letter.[1] After adjusting all the preliminaries I have written to Reay,[2] & have baited my hook with Scotch business, Ld Acton as Colleague, and H.M's approval.

I think your conversation with Rainy would be very useful. No doubt you will talk over the matter with the Lord Advocate, who knows so much. It appears to me that you might perhaps go so far on your own hook, or on yours and his, and not as from me, as to glance at a Bill (mainly) for the extinction of public stipends, and to point out that it would settle in rather a simple form 9/10 or 19/20 of the question of disestablishment for Scotland.

7. Fr.

Ch 8½ A.M. & H.C. Wrote to Mr P. Campbell—F. Leveson—Mrs Stanley—Ld Rosebery—Mr Asquith—J. Morley—D. of Sutherland—Ld Acton—Ed. Notes & Qu.[3]—The Queen—Mr Hazelhurst[4]—and minutes. Worked at St Deiniol's. Worked on Oxf. MS. The reading will be a difficulty with my present eyesight. Read Estourmel—Lawley's G. Bentinck. Helen read me Waverley.

To LORD ACTON, lord in waiting, 7 October 1892.   Add MS 44094, f. 212.

I am not at present willing to give up Occam. His case is for me like that of most of the eminent Oxonians of old date—I find them in the recognised authorities, but I cannot prove the case. Occam's birthplace was in the same district of Surrey as Merton: thence came Merton College which claims Occam (they spell the parish Ockham I think). It is most unlikely *at his date* that he was reared in Paris. His going there later on is ascribed to his being driven from Oxford on account of the troubles his opinions had excited. I have not *yet* learned [of] any case the other way.

2. Mr. Hallam Lit. Europe I. 22 cites a passage from Wood I. 159 which I cannot get at in my copy of Bliss's Edition.[5] Would you kindly see if it is accessible in the Athenaeum copy.

[1] Of 5 October, Add MS 44335, f. 238: importance of 'confiding the Scottish business to Reay' who has shown keen interest. Trevelyan was due for an interview with Rainy and others ('I shall be very cautious, and get their views without committing the Government in any respect').

[2] Unsuccessfully inviting Reay to be a Lord-in-Waiting, with responsibility for Scottish business in the Lords; Add MS 44549, f. 19.

[3] Pointing out that 10 St. James's Square, his house during the 1890 session, was once occupied by Lord Derby (as well as the elder Pitt); *Notes and Queries*, 8th series, ii. 267, 310.

[4] G. S. Hazlehurst; had sent his tract; see this day's letter.

[5] Anthony à Wood, *Athenae Oxonienses. An exact history of all the writers and bishops who had had their education in the most ancient and famous University of Oxford* [1500–1690], edited and continued by Philip Bliss, 4v. (1813–20).

3. Tennyson's death moves many and much and that justly.

He has done a very great work. The question of the succession comes before me with very ugly features. I have, as it happens, the old Poems & Ballads 1866.[1] They are both bad & terrible. Have they been dropped? If they have it is a reparation. Wordsworth & Tennyson have made the place great. They have also made it extremely clean. Southey who preceded was not small but was appointed against what was bigger. Before him was it not always small? I do not like the look of the affair.[2]

To H. H. ASQUITH, home secretary, 7 October 1892.   Add MS 44549, f. 21.

It seems that the Statute requires a Secretary of State (member of the Church of England) to be upon the Ecclesiastical Commission, & that the Home Secretary is usually the man. Will you accept—or if not find me a substitute among your distinguished brethren.[3]

To G. S. HAZLEHURST, 7 October 1892.   Add MS 44549, f. 22.

I thank you for your tract[4] and will not fail to peruse it; but I never give my signature in such cases, and my information [*recte* inclination?] is to believe that the time has not arrived when such questions of reunion can be effectually taken in hand.

To LORD ROSEBERY, foreign secretary, 7 October 1892.   N.L.S. 10025, f. 65.
'*Private.*'

On receiving your letter, I have decided, and likewise I loyally accept the gag.[5] But on the general question[6] I shall wish to speak to you, and possibly even to the Cabinet.

To Mrs. H. M. STANLEY, 7 October 1892.   Add MS 44549, f. 22.

I take it as a great mark of your kindness that you should write to me on Uganda and refer me to your husband's speech which has been, and will be, read so eagerly.[7]

The time does not permit me to add anything to the important announcement lately made by Ld. R. on behalf of the Government, and its acceptance by the Company; but I think you may rest assured of two things—one that we shall continue to consider very

---

[1] i.e. A. S. Swinburne, *Poems and ballads* (1866). Swinburne was an obvious but extremely problematic candidate. Gladstone tried to discover whether he had renounced the most notorious poems in this famous volume; see to Acton, 10, 17 Oct. 92.

[2] Acton replied, 8 October, Add MS 44094, f. 214, sending the à Wood reference from John Gutch's ed. of *The history and antiquities of the Colleges and Halls in the University of Oxford*, 2v. (1792–6), i. 160. He reported that Swinburne had not withdrawn the *Poems and Ballads*; he believed 'it will be difficult to do the right thing with the Laurel crown, and impossible to do anything with general consent'. He wrote again on 9 October, ibid., f. 216, mentioning that Tennyson 'made very little money until he became Laureate, when he rapidly became rich. . . . Has it occurred to you that the greatest Poet in England is a writer of exceedingly numerous Prose? [i.e. Ruskin]. The objection would be that he has also written a volume of Poetry.'

[3] Asquith replied, 10 October, Add MS 44516, f. 145; 'I think I had better eschew the Ecclesl. Commissionership. I was born & bred among Nonconformists, and though I am no longer among them, I think the Church might eye me askance'; he suggested Kimberley, 'who bids fair to be the pluralist of the present Cabinet'. The Commissionership was offered to G. Leveson Gower; Asquith, whose marriage in 1894 was by the Church of England rite, eventually accepted the post.

[4] 'The reunion of Christendom' (secretary's marginal note); no copy traced.

[5] Rosebery wrote, 6 October, N.L.S. 10025, f. 62, accepting the Garter, but 'ungraciously' requesting no further discussion of the matter.

[6] i.e. their general disagreement on Uganda.

[7] No letter traced. H. M. Stanley spoke in Swansea, *T.T.*, 4 October 1891, 5a, on the possible benefits of East African economic development to the British economy.

fully all the information that we obtain, and the other that the case in favour of occupation will be more fully & adequately represented than what there is to be said against it.

To the DUKE OF SUTHERLAND, 7 October 1892.   Add MS 44549, f. 21.

However reluctant to address you so soon after your recent bereavement, I offer as my apology that I write on a public matter.

If I should obtain your consent, it is my desire to submit your name to H.M. for the Lord Lieutenancy of the County of Sutherland.

As politics usually have a place in proposals of this kind, I shall not forego the mention of them, and I think it right to use the most explicit terms.

In point of party connection I have always looked upon you as an earnest Liberal: but I have never since 1886 been encouraged to regard you as sharing in the views of the bulk of the party with reference to the Irish question.

Should you accept the offer I now make I beg you to understand that it will be without any pledge or obligation on your part as to your political conduct either in or out of the House of Lords.[1]

8. Sat.

Ch. 8½ A.M. Wrote to Mrs Th. Tel.—Private Sec. Tel. and l.—Att. Genl—H. Tennyson Tel.—F. Leveson—Sir W. Harcourt—Mrs N. Lyttelton—& minutes. Worked on Oxford MS. An easier bag enabled me to spend most of the morning on Mr Rashdall's Proof sheets. Also read The Silver Domino[2]—and divers books. Worked at St D.s. Tea at the Rectory.

To Sir W. V. HARCOURT, chancellor of the exchequer,   MS Harcourt dep. 12, f. 116.
8 October 1892.

Your account of the rule of silent reserve combined with courtesy and general freedom agrees with the other reports, and seems to indicate a plan probably the best which the circumstances permit.[3] The same reticence does not hold good in my case, and sometimes I am tempted to wish it did.

The Queen would like to have the K. of the Belgians associated with us in Uganda but does not press it sharply. If we could get him into our shoes! With you I am prepared for a storm on this subject, and with you prepared to face it. Indeed I think the minute already adopted as the basis of a temporary proceeding leaves but very little choice to us as a Govt.

The Sutherland will is terrible. I have written to the Duke to offer the Lord Lieutcy without any stipulation as to politics. If he accepts it the Mistressship of the Robes might follow a while hence.

I am in the thick of the Granville Estate affairs, and bad enough they are. Hartington has behaved admirably wanted [sic]: but there is need of near £53000 to stave off difficulty from the Shelton Works and leave the Estate generally able to meet its engagements.

The Hothfield business is bad: and *she* has actually opened a correspondence with me upon it![4]

[1] Sutherland accepted after a little prevarication; see 11 Oct. 92 and Add MS 44516, f. 138.
[2] *The silver domino; or side whispers, social and literary* (3rd ed. 1892).
[3] Report from Balmoral, 4 October, Add MS 44202, f. 253.
[4] The Lordship-in-Waiting.

C. Bannerman has a good report of Captain Macdonald, very bad of Lugard.
I agree that we must consider the case of the Law Officers upon its merits.

To Hallam, LORD TENNYSON, 8 October 1892.   Add MS 44549, f. 22.

My telegram was necessarily brief; but the fact is that at this moment I am laden with very special duties beyond the heavy correspondence regularly entailed by my office.[1] I am bound by an old engagement to finish the preparation of a lecture on a wide subject in the Sheldonian Theatre at Oxford, and this raises for the present my daily work to a point so high that it will bear no postponement and no withdrawal.

I was deeply touched by your Father's unmerited recollection of me in the extremity of the last conflict.[2]

He and I had both lived into great loneliness, after beginning in the midst of large bands of friends.

Let me cite his own words[3]

> In the great cathedral leave him
> God, accept him; Christ, receive him.

Again let me express our earnest hopes that Lady Tennyson is not too hard pressed: and my not less earnest congratulations to you on your filial career; it has been that of a much more fine Æneas than the original.

9. S. 17 Trin.

Ch. 11 A.M. and [blank.] Wrote to Mr Fisher Unwin—The Queen—Mr Knowles—C. Higham—Tregaskis—Rev. Morris—Dr Luccock—Mr S. Laing—& minutes. Worked on Oxford MS. Read Laing's Origins—Capron's Antiquity of Man.

To J. T. KNOWLES, editor of the *Nineteenth Century*,   Add MS 44549, f. 22.
9 October 1892.

I sincerely sympathise with your desire and with your difficulties, for Tennyson had become like a great solitary tree in the forest where all the rest had died, such as I have seen more than once in Scotland.[4]

But also I cannot do it—I doubt if I could were I free, and with a possibility of concentration. But I am two removes from that state, which would be one of no better than bare possibility. First I have the work of my office; but the second is the *sealing* impediment; I have upon my hands the preparation for a lecture at Oxford on the 24th in the Sheldonian Theatre, with a very arduous subject, touching on Universities, which mentally & physically absorbs every hour that I can scrape together while retaining any capacity for work.

It is with much regret that I write this letter, but in such a matter to undertake with known incapacity to accomplish would be a profanation.

You will know better where to turn than I do. There is no suggestion I could offer you with confidence.[5]

[1] Hallam Tennyson invited Gladstone by wire to act as a pall-bearer; Add MS 44516, f. 130.
[2] See 6 Oct. 92n.
[3] From Tennyson's 'Ode on the death of the Duke of Wellington'.
[4] Knowles's letter, requesting a piece on Tennyson, untraced.
[5] Knowles himself wrote 'A personal reminiscence' of Tennyson for the *Nineteenth Century*, which greatly offended the Tennyson family; see P. Metcalfe, *James Knowles* (1980), 339–40.

10. M.

Ch. 8½ A.M. Wrote to Mayor of Bayonne[1]—The Queen—Hodder & Stoughton—
Ld Acton—Sir H. Ponsonby—J. Morley—Rev. Mr Mentin—F. Leveson—Sir H.
Acland—and minutes. Worked on MS for Oxford. Worked at St Deiniol's.
Finished Capron's remarkable book. Read Inheritance of the Kurts.[2] C. read
Waverley to me.

To Sir H. W. ACLAND, 10 October 1892.　　　　　　　MS Acland d. 68, f. 89.

　　You will I think more than most men realise the difficulty in which I am placed with
regard to the Laureateship. It is most desirable to keep it on the high moral plane where
Wordsworth & Tennyson placed it.
　　Is Ruskin impossible?
1. He would secure that capital object.
2. He has published Poems: he is a poet too in Prose.
3. What is the state of his health? I have been told perfectly entire in brain only not
capable of exertion. You probably know all about this, and I should much value your
judgment.[3]
[P.S.] Forgive me for troubling you with my Oriental Essay.

To LORD ACTON, lord-in-waiting, 10 October 1892.　　Cambridge University Library.

1. Why were you so transcendently kind as to copy out Wood?[4] The reference,
verified, was enough for me. Other men stint what one asks: you always broaden it.
2. I think you leave me quite enough standing ground for Ockham: and I think my
notices of his local origin have a small value.
3. But as to the case of Swinburne;[5] much worse I trow, than that of Ockham! I knew the
'Poems and Ballads' were alive but are bad ones still included? My copy (1866) of the
original has *62* Poems and 344 Pages.[6]
　　The licentiousness of Swinburne differs from all other known to me in the quality of
intensity. It is so earnest!
　　I must take time.
4. You speak I suppose of Th[eodore] Martin. I have only known him in his Translations;
which I think good.
5. I have used a freedom in asking the publishers to send you a copy of The Bookman for
Octr. on account of an Homeric article by Prof. Ramsay![7] For the sake of its extremely
luminous view of the origin and growth of that wonderful thing Hellenism: and not I
think for the sake of the acquittal it seems to pronounce on me.
[P.S.] I will make some inquiry about Ruskin.

---

[1] Thanking him for a history of the town; Add MS 44549, f. 22.
[2] See 21 Sept. 92.
[3] Acland replied, 12 October, Add MS 44091, f. 194: 'The case of Ruskin is very sad, & very difficult to describe with correctness. I have not seen him for some years. . . . He varies between excitement (less now than formerly) depression, and moderate intelligent intercourse. . . . He is a true
poet, of the rarest gentility, though he expresses himself in prose. The popularity of his writings is as
great as ever—or greater, as one knows by the great income he derives from them. . . . But I fear he
will do no more.' On 15 October, Acland sent a letter from Dr. Parsons, Ruskin's doctor at Amble-
side: ibid., f. 198. See to Acland, 15 Aug. 93.
[4] See 7 Oct. 92.
[5] i.e. for the Laureateship.
[6] See to Acton, 17 Oct. 92.
[7] See to Morley this day.

To J. MORLEY, Irish secretary, 10 October 1892. 'Secret'.   Add MS 44549, f. 23.

I value you very much your reply [sic] in my scrap of a Memorandum about Egypt.[1] Something said by you gave me the idea that you and R. were in harmony on that subject. Without some presumption of that kind I certainly should not like to moot the subject now. There will be a great advantage in being beforehand with any application from the French, which must come before very long. Especially as I imagine their demand for damages cannot be entertained. If my subjects are damaged by *your* subjects in a wild country, must they not take their chance?

An argument in favour of leaving out what you have spotted is that it has not I think been *tabled* before, and that it might suggest criticism which would not else have been thought of.

The Queen has written to me nicely about Tennyson. The succession[2] bothers me; I fear Swinburne is impossible.

I have used a freedom with you in causing to be sent you a number of the 'Bookman' for October[3] by reason of an article partly on me, and not, be assured, because it is favourable on the whole to me, but because of its singularly luminous view of the origin and constitutive elements of that great and immortal fact of Hellenism.

[P.S.] My great difficulty for Oxford is the delivery, in the present state of my eyesight. Thanks to you I have in a manner gone through Mr. Rashdall's sheets on Paris; very able & very comprehensive.

11. Tu.

Ch. 8½ A.M. Wrote to D. of Sutherland—The Queen—Mrs Bennett—Scotts— Mayor of Lpool—Watsons—Mr F. Leveson—Mr Marjoribanks Tel.—Sir H. Ponsonby—Mr Trotter—and minutes. Worked on writing out afresh my MS for Oxford. Worked at St Deiniol's. C. read Waverley to me. Read Pitt Correspondence[4]—Lloyd on Silver Crisis.[5]

To the DUKE OF SUTHERLAND, 11 October 1892.   Add MS 44549, f. 24.

I will write to the Queen about the Lord Lieutenancy, and many I think will be specially glad to see it when you have had, and I fear have, so much to go through.

I quite agree with you that people had better not suppose anything but the truth.

Were it a question of a formal covenant I should not personally object to making known to all interested, or even to the world, the entire paragraph (in preference to a part) which touches your politics just as it stands.

But there is I think no formal act in question; and what I advise is that both you and I should, as occasion offers, say that your political position is *in no way affected* by your acceptance of the Lord-Lieutenancy.

Kindly let me know if you approve.

[P.S.] I must add that it is a peculiar pleasure for me to do any act acceptable to the grandson of the Duchess Harriet whose memory is ever dear to me.

[1] See 5 Oct. 92n.
[2] i.e. to the laureateship.
[3] W. M. Ramsay, 'Mr. Gladstone on Homer', *Bookman* (October 1892), 15; a criticism of Gladstone's Homeric scholarship.
[4] See 20 Mar. 90.
[5] Untraced.

12. *Wed.*

Ch 8½ A.M. Wrote to Ld Ripon l.l.—E. Barnard—E.A. Floyer[1]—W. Downing—
M. Evans—Wms & Norgate—& minutes. Walk with Harry & visited Lane End
Colliery. Spent 2½ hours on my Bills & accounts: chiefly for St Deiniol's. A most
rare event! Worked on MS for Oxford. C. read to me. Read Effacement of O.
Penhaligon[2]—Chastel, Décadence.[3]

To LORD RIPON, colonial secretary, 12 October 1892.   Add MS 43515, f. 84.

If I understand you rightly the question which waits immediate decision in the matter
of Newfoundland[4] is
1. whether to send an agent for a financial inquiry into the capacity of the Colony to *sustain* a Guarantee
2. whether & how to make some immediate provision if it be necessary for the coming
winter, which would also come within the scope of the inquiry
I think with you that on this question if the Chancr. of the Exchequer agrees you need
not refer to the Cabinet. I make on it the following observations
1. In my view, any advance made for the winter distress should not be a separate grant
out and out but should stand for future consideration and become part of whatever it may
be decided to give or lend—Otherwise, you would have two pecuniary applications to
make to Parliament, and this seems inconvenient
2. Manifestly you want a strict as well as capable man to inquire. My *impression* is that Sir
Wm. Gurdon[5] is the kind of man wanted—they will know at the Treasury.
    3. I confess to not liking *primâ facie* a loan without interest—would it not be a rather
novel and a very awkward precedent. With respect to the general question, I presume we
should all agree that the union of Nfdd with the dominion [of Canada] is most desirable,
as well as that it is important to help onwards the settlement with France. Perhaps the
Union may be helped by our taking care to enlighten Nfdd on the weakness of her financial position. But, as to what is beyond this, it seems to me important that we should let
the two parties be, and especially, feel themselves to be the real independent agents.
Were we to assume ostensibly a primary part, and to enable them or either of them to say
'we did it to please you', we should be in danger of a false position. But this need in no
way disable us from tendering a warm assistance to the promotion of their common
desire.

13. *Th.*

Ch. 8½ A.M. Wrote to Ld Rosebery l.l.—Priv. Sec. Tel.—F. Leveson—Ld North-
bourne—Ld Acton—Sir W. Harcourt—The Queen—Mr Stuart Rendel—Dr
Granger—& minutes. Worked on Oxf. MS. Worked at St Deiniol's. C. read
Waverley to me. Read Oriel &c.—Mason's Bedell[6]—Chastel Destr. du Pagme.

[1] Ernest Ayscoghe Floyer, explorer and writer; in correspondence on Homer; see Add MS 44549, f. 25.
[2] E. M. Hewitt, *Effacement of Oriel Penhaligon* (1892).
[3] E. L. Chastel, *Histoire de la destruction du paganisme dans l'empire d'Orient* (1850).
[4] Memorandum on Newfoundland sent by Ripon on 9 October: Add MS 43515, f. 81.
[5] Gladstone's private secretary in his 1868–74 administration.
[6] Untraced.

To Sir W. V. HARCOURT, chancellor of the exchequer,   MS Harcourt dep. 12, f. 123.
13 October 1892. '*Secret*'.

In yours of yesterday[1] I entirely concur: & have written strongly to Rosebery in that
sense.

Also I have urged a smart rap over the knuckles for Portal or his friend whichever is
the guilty one.

To E. F. LEVESON-GOWER, M. P., 13 October 1892.   Add MS 44516, f. 164.

I sit down with a heavy heart to obey you & return your letter to Westminster.[2]

I think it excellent except the sentence which ends "quite reasonable": for my opinion
is obstinately fixed, & my belief is that in the mercantile world help would have been
forthcoming to avert a catastrophe.

I think Cobden was both saved & re-endowed if I recollect right & Tweedmouth I
believe paid in six figures to cover his brother. I admit these are not brothers: but no one
is asked to pay in six figures. My daughter in law is I believe of my mind.

The Duke of W. is distinctly a peg down with me, as Hartington is some pegs up. I am
sorry to think that if discredit comes, he may be a sharer as he would not like to show up
the rest.

I have sent back to you Mr B. Currie's letter, in a blank cover—I know your heart's
blood flows out with the ink.

You assuredly have nothing with which to reproach yourself.

To S. RENDEL, M.P., 13 October 1892.   Add MS 44516, f. 165.

1. Do you recollect my speaking to you about Welsh Rents, and did you take a note of
any particulars?

My recollections are very clear.

Wales (all) reduced 7%

Four Counties raised

Flint and Denbigh reduced 11%

I founded on Goschen. Possibly the paper is in London. Do not trouble about particulars:
only to say whether you recollect and how much.

The question will come up again in connection with the pressure for a Commission.

2. I am sorry you cannot come; but I understand your desire to get southwards. I should
like to have told you what communications I have had about the G[ranville] Estate. Two
persons before whom I brought the matter think strongly that the sole chance of getting
it through is by a recognition of special responsibility on the part of the relatives.

P.S. Since I wrote this, I have received a letter from F. Leveson which makes me very
despondent indeed.

To LORD ROSEBERY, foreign secretary, 13 October 1892.   Add MS 44549, f. 25.

I find in the Times of the 10th a most improper publication of a letter or extract from
Sir G. Portal respecting the evacuation of Uganda. It may be the act of him or his friend:
but I hope you will administer a sharp reprimand to the one, or secure the administration
of it by Portal to his friend if the fault be with the recipient.[3]

My eyesight now keeps me as a rule from all small print but I understand that Beach

[1] On Uganda, Add MS 44202, f. 261.
[2] i.e. letter, on the Granville estate, returned to the duke of Westminster.
[3] Rosebery replied next day, Add MS 44290, f. 14, that he had already asked Portal for an
explanation (telegram enclosed to Gladstone, but not found). See 15 Oct. 92.

has been speaking as if the late govt. had had no hand in this mess. When you kindly sent me the papers, intent merely on the meaning I did not ask myself whether they had been published. But I gather now that they have not. Viewing the attitude of Beach & the agitation in the Times is not the time come for the publication? I think the Cabinet would have desired it. See my second letter on other matters.[1]

14. Fr.

Ch. 8¼ A.M. Wrote to Lady Hothfield—Sir H. Ponsonby—Mr Baker—F. Leveson l.l.—Mr Murray—Mr Asquith—Ly Ribblesdale—The Queen—and minutes. Worked on Welsh Rents. Tea and conversation with G.G. Conversation with A. Gordon: come to examine the Herbert letters.[2] Read W. Morris's Gudrun[3]—and [blank.] Very tired: took an afternoon sleep.

To H. H. ASQUITH, home secretary, 14 October 1892.   Add MS 44549, f. 26.

I have read your clear & comprehensive paper & I agree in your conclusions.[4] The prohibition seems to me inadmissible. The proposal of a Committee is one thing as an appeal from the Executive, quite another if by the Executive as a measure of first instance. You will probably communicate with Harcourt & I think it would be well to let the Attorney General know. No need so far as I see for the Cabinet. J. Stuart & his wife are to be here next week, (a bit of *Solatium*).[5] Would you like me to speak to him in confidence. I suppose there are few spots if any, as to which it can be asserted, in London, that there is a positive & absolute legal right of meeting. But, there being a legal right to meet, I think that, in the huge space of London, there is some moral right to meet dispersedly & not to be tied to one spot. Your passage about Sundays would I think be less open to cavil if you altered the form of expression & said meetings would not be allowed except on the days which have recently become usual, or something of that kind.

15. Sat.

Ch. 8½ A.M. Wrote to Mr Meynell—Ld Rosebery l.l.l. & Tel.—Mr Lyall MP—Mr S. Laing—Mr Meynell—Mr Morley—Mr Cameron—& minutes. Drove into Chester & saw Mr Granger.[6] The effects of the accident have past: but he reports a slight decline in the sight of the available eye. This corresponds with my own perceptions. Conversation with Harry: Estate—& Granville Estate. Avoided reading by order. Worked 'some' on MS. 12 to dinner.

[1] Not printed. The Salisbury govt.'s correspondence is in *PP* 1893-4 lxii. 335 (January 1893).
[2] Gordon was working on his life of Sidney Herbert, published 1906.
[3] In William Morris, *The earthly paradise*, see 4 May 74.
[4] Asquith was due to meet a dpn. on 19 October from the Metropolitan Radical Federation on meetings in Trafalgar Square, a traditional place for such gatherings whose legitimacy was questioned following the disturbances in 1887-8; Asquith's compromise solution lasts to this day. See Spender and Asquith, i. 81 and Add MS 44516, ff. 162, 174.
[5] For Stuart's not being included in the government.
[6] The Chester eye surgeon; see 25 June 92.

To J. MORLEY, Irish secretary, 15 October 1892.   Add MS 44257, f. 15.

Labouchere's demands[1] are indeed extraordinary. He seems to think

1. That any requisite number of great appointments can be shifted in order to vacate for him the place he wants.

2. That the Foreign Secretary has nothing to do. It appears to me that your first duty is to undeceive him as to Rosebery—& I should like to say, were I in your place, that you will make it known to R. without whom you cannot presume to say a single word as to its being entertained, or entertainable; & that you think viewing the complex nature of the business as he has advanced it that you could do this with much greater advantage *viva voce*.

As far as I have gathered you do not see your way at all; still I think that you & I are hardly competent to shut the door absolutely without consulting some other colleagues—You would probably in writing protect yourself with sufficient reserves.

The two following remarks are without prejudice.

1. The P.C. difficulty wd. be less in high quarters, I think, if proposed by Rosebery; but has L. duly considered the splendours of a *G.C.B.*

2. As to the "domesticities" pray ask Houghton about the conjugal integrity of New York—I was much struck with an account he gave me here.

Ripon wd. be a good witness on this.[2]

[P.S.] The Queen wd. not like the abolition of the Laureateship with the Buckhounds!

To LORD ROSEBERY, foreign secretary, 15 October 1892.   Add MS 44290, f. 20.
'*Secret*'.

[Letter 1:]   Your proposed contribution to the Granville difficulty[3] is simply splendid, & far ahead of what (in my notion) a liberal equity demands—shall I add—or justifies.

The question whether the effort is to proceed rests I think practically with Hartington, & with the answer which Westminster may finally give him. The difficulty in that quarter has been to me quite unexpected.

As far as I am concerned I proceed upon the judgment & the character of Waterhouse. The Estate account, apart from the works, has never been made known to me: but that is I imagine a more simple affair. Mr Rendel has a signal competency to judge whether 53 m[ille] will save the works (Shelton). But his Chairman: must he not either say yes, or be silent.

His brother is coming here on Monday & probably knows his opinion. Shall I ask him whether he can properly tell me anything? *Rebus sic stantibus*, I shall in no way presume to commit you.

The Bankruptcy will I fear be a blow to the 'aristocracy'.

If it comes it will be mixedly[?] to the relations. If it is averted, this will be due to two individuals—Hartington & you. The act will have a sweet smelling savour.

P.S. Since writing this, Mr. S. Rendel's opinion has come before me: it is not quite consecutive but its colour certainly not bright.

[1] Sent by Morley on 14 October, Add MS 44257, f. 13: four demands, extracted from a 16 page letter: (a) he had decided to refuse office if invited, (b) the Queen would not have objected to him, (c) it is his 'fancy' to be ambassador to Washington, with a Privy Councillorship, but not a knighthood, to which he would object, (d) he proposed various other moves among the diplomatic corps. The affair reached the Cabinet, see 11 Nov. 92.

[2] Morley replied, 16 October, Add MS 44257, f. 17, that he had written 'my friend . . . an answer diplomatic enough to fit me for Washington myself'.

[3] See 20 Apr. 91, 12 May 92. Rosebery, 14 October, Add MS 44290, f. 17, thought bankruptcy better than paying money into a failing company, but felt that 'if you and Hartington are satisfied, I should be too. I will therefore give 2000£ towards making up the 53000£, on the same conditions as Hartington.'

[Letter 2:]   Add MS 44549, f. 26.

1. Portal's replies are strange enough—but I think they only call for such an answer or notice as you describe. 2. I confess it seems to me that the public will be misled till the Salisbury correspondence has been published, but as you do not think so[1] perhaps we had better let it stand until we meet when the Cabinet being already seized of the matter you might feel the pulse of others. 3. I think of Wed. 27th afternoon for Cabinet—if this day suits you. 4. I have suggested to the Queen that the remaining Lordships may stand over for a week or two or three. The Thurlow difficulty is not out of the way. I am choking off Lady Hothfield who evidently wants a Lordship as an instrument of putting down the rumours. She has as many lives as a cat.

16. 18 S. Trin.

Ch mg & evg. Wrote to Mr [E.T.] Cook (PMG)—and [blank.] Worked on Oxf. MS. Read Douglas Campbell on the Puritans[2]—Shuttleworth on Church Music.[3] Much conversation & discussion with Lucy [Cavendish].

17. M.

Ch 8½ A.M. Wrote to Mr Dougl. Campbell—Sir H. Acland—Ld Acton—Marchesa Teodoli[4]—Mr Morley—& minutes. Lots of guests. Interesting forenoon discussion on Temperance. Walk & talk Mr [James] Stuart. Finished at last writing my interminable Lecture. Read Campbell's Puritans—Teodoli's Under Pressure. Twelve to dinner.

To Sir H. W. ACLAND, 17 October 1892.   MS Acland, d. 68, f. 91.

I am indeed in your debt for your very interesting letter; and not least for the saddest part of it, which fully reveals the truth, and by the truth extinguishes all hope of Ruskin.[5] I do not at present know how I am to get through the difficulty of finding the proper successor to Tennyson. There is plenty of power still alive; but the incidents of it!

My lecture or address which is to explode at Oxford next Monday has cost me much labour; probably with very little fruit, and has been very hard to reconcile in any manner with my political daily work. However I am nearly out of the preparation now. I hope there is plenty of light for if not I know not how I shall manage the delivery, which will be perusal.

I am very sorry to read what you say of Romanes, who seems mentally to be a very strong man.
[P.S.] I return your enclosure. One other word about Ruskin when we meet.

To LORD ACTON, lord-in-waiting, 17 October 1892.   Cambridge University Library.
'Private.'

I have been able to get conclusive evidence about Ruskin: I am sorry to say it extinguishes all hope. He seems physically well but incapable of mental exertion.

[1] Rosebery, 14 October, Add MS 44290, f. 14, opposed publication at present. See 13 Oct. 92n.
[2] Douglas Campbell, of Cherry Valley, New York State, had sent his *The Puritan in Holland, England and America*, 2v. (1892); see Hawn P and next day's letter.
[3] H. C. Shuttleworth, *The place of music in public worship* (1892).
[4] Marchesa Lily Theodoli, novelist, had sent her *Scenes from Roman life. Under pressure*, 2v. (1892); see Add MS 44516, ff. 143, 328 and 29 Dec. 92.
[5] See 10 Oct. 92n.

You would much oblige me if you could find whether Swinburne by withdrawal and otherwise brings himself within the range of possibility.[1]

I understand W. W. Morris is an out and out Socialist![2]

L[ewis] Morris circuitously puts himself forward—here I can find no one to speak for him.

A certain Henderson[3] is a strong young poet: was imprisoned 3 mo for a Socialist riot, and dedicates to a friend now serving out a ten years sentence.

Austin, Buchanan, & other shadows flit in the distance.

[P.S.] I am glad there is to be a November *turn*.

To D. CAMPBELL, American historian, 17 October 1892.   Add MS 44549, f. 27.

It happened that I opened your work,[4] and read the deeply interesting preface before I had seen your letter[5] and ascertained to whom I owed the gift. Allow me now to offer you the special thanks it so well deserves.

The English race (I am a pure Scotchman) are a great fact in the world, and I believe will so continue; but no race stands in greater need of discipline in every form, and among other forms that which is administered by criticism vigorously directed to canvassing their character & claims. Under such discipline I believe they are capable of a great elevation and of high performances. And I thank you partly in anticipation, partly from the experience already had, for taking this work in hand, while I am aware that it is one collateral and incidental to your main purpose.

Puritanism again is a great fact in history, exhibiting so many remarkable and noble traits. It may perhaps be liable to the suspicion of a want of durability. During the last century it seems to have undergone in various quarters much disintegration and it is difficult to connect it historically with the Divorce Law of Connecticut;—but I am wandering into forbidden ground which my qualifications do not entitle me to tread, and I will close with expressing my sense of the value and importance of a work like yours and of the benefit which we in particular ought to derive from it.[6]

To J. MORLEY, Irish secretary, 17 October 1892.   Add MS 44549, f. 27.

1. I never heard of a more extraordinary suggestion, considering the authorship of it [than] that which you send me as proceeding from Labouchere about Uganda.[7] For us to send a Commissioner to superintend evacuation would be doing the most dangerous of all things, naively putting ourselves in the place of the Company by taking its duties into our hands.

2. Putting aside all other difficulties, which may be insurmountable, I am not at all sure that Labouchere would do the work of a mission[8] badly. I had no idea he was so young at 60.

3. Redmond's article[9] has afflicted me much. The man has surrendered himself to the miserable exigencies of an utterly false position. The mischief he can do would not per-

---

[1] Acton replied, 18 October 1892, Add MS 44094, f. 221, that Swinburne 'neither withdrew that volume of Poems and Ballads 1866, nor dropped it, nor purified it by omissions or alterations'; see 7, 10 Oct. 92.

[2] Acton confirmed this: 'the other Morris [i.e. other than Lewis Morris] . . . is quite flaring Communist, with unpleasant associations'; ibid.

[3] Fred Henderson, I.L.P. socialist and poet; mayor of Norwich 1939.

[4] See 16 Oct. 92.   [5] Of 6 September 1892, Hawn P.

[6] This letter printed in *T.T.*, 5 January 1893, 4e.

[7] Labouchere later moved an amdnt. to the Queen's Speech proposing a Commissioner to supervise evacuation; see 3 Feb. 93.

[8] See 15 Oct. 92n.   [9] See 1, 5 Oct. 92.

haps be formidable, were we very strong at every other point of the compass: but we have not upon the most favourable construction of our position, any strength to spare at any point. If the British portion of our plans namely a well constructed and pretty stout programme for this side of the Channel, were to fail, I certainly should be far from sanguine as to the general issue—I mean the immediate general issue; of the ultimate there can in no case be doubt, but that lies beyond my personal responsibilities.

3. [*sic*] The Laureateship bothers me mightily. Acton raised a hope by suggesting Ruskin, but on enquiry that hope flickered, and is dead. No light yet.

4. I have in a manner got to the end of my lecture; the remaining question is how to get through the delivery.

[P.S.] I am not quite sure whether your best address is Lodge or Castle.

18. *Tu. S. Luke.*

Dear Agnes's birthday. Ch. 8½ A.M. Wrote to Mr Marjoribanks—Rev. Mr Rashdall—Ld Rosebery—Prof. Romanes—Ld Sudeley—Lady Stepney—Murray—Sir H. Ponsonby—Priv. Sec. Tel.—and minutes. Further small work on Oxf. MS. Read it aloud to 6 or 8. 1 h. 20 min. Conversation with E. Talbot—Mr Geo. Rendel. Read 'Under Pressure'. Backgammon with SEG.

To E. MARJORIBANKS, chief whip, 18 October 1892.   Add MS 44549, f. 28.

Is it material that I should go to the Ld. Mayor's dinner? Will he be Liberal or anti-liberal? What am I to say? It is a horrid audience at the best. I am in this position: Clark forbids my going to evening banquets. I should require to get from him a special dispensation on special grounds.

Behind this lies another question, on which I replied, I think precipitately, without consulting you. It was some proposal to hold a celebration, I think a banquet, at the National Liberal Club, sometime in December. Mindful of Clark I begged off. I do not however feel sure that if the party were to be purely Parliamentary it might not be possible to make an useful & needful speech. It would perhaps be a safer occasion than what is known as a meeting of the party, which should never be held without a careful consideration of the conditions.

At your convenience let me know how these matters strike you.[1]

To Sir H. F. PONSONBY, the Queen's secretary,   Add MS 44549, f. 28.
18 October 1892.

I am anxious to be accurate about the marriage,[2] and at the cost of a day's delay I am sending to London for the Act of Settlement.

It gives me pleasure, but causes me no surprise to learn that the Queen was favourably impressed by the Lord Chancellor. He is, I believe, an excellent lawyer and I think him also very valuable as a sound political adviser.

It is very good of the Queen to give me credit for regularity in my correspondence. It would be most culpable on my part if, especially when not able always to commend to H.M. my political ideas, I were wilfully to fail or to be slack in any point of duty.

The Queen is also very kind about Canon MacColl. He is a really rather interesting specimen of the genus human being. A Pure Celt of Western Argyllshire. The qualities

---

[1] No reply found. After extensive discussion, the Cabinet named Ripon; see 2 Nov. 92.

[2] Marie, da. of the duke of Edinburgh, m. 10 January 1893 Ferdinand, Prince of Roumania. See next day and to Herschell, 9 Nov. 92.

which he curiously unites I never saw in any other human being. My opinion is that he ought to be put into a novel.

I visit Oxford on Saturday (Deanery) to deliver on Monday a rather formidable lecture about Universities in the Sheldonian Theatre. I need not say this was an engagement contracted long ⟨ago⟩ before the political crisis; and the preparation for fulfilling it has caused me much difficulty. I go thence to town.

To G. J. ROMANES, 18 October 1892.   Add MS 44549, f. 28.

The red gown is in London, but accessible; and shall certainly be forthcoming.[1]

It would be very kind if you would reserve for me two tickets besides my wife's.

I read out the lecture today for the purpose of more clearly ascertaining its monstrous dimensions. It can be cut down but not very largely. It took exactly an hour & 20 minutes.

Among my half dozen auditors was a distinguished Cambridge man, old fellow of Trinity,[2] who pronounced me fair in my comparisons affecting that quarter.

My little auditory want me to cite in extenso the two famous Geo I Epigrams of Trapp & Browne.[3] I object that they are too well known, at least to the resident academic body.

The excitement to which you refer is capable of explanation on grounds less flattering than self love would suggest. For a very old man is in some sense like a commodity walking out of a Museum or menagerie into the haunts of men.

I sincerely hope, after the rumours which lately reached me, that you have now entirely recovered your health & strength.

To LADY STEPNEY, 18 October 1892.   Add MS 44549, f. 28.

Thank you for your excellent letter.[4] It is I think a main use of the pamphlet to evoke criticism. I do not think I am greatly at odds with you. A quarter of a century ago I told John Mill of the Italian system: now, they say & quite recently adopted in New Zealand. The woman who is qualified registers, but votes only through a "near friend" whom she selects & puts on the register. I do not follow Crepaz in all things but think her work a real service. What I dread is the opening[;] the vista of changes, the *Verallgemeinung*[5] as she calls it.

[P.S.] The A. Gordons just gone south.

[1] Romanes wrote, 15 October, Add MS 44516, f. 178, that 'after a comically long discussion ... it was decided that, unless you have any objection, the *red* D.C.L. gown would be best ...'.

[2] i.e. James Stuart, M.P. (see 26 Oct. 78), staying at the Castle; HVB.

[3] Attributed to Joseph Trapp (1679–1747):

> 'The King, surveying with judicious Eyes
> The State of both his Universities
> To one a Troop of Horse he sent; for why?
> Cause that learn'd Body wanted Loyalty.
> To th'other he sent books, as well discerning
> How much that loyal Body wanted Learning.'

By Sir William Browne (1692–1774):

> 'The King to Oxford sent a troop of horse,
> For Tories own no argument but force;
> With equal skill to Cambridge books he sent,
> For Whigs admit no force but argument.'

See K. W. Campbell, ed., *Poems on several occasions* (1926), 75.

[4] Not found. See 3 Oct. 92.

[5] 'generalisation'.

19. Wed.

Ch. 8½ A.M. Wrote to Sir H. Ponsonby—Mr Bryce—Mayor of Lpool—Ld Acton—S. Lyttelton—and minutes. Studied the Acts of Settlement & wrote Memorandum on the Roumanian marriage.[1] Conversation with E. Talbot. At St Deiniol's with the ladies. A little work there. Read 'Under Pressure'—Newman on Universities.[2] Whist in evg.

To J. BRYCE, chancellor of the duchy, 19 October 1892.   MS Bryce 10, f. 125.
'Private.'

1. I am very glad to have the expression of your views[3] about Homer's Phoinikes, and to find we have so much ground in common.* Herewith I send you the Bookman containing an able and luminous article (I am not quite an impartial witness) by Professor Ramsay of Aberdeen which touches the same matters.[4]

2. The Laureateship is puzzling to the last degree. I welcome opinion as well as information from you. You would oblige me if you could let me know what are the *extremest* things W. Morris has said in the sense of socialism, and when.

3. I do not at all mislike your notion of communicating with Duffy, but please let it be absolutely as on your own behalf & not for the Govt. or under any commission from me.

*It was Col. Mure whose strong language first impressed me as to the necessity of much close work in detail upon the Homeric text, a thing in which the 'critics' were sadly deficient. I am conscious however of having at first written various things crude and untenable.

I am extremely concerned about the Norwegian troubles and I feel with you that the demand of Norway as it stands can hardly be sustained.[5]

20 Th.

Ch. 8½ A.M. Worked on Mem. for HM.[6] Wrote to Sir H. Ponsonby—Mr Rashdall—Ld Playfair—Ly Ashburnham—Mr Murphy—Sir E. Watkin—Press Assocn Tel. Again worked on Oxf. MS. Also on Pol. Mem. for HM. Read Under Pressure II—Newman on Univv.

[1] The position of Ferdinand of Roumania (see previous day) raised difficulties under the religious clauses of the Act of Settlement; mem. at Add MS 44774, f. 106.

[2] See 26 May 92.

[3] Of 18 October, MS Bryce 12, f. 75; Bryce suggested that if Swinburne was excluded from consideration for the Laureateship because, *inter alia*, of his 'tyrannicidal reference to the Czar a year ago', 'I hope you may not think that William Morris' "Songs for Socialists" ought to damage his claims in a similar way. Tho' he is a Socialist, I do not remember in them any incitement to violence'; Bryce also mentioned Morris's role in 'the anti-Turkish agitation of 1876–78'. A separate letter suggested Gladstone obtaining Gavan Duffy's views on the proposed constitution for Ireland; ibid., f. 83.

[4] See to Morley, 10 Oct. 92.

[5] Bryce replied, 26 October, MS Bryce 12, f. 85, that he had checked Morris's 'Chants for Socialists' [*sic*]: 'nothing to cause scandal . . . however I hear on good authority that it is practically certain that he would not accept the Laureateship were it offered'. On 28 October, ibid., f. 89, Bryce reported that Morris, whom he had privately sounded, had written that as 'a sincere republican' he was therefore unable to accept the post if offered. Swinburne being discounted, Bryce suggested Gladstone consider Coventry Patmore, 'not a great poet, still he is a poet, which some of the other aspirants are not'. Further correspondence with West on the Laureateship, ibid., f. 91 ff.

[6] Long memorandum for the Queen; see 28 Oct. 92.

21. Fr.

Ch 8½ AM. Wrote to Prof. Romanes—Ld Rosebery—H.N.G.—and minutes. 1–4¼. To Dee Bridge. Cut the sod and made speech at luncheon.[1] Will[2] (with his sisters) was there. More work on Mem. for HM. Finished Under Pressure—read QR on Govt.[3] Saw Gertrude.

To LORD ROSEBERY, foreign secretary, 21 October 1892.   Add MS 44549, f. 30.

It is as you say impossible to pass a judgment at once about the suggestion of attaching Uganda to Zanzibar,[4] but considered as an idea, I think it a good idea, & well worth examination. A native Govt. is far more likely to succeed than we are; and if cause can be shown for giving money, that is a definite matter, does not entail the impracticable, and need not load us with indeterminate responsibilities.

I would moreover say that it would be very desirable to collect as soon as may be any facts bearing upon the policy & practicability of the plan; and even to make soundings in Zanzibar itself with the Sultan's Govt. if you have there an agent tolerably unprejudiced or discreet. This would I think have to be mentioned in Cabinet.

[P.S.] Most happy to dine. A man's dinner I rather suppose.

22. Sat. [The Deanery, Christ Church, Oxford]

Ch. 8½ AM. Wrote to Gertrude G.—Ld Rosebery Tel—S.E.G.—Sir W. Harcourt—Sir T. Acland. 11½–4¼. To Oxford & the hospitable Deanery.[5] Large party. Conversation with Dean—Mr Romanes—Ld Acton—Dr [blank]—Mr . . . . Read Ed. Rev. on Govt[6]—Children of the Ghetto[7]—Estourmel Souvenirs.[8] Dinner & evening parties.

To Sir W. V. HARCOURT, chancellor of the exchequer,   MS Harcourt dep. 12, f. 127. 22 October 1892.

I acknowledge your letter of the 20th[9] with thanks and return your inclosure.

Yesterday I heard from R. and wrote to welcome the suggestion.

We must remember Nosey's proposal.

I am just telegraphing to R. to this effect—but adding that I do not think it creates any insurmountable difficulty.

I really was not aware that Uganda had been under the Sultan in any way. Your superior knowledge of the case promises to lead us out of the difficulty.

[P.S.] Inclosures herewith.

Running hastily over the valuable Uganda Mem. from War Office I see Zanzibar is the natural approach but I do not notice any mention of its *rule*.

---

[1] Cutting the first sod of the Wirral Railway, directly connecting Wales and Liverpool *via* Chester and Birkenhead; *T.T.*, 22 October 1892.

[2] i.e. W. G. C. Gladstone.

[3] *Q.R.*, cxxv. 538 (October 1892); by L. J. Jennings.

[4] Suggested by Harcourt; Rosebery was 'inclined to think it would be the best arrangement'; 20 October 1892, Add MS 44290, f. 25.

[5] i.e. staying with Francis Paget at the Deanery in Christ Church.

[6] *E.R.*, clxxvi. 557; A. Elliot on 'A "nebulous hypothesis"'.

[7] First volume of I. Zangwill, *Children of the ghetto*, 3v. (1892–3).

[8] See 29 Sept. 92.

[9] On Uganda, suggesting it be placed under the Sultan of Zanzibar; Add MS 44202, f. 263.

23. *19 S. Trin.*

Cathedral 10 A.M. and 5. P.M. Breakfast. Luncheon (Romanes)—Dinner: parties at all. Interesting but distracting. Read Newman on Univv. Saw Acton on points of my Lecture. Much interesting conversation as is in Oxford inevitable.

To A. H. D. ACLAND, vice-president of the council,   Add MS 44549, f. 30.
23 October 1892.

I think as we are to meet so soon I had better reserve in the main my reply to your letter;[1] but I will state so much as follows about Wales.

Disestablishment evidently stands No. 1; and I suppose that Land stands No. 2?

The landlords are busy, as it seems to me, in making a case for some Commission. If anything serious is to be done in these two matters, Wales will hardly be able to get any further time in the contentious line of business; but I imagine you do not contemplate any such demand.

All interests and all portions of the country are on the alert to get their share; some because they have done well, others in order that they may.

24. *M.*

Wrote to Univ. Ch. Chrstors [*sic*] & others. Read Newman on Univ. Visited the Pictures in Ch.Ch. Hall[2] with the kind Dean. Again went over my MS. $2\frac{1}{2}$–$4\frac{1}{4}$. Delivered my Lecture in the Sheldonian Theatre.[3] Light in front embarrassing. Audience excellent. Company at all meals. Magd. Chapel 6 P.M.

25 *Tu.* [*London*]

Chapel 8 A.M. Wrote to Bp Bath & Wells—Lady Aberdeen—Rev. Mr Stacey. Breakfast party: Mr Romanes. Visited Clarendon Press: most interesting—Bodleian—on 'Excerpts'.[4] Photographed by Miss Acland.[5] Saw Mr Jowett—Mr

[1] Of 20 October, Add MS 44516, f. 192, suggesting that the Cabinet discuss appointing a Commissioner, Acland proposing Owen Edwards, Fellow of Lincoln, Oxford, to inquire into plans for a University of Wales; he also raised matters about English secondary education.
[2] Which included Millais' third portrait of Gladstone.
[3] The first Romanes Lecture, published as 'An Academic Sketch'; see 31 Aug. 92. *The Times*, 25 October 1892, 10a, noted: 'He was in excellent voice, and each word and intonation was fully appreciated by every person in the crowded theatre. But in the early parts of the lecture there was an occasional interruption proceeding from the cheers of the crowd outside.' For the occasion, see Robert Blake, *Gladstone, Disraeli and the Queen* (Centenary Romanes Lecture, 1992).
[4] See E. W. B. Nicholson, 'Mr. Gladstone and the Bodleian' (1898): 'On Oct. 24, 1892, he delivered in the Sheldonian the first Romanes Lecture, and next morning came up into the Bodleian. He wanted to know what we could tell him about an old English book of prayers which he had at Hawarden, apparently a form of week-day service. We had nothing answering to his description, but after he had gone Mr. W. H. Allnutt was able to write and tell him that the book might be an order of prayer for Wednesdays and Fridays. During this his last visit he sat in the librarian's chair and discoursed aloud on the book, the whole book (only I fancy it was an imperfect copy), and nothing but the book, with as much earnestness as if he had been introducing an important measure in the House. I didn't remind him that there were unseen readers in the alcoves to right and left, for I knew that the readers would gladly exchange a few minutes' work for so memorable an experience.'
[5] Sarah Angelina Acland, 1849–1930; only daughter of Sir H. W. Acland; a well-known Oxford figure and a noted amateur photographer. The photograph is the frontispiece of this volume.

Romanes—Sir H. Acland—Vice Chancellor. Off at 4.34 to Downing St. Dined at Ld Rosebery's. Conversation with French Ambassador.

26. Wed.

Wrote to Mr Laing—Sir E. Watkin—E. Wickham—Mr Mundella—Mr Fenwick—Sir W. Farquhar—G.L. Gower—Rev. Count Povoleri—Wms & Norgate—Dr Reich[1]—Professor Holland—& minutes. Saw Sir A. West—S.L.—Mr F.L. Gower—Mr Marj[oribanks]—Sir W. Harcourt—G. Russell—Ld Acton. Dined at Mr Armitstead's. Read Divers pamphlets—Morrison on Crime.[2]

To Sir W. R. FARQUHAR, 26 October 1892.   Add MS 44549, f. 31.

It is indeed painful to differ from friends, especially from very old & most kind friends.[3] The Reform Bill of Ld. Grey made me, previously a follower of Mr Canning, into an orthodox Tory. The experience of life & public affairs led to my taking a wholly different view of the nature & value of liberty, & this has made me what I am. It is some consolation, in which affectionate friends may share to believe in what may be called involuntary error. But in your case I enjoy a solace which is much higher, for I believe that a political gap may have widened between us, but that in matters of a higher, a much higher import we have closely approximated, so far as I am able to judge.

As respects Uganda, our duty of course is to act, with due deliberation, upon the best evidence we can get. We have now to wait for the report of Capt. Macdonnell [sc. Macdonald] who was empowered by Ld. Salisbury to fulfil an important duty, in the accomplishment of which unfortunate delay seems to have occurred. Were my mouth open, I should have to be pretty free in answer, but happily I am bound by prudence to be silent. As regards Egypt & the Soudan, had my advice publicly given been followed, you would have had none of these difficulties great or small: & as regards Gordon, I must truly assure you that my difficulty is made greater in acquitting my friends & myself for what we did, than for what we did not do.[4]

To Sir E. W. WATKIN, M.P., 26 October 1892.   Add MS 44549, f. 31.

I think the question respecting the Channel Tunnel which you have put to me in your letter of the 22nd is one you are well entitled to raise.[5] It is one, however, which can only be decided by the Cabinet, and I must refer it in the first instance to the Bd. of Trade.[6] I think the recent movement of public opinion has been favourable; but I am not able to say whether it has been of such an extent as to warrant the return of the Executive to the position which it assumed at the first inception of the question; and again viewing the curious cleavage of political society upon this question, I am not able as yet to estimate the balance of personal opinions among my colleagues.

I need not tell you which way my own wishes lean; but manifestly I have no title to press them beyond a certain point.

I hope your rheumatism has departed or will soon depart.

---

[1] Emil Reich; on translations of Joseph Butler; Add MS 44549, f. 33 and *T.T.*, 26 October 1892, 9f, 28 October 1892, 4c.

[2] W. D. Morrison, 'The increase of crime', *N.C.*, xxxi. 950 (June 1892).

[3] Farquhar sent a cutting from *The Times*, 24 October 1892, of a letter from Lord Grey, and, recalling his son's death in the Sudan, hoped that the Sudanese policy would not be repeated in Uganda; Add MS 44155, f. 236.

[4] See 30 Oct. 92.   [5] Not found.

[6] Sent to Mundella this day, Add MS 44549, f. 31.

27. Th.

Wrote to Murrays—Bp of Bath & Wells—The Queen—Mr Goldwin Smith—Sir A. Clark—Lord Tennyson—& minutes. Saw Sir A. West—S.L.—Mr Asquith—Sir H. Lock—Ld Chancellor—Mr Bryce—Ld Kimberley—Ld Rosebery—Mr Fowler. Cabinet 2½–4½. Read Döllinger Conversations.[1]

Cabinet. Thurs. Oct. 27. 92. 2¼ A.M.[2] [*sic*]
1. Salaries of the Law Officers & their private practice.
   Determined on the merits to adhere. Chancellor will consider terms in which Mr. G. is to communicate.
2. *Opium*. Kimberley to meet the deputation.
   No hope from British Ex[chequ]er. Can there be an inquiry? To be con[sidere]d?[3]
3. Lord Mayors dinner—Cabinet wish me to attend.[4]
4. Directorships. Action & emolument should be suspended during terms of office. This to be made known. To stand over for a week.
5. Committee on Swaziland: Ripon, Kimberley, ⟨Harcourt⟩, Bryce, Acland.
6. Committee on incoming Bills—Local Govt.—London.

To Sir A. CLARK, 27 October 1892.   Add MS 44549, f. 33.

I have today mentioned to my colleagues the question of the Lord Mayor's Dinner, and the personal application of it—am I to go?
   I told them of your prohibition, and how I have abstained from public dinners for years. The case stands thus: they would like me to go unless you really think it mischievous. I think it rests with you to say aye or no.[5]
[P.S.] When we meet I should like to give you the history of the whole affair of my eye or eyes. I have been much pleased with Granger the Chester oculist.

To LORD TENNYSON, 27 October 1892.   Add MS 44549, f. 32.

I am afraid that I should have to adjourn any attempt to record my intercourse with your father[6] until after my resignation of my present office, & even then I fear it might have to compete with the demands of any unfinished work.
   I do not think that at any time during the last forty years I have ever found myself able when in office to give continuous thought to any subject outside public affairs.
   I will however allow myself the pleasure of referring to the first occasion on which I saw him. It was about the year 1837, when he called on me in Carlton Terrace.[7] This was an unexpected honour, for I had no other tie with him than having been in earlier life the friend of his friend to whom he afterwards erected so splendid a literary monument.[8] I cannot now remember particulars, but I still retain the liveliest impression of both the freedom & kindness with which he conversed with me during a long interview.

[1] J. J. I. Döllinger, *Conversations. Recorded by L. von Kobell*, tr. K. Gould (1892). See 5 Nov. 92. The frontispiece is a group photograph taken during Gladstone's visit to Tegernsee in 1886.
[2] Add MS 44648, f. 11.
[3] See 30 Oct. 92.
[4] See 2 Nov. 92.
[5] Clark's reply amounted to 'no'; Add MS 44516, f. 229.
[6] Hallam Tennyson requested 'a sketch of your lifelong acquaintance with my Father' for the memoir he was compiling; this letter is printed in *Tennyson. A memoir* (1897), i. 164.
[7] Not mentioned in the diary.
[8] i.e. Arthur Hallam.

I am greatly pleased to learn that you have undertaken the Life: doubtless an arduous task; but one to which your titles are multiplied as well as clear.

[P.S.] My occupation need not prevent my answering any question which at any time you might find occasion to put to me, if so be.

To Goldwin SMITH, 27 October 1892.   Add MS 44549, f. 32.

My attention has been called to a letter signed by you in the 'Times' of the 20th inst. and to its P.S.[1]

This P.S. has made it necessary for me to address you, and I hope you will excuse my doing it in the terms which were formerly, I think, usual between us.

In this P.S. you have impugned my 'veracity' on the ground that I said England imposed the Union on Ireland with an armed force of 130000 men. "Of course" you say I mean British force; and on this construction of your own (in my opinion one altogether irrational) you impugn my personal honour.

I spoke of the total force at the disposal of the Govt.; and it is well known to every student of Irish history that the Irish yeomanry were painfully prominent in the cruel proceedings of that period.

In the article from which you quote I repeated substantially a statement made by me in the XIXth Centy. (Oct. 1887) five years ago.[2] Dr Ingram writing in defence of the Irish Union had contended that in 1798 there were in Ireland 45000 regulars, besides artillery. In answer I quoted from Grattan's Life and Times the declaration of Lord Castlereagh in the House of Commons on Feb. 18. 1799 that the total force in Ireland was 137,500; a figure considerably beyond my recent statement.

These figures have been long before the world, & astonishing as they are, I am not aware that they have been, or can be questioned.

In July 1799, a few months later, Ld. Cornwallis declared that the force in Ireland, which I have seen stated at 125000 for a date near that month, was all required to preserve the peace and could not repel a foreign invasion.

[P.S.] You are of course at liberty to make public use of this letter.

P.S. I see your date is Toronto: I will therefore myself publish it.[3]

28. Fr.

Reperused for the last time & sent my so-called letter to the Queen on the situation. And wrote a covering apology. Also wrote to Ld Acton—M. Evans MP.—Sir A. Clark—Rev. Shirreff[4]—Mr R. Hutton—Sir W. Harcourt—Ld Rosebery—and minutes. Saw Sir A. West—Mr Murray—Mr A. Morley—Mr B. Currie —H.N.G. Worked at Lond. Library. Dined at Mr B. Currie's. Read Watson's Poems[5]—Döllinger Conversations.

Mr Gladstone presents his humble duty to Your Majesty, and offers his apologies for troubling Your Majesty with any remarks on what is commonly termed the political

[1] Ironic comments on Gladstone's 'historical veracity' in claiming, Smith said, the imposition of the Union through 130000 English soldiers.   [2] See 2 Sept. 87.

[3] This letter with Smith's reply from Toronto of 10 November is in *T.T.*, 22 November 1892, 3c.

[4] Francis Archibald Patullo Shirreff, missionary in C.M.S., had written to point out that part of Butler's *Analogy* had been translated into Hindustani; Add MS 44516, f. 227.

[5] W. Watson, *Poems* (1892); sent by R. H. Hutton; for this day's letter of appreciation, but at this time unable to respond to Hutton's request for a civil list pension to (Sir) William Watson, 1858–1935, see Add MS 44549, f. 34.

situation. On three previous occasions, when he has been called to assume the largest individual share of responsibility in your Majesty's Councils, he did not find anything of the kind to be necessary. On those occasions, he, with others, represented one of two great parties in the State (for in January 1886 the Liberal schism had not been developed), largely, though unequally, represented in all the different orders of the community. At the present juncture, the views of Your Majesty's actual advisers, although now supported by a majority of the people (to say nothing of the people of the Colonies, and the English-speaking race at large,) are hardly at all represented, and as Mr. Gladstone believes are imperfectly known, in the powerful social circles with which Your Majesty has ordinary personal intercourse.

Mr Gladstone humbly thinks it may not be inconvenient, on its own grounds, that he should attempt to lay before Your Majesty a representation of those views, not indeed in detail, but in their essential character: and not, as he trusts, in a polemical spirit, but with full and unconditional allowance to opponents of all that he would ask on behalf of friends. He desires, however, to begin with these two observations.

First that this Memorandum is submitted on his own sole responsibility; for he has felt that, if he sought the concurrence of his colleagues in its particulars, it might seem as if designed to interfere in some indirect manner with Your Majesty's absolute freedom of action. Whereas its sole object is that the existence of a certain view, as matter of fact, should be present to the mind of Your Majesty. He does not ask for any conclusion, or any observation, upon that view, from Your Majesty's practised judgment.

Secondly; that his reason for troubling Your Majesty at all is that, in his firm conviction, the controversy between parties, as it now stands, raises, and to some extent has already raised, a number of particular issues, and one general issue, reaching very far beyond the question whether Home Rule is or is not to be conferred upon Ireland; and that the raising of those issues is attended with inconvenience and may even be injurious to the safe and stable working of our Constitution. They have indeed, their immediate consequences; as it is feared that they may place the existing Ministry in relations of difficulty with the House of Lords. But it is only the prospect of consquences more remote, and longer-lived, which leads Mr Gladstone to deem these fit to be mentioned to Your Majesty.

The leading fact, to which he would point, is in his judgment a very painful one: it is the widening of that gap, or chasm, in opinion, which more largely than heretofore separates the upper and more powerful, from the more numerous classes of the community. Such an estrangement he regards as a very serious mischief. This evil has been aggravated largely by the prolongation and intensity of the Irish controversy.

But it began to operate, years before the present Irish controversy began in 1885-6. There were at least six ducal houses of great wealth and influence, which Mr. Gladstone had known to be reckoned in the Liberal party at former times, and which had completely severed themselves from it, before Irish Home Rule had come to be in any way associated with the popular conception of Liberalism.

But, after Home Rule had been proposed by the Government of 1886, the division of opinion in the Liberal party widened, and hardened. Some found in it an occasion, others a cause, for a separation from their former friends, which seemed to become hopeless when the promises made to Ireland in 1886, short of Home Rule, but yet of large breadth & consequence, passed gradually out of view. Further, this body of Liberals believed themselves bound to be habitual and steady supporters of a Tory government, and to vote against measures which in some marked cases had received their previous support.

Such was the character of this movement of Liberal dissent, that the supporters of the present Government in the House of Lords cannot be estimated at more than one tenth or one twelfth of that assembly. As regards landed property, Mr. Gladstone doubts whether Liberals now hold more than one acre in fifty, taking the three kingdoms together. In the upper and propertied classes generally, the majority against them, though not so enormous, is still manifold.

Yet, for the first time in our history, we have seen in the recent election ⟨for the first time⟩ a majority of the House of Commons, not indeed a very large, but also not a very small one, returned against the sense of nearly the entire Peerage and landed gentry, and of the vast majority of the upper and leisured classes.

On one side then of this gap there has been a large withdrawal from actual and working Liberalism. Has there been any corresponding change, in the opposite direction, on the other side of it?

On this subject Mr. Gladstone's personal experience has supplied him with considerable information. It cannot be doubted that there has been in the Liberal party, during the last six years, a large development of democratic opinions. The Liberal Associations now often term themselves "Liberal and Radical associations." The moderate Liberal (and by moderate Liberal Mr. Gladstone means such a person as Lord Granville or Lord John Russell) has not quite become, but is becoming, a thing of the past. There is to a large extent not only a readiness, but even a thirst, for conflict with the House of Lords. Mr. Gladstone does not rejoice in this development, and has done nothing knowingly to stimulate it. He believes that its main cause lies in the feverish atmosphere, which has been created by the prolongation and the fierceness of the Home Rule controversy; just as the fierceness of the Reform controversy of 1831-2 added immense force to the less developed Liberalism of that day, and might have carried popular opinions even to a dangerous excess, had it not happily been brought to a speedy close.

The farther the present prolongation is extended, the larger will be in Mr. Gladstone's belief the progress of democratic opinion generally both in the bulk of the Liberal party, and among the popular elements of the Tory party, so as to affect in various ways the public policy of the country; and this through the instrumentality of Tory, as well as of Liberal Governments, though through the two in differing degrees.

Mr Gladstone makes no undue assumption as to any unbroken continuity of the *present* preponderance; although it is possible that it might even be greatly enhanced by a conflict, under possible conditions, with the House of Lords. He is not speaking, however, of the balance of parties, but of the general movement of the country. He desires to lay before Your Majesty as a fact this movement of opinion, especially, but not exclusively, within the Liberal party. For the history of the last sixty years seems to show, that in the *direction*, in which the Liberal party moves, it is sooner or later found that the country has also moved.[1]

Considering the great importance which Mr Gladstone has attached to this growth of 'advanced' opinion and to its connection with the Irish controversy, he feels it but just to offer a single significant illustration.

When the opposition to Irish Home Rule acquired so much intensity, fervour, and compactness, it was met on the other side, among many other symptoms, by the appearance and rapid growth of a demand for Home Rule in Scotland, and later on in Wales. These developments have in no way been promoted by the leaders of the Liberal Party. In particular Mr. Gladstone will say for himself that he has used every effort in his power to temper, qualify, and restrain them, and has in Scotland incurred much obloquy thereby. In Parliament, he has steadily advised a greater deference of English members to Scottish opinion on Scottish questions, and he regards this as the most hopeful means of obviating a newly possible inconvenience. The sentiment appears to grow from year to

---

[1] A brief reiteration of the argument of the memorandum on the Lords and the 1884 Franchise Bill; see 19 Aug. 84.

year, and of late it has even made considerable head in Wales, and probably cannot be arrested except by a considerable deference on the part of Parliament to the specialties of Welsh opinion: opinion in Wales being more uniform than in any other portion of Your Majesty's Three Kingdoms.

The answer to all this would probably be that those, who have pressed forward a disturbing measure of Home Rule for Ireland, are responsible for all other disturbing measures engendered by the controversy. And this would be true, if it were admitted that Home Rule for Ireland is a disturbing measure. In the view of the present Liberal majority, it is not. In Mr Gladstone's view it is the direct opposite. This however is matter of opinion, on the one side and on the other. What appears to be matter not of opinion, but of fact, is that many disturbing measures, and disturbing tendencies, have grown and are growing, out of the controversy.

And though Mr Gladstone is firmly convinced that Home Rule is conservative, he is far from contending that it must of necessity always remain so. Should it, through the length and obstinacy of the struggle, expand into repeal of the Union, that is into the revival of the old and independent Irish Parliament, it might thus become very far from conservative.

Were it possible so to isolate the Irish Home Rule controversy that, while it was fought out as a separate issue, its continuance should not at all affect the general political situation, England (for it has been England alone which sustains this action) is powerful enough to carry on the controversy for a time indefinitely long. An Imperial crisis like that of 1782 would indeed bring it, as it brought the older Irish controversy, to a speedy but also a somewhat dishonouring end. In 1829 Ireland compelled the Duke of Wellington's government to give way to its fears of disturbance, after an obstinate resistance of many years. And Ireland is stronger now than she was then, in herself, and in the support so remarkably received from Scotland and from Wales. But the resisting party is stronger also, not only or mainly in the concentrated action of the upper classes, but because it, too, is based upon a wide franchise, and some amount of undeniably popular support. There is still subsisting in the country a limited remnant of that anti-Irish feeling, which was formerly intense, and which made it so difficult for Lord Melbourne to carry on his Government. Moreover the Tory party, naturally averse to most of the changes demanded by the Liberals, may as naturally regard the Irish controversy as a great impediment to those changes, an impediment which operates by absorbing the time and thus weakening the hands of the House of Commons. Nor do they seem to take into account what, in Mr Gladstone's view, is a fact they might be expected to appreciate; this namely, that, while Home Rule remains unsettled the Irish party must commonly constitute a steady and large addition to the Liberal force in the House of Commons, whereas the settlement may divide their forces, and must in any case largely diminish their ordinarily available voting strength at Westminster. Mr Gladstone therefore, well aware that his own time is short, does not confidently count upon success in bringing this great controversy to an early issue at a definite time. This may be, or may not. But he conceives it to have been already demonstrated, by the experience of the last six years, that the longer the struggle is continued, the more the Liberal party will verge towards democratic opinion. And indeed ⟨already⟩, in the mouths of many the word democratic has already become a synonym and a substitute for the word Liberal. An early settlement of Irish Home Rule would seem, then, to be the sole likely means of moderating this onward movement of Liberal opinion. At any rate the existence of that movement, and its activity, seem to him to have become plain in the eyes of all men.

In order to explain more completely the scope of this Memorandum, Mr Gladstone humbly deems it necessary now to add a very few words respecting his own views. These words are quite different from what has last been urged: as they have to rest in the main upon his own assertion, and can be valued only by those who believe in his sincerity.

He feels bound, however, to state that in his firm conviction the proposal of Home Rule is a proposal eminently Conservative in the highest sense of the term, as tending to the union of the three countries (whose moral union must surely be allowed to be at the least very imperfect), and to the stability of the Imperial throne and institutions. He terms the measure Conservative in exactly the same sense as he would term the repeal of the Corn Laws conservative, through its promoting the union of classes and giving a just contentment to the people. For twenty years before 1885, Mr Gladstone had laboured to the best of his abilities to make Ireland contented with the Union as it stands. Her condition has been immensely improved by legislative changes adopted before that date. But they have not made her contented with the Union. She has ceased, however, to ask for its repeal. That is to say she no longer seeks to have an independent Parliament, sovereign in principle. That subject might possibly revive under exasperation; but it is excluded from all present view. She is solemnly pledged by the voice of her constitutional representatives, to the acceptance of a 'subordinate Parliament', and to leave untouched the main and central aim of the Act of Union, which was to establish a single, instead of a dual, supreme authority. But, within the bounds thus established, she submits her prayer with an unvarying constancy, and in a perfect confidence that it must eventually and may soon, be granted.

To a measure of this kind Mr Gladstone made favourable reference in the House of Commons on the 9th of February, 1882, and especially in his letter to Your Majesty on the 13th of the same month. But he always anticipated grave evils, (which have now actually arisen,) from a great party conflict on the subject. In consequence of this anticipation, before the close of 1885, when it was more or less believed out of doors that the Government of Lord Salisbury intended to make a proposal in the sense of Home rule, he took upon himself the very serious responsibility of writing to offer them his support.

And at no time has he written or spoken of Home Rule as a measure favourable to the Liberal party except in so far as strength is to be derived (while it is perhaps oftener lost) from the promotion of a just cause, or a cause, believed to be just.

Mr Gladstone does not shut his eyes to the breadth of the allegations which are made, especially by those termed Liberal Unionists, on the other side. That the proposal of Home Rule destroys the Act of Union; that two millions of the Irish are opposed to it; that the assertions of the Irish people and their members cannot be believed; that they cannot safely be trusted with the same liberties as the people of Great Britain, but can only be ruled by the strong hand; each and all of these assertions are indeed not only weighty, but resistless, if they be true.

But it is not the object of this Memorandum to discuss contested assertions at all. Its object is to point out dangers and mischiefs tied on, as it were, to the prolongation of the Home Rule conflict. And these not only as they palpably exist at the moment, but as their increase is discernible in that progressive movement of the future, which it seems to be the special duty of an Adviser of the Crown, and not least of a very old adviser of the Crown, to forecast according to the best of his ability. Nor would Mr. Gladstone willingly be responsible for the omission to offer such a forecast, where the gravity of the case may seem imperatively to require it of him. Such considerations will, he believes, secure an indulgent appreciation of the motive with which he has taken upon himself, not to make any appeal to Your Majesty in the hope or anticipation of reply, but to lay these lengthened remarks at the feet of Your Majesty, and simply to submit them to Your Majesty's long experience and high discernment.[1]

October 28, 1892.

---

[1] Butchered, partial version in *L.Q.V.*, 3rd series, ii. 172. Fuller version taken from Gladstone's copy, in Guedalla, *Q*, ii. 446. The Queen found the memorandum 'very curious' and had to be prompted by her secretary into acknowledging its receipt; *L.Q.V.*, 3rd series, ii. 176.

To Sir W. V. HARCOURT, chancellor of the exchequer,   MS Harcourt dep. 12, f. 143.
28 October 1892.

1. I imagine that Rosebery will regard the Salisbury letter[1] as constituting a call for the publication of the correspondence in the F.O.
2. Your remarks on the Borneo Charter[2] are but too conclusive in principle though we were not there in immediate contact with any Foreign Power. But I should like to get up the departmental history. I am under the strong belief that the Cabinet knew nothing of these perilous particulars, & only gave an (unwilling) assent to the principle.
3. I will try to see Rosebery soon, and find whether he can be made willing to publish. Salisbury's letter in the Times is certainly a challenge.
4. I think I stated the case of the Dinner impartially to Clark. But he kicks very much against my attending.

To LORD ROSEBERY, foreign secretary, 28 October 1892.   Add MS 44549, f. 33.

Could you come to see me some time before the Cabinet on Monday? I want to tell you what Waddington said to me on Tuesday at your house—not much but earnestly spoken. I should like to see what you are putting in train for the Cabinet, or preparing to put in train, and to speak about Salisbury's letter in the Times of today. I do not think anyone speaking on the 9th for the Govt. could well pass over Uganda, or could take that letter as an ingenious, or other than a misleading, statement of the case.[3] How are the precedents in the F.O. as to publication in the Gazette, or otherwise than by Blue Book?
[P.S.] Oh that Borneo Charter!

29 Sat.

Wrote to Dr Moore—Abp of Canterbury—Ld Rosebery—Mr Reynolds—Mr A. Galton—Mr Poole—Sir R. Phillimore—Count Povoleri—& minutes. Saw Sir A. West—Sir W. Harcourt—Ld Chancellor—Mr Morley—Edw. Hamilton. We dined at Mr Armitstead's. Wrote Mem. on the business of the coming Session.[4] Read as yesterday.

30. 20 S. Trin.

Chapel Royal noon and afternoon. Worked hard on my notes to Oxford Lecture & dispatched them. Saw Ld Acton—Ld Spencer. Wrote to Mr Asquith—Ld Acton—Mr Hare. Read Paterson Smyth, 'How God inspired the Bible'[5]—and Döllinger Conversations. Tea and conversation with the Farquhars.[6]

[1] Letter from Salisbury, *via* his secretary, in *T.T.*, 28 October 1892, 6a: his govt. 'had not determined on the evacuation of Uganda, but, on the contrary, always contemplated retaining it . . .'.
[2] On 27 October, Add MS 44202, f. 265; the Borneo Charter details 'identical with those of the E. African Charter', and an 'unfortunate pilot balloon' restricting liberal comment.
[3] Rosebery replied this day, Add MS 44290, f. 30, that he would come but that Uganda 'is hardly ripe for treatment as I am afraid there may be difficulties in the way of handing it over to Zanzibar . . .'.
[4] See 31 Oct. 92. Harcourt this day told Gladstone of a dinner on 27 October when those attending (himself, A. Morley, Fowler, Bryce, Trevelyan, Acland) decided to suggest a full Queen's Speech, not limited to Irish government; see Stansky, 16.
[5] J. Paterson Smyth, *How God inspired the Bible* (1892).
[6] i.e. Sir W.R. and Lady Farquhar; see 26 Oct. 92.

31. M.

Wrote to The Queen l.l.—Attorney General l.l.—Mr Rendel—& minutes. Ten to dinner. Cabinet 2½–5. Saw Mr Asquith—Ld Rosebery—Sir A. West—Mr Stuart Rendel—Ld Rosebery. Conclave on the Directorships. Read Watson's Poems. Finished Dollinger Conversations.

Cabinet. Monday Oct. 31. 92. 2½ PM.[1]
1. Sir A. Clark's advice—W.E.G. not to attend [the Lord Mayor's dinner].
2. Sir H. Ponsonby's letter on dynamitards: facts recited.[2]
3. Commn. to inquire what land is available for the extension of Crofter holdings agreeably to the Report of the Crofters Commission & to the legislation of 1886.
4. Registration Bill considered: as to Registration Officer's capacity and the double powers. The preparation of this Bill was referred to a Committee as within.[3] Also Local Govt. Bill—and London Council Bill.
5. Welsh Suspensory Bill. Scotch Extinction of Stipends Bill to be taken up by *Government*. But this may be reconsidered.

Secret.   *Session of 1893*[4]
1. We are pledged to introduce and carry through the Commons a Home Rule Bill for Ireland which under any circumstances will make a heavy drain on our available time in the Session of 1893. Of this Bill I propose to speak to the Cabinet after dealing with other & chiefly less arduous measures.
2. We may without doubt ask and get the whole time of the House whenever this Bill, from the second reading onwards, is on the Orders of the day. But in 1881 the Irish Land Bill took over fifty sittings, as I think: we shall be happy if we get the H.R. Bill in as few; and this comes near half the Session. Independently of the fact that Supply has lengthened since that date.
3. I suppose it to be our capital object, given the pledge already named, so to use the Session of 1893 as to secure on behalf of Great Britain the best legislative fruit we can, and also to strengthen ourselves, in the highest degree we can, for following Sessions and occasions.
4. On other words to use in the most economical manner that is possible the half-session available for British purposes.
5. It seems to me that our capital aim should be to pass through the House of Commons as large a number of good Bills as we can and to send them to the Lords. If they are accepted absolute good will be done. If they are rejected, relative good will be done, and our hands strengthened in the country as against the resistance of the House of Lords.
6. I think it bad policy to introduce Bills without a *reasonable* hope of passing them. To name them in the speech and lay them on the table may for the moment warm the blood of sectional partisans: but it cools again with speed as it becomes plain that there never was a fair hope of progress: the Government is discredited by miscalcula-

[1] Add MS 44648, f. 12. Gladstone told the Queen this day, CAB 41/22/15: 'The particulars of a Bill for granting to Ireland the controul of affairs purely Irish have not yet been considered, but the introduction and prosecution of a measure of that kind is taken for granted throughout.'
[2] Rumour that the govt. intended to release them; denied; Guedalla, *Q*, ii. 452.
[3] Kimberley, Ripon, Fowler, Asquith, Trevelyan, Lefevre, Ld. Chanr. for Registration; Add MS 44648, f. 17.
[4] Holograph, initialled and dated 31 October 1892; Add MS 44774, f. 112.

tion; and the House may justly resent the waste of its time in discussion without result. But this of course will be decided by the Cabinet in cases as they arise.

7. In order to obtain a maximum of practical effect, let us consider the various modes of putting Bills forward.

8. First I would consider as Class I such Bills as are not likely to raise very great differences of opinion, and as we might hope rapidly to pass into Grand Committee. I take the introduction of the Irish Bill as the first business after the Speech. A fair interval after that stage and before the second reading would be demanded. It seems to me that the best use of that interval would be to spend it in passing such Bills through 2 R. and into the Grand Committee. This need not of course preclude the *introduction* of more contentious Bills.

9. A limited time for carrying some of those Bills might be found between 2 R. of the Irish Bill and its Committee. But I cannot anticipate a great deal of clear fighting space until the Irish Bill had been disposed of in the Commons.

10. In order to economise our means, I have suggested the early use of Grand Committees. I suggest further Reselection by preference, where it can be done
    a. of short and even single clause Bills.
    b. using the aid of Private Members with such Bills as they could properly press forward in their own names with the promise of aid from the Government later on if required.
    c. Introduction of Bills in the House of Lords.

11. I do not know whether we shall require to undertake any Bill both long and contentious, besides the Irish Bill, except the Local Government Bill, which I fear we could not wholly divest of that character. This I conceive we should have to *press*, after the Irish Bill. There is no tactic so bad as that of endeavouring to work two large Bills at once or what is called pari passu.

12. In any view of the matter, there is plenty to do.

Tues. Nov. One. 92.

Wrote to The Lord Mayor—The Queen—Rev. A. Fawkes[1]—Mr Turton[2]—Mr H. Hart l.l. & tel.[3]—Ld Reay—J. Watson & Smith—Ld Rosebery l.l.—& minutes. Saw Mr Hamilton (painter)—Sir A. West—Mr Morley—Mr Marjoribanks—Ld Spencer—French Ambassador—Rev. E. Talbot—Mr Knowles l.l. Read Watsons Bridges[4]—Hamilton on the Laureateship.[5] Eleven to dinner.

To LORD ROSEBERY, foreign secretary, 1 November 1892.   N.L.S. 10025, f. 114.

[Letter 1:]   The Waddington conversation has not been at all confined to the limits of the *sofa* this day week as you see from my No 3.

No 1. Uganda: is 'rather a burning question.' It would not however burn if we without waiting for the Macdonnell report are prepared at once to acknowledge a responsibility in principle for losses and grievances brought about by the wrongful conduct of the Company. I said I felt sure that on this question, whether we can make a more or less abstract

---

[1] Nonconformist; had sent an article on Gladstone's lecture; Add MS 44549, f. 35.

[2] Declining E. Turton's request for a baronetcy; Add MS 44549, f. 35.

[3] Printer to Oxford University (see 25 Sept. 86); on the Romanes Lecture.

[4] Possibly G. W. Watson, *A practical and theoretical essay on oblique bridges* (1839 and other eds.).

[5] Walter Hamilton, *The Poets Laureate of England. Being a history of the office of Poet Laureate, biographical notices of its holders and a collection of the satires, epigrams and lampoons directed against them* (1879).

acknowledgement of responsibility, or cannot do it till we know the facts, a speedy answer could be given him.

2. The non-burning question of spheres of influence between Burmah & Cochin China is he supposes in motion, and easy of solution.

3. Egypt! He inquires *whether we are prepared for a friendly conversation*, or whether such conversation is barred. If we are so prepared he thinks that his Government would be prepared to indicate a possible basis of settlement.

He laments that the old Granville arrangement was intercepted [*sc.* interrupted?] (about 1882?) as I suppose all do. He thinks that on the Drummond Wolff failure both French & English Governments committed faults.

Without any indication from myself, I promised to procure him an answer on this question also.

I had not the smallest expectation of his touching this No 3, but of course did not state surprise.

[Letter 2:]   '*Secret*'.   N.L.S. 10025, f. 116.

Astonished at what Waddington said here, I am yet more astonished that he did not say it across the way.[1] I think we can set this straight a little further on. I am under no pledge to be myself the giver of any reply. What I should like, and what I think you would like, is that it should at once be considered whether we ought at once to admit in answer to the circumscribed terms of his question that viewing the terms of the Charter there *may* be a liability: much as you originally intended.

[P.S.] You understand that there was no mention here of Madagascar.[2]

Wed. Nov. 2.

Wrote to The Queen—Ld Rosebery—Mr S. Rendel—Mr Fowler—Mr C. Bannerman—Sir H. Ponsonby—& minutes. Agreeable dinner at G. Russell's. Saw Ld Chancellor—J. Morley *cum* Ld Spencer—Sir A. West—Mr Bryce—Rev. Scott Holland—Mr Henderson—Rev. Stanton. Read N.C. Poems on Tennyson[3]—Hamilton on Laureateship—Tennyson's Posthumous Vol.[4]

Cabinet. Wedy. Nov. 2. 92. 2½ PM[5]

2. Mr. Fowler. Commission on whether we shd. have changes in the ⟨working⟩ system of the Poor Law for persons whose destitution is due to old age.[6]

1. Who attend the Lord Mayor's dinner? Ld. Chancr.; Ripon; Mundella; Spencer; Asquith; C. Bannerman; Morley.
   Ld Ripon will return thanks.

3. Bills discussed—Temperance (Veto) most.

[1] Rosebery this day, Add MS 44290, f. 35, reported a talk with Waddington: 'He mentioned that he had just been to see you. With me he only dwelt on Uganda and the sending of coolies to Reunion! Not a word of Egypt. Surely this is strange diplomacy.'

[2] Rosebery replied this day, Add MS 44290, f. 37: 'I see no special cause for haste in the Uganda matter. We must at any rate await Herschell's opinion as to our liability.'

[3] Poetic tributes to Tennyson by his friends, including Huxley; *N.C.*, xxxii. 831 (November 1892).

[4] *Death of Œnone* (1892); Tennyson corrected the proofs on his deathbed.

[5] Add MS 44648, f. 13.

[6] Established in December 1892 as the Aberdare Royal Commission on the Aged Poor; see *PP* 1895 xiv and *Life of H. H. Fowler, by his daughter* (1912), 261–2. Draft of terms of reference in Add MS 44516, f. 232.

4. Presidential Armies: distinction to be abolished.
    Ld K. may frame a Bill.[1]
5. Spencer mentioned Gurdon's[?] wish—Cattle from Canada to be prohibited for a time.
Ripon urges there is no pluropneumonia in Canada.

H.O.	Employers Liability
	Conspiracy
B.T.	Railway Servants
	Report of Accidents

One man one vote: Chancellor, Harcourt, Asquith to consider best form of *one man one vote*.[2]

To H. CAMPBELL-BANNERMAN, war secretary,   Add MS 41215, f. 42.
2 November 1892. '*Early*'.

I think that the subject on which you have written to me (the two battalions of Guards)[3] important as it is, fall[s] within the class of Treasury questions in the first instance and would only come to the Cabinet in cases of such differences between you & the Chancellor of the Exchequer as could not be accommodated without that resort. I advise therefore that you should communicate with him.

To LORD ROSEBERY, foreign secretary, 2 November 1892.   N.L.S. 10025, f. 119.
'*Immediate*'.

On the back of Waddington's double request of yesterday—and though he uttered no complaint he seemed to *think* we had been slack—came the Rhodes Telegram and the important and comprehensive dispatch from Portal. Will not these require early consideration—shall you be ready to mention them on Friday, or even today?[4]

If the Zanzibar plan proceeds in any form, it suggests that there will be a network of questions and a case or cases of *do ut des*.

I think that one of Waddington's questions should be answered (through you) soon?

I apprehend that France has a perfect title to raise the Egyptian or any other question when she pleases: but that in asking our consent she signifies her desire to solve it in friendly concert.

(That cipher between Khedive and Sultan almost haunts my dreams)

3. *Th.*

Wrote to Ld Chancellor—Mr Rathbone MP—Watsons—Mr Allnutt—Mr Hart (Univ. Press)—and minutes. Worked at Lond. Library. Saw Sir A. West—Mr Marjoribanks—J. Morley. Read Chained Books[5]—Hamilton on Laureate.

[1] In April 1893 Kimberley introduced a bill amalgamating the armies of the Madras and Bombay Presidencies; see H. L. Singh, *Problems and policies of the British in India* (1963),155.

[2] These bills are on an undated holograph; Add MS 44648, f. 18.

[3] On 1 November, Add MS 44117, f. 99, on restructuring of the home/abroad system of battalion organisation, which would involve '*the raising of two new battalions of Guards*'.

[4] Rosebery replied this day, 1.40 p.m., Add MS 44290, f. 38: 'I have only just received your note. I think we had better postpone F.O. questions till Friday—and should prefer that you should answer Waddington yourself on any points he raised with you.' For Rhodes, see 4 Nov. 92.

[5] W. Blades, *Books in chains, and other bibliographical papers* (1892).

To LORD ROSEBERY, foreign secretary, 3 November 1892.   N.L.S. 10025, f. 122.
Uganda I suppose now presents several aspects pressing in various degrees[1]
1. French query as to our responsibility
   next
2. Rhodes on Telegraph
   and
3. This, I imagine, inextricably mixed with the alternatives in the Portal dispatch, one only of which I suppose capable of being entertained.
   But you are far more competent than I to give the order.
   I should be very glad if we could also answer the preliminary Egyptian question?

4. Fr.

Wrote to Ld Rosebery—The Queen l.l.—and minutes. Saw Sir A. West—Mr Morley—Ld Ripon—E. Wickham—Ld Rosebery—Sir W. Harcourt *cum* Ld Kimberley respecting Ld R. and French Ambassador. Cabinet 2½-5. Dined at Lansdowne House with the Astors.[2] Read Hamilton on Laureateship. Our Cabinet was not comfortable. Rosebery is abnormally excited by the conduct of Waddington. Conversation with Dr Nevins—Mrs Astor—Mrs Sandys.

Cabinet. Friday Nov. 4. 92. 2¼ PM.[3]
1. Resolution of Irish Board of Education respecting emblems in schools.
   To write according to head 3 of his Memorandum explaining that there is no recessing from the pledge as to Conscience Clause.
2. Ld Kimberley to return thanks for H.M. Govt. on the 9th.
3. Refusal of Mr. Rhodes. To stand over till Monday.[4]
4. Uganda. Ld Rosebery wishes for a Commissioner. Discussion & long arg[ument] on Treaties. To resume on Monday.

To LQRD ROSEBERY, foreign secretary, 4 November 1892.   N.L.S. 10025, f. 128.
'Early'.
   I hope you will allow matters to fall into their usual and proper channel for communication with the representatives of Foreign Powers, now that Waddington's proceeding is a thing of the past. That proceeding was twofold
1. His speaking to me on the Uganda matter already opened with you
2. His opening the subject of Egypt with a general question, when it had not yet been submitted to you.
   Of these steps the second is I suppose the strongest.
   According to my experience it constantly happens in other departments of the Government that persons of more or less authority bring *first* before me matters proper to be treated in those departments. My object uniformly is to get them at once into the proper hands, and let them be prosecuted departmentally or in concert, as the case may be.

[1] See 1 Nov. 92n.
[2] See 15 June 92.
[3] Add MS 44648, f. 19.
[4] Rhodes the previous day offered to administer Uganda in exchange for a subsidy of £25,000 *per annum*, and to link Uganda at once with Salisbury by telegraph, eventually extending it to Cairo, with no charge to the British government; see R. I. Rotberg, *The Founder* (1988), 510, and to Rosebery, 12 Nov. 92. The Cabinet does not seem to have considered the matter further. Gladstone made no mention of it to the Queen on 4 or 7 November.

Certainly this is more rare in the case of the Foreign Office, yet it has happened. I remember a marked instance. Bernstorff, when Prussian Ambassador, brought to me the important communication which Bismarck had instructed him to make about the Benedetti Treaty in 1870.[1]

This would be highly inconvenient, as I think you will see, if the first step were followed up by a second and a third in prosecution of the business. But it never has been so. The matter passes at once to the Foreign Minister and with him remains. It might be difficult to formulate a complaint, and all practical inconvenience is put aside by my following the course usual in other cases.

But there remains the strange fact of his silence with you in regard to Egypt; which I can neither defend nor explain. If however in this there be some appearance of disparagement, it seems to me that the case would be aggravated, not mended, were I to make the return communication. Let us suppose him—the extreme supposition—to be ready to claim the right to address the Prime Minister, if and when, as an Ambassador accredited to the Queen, he thinks proper. But we the British Government, provided I have given due attention to the matter, are surely entitled to choose our medium of answer, and it seems to me that without raising any question as to his title we shall do best to keep, everyone, within the limits of his own attributions; and that by doing otherwise *we* should disparage our own foreign Minister.

I am sorry to trouble you with so long a note, but I thought it might be less inconvenient than my asking to see you on a matter which I hope we may avoid mentioning i.e. reciting in Cabinet & on which I hope for your concurrence.[2]

[P.S.] I should like the Cabinet to know the patience & courtesy with which you have proceeded in the case of Madagascar.

5. Sat.

Wrote to Sir W. Harcourt—Sir H. Ponsonby—Lady Marr—Fr. Döllinger[3]—A. Reader—Abbot of Monte Cassino. Saw Sir A. West—Sir W. Harcourt—H.N.G. Anxious reflections on the last & the next Cabinet. Read Prometheus (Bridges)[4]—Hamilton's Laureateship. Tea with Lady Granville at Kensington: told her of *my* infinite loss in her husband.

To Fraulein DÖLLINGER, 5 November 1892.   Add MS 44549, f. 36.

Pray accept my best thanks for the new record in the 'conversations'[5] of your venerated uncle. Of such a man we cannot have too many records, and in these particular recitals I note two special developments. The first that of his early years, which had been wholly unknown to me. The second that of the fervour of his inner life, which he seemed studiously to keep in the shade, avoiding exterior manifestations, as is common I believe with spirits of a high order. Both these are of rare interest, and I desire to make my thanks warm in proportion.

[1] See 19 July 70.
[2] Rosebery replied, 4 November, Add MS 44290, f. 41, that he had 'nothing to say' in Cabinet about Egypt, and that Waddington 'had no right to go to you about Uganda. I had assured him that the subject of our liability had been referred to the Chancellor.... Either he believed me or disbelieved me; if the latter, we cannot go on dealing with each other.'
[3] Johanna Döllinger, the theologian's niece. See this day's letter.
[4] R. S. Bridges, *Prometheus the fire-giver* (1883).
[5] See 27 Oct. 92 and Add MS 44516, f. 242.

To Sir W. V. HARCOURT, chancellor of the exchequer,   MS Harcourt dep. 12, f. 152.
5 November 1892.

I agree in the limited praise of the new coinage,[1] and especially in the limitation of the praise.

As to the 'reverse' of the florin and the shilling, narrowness of knowledge does not allow me to speak with confidence, but I seem always to have seen on a coin a *central* object, which constituted an unity, not a collection of objects which destroy it. But I quite understand that the matter is past praying for.

6. *21 S. Trin.*

Chapel Royal Noon and 5½ P.M. Wrote to Sir W. Harcourt—Ld Rosebery l.l.—J. Morley. Saw J. Morley & made him Envoy to Rosebery. He is on the whole from great readiness, joined with other qualities, about the best stay I have. Read Euchologion[2]—Czar Persecutor (Stundists)[3]—Andrewes Devotions, the S.P.C.K. Edition[4]—and other Tracts.

To LORD ROSEBERY, foreign secretary, 6 November 1892.   N.L.S. 10025, ff. 133–6.

[Letter 1:] I am sure there would be a sincere desire to close with a wish which you seriously entertain, and I have (as in duty bound) been thinking how any risks accompanying the dispatch of a Commissioner to East African [*sic*] can be minimised, and benefit derived from the mission.

On the one hand I take it for granted that any one to be useful there should be a man absolutely without prepossession, firm in character as well as loyal and with some political faculty and (if possible) experience. He should be plainspoken as to all advantages and all difficulties.

If such should be the man, then come his instructions. And here as it seems to me detail would be dangerous as ⟨exhibiting⟩ likely to exhibit preference. Would it suffice to refer to him the printed papers and correspondence, including the official declarations of the late Ministry in Parliament—to desire him to assume the recent letter of the Cabinet as his point of departure; to master to the best of his ability the physical social and political facts of the country, its relations to the other tracts or regions embraced in the Company's treaties, and its prospects under its present or any indigenous government; and to offer such suggestions as might commend themselves to his deliberate judgment.

I am very sensible that the reports of such a Commissioner might abridge the liberty of action now possessed by those who think as I do of the prevailing earth-hunger. But, for me personally, that problem must before long find its solution in a way independent of Commissions and Commissioners, a solution approaching at a moderate pace, but assuredly one which does not slacken.[5]

[1] Harcourt, 3 November, MS Harcourt dep. 12, f. 148, wrote that the new designs 'have been settled by the late Govt. with the Queen so we have no responsibility for them'; he noted that *Indiae Imperatrix* appeared for the first time, at the Queen's insistence.
[2] Copy of the Orthodox liturgy, sent by Olga Novikov; see Add MS 44549, f. 36.
[3] E. B. Lanin [i.e. E. J. Dillon], 'The Tsar persecutor', *C.R.*, lxi. 1 (January 1892).
[4] P. G. Medd, ed., *The Greek devotions of Lancelot Andrewes* (1892).
[5] Rosebery, 7 November, Add MS 44290, f. 44, argued that the Commissioner's instructions would probably have to be submitted to Parliament, that there was a danger of 'irritating almost equally evacuationists & retentionists', and that the Commissioner would require defence, so that 'his residence in Uganda will partake of the character of an occupation'.

[Letter 2:] '*Secret. No. 2.*'   If it should occur to you that I can in any way be made useful as to the Waddington business, I hope you will frankly let me know. It is to *me* additionally perplexing for a reason I will now briefly state.

He is in the habit of going into Lancashire and has offered himself as a guest at Hawarden. This I think has been hanging on for a couple of years. Last year it was interrupted. A month ago or so he renewed it: and we agreed to propose a date when these Cabinets come to their temporary termination.

This is at present a little embarrassing. But I hope a solution will be found.

I should like to tell you a story of an experience of my own with a foreign Minister, Motley. But I spare you now.

Let me add however a collateral word. I cannot abate what I have said about Waddington's reticence: and I also put aside for the moment what you told me of Madagascar. But you would wish to deal with all facts at their just value; and it strikes me that in the two matters of Uganda and Egypt the conduct of the French Government is in substance friendly. For as to Uganda, they might have sent an agent (without official character I suppose) to learn their side of the missionary case, instead of simply leaving us to inquire. And as regards Egypt—they might I presume have at once reopened the correspondence instead of asking us beforehand whether we were willing to concur in it. I hope therefore that whatever happens it will not be necessary to *fret* Waddington's principals.[1]

P.S. I have seen Morley—found he was going to you—he thereby knows the contents of this—& of *No 1.*

7. M.

Wrote to Ld Rosebery—The Queen—M. Waddington—and minutes. Saw Mr Morley—Do *cum* Sir W. Harcourt—Ld Kimberley—Mr Acland—Ld Chancellor—Ld Cobham. Eleven to dinner. Cabinet $2\frac{1}{2}$–5. Important work done. Read Laureateship finished—Tennyson's latest vol—do: of special interest.[2]

Cabinet. Mond. Nov. 7. 1892. $2\frac{1}{2}$PM.[3]

1. The Prince of Wales to have information as to Cabinets on the same footing as heretofore.[4]
2. Liability for losses according to French subjects through the wrongful acts of servants of the Co. & not satisfied by the Co. itself. Agreed that we acknowledge in very guarded terms a contingent liability.
3. As to sending a Commissioner to Uganda
   as to his guard & security.
   Company to be asked to remain on the ground for a time as the best means of enabling the inquiry to go forward on wh. wd. be founded our deliberations as to the future.
   Ridgeway West [*sic*]: reserved for consideration.

[1] Waddington requested an interview with Kimberley. Rosebery replied, 7 November, Add MS 44290, f. 46: 'He will soon begin sapping the Colonial Office and possibly besieging the Admiralty. I suggest that you send him what answer you please about Egypt with a gentle reminder that the most convenient course is to treat foreign policy through the Foreign Office.'

[2] See 2 Nov. 92.

[3] Add MS 44648, f. 20.

[4] The Queen queried whether Salisbury had briefed the Prince on Cabinet decisions and, finding that he said he had not done so systematically, arranged that the Prince should only receive information on 'any very important decision'; see *L.Q.V.*, 3rd series, ii. 178 ff.

Not named in Cabinet. Nov. 7. 92.[1]
1. The reply. That any communication by the French Government of its views on Egypt will be met by Ld Rosebery on the part of the British Government in the same friendly spirit in which we are confident that it will be received. R. agrees.
2. By whom to be communicated. R. declines. Agrees to WEG.

[Note to Rosebery:] I understand you to think my answer to Waddington respecting Egypt, which you have seen, should be sent without mentioning it in Cabinet?
    This I think would be quite proper.
        (assented to).
            N.7. 1892[2]

8. *Tu.*

Wrote to Ld Rosebery Tel.—G.L. Gower—Mr Rathbone—Mrs Bolton—Tregaskis—Mr Acland—The Queen—and minutes. Saw the two Deans of Gl[oucester] & Winch[ester] on the Cathedrals. Saw Sir A.L. West—S.L.—Mr Marjoribanks—Welby. Twelve to dinner. Read Lugard on the war[3]—Books in Chains &c.[4]—Dickinson on France[5]—D. Wilson on Atlantis.[6]

To Sir W. V. HARCOURT, chancellor of the exchequer,   MS Harcourt dep. 12, f. 153.
8 November 1892.
    I have reflected much on our conversation yesterday and not liking to delay till tomorrow I have written to him two letters, such as I think, under the circumstances, you would approve.

9. *Wed.*

Wrote to Mr Morley—Sir W. Harcourt—Hon. R. Noel—Sir H. Ponsonby—Ld Chancellor—Pr. of Wales Tel.—and minutes. Wrote on Homer. Worked on Acts of Settlement. Saw Chinnery—& others. Saw Sir A. West—Mr F.L. Gower—Mr Murray. Read The Inspector[7]—Books in Chains—Irish Military History.[8] Evg. at home.

To LORD HERSCHELL, lord chancellor, 9 November 1892.   Add MS 44549, f. 38.
    Is it quite certain that the following points have been fully considered (*re* Princess Marie's descendants):[9]
1. Is there a general definition in law of a Protestant,
2. or in usage?

[1] Add MS 44648, f. 21.
[2] Gladstone's holograph; Add MS 44648, f. 24.
[3] F. D. Lugard, 'British officials and French accusations', *F.R.*, lviii. 689 (November 1892).
[4] See 3 Nov. 92.
[5] G. L. Dickinson, *Revolution and reaction in modern France* (1892).
[6] Daniel Wilson, *The lost Atlantis; and other ethnographical studies* (1892).
[7] Perhaps N. V. Gogol, *The Inspector-General* (1892).
[8] Probably M. O'Conor, *Military history of the Irish nation, comprising a memoir of the Irish Brigade in France* (1845).
[9] Legal problems raised by her impending marriage to the Orthodox Ferdinand of Roumania. See to Ponsonby, 18 Oct. 92.

3. If it be said a Protestant is a Western Christian who disagrees with and is separated de facto from the Church of Rome, this definition would cover (1) the old Catholics, (2) the Church of Utrecht, neither of which would, I believe, accept the name of Protestant. What then is the true legal definition?

4. It seems to me as an outside ignoramus that the two Acts of 1 Will. & Mary (1. for establishing the coronation oath, 2. for settling the succession to the Crown)[1] are oddly but substantially related. This Act of Settlement is wholly penal, negative, and anti-roman; it enacts that the Sovereign shall be protestant, but without defining the word it ascertains the fact by the stringent Declaration from 30 Charles II. Is that Declaration still imposed upon the Sovereign at Coronation? If it is, it is amply & directly sufficient of itself to exclude not only Romans, but Orthodox (this not by its condemning transubstantiation but by its condemning Invocation). In this case cadit quæstio.

5. Besides this Act for maintaining the Coronation Oath requires the Sovereign to maintain the Protestant Reformed religion established by law. But it points to no Protestantism other than that of the Established Church; and even of this it does not require the profession.

So that thus far the intention manifestly being to have a Protestant throne, Protestantism had only a negative definition by renunciation.

6. But when we come to 12–13 Will III[2] we find a more complete arrangement. Nothing is done to derogate from the affirmative provision already established for the Succession. But a new affirmative provision appears. The sovereign must join in Communion with the Church. May it not be said that for the purposes of the Act this provides a statutory definition of Protestantism? and that it attempts no other? and that it might be hard to exclude a person complying with this condition by *virtue* of the enactment that the Sovereign is to be Protestant? What right would there be to interpret the law penally against a person fulfilling its only defined positive condition, by virtue of a form to which the Legislature has not thought fit to annex any other definition?

7. It being borne in mind that if dissent from the Pope be the popular idea of Protestantism, the Orthodox dissent from him rather more strongly than we do, i.e. in the Nicene creed itself.

A curious question arises whether a Stundist[3] could succeed. They believe rather less than a quaker; so that if limitation of belief (which is far from the historical and original meaning) were the condition they might qualify; but then they are Easterns.

All this, which may be quite worthless, tends to the conclusion that there is no absolute barrier to exclude an Eastern from the Throne (if willing to communicate and take the coronation oath) unless it be in the Declaration of 30 Car. II.[4] The importance of the topics in themselves inevitably leads into considerations which are minute perhaps slippery.[5]

To Sir W. V. HARCOURT, chancellor of the exchequer,   MS Harcourt dep. 12, f. 156.
9 November 1892.

Many thanks.[6] On the surface Lugard seems to make a case against the R.C.s. I hope he has right on his side.

The Number suffered some damage on its way to me.

---

[1] 1 Will. & Mar. c. 6 and Sess. 2, c. 2 (known as the Bill of Rights).
[2] 12 & 13 Will. III, c. 2; the Act of Settlement.
[3] The Russian evangelist, quasi-Baptist, sect in which Gladstone was interested at this time.
[4] The 'Declaration' in the Second Test Act, 1678, 30 Car. II, St. II, c. 1.
[5] No reply found.
[6] Harcourt sent a copy of Lugard's article in the *Fortnightly*; Add MS 44202, f. 281.

To J. MORLEY, Irish secretary, 9 November 1892.   Add MS 44549, f. 37.

1. Please to consider whether you can make any preparatory inquiry during your present visit to Dublin on the admissibility of Delegation—which of course means enumeration without a comprehensive covering clause. If you could, & if the reply were such as is anticipated, it might promote expedition on a matter where I believe there is really no option.[1]

2. To return to my old notion about recruiting for the Constabulary. Comparing this date with ten years back, we have first a diminished population, secondly enormously diminished crime. Is the Constabulary now at the same figures (a) of number (b) of experience (or a higher one). I cannot help imagining that without announcing any new principle there must be a case for reduction. Every farthing of relief in charge which we can give will help to ease the financial part of the coming Bill. If you do not see your way to any measure yet, would you cause a note of the leading facts (such as I have named) to be prepared.

10. Th.

Wrote to Scotts. Worked on arranging my papers a little in their new home. Saw Sir A. West—Mr Murray—Ld Spencer—Mr Morley (Irish Bill). Wrote Mem. on Heads of Irish Bill.[2] Dined with Mr Knowles. Conversation with Mr K.—with Abp Vaughan[3]—with Sir J. Adye—& especially, most interesting, with Mr Vincent Horsley.[4] Read Irish Mil. Hist.—The Inspector. Wrote heads of Irish Bill.

11. Fr.

Wrote to Mr H. Hart—Atty General—Rev. Williams[5]—Rev. Williams—Mr Chinnery (BP)—Mrs Bolton (BP)—J. Morley—The Queen—and minutes. Harcourt came early & poured out antiIrish opinions, declaring himself pledged to them. Saw Ld Kimberley—J. Morley l.l.—J. Bryce—Sir A. West—S.L. Cabinet 2½-5. One person outrageous. Framed propositions on Irish Bill & sent them to J.M. Dined with the Wests. Finished The Inspector—Read Books in Chains—Milit. Hist. Ireland.

Cabinet. Friday Nov. 11. 92. 2½PM.[6]
2. Welsh Land. Commission? Favour inquiry.[7]
3. Labouchere's desire to be made a Foreign Minister.[8]
    Extra-Cabinet conversation.

[1] Morley replied this day, Add MS 44257, f. 25, that he had not gone to Dublin, but was working on 'the points to be changed in the Bill of 1886'; he would send a note on the constabulary.
[2] See next day.
[3] See 5 Aug. 61.
[4] Probably Victor Horsley, opponent of anti-vivisectionalists; *T.T.*, 28 October 1892, 5f.
[5] Robert Williams of Dolwyddelaw; on a Welsh tr. of Butler's *Analogy*; Hawn P and Add MS 44549, f. 38.
[6] Add MS 44648, f. 28. There is no number '1'.
[7] There are some illegible jottings next to this item.
[8] Labouchere hoped to be minister in Washington; Rosebery prevented the appointment; James, *Rosebery*, 256-8. Rosebery had the correspondence on the subject privately printed (ibid., 258) and had to bear the consequence of his refusal in Labouchere's public taunts. See to Morley, 15 Oct. 92.

3. Poor Law Guardian qualification. Reduce qualification: £5 adopted—a short Bill to follow.
4. Ld Rosebery authorised to learn informally whether E. African Co. will consent to a prolongation of the time.
5. Remaining bills (other than Irish) considered & list closed.

[Propositions on the Irish Bill]
1. That the Supremacy of Parliament be preserved entire.
2. That except as to reservations contained in the Act, affairs distinctively Irish be handed over to the Irish Parliament.
3. That Customs and Excise and them only be excepted from the taxing power of Ireland.
4. But that all Irish receipt whatever be handed to a British Receiver General.
5. That the said Receiver General pay into the British Exchequer as a first charge the Irish share of the Imperial contribution, together with any other charges expressly imposed by the Act.
6. That provision be made for supporting his acts by judicial authority and if necessary by force.
7. That rules be laid down for determining what is Irish and what British revenue, in cases when local receipt cannot be taken as a test.
8. That the Veto and other restraining powers of the Viceroy and the Crown be exercised in the same sense and spirit as under the Canada Dominion Act.
9. That the responsibility of the Executive be left to be determined by the full working of the Irish Parliamentary institutions.
10. That all ordinary administrative power shall be under Irish controul saving temporary and express exception as to the Judiciary, and the Constabulary force.
11. That the functions of the Viceroy be regulated and exercised as under the Canada Dominion Act.
12. That the percentage contributed by Ireland be fixed for [20?][1] years & thereafter until, upon an Address to the Throne from the Irish Parliament, the Imperial Legislature shall otherwise determine.[2]

SECRET.   *Home Rule Bill of 1893.*[3]
                              HEADS FOR CONSIDERATION.

1. Insert the words   1. OUGHT the supremacy of Parliament to be expressly asserted
in the Preamble.   either in the Preamble of the Bill, or otherwise?
2. Alternative   2. Ought the functions of the Viceroy to be defined as in the Bill
form—   of 1886, or as in the Canada Dominion Act or otherwise?
(1.) As in 1886.   3. Ought the Irish Legislature to be excluded—
(2.) As in   (*a.*) From creating an established or preferred religion?
Canada Act.   (*b.*) From imposing a national poor-rate?
                        (*c.*) From administering criminal justice, otherwise than according to established principles, as in the United States?

[1] Gladstone's brackets.
[2] Holograph marked 'Secret', dated 11 November 1892; Add MS 44774, f. 118. Copy sent to Morley; see secretary's docket, Add MS 44257, f. 30. For Morley's comments, see 12 Nov. 92n.
[3] Printed with marginalia for the Cabinet, 14 November 1892; MS Harcourt dep. 162; no holograph copy found. The marginalia clearly reflect decisions, but they cannot be the Cabinet's, as it had not discussed the mem. by 14 November.

Draw clause or clauses both ways.	4. Ought its powers to be given, as in the Bill of 1886, by the reservation of Imperial subjects and the grant of the rest—or as in Canada, by enumeration with a comprehensive clause at the close for all private and local matters?
Postponed.	5. Ought there to be— One Order of Chamber; Or as in 1886 two, capable of voting as one; Or two absolutely; Of what numbers; And how chosen or appointed?
Postponed.	6. Ought Ireland to be represented at Westminster by persons separately chosen, or by persons already elected to the Irish Parliament? By the whole of those persons, or a part? Shall they vote on all subjects, or a part?
No instructions.	7. Ought any proposal we may make for representation at Westminster to be proposed as an essential part of the Bill?
By a fixed proportion of the Imperial expenditure	8. Ought Ireland to contribute to Imperial charges by a fixed sum, or by a fixed proportion or percentage of such charges?
Yes.	9. Ought such percentage to be fixed for a substantial term of years, say twenty, and thereafter until Parliament shall upon an Address to the Crown from the Irish Legislature otherwise determine?
Yes; or an equivalent.	10. Ought the clause which restored the whole of the Irish Members to voting power on any proposal to alter the terms of the Bill to be retained?
Yes.	11. Ought it to be provided that, for a short term of years—

(*a.*) No Judge of a Superior Court in Ireland shall be appointed without the counter-signature of a Secretary of State?

(*b.*) The Viceroy shall have the control of the Constabulary, the charge voted by the Parliament, with due reservation of existing rights, and, on the other hand, of authority to establish local police?

(*c.*) The entire right of legislation on land and land purchase shall be retained by the Imperial Parliament?

W. E. G.

10, *Downing Street, Whitehall,*
November 11, 1892.

To H. HART, Printer to Oxford University, 11 November 1892.   Add MS 44549, f. 38.

You may remember that when the beautiful Indian paper was shown me at the Press[1] I referred to Japan as the great storehouse of knowledge in relation to all manufacture from vegetable fibre. It may interest you to see the enclosed. It was given to me last night by Mr. Knowles, the Editor of the *Nineteenth Century*. I send it exclusively as a specimen of Japanese production, and not for what has been put on the surface.

To J. MORLEY, Irish secretary, 11 November 1892.   Add MS 44549, f. 38.

The inclosed brief Memorandum shows the order in which I think it might be most expedient to submit the chief points of the H.R. subject today. Please to examine before you come. There are a few references with which we ought to be prepared.

[1] See 25 Oct. 92.

12. Sat [*Hotel Metropole, Brighton*]

Wrote to Tregaskis—Ld Kimberley—S. Rendel—Mr Morley—S.L. Tel. 10 A.M.
The blackest darkness. At 1½ we were in summer light & even warmth at Brighton. (Metropole).[1] Worked on Irish Bill. Walk with Mr R. Noel.[2] Read Bigotry & Progress[3]—Books in Chains (finished).

To LORD KIMBERLEY, lord president and Indian secretary,   Add MS 44549, f. 39.
12 November 1892.

There is no doubt that last evening you kicked against a great stumbling block. I do not know whether it is new to you.[4] It has been continually before me for the last 6 years: nobody has suggested any means for getting it out of the way. The highest function of the H. of Commons is to change the Executive. An English member we will say moves an Address to the Crown to the effect simply that the existing Ministers do not possess the confidence of the House. The considerations on which the motion rests need not be & commonly are not stated. On this motion are the Irish members to vote?

No doubt you might by contrivances not perhaps very simple in their working exclude them from large number of subjects. I assume that this could be done by a Committee: Seats on which would I think be most unpopular. But would not the upshot of this exclusion be that you would shut them out of the smaller & lower questions & leave them to the higher? And may it not be asked is it worth while? There are pretty strong cases of anomaly already. A Jew or a Hindoo (if our friend is one), probably a Brahmin, votes on the question of a new distribution of Chapters of the Bible in the Services of the English Church. But this & other anomalies are cured by good sense or are not felt. I cannot sustain in argument any right of the Irish to vote upon questions purely English Scotch & Welsh. I do not deny that you might erect & possibly work a machinery of exclusion from the lower questions. This is a question for consideration.

But I have looked in vain at the question which alone is much worth looking at. If you can find a good working answer to the question I put in the earlier part of this letter, you will do good service to the cause. The problem has baffled me. If it baffles all I am ready to face the inconvenience. It would be much less than we now endure if by smaller numbers.[5]

To J. MORLEY, Irish secretary, 12 November 1892.   Add MS 44257, f. 31.
'*Secret*'.

The paper[6] I sent you last night was not meant to raise *any* point new to you. It struck me however that if minds continue to be so stuck *abroad* as they were last night (I hope

---

[1] Opened in 1890, on the sea front.
[2] The poet (see 20 July 74), who had sent Gladstone volumes of his poetry, perhaps fishing for the Laureateship; see Add MS 44549, f. 37.
[3] *Bigotry and progress. A metaphysical romance* (1888).
[4] Kimberley wrote this day, Add MS 44229, f. 58, in a letter which crossed Gladstone's (ibid., f. 60) on Irish members in 'the Imperialist Parliament . . . is it really impossible to mark off the questions on which they should be restrained from voting? . . . The more I think of it, the more I fear that our Bill will be wrecked in the Commons, if the Irish are allowed to vote on all questions. Labouchere has in 'Truth' declared himself unequivocally opposed to any such provision, and determined to prevent its passing. Will he not get members enough from our side to follow him to secure with the help of the Tories our defeat?'
[5] Kimberley's reply next day, ibid., f. 62, argued the case against an 'inequality of rights. The British members by such a provision are placed in a position of inferiority as regards Parliamentary functions from the Irish members. . . . Reduction of the number of Irish members would palliate the inequality, but it is open to the charges of unfairness to Ireland. . . .'   [6] See 11 Nov. 92.

and think a draft bill may bring them together) it might be wise to be prepared with a set of propositions, for that contingency only[,] which though not in draftsman's language, are divergent enough upon main points and if adopted might suffice to prevent aberration. I drafted them mainly for contingencies.

But also a little for preparation. I think of showing them to Spencer. And perhaps you could advise me, if by return so much the better, whether to show them to the Chancellor, to which I also incline.[1]

It [*sic*] was anxious[?] to see Kimberley kick against a point of difficulty as if it had been a discovery or novelty: it having been commonplace of our thoughts for six years.

I have written this on the rail (not firstrate in smoothness) to Metropol Brighton. Due in London Monday afternoon.

To S. RENDEL, M.P., 12 November 1892. '*Private*'.   Add MS 44549, f. 39.

Observing facts about Welsh land as well as I can, I have spoken to my colleagues. We are all of opinion that there is a case for enquiry.

We reserve the question what the instrument of Enquiry should be. It might be a Commission, or a Committee; we are pledged to more than one Commission already; and Commissions cannot be greatly multiplied without discredit & weakness. But quite apart from this I incline to think that a Committee is, viewing the nature of the case the better and the safer instrument. It is not the Irish case over again; a Commission might look as if it was. All opinions can be better represented on a Committee; and the miscellaneous & murdered state of the facts will I think obtain perhaps a fuller and fairer exhibition.[2]

I mark the letter private, but the opening sentences are for communication at your discretion.

I hope you are enjoying Valescure and have tasted or are about to taste Malfrey Coffee. I write at $10\frac{1}{2}$ am. Half an hour ago the atmosphere was as black as moonless midnight. It is hardly better now. Pray remember us to M. Martin if you have the opportunity.

[P.S.] We are going to escape from this cavern if we can and spend Sunday at Brighton.

To LORD ROSEBERY, foreign secretary, 12 November 1892.   Add MS 44549, f. 39.

I am sorry we did not dispose of Rhodes when I suggested considering his case on Wednesday.[3]

The Cabinet separated last night with the full understanding that they were not to be summoned again.

What question, in terms, is put by Rhodes to the Govt.? Should not this be drawn into form either from his letter (which I shd. hardly know how to do) or by a request to him.[4]

The difficulty perhaps lies here that we can hardly make public to the world through him the decision to send a Commissioner.

We could judge better if we knew precisely to what he asks an answer.

I am off to Brighton for Sunday: & return not later than Mon. afternoon.

---

[1] Morley replied, 13 November, Add MS 44257, f. 35, that it was unlikely that the propositions would be wanted, as they only applied 'in case minds shew themselves floating and incoherent'; he suggested retaining the 1886 wording for No. 2, and doubted the wisdom of placing the Receiver Generalship 'among fundamentals', given likely Irish reaction.

[2] Despite this, the Carrington Commission on Welsh land was appt. 1 April 1893; *PP* 1894 xxxvi.

[3] Rosebery, 11 November, Add MS 44290, f. 48: 'I cannot delay giving Rhodes an answer about his telegram.' See 4 Nov. 92 and *PP* 1893–4 lxii. 371.

[4] Rosebery replied, 12 November, ibid., f. 49: '. . . I do not think it possible to refuse Rhodes's request. It amounts mainly to this—that I should ask the farmers to give him facilities for passing through their territory, though of course he wants some sanction from us for settling in Uganda.'

13. 22 S. Trin.

St Paul's mg & evg. The crowds most kind: not very convenient. Wrote to Lady Sherbrooke—Mr Morley Tel. l.l.—Ld Chanc.—Rev. Mr Owen—Mr Marjoribanks—Priv. Sec. Tel. Saw Mr Marjoribanks—Mr A. Morley—H.J.G. On Pier: also drove: walking impossible. Read Things to Come[1]—Progress & Bigotry—Falding on The Ministry.[2]

14. M. [*London*]

Wrote to Ld Rosebery l.l.—Ld Kimberley—and minutes. Morning spent chiefly on Pier and drive. Saw Ld Chancellor—Sir A. West. Worked on Irish Bill. Back to London in afternoon. Dined with Childers. Saw Mad. Albani & divers politicians. Read Progress & Bigotry—Dickinson on France.[3] Our kind friend[4] went on to Riga.

To LORD ROSEBERY, foreign secretary, 14 November 1892.   Add MS 44549, f. 40.

As to Rhodes[5] I apprehend there can be no objection to your applying to the German Govt. as he desires. But I apprehend nothing can be told him as to what we have said or done since the published (3 months) letter to the Co. until you send the letters of which the purpose (and perhaps purport) have been agreed on.[6]

15. Tu.

Wrote to Ld Spencer—J. Morley Tel. and l.l.l.l.—Rev. Mr Temple—Mad. Novikoff—Ld Ripon—and minutes. Dined at Ld Spencer's. Saw Sir A. West—S.L.—Ld Spencer l.l.—Mr Marjoribanks—Adm. Hoskins—Ly Spencer—Ld Acton. Worked much on retention plans & figures. Read Progress & Bigotry—Wiesemann [*sic*] on Mary Stuart.[7]

The Schedule is not yet drawn out: but the important facts are these
1. If Parliament provides for each County & Town in Ireland (together with one representative for the University) one representative at Westminster, and one further representative for each 75000 (or part of 75000) of population over the first 75,000, the result as I reckon it will be that Ireland will be represented at Westminster by 80 members.
2. The number of members to which she is entitled in the ratio of her population to the population of the United Kingdom is I believe 74.
3. If Parliament entrusts to the members for each of the four Irish Provinces the duty of choosing their representatives, subject to the rule stated above, the only difficulty which need be taken into account is perhaps the case of Ulster: where, if each man gave a party vote throughout the returns would be Nationalists only 8 against 18 opponents, whereas in Parliament they are now 14 against nineteen.

[1] 'Things to come': Essays towards a fuller apprehension of the Christian Idea (1891).
[2] F. J. Falding, The Christian ministry and modern thought (1892).
[3] See 8 Nov. 92.   [4] Probably Madame Novikov.
[5] See 12 Nov. 92n.
[6] Rosebery replied, 15 November, Add MS 44290, f. 52: 'I told Rhodes last night that I would use my best offices with the German Government, but that I could tell him nothing about Uganda.'
[7] L. Weisener, Marie Stuart et Comte de Bothwell (1863).

4. But if it was provided that in any province the minority vote should be compulsory on the demand of one third (or less) of the members, then each person could only vote for one less than the number in each case to be chosen. The result would then be (on the same supposition as before with respect to party voting)

Nationalists   11
Tories and D[issentient] L[iberals]   ... 15
which would be fair enough[1]

To J. MORLEY, Irish secretary, 15 November 1892.   Add MS 44549, f. 40.

[Letter 1:] 1. On the memorandum written for contingent use,[2] I agree in substance with all you say. The word distinction was borrowed for a purpose but the words of 1886 are better.

2. I am however, sorry that you anticipate Irish opposition to the Rec: Genl:—It was not heard of in 1886 or since so far as I know.[3] This can stand over till we meet.

3. I have been working hard & I hope not quite unprofitably upon the two knottiest points in the whole affair, those of the numbers for retention, & the limitation of voting. Before you come over I hope to have got them into form & to have ascertained one or two good opinions upon them.

4. I mentioned to the Chancellor last night, & he & Spencer have both seemed to agree, that we may do well to import into the draft to be laid before the Cabinet, for the sake of completeness but with a distinctive mark some portions of the Bill of 1886 which might be termed uncontested, or which at any rate we can assume as points of departure.

If you approve of this generally can you be here so as to assist in doing it, or shall I try my hand at once. Should you be able to answer this by telegraph please do it: if none comes I shall know the reason.

[Letter 2:]   Add MS 44257, f. 39.

I think it would be very desirable that you should feel the pulse of the Nationalist leaders in a preliminary way & on your own behalf as to a. enumeration of powers
                                        b. numbers at Westminster
                                        c. voting at Westminster.
I have been working pertinaciously on b, and the results are curious and I think rather promising.
[P.S.] (Please let me have a copy of this.)

To LORD RIPON, colonial secretary, 15 November 1892.   Add MS 43515, f. 91.

I understand that not only Rhodes, but the Cape Govt. as otherwise represented are ready to undertake (and that at a largely reduced charge) the administration of Bechuanaland. The charge as it stands appears to be extravagant and could hardly (as I should think) have been agreed to by a Liberal House of Commons. But quite apart from this it seems to me to be in principle a great object to get the territory away from absolute Crown Government and put it under the authority which is local and which rests on a representative basis: and I think that if you can manage to bring about a result of this kind you will achieve what is in every sense a good measure.[4]

[1] Initialled and dated 15 November 1892; Add MS 44774, f. 133.   [2] See 11, 12 Nov. 92.
[3] Though see to Morley, 19 April 86 and above, x. cliii.
[4] Ripon replied this day, Add MS 43515, f. 93, that Rhodes's proposals were not yet available in writing, but were expected soon; they were understood to deal only with the Crown colony of Bechuanaland, not the much larger Protectorate; it would have been useful if Rhodes had made his proposals 'to me instead of to Harcourt'.

16. *Wed.*

Wrote to J. Morley l.l.–Ld Chancellor–Ld Spencer–Mr S. Rendel l.l.–Mr Mayhew–Mr Wilberforce–& minutes. Worked on Irish Bill & papers. Saw Sir A. West–Mr Murray l.l.l.–E. Hamilton–Ld Ripon. Hard day: brain overdone. Dined with Mrs Sands. Read Watson's Poems[1]–Progress & Bigotry.

Queen Nov. 16[2]

1. List of Bills in preparation.
2. Home Rule has an empty meaning.
3. A Conservative measure not destroying the Act of Union.
4. Assertions of Irish believed.
5. No use in discussing whether the Irish shd. have the same liberties.
6. Ignorant as to evicted T[ennants] Commission.

To J. MORLEY, Irish secretary, 16 November 1892.   Add MS 44549, f. 41.

Shall we say 11 on Saturday forenoon–Silence will mean consent. I am to see Jenkyns and the draft on Friday; but will take good care then.

Today I have had a head splitting discussion with Hamilton. He says the machinery as to the Receiver General cannot be improved. But he sees difficulties in the financial question which I hope we shall be able to overcome.

Seeing in the Cabinet some disposition towards restrained voting and full numbers (i.e. full rateably to population) I have been working on a scheme by which I bring out 81 Westminster members for Ireland: but I do not know how to manage Ulster without introducing the minority vote in the choice of the 81 by provinces.

17. *Th.*

Wrote to J. Morley–E. Hamilton–Ld Acton–Ld Chancellor–Ld Rosebery–Sir W. Harcourt–M. de Steding [*sic*][3]–& minutes. Read Progress & Bigotry–Ch. Qu. Rev. on Crime. Saw Sir A. West–Mr Murray–E. Hamilton–Mr Fowler–Ld Ripon. We drove to W. Hampstead for tea with Mrs Th.

To Sir W. V. HARCOURT, chancellor of the exchequer,   MS Harcourt dep. 12, f. 159.
17 November 1892.

This is my Mem. of the results as to Bills, up to this date, so far as I can carry it. The allocation I have put in pencil.[4] At the next Cabinet I should like to complete, & verify. Please return, keeping any copy you think proper of this rough document.

18. *Fr.*

Wrote to Mr Stanford–Ld Chancellor–Mr Hutton–Sir W. Harcourt–Sir T. Acland–The Queen (long)–& minutes. Saw Sir Alg. West–Sir H. Jenkyns 11–1.

---

[1] See 28 Oct. 92; this copy sent by H. H. Asquith, with the comment: 'Unless my ear is at fault, he has the true ring; ... he seems to me to be, in performance, not behind, and, in promise, far in front of, all available competition [for the Laureateship]'; Add MS 44516, f. 260.

[2] Holograph; Add MS 44774, f. 143. Notes on the Queen's letter sent this day from Balmoral (Guedalla, *Q*, ii. 454) commenting on Gladstone's mem. of 28 Oct. 92; for Gladstone's reply, see 18 Nov. 92 and Guedalla, *Q*, ii. 455.

[3] Reading uncertain; nephew of Baron Nisco, the last volume of whose works he had sent; see Add MS 44549, f. 42.   [4] Harcourt approved it; Add MS 44202, f. 284.

—Turkish Ambassador—Mr Murray—Mr A. Morley. Saw Cavendish. Dined at A. Morleys. Read Myers's St Paul[1]—Progress & Bigotry.

To Sir W. V. HARCOURT, chancellor of the exchequer,   MS Harcourt dep. 12, f. 160.
18 November 1892.
   The points were three on the draft of Instructions to the Commissioner:
1. I should agree, but with the utmost reluctance to 'and the liabilities' &c.
2. It seems to me that administering & administration are words with poison in them, as tending *to insinuate a foregone conclusion* which is I think what the Cabinet did not mean to do,—I should like better the original draft with the single change of 'dealing with' instead of administering. This is agreed to by Rosebery.
3. The amendment on p. 2 seems to have been forgotten? It would not I think in any way clash with any one's views & the old controul is more than ample.

To LORD HERSCHELL, lord chancellor, 18 November 1892.   Add MS 44549, f. 42.
   It was when I arrived at the result of 18 & 8 for Ulster that I was driven upon the minority vote as the lesser evil. For surely we could not expect that the Nationalists who are now as 7 to $9\frac{1}{2}$ to become 4 to 9 in the Imperial Parliament. The minority Vote is not wholly unsuited to indirect election, and was inserted in the University Acts. Also it seems adapted (if there is indirect election) to the possible beginning of distinct parties hereafter in any of the other three provinces.

19. Sat.

Wrote to Ld Brassey—Hon. Rev. Northcote—Dr. Ginsburg—Rev. E. Wickham—Mrs Cavendish BP.—Mr Rathbone MP. 11–12. Spencer and J.M. on Irish Bill. 12–1$\frac{1}{2}$. The same with Sir H. Jenkyns. Saw Sir A.W.—S.L.—Ld Ribblesdale—Mr Asquith.—Alfred Lyttelton. Read Bigotry & Progress—A Solution of the Irish Question[2]—Wiesemann's Marie Stuart.

      Sketch for Cabinet agreed on in conversation. N. 19. 92.[3]
Propose Committee—and why.
assumed—Percentage of revenue.
           1. supremacy—in some form.
Query is there a   2. Enumeration or reservation as in 1886.
general inclin-   3. Retention by direct election.
ation of Cabinet   4. Full numbers? limitation of powers?
           5. One chamber or two?

20. 23 S. Trin.

Chapel Royal mg and aft. Wrote to Sir W. Harcourt—Ld Kimberley—H.N.G. Read P. Smyth on Bible[4]—Progress & Bigotry (finished)—Forbes Winslow, Inebriates[5]—Roch Hierurgia.[6]—Lantsheare on Hittites.[7]

[1] F. W. H. Myers, *St. Paul. A poem* (1867).
[2] Untraced; many of this title, but none recent.
[3] Add MS 44648, f. 34. See 21 Nov. 92.
[4] J. P. Smythe, *How God inspired the bible* (1892).
[5] One of F. B. Winslow's many writings on insanity and suicide.   [6] Untraced.
[7] L. de Lantsheere, *De la race et de la langue des Hittites* (1891).

To H. N. GLADSTONE, 20 November 1892. '*Secret*'.   Hawarden MS 902, f. 202.

Dearest Harry,

I inclose to you a letter I have just had from Kimberley.

I am inclined to think the Indian Committee has been wrong in suspending its sittings, and ought to have continued to take evidence though it might not have been right to proceed to a report.

Kimberley is right I think in anticipating that the Indian Government will bring pressure to bear upon us & we shall run the risk of haste & imprudence if a silver panic arises.

I intend for the present to advise what I have mentioned on my first page. What do you say? Your affte. Father   W.E. Gladstone.

21. M.

Wrote to Ld Rosebery l.l.—The Queen—and minutes. Dined with the A. Lytteltons. 11-1. Conclave on Irish finances. $2\frac{1}{2}$-$5\frac{1}{4}$. Cabinet:—Comm. appointed—more daylight—D.G. Saw Ld Kimberley—Agnes G.—Mr F.L. Gower—Sir A. West—Ld Rosebery. Read King Lear. In the morning I was depressed: & rested on "The trial of your faith which is much more precious than gold that perisheth".[1] But then the skies brightened, and the wheels began to run.

Cabinet. Monday Nov. 21. 92. $2\frac{1}{2}$PM.[2]
1. Meeting of Parliament. Tues. 31st. Jan.
2. List & allocation of Bills. (Change as to Scotland)
3. Committee of Cabinet for preparation of an Irish Government Bill proposed by WEG.[3]

    WEG; Spencer; Chancellor; Morley; Bryce; and Bannerman.

Monday Nov. 21. 92. [Notes for Cabinet Committee][4]
1. Committee not authorised to withdraw from the bill a direct assertion of the supremacy of Parliaments & Acts of Parliament.
2. Retention of full numbers not 203[?]
3. Full numbers rateably & [blank]
4. Voting power to be limited, or not?
Much discussion on these points: which remain with the Committee.
Direct Election preferred.
One or Two Chambers. Leave in some degree to the Irish.
Query leave the Irish Peers out—Leave alone.
C[ommittee] either to reserve.
N.B. protection of minorities—to be borne in mind.

Bills referred to Committees of Cabinet.[5]
1. Local Government—Committee.
2. London County Council—Rosebery & Fowler.
3. Registration—Committee.

[1] Version of I Peter, i. 7.
[2] Add MS 44648, f. 30.
[3] Note passed in Cabinet: [Gladstone:] 'Bannerman? or Asquith? Please *tick*.' [Spencer:] 'Bannerman, who may protest when Asquith might be suggested'; Add MS 44648, f. 31.
[4] Add MS 44648, f. 32.
[5] Undated holograph; Add MS 44648, f. 35.

4. Single Vote (one m. one v.): Chancellor, Home Secretary, C[hancellor of] E[xchequer].
5. Temperance—Local Veto—Committee.

Bills to be prepared.[1]

Employers Liability: H[ome] O[ffice].
Conspiracy: Robertson? Chr. & Home Sec. to prepare.
Church in Wales & Suspensory Bill: H.O.
Church in Scotland. H. of C.[2] Extinction of Stipends from public sources on vacancies or
  Suspensory Bill: WEG with Sir G. T[revelyan] & Ld. Advocate.
Primogeniture (H. of Lords):[3] Chancellor
⟨Single Vote⟩
Factory & Workshop: H.O.
Railway Servants   ⎱
Report of accidents ⎰ H.O. and B. of Trade
Compulsory Registration of Land on Transfer: Chancellor to have Bill in preparation for
  committee[?]
Court of Criminal Appeal: Chancellor, H. of Lords.
Shortening of Parliaments: Bryce.
Charge Election expences on the Rates: Fowler

In the hands of independent MP: University Representation (Bryce to see Mr. Roundell).

To LORD ROSEBERY, foreign secretary, 21 November 1892.   N.L.S. 10025, f. 175.

I agree with you[4] in recognising the importance of Portal's letter, and my first inclination is to a favourable view of its basis.

The Cabinet today is devoted (after one or two *short* matters) to Ireland and this could
not now be postponed,

We could meet again for this letter tomorrow or Wednesday—

Much depends upon the question what sort of man is Portal. Clearly a clever & con-
structive one but I should like to know more—& you will have the means of learning.

Does not this again place you and Harcourt nearly at the same point of view? And, he
being so much involved as Finance Minister would not the interval be well employed (if I
am right as to the position) in helpful communications with him which might smooth our
course.[5]

22. Tu.

Wrote to Sir H. Jenkyns—Ld Kimberley—Sir W. Harcourt—& minutes. Cabinet
Comm. on Irish Bill 11–1¾. Saw S.L.—Sir Alg. West—Sir W. Harcourt—Ld
Acton—Mr Irving—Miss Terry. Lyceum Theatre, King Lear. *She* admirable: he
of great power & skill, but wanted measure. Read King Lear—Rev. Neil on
Palestine.[6]

---

[1] Undated holograph; Add MS 44648, f. 36.
[2] i.e. to be introduced in the Commons.
[3] i.e. to be introduced in the Lords.
[4] No letter from Rosebery found.
[5] Note from Rosebery proposing, with Harcourt's agreement, to offer Portal the Commissionership, 29 November, Add MS 44290, f. 54. Gladstone's telegram concurred (passage suggesting his
relative in India, i.e. N. G. Lyttelton, deleted in draft); ibid., f. 56.
[6] J. Neil, *Palestine explored* (1882).

Retention. Argument on the numbers[1]
For the *whole* number

1. Simplicity in drawing the act.
2. Avoidance of the necessity of a special clause to provide for the return of the whole body to Westminster if and when it shall be proposed to alter the act.

For a *diminished* number

1. The inconvenience of possible interference in votes of confidence (which may be founded on considerations wholly British) or the like will be diminished by serious reduction.
2. The object of hearing the voice of Ireland will be gained by a reduced number, for it will be a reduced copy of the Irish House, and will express its wants and wishes.
3. Inasmuch as Ireland is generally without practice in self-government, it might be a burden more than a privilege to her were we to point in the Act of Parliament to the attendance of a large number of Irish members at Westminster.
4. We do not propose by the Bill to stereotype the numbers of the Irish House. Their number may in deference to Irish wants or desires be enlarged, and even considerably enlarged, from the present number of 103, even if they should start with one so small. But to have such a total number empowered to vote at Westminster would be a serious, probably even an intolerable inconvenience.
   Limitation therefore in some form appears to be indispensable.
5. There is yet a further, and in the mouth of opponents an extremely strong objection to the retention of the Irish Members *en bloc*. It is that Ireland is now represented considerably & alas from year to year increasingly, beyond her numerical claim as a portion of the United Kingdom. I know not what sufficient plea to urge in answer to this objection.

To Sir W. V. HARCOURT, chancellor of the exchequer,   MS Harcourt dep. 12, f. 170.
20 November 1892.

Your illustration is perfectly fair.[2] I will make it known to the Committee. For myself I am sea-sick with 'retention' and the whole Cabinet seemed yesterday to be much in the same plight.

23. *Wed.*

Wrote to The Queen l.l.—Mayor of Liverpool. Comm. on Irish Bill 11–2. Cabinet 2½–4¾. Something of a scene with Harcourt at the close. Tea with the Labouchere's & conversation—Ld Acton—Hon. S.L. Read Neil on Palestine—Ld Wastwater.[3] Wrote (late) Mem—for Finance of Bill: & lost my sleep till 5.

Cabinet. Wed. Nov. 23. 1892. 2½PM.[4]
1. Uganda. (Demands of the Co.). The three printed Resolutions adopted. Ridgway if possible. Second[?] to Portal.

[1] Secretary's fair copy, initialled and dated 'N. 22' by Gladstone, of a draft with deletions; Add MS 44774, ff. 129, 131.
[2] Suppose the Home Secretary's salary was proposed for reduction because of his comments on Trafalgar Square meetings or release of political prisoners: would the Irish M.P.s vote or not?; MS Harcourt dep. 12, f. 168.
[3] S. Bolton, *Lord Wastwater*, 2v. (1892).
[4] Add MS 44648, f. 37.

[Printed resolutions:][1] 1. That it is desirable that the evacuation of Uganda by the company should now proceed without further interference from the Government.

2. That a Commissioner be appointed for the purpose of reporting on the actual state of affairs in Uganda, and the best means of dealing with the country.

3. It would be the duty of Sir G. Portal,[2] whether he go as commissioner himself or not, to provide a suitable force of Zanzibaris.

2. Poor Law Commission. Add to the terms of appointment: 'whether interference would otherwise be afforded in these cases'.[3]

3. Swaziland. Ripon reported conclusion of Commee. Loch should be empowered to learn the case of the Transvaal—any arrangement to be subject to our assent.

4. Channel tunnel. If Private Bill introduced, question to be an *open question*.

5. L.C.C. Bill. Bill to be enlarge[?][4] the power will come in. They must frame their taxation Bill—we shall have every desire to consider it favourably. Rosebery & Fowler to consider further.[5]

6. Scottish Crofters' Commission. Cabinet.

SECRET   *Committee of Cabinet on Irish Home Rule Bill.*[6]
          First day's work 1–17. Second 18–21.

1. Date for the operation of the Act 1894.

2. The 103 actual Irish members then to become the first [Irish House of Commons?][7] under the same conditions as if they had been elected under the Act.

3. In preparation for that date, an Election to be held for the choice of Irish representatives to sit at Westminster, who would take their seats on the next following summoning of Parliament.

4. The Election to be by the present constituencies as exhibited on the Register.

5. And on the basis of the representative areas as described in the Schedule concerned. Each area to have one representative.
   And also one additional representative for any excess of population over 75000, and further for each 75000 or portion thereof but in no case to exceed the present number of members at present fixed by law, therewith[?] yielding about 80 members.

6. All other particulars governing the election to be fixed by H.M. in Council.

7. Any such Order in Council to be laid on the Table, to take no effect until 40 days therefrom, ⟨and⟩ nor thereafter in case of an adverse address from either House of Parliament. And *toties quoties*.

8. The position of the members so chosen would be the same as that of all other members of the House of Commons, except so far as in this act otherwise provided.

---

[1] Printed resolutions stuck onto this day's letter to the Queen; CAB 41/22/21.

[2] Portal was appointed Commissioner; see *Africa and the Victorians*, 319 and Perham, *Lugard*, 429 ff. Frank Rhodes was one of the assistant commissioners; see Rotberg, *The Founder*, 512.

[3] A typed draft reads: 'To consider whether any alterations in the system of Poor Law Relief are desirable in the case of persons whose destitution is occasioned by incapacity for work resulting from old age, *or whether assistance could otherwise be afforded in these cases* [Gladstone's italics]'; Add MS 44648, f. 40.

[4] Word largely blotted out.

[5] This became the London Equalization of Rates Bill (lost in 1893, passed in 1894); see 23 Jan. 93 and J. Davis, *Reforming London* (1988), 168.

[6] Undated holograph; Add MS 44648, f. 42.

[7] Gladstone's [ ], here and in the rest of the memorandum.

9. Where the number allotted to a representative area exceeds two, such elector shall be entitled to vote only for a number less by one than the full number of members so allotted.

10. The constitution of any Irish House of Commons including the first may be altered by Irish Act.

11. There shall be a Senate of [fifty four?] members.

12. In any Irish Act altering the numbers of the Irish House of Commons the proportion of members established by this Act between the two bodies shall be preserved, and the proportions of the three divisions of the Senate hereinafter established.

13. The Senate shall consist of
one third nominated by the Crown,
one third elected by the constituencies [but possessed of a property qualification],
one third so elected from among the Irish Peers only.

14. All then to sit for double the term of years appointed as the maximum term for the House of Commons and to be resident in Ireland.

15. And to be resident in Ireland.

16. Vacancies in any of the three sections to be filled by the ⟨same⟩ authority which made the original choice.

17. Power to the Crown by Order in Council, on the same conditions as above, to distribute the areas of representation for the Electors ⟨of the several⟩ within the several provinces of Ireland of Senators as above specified.

WEG

18. Deadlock. Clause 23 of 86[1] leaving out whichever period is longest: and adding to 21 'deliberate &'

19. For a term of 20 years provisions herein respecting Senate not to be alterable by Irish Parliament, (except on the point of numbers without altering [*sic*][)]. No restriction after 20 years.

20. (Clause 10 sect 6 of 86) partial renewals at 3, 6, and 9 years of each of the three sections. Priority to be determined by lot.

21. As to limitations of voting powers of Irish members. see Fourth Day's report.

24. Th.

Wrote to Sir W. Harcourt—and minutes. Comm. of Cabinet 11-1¾. Good progress. Saw S.L.—Italian Ambassador—Mr Schnadhorst. Read Ld Wastwater —How we lost Australia[2]—Neil's Palestine. We dined with Sir H. Farquhar. Duke of Fife, Randolph [Churchill], and others, all agreeable. Saw Chinnery.

Third day's work. (Thurs.)[3]
Cabinet Commee on Ireland Nov. 24. 92.

1-13

1. Provision of 1886 respecting the return of the 103 members on any proposed change in the Bill to be dropped.

2. Supremacy. Words to be retained in Preamble substituting 'supreme' for full.

3. Describe the Senate & House of Commons (?) as "the two Houses"

[1] i.e. of the Government of Ireland Bill, 1886.
[2] *The battle of Mordalloc, or, How we lost Australia* (1888); imaginary, futuristic battle between Russians, Chinese and Australians.
[3] Add MS 44648, f. 46.

4. Veto. Adopt Sections 5 to 7 of Canadian Act striking out Instructions & reducing 2 years to Preamble.
7. Retain Cl. 26 ⟨subs. 4⟩ of Bill of 86[1]
8. Do Clause 7 sect. 1.[2]
   and subs. 2. to run 'The Lord Lieut. shall exercise'.
9. Finances, See Mem. herewith.
10. Reserve Imperial Controul of Telegraphs for matters of defence, public security & the like.
    International obligations to be second.
11. Invest Judges of Exchequer with ⟨executive⟩ special & final power over all Imperial matters: and to be appointed on joint recommendation of Ld Lieut. & Sec. of State.
12. For [10?] years, no [sc. any] appointment of any Judge of Supreme ⟨to be appointed in⟩ shall be countersigned by the Secretary of State.
13. R.I. Constabulary to remain under the controul of the Lord Lieut. for five? years— Dublin Police until Irish Legislature otherwise provide.

                                                    WEG N. 24. 92.

Finance

1. Draw provisions in concert with the Treasury for ascertaining, by the respective transfers of receipt, the true revenue of Great Britain and of Ireland severally.
2. Provide that Ireland's revenue be saddled as a first lien with [1/20] of the Imperial charges [to be scheduled in the Act]
3. And with [750m?] on account of Constabulary charge. All reductions from the present expenditure down to that sum to be divided equally between the two Exchequers: below that sum to go to the credit of the Irish Exchequer only.
4. Revenues of Customs and Excise to remain under Imperial Controul. ⟨Also of Post Office and of Telegraphs.⟩
5. Court of Exchequer to enforce processes (as in 1886) and to be constituted specially with that view.
6. Processes in fiscal cases to be supported by the civil and if need be the military force.
7. Financial provisions may be altered after [20][3] years by the Imperial Parliament in conformity with Address from Irish Legislative Body.
8. Transfer Irish Postage and Telegraphs to the "two bodies" both as to revenue & charge, but disable them from raising postal rates

To Sir W. V. HARCOURT, chancellor of the   MS Harcourt dep. adds. 10, f. 215.
exchequer, 24 November 1892.

I have received from Rendel a representation corresponding with that of Ellis.[4] Nothing has been said or done to fix Committee as against Commission. But I am desirous to declare nothing at present when we are just announcing two other Commissions and have another sitting in Dublin.

---

[1] Clause dealing with the powers of the Lord Lieutenant, including prevention of their alteration by the Irish legislature.
[2] On the Executive Authority.
[3] The 1886 Bill had fixed the financial contribution of Ireland as a fixed, money sum for 30 years.
[4] For a Royal Commission on Welsh land; a select cttee. not sufficient; Add MS 44202, f. 287.

25. *Fr.* [*Windsor Castle*]

Wrote to Ld Rosebery—Mr H. Gardner—S. Rendel—Sir W. Harcourt—J. Morley—The Queen—Sir H. Jenkyns—Sir H. Ponsonby l.l.—and minutes. Saw Kimberley—Rosebery—Sir H. Ponsonby—Sir J. Cowell—Mr Rhodes—S.L. Full time audience of H.M.—See Mem. of topics. Cabinet Comm. 11-2¼. We finished, D.G. Read Lord Wastwater. Dined & slept at Windsor.

Topics[1]

1. Inquiry for the Queen's health.
2. The fogs of London & Windsor.
3. The Laureateship. W. Watson[2]
4. The Dowager Duchess of Sutherland: The Duke's state as to money
5. The Roumanian marriage. The Pope's dispensation has been given. Marriage of the present King & punishment of the Priest.
6. Lord Acton: not yet personally known to the Queen
7. Condition of Lady Kimberley
8. Has Mrs Gladstone still a nephew who is a master at Eton.
9. Dean Wellesley & Mr A. Claybon.
10. The Dean of Peterborough.
11. Health of the Bp of Rochester.
12. Agricultural distress (H.M. seemed half inclined to lay it upon "large importations")
13. Commission thereupon—(not desired—).

These are all or mainly all the topics of conversation introduced at the Audience tonight. From them may be gathered in some degree the terms of confidence between H.M. and the Prime Minister. Not perhaps with perfect exactitude, as she instinctively avoids points of possible difference. But then it seems that such are now all points.

Comm. of Cabinet on Govt. of Ireland Bill.[3]
Fourth Day. Friday Nov. 25. 92

1. Limitation of voting.
   a. Disability to affect Representative Peers
                Irish Representatives
   b. Applies to any Bill which is confined to Great Britain or some part thereof
   c. And any vote in Supply to which Ireland does not contribute
   d. Any motion or resolution referring to any such Bill or vote
   e. Standing orders to be made accordingly
   f. Such Standing Order may include any motion or Resolution declared in the Order to ⟨be⟩ concern only Great Britain or some part thereof
   g. Nothing herein is to prevent Irish members from voting on any matter which is by this act reserved to the imperial Parliament.
2. *All* Irish appeals to be to the Judicial Committee [of the Privy Council] only.

[1] Initialled and dated 25 November 1892, Add MS 44774, f. 163.
[2] The Queen and Gladstone then agreed to leave the laureateship vacant. In 1896, Salisbury appointed Alfred Austin.
[3] Add MS 44648, f. 50.

3. Depart from Bill of 1886 as to Viceroys power of appeal to Judicial Committee on constitutionality.[1] But
  Where Viceroy vetoes as *ultra vires*, appeal allowed· to Judicial Committee on address of either House.
  Where Viceroy has assented question of ultra vires may be raised & referred to Judicial Committee on the application of any two County Councils (if such shall be established in Ireland) or Town Councils of towns having a population [blank.]
  Ld. Chancellor.
4. Enumeration v. reservation.
  Enumeration to be subjects retained of Imperial [blank]
  Enumeration of delegated powers as within A[2]
(5. (Sir R. Welby attended.)
  Excise management & collection to be Irish: all monies to be paid to a British Receiver, or else by warrants of the Lord Lieutenant
A.
The Irish Legislature may make laws for the peace welfare & government of Ireland in respect of the following matters
  Property & Civil Rights & the Criminal Law.
  Municipal Institution & Local Government
  Administration of Justice Civil & Criminal
  Education
  Other matters of a local or private nature whether applying to the whole of Ireland or ⟨not⟩ any part thereof

To LORD ROSEBERY, foreign secretary, 25 November 1892.   N.L.S. 10025, f. 181.
  I presume, & will take for granted unless I hear to the contrary that Ribot's suggestion of arbitration does not require an immediate reply. It is not so far as I see an unfair one: but I should like its standing over until there shall appear to be a *dignus vindice nodus*.[3] This however is not meant to convey to carry any possible opinion.
[P.S.] We hope to go to Hawarden tomorrow evening.

26. Sat. [Hawarden]

Wrote to Mayor of Lpool—Sir H. Ponsonby—J. Morley—& minutes. Returned to D. St. 11¾. Saw S.L.—J. Morley. 1½-6½. To Hawarden. Finished Ld Wastwater. Read Tib[4] and Le Cardinal Manning.[5]

To J. MORLEY, Irish secretary, 26 November 1892.[6]   Add MS 44549, f. 44.
  I do not know & have no legitimate means of learning what are Mr. Redmond's views of the H.R. question, & of the effects produced & to be produced upon its fortunes by the action of the group of members which he leads. His own proceedings are difficult in my

[1] Clause 25 of the 1886 Bill dealt with the Lord Lieutenant's power to refer questions of constitutionality to the Privy Council.
[2] i.e. those listed at the end of this memorandum.
[3] Difficulty that requires the intervention of another to solve it.
[4] Mrs. George Ferme had sent her novel, *Tib* (1892), published under the pseudonym of George Douglas; see Add MS 44549, f. 46.
[5] One of many popular lives.
[6] Part in Morley, iii. 494 (disguising the criticism of Redmond).

mind to reconcile with his tone & method when he was a member of the united Irish party.[1]

It appears to me that his present proceedings, & his severance from the main body are consistent & in that sense warrantable upon any one of three grounds & three only
1. That it is desirable for the sake of Ireland to break down the present effort (the fruit of seven years' labour).
2. That the personal quarrel such as it seems to us rests upon such high grounds of offence given & taken as to require that the question itself should be left to *take its chance*.
3. That we have such a surplusage of means of action at our command that we can afford to waste a few of them without impairing the likelihood of success.

None of us are [*sic*] entitled to say a word on the first two of these considerations: but on the third our information & means of judgment are better than his. I hope he does not lean on it: for it is a sheer & miserable delusion.

Until the Schism arose, we had every prospect of a majority approaching those of 1868 & 1880. With the death of Mr Parnell it was supposed that it must perforce close. But this expectation has been disappointed. The existence & working of it have to no small extent puzzled & bewildered the English people. They cannot comprehend how a quarrel to them utterly unintelligible (some even think it discreditable[2]) should be allowed to divide the host in the face of the enemy: & their unity & zeal have been deadened in proportion. Herein we see the main cause why our majority is not more than double what it actually numbers & the difference between these two scales of majority represents as I apprehend, the difference between power to carry the Bill as the Church & Land Bills were carried, into law, & the default of such power. That Mr. Redmond is mad is the conclusion some would like to draw. But we have no right to draw conclusions: we can only state facts, & estimate contingencies to the best of our power.

The main mischief has already been done: but it receives additional confirmation with the lapse of every week or month.

The demands in his article were such as might more reasonably be made by some inhabitant of another planet, if we estimate them with reference to the present issue. But if he proceeds upon a superior knowledge to ours of Ireland, & sees clearly that the postponement of the issue is for Ireland's good, then he may be giving proof, incomprehensible to us because of our ignorance, that he is a statesman of Patagonian stature.

27. *Adv. S.*

Ch mg & evg. Read the Lessons mg. Wrote to E. Wickham Tel.—Sir R. Welby—Ld Acton—and [blank.] Unpacking. Read Conversion of a Bp.[3]—Did Moses write the Pent.[4]—Bp of Winchr Pastoral.

28.

Heard every hour strike thro' the night except one oclock. Church $8\frac{1}{2}$ AM. Wrote to Canon Furse—E. Wickham—Ld Spencer—Sir R. Welby—Bp of Winchester—and minutes. Read Tib—Life of Mrs Beecher Stowe[5]—Poems of Cr Wilson[6]—Theron the Socialist.[7] 5-6. Tea & conversation G.G.

[1] For Redmond's article, see 1, 5 Oct. 92.
[2] The copyist wrote 'discretable'; 'discreditable' seems the more likely reading, if a little weak.
[3] Possibly E. B. Maxwell, *Bishop's conversion* (1892).
[4] F. E. Spencer, *Did Moses write the Pentateuch after all?* (1892).
[5] C. E. Stowe, *Life of Harriet Beecher Stowe* (1889).
[6] Perhaps Claude Wilson, *Sonnets to the Queen and other poems* (1880).
[7] Untraced; unlikely to be J. Hervey, *Theron and Aspasio*, 3v. (1755).

29. Tu.

Better night D.G. Ch. 8½ A.M. Wrote to Ld Coleridge—Ld Rosebery Tel.—Mrs Ferme (writer of Tib)[1]—and minutes. Saw Mrs Grenfell & Mrs Wortley. Read Tib (finished)—Cusack's Life[2]—Morley on Snakes.[3] Drive with C. Backgammon with S.

30. Wed.

Ch 8½ A.M. and Holy Commn. Also 7.25 PM. Wrote to Lucy Cavendish—Dr Hunter MP—Rev. Mr Eales[4]—Mr Marjoribanks MP—Mr M. Müller—Mr Murray. Drive with C. Read Dryden's Wild Gallant[5]—and [blank.]

To Dr. W. A. HUNTER, M.P., 30 November 1892.   Add MS 44516, f. 285.

I can at once assure you that your letter and its enclosure shall be referred to the Cabinet,[6] which will I am certain consider them with the care which their importance and that of their subject demands.

You justly observe that the plan will not satisfy the Scottish Home Rulers as a receipt in full—I presume from this that there may be *some* among the subscribing members who would only accept it without prejudice.

Even those however should without doubt give it a fair trial if Parliament were inclined to so large a concession. And I shall assume, unless I hear to the contrary, that the bulk of the subscribers put it forward as (I will not say a final, for the word invites cavil but) a definitive settlement.

To E. MARJORIBANKS, chief whip, 30 November 1892.   Add MS 44332, f. 236.

I send you a copy of my letter to Dr Hunter.[7] It contains what you advised and a little more. It would be absurd for the Cabinet to entertain the subject—which will at best embarrass them—if the plan is propounded as a mere stepping stone.

Even after allowing for official men, there are a good many Liberal names absent? Are these men who will not go so far?[8]

Thurs. Dec One 1892.

Ch 8½ A.M. Read Dryden Wild Gallant: what a heathenish play! And Defence of his Essay.[9] Wrote to Mayor of Lpool—Canon Furse—S.L.—Mr Tollemache—Mr Murray Tel—Mr Asquith L. & Tel.—Ld Rosebery Tel.—Sandycroft Reading Room. Worked on books & papers. Read also Blanche Lady Falaise[10]—Much conversation on Deanery of Peterborough.

[1] See 26 Nov. 92. Note of thanks and criticism at Add MS 44516, f. 279.
[2] Perhaps M. F. Cusack, *Life inside the Church of Rome* (1889).
[3] Untraced.
[4] Samuel John Eales, vicar of Salisfield, on the Romanes lecture; Add MS 44516, f. 273.
[5] J. Dryden, *The wild gallant*, first performed 1663; see 7 Sept. 42.
[6] Proposal for a committee on Scottish business; letter and paper untraced; see item 7 of cabinet on 17 Dec. 92.
[7] See previous letter.
[8] No reply found.
[9] J. Dryden, *Essay of dramatick poesie* (1668).
[10] J. H. Shorthouse, *Blanche Lady Falaise: a tale* (1891).

To H. H. ASQUITH, home secretary, 1 December 1892.   Add MS 44549, f. 47.

Undoubtedly the letter from Knollys[1] seems to have the unemployed for its objective: but if you can turn it towards the Poor Law Commission with good collateral arrangements, the plan would be a good one. The Prince's presence would tend to keep a certain person in order. It will make the choice of a Chairman a still more serious matter. If you see Fowler tomorrow, ask him whether Aberdare might not be worth thinking of.[2] I am glad to hear your *one & one* Bills (you will be clever if you can invent a new title) are all short.[3] Under the circumstances, when you are preparing a victim for slaughter, the argument in favour of the shortest & simplest form seems strong.

Frid. 2.

Ch. 8½ A.M. Wrote to Sir H. Ponsonby—Mrs Kinnaird—Mr Fowler—Sp. Lyttelton—Mr Cross—and minutes. Saw Rev. Mr Allen. Read up Liverpool Hist. in utter deadness & reluctance of mind.[4] Read Blanche Lady Falaise—Life of Aspinall[5]—'The famous Whore'.[6]

To Mrs. KINNAIRD, 2 December 1892.   Add MS 44549, f. 48.

All subjects associated with the name of Arthur Hallam are of deep interest to me, & it appears that I can to some extent reply to your inquiry.[7] From memory I can say positively that he published poetry in the *Eton Miscellany* in the year 1827. It does not seem to have been republished in the Privately Printed remains.[8] Whether it appears in the published volume I do not know. The Eton Miscellany would I presume be found in the British Museum. I have it, not however in the house: but if there is difficulty in getting at it in town I think I could look it up.

To J. W. CROSS, 2 December 1892.   Add MS 44549, f. 49.

I thank you much for your kindness. The Volume arrived today & I was able to read a part. Nothing can be more acceptable to me than what begins with Dante and ends with a *ding* into bimetallism.[9] I was also greatly interested in the sketch of New York Society, a subject of real moment. Be assured I have not forgotten our pleasant meeting at Grasse.[10]

3. Sat.

Ch. 8½ A.M. Wrote to S.L.—The Queen—.....—& minutes. 11½–5¼. Expedition to Liverpool to receive the freedom. Day fine (between one of fog & one of

[1] Untraced letter to Asquith volunteering the Prince of Wales as a Commissioner; see Asquith to Gladstone, 30 November, Add MS 44516, f. 281.
[2] The Prince was appointed a Commissioner and Aberdare the Chairman.
[3] Ibid.; '"One Man one vote" is more troublesome than it sounds. We have now five alternative schemes, all very short, but none of them free from objections.'
[4] For his speech next day.
[5] W. Lewin, *Clarke Aspinall* (1892).
[6] G. Markham, *The famous whore, or noble courtizan* (1609); on Paulina, 'the famous Roman courtizan'.
[7] Not found.
[8] See 9 Jan. 62.
[9] J. W. Cross, *Impressions of Dante & of the New World, with a few words on bimetallism* (1893).
[10] See 5 Feb. 83.

snow). Perhaps about 80,000 in Hall & Streets. Spoke 45 m St G[eorge's] Hall[1]
10 m Town Hall. All most kind. Read B. Lady Falaise—and [blank.]

4. 2 S. Adv.

Ch 11 AM with H.C. & admirable Sermon from H. D[rew]. Wrote to Lord
Chancellor—H. Fowler—Ld Rosebery—A. Morley—and minutes. Read Moss,
Xty & Evoln.[2]—Lily, The Great Enigma[3]—. . . . . of the Religions.

5. M.

Ch. 8½ A.M. Wrote to Mayor of Liverpool—Agnes Wickham—J. Morley—Dean
of Gloucester—and minutes. Wrote Mem. on Irish Bill. The snow came to 8 in.
Business with Mary. Read Blanche Lady Falaise (finished)—Life of Cervantes[4]—
Finished Paulina.[5] Whist in evg.

Notes on Mr Morley's Report dated Dec. 1. 92.[6]

1. Supremacy. In their own interest the Irish will have to yield, and the sooner they see it
   the better.
       There is something of equity, as well as evident policy, in the demand for some
   words on the Supremacy. Declarations of Parnell, and I apprehend of others, before
   1886, were quite capable of being interpreted into separation; and any honest
   jealousies thus aroused have a title to satisfaction.
2. I need not remark on Enumeration. Would it not be well for you to write to the Chancellor on this subject? Before the close of the Committee he intimated in my hearing
   that he might be willing to give way, if pressed. I think he is the person in the best
   position for maintaining the unanimity of the Committee.
3. Veto. There is a good deal of force in the Irish pleas taken in the abstract. In my
   opinion however they are quite wrong. *Solvitur ambulando.* The Canadian system has
   been at work for a quarter of a century, and has proved itself compatible with perfect
   autonomy. On this account it is for their interest to take it. We can argue strongly for
   this on the ground of its working. But any new words or plan we may propose will give
   rise to great, and perhaps very dangerous difficulties. Suppose the Canada words are
   moved against us, and sustained by reference to the perfect practical freedom they
   have allowed? What will be our reply? I do hope our friends will accord to us some
   authority in arguments of Parliamentary tactic.
       New constitutional formulae or forms are not desirable. In London I had much con-
   versation with the *three* on the Veto. I pointed out to them the case of Canada; and

---

[1] *T.T.*, 5 December 1892, 8a; a confident assertion of the triumph in the next century of Liverpool
as the centre of world commerce.
[2] A. B. Moss, *The bible and evolution* (1890).
[3] W. S. Lilly, *The great enigma* (1892).
[4] J. F. Kelly, *The life of Miguel de Cervantes Saavedra* (1892).
[5] See 2 Dec. 92.
[6] A secretary's copy, dated 5 December 1892, original untraced; Add MS 44774, f. 175. Morley
had sent the 'Minutes of Conference at Shelburne Hotel. Dec 1. 1892' attended by Blake, Sexton,
Healy, Dillon and Davitt; ibid., f. 168. The conference thought a declaration of supremacy 'quite
superfluous & very obnoxious' but if made, to be put in the preamble; it criticized any change from
the policy of 1886 on reserved rather than enumerated powers; it objected to any addition to the
veto powers of 1886 and regarded proposals for a Senate as 'fantastic'; it contended that the constabulary was an Imperial expenditure and that Ireland ought 'not to pay more than $\frac{1}{25}$ or 4 p.ct.'.

expressed very strongly my opinion that Ireland ought not to have less, and could need no more. *They* appeared to me at that time warmly to concur. I feel assured we can carry this plan. I do not see how to answer for carrying any other.

4. *Peers chosen from Peers*. Waiting the production of the Irish scheme, I am sensible that the present plan on this subject has the aspect of a *fad*, though it is none; and at any rate that we cannot force it on the Irish, for there would be no Liberal support for it against them.

5. *Finance*. What Parnell asked in 1886 *from me*, when he did not know of the irregular excess in Irish Local Receipts, was *5 per cent*. With $\frac{1}{8}$ of the representation, and $\frac{1}{8}$ of the population, $\frac{1}{20}$ of the charge (as against $\frac{2}{17}$ in 1800) does not seem much. Look at the proportions of Income Tax and Death Duties. I rather think however that the Irish view would get some amount of support from our permanent civil officers, who have not converted me.   WEG Dec. 5. 92.

To R. D. HOLT, mayor of Liverpool, 5 December 1892.   Add MS 44549, f. 48.

I thank you for your most kind note, & I greatly rejoice if we were able in our share of the celebration of Sat. to manifest the pleasure & the gratitude, which both the particular favour conferred, & the general manifestation made by the town of Liverpool could not but awaken. The conduct of all persons, from the head of the municipal community downwards was such as can never be forgotten: & all the executive arrangements gave the utmost scope for the exhibition of public feeling. At my time of life such a day seems to partake of the character of a farewell; but in whatever light it be viewed nothing could be more touching or more cheering. Accept my personal thanks, with my wife's, to yourself & Mrs. Holt.

6. *Tu.*

Ch. 8$\frac{1}{2}$ A.M. Wrote to Canon Temple—Ld Rosebery l.l.—Mrs L.—Ly Sherbrooke—The Queen—Señor Lazara[1]—Mr Bryce—Sir H. Jenkyns—Ld Coleridge—& minutes. Took the guests to my Library St D[einiol']s. Saw also Mr Williamson. Read Life of Cervantes—Westm Rev. on Tom Paine[2]—..... on Irish Finance. Whist in evg.

To J. BRYCE, chancellor of the duchy, 6 December 1892.   MS Bryce 10, f. 127.

I thank you for your letter.[3]

As a first step I have desired that the Scotch memorial may be sent round to those Ministers who are associated with Scotland, also to the Lord Advocate.

The question raised is a grave one and we must endeavour to draw to it the most serious attention of the Cabinet.

It would be a great public good achieved if we could by any fair measure satisfy & appease the Scottish national desire.

---

[1] Giving his permission to translate some of Gladstone's writings into Spanish; Add MS 44549, f. 49.

[2] *W.R.*, cxxxviii. 483 (November 1892).

[3] Of 5 December, MS Bryce 12, f. 99: 1. Bryce had sounded C. Roundell 'regarding a Bill to extinguish University representation in Parliament', which Roundell agreed to introduce; 2. Bryce enclosed a mem., ibid., f. 101, supporting the idea of a Grand Cttee. for Scottish Bills; 3. he reported proposed Swedish concessions to Norway in the office of the Foreign Minister.

The concession you report on ⟨behalf⟩ the part of the Swedes appears to be very large indeed.[1]
[P.S.] Roundell—all right.[2]

7. *Wed.*

Ch. 8¼ A.M. Wrote to (H.) Ld Tennyson—Mr Friedlander[3]—A. Morley—Mr Asquith—Mr H. Hart—and minutes. Examined Gehrings Index Homericus.[4] Read Life of Cervantes—Drummond Wolff's Notes.[5] Long conversation with French Ambassador, who was called away. Also with Max Müller who came in evg.

To LORD TENNYSON, 7 December 1892.   Add MS 44549, f. 49.

I am afraid that your Father's letters to me stand in their chronological places among a mass of many thousand.[6] If you know the *date* of any which you wish to see, by it I could get at them. Otherwise I fear it could only be done when I am in a condition to sort & classify the mass. My earlier letters are classified: & *if* I find any of your Father's I will send them for your use. You have a very important work in hand as his Biographer & I am sure you will bestow upon it the very best of your labour.

8. *Th.*

Ch. 8¼ A.M. Wrote to J. Morley L. & tel.—Archbp of Canterbury—Mr Fowler l. & tel.—Mr Weld Blundell—Miss V. Woods[7]—& minutes. Wrote Mem. on Irish Conferences.[8] Long & interesting conversations with M. Müller: who is most kind: too negative: antiDarwinian. We visited St Deiniols. Reading (much as usual).

To E. W. BENSON, archbishop of Canterbury, 8 December 1892. Add MS 44549, f. 50.

Even apart from the strong opinion expressed by Your Grace in your letter of the 4th[9] I am sensible and the Cabinet have been sensible, that there is much to be said in favour of appointing some clerical members to the Commission on Poor Law Relief. The question was however distinctly considered by the Cabinet, and they arrived at a negative conclusion. And this not from any insensibility to the weight of clerical knowledge and

[1] Bryce replied, 10 December, ibid., f. 104, reiterating the urgency for progress on the Scottish Cttee.
[2] Roundell was appointed to the Royal Commission on the Aged Poor.
[3] S. Friedlander, in correspondence on early Hebrew poetry; Add MS 44549, f. 49.
[4] The 1st v. of *Index Homericus. Composuit A. Gehring*, 2v. (1891–5).
[5] Sir H. D. Wolff, *Some notes of the past 1870–91* (1893).
[6] Hallam Tennyson asked, 'Could you kindly let me have copies of my Father's letters to you? They would be very valuable for the Memoir. And if you ever feel inclined (only for an hour) to dictate any reminiscences to your Secretary—you would not be sorry—and I should be glad'; 5 December, Add MS 44516, f. 300. There are a number of Gladstone's letters in Tennyson's biography, but no 'reminiscences'.
[7] Virna Woods of America had sent her 'lyrical drama', *The Amazons* (1891); see Add MS 44549, f. 50.
[8] Not found, unless a revision of that of 5 Dec. 92; Morley's paper on Irish M.P.s' views on an Irish Senate arrived this day, Add MS 44257, f. 49.
[9] Not found. There were no clerical Commissioners.

judgment in the matter. Nor, except in a secondary degree, from the inconvenience of having to meet somewhat similar claims on behalf of R. Catholics & Non Conformists.

The categories under which strong recommendations are urged upon us for enlarging the body (including the ladies who exhibit an energetic activity) are so numerous, & with so much apparent support, that we are in sight of the danger of converting our Commn. into a little Parliament.

But so far these claims have not been accepted. Yet not I think mainly on the ground of the inconvenience attendant on further adding to numbers already somewhat large. This Commission will probably open up some extremely large and not less difficult & delicate questions of public policy. Much aid may be hoped from the Commission *towards* the solution of these questions. But it is not here, as it is in many cases, where the solution itself may mainly or largely be referred to the Commission. The questions are such that neither Govt. nor Parlt. can escape from bearing the main weight of responsibility.

This being so, my conclusion I confess is that the Commission ought not to be constituted, generally speaking, on the basis of representation of class; that it should be composed rather of what may be largely defined as public men; and that in such a case as this the position of witnesses will give a more free, beneficial, & effective opportunity than any other for bringing to the front sentiments & judgments most important in themselves, yet liable in their formation to be affected by influences partial in their character, and very distinct from those which will have, in all likelihood to guide the final judgment.

To H. H. FOWLER, president of the local government board,   Add MS 44549, f. 49.
8 December 1892.

I wrote yesterday about the letter to the Prince of Wales, & telegraphed today about Aberdare. I will now at once reply to the archbishop: & so I proceed to the ladies. And what strikes one first is this: that you & I are politically competent to decline their aid, but if we think it should be accepted, the acceptance would be so much of a measure in itself that we should have to consult the Cabinet: & I doubt whether the C. would agree.[1]

I understand you to be *willing*, but not *anxious*. For my part I am shy of it. As you say the questions to be opened, certainly or probably are questions of public policy, & not only so but of very high & difficult public policy. I own that I would rather give the ladies their first canter on some subject less arduous, & where there would be less danger of their being led astray by the emotional elements of the case.
[P.S.] As to Fenwick I have nothing to say in an opposite sense: but I advise your consulting the late & present Whips.

9. Frid.

Ch. 8½ AM. Wrote to Abp of Canterbury—Mr Lefevre—Herbert J.G.—Lady Stradbroke—Mr Fowler Tel.—S.L. Tel.—Sir W. Forwood[2]—Ld Rosebery—and minutes. Read Life of Cervantes[3]—Edward the Confessor.[4]

J. Morley came in evg: long conversations. He is a great stay in Rosebery troubles which are renewed.

[1] Fowler reported, 7 December, Add MS 44516, f. 303, on a dpn. at the request of Lady Carlisle and Lady Aberdeen 'asking for the appointment of one or more Lady Commissioners. I stated that I would lay their views before the Government.' There were no female Commissioners.
[2] Regretting his inability to open a railway at Liverpool. Sir William Bower Forwood, 1840–1928; Liverpool railway developer, mayor and magistrate.
[3] See 5 Dec. 92.
[4] Perhaps Bassanio, *Edward the Confessor* (1886); a drama.

To E. W. BENSON, archbishop of Canterbury, 9 December 1892. Add MS 44549, f. 51.

Ld. Ripon has to recommend to H.M. a Bishop as Prelate of the Order of St. Michael & St. George.

It seems admitted that it should be a Colonial or overseas Bishop. Bp. Hills has been mentioned. He stands at Oct. 76; which probably means another vacancy soon.

Would your Grace advise a senior Bishop; or one of the most distinguished? In the latter category should Bp. Copleston be thought of? I am now not well acquainted with the personnel of the Colonial Episcopate. And I am not quite certain as to an Indian Prelate's being available, but Bp. C. is still I believe at Ceylon.

Any suggestion from Your Grace would I am sure be acceptable.

To LORD ROSEBERY, foreign secretary, 9 December 1892.   N.L.S. 10025, f. 197.

I am sorry there is such a pressure for the despatch of instructions to Portal, for a little interchange of ideas might remove what is possibly a misapprehension on my part. My impression was, & I think it was the impression of the Cabinet, that Portal's mission was to be specially based upon the recent communication from him which was submitted to them, and which put forward as his main idea that Uganda should be brought into union with Zanzibar.

But I do not find in your draft of instructions any reference to this which according to my idea was to be their capital point. I think that anyone reading the draft would have no idea that Zanzibar was any way in question.

If I am right surely this is a gap which ought to be supplied?

John Morley on his Newcastle trip has offered himself here, but will not arrive before post. I will however show him the draft (as it is in machine type, & you have therefore other copies) together with this note (i.e. a copy of it) and he may be able in some degree to verify my recollection or the reverse.

I have noted within three points of detail[1] but of course the main point is that of Zanzibar.[2]

To G. J. SHAW LEFEVRE, first commissioner of works,   Add MS 44549, f. 50.
9 December 1892.

Many thanks for your interesting paper.[3] If you reckon 1885 as an Irish case, then I think you can hardly reckon 1846 which was the converse.

Of course it is to be borne in mind that the Irish representation only became a broad & working system after the Ballot Act.

To LADY STRADBROKE, 9 December 1892.   Add MS 44549, f. 51.

Indeed I sympathise with you[4] strongly as to the distress of agriculture which we are feeling here as elsewhere. I feel with & for it not the less because I do not yet fully understand why the prices of stock should be ruinously low in a year in which the root

[1] Points listed in N.L.S. 10025, f. 200.
[2] Rosebery this day, Add MS 44290, f. 64, replied: '. . . I took your own words "the best means of dealing with the country". To those I have now added "whether through Zanzibar or otherwise".' See to Rosebery, 21 Oct. 92.
[3] Lefevre, 7 December, Add MS 44153, f. 295, sent a long mem., dated 7 December, 'on the changes of Government during the present century, shewing that there has never been resignation on a purely English or purely Scottish question. It also shews that no measure affecting England only has ever been passed through the House of Commons in opposition to a majority of the English members . . .'; Gladstone's annotations disagree with a number of Lefevre's facts.
[4] No letter found.

crops were good almost beyond example. Might it not be useful in some degree if the farmers could not have more organisation among themselves to secure their getting fair terms from the middle, or next-middle, man? You will have observed that their acting friends do not much advise them to rely upon the restoration of protection.

10. Sat.

Ch. 8½ AM. Wrote to Mr H. Gardner—Geo Russell—S.L. Tel.—Ld Spencer—Bp of Gibraltar—and minutes. A day of hard work, followed by a night sleepless till near 5. A.M. Worked with Morley—so genial & effective. Showed him St Deiniol's. Read Cervantes finished—Edw. the Confessor. Saw the Tomkinson party.

11. 3 S. Adv.

Ch. 11 A.M. and 6½ P.M. Wrote to Sir W. Harcourt—The Queen l.l.—S.L. l. & tel.—Ld Rosebery l.l.—Mr Fowler—Ld Spencer l. & tel. Saw J. Morley mg: who left for Dublin. Saw S.E.G. Read Lilly's Great Enigma—Dr Fry's Social Tract.[1] We determined on making a trip to Biarritz.

To Sir W. V. HARCOURT, chancellor of the exchequer,   MS Harcourt dep. 12, f. 176. 11 December 1892. '*Private*'.

I have not been sleeping very steadily of late and after consultation with Clark & agreeably to his views have arrived at the conclusion that a short run to Biarritz, occupying a fortnight to three weeks will be admirable as a measure of precaution, and of preparation for coming labours. It will not I think entail any interferences with Cabinet arrangements, but I do not like to take the step without seeing my colleagues & I am summoning the Cabinet for Saturday. I hope the Committee on the Irish Bill will terminate its labours on Friday. I write in order that you might not be startled by any unexpected summons.

You will receive a short Circular on our progress with the Irish Bill.
[P.S.] I think my plan had better not be mentioned outside the Cabinet at present.

To LORD ROSEBERY, foreign secretary, 11 December 1892.   N.L.S. 10025, ff. 208–11.

[Letter 1:]   I have received your letter and *thank* you for the alterations you have made. I think however you will see that we have not yet quite got on the right ground, according to the decision of the Cabinet. I need not enter into detail. But you will remember that the Cabinet adopted on the 23d of November three propositions which were laid before it in print. I reported them to the Queen on that day "as the basis on which Lord Rosebery will now, after the report of Sir G. Portal, and his recent correspondence with the E. African Company, proceed to his next steps with reference to Uganda."

When I suggested, as an amendment on a form laid before me the phrase "the best mode of dealing with the country"[2] I did not consider that we were in any way modifying (as indeed we could not) the proceedings of the Cabinet, or depriving Portal's ideas about Zanzibar of the degree of prominence that (I conceived) had been given them. My impression is that if I am right it will be proper by a subsequent paper (for I infer from

[1] T. C. Fry, 'A social policy for Churchmen' (1892); produced by the Oxford University branch of the Christian Social Union.
[2] See to Rosebery, 9 Dec. 92n.

your letter that you dispatched your first instruction, as amended on Saturday) to develop the reference you have made to Zanzibar.

I have sent for the three propositions, and *if* I find they require me to add to or modify this I will write again tomorrow.[1]

[Letter 2:]   In conversation with Clark, & agreeably to his views, (urged also in the same direction by Morley who has been here and is just gone off to Ireland) I have arrived at the conclusion that I ought to seek rest & air abroad for two or three weeks as a measure of prevention, and of preparation for the approaching work in and after January; in consequence of irregularity of sleep; which, warned by previous experience, I believe it is prudent and needful to deal with in its early stage.

Please not to mention this at present beyond the Cabinet. I did not think I could do it except after communication with them, and I have summoned a meeting for Saturday.[2] [P.S.] When we meet we had better speak about a note naming you which I have had from West.

To LORD SPENCER, first lord of the admiralty, 11 December 1892.   Althorp MSS K8. '*Private.*'

We have for some time been in consultation with Clark on the question whether a run abroad was necessary for me in order to have a fair prospect of meeting the coming work. The sleeping power was not so assured as might be wished and hence the consultation. I have now most reluctantly been brought to the conclusion that I ought to go. Morley's presence here has helped to this conclusion. I therefore propose the *Committee* should meet in D. St. on Friday at 3 and the Cabinet on Saturday as it is necessary to act in such a matter, as I think, with their concurrence. I feel the hardship I inflict upon them through the inevitable conditions of my advanced age.

[P.S.] Perhaps this had better not be mentioned outside the Cabinet at present and within it only as a measure of precaution and preparation.[3]

12.

A good night D.G: but prudence kept me at home. Wrote to Ld Ripon— Warden of Trin. Coll.—Ld Rosebery Tel. Walk & rest after it: now becoming a necessity. Children's Charades. Read divers—and Cowley's remarkable Tract on Divorce[4] & topics akin—Godwins Mandeville.[5] Framed my plan for distributing £12000 more to my children: i.e. six of them.[6] Worked on books.

[1] Rosebery replied, 12 December, Add MS 44290, f. 69, that 'there is nothing in the three points to which the Cabinet agreed with reference to administration by Zanzibar.... I have been racking my brain to try and remember any decision of the Cabinet in that direction without success ... though I personally do not object to it, I think the allusion to Zanzibar already inserted goes beyond the Cabinet.' Rosebery was right about the Resolutions; see 23 Nov. 92.

[2] Rosebery replied sympathetically next day, Add MS 44290, f. 70, but emphasising the need for proper discussion in Cabinet of the Irish Bill and hoping for at least two Cabinet discussions of it before Gladstone left.

[3] Spencer replied sympathetically next day; Add MS 44314, f. 61.

[4] C. Cowley, *Our divorce courts: their origin and history* (1879).

[5] W. Godwin, *Mandeville. A tale of the seventeenth century in England*, 3v. (1817).

[6] i.e. all the living children.

To LORD RIPON, colonial secretary, 12 December 1892.   Add MS 44515, f. 95.

I have received & read as well as I could the batch of papers on the Solomon Islands. (You may be puzzled by my reservation: but the transition from *good* manuscript to indifferent typewriting is a *disastrous* one for persons of limited visual power like myself).

You will I think agree with me that as there is a Cabinet on Saturday you would do well to mention the subject there.

Besides the condition properly inserted in the proposal for ascertaining that the ground is in no way pre-occupied you will doubtless assure us that there is no reason for believing the natives unwilling to be under our Protectorate.

There seems to be weight in the argument on the Labour traffic, & the coaling stations of the Admiralty are also a fact in the case. Should France object, & be able to show any *primâ facie* case in support of objection, then I think we should go to arbitration.

The whole subject is as you show very unpalatable, but we must endeavour to deal with it as equity may require on a consideration of all the facts. I attach real weight to your judgment on it.[1]

13. Tu.

Ch. 8½ A.M. Wrote to Rosebery l.l.—(one of them an apology)—J. Morley—Sir A. West—and minutes. Read Mandeville—Mivart in N.C.—Traill on Tennyson—Mrs Gell on Girlhood &c.[2] Drive with C.

To J. MORLEY, Irish secretary, 13 December 1892.   Add MS 44257, f. 59.

1. Please to take notice that I am due to leave Sandycroft at 9.40 on Friday, Chester 9.55 and that if I find you in the train it will be for much pleasure and profit.

2. I have telegraphed to London to circulate the Bill to the Committee with the Finance as the Committee left it. I cannot well conceive how they could think in London of anything else.

3. I have cried peccavi to Rosebery. On seeing "the three propositions" I found them less pointedly Zanzibarish than *I* had supposed—& you also if I mistake not, my wishes remain unaltered [*sic*].

My youngest daughter goes with me to London & Biarritz.

To LORD ROSEBERY, foreign secretary, 13 December 1892.   N.L.S. 10025, ff. 222-5.

[Letter 1:] I am *so* sorry that my telegram yesterday did not spare you the trouble of writing.

It is in my view a serious offence to aggravate causelessly the occupations of a much occupied man: & this is just the offence I have to confess. *Peccavi*.

My recollection (confirmed by J. Morley's) was that on the 23rd the Cabinet gladly accepted Portal's communication as opening probably the best and safest channel for the proposed inquiry; without at all shutting out the examination of others. But I thought this preferential position had been exhibited in the three adopted propositions, which on receiving them yesterday morning I found it had not. The Resolutions establish no claim, though they may have a wish. I hope and think it probable that Portal will make early and exhaustive examination into the practicability of the idea he has suggested. Pray understand that I no longer feel myself warranted in making any request: as the Americans say, the bottom is knocked out of my case for it: and I am very sorry for the trouble given you by my letter of Sunday.

---

[1] No reply found.
[2] All in *N.C.*, xxxii. 899, 930, 952 (December 1892).

[Letter 2:]　Clark is coming here tomorrow. I hope there will be little difficulty in dealing with the matter. There are others, not serious in themselves, but serious with reference to the office I hold, which if I get sight of you on Friday at 6 or 7 oclock I may mention for a minute or two. Perhaps you will then tell me whether you have arrived at a definite conclusion about the Leadership in the House of Lords. The difficulty you present appears to be that of being in two places at once. Salisbury however in some manner contrived it? Your wish must rule.[1] I do not know whether there will be any bill-work ready for the Cabinet on Saturday but there are one or two matters at least for which it will be convenient, including the Solomon Islands.

14. Wed.

Ch. 8½ A.M. Wrote to Abp of Canterbury—Mr Fowler—Ld Ripon—Watsons—Scotts—H.N.G.—& minutes. Walk with Helen. Viewed Home & Asylum. Read Mandeville—Momerie on Future Religs[2]—Sanday on Huxley.[3]

15. Th.

Ch. 8½ AM. Wrote to Ld Rosebery—Murrays—Mr Poulis—and minutes. Preparations (sorrowfully made) for departure. Yesterday evening a medical hour with Sir A. Clark. This forenoon another. He reports wonderfully. Read Mandeville (finished)—Rendall's Address[4]—Pater's Epicurean.[5]

To H. POULIS, 15 December 1892.　　　　　　　　　　Add MS 44549, f. 52.

　I fear I cannot aid you in your main purpose.[6] I heard of Mr F. Newman[7] when I was an undergraduate (1828–31) a man of great talent, especially of mathematical talent, unable to take holy orders as he dissented from the Prayerbook. As to the time of his being in or out of Oxford I cannot speak. He was not in my day a *figure* for the University at large. Of the Plymouth Brethren I had no original knowledge whatever, nor have I any, but I observe their power, as a moral attractive force, in juxtaposition with the Established Church of Ireland. Of the tongues I know something but this subject hardly came within the precinct of the University.
[P.S.] I had a great esteem for Mr F. Newman but of late years he has I think avoided all communication with me.

16. Frid. [London]

Off at 9.25. D[owning] St. 2.40. Saw Sir A. West—Mr Marjoribanks—Ld Spencer—Mr Morley (in train)—Ld Acton. 3–7. Cabinet Committee on Irish Bill. Ld Acton & Mr Armitstead dined. Read Herodotus, first Chapters.[8] A

[1] Rosebery declined leadership of the Liberals in the Lords: 'putting aside the intellectual disparity [between himself and Salisbury] there is a vast difference between leading a party of 500 peers and a party of 25'; the evening work might revive his insomnia; 14 December, Add MS 44290, f. 73.
[2] A. W. Momerie in *F.R.*, lviii. 834 (December 1892).
[3] W. Sanday, 'Professor Huxley as a theologian', *C.R.*, lxii. 336 (September 1892).
[4] Perhaps M. C. Rendall, 'Gladstone's foreign and colonial policy. An address . . .' (1884).
[5] See 4 July 85.
[6] No letter from Poulis traced, and Poulis himself unidentified.
[7] i.e. F. W. Newman, J. H.'s brother, later a unitarian; see 7 Feb. 57n.
[8] Start of a study of Herodotus' *History* (which includes a speculative description of the source of the Nile and the Ruwenzori mountains, the boundary of Uganda and the Congo). See 29 Aug. 28.

bold venture—also divers. Wrote to Sir W. Harcourt—Mr Fowler—and minutes.

To Sir W. V. HARCOURT, chancellor of the exchequer,   MS Harcourt dep. 12, f. 183.
16 December 1892.

With regard to the Memorandum you have just circulated,[1] it appears to me that as a first step it might be well if Lefevre were to endeavour informally and privately to ascertain what may be the interior views & the real policy of the London County Council in a proceeding apparently not less gratuitous than inconvenient in possible consequences.

An inquiry of this kind might assist the Cabinet materially in approaching the question. Rosebery would I imagine best know whom Lefevre ought to approach.

17. Sat.

Wrote to The Queen—C.G.—and minutes. Cabinet 12-2. Saw HNG (on distribution)—Sir A. West—Mr Asquith—Mr Morley—Ld Spencer—Ld Acton. Dined at Mr Armitstead's. Read Herodotus—Miss Weston.

Cabinet. Sat. Dec. 17. 92. Noon.[2]
1. My journey to Biarritz. Sir A. Clark mentioned: general assent.
2. Protectorate over Southern Solomon Islands. Accepted with some reluctance.[3]
5. Agricultural Distress:[4] inquiry by Commission ⎫
                                     by Committee ⎭
Roundell's letter: referred to Cabinet Committee on Local Govt. which includes rural reforms.
4. Aged Poor: Commission. Archbishop's request & argument[?] named. Cabinet adheres.[5]
7. Request of 35 Scottish MPs.
[6]Committee of 30. By resolution. With the addition of such English & Irish members specially interested by office or otherwise in the subject of the Bill as the House may select.[7]
Proposed by Hunter.
Whatever Scotch Bill conference[?] for the purpose might offer.
3. Wages in Govt. spending departments. Meetings of representatives of spending Departments at B. of Trade already held: to be continued & to collect the facts.

[1] Printed for the Cabinet; on need for a policy on rates of govt. wages and a decision on whether 'it is desirable that the minimum rate of wages in government departments should be raised to a point considerably above that of other employers of labour'; copy in MS Harcourt dep. 12, f. 181.

[2] Add MS 44648, f. 53. Most of the headings were written out before the meeting in the order printed above; the numbers were added, probably during the meeting, to show the order of discussion.

[3] Ripon was given permission to inaugurate a protectorate provided that there was no sign of foreign action or unwillingness on the part of the islanders; the protectorate was later considerably expanded; see W. P. Morrell, *Britain in the Pacific Islands* (1960), ch. xii.

[4] Gladstone told the Queen that while a Commission was desired, the Cabinet Cttee. was considering legislative improvements; CAB 41/22/22.

[5] Benson requested Anglican representation on the Commission; Fowler objected as there would have to be Roman Catholics and Nonconformists also; Add MS 44516, f. 303.

[6] Rest of this point is on a separate sheet.

[7] This sentence is in Asquith's hand.

4. Mr Morley finds it necessary to contemplate a change in the office of undersecretary. Tasmania to be offered to Gormanston—B. Guiana to Ridgway.[1]

8. London Co. Council want 12 improvement[?] Bills.[2] Govt. to abolish restrictions—they must work their own finance. Rosebery, Fowler, Asquith to arrange to meet a deputation from the county council.

To H. D. GARDNER, president of the board of agriculture,   Add MS 44549, f. 53.
17 December 1892.

You will have heard I made no doubt of the expression of opinion which has been conveyed to the Govt. by Mr Roundell on behalf of a large number of Liberal members representing rural constituencies.[3] This does not require any positive decision at the present moment against inquiry should it seem desirable, but it puts into the foreground that preparation of measures of rural reform which have already been to a given extent under consideration.

To Mrs. GLADSTONE, 17 December 1892.   Hawarden MS 780, f. 215.

Beloved C. On a card to Mary late last night I explained that all my time from arrival until well past seven was occupied. As I had a few minutes available before dinner I walked as far as Lord Derby's door to inquire for him. The answer was 'nothing pressing: last account a little better[']. But the use of such words seems to show that even the 'establishment' is aware of the very grave nature of the case.

The Cabinet Committee of four hours yesterday, and the Cabinet of two hours today, both went perfectly well: plenty of serious matter but nothing sharply contentious or critical as among ourselves.

We dine with Mr Armitstead today, A. Morley Monday. The plan now is to leave London on Sunday afternoon but spend the day and night at Folkestone which is almost as good as Biarritz and then to go forward on Wednesday so as to take the benefit of the *fast* train which goes three times a week, Mond. Wed. & Frid. and cuts four hours off the journey. Your generous conduct in going to Seaforth is really the only impediment to our taking Monday: but I think we should do very well as we are.

It seems that Mr A. is very desirous that I should have a Private Secretary and there are various other reasons which have made me yield & Mr Shand will go but will not be member of the party.

Nothing could be easier than the journey yesterday. It gave ample opportunity for talk

---

[1] Gormanston was to be transferred from British Guiana to Tasmania, to make room in the former for West Ridgeway, who could then be transferred from the Irish Office. The manoeuvre failed; a place was found for Ridgeway as Governor of the Isle of Man in 1893. Jenico William Joseph Preston, 1837–1907; 14th Viscount Gormanston; governed British Guiana 1887–93, Tasmania 1893–1900.

[2] B. F. C. Costelloe's mem. of 15 July 1892 listed 13 subjects on which the L.C.C. hoped for action from an incoming liberal government; at least 12 of these would have required bills; they include amendment of 1888 Local Government Act, women councillors, police administrative arrangements, consolidation of Building Acts, valuation reform, housing reform, local taxation reform, technical education, unification of City and County govt., district councils, schools boards, dockland trust, land reform. See *L.C.C. Official Reports*, vol. III, no. 52 (Local Government and Taxation Committee).

[3] Gardner reported, 14 December, Add MS 44516, f. 316 that 'the present agitation is no doubt considerable . . . I am sorry, therefore, that my suggestion of a Commission has not been favourably received'; he gave an account of a dpn. from 8 liberal M.P.s, requesting a Royal Commission on Agricultural Holdings.

with Morley. No Hall at Euston!!! But the Phillimore Carriage!!! in which we came at a good pace and I feed the coachman, or rather fed him, at any rate fee-ed him. There was such a crowd on the platform that to get me out of the way was the first object.

It is sad to lose Xmas and New Year at Hawarden but I think that we are going where duty leads us.

On Monday at 11.30 I am to call on the Prince at Marlborough House. Love all round, and to Dossie least of all, but not least of all to Dossie. I hope Mr Mowat is all right again & am ever your affte. WEG

More appetite for luncheon today than for a week. Good night the last.

18. 4 S. Adv.

Chapel Royal mg (Gospel according to Rogers) & aft. Saw Sir A. Clark—Ld Carrington—Sir A. West—Mr Morley. Dined rather reluctantly with Ld Carrington to meet P. of Wales and Duke of York. Read Bp Sandford's Sermon—Pollock on Renan X[1]—Hutton on Renan +.[2] Wrote to Mr Morley.

19. M.

Wrote to The Queen—Mr R. Owen—Mr B. Currie—and minutes. Dined at Mr A. Morley's. Worked on books & papers. Saw Sir A. West—Mr Morley—Ly D. Neville—Sir W. Harcourt. Read Herodotus. Made trials of novels & books for the journey.

20. Tu. [Folkestone]

Wrote to The Queen—Mrs Thistlethwayte—and minutes. Saw Sir A. West—Sir E. Watkin—Mr Morley—H.N.G.—Vicar of Folkestone. Travelled to Folkestone. Saw the beautiful Church. Attended service 5.30 PM. Read Herodotus I.—The Heir to Millions.[3]

21. Wed. [On train]

Wrote to Mr Fowler—Mr Leveson Gower—The Queen l.l.—& minutes. Off at 11¾. Travelled all night to Biarritz. The Nord too rough for reading. Saw Ld Dufferin & others at the station in Paris. Read the Clio.[4]

To H. H. FOWLER, president of the local government board,   Add MS 44549, f. 55.
21 December 1892.

In a momentary famine of paper I reply to your note by advising that you should make known to Sir H. Ponsonby the reasons which have led you to recommend Mr Arch,[5] & the absence so far as you know of just causes of objection—& the view of the Cabinet that he was a fit & proper person: if, as I rather believe, he was mentioned there—& trust that if there be facts unknown to you which render him unfit H.M. will be graciously pleased

---

[1] F. Pollock, 'Some recollections of Ernest Renan', *N.C.*, xxxii. 711 (November 1892).
[2] R. H. Hutton, 'M. Renan and Christianity', *National Review*, xx. 301 (November 1892).
[3] E. Fawcett, *The heir to millions*, 2v. (1892); see 24 Dec. 92.
[4] In Herodotus, book i.
[5] Asquith, 20 December, Add MS 44516, f. 326, wrote that Ponsonby had telegraphed him that the Queen objected to J. Arch being on the Aged Poor Commission; Arch was none the less appointed.

to inform you, or (say) cause you to be informed. Should there be real cause, or should H.M. have invincible objection I suppose the matter would not be worth a contest, *but* the objection should not I think at once be accepted without any reasons. Possibly Arch may have used disrespectful language about Royalty.

22. Th. [*Grand Hotel, Biarritz*]

We reached the *Grand* at Biarritz at 7 A.M. and got some sleep. It was daylight before 7 and a brilliant morning. I was however troubled with lumbago and kept very quiet. Wrote to Lady Aberdeen. Read as yesterday.

23 Fr.

Wrote to Mr R. Brett—Rev. Mr Ingram—. . . . . . .—and minutes. Drove to the Adour. Read as yesterday, and Brett's [blank.][1] Daylight at 5. P.M. We seem to gain *at least* 1½ hour as compared with London. Saw Mr Shand.[2]

24. Sat.

Wrote to Sec. Bayonne Library—Mr E. Fawcett[3]—Mr . . . . .—and minutes. Read Herodotus—Mr Brett—Mismer Monde Mussulman[4]—Curate of Rigg.[5] Drive with the party. Lumbago intruding. Saw Mr Shand.

25. Xm Day.

Ch 11 AM and H.C.—Rain frightened me [from going out again] in aft. Read Curate of Rigg—Whyte's Lecture on Law[6]—Lecture on St Peter[7]—Pollock on the P. Church History.[8] Saw Mr Shand.

26. (St Steph.) M.

Wrote to E. Fawcett—& minutes. Lumbago better. Sleep I hope re-established. The sea, as ever, glorious. Drive with the party to the Games. Heard the admirable band of the 19th. Read Herodotus—Footprints of Statesman—A sacrifice to Honour.[9] Backgammon all these evenings with Mr A[rmitstead]. Saw Mr Shand.

[1] R. B. Brett had sent his *Footprints of statesmen during the eighteenth century in England* (1892); see Add MS 44549, f. 53.
[2] Shand (see 18 Aug. 92) accompanied Gladstone to Biarritz. He appears there to have acted as a genuinely *private* secretary, possibly paid for by Armitstead; his appointment was the subject of some dispute in the Gladstonian court; see West *P.D.*, 92. He retained a connection with the family after Gladstone's death.
[3] Edgar Fawcett, American novelist. See 26 Dec. 92.
[4] C. Mismer, *Souvenirs du monde musulman* (1892).
[5] *The curate of Rigg: a sketch of clerical life* (1890).
[6] Untraced; perhaps by Alexander White.
[7] Perhaps *Leaves from the life of the Apostle Peter* (1892).
[8] Untraced.
[9] Untraced.

Rel[igion].[1]

Without the law there is no sin, says the New Testament: and, in proportion as the Law is lofty pure and clear, the sin is wider, deeper, more intense, more poisonous to the whole being of the sinner.

We read in the first Book of Herodotus strange and horrible things concerning the use of women among Lydians, Assyrians, Massagetae. And yet, with and by them, it does not appear that the whole being of these nations was destroyed. There remained in part what was noble and manful. But the sins of Christians are far beyond those of heathens. It seems as if the force of depraved imagination had, *materially*, carried them much further. But besides extension of the range it seems as if they went deeper into the man, got at the very centre of his being, made him tenfold a rebel, placed him in greater nearness to the evil ones. *Corruptio optimi pessima*[2] is not a mere figure of speech.

To E. FAWCETT, 26 December 1892.   Add MS 44549, f. 54.

I thank you both for the work which you have been good enough to present to me[3] and for the kind words with which you have accompanied it, unduly self disparaging though they are.

The purpose of your book is I understand to draw a portrait of the social life of America, or at least of New York which I take to be at present its chief social centre; and this purpose is one, as I have long considered, of the very highest interest for the world at large, and especially for the English speaking portion of it. On this account also I feel myself your debtor, though the picture you have given is a somewhat painful one in some of its highest aspects.

27. *Tu. St J.*

Wrote on Olympian religion. Read Herodotus. Drive to Bayonne & cardleaving. Saw Mr Shand—Freiherr von Rammingen. Read also A Sacrifice to Honour— Monde Mussulman—finished Mr Brett. Backgammon with Mr A.

28. *Wed.*

Wrote to Mrs Walker—J. Morley—and minutes. Long and pleasant drive to Cambo & its beautiful river glen. Capped verses with C. Saw Rev. Mr Broad[4]— in rather broken health. Saw Mr Shand. To Bayonne for calls of ceremony &c. Backgammon with Mr A. Read Herod.—finished a Sacrifice to Honour: a singularly bad tho' evidently well meaning novel. A little done on Hor[ace] Od. Transl.[5]—But how difficult!

To J. MORLEY, Irish secretary, 28 December 1892.   Add MS 44257, f. 69.

Since hearing of the outrage in Dublin[6] (wh. was not known here by the first telegram to Sir J. Pender till 40 hours after it had happened[ )], I have been impelled to write & yet

---

[1] Holograph dated 26 December 1892; Add MS 44774, f. 190.

[2] The corruption of the best is the worst: the fallen saint is the worst kind of sinner.

[3] See 20 Dec. 92.   [4] G. E. Broade, anglican chaplain in Biarritz; see 20 Dec. 91.

[5] See 14 July 92.

[6] 'a dynamite explosion close under the walls of the Castle [in Dublin]', and a constable, Synnott, killed by it; reported by Morley by letter on 25 December, Add MS 44257, f. 64, with the comment, 'This is, I believe, the first occasion on which life has been lost by dynamite in the United Kingdom. . . . Tho' its political significance is not very great, its effects on British opinion cannot be good. . . .'

held back by understanding so little of it except our strong sympathy with you personally, for it is indeed trying at a time when you are in the midst of such hard & grave work, from which none can relieve you: & then its being on your birthday though on the latest hour of it seems to give it an edge.

I read the first sentence of the Article in the "Times", so base & therefore so appropriate,[1] & got no further—it is however well that if this was to happen it did not happen on the back of a Ridgway removal, or an Egan release.

What strikes me as strange is that the assassins (for all dynamiters are such) should seem to have had in aim the rank & file of the police (if so it be) & not to have aimed at higher game.

Doubtless either Nationalists or Parnellites would be delighted to help in detection, if they could—& with reason. It is a serious blow to them & a blow to Ireland & to us mainly through them. As to the true agencies at work, I suppose we have to look to America, where the dregs of Irishism (our creation) safely skulk. Now to baser matter. I have confidence in the Sea & it is ever kind to me.

I have been bothered a little with lumbago due to my laying aside my fur (I think furs not a little dangerous) but it is better, & my sleep is *good*. We are going off to Cambo for a drive & having made the Rammingen acquaintance are in for an interview tomorrow.[2]

The Paris news has been deplorable. I presume the state of things there holds back any application about Egypt.

29. Th.

Wrote to Mr Rolfe—Mrs Ad. Acton—M. Dvar—Marchesa Theodoli[3]—and minutes. Visit to Princess L. Von Rammingen. Very particularly pleased. Tea with the Stapyltons. Saw Sir J. Pender—Mr Shand. Visited Q. of Serbia's new house. Backgammon with Mr A. Read Herod.—Monde Mussulman—Tannhäuser[4]—L.T. on Ld Tollemache.[5]

Eighty three birthdays! What responsibilities have old men as such for prolonged and multiplied opportunity. And what have I, as among old men. What openings, what cares, what blessings, and what sins. Even this trip, this place, is no small addition. May God at the length give me a true self knowledge. I have it not yet.

30. Fr.

Wrote to The Speaker—Mr Tollemache—Mr Howorth MP.—Mr Fullarton—& minutes. Read Euterpè[6]—Monde Mussulman—Tannhäuser finished much

---

[1] Probably the leader of 27 December 1892, which argued that Synnott's death was the result of Gladstone's 'yielding to terrorism . . . [home rule was] a recognition of the *chanteur* and the blackmailer' [in fact in the third sentence].

[2] Morley replied, 30 December, Add MS 44257, f. 71, that 'the opinion among the police experts is that it is undoubtedly the work of a small low gang, upon whom they will clap handcuffs in reasonable time. We are all perfectly cool and steady here [Dublin]. . . . The Parnellites are undoubtedly the persons most hardly hit by the crime in Ireland; but we shall suffer to some extent in England.'

[3] Regretting his inability to review her *Scenes from Roman life. Under pressure*, 2v. (1892), which had sold badly; see Add MS 44549, f. 54. See 17 October 92.

[4] R. W. M. Fullarton, *Tannhäuser* (1893); sent by the author; see Add MS 44549, f. 54.

[5] L. A. Tollemache, 'Lord Tollemache and his anecdotes', *F.R.* lviii. 74 (July 1892).

[6] i.e. in Herodotus.

pleased. Backgammon with Mr A. Mr Webster came.[1] Walk with him. Concerned not to find him in greater strength.

31. Sat.

Wrote to Ld Rosebery—A.E. West—Dr Robertson—Mr D. Nutt—Mr Coates[2]—& minutes. Drive to luncheon with Mrs Dundas, near St Jean de Luz: noble view.

And so is drawn the curtain of the year. For me in some ways a tremendous year. A too bright vision dispelled. An increased responsibility undertaken, with diminished means. That *I* of all men should have come to a position which in its way is perhaps without parallel. But the *stays* are wonderful, almost incredible. The fountain of mercies still inexhaustible. *Cum Te patiar*.[3] Lead me through duty into rest.

---

[1] See 5 Jan. 92.
[2] Declining C. H. Coate's invitation again to stand for the Rectorship of Edinburgh University; Add MS 44549, f. 54.
[3] 'I will suffer with Thee.'

Biarritz January 1893.

1 S. Circumcision.

Ch 11 A.M. with H.C.—5½ P.M. Wrote to Duke of Argyll—Sir W. Harcourt—K. & Q. of Belgians Tel. Read Robertson, Religion of Israel[1]—Loraine, Battle of Belief.[2] Walk with party.

To Sir W. V. HARCOURT, chancellor of the exchequer,   MS Harcourt dep. 13, f. 1.
1 January 1893.

Many thanks for your letter,[3] and the good wishes, which we not less heartily return.

This is indeed so far as I can judge a place of great sanitary methods: indeed the sea is always kind to me.

I have reflected with sorrow on the menacing prospects of the Estimates which you mentioned to me. Must you altogether renounce the hope of getting them somewhat restrained? Both the heads are men who I think might not dislike being supported against professional oppressors.

The thing really to be dreaded is that we may cease to pay off debt. As long as the process of liquidation is continued at a tolerable or at least appreciable rate, the evils of extravagance though great are within bounds.

I see you do not mean to come up till the 10th. In this matter I *dress* to your model and shall now adjust my plans accordingly. I had meant to be a little sooner. But I thankfully accept the elongation: and I really believe our work is well forward.

You seem to have had severe weather. The days of the old open winter seem to have gone away altogether. So much the worse for us old folks already frozen within.[4]

2. M.

Wrote to J. Morley l. & tel.—Mr Menken—Dr Greenhill—Mr Reader—& minutes. Read The Medicine Lady[5]—Herod. Euterpe—Thalia[6]—Reports on the Dover borings[7]—Monde Mussulman.[8] Thermometre 28% & cold wind. Dined with the Tollemaches: much conversation.[9]

To J. MORLEY, Irish secretary, 2 January 1893.   Add MS 44257, f. 73.

Having just received yours, I telegraph to say I am due in London on 10th. This has resulted from a letter of Harcourt's in which he tells me that he means to go up "about" the 10th. I have replied that I "dress" to him in this matter.

[1] J. Robertson, *The early religion of Israel* (1892).
[2] N. Loraine, *The battle of belief* (1891).
[3] Of 29 December, birthday greetings; Add MS 44202, f. 298.
[4] Harcourt replied, 4 January, MS Harcourt dep. 13, f. 3, that his efforts had failed to prevent a War Office 'excess of at least £250,000 and the Admiralty of £50,000' in supplementary estimates.
[5] L. T. Meade, *The Medicine Lady*, 3v. (1892–3).
[6] i.e. in Herodotus.
[7] i.e. on borings for the proposed Channel Tunnel.
[8] See 24 Dec. 92.
[9] Recorded in Tollemache, *Talks*, 70.

As regards the explosion[1] it will do good (except as to the slaughter) if it at length brings home to the Parnelite mind the insane folly of their course. In England it is indeterminately but really bad. It is one of a series of taps of the hammer, each of them small, but all driving the nail the wrong way. The rascal "Times" knows its business.

I am glad you are well & I hope Mrs. Morley is also well & pleased with Ireland up to the deplorable outrage. It would be unfortunate were Sexton to get at Welby's personal opinion that we ought not to take from Ireland as Imperial Contribution more than what is now the residue of her taxes after defraying the enormous Civil charges at the present rate.

That is to say that besides making a clear income for her of 400m per ann. at Imperial cost, we are to abjure the whole benefit (so I think it would come out) of the very large economies which will almost spontaneously be made.

3. Tu.

Saw Mr Shand & worked on minutes. To Bayonne for calls. Read Thalia—Medicine Lady—Michaud, La Theologie[2]—Monde Mussulman (finished). Visited the Club with Mr A[rmitstead]. Weighed and was recorded 12.9 Proh pudor.

4. Wed.

$10\frac{3}{4}$–$4\frac{1}{2}$. To Sarre.[3] A beautiful spot, Mr Webster's family & home most cheering, most edifying. Saw Mr Shand & wrote minutes. Read Thalia—Medicine Lady—and [blank.]

5. Th.

Wrote to Mr Mayhew—Lady Napier—Mr Howell—Mr Stanley—Mr Mayhew—and minutes. Saw Mr Shand. Walk with the party. The easterly winds seem to have taken all the distinctive character off the sea for the moment. Read Thalia—The Medicine Lady—Rev. Myers on Poets—not over clerical![4]

To Sir W. V. HARCOURT, chancellor of the exchequer,   MS Harcourt dep. 13, f. 5.
5 January 1893. '*Private.*'

I send you herewith a Review containing an article on Uganda,[5] a *glance* at which I think you may find really refreshing. But you will notice that the writer is not bold enough to give his name.

I have summoned a Cabinet for the 11th at 3, which I hope you may not find too early. Cold enough here though less than with you.

To LORD KIMBERLEY, lord president and Indian secretary,   Add MS 44549, f. 55.
5 January 1892.

I only postponed speaking to you definitely on the Leadership in the Lords because I had one or two previous references on the matter still to make. I am now in a condition to

[1] See to Morley, 28 Dec. 92.
[2] E. Michaud, *La théologie et le temps présent* (1893).
[3] i.e. Sare, where Wentworth Webster (see 5 Jan. 92) was anglican chaplain.
[4] Rev. F. W. H. Myers, 'Modern poets and the meaning of life', *N.C.*, xxxiii. 93 (January 1893).
[5] Identified from secretary's docket as Philo-Africanus, 'Uganda', in *Imperial and Asiatic Quarterly Review*, v. 55; praising the decision to send a Commissioner and refuting point-by-point the argument for annexation.

ask that you will agree to continue, or resume, whichever it may be, the duties of the office which I fear will not be in all respects less arduous from the fact that its followers are few. Be they what they may I am confident that they will be discharged by you in such a way as to win the confidence & approval of all our friends, & not of our friends alone. You will I have no doubt make known to me from time to time all that may require it, & as to any matters now depending, I shall be happy to see you as soon as you can make it convenient.[1]

6. *Fr. Epiph.*

Dearest C.s birthday. We sent together to Early Communion. Seemingly I caught some cold. Saw Mr Shand—Sir W. Des Voeux.[2] Went to bed at 3 P.M. & worked by Salicine.[3] Read Thalia—Medicine Lady—Tried again at Horace's Odes for translation.

7. *Sat.*

Bed till 3.30. Wrote by dictation to Sir W. Harcourt—D. of Argyll—Mr Mundella—Mrs Rendel. Mr Tollemache dined. Much conversation with him.[4] Backgammon with Mr A: yesterday & today.

To Sir W. V. HARCOURT, chancellor of the exchequer,   MS Harcourt dep. 13, f. 6.
7 January 1893.[5]

I am much concerned to learn from your letter of the 4th[6] that the plague of Supplemental Estimates is upon us—in any case they are awkward, but if they form real additions to the outlay originally contemplated they are mischievous in the highest degree & tend insidiously to undermine the rights of the H. of Commons.

If as I have heard the late government seriously set their face against them, they deserve great credit for it & it will be deplorable if we depart from a good precedent set by them.

I should be glad if you would call for a return showing the amount of Supplemental Estimates & also of Army & Navy Expenditures during the past 10 years.

If the figures justify your apprehensions can we not make some expostulation with the Heads? You may depend upon my earnest support whatever it may be worth.
[P.S.] A little cold: it is departing from me.

8. *1 S. Ep.*

Reluctantly kept the house in view of the journey: & my bed till 4 P.M. Read Bungener Sermons sous Louis XV[7]—Medicine Lady (finished)—Robertson Religion of Israel. Prayers solitary.

---

[1] Kimberley wrote on 10 January, Add MS 44229, f. 69, of his amazement at an announcement that he was to give a dinner as leader of the House of Lords; he had made every endeavour, unsuccessfully, to persuade Rosebery to take the leadership, 'believing it to be most important for the interests of the Govt. that he should lead'. On 12 January, ibid., f. 71, he wrote that, Rosebery having definitely refused, 'I feel I have no alternative but to conform to your wishes'.
[2] Sir (George) William Des Voeux, 1834–1909; retired colonial governor.
[3] Medicine obtained from willow bark, used as a substitute for quinine.
[4] See Tollemache, *Talks*, 78.
[5] Written by amanuensis, signed by Gladstone.
[6] See 1 Jan. 93n.
[7] L. L. F. Bungener, *Trois sermons sous Louis XV*, 3v. (1850): a novel.

9. M. [On train]

Rose at ten; had profited both by medicine and rest: able to face the journey. Off at 5.30 P.M. Packed. Saw Mr Shand—Mr Tollemache. Read Herod. (finished Thalia)—Hoche et l'Irlande[1]—Sermons sous L. XV. Worked on Horace a little.

10. Tu. [London]

Rough rails: we fared tolerably but variously in sleep. Breakfast in Paris. Passage passable. Downing St 6.30. Saw Sir A. West—Herbert G. Worked on Horace. Read Hoche et l'Irlande. And thank God for the manner in which Biarritz has done its work for me. My sleep is quite restored.

11. Wed.

Wrote to Mr Cook—Sir W. Harcourt—Ld Kimberley—The Queen l.l.—& minutes. Saw Sir A. West—Private Secretaries—Sir W. Harcourt—Ld Ripon—Mr Morley l.l.—Ld Chancr—Ld Kimberley—Herbert J.G. (on Lecture). Cabinet 3–5½. 7 to dinner.

Cabinet. Wed. Jan. 11. 1893. 3 PM.[2]
1. Sir W. Harcourt gave notice of a probable deficit of 1¾ ⋒.
2. The Irish Bill: Preamble & Sections 1–5.

To Sir W. V. HARCOURT, chancellor of the exchequer,   MS Harcourt dep. 13, f. 9.
11 January 1893. '*Immed.*'
  1. Please to say 1 o'clock.[3] I shall have more leisure.
2. On the forecasts I will only say that they only have full authority, I think, at a later date, & when including the views of the Revenue Departments. But I quite agree that they may have their use at the present moment.
3. Please to read an able letter from the Speaker which however requires no present action.
4. I shall be glad to speak to you on the Lords Leadership. See Kimberley's letter.
5. Also about a supposed or asserted intention of Labouchere to move an amendment on Uganda.[4]

12. Th.

Wrote to J. Morley—The Speaker—Ld Rosebery—Ld Norton—Mr A. Acton—Mr Max Muller—Sir A. Clark—Mr Armitstead—and minutes. Saw Sir A. West—Mr Morley—Ld Kimberley. Visited Mr Adams Acton's Studio to inspect the two

---

  [1] Probably G. Escaude, *Hoche en Irlande 1795–1798* (1888).
  [2] Add MS 44648, f. 58. 'The Cabinet agreed to the first five Clauses of the Bill after close attention and with some amendments'; CAB 41/22/23.
  [3] Harcourt wrote at 11 a.m. to request a decision: 'I have a *very bad* financial outlook to deal with', a deficit calculated by Hamilton as £1,720,000; 'I am being pushed on all sides by all my colleagues for increased expenditure. I will ask leave at the commencement of the Cabinet today just to state the figures of E. Hamilton'; Add MS 44203, f. 10.
  [4] Harcourt replied next day, ibid., f. 12, that that day he learned Labouchere planned a motion in concert with Dilke. See 3 Feb. 93.

small busts.[1]. Read Sermons sous Louis XV—Hist. of White's Club.[2] Saw Lucy Cavendish.

To R. W. BUCHANAN, 12 January 1893. '*Private.*'   Add MS 44549, f. 57.

I thank you sincerely for your kind gift.[3] It reaches me not at the most fortunate moment of the year, for this is a time of much pressure in preparation for the Session. It will not however be my fault if I do not soon make myself I dare not say master of it but well acquainted with it, so far as failing sight & the fogs of London will permit. I agree with you that Humanity has need of supreme pity, & rejoice that you stand on the basis 'opposed to the material'. For my own part however, while not expecting on this side the tomb any solution of the problems deep & wide that surround us, I am rooted in historical Christianity, elastic enough for me, not only as a working hypothesis but as a working remedy.

To Sir A. CLARK, physician, 12 January 1893.   Add MS 44549, f. 55.

Biarritz has been very kind to me and the sleep has been completely restored.

I venture to send to your door (it will I hope be on Saturday) a modest but we think excellent bust of me by Mr. Adams Acton.[4] I hope you will kindly give it a place as another favour to an old & obliged patient who has profited so much by your care your skill & your inexhaustible fund of kindness. Pray do not trouble to reply, but graciously admit the intruder.

To J. MORLEY, Irish secretary, 12 January 1893.   Add MS 44549, f. 55.

Here is a correspondence between Harcourt & Chamberlain which requires attention without delay. And a Memm. of mine about the Irish members. I am clear that they ought to change & if they do not change *they* will create a very disagreeable dilemma. Cannot they do what O'Connell did? He sat on the Opposition side during the Grey Govt.—on the Govt. side below the gangway (mostly, if not always) during the Melbourne. Can you see me on this?

13. Fr.

Wrote to The Queen l.l.—Sir W. Harcourt—Mr Downing & minutes. Cabinet 2½-5¼. Saw Sir A. West—Mr M'Carthy *cum* Mr Morley—Mr Morley. The difficulties of retention are more & more felt: but we have no choice. Read Hoche et l'Irlande—Sermons sous Louis XV. Garrick Theatre in evg.[5]

Cabinet. Friday Jan. 13. 93. 2½ PM.[6]
1. Number of Irish members at Westminster to be proportional to population.
2. Shall the Irish members be excluded from voting (on general terms) on exclusively British questions. Agreed to.
Harcourt, Fowler, Asquith, Acland, *dissentient*.

[1] 'Sculpture Portraits' of Gladstone (replicas costing £67.10.0 made from 'the model made in Rome in the year 1868') by J. Adams Acton for Sir A. Clark and G. Armitstead; see Adams Acton to Gladstone, 13 January 1893, Add MS 44517, f. 10.
[2] W. B. Boulton, *The history of White's*, 2v. (1892).
[3] A copy of his most recent poem, *The Wandering Jew. A Christmas Carol* (1893), 'in which I have endeavoured to express in a sort of colossal cipher the present position of Christ in relation to Humanity'; Add MS 44517, f. 7.
[4] See note 1 above.
[5] To see R. C. Carton's comedy, 'Robin Goodfellow', with Hare, Forbes Robertson and Norreys.
[6] Add MS 44648, f. 59.

Question reserved between a higher qualification and nomination.
Home rule the neutral[?] change at Westminster.
  consequential
  exceptional

To Sir W. V. HARCOURT, chancellor of the exchequer,   MS Harcourt dep. 13, f. 11.
13 January 1893. '*Private.*'
1. I return the Chamberlain correspondence. His case is strong. We are however trying
whether the Irish will finally refuse to move.[1]
2. I should be very glad for a word about L. & Uganda. Stanley wishes for the Company
but disapproves of Government occupation.[2]

14. Sat

Wrote minutes. Wrote paper on Irish Finance. Saw Sir A. West—Mr Morley—
Do cum Sir [blank] Jenkins[3]—Do cum E. Hamilton & Sir R. Welby—Lady Stan-
ley. Drive with C. Read Sermons &c.—Bp Coplestone on Buddhism[4]—History of
White's.

That the only justifying ground of taxation is to meet public charges of necessity or high
utility.
    That the first duty of the taxing authority is to ascertain on this basis the amount of
public charge and then to find the best means of raising the revenues necessary to meet
it.
    That in the case of the Bill for the government of Ireland our first financial duty is to fix
on equitable grounds the contribution which Ireland ought to make towards Imperial as
distinct from local expenditure because this concerns the obligations to the Empire as a
whole, and because the purposes of Imperial expenditure are matters of primary necessity viz.
Obligations of honour as to the National Debt
Provision for safety by national Defence
Provision for the supreme power which is necessary for the organised existence of the
nation.
    That the contribution of Ireland to Imperial expenditure should be governed by an
equitable consideration of comparative resources.
    That the most convenient form for it is a quotal part rising or falling with the increase
or decrease of the Imperial charge.
    That after Ireland has been credited with the whole of the revenue which she yields,
and debited with her share of Imperial charge, the next step in order is to consider
whether the residue is sufficient to meet the local charges, including the new Government which is to controul her local Affairs.
    Estimating the local charges according to the present provision excepting as to the
Constabulary which Great Britain was to provide in 1886, with a contribution of one million from Ireland, and taking the Imperial quota due from her at one twentieth part, it

[1] On seating in the Commons.
[2] See to Harcourt, 11 Jan. 93n.
[3] Sir John Jones Jenkins, 1835–1915; of Swansea, liberal (unionist) M.P. Carmarthen district
1882–86, 1895–1900; kt. 1881.
[4] R. S. Copleston, *Buddhism, primitive and present, in Magadha and in Ceylon* (1892)

appears that the revenue she yields will after meeting these charges leave only a surplus of £48,000.

If as is plain such a sum is quite insufficient for providing her new domestic government, and if for this purpose so large a sum as £400,000 is reasonably required, it follows that under the new arrangement a sum of £350,000 and upwards per ann. has to be provided at the expence of Great Britain for the pecuniary benefit of Ireland.

It is submitted that this payment should be so adjusted that it may be gradually recouped out of savings on the present enormous charges of Irish civil Government. If instead of one million we take only £750m from Ireland for police, we add £250000 to the sum available for the charges of the new Government. If we also relieve Ireland for a time of a portion of her contribution to the Sinking Fund, by making it $\frac{3}{8}$ instead of $\frac{6}{8}$ per Cent, that contribution being at $\frac{6}{8} = £250000$, we thus obtain a further sum of £125000 per ann. and raise the sum available for the new Irish Government to £423,000 per ann.

Great Britain would be gradually relieved from this charge, as the cost of the Constabulary was progressively reduced. When it had been reduced by more than £375000 per ann. Great Britain would begin to gain by the new arrangement. The Sinking Fund under which Ireland would only pay $\frac{3}{8}$ per Cent, would cost Great Britain an increase of 125m forming part of the £375m.

When Mr Goschen's reduction of interest on the three per Cent takes final effect at a fixed date (in 19[blank]) the Irish contribution should be readjusted so as to equal the 250m now paid by Ireland.

Of the additional charge of 625m Ireland would be recouped (about 70m?) by her share of the reduction then arising in Debt charge.

All further means, if any, required for the internal government of Ireland must be found (a) by economies (b) in growth of revenue, (c) in new taxes.

WEG Jan 14. 92 [sc. 1893][1]

15. 2 S. Epiph.

Ch. Royal mg. Guards Chapel evg. Saw Canon MacColl—Sir A. Clark. Read Sermons &c.—Bp Westcott on Gospel of Life[2]—P. Vannutelli on Russian Ch.[3]

16. M.

Wrote to Mr Godley—Mr Hibbert—The Queen—Sir W. Harcourt—Ld Rosebery—and minutes. Dined with Mr Morley. Cabinet Committee 12–1$\frac{3}{4}$. Cabinet 2$\frac{1}{2}$–5$\frac{1}{4}$. Sir W. H. pursued his usual lines in the usual way. Special conversation afterwards with J. Morley. Saw Sir A. West—Mr Morley—Sir W. Harcourt—Ld Kimberley. Read Hoche et l'Irlande. Read 'Sermons' (finished) & Irlande.

Cabinet. Jan. 16. 93. Mond. 2$\frac{1}{2}$ PM.[4]
1. Egypt. Telegraph to Ld. Cromer.[5]
2. Irish Bill.
   Exclusion Clauses (now 6, 7). Clause 7 as recommended agreed to.
   Alteration of Legisl. Clause. Old Clause 6 adopted—with new restraints.

[1] Holograph; Add MS 44775, f. 13.   [2] B. F. Westcott, *The gospel of life* (1892).
[3] V. Vannutelli, *Studio comparativo fra l'Oriente e l'Occidente* (1892).   [4] Add MS 44648, f. 62.
[5] Cromer had reported Abbas II's '*coup d'état*, which swept all the Anglophile Ministers out of the Cabinet, and which was manifestly intended to deal a decisive blow to British influence'; this day's Cabinet informed Cromer: 'We cannot, therefore, sanction the proposed nomination of Fakhry Pasha'; Cromer, *Abbas II*, 22–4. See next day.

⟨Police⟩
Council—composition of. General conversation.
3. Finance. Preliminary conversation. Harcourt read his paper of objections.[1]

To Sir W. V. HARCOURT, chancellor of the exchequer,   MS Harcourt dep. 13, f. 21.
16 January 1893.

We have to consider today in Cabinet-Committee matters connected with retention. If we get through rapidly as I *hope* we may for hard work was done on Saturday—I shall be at your command before the Cabinet.

With others I have worked hard to get the Finance of the Irish Bill into such a shape as to present to you the points most essential for your consideration without a mass of detail which you will learn elsewhere.

I now confine myself to main propositions.

There are two *essentials*.

1. What quota should Ireland pay under a standing provision of the Bill towards Imperial Expenditure.

2. What balance shall we by *manipulation* of present charges provide for her (wholly or mainly out of the British pocket) to enable her to start her Local Government.

(I personally am in favour of reimbursing eventually, under the machinery of the Bill[,] the British pocket).

My opinion also is that detailed negotiation on particulars of Finance between the Cabinet and the Irish is impossible—& that the Cabinet should at once present to them not quite but something near an *ultimatum.*

To LORD ROSEBERY, foreign secretary, 16 January 1893.   N.L.S. 10026, f. 3.
'*Immediate.*'

It has long been on my mind that a conspiracy against the occupation was brewing in Egypt. The French communication has I presume been delayed by internal affairs. An attempt is now made with boldness apart from French aid.

I am clear that the Cabinet should be consulted—& that you must have precedence of the Irish Bill.

It would be well to present to them the extract from Ld. Granville to which Cromer refers.

His principle seems sound & necessary. But what are our executory means? Do his words[2] on the opposite side include the use of force? *Here* difficulty might arise; we are in Egypt under the old dual understanding of Salisbury's, to support a native Government or some such phrase.

17. Tu.

Wrote to Mr Morley—Sir H. Ponsonby—The Queen—Ld Rosebery l.l.l.—and minutes. Ten to dinner. Alarming proposal from Egypt. Sudden Cabinet 5 PM—6½. Saw Sir A. West l.l.—Sir W. Harcourt—do *cum* Ld Rosebery—Mr Marjor.—Mr Asquith—Mr Morley—Mr Bowen. Read Hoche et l'Irlande.

[1] In MS Harcourt dep. 162; see 19 Jan. 93n.
[2] 'to take—charge essential that the K. . . whatever cost.'; secretary's note on the copy in Add MS 44549, f. 56.

Cabinet. Tues. Jan. 17. 93. 5 PM. (Summoned 3 PM.).[1]
On reply & proposal from Lord Cromer.[2] Plan universally disapproved. Two telegraphs adopted in preference to W.E.G.'s. Suggestion for fear Khedive should catch at 'the Powers'.

[*Gladstone's draft*:]
In the event of Khedive's refusal to withdraw[:] Inform him in view of our present responsibilities for the peace and safety of Egypt, and as we cannot agree to his proposal, or be bound to recognise or adopt any of its consequences, that it is in our opinion his absolute duty to postpone until after a reasonable time has been given for the Queen's Government to consult the Powers on the fundamental change in the situation of Egypt which would be brought about by persistence in the present intentions of the Khedive to depart from the line of conduct which through the last ten years has been pursued by his predecessor and himself. Should the Khedive decline this proposal he must be held solely responsible for the grave consequences which may follow.

Egypt[3]
We went to Egypt with a military force to give our support to a native government.

That support has been given against the rebellion of Arabi, and against aggression from without.

We could not have undertaken this responsibility except for a Government whose measures in all leading particulars we could approve and defend.

For ten years, by the free consent of the Khedive, and without loss of his dignity, we have enjoyed the necessary share in the direction of the government, have been consulted in all matters of importance, and have maintained the peace and safety of the country: in connection with which there have been effected great financial reforms, and a marked increase in prosperity.

The present Khedive departing from the course pursued for ten years has decided on a change by the dismissal of the Prime Minister, which we think to be of vital importance and which we entirely disapprove. This has been done without consulting us.

Lord Cromer proposes to take military possession of the offices and to undertake their provisional administration should the Khedive persist in his resolution. He also proposes to take possession of the Telegraph and thus to place under our controul all international communications which might be conducted through it.

This is to take possession of the country.
But 1. We went to Egypt engaged to *support* a native government.
    2. Every question of the disposal of territory within the Turkish Empire is reserved to the Great Powers by the Treaty of Paris. Consultation with the Powers seems to be required

[1] Add MS 44648, f. 65.
[2] On this afternoon, Cromer reached an agreement with Tigrane Pasha: Fakhry Pasha (regarded as Anglophobe) was to be dismissed, with Riaz Pasha becoming Prime Minister, and the Khedive was to make a public statement of his wish to cultivate friendly relations with Britain and his willingness to adopt British advice. Next day, Cromer saw the Khedive: 'matters were settled in conformity with the arrangement made on the previous evening'; Cromer, *Abbas II*, 27; Riaz Pasha in fact proved to be strongly Anglophobe. Cromer's tel. no. 22 requested that if the Khedive refused to dismiss Fakhry, military possession should be taken of the offices, the telegraph seized, and provisional ministers appointed; 'the Cabinet deliberated, and felt that these proposals were not only of a very extreme character but open to much doubt and objection on the grounds of law not less than of policy'; CAB 41/22/26.
[3] Initialled and dated, at the end, 7 January 1893, and, at the start, 17 January 1893 (the latter being the more probable); Add MS 44775, f. 28.

To J. MORLEY, Irish secretary, 17 January 1893. '*Secret*'.   Add MS 44257, f. 77.

I wish to supply a word which ought not to have been omitted in my conversation with you after the Cabinet. It is with few men only that such conversations are possible, & they ought when they occur to be complete. The omitted word is this that you continue to be as you have been all along a prop & main prop to me in a task which adventitious as well as natural causes at present render especially arduous.

[P.S.] I ought also to ask your pardon for liberty taken, & to say that in my case free speech is really the measure & the proof of confidence.

To LORD ROSEBERY, foreign secretary, 17 January 1893. 'No. 1.'   N.L.S. 10026, f. 9.

[Letter 1:]   With regard to Harcourt's paper, I would suggest your asking to see the MS which he read to the Cabinet: all the others heard it throughout. I shall be very glad if it can be printed before tomorrow's Cabinet but some rumour has reached me that the printers are very hard pressed. I have written some thing on the finance but I do not think of having it printed. In the main it is conversation to which we must look.

[P.S.] The *long* report with the demands of the Irish members makes the heavy demand as I imagine on the press.

[Letter 2:]   I have concurred freely in the two telegrams sent tonight to Lord Cromer, and this note will require no notice, but I wish you to know that one motive which led me to suggest sending a positive proposal to Lord Cromer was my belief that it would place him personally in less difficulty as the instrument of our policy, than our putting his measure aside without giving him any other. However if he takes kindly to the request for suggestion the purpose may be gained.

18. Wed.

Wrote to The Queen—Sir W. Harcourt—Mr Lambert MP—Mr Beaufoy MP.—& minutes. Saw Sir A. West—Mr Marjoribanks—Mr Morley ($2\frac{1}{2}$ hours) l.l.—Ld Chancellor (from Osborne)—H.N.G. (from Valescure). Cabinet $2\frac{1}{2}$-5. Wrote Mem. on Harcourt's financial plan: proposed in a spirit of furtherance. Read Hoche et l'Irlande—Irish Documents 1795-1804.[1]

Cabinet. Wed. Jan. 18. 93. $2\frac{1}{2}$ P.M.[2]
1. Speech Council: ask Jan. 30.
2. Khedive's proposal of Riaz Pasha accepted.[3] Rouillet—Private Secretary—to have him for 3 months.
   Ld Rosebery pointed out venom[?] of pressure.
   a. refusal to recognise.
   b. Support of investiture at Constantinople.
   c. Increase army of occupation.
   Ld R. will telegraph satisfaction—take note of K's position[?] & desire C[romer] to communicate it.
3. Harcourt's plan—to give them $5\frac{1}{2}$ ₥ & taxing[?] power other than Customs & Excise.

[1] J. T. Gilbert, *Documents relating to Ireland, 1795-1804* (1893).
[2] Add MS 44648, f. 68.
[3] This day's telegrams printed, with Gladstone's annotations, at Add MS 44635, f. 92.

18 January 1893.[1]

Cabinet determines principles as follows for

✓ 1. Constabulary.

✓ 2. Savings for civil service.

✓ 3. Constitutional questions. Omit Clause 2 & 3: final alteration if possible.

✓ 4. Who shall be the first Irish legislature. Cabinet[?] thinks there should be re-election. If Irish MPs greatly oppose, we may consider[2]

    5.✓ Savings for Judges.

    6.✓ Appointment of new Judges during a term—7 years.

    7.✓ Cl. 35 (Power of Irish Parlt. to alter)

    8. + Constitution of the Electorate for Council.

        nomination gone[?]. constituency $\frac{1}{3}$ to $\frac{1}{2}$ the present constituency.

✓ 9. Renovation of a Land Act.

+ Not to exceed 36 & then joint voting to get rid of deadlock.

Advantages of Sir W. Harcourt's plan.

1. It relieves Ireland from the inconvenience which might attend changes of Customs and Excise Duties by Imperial authority, in their operation on the immediate financial wants and supplies of Ireland to which they might not be adapted.

2. It relieves the operation of the Bill from an encumbering process of scrutiny in order to ascertain from time to time the amount of difference between the true revenue of Ireland and the amount locally collected there.

3. It gets rid in the main, though not altogether of what may be called a dissight in the plan of the Bill under which the Viceroy would have to make frequent payments out of revenues collected and recognised as Irish to the English Exchequer.

4. It greatly simplifies the account between the two countries as the transaction would assume the form of a lump sum subject to two deductions only.

    a. (I assume, and I believe to be needful) the deduction of the estimated or ascertained amount of the Direct taxation, or taxation outside Customs & Excise, which I apprehend, should be handed over bodily to Irish authority.

    b. sums due for interest of advances,

        interest on Loans

        and the like.

        Both deductions resting on a very clear basis

5. It gets rid of the subject of the *quota* which in its nature affords much room for debate, and differences of opinion as to the means[?] by which Irish capacity to contribute to Imperial expenditure should be measured

6. A considerable abbreviation might probably be expected in a thorny and important portion of the Bill and the field of debate narrowed accordingly.

7. There would I think be considerable advantage, since we cannot hold by the proposals of 1886 on finance as they stood, in cutting ourselves clear, so to speak, of the wreckage, and so disembarrassing the case of much needless and perhaps injurious argument.

Disadvantages of the same plan

1. During the term of years for which the plan would operate without change, Ireland would take no benefit from any increase in the receipts from the Customs and Excise.

---

[1] Add MS 44648, f. 69.
[2] Final word illegible.

2. She would have no forcible motive for economy in the collection and administration of the Excise as the proceeds of the duty would only swell an Imperial fund.

3. It would impose a heavier burden upon the British taxpayer, who would have to find an available balance to the good of nearly the same amount for Irish government to start with, without any process of recouping from economies in the Constabulary by such as is provided by the Bill.

4. Might not some difficulty arise as to the constabulary? We are to pay to Ireland the whole cost of it: she is to vote for it as much as she pleases. Can we make sure of its being efficiently supported? This point I think requires attention.

5. The annual payment to Ireland would be reconsidered at the end of a short term of years: but it does not appear by what rule the readjustment would be guided: The payment is now to be determined by the ascertained amount of actual Irish charge for local purposes. This test would evidently disappear. What other would be available in lieu of it? The answer to this demand might be offered *alors comme alors*. It would not be satisfactory in point of reason. But the date when a solution of the problem would be wanted is somewhat distant. Would its distance perhaps induce disposition to acquiesce in an incomplete arrangement?[1]

To Sir W. V. HARCOURT, chancellor of the exchequer,   MS Harcourt dep. 13, f. 23.
18 January 1893.

On the Chamberlain letter

1. Is it necessary or convenient to refer to the *motives* of the Irish members in refusing if they refuse to cross.

2. I have never known an *arrangement* by the Government as to retiring Ministers: only the operation of an usage.

3. I strongly believe this usage was acted on by Mr Huskisson and his friends in 1828.
   These are the only observations that occur to me.

19. Th.

Wrote to Ld Spencer—Sir W. Harcourt—Scotts—Ld Kimberley—Mr Mundella—Sir H. Ponsonby—& minutes. Dined at Sir A. West's. Drive with C. Finished Hoche et l'Irlande. Read Irish Documents 1795–1804. Saw Sir A. West—Mr Morley—Do *cum* Welby & Hamilton. Worked on Irish Finance.

To Sir W. V. HARCOURT, chancellor of the exchequer,   MS Harcourt dep. 13, f. 30.
19 January 1893. '*Immediate*.'

I noted down last night what at first sight seemed to me the advantages of your plan, and the difficulties. I send my notes to run the gauntlet of Welby and Hamilton and pass

---

[1] Initialled and dated 18 January 1893; Add MS 44775, f. 32. Harcourt wrote this day, Add MS 44203, f. 15, objecting 'to the Irish financial scheme I hear propounded'. See Harcourt's mem. of 16 January, MS Harcourt dep. 162, arguing the proposed arrangement in the Bill 'involves a constant financial conflict between the two Parliaments' because indirect taxation for Ireland would be Imperially determined but direct not, and Britain would be unable to increase Irish direct taxation in wartime. Hamilton criticised Harcourt's alternative as limiting the authority of the Irish Parliament to the Postal Revenue; mem. of 20 January, MS Harcourt dep. 160, f. 26.

them on to you. There is one of a practical character about the Constabulary but there may be ways of surmounting it. Unquestionably the suggestion has in my eyes many advantages.

20. Fr.

Wrote to The Queen—Ld Rosebery l.l.l.—and minutes. Cabinet $2\frac{1}{2}$–$5\frac{1}{2}$. Saw Sir A. West—Mr Morley l.l.—Sir W. Harcourt—Then together—Mr Hamilton. Read Pearson.[1] Rosebery brought his boys "to ask my blessing". They go to school tomorrow.

Cabinet. Friday Jan. 20. 93. $2\frac{1}{2}$ P.M.[2]
1. Pope's Episcopal Jubilee. Salisbury's precedent. Advised[?] not propose to take any step.
2. Rosebery reported the French *protest*.
    Read the Cromer Telegrams.[3]
    Note[?] framed by Harcourt & amended—not a moment to apply pressure—words written by Rosebery amended and sent.
3. Local veto Bill. Minimum notice of 12 months.
We shall be prepared if necessity shall arise to increase the British garrison in Egypt but as we do not think the time propitious for an announcement[, Cromer to] request authority before making it.[4]

1 All Irish Revenues except the Revenue of Customs to be collected by the Irish Government.
2. The Revenue of Excise to be collected for account of the Imperial Exchequer.
3. But Ireland to be credited with 25% on all sums in excess of the present amount.
4. Excise & Customs duties to be regulated by Parliament and paid to the Exchequer.
5. Six millions to be allowed to Ireland to meet all the civil charges and provide a free[?] working balance: subject to the following conditions.
    (a) against it is to be charged the present amount of taxes received from Ireland, other than Customs & Excise; taken at £1250000.
    (b) special provisions in respect £1500000, the portion of the six millions allowed in respect of Constabulary.
    (c) There may also be charged against it items due from Ireland on other than Revenue Accounts.
6. All taxing powers except Custom & Excise to be given to Ireland.

Financial bearings

1. The present Irish Revenue being taken at 8ᵐ and Great Britain undertaking a charge of 6ᵐ will retain from Irish sources an annual sum of 2ᵐ available for Imperial Expenditure.
2. Ireland will have by way of free balance for commencing her domestic Government

[1] C. H. Pearson, *National life and character: a forecast* (1893).
[2] Add MS 44648, f. 70.
[3] Cromer reported Riaz Pasha's hostility and asked for an increase in the garrison; Cromer, *Abbas II*, 34, 37–8.
[4] Draft in Gladstone's hand, dated this day; Add MS 44648, f. 71. The Queen was informed of this decision; CAB 41/22/28.

1. Difference between 6m & the present amount of Civil Charges: 360m.
2. All retentions of Civil charge *including Constabulary* between the passing of the Act and the first balance-sheet, say 100m
3. Increments of Excise
4. All future economies on any of the existing heads of charge[1]

To LORD ROSEBERY, foreign secretary, 20 January 1893.   N.L.S. 10026, ff. 18–27.

[Letter 1:] Pray postpone the subject, a most formidable one, of your letter of 19th[2] just received until we settle the finance of the Irish Bill which at this moment absorbs nearly all time & attention.

I am not quite sure whether your proposed increase is to meet danger on the *frontier*.

Pray *refer* to a debate of last year on motion by Labouchere to reduce the force in Egypt. It has important bearings on the present.

[Letter 2:] I like the way in which you performed your difficult task with Waddington; and I do not know how far you are bound in your written recital by terms actually used: but I think there is some inconvenience in placing on record a statement that we intervened in Egypt to prevent maladministration. For is it historically accurate? At least if it speaks of our material intervention. If it means our intervention in concert with France to prevent the maladministration of Ismail it is I suppose perfectly true but wants a word or two to shew that it does not refer to the military occupation merely in order to prevent misapprehension. Query (if I am right in my construction) insert "in concert with France"; or any thing distinctive.

[Letter 3:] 1. I have just got your answer.[3]
2. The 'two telegrams'[4] you refer to were *not sent to me from F.O.*—I think by some mistake. Your letter was consequently in some respects hard to understand.
3. I should have thought it would be for you to have some prior communication on the military question.
4. Cromer seems to have in his head the putting down [of] treaty rights (such I believe they are) of the Khedive by British force; the threat of it is the same thing. There are two ways. One force: the other law or the Powers. I thought the Cabinet wholly leant to the latter.
5. Irish Finance cannot come to Cabinet today. I fear you will find your proposed use of it will not remove difficulties.

21. Sat

Wrote to E. Hamilton—Ld Rosebery l.l.l.l.l.—The Queen—Sir W. Harcourt l.l.— Mr C. Bannerman—and minutes. Saw Sir A. West—G. Murray—Mr Hamilton— Mr Purcell—Mr Bryce. Drove with C. to tea with Mrs Th.—5½ miles. Read Hist. of Gray's Inn.[5] A day of much and varied anxiety. But some blessed words of Scripture came to me ever and anon to give the needed support. Dined at Mr Bryce's to meet Mr Blake.[6]

[1] Holograph, dated at the head of the page 20 January 1893; Add MS 44775, f. 40.
[2] Add MS 44290, f. 80: 'it will be necessary to strengthen the Egyptian army of occupation as soon but as unobtrusively as possible'; need for immediate Cabinet discussion.
[3] Dated this day, Add MS 44290, f. 84.
[4] From 'Baring' (i.e. Cromer); ibid.
[5] Probably W. R. Douthwaite, *Gray's Inn* (1886).   [6] See 24 Apr. 93.

To Sir W. V. HARCOURT, chancellor of the exchequer,   MS Harcourt dep. 13, f. 49.
21 January 1893.

I have read your able paper[1] but I think Hamilton's new manipulation carries us altogether *past* all or nearly all the objections to your plan or to my suggestions. I hope it will have your favourable consideration.[2]

To LORD ROSEBERY, foreign secretary, 21 January 1893. 11½ P.M. N.L.S. 10026, f. 45.

1. I send you Bannerman's letter on today's telegrams from Egypt.
2. I cannot tell who are in town except two or three. Harcourt is at Malwood. By telegraphing they may doubtless be brought up tomorrow, and a Cabinet held as early as you please on Monday; at 12, 11, or 10.
3. The safety of the garrison is obviously vital: but, as Bannerman observes, General Walker has not today spoken I should advise sending by telegraph two inquiries (1.) Does Cromer apprehend disturbance of public order? (2) Is Walker prepared, or not, under arrangements already made, to be as usual responsible for the safety of the garrison?
You would have your answers tomorrow, or, without doubt, in good time for any Monday Cabinet.[3]
4. That unhappy proposal for political intimidation seems to make it especially necessary to keep clear from misunderstanding the military nature of any proposal which may on a certain supposition have to be adopted. We can then with perfect honour assign to it the proper construction.
5. Pray read, as soon as you can, the authoritative account of the British occupation given in the Queen's Speech of Feb. 14. 1883.

22. 3 S. Epiph.

Chapel R. mg. Guards Chapel evg. Wrote to The Queen—S.E.G.—Ld Rosebery. Saw Ld Spencer—do *cum* Mr Campbell Bannerman—Sir A. West—Sir A. Clark. Read Sermon sous Louis XIV—Montefiore Hibbert Lect.[4]—Notes on Deuteronomy.

To S. E. GLADSTONE, 22 January 1893.   Add MS 44549, f. 58.

I have received your very judicious letter on the Liberal Churchman's Union[5] now projected. I am aware of no foundation for the statement that "I am *not* keenly anxious for the Union to be established" beyond this that I do not take part in associations beyond the line of my own immediate duties & that it is not my practice greatly to stimulate others as to acts for which I am not to share the responsibility.

---

[1] Harcourt's paper, dated this day, MS Harcourt dep. 13, ff. 32–48, proposed that 'the rate of taxation for the whole Kingdom would be settled as now by the Imperial Parliament, the proceeds as now would go to the Imperial Exchequer, the only change introduced by Home rule would be the important one that the Irish Parliament would have the disposal and control of the sum total of Irish expenditure . . .'.
[2] Harcourt wrote again this day that he had now read Hamilton's plan, 'the best "Arrangement in Home Rule" we have yet reached'; Add MS 44203, f. 19.
[3] Rosebery wrote this day, Add MS 44290, f. 87, that Cromer could not wait till Monday: 'It is clear that he can no longer answer for order and I think that under the circumstances the Cabinet yesterday implied that they would give the troops. . . . I am apprehensive of waiting till Monday afternoon. . . .'
[4] C. G. Montefiore, *Lectures on the origin and growth of religion* (1892).
[5] Established as the Modern Churchmen's Union 1898 by Hastings Rashdall and others.

But I fully understand the feeling of necessity for such an union which has evidently prompted the movement: I regard it with sympathy, & cordially wish it success. This need not be treated as a secret. I may add, but not for the same free communication, what you already know, that I think the time has come when it is my duty in my own action to have some regard to this fact of Liberal Churchmanship. I have from you another, older, & more interior letter, to which I have not yet answered, though I felt & feel it much & with pleasure, simply because my mind has been too much pressed to allow me to collect myself sufficiently for the purpose of answering such a letter.

To Sir W. V. HARCOURT, chancellor of the exchequer,   MS Harcourt dep. 13, f. 53.
22 January 1893.

1. Though it is annoying in this matter of Irish Finance that the figures shift as in a Kaleidoscope, I hope they are now arriving at their *assietee*. I am *greatly* pleased with Hamilton's new adaptation of your plan which retains, perhaps even increases, all its great advantages, especially that of giving the Chancellor of the Exchequer a *perfectly free hand*.

2. Morley had $3\frac{1}{2}$ hours with the Irish last night. I understand him to report that they deem it vital that they should have all taxing powers outside Customs

Excise
P.O. & Telegraphs

and all levying power except Customs.

3. We ought not to agree to this *because* the Irish demand it if it is impolitic. I am however fully convinced that both these provisions are politic; and that we should make a great mistake in the interest of Great Britain were we to undertake any levy of *internal* monies in Ireland.

To J. MORLEY, Irish secretary, 22 January 1893.   Add MS 44549, f. 58.

The Cabinet as we see have to decide for themselves a great question of equity which is two-sided. What can we fairly ask Ireland to receive. What can we fairly ask Gt. Britain to pay? I certainly think that if they find for Ireland a free balance of £500,000 per ann. they will ask the English tax payer as much as equity will warrant—& as much (though this is a subject open to many chances) as the H. of Commons is likely to accept. I see no likelihood whatever that the C. will agree to more, & I conceive that they have given you a commission accordingly. I apprehend that they do not desire to limit the liberty of the Irish National party to move in Committee whatever they may feel it their duty to propose.[1]

To LORD ROSEBERY, foreign secretary, 22 January 1893.   N.L.S. 10026, f. 52.

I think it will a little relieve your mind to learn that a ship laden with a homeward battalion is believed to be at Suez and that Lord Spencer in concert with Bannerman and me (not at all as implying alarm) has telegraphed to detain it at least until tomorrow night.

Bannerman thought he ought to telegraph to Walker. He has also seen the Duke of Cambridge. It seems that the really valuable military opinion is that of Grenfell who is in Paris: expected at the War Office on Tuesday, & might I suppose be quickened.

23. M.

Wrote to The Queen—E.Hamilton—J. Morley l.l.—C. Bannerman—Ld Rosebery—and minutes. Drive with C. Saw Sir A. West—J. Morley—Sir W. Harcourt

---

[1] No reply found.

—E. Hamilton—do *cum* Sir R. Welby—Mr Asquith. Read Austin's Transl.[1]—
Ireland Documents. Cabinet 12–1½ Egypt and 4–5¾ Irish Finance, chiefly.

Cabinet. Monday Jan. 23. 93. Noon.[2]
1. Queen's letter—read.[3]
2. W.E.G. read Speech Paragraphs of 1883 concerning Egypt.[4]
3. Two telegrams of Lord Rosebery amended and agreed to. 1. For Crown. 2. For the
   Powers.[5]
The situation was recognised as a *crisis* not yet having assumed a permanent character.
(The general sentiment was that if the severance in spirit of Native & British Govt.
became chronic, the situation in Egypt would be fundamentally changed, & the Powers
would have to be called in.)
4. Irish Finance. (Aftn.) (Non quorate). Scheme considered & adopted.
5. Metropolis. Vide.[6]

[Egypt:][7] 1. The present situation is temporary. 2. Absolute duty to provide for order &
safety. 3. If the split with Khedive is prolonged & assumes a chronic form, our position
will be fundamentally changed and the Powers must come in.

Measures adopted. Jan. 23 [1893][8]
1. Send in the cavalry as intended.
2. Detain ⟨provisionally⟩ the battalion which they were to replace.
3. And the battalion now in troopship on the way home for a short time.

After Cabinet Jan. 23. 93. Demands of L.C.C.[9]
1. Bill for increase of their general powers we to approve.
2. Bill to equalize the rates in the metropolis. To examine.
3. City to be thrown into the mass. SMALL Royal Commission.[10]

To H. CAMPBELL-BANNERMAN, war secretary,	Add MS 41215, f. 44.
23 January 1893. '*Secret*'.

  I think you will agree with me that the sending of men of war at this time to Alexandria
should force be needed would be open to grave objections as recalling the memory of the

----

[1] Perhaps S. Austin, *Characteristics of Goethe . . . with notes, original and translated*, 3v. (1833).
[2] Add MS 44648, f. 74.
[3] Letter of 21 January apparently before receiving that day's Cabinet letter; she complained at
the Cabinet for ignoring Cromer's requests for reinforcements, reminding it of the Gordon disaster
and requesting Gladstone to read the letter to the Cabinet; Guedalla, ii. 460. He did so, telling the
Queen, CAB 41/22/29, that her letter 'was heard he need hardly say in a spirit of deep deference
and respect, but the case has been so far advanced by the subsequent circumstances that as Your
Majesty will find the Cabinet have now gone beyond the point to which Your Majesty desired that
they should advance'.
[4] Announcing 'withdrawal of the British troops . . . as expeditiously as a prudent consideration of
the circumstances will admit' and a 'full provision . . . for the exigencies of order'; *H*. 276. 3 (15 February 1883).
[5] Announcing reinforcement of the garrison; Cromer, *Abbas II*, 38.
[6] See below.
[7] Separate holograph mem. dated this day; Add MS 44648, f. 75.
[8] Add MS 44648, f. 77.
[9] Add MS 44648, f. 76. The Rates Equalization Bill; see 23 Nov. 92 and J. Davis, *Reforming London*
(1988), 168.
[10] Royal Commission on Amalgamation of the City and County of London, *P.P.* 1894 xvii–xviii.

bombardment [of 1882] and suggesting to hostile, perhaps even to impartial judges some intention of renewing it under possible circumstances.[1]

This 'without prejudice' to any other topic.

To J. MORLEY, Irish secretary, 23 January 1893.   Add MS 44257, f. 82.

Though I must not speak positively I am by no means certain that we might not re-introduce the quota into our plan so as to avoid all the objection about war-taxation; of course it must be without disturbing the £500,000. I will endeavour to see Welby & Hamilton early and if I find the idea breaks down I will telegraph to you I hope not later than noon.

24. Tu.

Wrote to J. Morley Tel.—Ld Kimberley—Mad. Novikoff. Dined at Mr Armit-stead's. Saw Sir A. West—Sir R. Welby *cum* Mr Hamilton—Mr Marjoribanks—Ld Rosebery—Mr L. Harcourt. Read Weir Mitchell's tragedy[2]—Sewell's Dante and Swedenborg.[3] Drive with C.

25. Wed.

Wrote to Mr Acland—Mr Carvell Williams—Ld Aberdeen—The Queen—Sir A. Gordon—& minutes. Cabinet $2\frac{1}{2}$-$4\frac{1}{2}$. Saw Sir A. West—Ld Spencer *cum* Mr A. Morley—Ld Rosebery—Att. General. Dined at Gray's Inn. A most kind reception.[4] Most curious custom here: all partake of bread morsels and wine before dinner. Read Count Serebryani[5]—Sewell on Dante &c.

Cabinet. Wed. Jan. 25. 1893. $2\frac{1}{2}$P.M.[6]
1. Request from Marjoribanks for Cabinet aid in elections. A.M. to report to him. He may attend.[7]
2. Transfer Clause as per Herschell.

26. Th.

Wrote to Sir W. Harcourt—Ld Rosebery—& minutes. Dined with Misses Monk. Saw Sir A. West—Mr Herbert Gardner—Mr Morley—Do *cum* Sir R. Welby—Also Miss Monk—French Ambassador (private)—Sir W. Phillimore—Lady Holker. Drive with C. Read Serebryani—Ireland Documents—Scotch Home Rule.[8]

[1] On 22 January, Add MS 44117, f. 112, Bannerman told Gladstone of the Duke of Cambridge's proposal to 'send a man of war or two to Alexandria. I am sending his notes to Spencer, as they deal with his affairs.'
[2] Probably S. Weir Mitchell, *Characteristics* (1892).
[3] F. Sewall, *Dante and Swedenborg, with other essays on the New Renaissance* (1893?).
[4] See *T.T.*, 26 January 1893, 10a.
[5] A. K. Tolstoy, *Prince Serebryani. An historical account of the times of Ivan the Terrible and of the Conquest of Siberia*, tr. J. Curtin (1892).
[6] Add MS 44648, f. 82.
[7] Marginal note reads: 'Stand over until after Hudd[ersfield] and Ha[lifax]'; i.e. a request from the Chief Whip for Cabinet members to assist at by-elections; the liberals lost Huddersfield by 35 votes, but held Halifax. See to Marjoribanks, 1 Feb. 93.
[8] W. Mitchell, *Is Scotland to be sold again? Home Rule for Scotland . . . with a retrospect of 1891 and 1892* (1893).

To Sir W. V. HARCOURT, chancellor of the exchequer,   MS Harcourt dep. 13, f. 55.
26 January 1893.

I thank you for your enclosures and I agree with you that the agricultural depression should be noticed in the Queen's Speech.[1]

I have seen John Morley about Ireland, and have also conversed with Gardner who is quite in tune with us: and I am inclined to ask for a paragraph such in effect as I inclose. Please to return it.

[P.S.] I have not supposed that either trade or revenue require specific notice.

To LORD ROSEBERY, foreign secretary, 26 January 1893.   N.L.S. 10026, f. 58.

Many thanks for the draft which I return.

I suppose it can hardly be called an incident, though it is a main element in the present state of facts, that the Khedive's breaking up the rule of harmony could not but create uneasiness in the popular mind, and tend to set him up as a conflicting force & destroy the harmony without which dualism is intolerable.

I suppose Waddington is still for the purposes of common intercourse an Ambassador without shock [sic] or prospect of recall. This I name only because I may see him this evening in the house of his relations the Misses Monk.

27. Fr.

Wrote to The Queen—Sir H. Ponsonby—Sir W. Harcourt l.l.—Mr Marjoribanks—Mr Morley—Mr Beaufoy—Mr Ponsonby—Mr Lambert—and minutes. Saw Sir A. West l.l.—Mr Lambert cum Mr Beaufoy—Mr Marjoribanks—Ld Spencer +—J. Morley +—A. Morley. Worked on the Draft Speech. Cabinet 2½–4¾: amended & adopted it. Read Serebryani—Ireland Papers.

Cabinet. Frid. Jan. 27. 1893. 2½ PM.[2]
1. The Cabinet met to consider draft of the Queen's Speech. It was amended & agreed to.
2. Certain Ministers agreed to go to Osborne on Monday.

To Sir W. V. HARCOURT, chancellor of the   MS Harcourt dep. 13, ff. 59–62.
exchequer, 27 January 1893. '*Private.*'

[Letter 1:]   I find from communication with Osborne that the Queen attaches value to the continuance of a constant nightly report of Parliamentary proceedings, to be given as soon as may be convenient.

On the other hand I am afraid it will not be physically possible for me to continue the practice of steady attendance on all evenings until the close of business so as to be in a condition to make this report.

I am reluctant to attempt the imposition of a burden upon others but there seems to be a necessity for making some new provision.

Would you think me unreasonable if I begged you to undertake this reporting to the Queen, except on nights when the Irish Bill is on: for these nights I think I ought to retain my responsibility and do the best I can to meet the case.[3]

---

[1] Suggested in previous day's note, with a formulation from 1836; Add MS 44203, f. 21.
[2] Add MS 44648, f. 85.
[3] Harcourt this day readily agreed, Add MS 44203, f. 30. Gladstone continued to write the reports of Cabinet meetings.

[Letter 2:] I will put words to exclude all possible reference to the rates but does not the conduct of the landlords in the reduction of rents deserve a little acknowledgement?

The reason I noticed a possible temporary character is that the most prominent feature of the distress namely the price of Stock is so obviously temporary.

But these points can be easily disposed of.

28. Sat.

Wrote to J. Morley—Sir W. Harcourt—Mr Beaufoy—Sir H. Ponsonby—& minutes. Saw Sir A. West—Mr Morley—M. Waddington. Worked on Home Rule. Read Serebryani (finished)—Isaac Eller's Money[1]—Ireland Papers. Drive with C. Dined at Ld Reay's.

29. Septa S.

Chapel Royal mg. St James's evg. Wrote to The Queen (Tel.)—Bull & Auvache. Saw Sir C. Tennant—Sir W. Phillimore—Sir A. Clark. Conclave on the Queen's Telegram. See Notes. Read Harrison on Scepticism &c.[2]—Sermon sous Louis XIV[3]—Q.R. on Bp Lightfoot[4]—Westcott Gospel of Life.[5]

Immediate: Please to come here at 3.30.[6]

Ld Kimberley✓
Lord Spencer✓
Sir W. Harcourt✓
Mr Morley✓

Awkward telegram.
Have we authority?
Bill of 1886 was "to amend the provision for the future Govt. of Ireland"
As to the other point H.M. might be satisfied on knowing it is only to five years
Message only arrived last night hard upon midnight.

WEG Jan 30 [*sc.* 29]. 93.

30. M.

Wrote to Ld Rosebery—Mr T.E. Ellis MP—The Queen—Mr Walpole—Sir H. Ponsonby—& minutes. Short drive with C. 12-2. Conclave on Bill. Saw Sir A. West—Mr Renald—Mr Morley—Mr Lambert—The Speaker—Ld Acton—Mr Marjoribanks.

Official dinner & evening party. 8-11. I feel, what? much troubled & tossed about: in marked contrast with the inner attitude on former like occasions.

Read Sermon &c.—Mr Eller's Money—Ireland Documents.

[1] A. Dean, *Isaac Eller's money* (1893).
[2] A. J. Harrison, *Problems of Christianity and Scepticism* (1891).
[3] See 8 Jan. 93.   [4] *Q.R.*, clxxvi. 73 (January 1893).
[5] See 15 Jan. 93.
[6] Holograph; Add MS 44775, f. 58. The Queen's telegraph, dated 28 January, read: 'I cannot say the measure will be for the *better* government of Ireland. Can you leave out "better" and also leave out reference to short Parliament.' (Guedalla, *Q*, ii. 462. Gladstone's reply, dated 29 January and following this day's conclave, agreed to return to the 1886 formula, but did not yield on the 5 year term for the Irish Parliament (ibid.).) The Queen's Speech read: '... to amend the provision for the Government of Ireland'; 4 *H* 8. 4.

To LORD ROSEBERY, foreign secretary, 30 January 1893.   N.L.S. 10026, f. 61.

I met Waddington on Saturday at Reay's.

He announced his coming retirement from the diplomatic body.

Did not defend Khedive except by saying it was due to Cromer's want of tact in treating him.

Said French Agent (Consul?) endeavoured to dissuade Khedive.

Told some one else, as I understand, that we could not do otherwise than increase our force.

According to Ford's[1] last Telegram, the Sultan seems to have surpassed himself. Perhaps he may give you some such opening as you have I think desired.

31. Tu.

Wrote to Sir W. Harcourt—& minutes. Drive with C. H. of C. 4–11½. Spoke 50 m in reply.[2] Much tired. Saw Sir A. West—H.N.G.—Mr Marjoribanks—Mr Murray —Ld Rosebery. Read Sermon &c.—Jersey Correspondence 1796[3]—Pr. of Wales Debts 1797.[4]—Dilke on Uganda.[5]

To Sir W. V. HARCOURT, chancellor of the exchequer,   MS Harcourt dep. 13, f. 66.
31 January 1893.

I return Channing's letter.[6] Perhaps the good reception thus far of the Speech may have modified your view. But in any case I shall be most ready to answer any question about payment of members in the sense which appeared to satisfy the Cabinet the other day when we spoke of it.

Wed. Feb. One. 1893.

Did not rise till 10.30. Now that I have taken the plunge I feel slightly more at home. Wrote to Mr Marjoribanks—Lady Hayter—Ld Rosebery—and minutes. Cabinet Comm. Irish Bill 2½–4½. Saw Sir A. West—Mr Marj.—Ld Acton—Mr Scott Holland. Dined with the Harcourts. Read Sermon &c.—Jephson on Irish Bill.[7]

To E. MARJORIBANKS, chief whip, 1 February 1893.   Add MS 44549, f. 60.

I feel no doubt as to the actual proceeding in the Cabinet on the question of Cabinet Ministers at bye elections.[8] The Cabinet thought that there was no personage of corresponding position on the other side in the elections immediately pending & that this of itself was quite decisive as to those elections.

There was no decision express[ed] or implied as to what might happen in a case such

[1] Sir Francis Clare Ford, 1830–99; ambassador to Spain 1887, Turkey 1892, Italy 1893.
[2] A sharp reply to Balfour; 4 *H* 8. 108.
[3] G. B. Villiers, *The correspondence between the Earl and Countess of Jersey and . . . Dr Randolph* (1796).
[4] *A review of the conduct of the Prince of Wales* (1797).
[5] Sir C. W. Dilke, 'The Uganda problem', *F.R.*, lix. 145 (February 1893).
[6] In MS Harcourt dep. 13, f. 68, on need to announce payment of members in the Queen's Speech, not in April.
[7] H. L. Jephson, 'Passing the wit of man [on Gladstone]', *N.C.*, xxxiii. 189 (February 1893).
[8] Marjoribanks, 21 January, Add MS 44332, f. 238, asked 'your formal sanction to a plan' for a speech by a Cabinet minister in each of the six constituencies with by-elections.

as that now presented by Chamberlain at Walsall: I do not say that there was any particular indication in favour of a Minister's going, but the question certainly remained open.

To LORD ROSEBERY, foreign secretary, 1 February 1893.   Add MS 44549, f. 60.

I entirely agree with you about the Telegram:[1] *cela donne à penser*. I think that inveterate liar [the Sultan] exaggerates, perhaps much exaggerates, all that he says about the Triumvirate: but all he can do will be done & without scruple. While I am deeply impressed, I am not ripe enough in results to ask you to consider any suggestion: but I hope you will ask yourself what we asked of Cromer as to the Khedive: what are your means of pressure? It is well that the plot contains as one of its elements intermediate peace. If the French proceed in a spirit of courtesy a correspondence with them might turn out to be the most dignified of the various paths.

Balfour made a singular declaration last night, undoubtedly in direct concert with Salisbury. It was that the *difficulties* & *dangers* of the occupation had been increased: but that this did not mean it ought to terminate sooner. This last bit in an explanation.

2. Th. Purifn.

Wrote to The Speaker—Ld Rosebery—Mr Mundella—and minutes. Saw Sir A. West—Mr Marj. H. of C. 3¾–8¼.[2] Read Sermon &c.—Pitt's Speeches[3]—Some Aspects—Timon of Athens.

3. Fr.

Wrote to Dr Richter[4]—Prince of Saxe Meiningen[5]—The Macdermott[6]—Mr Morley—Mr Stanhope—Mr Whitbread—Mr Mellor—and minutes. Saw Sir W. Lawson—Sir A. West—Mr Marj.—Sir W. Harcourt. Conclave H. of C. 3.15. Read Richter's Cyprus—Timon of Athens. H. of C. 3–8 and 8¾–11½. Spoke ½ h on Uganda.[7]

4. Sat.

Wrote to The Speaker—Ld Rosebery l.l.l.—and minutes. Worked on Ireland. Saw Sir A. West—The Macdermott—Mr Murray—Mr Rendel—Sir W. Harcourt. Read Timon of A. (finished)—Mr Eller's money dismissed.—The Fate of Fred. Lavers[8]—Irish Debates, 1792–3. Drove with C. to see the Hampstead Cottage.[9] Ten to dinner.

---

[1] Telegram from Ford, sent by Rosebery this day, Add MS 44290, f. 102, with the comment: 'Italy is the key of the situation and Italy is not such a fool as to join this triple conspiracy. . . .'
[2] Questions; intervened during disorder in the Queen's Speech deb.; 4*H* 8. 266.
[3] See 15 June 32.
[4] Max Hermann Ohnefalsch-Richter, German archaeologist, had sent his *Kypros, die Bibel und Homer*, 2v. (1893). This letter of comment is reproduced in facsimile in Reid, *G*, 147.
[5] Bernhard, Duke of Saxe-Meiningen; see Add MS 44517, f. 33.
[6] Hugh Hyacinth O'Rorke, known as The MacDermot and 'Prince of Coolavin', 1834–1904; Irish solicitor general 1886, attorney general 1892–5.
[7] On Labouchere's amndt. for evacuation of Uganda; 4*H* 8. 478.
[8] A. Morrison, *The fate of Fred Lavers* (1893).
[9] The cottage rented by H. N. Gladstone; see 11 Mar. 93.

To LORD ROSEBERY, foreign secretary, 4 February 1893.   N.L.S. 10026, ff. 75–81.

[Letter 1:]   Some confusion has perhaps & naturally grown out of the proceedings of Labouchere & the Opposition who resolutely discussed Uganda last night without knowledge of the papers.

As far as I have seen them, the instructions of Lord Salisbury to Portal March 22. 92 in Par. 7 of p 2 and your instruction of Dec. 10 92 par. 8 place the case of Portal as to his powers on a satisfactory footing.

I myself used last night a careless expression that he would be sure to act in the interest of peace & order 'unofficially[']: what I meant was outside his Commission of *inquiry*.

You mention Salisbury's commission & say he has with him a staff for the administration of Uganda pending con[sideratio]n of his report.[1] I find no such information in the papers but perhaps you use the word administration as meaning what is indicated in your Par. 2.

No doubt you will be here on Monday when we can confer if need be.

[Letter 2:]   I return your draft reciting conversation with Waddington. I quite understand with you that negotiation about Egyptian evacuation cannot well proceed within the shadow of the recent events: & so I hope you would yourself interpret the word moment. I should like to avoid if possible any controversy with France upon the question of time.

It is difficult to make out determinately a separate title for France to raise the question but I suppose any of the Great Powers is entitled, & certainly we have had much separate communication with France on the matter in former years: & perhaps the alternative of the Suzerain is practically no better.

Mr Villiers will have informed you of the accidental omission in the Uganda papers which Harcourt discovered today.

I am obliged to postpone the Cromer draft of today[2] until daylight: will it not probably be one for circulation.

5. *Sexa S.*

Chapel Royal mg & H.C.—do evg. Wrote to Sir W. Harcourt—Mr Chamberlain—Mrs Astor—Ld Rosebery l.l. Notwithstanding the blessings of today, in returning from the sacred precincts I feel both depression & worry. Saw Sir A. Clark. Read Sermon &c.—Dr Hutton's Address[3]—Michaud's Revue Internat. de Theologie[4]—Prudenzano, S. Francese.[5]

---

[1] Rosebery had written this day, Add MS 44290, f. 104, that he had 'never breathed that august air [of the Commons] and am therefore a bad judge of times and seasons, but I cannot understand the difficulty of giving the assurance asked for by Balfour and Chamberlain. Portal goes up with the fullest powers. He is already under his Salisburian commission commissioner for the sphere of influence, he has a staff with him expressly to make provision for the administration of Uganda pending the consideration of his report, it was certainly not in the contemplation of the Cabinet that he should go as a mere reporter . . . but I am afraid that some such impression has been produced. . . .' For papers on Uganda (just published) see 23 Sept., 13 Oct. 92.

[2] See to Rosebery, 6 Feb. 93.

[3] Perhaps A. W. Hutton, 'Principles and politics. A lecture' (1891).

[4] See 3 Jan. 93. Michaud's piece was printed as a pamphlet and as an article in *Revue Internationale de Théologie*, i. 83 (January–March 1893).

[5] F. Prudenzano, *Francesco d'Assisi e il suo secolo considerato in relazione con la politica . . .* (1857), sent by the author; Add MS 44517, f. 5.

To J. CHAMBERLAIN, M.P., 5 February 1893.   Add MS 44549, f. 62.

I thank you for your note.[1] Tomorrow however with the Papers on Uganda in your hands, you will obtain a fuller and clearer view, than I was able from memory to give to Mr. Labouchere on Friday, of the position of Sir G. Portal & his means of action. The recent instructions, to be fully understood, have to be compared with p. 2 of the Africa No. 4 of 1892 which shows the authority conferred upon him by his original commission and not since withdrawn.

To Sir W. V. HARCOURT, chancellor of the exchequer,   MS Harcourt dep. 13, f. 70.
5 February 1893. 'Secret'.

This is the draft of a dispatch to Cromer which it was arranged that Rosebery should prepare.

I should like to know how in a general way it strikes you.

My impression is that two or three passages might be modified with advantage, and that it would be well to add something which would show that we contemplated a gentle and careful exercise of our very invidious though under the circumstances necessary powers.

I should think the Cabinet would expect to see this important paper in draft?[2]

To LORD ROSEBERY, foreign secretary, 5 February 1893.   N.L.S. 10026, ff. 84-8.

[Letter 1:]   Uganda. Most unfortunate that we have not had your Uganda Memorandum.

If a question is put to me tomorrow had I not better read the relevant points of the Portal Commission and your instructions—& say he has no instruction to come away & will doubtless use his own best judgment, probably leaving some one to represent him if he does?[3]

[Letter 2:]   Would you come here on returning to town tomorrow—or at any hour before H of C. which may suit you—and let us go over the Cromer dispatch—when I would suggest for your consideration points that I think might be taken in the Cabinet: for on reflection I think the papers will have to be seen there.

I think every thing fundamental stands well and will be accepted; there are however points of expediency and expression—

And I would offer this suggestion: to put in a sentence or short paragraph to the effect that our necessary but strong and also invidious powers will be exercised with all possible care and consideration for the feelings of Egyptian authorities and people.

6. M.

Wrote to Keeper of Printed Books [British Museum]—Ld Rosebery—& minutes. Read Sermon &c. (finished)—Fate of F. Lavers. Saw Sir A. West—Ld Rosebery—Mr Morley—Mr Marj.—Mr Murray—Sir W. Harcourt—Mr Hamilton. Drive ½ h. H. of C. $3\frac{3}{4}$-$8\frac{1}{2}$.[4]

[1] Of 3 February, Add MS 44126, f. 195, withdrawing his tabled question as Gladstone had answered it in the course of his speech on 3 February.
[2] Harcourt this day returned the draft (not found) with comments in blue pencil; Add MS 44203, ff. 37, 39.
[3] Draft by Rosebery for answer to Chamberlain's question, Add MS 44290, f. 110.
[4] Queen's Speech; 4H 8. 559.

To LORD ROSEBERY, foreign secretary, 6 February 1893.   Add MS 44549, f. 63.
Many thanks;[1] and in return I will certainly contract my front as much as possible.
1. on the protest.[2] You desire to be explicit. But what is your meaning? Have we defined
in our own minds what the "further action" should be; and are we agreed on it? I lean to
the belief that if we definitely break with Egypt there is no safe alternative but the
Powers. I do not ask the Cabinet to say so. But the words "further action" will I think be
interpreted in the sense of Cromer's recommendations, and I apprehend the Cabinet are
much disinclined to Cromer's ulterior policy. Perhaps I did not fully enough explain
myself this morning.
2. on p. 6 I understand you to reserve your judgment on the para:, but to agree with me
about the words I have underlined that they are not suited to a despatch.
3. on "fresh intervention" I cannot certainly read your words, but I see enough to accept
fully the meaning.
[P.S.] I thought it would be well to show Harcourt the papers: he said he would write to
you. He has the draft.

7. Tu.

Wrote to Maire de Bayonne—Ld Justice Bowen—and minutes. H. of C. 3–8 and
9½–12. An anxious evening but with a good ending.[3] Saw Sir A. West—Mr Murray—Mr Marj.—Mr A. Morley. Read F. Lavers (finished)—and Union debates
and pamphlets.

Mr Asquith[4]
Mr Mundella

    Lowther's motion.[5]
If this goes into full debate, I hope you (vos) will be prepared to deal with it.
    Might it be expedient for me to say a few words in the hope of shortening?
    To the following effect
1. If L. produces facts or presumptions, to say we shall not object to inquiry with a view
    to full knowledge
2. More doubtful. If the prevailing misconceptions are extensive, would it be safe to allow
    inquiry in order to dispel them?
                                                              WEG 7 F. 93

[Asquith's reply:] Mr Gladstone: I think it would be very desirable that you should say a
few words at the outset to the effect of (1). Inquiry is all that our people who might otherwise support Lowther really want, and as 5 years have passed since the matter was last
investigated (in 1888), & the volume of immigration has in the meantime undoubtedly
grown, there is a plausible case for further inquiry.
                                                          H. H. A[squith]
                                                7 Feb 93

[1] Rosebery sent comments on Gladstone's amendments to a draft dispatch to Cromer; Add MS
44290, f. 113; see 5 Feb. 93. For the dispatch, finally sent on 16 February, see PP 1893–4 cxi. 1123.
[2] Rosebery wrote: 'On page 4 I find my principal difficulty. I think the words "that your protest
would have been supported, if necessary, by further action" represent not less than the truth.
Whereas the words which you suggested do not convey to my mind any distinct meaning at all.'
[3] Keir Hardie's amndt. on unemployment and depression defeated in 109:276; 4H 8. 770.
[4] Holograph, with replies from Asquith and Mundella on the same sheet; Add MS 44775, f. 62.
[5] On alien immigration; see 11 Feb. 93.

[Mundella's reply:] I think it would be very desirable that you should speak in the direction of inquiry. The whole question is much exaggerated and misunderstood and good will come of *full knowledge*

A M[undella] 7 Feb.

8. *Wed.*

Wrote minutes. Read Richard Cable[1]—Walpole's Isle of Man.[2] Saw Sir A. West—Mr Marj. l.l.l.—Ld Spencer—Sir W. Harcourt—Mr Stewart—Mr Arch. H. of C. 12–2 and 3–6. Spoke on the Collins motion.[3] Dined at Marlb. House. Conversation with P. of Wales—D. of York—Abp of Canty—Ld Rosebery. Saw Sir A. Clark: very encouraging.[4]

9. *Th.*

Wrote to Mr Morley—Sir W. Harcourt—The Queen—Walter James—and minutes. Saw Sir A. West—Mr Marj. l.l.—Mr Hamilton—Mr Morley. H. of C. 4–8¼. Asquith admirable.[5] Backgammon with Mr A. Read Rich. Cable. Worked on Ireland. Drive with C. Saw Sir A. Clark.

To Sir W. V. HARCOURT, chancellor of the exchequer,   MS Harcourt dep. 13, f. 73.
9 February 1893.

The question of members' payment is a grave one in a party point of view and may have grave results.[6] But for today & for Mr. R. Wallace I think my only duty is to keep Reid and his coadjutors in the ⟨first⟩ place of priority and not to let him usurp it by an answer today.
[P.S.] I assume it to be your opinion that if & when done it should be done by legislation & not by Vote in Supply.[7]

To LORD NORTHBOURNE, 9 February 1893.[8]   Add MS 44517, f. 39.

Absorbed and distracted as I am at this time by the pressure of business, I cannot longer delay saying a few words on your dear Father's death. It is to me, as it is to my wife, an event which reaches back so far. With it seems to totter the fabric of more than half a

---

[1] S. Baring-Gould, *Richard Cable, the lightshipman*, 3v. (1888).
[2] Sir S. Walpole, *The land of Home Rule. An essay on the history and constitution of the Isle of Man* (1883).
[3] On relief for agriculture; 4*H* 8. 774.
[4] Perhaps a reference to his own health, or to Clark's, the latter having been seriously ill.
[5] Asquith spoke on treason-felony convictions, Gladstone on business of the house; 4*H* 8. 909, 943.
[6] Harcourt wrote this day, Add MS 44203, f. 41, having noticed a question down for Gladstone; he felt it 'a most critical matter . . . if the Radical Party are not satisfied in respect of it the majority will be most seriously shaken. I do not know any question which is more certain to break up the united action of the Party.'
[7] Harcourt replied this day, ibid., f. 43 that he had 'rather assumed' such an important change would be made by Statute but 'if you doubt this of course the matter ought to be very carefully considered and I should say ought to be a Cabinet question'; he hoped money might be reserved in the Budget, £100,000–£150,000 for the present year.
[8] Gladstone's god-son, i.e. the 2nd Baron Northbourne, whose father, formerly W. C. James, d. 4 February. This letter is a typed copy, evidently sent by Northbourne to Morley for his biography.

century's recollections, which for me began in the winter of 1838[1] when your Mother in her youthful beauty was enjoying Rome as it could then be enjoyed, together with her parents. Unless memory deceives me that winter laid the foundations of his marriage, as it did of mine—and it is united with his present death by a long unbroken line of his warmest friendship. Even from out of the chaos of business I look back along it and see how bright it stretches into the distance along the waste of years. If the responsibilities of a man are to be measured, in some not inconsiderable part at least by the excellence of his parents, then you my dear Walter have them in such [blank] as is shared by few. A long life has in my case been coupled with a wide acquaintance: but among all the friends I have known I could not, [in] the light of this our Christian civilisation, easily point to a more happy or more normal life and death than that of your Father. I feel indeed as if I ought not to be here and writing about him but rather to have preceded him. Here however I am, and being here I feel that this honour[?] has been given you by God, that in your case the pains of privation, which I know must be sharp, are singularly set against what I may almost call a far more exceeding and abundant store of consolation which we remotely though warmly, and you in close proximity, and almost without limit must draw from the retrospect of his gifts his virtues and his graces. Peace be with him, the peace of the just, the peace of his Redeemer; and what can I wish for you and yours but the heart and the strength to follow him.

10. Fr.

Wrote to J. Morley—Lady Hayter—and minutes. Saw Sir A. West—S.L.—Mr Marjoribanks—Sir W. Harcourt—& minutes. Dined with Miss Peel. 8-10. H. of C. $3\frac{1}{2}$-8 and 10-$1\frac{1}{2}$.[2] Worked on Irish question. Read Rich. Cable.

11. Sat.

Wrote minutes. Worked much on Irish question. H. of C. $12\frac{1}{4}$-$2\frac{1}{2}$ and 5-6. Spoke on Lowther's motion about aliens.[3] Saw Sir A. West—Mr Marj.—Mr Morley—Abp of Canterbury. Dined at Ld J. Bowen's. Saw Welby & Hamilton on the Irish Finance. Read Richard Cable.

12. Quinqua S.

Chapel Royal mg & evg. Dined at Mr Rendel's. Saw Ld Oxenbridge—Lady Breadalbane—Sir A. Clark—Sir A. West. Worked on Irish financial notes. Read H.S. Revised Version—Montefiore Hibbert Lecture[4]—Chadwell Purgatorio.[5] Wrote to E. Hamilton.

13. M.

Wrote to The Queen—J. Morley—Sir W. Harcourt—and minutes. Drive with C. $\frac{1}{2}$ hour. Saw Sir A. West—Mr Morley—Mr Hamilton—Sir A. Clark—Mr Marj.

[1] See 15 Jan. 39.
[2] Queen's speech; 4H 8. 1066.
[3] Gladstone met Lowther's motion for an Aliens Bill with an offer of inquiry; the motion was defeated in 119:234; 4H 8. 1174.
[4] See 22 Jan. 93.
[5] C. L. Shadwell, The Purgatory of Dante . . . introduced by W. Pater, 2v. (1892-9).

H. of C. 3½–7. Spoke 2¼ h on Introduction of Irish Bill.[1] I felt very weak having heard every hour (or all but one) strike in the night. I seemed to lie at the foot of the Cross, and to get my arm round it. The House was most kind: and I was borne through. The later evening I spent on the sofa.

To Sir W. V. HARCOURT, chancellor of the exchequer,   MS Harcourt dep. 13, f. 76.
13 February 1893.

Some of your words are alarming[2] but I do not think anything has been done to commit you. Nothing of that kind need be said tonight: and I have summoned the Cabinet for tomorrow.

14. Tu.

Wrote to The Queen l.l.–& minutes. Cabinet 12–2. Read Rich. Cable. Saw Sir A. West–Mr Marj.–Mr Morley–Ld Kimberley–Mary & H. Drew (on the Norwich resignation.)[3] Fourteen to dinner. H. of C. 4–7¾ (Irish Bill).[4]

Cabinet. Tues. Feb. 14. 1893. Noon.[5]
1. Irish Bill, Finance. Duties of Excise.[6]
2. East India Juries.[7]
3. First Lord of the Admiralty. To sign statement?[8]
4. WEG's answer to G. Hamilton.[9] No–not to commit[?] Govt. as to any obligation–leave the matter open.

15. Ash Wed.

Ch Royal 11–1. Saw Sir A. West–Ld Chancellor–Mr Morley–Ld Acton–Mr Marj.–Sir A. Clark. Drive with C. & Walk. Wrote to Princ[ipal of] Lampeter–Sir W. Farquhar–Mr Morley–& minutes. Read Rich. Cable–Roden Noel Essays.[10]

To Sir W. R. FARQUHAR, 15 February 1893.   Add MS 44549, f. 64.

The whole tone & terms of your letter[11] bear witness to the pain you have suffered in writing it, & in arriving at the decision which it announces. I think the best & most

---

[1] Introduction of G[overment of] I[reland] Bill; 4*H* 8. 1241.
[2] Strong letters of 12 and 13 February on proposed changes 'without my knowledge' to the excise clauses of the G.I. Bill; Add MS 44203,. f. 45.
[3] Possibly an opportunity for preferment of H. Drew; if so, it came to nothing.
[4] And spoke on business of the House; 4*H* 8. 1397.
[5] Add MS 44648, f. 86.   [6] Memoranda at ibid., ff. 87–9.
[7] Illegible comment follows.
[8] Could Spencer as a peer sign the annual statement on naval policy and expenditure? The Cabinet decided he could; CAB 41/22/34.
[9] On whether liberals would legislate on Irish land; 4*H* 8. 1391.
[10] R. B. W. Noel, *Essays on poetry and poets* (1886).
[11] Of 11 February, Add MS 44155, f. 238, on Welsh disestablishment, concluding: 'Many of your political acts have grieved me most sorely, but I have loved you with the strongest affection & that you should now attempt to strike down the Church you taught me to love breaks my heart.' It was to Farquhar's sister that Gladstone proposed marriage in 1835; see 3 Sept. 35 ff.

grateful return I can make for this leniency is to say nothing about my own pain in receiving such a communication from my oldest living friend. And also to assure you that it has no effect whatever upon my old lifelong sentiments towards you except to enhance them. If I accept your judgment it is to be borne in mind that I have no title to appeal against it. But I may possibly write you a separate letter to show first that my position on the Welsh Church is not so much altered as you suppose: secondly that it is an unnatural & strange thing for those who are united as to *Church* to stand aloof from one another by reason of any differences about Establishment. God bless you & yours now & ever.

To J. MORLEY, Irish secretary, 15 February 1893.   Add MS 44549, f. 64.

I think that if you show the Bill to the three Irish members named[1] you should do it under protest, for I am convinced that it is impolitic & imprudent. Not that it will wreck the measure but it will furnish a fresh aim in debate against it. If you ask Mr Dillon he will tell you that I told him this yesterday in strong terms & that he made no sort of protest against it. If they insist I do not say you can resist: but I cannot be a willing party, & this reluctance is not in our interest but in the interest of Ireland as connected with Parliamentary tactics.
[P.S.] Remember that an alteration of arrangement is in question—on which I hope you will be kind enough to speak to me early tomorrow. If the Bill be shown we shall have a mouse made into a mountain.

16. Th.

Wrote to Mr Reid MP—Mr Morley—Sir W. Harcourt l.l.—and minutes. Cabinet at 2.30 and again at the House in evg. H. of C. 4–8.[2] Dined at Spencer's to meet the Duke of York: who is not only likeable but perhaps loveable.[3] Saw Sir A. West—Mr Marj.—Mr Morley—Mr A. Morley.

Cabinet. Thurs. Feb. 16 [1893]. 2½ PM.[4]
1. Newfoundland. Ld Ripon to inform them that if they do not legislate for the purpose provided (and defeated in Newfoundland) we must.
2. Harcourt. There is no plan of a separate finance for Ireland which is not destructive of the finance of Great Britain.
   Cabinet considered language of clause relating to the contingency of augmented Excise.
Resumed at 6¼ in the H. of C.
Resolved at 8 P.M. to propose to Irish leaders through Mr. Sexton that the Clause should at present stand so as to give the whole proceeds to the British Exchequer but should be subject to reconsideration in the interests of Ireland.
   (I left my seat at 7.45 to join the Cabinet & found them indisposed to any qualification at present—apparently for fear of clashing with the finance of the year.)
   [( ]Late at night I received Mr A. Morley's report—herewith.)[5]

[1] Morley wrote, 16 February, Add MS 44257, f. 85: 'Dillon is very urgent that he and Sexton and Blake (nobody else) should be allowed secretly to run through the Bill before it goes to press. There would be no communication to the party. Their only intention is to guard against any slip of phrase.'
[2] Spoke on breach of privilege by Lord Wolmer; 4H 8. 1593.
[3] i.e. the future George V.
[4] Add MS 44648, f. 89.
[5] Not found.

To Sir W. V. HARCOURT, chancellor of the exchequer,   MS Harcourt dep. 13, f. 85.
16 February 1893.

[Letter 1:]   As regards the English part of your letter,[1] I observe first that the Cabinet has not yet adopted the Defence Estimates for the coming year. They are invariably brought before the Cabinet when ready.

It would be quite premature to arrive in the middle of February at binding decisions on a Budget. But my present impressions, on the case you have sent me, are against moving on Excise when the Death Duties promise in the lump i.e. in the rough to fill up the void formidable as that void is.

[Letter 2:]   MS Harcourt dep. 13, f. 87.

As regards the Irish part of your letter[2] it seems to me altogether too late to attempt alteration of the Bill as it now stands and as it was fixed by the Cabinet after repeated and long deliberation. How could Morley go now to the Irish and alter matters on which we are for the present committed to them? I have publicly announced that the Bill is ready and the serious delay in its circulation, which must result from our reopening now, would of itself terribly discredit both the Government and the question of Home Rule.

There are the alternatives of quota and lump sum, neither of which you recommend, but which are now, especially the quota, excluded absolutely by any [?every] public declaration yet made.

[P.S.] Pray see Morley if necessary on the subject of the understanding with the Irish. The Cabinet might meet ⟨in my Room⟩ this afternoon if you desired it. There is one point (but I do not know what Morley would say to this) that perhaps is open to consideration, whether the word imperial fully expresses our meaning which I take to be for purposes not confined to Great Britain.

To R. T. REID, M.P., 16 February 1893.   Add MS 44549, f. 65.

Your colleagues Dr Hunter, Mr Picton & Mr Fenwick were kind enough to call upon me[4] yesterday when I made known to them my answer to the inquiry which you had previously made on their behalf. I understood when they withdrew that they would deliberate upon the question whether they would take any & what further steps, & I do not doubt that I shall in due time learn your & their intentions. In the meantime I will write to Mr Wallace who has a question on the paper for today to tell him I have seen the gentlemen to whom I previously referred & that I deem it probable I shall have a further communication from them. In the meantime I am not prepared with any definite reply.

17. Fr.

Wrote to Mr Reid MP—Mr Wallace MP—Ld Ripon—Col. H. Vincent—Sir A. Gordon—The Queen l.l.—& minutes. H. of C. $3\frac{3}{4}$-8 and $10\frac{1}{4}$-1. A spirit of warmth

---

[1] Long letter of 15 February, Add MS 44203, f. 49; Hamilton now estimating an actual deficit of £1,665,000, i.e. 'near upon £2,000,000'; Harcourt expects £1,500,000 from 'extended and graduated Death Duties' and £500,000 from increased Excise.

[2] Harcourt (see note to previous letter) argued 'it would be possible even now to remedy the fatal blot as to the *Excise Revenue*—perhaps the most important of all sources of Income from Ireland'. He docketed this: 'wrote that I gratefully accept Cabinet for this afternoon'.

[3] Deputation on payment of members.

certainly pervades the majority.[1] The Bill brought in amidst enthusiastic demonstrations. Saw Sir A. West—Ld Spencer—J. Morley. Read Rich. Cable.

To Sir A. H. GORDON, 17 February 1893.   Add MS 44549, f. 65.

I received yesterday your book & I thank you very much for it. I have sedulously applied all my fragments & scraps of time to reading the latter chapters; & I am greatly delighted. You have I think, so far as I have gone, done much for the public, much for your own reputation. But more than this you have embalmed the sacred memory of your father, & have made known to the world, with scarcely less of art than of affection, a rare, most attractive & most remarkable personality. I think that from the date of this publication, Ld Aberdeen will hold a new & loftier place in the estimation of the country, one however in no way beyond his deserts, for indeed it is not very easy to see how these could be exceeded.

It was not to be expected that in writing his biography you should write the biography of others, or that you should always know all the converging influences which have determined their course. Some of the points at which you come into contact with me are treated in a manner which reminds me that I must if I can put my own narration on paper. You have already helped me in tracing my own mental history about the franchise & evidently I did not like its extension so late as in the autumn months of 1852. But I am curious to know who was the one Peelite in the Cabinet who argued with the Whigs in opposing the extension. Naturally I suspect you of meaning me. But if so I *think* you are wrong, & I should like to know your evidence. Unquestionably, when the Palmerston resignation took place, I was entirely against him, & I went with Newcastle to induce him to withdraw the resignation. I am confident that I was on the side of extension from the time when the question came up for discussion in the Cabinet. There is another passage in p. 20 about the history of the Naples letters where my recollections are in sharp conflict with your statement. My story—& I had occasion to tell it to the H. of Commons near (I think) 30 years ago—is that I never intended an appeal to Parliament or the world at that stage, that I looked to Ld. Aberdeen from the first, & was most pleased & grateful when he met my wish. Perhaps you have proof which will overthrow me. But of one thing I am certain. When Henry Lennox came back from Italy & said he followed my example in at once coming to Parliament I said he had done the very reverse of what I had done, as I never thought of going to Parliament or the world without trying first to give the Neapolitan Govt. an opportunity of mending its ways without noise. This is of course quite distinct from my subsequent proceeding to publish at the close of the season & near the close of the Session without first asking your Father's leave. I think that perhaps the climax of your work is the very remarkable account of the correspondence in the autumn of 1852.[2]

To C. E. H. VINCENT, M.P., 17 February 1893.   Add MS 44549, f. 65.

I thank you for your letter[3] and I clearly understand that the purpose of your desire to confer with me is that you may recommend to the Govt. a method of trade legislation which would impose differential duties on the importation of foreign commodities into this country.

I fear that my seeing a deputation on such a subject would lead to misapprehension, & to disappointment. It would hardly do less than convey to the public the idea that there

[1] Government of Ireland Bill [G.I. Bill] brought in; 4*H* 8. 1717.
[2] Gordon replied on 19 February, defending his case with quotations; Gordon's letters about this book, but not Gladstone's, are in *T.A.P.S.* new series li, part 4 (1961), 103 ff. Sir A. H. Gordon, *The Earl of Aberdeen* (1893).
[3] Not found. Vincent was a well-known protectionist.

might be circumstances under which I might be ready to recommend to my colleagues the adoption of such a plan. But since I am compelled to regard the plan as unjust to the mass of the community, unfavourable to the industry and enterprise of the country, and subversive of the legislation which it cost us 20 or 25 years to accomplish, you will perceive that with these opinions I am precluded in principle from the discussion of such a plan, and were I to receive a deputation in its favour, I might be justly charged with acting under false appearances and giving encouragement to expectations which I did not mean to fulfil.

You will therefore I am confident excuse me on these grounds from receiving the deputation.

18. Sat.

Wrote to The Queen—Sir W. Harcourt—Sir A. Gordon—Mr Rathbone MP—Ld Rosebery—& minutes. We drove to Harry's Cottage for 5 P.M. Tea. Walk to the Flagstaff: most striking. Saw Sir A. West & others—Mr Labouchere. Dined at Mr Knowles's. Read Life of Ld Abn—Rich. Cable.

To Sir W. V. HARCOURT, chancellor of the exchequer,　　MS Harcourt dep. 13, f. 93.
18 February 1893.

I agree with you as to the Channel Tunnel[1]
1. That it should be an open question for us
2. That the responsibility for authorising should not be with the Treasury.
  I think also
1. that the whole question of principle will be raised upon this Bill and if so that the judgment of Parliament upon it ought to [be] given once for all
2. That the matter of authorisation might properly and in accordance I think with usage be given to the Board of Trade
3. As regards the Departmental intervention of Admiralty and War, it seems to me that *usage* if clear ought to govern. If they have intervened as Departments heretofore I do not wish to exclude them; if they have not I do not think a new precedent should be made. The proposed reference seems quite right if usual.
4. The statement of Sir Courtnay Boyle omits to state that when the Liberal Board of Trade opposed the Bill by direction of Cabinet the opposition was purely circumstantial and the question of the merits was expressly excluded.

19. 1 S. Lent.

Chapel Royal mg & evg. Drive with C. Wrote to E. Marjoribanks. Saw Sir A. Clark. Read Bp Westcott—Muir, Caliphate[2]—Montefiore Hibbert L.—and [blank.]

20 M.

Wrote to Mrs Th.—The Queen l.l.—Lady Lindsay—Mr Rendel—Abp of Canterbury—& minutes. Attended the Levee at 2 PM. Saw Sir A. West—Ld Acton—Sir

---

[1] Harcourt wrote, 17 February, Add MS 44203, f. 55: '*Ecce iterum* Watkin & the Channel Tunnel. . . . I belong to the "old fogey" party on that question not from fear of invasion in time of *War* but of *Continentilisation* in time of *peace*'; he suggested it be not 'made rigidly a Government question' and that Parliament not the Treasury should give the authority to complete the experimental tunnel.
[2] Sir W. Muir, *Caliphate: its rise, decline and fall* (1891).

A. Clark—Ld Rosebery—Mr Rathbone MP.—The Turkish Minister. H. of C. 4 PM—6½.[1] Dined at Grillion's. Read Richard Cable—Life of Ld Aberdeen.

21. Tu. [Windsor Castle]

Wrote to Sir A. Gordon—Mr Bryce—Mr Courtney—and minutes. Off to Windsor at 4.40. Saw Sir A. West—A. Gordon—Mr Murray (RB)—E.W. Hamilton—Bp of St Asaph—Sir A. Gordon—Mr Marj.—Ld Acton—Sir J. Cowell—Sir H. Ponsonby—Audience of H.M. and conversation with Empress Frederick. Also with Sir M. about the Websters.[2] Read Life of Ld Aberdeen—Rich. Cable.

To Sir A. H. GORDON, 21 February 1893.   Add MS 44549, f. 67.

I must be brief today in reference to your letter. Of course I have had no opportunity of referring to any sources of my own.

As to Naples I think that Ld. Aberdeen could not be expected to give in his letters to third persons a full account of my position: nor are these letters inconsistent with the truth (according to my version of it) though they do not tell the whole truth. The supposition with which they seem to harmonise is this that I was fully persuaded an application of some kind would be necessary but my first wish was to make it through Ld. Aberdeen & Austria if he would consent as he most kindly did consent. But your statement is that I intended to make my appeal direct & was only converted by Ld. Aberdeen to the idea of using his intervention.

This is a trivial point.

About the other point I am less clear & I care less. Only I would say the impressions, that is to say the suspicions, of political men (except Ld. Aberdeen) are worth little, & those of Graham, admirable as he was in so many respects, are perhaps worth the least of all. I never contemplated personal reunion with Ld. Derby. Collective reunion I may have desired for I thought the proceedings of the first Palmerston Govt. so bad (& this in a great degree from a liberal point of view) that I regarded with satisfaction the Derby Succession in 1858, & this also is the fact that for a long time, certainly in 1858 I had a great weakness for the small boroughs (so had Brougham) which had returned almost all our statesmen in their political youth.

22. Wed. [London]

Returned to town by the 10.20. Wrote Autobiog.[3] Wrote to Ld Northbourne—Mr Bryce—Sir W. Harcourt—and minutes. C. & Mary now both laid up. Saw Sir A. Clark—Sir A. West—Mr Bryce—Mr Asquith—Mr Morley—The Speaker—Abp of Canty—Mr Mundella. Dined at the Speaker's. Meeting of Trustees of B. Museum at 1.15. Read Rich. Cable—Finished Life of Ld Abn.

To Sir W. V. HARCOURT, chancellor of the exchequer,   MS Harcourt dep. 13, f. 95.
22 February 1893.

Have you agreed with the War Sec. on the Army Estimates? If so a very short time would suffice for a Cabinet tomorrow before the House.

[1] Questions; registration of electors; 4 H 8. 1875.
[2] Perhaps the Anglican clergyman he was assisting; see 9 Jan. 92.
[3] Unclear which part; *Autobiographica* contains nothing from this time.

23. Th.

Wrote to Mr Asquith—Sir W. Harcourt—Mr Morley—The Queen l.l.l.—Archbp of Canterbury—and minutes. Read Rich. Cable. Saw Sir A. West—Mr Marj.—Mr Acland—Mr Morley—Mr Rendel—Mr Asquith. Cabinet 2¼-3. Labour MP.s Deputn at 3.[1] H. of C. 4–7¾ and 9½-12½. Spoke 30 m at 11.30.[2] Pity the sorrows of a poor old man. C. has a *very light* influenza.

Cabinet. Thurs. Feb. 23. 1890 [sc. *1893*]. *2¼ PM.*[3]
1. Estimates—Mil[itary] & Naval.
Army 171 m[ille] increase } *Yes. Nem. con.*
Navy   the same
2. Welsh Suspensory Bill. more limited construction of the progress in view adopted and the Eccl. Commn. left out.
3. Bryce—Appt. of Duchy Magistrates. Cabinet agreed to the revocation of the Dufferin Minute. Chancellor of Duchy will now be responsible as before 1871.
4. Morley & the corresp. with the Welsh members. *Postpone.*

To H. H. ASQUITH, home secretary, 23 February 1893.   Add MS 44549, f. 68.
With reference to your amended notice for today, & on the wording:[4]
1. Our friends will like the assertion implied in 'Church of Engld.' but will not our opponents also make much of it as showing that the Bill is part of a latent design against the Church of England & will not this tell?[5]
2. Have you ascertained that the Dioceses of Wales nowhere go beyond Wales & Monmouthshire?
3. Did not you intend to confirm [*sc.* confine] the Bill to the range of *public* patronage. Otherwise you at once affect the market value of recognised private property in advowsons.

24. Fr.

Wrote to Ld Ripon—Mr Everett M.P.—and minutes. H. of C. 3¾-8.[6] Saw Sir A.W.—Sir A. Clark—S.L. on preferments—Abp of Canterbury—Dr Richter—Mr Rendel. Read Tucker's Eton[7]—American Epitaphs. Poor?[8]—Finished Richard Cable. H. of C. 4–8 and 9½-12½. Spoke 1½ h. on Wales Susp. Bill.[9]

[1] No account found.
[2] Introduction of Welsh Suspensory Bill; 4*H* 9. 277.
[3] Add MS 44648, f. 90.
[4] Welsh Suspensory Bill (modelled on Gladstone's Irish Suspensory Bill of 1868), sent by Asquith; Add MS 44517, f. 48.
[5] Asquith replied, 23 February, Add MS 44517, f. 50, that 'I do not see how else to define the bishoprics &c. with which the Bill deals than as "Church of England". We cannot conceal the fact that, pro tanto, that Church is to be affected. The Bill is to be confined to public patronage . . .', and that he was inquiring *re* boundaries.
[6] Private business; 4*H* 9. 289.
[7] W. H. Tucker, *Eton of old; or, Eighty years since 1811–22* (1892).
[8] Probably J. R. Kippax, *Churchyard literature: a choice collection of American epitaphs* (1877).
[9] Not debated this day; presumably a reference to his speech of 23 Feb. 93. This phrase is written in sideways to the diary text, in red ink.

25. Sat.

Wrote to Rev. S.E.G.—Mr Everett MP—Sir A. Gordon—Mr F. Harrison—
.... MP—and minutes. Went to Lyceum to see [Tennyson's] Becket. Capital. Saw Mr Irving—Miss Terry—Miss Ward.

Burned my box of Mrs Thistlethwayte's older letters. I had marked them to
be returned:[1] but I do not know what would become of them. They would lead
to misapprehension: it was in the main an one-sided correspondence:[2] not easy
to understand.

Saw Sir A. West—Mr S.L.—Drove to tea with Mrs Th. Read Orthodox[3]—Mr
Harrison on Home Rule[4]—Tennyson's Becket.[5]

To Sir A. H. GORDON, 25 February 1893.   Add MS 44549, f. 68.

I think there is force in what you say.[6] What I may truly allege is that the first extract from
your Father ascribes to me an intention which I never could have entertained, namely
that of publishing or going to Parliament, although knowing that the first effect wd. be to
worsen the lot of those actually imprisoned.

A general has the right and duty to stake the fates of his men. An authorised Civil
Agent might have some similar right. As a volunteer I always felt that I had none; and I
greatly disapproved of what I understood to be Mazzini's line in this matter. Accordingly
I have always sought to avoid what would in any way aggravate the lot of victims.

A paragraph about the middle of your letter, beginning "I do not know that" is I think
quite true. But undoubtedly what my desire was set upon was to obtain your Father's
intervention. The other (appeal to the people, the *public*, for I am not aware of having
thought of Parliament) was a forlorn hope.

To W. MATHER, M.P., 25 February 1893.   Add MS 44549, f. 68.

I think that on a former occasion I apprised you of the great interest with which I
regard your proposals as to the miners hours.

I found among the miners of Midlothian a great difference of opinion marked by
districts. I suggested the idea of Local option & it seemed at first sight to be favourably
received.[7]

26. 2 S. Lent.

Chapel Royal mg. Guards Evg. Wrote to The Queen—Mr Asquith. Saw Ld
Spencer—Sir A. Clark. Read (new) Sermon Sous Louis Quinze[8]—Life of Wicliff.[9]

To H. H. ASQUITH, 26 February 1893. '*Secret*'.   MS Asquith 9, f. 35.

The inclosed is in no way formidable except that it will entail on me the necessity of
writing rather a long letter.

---

[1] i.e. after his death.
[2] Meaning, presumably, that the substantial letters were those written by him. His letters to Mrs
Thistlethwayte were obtained by the Gladstone family solicitors after her death; see above, v. lxii.
[3] D. Gerard, *Orthodox* (1892).
[4] F. Harrison, 'Notes on the Home Rule Bill (No. 1) Clause Nine', *C.R.*, lxiii. 305 (March 1893).
[5] See 10 Dec. 84.   [6] See 21 Feb. 93n.
[7] No correspondence found.
[8] See 8 Jan. 93; perhaps one of the various new eds. in the 1850s.
[9] L. Sergeant, *John Wyclif, last of the schoolmen and first of the Reformers* (1893).

Can you supply me with any explanation, such as it would be useful to submit, on the reference to you in the second page.[1] It is not a matter of necessity but I thought it possible you might like to say something.

25 February 1893 (Windsor Castle)

The Queen was much surprised to find on reading the report of the debate in the House of Commons on Thursday night that, what Mr Gladstone did not sufficiently explain, and therefore led her to suppose was only a bill for suspending claims founded on vested church interest in Wales—was as Mr Asquith admitted, the first step towards the disestablishment and disendowment of the Church of England!!

There is no 'Church of Wales' and therefore this measure is in reality directed against the whole Church! The Queen thinks Mr Gladstone cannot have fully considered this, and she must say this is a very serious step and one which she cannot help contemplating with great alarm.

She now recognises the force of the protest of the deputation of Convocation received on Thursday in their address, in the answer to which she was advised to ignore the remonstrance of the Bishops and Clergy against this calamitous proceeding.

Surely Mr Gladstone cannot be aware of the strong feeling of uneasiness and apprehension which the Home Rule Bill produces and to add this measure to it is most unfortunate. Had the Queen known the real intention of the Government she would not have passed over in silence the protest of the Bishops and Clergy.

The Queen trusts Mr Gladstone may yet pause before taking so disastrous a step as to attempt to disestablish part of the English Church of which she is the Head, and of which she always thought Mr Gladstone was a loyal member.

(To Mr Gladstone: underlining omitted.)[2]

27. M.

Wrote to Mr Fowler—Mr Asquith—The Queen—Abp of Canty—Mrs Th.—Ld Kimberley—& minutes. H. of C. 4-7¾.[3] Dined at Grillion's. Saw Sir A. West—Mr Bryce—Mr Marj.—Mr Stanhope—Ld Knutsford. Finished 'Orthodox'—Read Our Foreign Competitors.[4]

To J. BRYCE, chancellor of the duchy, 27 February 1893.   MS Bryce 10, f. 131.

I do not think the Cabinet could well consider the adoption of an important change such as you propose in connection with the involved case of Lancashire,[5] or as an executive measure simply. I do not see very strong reasons why under the circumstances now prescribed by the case you should not quietly retrace the steps taken by Dufferin.

We could then here quietly await the advent of legislation on the subject which is an important one.

[1] Asquith replied this day, Add MS 44517, f. 56: '... It is difficult to follow the processes of the Royal mind'; the Bill was self-evidently 'a preliminary step to disestablishment & disendowment'; the reference to Asquith was 'quite inaccurate. I was careful to limit myself to the statement that the Bill was the prelude to disestablishment so far as the four Welsh dioceses are concerned.'
[2] Secretary's note.
[3] Questions; moved motion for morning sittings; 4H 9. 445.
[4] J. Baker, *Our foreign competitors* (1892).
[5] Not found. See 23 Feb. 93.

28. *Tu.*

Wrote to Rev. Mr Dampier[1]—Sir H. Ponsonby—and minutes. Worked by meditation on the question of bimetallism. 14 to dinner (M.P.) H of C. $3\frac{3}{4}$-$7\frac{3}{4}$ and $10\frac{1}{2}$-$12\frac{1}{2}$. Spoke 1 h (so they told me) on Bimetallism.[2] Read 19th C. on Crime—And on A. de Musset.[3] Saw Sir A.W.—Mr Murray—Mr Marj.—Sir W.H.

WED. MCH ONE 1893.

Wrote to Abp of Canterbury—Madame Waddington—Ld Bute—Mr Weld Blundell—J. Morley—W. Downing—& minutes. Dined at Mr Gardner's. Saw Sir A. West—Mr Marj.—Dean of Peterborough—Lady D. Nevill—Lady W. Gardner —French Ambassr—& Madame W. Saw Two [R]. Read Tucker's Eton—and Carnè Fondateurs.[4] Worked on books.

To Sir W. V. HARCOURT, chancellor of the exchequer,   MS Harcourt dep. 13, f. 98.
1 March 1893.

It is I who have to thank you[5]
1. for a capital speech
2. for supplying me, on the bench, with the best half of mine.
The opposition made a failure in a tricky course: Goschen has the chief discredit: the second time in two days!
Marjoribanks did well; helped by your instruction.
A different result would have been a beginning of sorrows.
Douglas said in the lobby before the Division 'The Govt will be in a very tight place'
Under Clark's advice I propose to play truant probably at Brighton from Friday after the meeting of the House to Tuesday morning.

2. *Th.*

Wrote to Mr D. Nutt—Ld Kimberley—and minutes. H. of C. $4\frac{1}{4}$-8.[6] Ten to dinner. Drive with C. Saw Sir A.W.—Mr Morley—Mr Asquith—Mr Marj. Read Carné—Miss Lambert on Becket.[7]

3. *Fr.* [*Lion Mansions, Brighton*]

Wrote to Rev. S.E.G.—Ly Aberdeen—and minutes. Saw Sir A. West—Mr Marj.— Mr Asquith—Siamese Amb. & Capt. V.—Miners 8 hours Depn[8]—Sir W. Harcourt *cum* Mr M. H. of C. $3\frac{1}{4}$-$4\frac{1}{4}$.[9] Then off to Brighton (Lion Mansions—for

---

[1] Offering a rectory to Augustus Dampier, rector of Gillingham, Beccles, which he evidently declined; Add MS 44549, f. 69.
[2] 4*H* 9. 606.
[3] *N.C.*, xxxiii. 480, 525 (March 1893).
[4] L. J. M. de Carné, *Les Fondateurs de l'unité française*, 2v. (1856).
[5] Harcourt wrote this day, Add MS 44203, f. 61, congratulating Gladstone on his speech.
[6] Lawlessness in Co. Clare; 4*H* 9. 840.
[7] A. Lambert, 'Aspects of Tennyson: the real Thomas Becket', *N.C.*, xxxiii. 273 (February 1893).
[8] Given the absence of agreement about the 8 hour day, Gladstone stated the govt.'s unwillingness to enforce it in areas where it was not already agreed upon, or 'to go further in the way of compulsion than to permit it by local option'; *D.N.*, 4 March 1893, 5.
[9] Estimates, 4*H* 9. 980.

quiet).[1] Read Carné Fondateurs—Introduction—Pearson, Forecast[2]—Sir D. Wolff, Notes.[3] Backgammon with Mr A[rmitstead].

4. Sat.

Wrote to Mr Marj.—Ld Kimberley—Mr B. Currie—& minutes. Backgammon with Mr A. Acton came: also Morley. Drive inland. Pier & salt air in perfection. Wrote on Manning.[4] Read Alexandrana[5]—Pearson, National Life R.—Wolff 'Some Notes': thin—&c.

To B. W. CURRIE, banker, 4 March 1893.   Add MS 44549, f. 70.

I received your kind note[6] about the Austrian loan on Tuesday as I went to the House, and I fully intended to cite it. But my sight is now impaired so that when speaking I obtain hardly any assistance from ordinary written notes, and have to depend almost entirely upon memory alone; but in this instance memory played me a trick and completely failed.

I hope the general result has been this: aggression produced a recoil: The H. of C. has recorded its opinion against the reassembling of the Conference; and one of the many impostures current, if not killed, has been so far scotched at least that it can hardly lift its ugly face again for some time to come.

To LORD KIMBERLEY, lord president and Indian secretary,   Kimberley MSS.
4 March 1893.

I was much impressed some years back with a report of Colonel somebody (alas my name-memory) on Indian forestry. The point started was whether this could hereafter solve the question of the frontier.
The steps I think were
1. Planting on the S. side of Hindoo Kuch.
2. Extension to the North side.
3. Increase of cultivable soil and modification of climate in Afghanistan.
4. Consequent change of the habits of the people to settled life and to agriculture.
5. The constitution of a solid nation & a *living* barrier.
If you do not know the report it is worth looking back to. It must be well known in the Office. The upshot is a desire for the extension & efficiency of the Indian Forestry Department.

To E. MARJORIBANKS, chief whip, 4 March 1893.   Add MS 44549, f. 70.

I do not know whether you have at command a really clever and biting pamphleteer. If you have I think there is a capital field opened in the Unionist proceedings of the last few days; and it might be entitled "a week of friction".
It is an ascending scale:
1. There is the paltry proceeding by which when we sought to save perhaps 20 hours, they discounted us by wasting 2 or 3 in worthless discussion, and by the thinnest pretexts supported their voting in the direct contrary way to the liberals last year. All in hope of a good division which failed.

---

[1] See 30 Mar. 85; on this occasion, probably paid for by Armitstead.
[2] See 20 Jan. 93.   [3] Sir H. D. Wolff, *Some notes of the past, 1870–1891* (1893).
[4] One of various papers of recollection, in *Autobiographica*, i.
[5] Untraced.
[6] Not found. For the bimetallism debate; see 28 Feb. 93.

2. Then the yet more paltry shift of Tuesday, and the resolution which involved nothing, all in the same hope, and with not merely failure but a disastrous & smashing result.
3. Then on Thursday the "urgent" debate for some three hours on Co. Clare which has slept all these years, though three times in succession the Judge of Assizes has denounced the state of things.
4. Last and worst the impudent assault on the chair. All with two special ulterior aims; (a) to obstruct business, (b) to clog the H.R. Bill and mix it up with the Budget after Easter, in the hope of its not reaching the H. of Lords.

I do not know whether Paul could do this.[1]

The more I think the more I am impressed with the vital necessity of the 2d. reading before Easter.

5. S.

St Paul's with H.C. mg. But in evg prayers with C. I did not like to create an evening concourse by going to Ch. Wrote to Lady Harcourt. Read Mad. de Crespigny[2]—Life of Wiclif—From Darkness to Light[3]—and Tracts. Much conversation with A[cton].

To E. MARJORIBANKS, chief whip, 5 March 1893.   Add MS 44549, f. 71.

I had no idea you could or would extend my leave until tomorrow, but I think it right to accept the permission for Brighton has done me marked good in a department where it was required.

The web of obstruction seems to have been cunningly & widely woven: we must hold above all by our first & main subject the Irish Bill: if we win in this there will perhaps be a remission of friction in other matters.

6. M.

Wrote to Priv. Sec. (Tel.). Pier airing & drive. Ld Acton left us. Backgammon with Mr A. Read Alexandrana—Pearson—and Bourget Cosmopolis.[4] Marked improvement from Brighton climate in the department requiring it.

7. Tu.

Wrote to Mr Marj.—Mr [blank]—Sir J. Paget—Marquis of Bute. Pier airing. Drive by Rottingdean and race course. Saw Rev. D. Robertson. Backgammon with Mr A. Read Pearson, National Life—Bourget Cosmopolis.

8. Wed. [London]

Wrote to The Queen—Mr Reid—Mrs Bolton B.P.—Mr Armitstead—and minutes. Off at 9½ to London. Cabinet 12–2¼. Saw Sir A. West—Mr Marjoribanks—Ld Curzon—& others. Drive with C. Dined at Ld Tweedmouth's. Finished Alexandrana—Read Ville Hardouin Conquete de Constantinople.[5]

[1] Marjoribanks replied next day that he would 'induce' H. Paul to 'do the work you suggest'; Add MS 44332, f. 243.
[2] Perhaps C. de Crespigny, *A vision of great men, with other poems and translations* (1848).
[3] A. A. I., *From darkness to light* (1872).
[4] P. C. J. Bourget, *Cosmopolis* (1893); a novel.
[5] G. de Villehardouin, *La conquête de Constantinople*, ed. E. Bouchet, 2v. (1891); first published 1584.

Cabinet. Wed. Mch. 9. [sc. 8] *1893. Noon.*[1]

1. Loss [*sic*] Chancellor's Primogeniture Bill. Not to be renewed *in Land Transfer Bill*.
2. State of Business in H of C. Change 2R to Thurs. 16. oppose Hobhouse's motion[2] but intimate [blank space left]
3. Morley reported ferment increasing in Belfast. Fear that the Orange leaders may be unable as the Bill proceeds to restrain their followers—no fear of "an organised rising". Buller not alarmed. Wolseley in good heart.
   Since 86 Protestant provisions[?] of R.I.C. in Belfast.
4. Also outrages are increasing.
   Au. to Feb. 92–3   Agrarian—13%
   —   −35
   (But 11 v.g. for Series Jan. & Feb.).
   Nonagrarian 645 incr. to 719—11 per cent.
   & Serious 85 to 101.
5. Change of venue. Two Kings Bench Judges having spoken as to its necessity. Court will probably be more willing to give. (Sir W.H. it shd. be judicial rather than *executive*)
6. Evicted Tenants. Recommendation of Commission we agreed to. Facts to be further examined—including Church Surplus Fund.

9. *Th.*

Wrote to Mad. Novikoff—Dr Hutton—Dean Liddell—and minutes. H. of C. 4¼–7 and 11¼–1¼.[3] Saw H.N.G.—Sir A. West—Mr Marj.—Ld Aberdare—Mr Atkin & his two young black protégés[4]—Sir W. Harcourt. Read Ville Hardouin—Pearson. Worked on list of colleagues.

To Rev. Dr. G. C. HUTTON, 9 March 1893.   Add MS 44549, f. 71.

With reference to the important subject of your letter, I may confidentially inform you that we have not yet obtained sufficient information as to the views of the representatives of Scotland but we hope soon to possess it & resolve on our course accordingly. You will however observe that obstruction is aiming at & obtaining new methods & proportions.

10. *Fr.*

Wrote to The Queen—Mr Morley—Ld Bute—C.G.—& minutes. Dined at Mr Rendel's. Finished list of [Cabinet] colleagues: *sixty nine to this date*. Saw Sir A. West—Mr Marj.—Mr Murray—Mr Caine—Sir W. Harcourt—Mr McCarthy—also T.P. O'Connor on Irish attendance. Audience of the Queen at 3¾ PM. A form as usual, indeed I fear a sham. Read Ville Hardouin. H. of C. 2½–7½ (less the Audience) and 9½–11¼. Spoke at both sittings.[5] On the main business a bad day.

11. *Sat.*

Wrote to A. Arnold—Sir H. Ponsonby—C.G.—Mrs Bolton—and minutes. Saw Sir A. West—Mr Marj.—Sir W. Harcourt—Mr Perkins—Ly Aberdeen—Mr Morley—

[1] Add MS 44648, f. 92.
[2] Hobhouse's motion of difficulties of 'unofficial members' amended in ink by Gladstone; Add MS 44648, f. 74. See 10 Mar. 93.   [3] Army administration; 4*H* 9. 1538.
[4] Not further identified.   [5] On Scottish disestablishment; not found.
[6] On Saturday sittings, and on Hobhouse's motion on unofficial members' business; 4*H* 9. 1648, 1674.

Ld Aberdeen. Conclave on business. Dined at Ld Kimberley's to settle list of sheriffs. H. of C. 12½–1¼; 3–7½.[1] Read Villehardouin. Off to Harry's Hampstead Cottage at 11.

To Mrs. GLADSTONE, 11 March 1893.[2]   Hawarden MS 780, f. 219.

In my note of yesterday I described the formal and menacing character of my audience at Buckingham Palace: but I ought to have mentioned that she inquired somewhat kindly after your health. But a painful sense of unreality pervades these conversations and the public announcement of an audience hoodwinks the public.

I was glad to hear that your journey was satisfactorily accomplished.

Here I have nothing good to report. The audacity of organised obstruction has reached a height hitherto unknown. The badness of our divisions yesterday, which has greatly worsened the situation, were [*sic*] almost entirely due to the absences of Irish members on a set of questions which in substance and reality belonged to the vital fortunes of the Irish Government Bill. These absences were not sixteen but twenty two: and our divisions instead of being 21, 22, 27, ought to have been 43, 44 and 49, which would have borne an entirely different aspect.

The arrangement for going to Hampstead,[3] now fixed, has not proved appropriate for the time—after attending most of the day I am even at half past six totally uncertain how long I or how long the House may have to sit between this time and midnight, or whether I can attend the official dinner for pricking the sheriffs. It is now extremely difficult to say whether we can have the second reading of the Bill before Easter. In fact practically we despair of it, and shall have to put forward some of the English Bills as the best substitute in our power to use.

I saw the Aberdeens this morning and they seem to have won[?] fresh evidence through Ld Stanley's[?] eldest son of the intention to resign the Governorship of Canada not later than in July or August.

As the little children say, I think I must now come to an end: in truth I write amidst such distraction and can hardly say whether there is anything in the way of further news: except it be that Harcourt and Fowler are gone to Windsor this morning, and that for once a Wesleyan Methodist will have to make his way back to town on a Sunday. Ever your Affte. WE Gladstone

12. 4 S. Lent.

ChCh. Hampst. mg & aft. Herbert came. Music in evg. Read Gore's Mission of the Church +[4]—Life of Dr Webster[5]—Life of Wiclif (Sergeant).

13. M.

Off at 10.15: a slight cold. Saw Sir A.C., who ordered me to bed forthwith. Wrote to Rev. Mr Owen—Mr . . .—Mr Morley—and minutes. Saw Scotts—Sir A. West—Sir A.C. (2°) in evg. Read Villehardouin—Arnold's Adzuma[6]—Tucker's Eton.[7]

---

[1] Spoke on army administration; 4 *H* 9. 1799.
[2] Part in Bassett, 257.   [3] To stay with H. N. Gladstone.
[4] C. Gore, *The mission of the Church. Four lectures* (1892). See to S. Gladstone, 20 Mar. 93. On 29 March, Gladstone asked Murray, the publishers, for 20 copies to distribute; Add MS 44549, f. 76.
[5] Perhaps H. E. Scudder, *Noah Webster* (1881).
[6] Sir E. Arnold, *Adzuma; or, the Japanese wife. A play* . . . (1893).
[7] See 24 Feb. 93.

14. Tu.

Bed all day. Saw Sir A. Clark twice—Saw Sir A. West for business and minutes. Read as yesterday—finishing Tucker's Eton.

15. Wed.

Rose after dusk, and dined: we had only Lucy and Morley. Saw Sir A. West—S.L.—Sir A. Clark twice (he is well satisfied)—Ld Rosebery. Read Villehardouin (finished)—Schoolmaster's Romance[1]—Adzuma (finished).

16. Th.

Wrote to Mr Morley—Sir H. Ponsonby—S.E.G. l.l.—Mr Whitbread MP—Mr Wallace MP—Sir M. Biddulph—& minutes. Backgammon with Mr A. who dined. Saw Sir A. West—Mr Marj. *cum* Sir W. Harcourt—Mr Bryce. Read Pearson—Romance of a Schoolmaster.

To J. MORLEY, Irish secretary, 16 March 1893.   Add MS 44549, f. 73.

I do not very well see what change as to finance we can at this juncture determine upon;[2] the revenue & charge of the coming year being an essential element for our final plans. We have laid down broadly the principle of equitable contribution. We have implied that the case of war contribution has been left in view. And we have actually in hand (so to speak) by subsection 5 of Clause 10 which imposes on Ireland, as it stands, much more than in ordinary circumstances she ought to pay. You may have definite ideas, but I am for the present wholly without them. Even the question between *quota* & *fund* will I suppose have to await its final decision in the Committee. It involves no fundamental principle.
[P.S.] See my Speech p. 24 herewith. The passage is not long but is rather comprehensive.

17. Fr.

Wrote to H.M. Gilbert—The Queen—Messrs [blank]—and minutes. H. of C. $2\frac{1}{4}$–$4\frac{1}{2}$.[3] Saw Sir A. West—S.L.—Sir W. Harcourt cum Mr Marj.—Mr Whitbread M.P. Conversation with Ly Thealby [*sic?*] (O.F.)[4]—Ly Ampthill (Ld Beaconsfield). Read Pearson—Romance &c. Dined at Baron F. de Rothschilds.

18. Sat. [The Durdans, Epsom]

Wrote minutes. Off at 4.30 to the Durdans.[5] Much conversation. Saw Sir A. West—E.Hamilton. Read Toland on Events in Prussia & Hanover[6]—Pearson (finished)—Newark Election 1790.[7]

---

[1] E. de Amicis, *Romance of a schoolmaster*, 3v. (1893).
[2] Apparently an answer to an untraced letter or conversation; Morley's letter of 14 March, Add MS 44257, f. 89, did not raise the financial question.
[3] Misc. business; 4 *H* 10. 437.
[4] Presumably on the Oak Farm bankruptcy of 1847.
[5] Rosebery's house by the racecourse at Epsom.
[6] J. Toland, *An account of the courts of Prussia and Hanover* (1705).
[7] Not found.

19. 5 S. Lent.

Ch. mg & Parish Ch. aft. Saw the Vicar. Read Gore's remarkable & admirable 'Mission of the Ch'.[1] Read the Golden Bottle[2]—Sergeant's Life of Wiclif. Wrote to S.E.G.—J. McCarthy.

20. M. [London]

Back to London by the 11.9. Wrote to Sir H. Ponsonby—Mr S. Karr MP.[3]—Mr Pearson—Mr Reader—Rev. S.E.G.—Mayor of Newark—and minutes. Dined at Ld Brassey's. Saw Sir W. Harcourt—Mr Marj.—Sir A. West—Mr Waterfield—Mr Bryce—Sir W. Harcourt. H. of C. 4–8¼. Spoke upon (la maledetta)[4] Uganda.[5] Read Romance &c.—Hist. Helene de Ligne.[6]

To S. E. GLADSTONE, 20 March 1893.   Add MS 44549, f. 73.

1. I have written to recommend Mr. Sheepshanks.[7]
2. However respected and respectable the Rector of Liverpool[8] may be, he is not a man up to the mark which in my view qualifies for the Cathedral preferment in the gift of the Crown.
2. I have been reading with great delight Mr. Gore's 'Mission of the Church'.[9] I do not know when I have seen so much matter in so small a book and in general so admirably stated. If you have it not I should like to give it you.
   Is it true that he keenly desires parochial preferment?[10]
   In one shape or other he ought to be advanced and I should be glad if he resigns his present employment. He is a much broader man than Dr. Pusey, with rather a different work to do—and the association with the name does him some injustice.

21. Tu.

Wrote to Ld Reay—Rev. Mr Sheepshanks—Sir H. Ponsonby—Mr Marj.—Archd. Denison—& minutes. H. of C. 2½–5½.[11] Drive with C. Saw Sir A. West—Sir W. Harcourt—Mr Marj. Read the Grande Dame—O'Neill Daunt Hist of Ireland.[12]

22. Wed.

Wrote to J. Bryce—Ld Kimberley—W. Wright—Philad. Meeting Tel.—and minutes. H. of C. 12¼–1¼. Spoke on Uganda.[13] Saw Sir A. West—Mr Marj.—Mr

[1] See 12 Mar. 93.   [2] I. Donnelly, *The golden bottle* (1892).
[3] Apparently *sic*; none of this name.   [4] 'The hateful'.
[5] Clashing with Labouchere, who moved a reduction in the vote for Portal's mission; 4 *H* 10. 549.
[6] L. Perey, *Histoire d'une grande dame au XVIIIᵉ siècle. La Princesse Hélène de Ligne*, 2v. (1887–90). She was also known as Helen Potocka.
[7] Appointing John Sheepshanks, 1834–1912, to the see of Norwich.
[8] Alexander Stewart, rector of Liverpool since 1870; Gladstone owned the advowson, but bought it after Stewart's appointment.
[9] See 12 Mar. 93.
[10] Gore (see 11 Jan. 85) was then Librarian of Pusey House in Oxford; later in 1893 he became incumbent of Radley, a small parish near Oxford, where he was not happy.
[11] Spoke on business of the House; 4 *H* 10. 677.
[12] See 30 June 86.
[13] Again clashing with Labouchere; 4 *H* 10. 772.

Meux—Sir W. Harcourt—Mr Fowler. Saw Grandt [R?]. Pleasant dinner at Mr Whites. Much conversation with Mrs White—Duchess of Sutherland—W. Richmond—& M. Jusserand. Read Princesse C. de Ligne—O'Neill Daunt.

23. Thurs.

Wrote to Sir E. Grey—Mr Blunt—Mr A. Reader—Mr Matthew[1]—& minutes. H. of C. $4\frac{1}{4}$–8. Minds are in a lively state.[2] Saw J. Talbot (jun.)—Sir A. West—Mr Marj.—Sir R. Welby *cum* Mr H.—M. Jusserand—Mr Spicer—Mr Whitbread. Fourteen to dinner. Read Grande Dame—Field, Atlantic Telegraph.[3]

24. Fr.

Wrote to The Queen—Ld Kimberley—& minutes. Drive with C. Evg at home. Cabinet 12–$1\frac{3}{4}$. H. of C. $2\frac{1}{4}$–4.[4] Saw Sir A. West—Mr Marj.—Mr Rathbone—Mr Massingham. Read Grande Dame—Congested District Report.

Cabinet. Mch. 24. 1893. Noon.[5]
1. Agreed to give Monday for motion arraigning the Irish Govt. by Balfour.
2. Plan for taking time after Easter.
3. Harcourt's Finance.
   1892–3 Est. Surplus 4 m[ille]
   1893–4 Est. Deficit[?] 1m͡: Rev[enue]—750 m[ille]
                    (1,088m)
   Action of H. of C.—1d I[ncome] T[ax] + Treasury Chest 250 m.
4. Contagious Diseases India.
   Stansfield [*sic*] proposal.
   K[imberley] agrees as to the tabling of the evidence & to be publshed. K. to send me[?] a paper[?][6]
4.[*sic*] Payment of members tonight.
   W.E.G. said he proposed to take no part.
   Further talk to be at $6\frac{1}{2}$.[7]
5. To meet again on Tues. unless H. agrees to I.G. Bill on Thurs.

25. Sat.

Wrote to S.E.G.—Ld Kimberley—Mad. Taine—Mr Stansfeld—Ld Acton—and minutes. Dined at Ld Breadalbane's. Saw Sir A. West—Sir W. Harcourt—Mr

[1] Charles Matthew, probably editor of a periodical, on reprinting Gladstone's youthful translation of Hecuba; Add MS 44549, f. 74.
[2] D. P. Barton moved the adjournment on the case of the Fenian, John Foley; 4 *H* 10. 801.
[3] C. W. Field, *The Atlantic telegraph* (1856).
[4] Series of exchanges in question time; 4 *H* 10. 903.
[5] Add MS 44648, f. 95.
[6] Note passed in Cabinet reads: [Gladstone:] 'Have we any remaining difficulty about Contagious Diseases India?' [Kimberley:] 'I should like to have it mentioned here'; Add MS 44648, f. 96.
[7] Gladstone told the Queen, CAB 41/22/37: 'The members of the Cabinet in general appear favourable to the payment not only of members who need this aid for the fulfilment of their duties, but of all members. They do not think however that this can be accomplished at the present time.'

Marj.—Ld Spencer—Ld Acton—and many at Ld Breadalbane's. Also Mr Morley *cum* Ld S. Read Helene de Ligne—Atlantic Telegraph.

To J. STANSFELD, M.P., 25 March 1893.[1]   Add MS 44549, f. 74.

I am very glad to think that in this important matter of the Contagious Diseases Acts arrangements in India we have virtually come in sight of the goal & are about to touch it. As to expediting the business so as to dispose of it during the present Session we are entirely of your mind. As to the point of publicity we agree to your proposal that the evidence of your witnesses shall be put into authentic form before the Committee, that evidence in that form to become public after the Indian Govt. has had its opportunity of reply so as to bring the matter finally to a head. We do not feel we can ask ⟨you⟩ to impose upon you & your friends any obligation to treat the matter as confidential. At the same time we hope, & indeed anticipate, that they will maintain as much reserve, about all *ex parte* statements as they may feel that they properly can.

26. S.

Ch. Royal mg & St James's evg. Saw Abp of Canterbury—The Breadalbanes. Read Faith Healing[2]—Westcott, Divine Life[3]—..... on Systematic Theology—&c. Wrote to H.N.G.—The Queen.

27. M.

Party Meeting 12–1¼. Excellent: most opportune.[4] H. of C. 4–8, 8¾–11½. Spoke a second time.[5] Well tired. Saw Sir A. West—Mr Marj.—and others. Read Helen *Potocki*.[6]

28. Tues.

Wrote to S.E.G.—Hon Mrs Talbot—Sir J. Lacaita—& minutes. Saw H.N.G. (Indian Currency) mg, & evg. Conclave on do H. of C. at 6. Deputations on Irish Govt at 12, and at 1. Replied to each in a kind of speech.[7] Saw Viceroy of Ireland—Sir A. West—Mr Murray—Mr Marj. Read Helen Potocki—Land of Ararat.[8] Worked on books. H. of C. 2–4 and 5¾–7¼.[9]

---

[1] See also letters to Kimberley, 21, 24 March 1893, Add MS 44549, f. 74, on difficulties of accommodating a Select Cttee. in the Commons; a department cttee. was appointed, leading to the amendment in 1895 of the Cantonment Act 1889; see J. L. and B. Hammond, *James Stansfeld* (1932), 272 ff.

[2] J. M. Buckley, *Faith healing* (1892).

[3] See 15 Jan. 93.

[4] Emphasis on the need for party reticence and discipline during the Session; *T.T.*, 28 March 1893, 11a.

[5] On business of the House; Balfour followed with his motion on governmental incompetence in Ireland; 4*H* 10. 1201.

[6] See 20 Mar. 93.

[7] Unionist deputations from the Belfast Chamber of Commerce and from City of London bankers and merchants; reports in *Freeman's Journal*, 29 March 1893, 5–6.

[8] A. Macdonald, *The land of Ararat; or, up on the roof of the world* (1893).

[9] Misc. business; 4*H* 10. 1359.

To Sir J. P. LACAITA, 28 March 1893.   Add MS 44234, f. 222.

On receiving your letter of the 19th with its inclosure, I felt that it wd. be difficult to comply with the request which the Editors of the Ricasoli papers had done me the honour to make;[1] but I also felt that I ought not to reply without carefully examining the question.

I am sorry to say that the result of that examination is unfavourable. It is plain that the Pope was the principal party to such a conversation. It might be questioned whether I was authorised even to make known to Baron Ricasoli its purport, though this was done in confidence & because I thought at the time that it was in the interest of all parties concerned. Clearly I have not acquired by the lapse of time any title to carry the matter further. The main question I fear is still a burning question.

I could not even for myself venture to treat it without reserve, much less am I authorised to make *myself* the spokesman of His Holiness.

There are other considerations leading to a similar conclusion, but I have said I fear already enough to warrant & demand it. In conveying it please to convey also my regrets & my sincere respect.

I trust you are rallying to full strength & will soon be among us.

29. Wed.

Wrote to Mr Tollemache—Mr Bryce—Messrs Murray—Mrs Grandt—Mr Hinshelwood[2]—Mr T.W. Russell MP.—& minutes. H. of C. 12–2 and 5–6¼.[3] Backgammon with Mr A. Saw Sir A. West—Mr Marj. Worked on books. Alas no Church—on this great day. Read Helen Potocki.

30. Th. [Brighton]

Wrote to J. Westell—Mr Dowling—Mr Ivory—Keeper of Printed Books—Mr Roden Noel—Ld Rosebery—and minutes. House of C. 3½–5½.[4] Worked on books. Saw Sir A. West—Mr Marj.—Mr Murray—Mr Westell. Reached Brighton at 8 PM. Read Chamberlain in NC[5]—The German Emperor &c.

To LORD ROSEBERY, foreign secretary, 30 March 1893.   N.L.S. 10026, f. 101.

Thanks for your suggestion.[6] Alas that I should need a monitor.

What a *farce* apart from any thing else are these attacks on *England* in *Belgium*. Can you not in some reply to Monson infuse a gentle touch of irony? The merest soupçon. [P.S.] I cannot help *wishing* we could use "good offices" (vide Pacifico case) between Sweden & Norway. So far as I yet know, Norway has a strict *right*, but is making a bad use of it.

[1] Request *via* Lacaita for publication of Gladstone's mem. of his conversation with Pius IX on 22 Oct. 66 (sent to Ricasoli on 5 Jan. 67); Gladstone consulted Acton on 25 March, Add MS 44549, f. 75. It was later published in Lathbury, ii. 395 and above, vi. 472.

[2] A. Ernest Hinchelwood had sent his *Through starlight to dawn* (1893); Add MS 44549, f. 76.

[3] Spoke on privilege, business of the House, revenue depts.; 4*H* 10. 1403, 1409, 1486.

[4] Questions; business of the House; 4*H* 10. 1505, 1512.

[5] J. Chamberlain, 'A bill for the weakening of Great Britain', *N.C.*, xxxiii. 545 (April 1893).

[6] Not found.

31. Good Friday.

11–3 Chapel Royal: admirable Sermon from Rev. W. Wakeford:[1] then to St
Paul's. Wrote to S.E.G.—Mary Drew—& minutes. Read New Catholic Church[2]—
Difendiamo la famiglia[3]—Xt in the Two Testaments[4]—D'Antraigues.[5]

Sat. Easter Eve Ap 1. 93.

Wrote to T.W. Ellis MP—Mr Tollemache—A. West—Miss Hwyl(?)—and
minutes. St James's Ch. 10½ A.M. Read D'Antraigues—The Heroine of 49.[6]
Backgammon with Mr A.

2. Easter Day.

Early celebration Ch Royal. Morning service in the Dome:[7] 3000 Volunteers.
Chapel Royal Evg. Wrote to Bp of Chichester—Mrs Sands—Sir W. Farquhar—
S.E.G. Read Orr 'God & the World'[8]—19 Cent. on Future retribution[9]—Bp
Ridding's Charge.[10] Airing on the old Pier.

3. M.

St James's Ch at 10.30 AM. Wrote to Mr Sheepshanks—Mr Marj.—Rev S.E.G.—
Mr Trumbull—The Queen—Mr Murray (Tel.)—and minutes. Read Courtenay
[on bimetallism] in N.C.—King of Sweden in do[11]—D'Antraigues—Heroine of
1849. Backgammon with Mr A[rmitstead]. The Actons came. Much conversation.

To S. E. GLADSTONE, 3 April 1893.[12]   Hawarden MS 840, f. 4.
Dearest Stephy,
   I have read your letter with deep interest. It raises you, if this be possible, still higher in
my estimation. The idea of your severance from Hawarden Rectory is from many points
of view frightful. But I must admit there is great force in your reasons. Especially do I
enter into and adopt your desire for some mental leisure & opportunity of refreshment &
enlargement. I think it was observed in the case of so rich a man as Bp S. Wilberforce that
he suffered from not importing in due proportion to what he exported. Further I see that
in being *trans*ferred you do not wish to be *pre*ferred. My opinion is that preferment is in
the Providence of God to be at some time your lot: but *you* as my son could hardly
receive it from me as Minister with advantage of propriety. But within the most modest

[1] William Wakeford, curate of St. Saviour, Eastbourne. Gladstone gathered information on him
with a view to preferment, but found none; see Add MS 44549, f. 77.
[2] J. Morris, *Catholic England in modern times* (1892); see 14 May 93.
[3] Untraced.
[4] Perhaps A. M. Fairbairn, *Christ in the centuries and other sermons* (1893).
[5] One of the various works on the French revolution of E. L. H. A. de Launay, Count d'Antraigues.
[6] Untraced.
[7] Part of the stables of the Royal Pavilion, converted into a concert hall.
[8] J. Orr, *The Christian view of God and the world* (1893).
[9] Mivart in *N.C.*, xxxiii. 637 (April 1893).
[10] G. Ridding, 'The second visitation charge' (1893).
[11] *N.C.*, xxxiii. 1710 (April 1893).
[12] Secretary's copy.

limits there are diversities of choice. On the one side are congregations like that of Mr Sheepshanks with much religious life (as I gather), but well to do: on the other side are charges where the poor, & the *people* decidedly preponderate. The former class would I think give you more mental leisure. But I should much like to know in which direction your choice inclines.

2. As you have followed Mr Sheepshanks business thus far, I send for your perusal an excellent letter from him. But I do not think that as representing the Crown I could enter into the arrangements which he suggests.

3. I have just written to recommend Mr Davenport Jones. Might you not at the proper time recommend him to study the Squire's wishes & prepossessions as far as he properly can. Ever your affecte father   WEG
Blessings & Blessings for the birthday.

4. *Tu.*

Wrote to A. West—Sir H. Ponsonby—Sir G. Trevelyan. Saw Mr P.M. Campbell —Ld Oxenbridge—The Roth family—Ld Acton. Read D'Antraigues—The Heroine of 1849. Backgammon with Mr A.

5. *Wed.*

Wrote to Ld Rosebery—Ld Ripon—Mr Leggatt[1]—S. Ln Tel.—Mr Seymour Keay—and minutes. Saw MacCurran (intruder)—Supt of Police—Sir U. Shuttleworth—Mr G. Russell. Backgammon with Mr A. Read as yesterday. Worked on Irish question: for debate tomorrow.

To LORD RIPON, colonial secretary, 5 April 1893. '*Immediate*'.   Add MS 43515, f. 104.

Is there any *Statute*, or other *law*, which prevents the self-governing Colonies from intervening on their own account in Diplomacy, and Foreign relations? E.g. Canada with U.S.

To LORD ROSEBERY, foreign secretary, 5 April 1893.   Add MS 44549, f. 78.

I could have wished to answer today your interesting & I think most reasonable letter just received,[2] but I have run the early post hard in reading and considering the astonishing despatch & letters from Sir G. Portal.

The good point is that he seems to show very well in them. They seem also to raise very important matters for consideration.

One suggestion they carry to my mind is that after he has framed his report one of the alternatives for his consideration should be his bringing it, or coming himself sharp upon its heels. Excuse bad writing.

[P.S.] If you think the papers require a Cabinet at once, it could be on Friday at 12.[3]

6. *Th.* [*London*]

To London by 9.45. Worked on papers for debate. Wrote to Sir W. Farquhar— Rev. C. Hargrave—Ld Rosebery—Rev. Mr Barker—The Queen—and minutes.

[1] T. G. Leggatt, on translating Horace; Add MS 44549, f. 78.
[2] Replying ('terribly slow') to Gladstone's of 30 March; Add MS 44290, f. 119.
[3] Rosebery replied, 6 April, ibid., f. 121, that Portal's letter was private, and therefore could not be publicly acted on: 'The charges against the Company's officials are grave, but I do not see that we could deal with them at this juncture'; Rodd to request Portal to report officially.

H. of C. $3\frac{1}{2}$–8 & $9\frac{3}{4}$–$11\frac{3}{4}$. Spoke $1\frac{1}{2}$ h. on moving the second reading.[1] Saw Sir A. West—S.L.—Sir G. Trevelyan—Mr Marj.—Mr Asquith—Sir W. Harcourt. Read D'Antraigues—Heroine of 1849 finished.

To LORD ROSEBERY, foreign secretary, 6 April 1893.   Add MS 44549, f. 78.

The drift of my letter was simply to open the door for meeting any possible desire of yours—I do not think an Uganda Cabinet is necessary now. It is I think needful that Portal should report as you have instructed Rodd to tell him. Might he not also be told to consider what I suggested, the possibility, in view of these grave charges, of his coming home about them? and bringing or preparing his witnesses.

7. Fr. [Brighton]

Brighton at $7\frac{1}{2}$ P.M. Wrote to Mr G. Bowles MP.[2]—Scotts—Mr B. Currie—Mr Westell—The Queen—& minutes. H. of C. $3\frac{1}{2}$–$5\frac{1}{2}$.[3] Saw Sir A.W.—Mr Marj.—Mr B. Currie—Mr M.—Mr A.M. Read Newb. H. Magazine[4]—Voice from the South.[5]

8. Sat.

Wrote to Private Secret. Tel.—Ld Breadalbane—Mr Sheepshanks—Rev. Dr. Cox—S.E.G. l.l.—Rev. R. Barker—Sir W. Harcourt—& minutes—Mr Brodrick MP. Drive: visited the noble Churches St Martin & St Bartholomew.[6] Backgammon with Mr A. Read Lyall's India[7]—Voice from the South.

To S. E. GLADSTONE, 8 April 1893.[8]   Hawarden MS 840, f. 6.

Dearest Stephy,

The whole idea of severing you from the charge, let alone the House, is a wrench, and a rend; and separates bone and marrow. It is moreover a very complex business; & the succession is most formidable. What I think is this. We should hope, if you will have us, to come to you, and at any rate to Hawarden, at Whitsuntide: when we can prosecute this subject in free conversation.

In the meantime, pray understand I do not seek to be a part in *propelling* you to resign Hawarden.

But if God guides you to that conclusion—and if you arrive at it I shall feel assured that it is by His guidance—and if the immediate object of your contemplation shall be rather a temporary than a permanent cure—pray consider, and not for a rapid reply, whether the following suggestion has anything in it.

I am very anxious to constitute and set going my Hawarden or St. Deiniol's trust. Partly I want the Library worked into shape, set upon orderly and systematic lines. But this is not the *main* thing, for it might be done by various kinds of people quite *subordinately*, of course if they have in them a spice of Bibliographical taste. But while the Library is in

---

[1] G.I. Bill 2°R; $4H$ 10. 1597.

[2] Thomas Gibson Bowles, 1843–1922; tory M.P. King's Lynn 1892–1906; later a free trade liberal.

[3] G.I. Bill, 2°R; $4H$ 10. 1717.

[4] *Newbery House Magazine*, viii (April 1893).

[5] D. Defoe, *A voice from the South* (1707).

[6] Built in 1881 and 1875 respectively.

[7] Sir A. Lyall, *The rise and expansion of the British Dominion in India* (1893).

[8] Secretary's copy. No reply traced.

some sense the foundation, I want to build upon it an institution: a Clergy House, a House of Rest & refreshment not rigidly confined to our own Clergy, a House of Study for the glory of God and the culture of men, a House of Mission perhaps for Liverpool, a House of help perhaps for the parish of Hawarden, and of course a House of Prayer and worship. *Could not you* perhaps undertake the quiet & cautious modelling of all this? Could not you become the first head of my Trust? We should have much Counsel and I think sweet Counsel upon it.

You see my position is this, that while I continue in this life of contention I have not brain free to prosecute the subject unaided, or to take the 'labouring over'. But in association I think we could get on, and you would have a full share of influence.

The consideration where you were to dwell will of course come up if the notion is entertained. So will remuneration; but you must certainly have something, and not *less* than £300 a year. Ever your affte. Father W.E. Gladstone

The inclosed is most interesting. Can you give us the communicants for the whole Parish?

In no case send me a rapid negative I pray.

To Sir W. V. HARCOURT, chancellor of the exchequer,   MS Harcourt dep. 13, f. 99.
8 April 1893.

I am very glad that you have had the curious question of the Chiltern Hundreds thoroughly worked out.[1]

1. The statement as to me in p. 32 corresponds with my recollection.

I could add to it as follows.

It fell to me to appoint (I think) Mr Roupell MP[2] to the Chiltern Hundreds and this on account of his "shining virtues" if I recollect the words aright.

This being so I was rather disgusted when the case of [Edwin] James turned up.[3] I am not sure that we knew any facts at the time, but it *smelt* very ill, a strong suspicion of blackguardism hanging about him.

Accordingly I tried to move the Palmerston Cabinet to let me propose a change in the system: But that Cabinet unless under pressure or with inducement (which was not thought to include improvement) was commonly immovable. So it was on this occasion.

So I did the only & poor thing left to me, by striking out the shining virtues. It was not my *object* to enlarge any discretion, but only to remove a scandal.

2. I have no trustworthy recollections in the stamping and sealing. But I vaguely think
a. that I did nothing except to sign
b. that the paper carried no stamp.

I think that Sir C. Ryan, the present Auditor General, who was my Private Secretary 30 years ago, would probably have a readily available recollection on the subject.

The paper appears to be most careful & most curious

Lord North in p. 24 is indeed Lord North all over.

[1] Mem. on the Chiltern Hundreds sent, 7 April, by Harcourt; Add MS 44203, f. 69.
[2] William Roupell, liberal M.P. Lambeth 1857-62; took Chiltern Hundreds April 1862; convicted of forgery September 1862.
[3] In the case of Edwin James (d. 1882; liberal M.P. Marylebone 1859-61 when took Chiltern Hundreds with debts of £100,000), Gladstone had altered the wording of the Warrant.

9. 1 S.E.

St Martin's mg (10¾–1¼) with H.C., St James's evg (*crammed*). Wrote to Mrs Sands—Mary Drew—R. Cameron—and minutes. Read Chapman on Genesis[1]—Luccock's Ch of Scotland[2]—Revue Internat. de Theologie.[3]

10. M. [*London*]

In D. St at 2.50. Wrote to The Queen—Dr Ginsburg—& minutes. H. of C. 3½–7¾.[4] Dined at Grillion's. Saw Sir A. West—Mr Marj.—H.N.G.—A. Morley—Ld Acton. Read Voice from the South—Beust's Memoirs.[5]

11. Tu.

Wrote to Rev. Barker—U.S. Minister—M. Drew—Ld Acton—The Queen—and minutes. H. of C. 3½–7¾ and 9¾–12.[6] Saw Sir A. West—Mr Marj.—and others. Read Voice from the South (finished).

12. Wed.

Wrote to Ld Rosebery—Watson & Smith—H. Drew—Mr Sheepshanks—A. Morley—and minutes. Conclave on course of the debate. Saw Sir A. West—Mr Marj.—Mr Mundella—Mr Story—Dr Cameron—Saw W. Wickham: a dear boy. Conversation with Mr Healy on Ireland. Dr Ginsburg on my rare books. Read experimentally in various works. Fourteen to dinner.

To A. MORLEY, postmaster general, 12 April 1893.   Add MS 44549, f. 80.

I am sure you will consider how difficult it would be for me to make a statement to the Queen conveying Wolverton's resignation on Ulster grounds.[7] I should have to state as follows—1. that the pretensions of Ulster to rebel were fully announced 6 or 7 years ago, & also the opposition of the parties (untruly) named "Ulster" to the Bill. 2. That the majority returned to Parlt. by the entire country was larger than agst. Home Rule. 3. That under these circumstances Wolverton received me on a political visit, & gave me a warm & valued welcome acknowledged by me in a speech. 4. That he afterwards accepted office from H.M. 5. That there is *no* change *no* new fact of moment since 1886, except that the Parliamentary minority has been turned into a majority. If under such circumstances I were to report to the Queen that he was going to resign on Ulster grounds, would it not seem like an accusation of some kind against him? None of this would apply if (office being found irksome) he were a few months hence to resign on Bank reasons or any others not political. Make as much use of this letter as you think proper.

[1] C. Chapman, *Pre-organic evolution and the Biblical idea of God* (1891).
[2] H. M. Luccock, *The church in Scotland* (1892).
[3] Perhaps A. Kiréeff (probably a relative of Olga Novikov) on infallibility in *Revue Internationale de Théologie*, i (April 1893).
[4] Made various interjections in Chamberlain's speech on G.I. Bill 2°R; 4*H* 10. 1833.
[5] Count F. F. von Beust, *Memoirs*, 2v. (1887).
[6] Interjected in G.I. Bill 2°R; 4*H* 11. 69.
[7] 4th Baron Wolverton resigned as lord-in-waiting. Morley reported, 11 April, Add MS 44254, f. 244, that Wolverton's difficulties were Ulster and his membership of the govt.'s adverse affect on his Irish [banking] clients; Morley felt he disliked his post and wanted an excuse to leave.

13. Th.

Wrote to The Queen–.......–& minutes. Deputation on Imperial Federation 12½–1½. H. of C. 3¾–8¼ and 9¾–11¾.[1] Saw Sir A.W.–Mr Marj.–Mr Bryce–Mr Story. Read ....

1. Position of Colonies not self-governing.
2. Adjustment of Imperial burdens–on what basis
   Securities for the punctual and steady working of a financial system
   Prerogatives of peace & war: is it to be devolved upon the Council?
   Decisions in Emergency. Are the Colonial members to be invested with powers or must they refer?[2]

14 Fr.

Wrote to W. Rider–Dr Richardson–The Queen–Mr Reader–& minutes. H. of C. 3¾–8 and 9¾–11¾.[3] Saw Sir A. West–Mr Marj.–Mr Morley. Read L. Waterton (= O)[4]–Tiltyard of Life[5]–Bourinot on Canada Govt.[6]

15. Sat.

Wrote to Ld Rosebery–Empress Frederic–Mad. Novikoff. Rose at 10.30 after a slight stomach-attack. Read Tiltyard &c.–Geffckens British Empire[7]–Cavour's [Thoughts on] Ireland.[8] Dined at Hampstead with the Harrys.

To LORD ROSEBERY, foreign secretary, 15 April 1893.   Add MS 44549, f. 81.

I send a letter of some weight from Dilke which has just reached me.[9] Please let me have it again as soon as may be, for I should like Harcourt, & also Morley to see it soon.

I do not understand how to reconcile Cromer's confident belief that the masses in Egypt are attached to the occupation, with his reports of the Khedive's popularity, or with Hook's representations as to the danger of Englishmen who are engaged in collecting revenue.[10]

---

[1] G.I. Bili 2°R; 4*H* 11. 212.

[2] Notes for meeting with deputation of the Imperial Federation League, Add MS 44775, f. 118, with list of members in the deputation, and of those sending apologies, ibid., f. 116. Report of meeting in *T.T.*, 14 April 1893, 11b.

[3] G.I. Bill 2°R; 4*H* 11. 335.

[4] Untraced.

[5] Ibid.

[6] Sir J. G. Bourinot, *Federal government in Canada* (1889).

[7] F. H. Geffcken, *The British Empire* (1889).

[8] See 25 Dec. 68. Henry Chaplin referred him to this work as the source for his quotations in his speech on 13 April; see Chaplin to Gladstone, 14 April 1893, Add MS 44517, f. 114.

[9] Long letter from Dilke, 14 April, copy in Add MS 43875, f. 287 (holograph untraced), deploring the continued occupation of Egypt and announcing 'I shall have to bring the question before the House of Commons' (see 1 May 93).

[10] Rosebery replied next day, Add MS 44290, f. 123, with thanks: 'It is interesting and able, bar perhaps the Crokerian assumption of an omniscience and precision which he does not possess. No one is more sensible than I am of the delicacy and perplexity of our position in Egypt. Were we out of it I should on the whole rejoice. . . .'

16. 2 S.E.

Chapel Royal noon, & afternoon. Much conversation with E. Wickham. Read Vicar of Elliswold[1]—Denison, Notes(?)[2]—Saphir on Scripture[3]—Robertson, Religion of Israel.[4]

17. M.

Wrote to Dr Cameron—Ld Rosebery—The Queen—Mr Higham—Mr E. Hamilton—and minutes. Saw A. West—Mr Marj. l.l.—Mr Morley—Sir R. Welby. Dined with Sir R. Welby. Sat till 11.30. Saw one [R]. Read Vicar of Ellismond—Jones on the Sun.[5]

To LORD ROSEBERY, foreign secretary, 17 April 1893.   N.L.S. 10026, f. 125.

In my last note I made an omission. I was struck by Cromer's expression 'there has been no explosion so far'. Should such a thing happen, which God forbid, might it not be said 'he gave you warning'. But the *counsel* given by him last autumn was 'stay as you are'. I for one should much like to know whether the counsel then given still stands in full force?

Even apart from it (and it was of course a fact of importance), two causes will I think account for the past time.

1. As you observe, the Khedive's escapade.

2. The incessant ministerial troubles in France, which have I suppose delayed the action indicated by Waddington, but which might issue in some movement of a less friendly character, made *ad captandum*.

But I think that after a certain number of months, marked only by quiet & fair speeches, No. 1 would naturally cease to operate.

I have a notion of the manner in which the Salisbury convention might perhaps be modified.

I think, or rather fear, the terms of Dilke's letter[6] do not permit my sending it round to the Cabinet:[7] but I am much in harmony with your note on it.

18. Tu.

Wrote to Scotts—W. Ridler—Messrs Sotheran—The Queen l l—Ld Aberdeen Tel.—and minutes. H. of C. $3\frac{3}{4}$-$7\frac{3}{4}$ and $9\frac{3}{4}$-12. Morley, capital speech.[8] Backgammon with Mr A. Saw Sir A.W.—Mr Marj.—Mr Murray—Sir C. Dilke (Egypt). Read 'Daughters of men'.[9]

[1] W. Damer, *The Vicar of Ellismond* (1892).
[2] G. A. Denison, *Supplement to Notes of my life, 1879, and Mr. Gladstone, 1886* (1893); sent by the author.
[3] A Saphir, *The divine unity of Scripture* (1892).
[4] See 1 Jan. 93.
[5] John Jones, *The sun a magnet* (1880).
[6] See 15 Apr. 93n.
[7] But see to Rosebery, 24 Apr. 93.
[8] On G.I. Bill 2°R; 4*H* 11. 627.
[9] H. Lynch, *Daughters of men* (1892).

Sir C. Dilke's motion on Egypt is an amendment on the motion for going into Committee of Supply.

The answer I think must turn, mainly & substantially, on the obvious impolicy of tying the hands of the Government, in a matter where so many Powers, independent of us and of one another, are concerned, by a preliminary resolution in whatever terms it might be couched.

I think we might safely acknowledge the principle & spirit of Salisbury's proceedings in the matter of the Drummond Wolff Convention and give them due credit. But observe that the rejection of such a Convention leaves matters not precisely as it found them.

Certain proceedings in Egypt which marked the close of January, and which were noticed in the speech from the Throne, made the careful maintenance of existing relations in Egypt for a time not only the paramount but the exclusive duty of the Government. But we will not regard such occurrences as affecting in any manner, if the sequel be satisfactory, the fundamental considerations which bear upon this subject of the occupation.

Our acknowledgments of the temporary nature of the occupation ought not to be diluted by pleas which would admit of its indefinite prolongation. And it would be right to mention the summary communication with Mons. Waddington in the Autumn and the nature of such communications as have taken place between the Foreign Secretary and the Turkish Ambassador.

The nature, and the present situation, of the question forbid the Government to enter into further explanations at the present juncture. They are fully sensible of the gravity of those considerations, both of interest and of honours with which they have to deal but they are bound to reserve a free discretion as to all particulars belonging to the time and manner of applying them.[1]

19. Wed.

Wrote to Ld Kimberley—Mr M'Geagh[2]—and minutes. Saw Sir A. West—Mr Marj.—Mr Fowler—Mr Roundell—Ld Chancr—Mr Hobhouse—Mr Jebb. Miners Deputn $12\frac{1}{2}$-$1\frac{3}{4}$.[3] H. of C. at 5. Drive with H. Dined at Mr Roundell's. Read Q.R. on Reaction[4]—Germ Growers.[5]

20. Th.

Wrote to The Queen—Sir F. Leighton—& minutes. Revised Mem. on Egypt. Saw Sir A. West—Mr Marj.—Sir W. Harcourt—Ld Rosebery (Egypt X.) H. of C. $3\frac{3}{4}$-8.[6] Conclave on Regn Bill and order of business. Read Germ Growers: which passes into nonsense. Much exhausted in evg.

[1] Holograph, dated [18?] April 1893; Add MS 44775, f. 139. See 1 May 93 for Dilke's motion.
[2] Robert MacGeagh, ex-president of Ulster Liberal Unionist Assoc., on Gladstone's self-removal as executor of J. Hope (Scott) on his conversion to Catholicism; *T.T.*, 4 May 1893, 12c.
[3] Dpn. from Miners' National Union, introduced by J. Wilson, M.P., and representing miners in Northumberland and Durham, opposing the Eight Hours Bill; *T.T.*, 20 April 1893, 12a.
[4] *Q.R.*, clxxvi. 549 (April 1893).
[5] Untraced.
[6] Questions; G.I. Bill 2°R; 4 *H* 11. 781, 785.

Secret.   *Provisional*[1]

The Queen's forces will be withdrawn from Egypt within (two years) from an early date (say [blank]) provided that

1. There shall not at the time for evacuation be any sign of apparent danger in the measure.
2. The Turkish Commissioner shall also be withdrawn.
3. No other Powers shall take the place of Great Britain or maintain or station any force in a manner such as to exercise any political influence upon Egypt.
4. Provision shall have been made at a Conference of the six Powers deliberating together with the Suzerain Power for the right of re-entry which is to be lodged in the hands of the Queen only.

The Queen's Government will acknowledge such provision as satisfactory provided that

1. The right of re-entry shall not be subjected to any specified limit of time.
2. Nor to other conditions entailing a variation from the present form of occupation.
3. But the right of re-entry shall only be exercised in case there shall in the judgment of the British Government be grave danger menacing the native Government of Egypt.
4. And shall be subject to termination upon a notice of not less than one year if at a conference composed of the six Powers together with the Suzerain Power a majority of the seven Powers assembled shall so determine, and shall make such provision for the security of Egypt as in their judgment the case shall require.
5. Also the British Government shall be entitled, but not bound, at any time to withdraw its forces of its own motion if in its judgment this can be done without prejudice to the native Government of Egypt.

To Sir F. LEIGHTON, president of the Royal Academy,   Add MS 44549, f. 82.
20 April 1893.[2]

My abstention from your great Festival is as you know purely medical in its grounds.[3] As it is, unlike the Lord Mayor's Festival, non-political, I think that your choice of a guest to return thanks for the Ministers should be entirely your own. I need not therefore refer to any particular & have not the smallest objection to offer.

21. Fr.

Wrote to The Queen—Cawthorn & Hutt—and minutes. Worked on Home Rule papers & notes. Saw Sir A. West—S.E.G.—Mr Marj.—J. Morley. Read Julius Caesar. H. of C. 3¾-6½ & 9¾-1½. Spoke from 11.5 to 1 A.M. Majority 43.[4] What a poor creature I felt. Eight to dinner: and backgammon with Mr A.

22 Sat.

Wrote minutes. At 2 PM attended the Bradley marriage in the Abbey.[5] Then to Mr W. Richmond's (5 m distant) saw his St Paul's work, & came to comprehend

---

[1] Secretary's copy, dated 20 April 1893; Add MS 44775, f. 128; scrappy holograph draft at ibid., f. 126.
[2] Written after consultation with Kimberley and Harcourt.
[3] Request from Leighton to speak at the Royal Academy dinner; Add MS 44517, f. 118.
[4] 2°R of G.I. Bill carried in 347:304; 4H 11. 1007.
[5] Marriage of Emily Tennyson Bradley, da. of the dean of Westminster, to Alexander Murray Smith.

his noble undertaking.[1] Saw Sir A. West—Lady Compton—Conversation with S.E.G. Backgammon with S.E.G. Read Julius Caesar—Westm. Rev. on Disestabl.[2]—De Tabley's Poems[3]—and [blank.]

23. 3 S.E.

Chapel Royal mg. All Saints aft. Both with the S.E.G.s. Saw Sir A. Clark who counsels serious examination of the eye. Also Lucy—and S.E.G. Read Joshua 2-8—Orr on World-Survey[4]—Robertson. Rel. of Israel—and Zahn.[5]

24. M.

Wrote to Hon. E. Blake[6]—Mr Stansfeld—Rev. Mr Fuller—Ld Rosebery—& minutes. H. of C. $3\frac{3}{4}$-$7\frac{3}{4}$ (Budget: H. largely read his speech).[7] Attended the Levee. Saw Sir A. West—Ld Kimberley—Ld Rosebery—The Speaker—Mr Evans MP—Mr Mills. Saw Burdett [R]. Dined at Grillion's. Read Odyss. X—De Tabley's Poems.

To LORD ROSEBERY, foreign secretary, 24 April 1893.   N.L.S. 10026, f. 131.
    I have just put into circulation the Dilke letter.[8]
    I ought to have told you that we bring on Supply (of necessity) before Committee on Home Rule Bill: and I conclude that Dilke will feel himself bound to raise the Egyptian question, though probably in the considerate spirit of his letter. There will be difficulty if so, in meeting him: unless any one should traverse him in the sense of indefinitely prolonged occupation.[9] Of this a contingent intimation has I think been conveyed to Harcourt by Lawson.

25.

Wrote to Abp of Canterb.—Ld Rosebery—Mr Blake—Mr Lyttle *cum* Mr Tripp—and minutes. H. of C. $3\frac{3}{4}$-$7\frac{3}{4}$.[10] Saw Sir A. West—Mr Marj. l.l.—Mr Asquith—Conclave at H. of C. on Registration Bill. Ten to dinner. Backgammon with S.E.G. Read Od. X—Julius Caesar & Macbeth.

---

[1] W. B. Richmond's mosaics which decorate the ceiling of St. Paul's, then in preparation in his studio in Hammersmith; Richmond's letter of invitation, hinting at Gladstone's support for fund-raising, is at Add MS 44517, f. 121.
[2] *W.R.*, cxxxix. 386 (April 1893).
[3] J. B. L. Warren, Lord de Tabley, *Poems romantic and lyrical* (1893); second series.
[4] See 2 Apr. 93.
[5] Probably T. Zahn, *Das apostolische symbolum* (1893).
[6] Edward Blake, 1833–1912; formerly prime minister of Ontario; home rule M.P. S. Longford 1892–1907. An important influence on the G.I. Bill. See Add MS 44549, f. 82.
[7] 4*H* 11. 1027.
[8] See to Rosebery, 15 Apr. 93.
[9] Rosebery replied, this day, Add MS 44290, f. 125: '. . . I could not use or be a party to using language which pointed to "definitely limited occupation", until I was much more certain than I am now that evacuation does not simply imply leaving the results of all our labours in Egypt at the mercy of a petulant boy who is extremely indisposed to us.'
[10] Employers' Liability Bill; 4*H* 11. 1176.

To E. W. BENSON, archbishop of Canterbury, 25 April 1893.   Add MS 44549, f. 83.

I had serious designs upon Your Grace which were deferred by your non-appearance at Grillion's dinner.

The main one was to deposit with Your Grace a statement which calls for no reply unless and until the proper time arrives.

It refers to the depressed state of clergy incomes, and I only wish to say that if Your Grace should consider that this subject requires at this period a public effort & appeal I beg to be remembered as one prepared to join in the undertaking at least by my subscription. I take it for granted that such an effort if undertaken should not be on an insignificant scale, but should aim at raising a considerable sum,—not less I should say than half a million.

I had one or two other enquiries to make which will very well keep.[1]

26. Wed.

Wrote to Mr Dowling—Duke of Fife—Sir A. Clark—Sir W. Whiteway[2]—& minutes. Dined at Mr Rendel's. H. of C. 2½-5¾.[3] Saw Maharajah of [blank] *cum* Ld Reay. Saw Sir A. West—Mr Murray—Sir W. Harcourt—Mr Marj.—Mr Bilson —Ld E. Fitzmaurice. Read Florine[4]—Macbeth—Bradlaugh Channel Tunnel.[5]

To the DUKE OF FIFE, 26 April 1893.   Add MS 44549, f. 83.

I thank you very much for your letter,[6] & my reply need not, & I hope will not, bear any thing of a controversial aspect. I was not sanguine enough to believe, in the absence of evidence, that your opinion on the question of Home Rule for Ireland had undergone a favourable change. But what I am glad to learn is that you still cherish the hope of reunion with the Liberal party. Though I can never witness the event I cherish that hope also, at all events in the H. of Lords. When the schism occurred in 1886 I made earnest efforts, in the H. of Commons, towards maintaining Liberal cooperation on questions other than Home Rule. But if there was a corresponding desire on the other side (& this there may have been), its operations must have been checked by difficulties: at any rate the result of my efforts was total failure. The consequences within the walls of the H. of Commons have been decisive. The position of "Liberal Unionists" in the Lords has been happier. One or two Peers have gone so far as to express a desire to receive our 'Whips' except on Home Rule or matters connected with it. So that the Peers have not been severed from the bulk of the party in the same sense, or to the same extent, as in the Commons. Here is an omen of possible good in the future, in a matter outside my

[1] Benson replied on 1 May, Add MS 44109, f. 233, proposing a meeting, and on 6 May sent the 'Report of the Committee on diminished incomes of the Clergy' to the Upper House of Convocation; ibid., f. 236.
[2] Sir William Vallance Whiteway, 1828-1908; premier of Newfoundland 1878-85, 1889-94 (unseated for corruption), 1895-7.
[3] Registration Bill; 4*H* 11. 1225.
[4] A. Kay, *Florine, a dramatic poem* (1858), or W. B. MacCabe, *Florine, princess of Burgundy* (1855 and later eds.).
[5] C. Bradlaugh, *The Channel Tunnel: ought the democracy to oppose or support it?* (1887).
[6] Of 25 April, Add MS 44517, f. 93, regretting the liberal schism, stating that he used to attend Unionist meetings until his marriage, and that 'it is only honest to confess to you that my opinions on Home Rule have been rather confirmed by time and consideration . . . but I still cherish the hope [of] witnessing the reunion of the Liberal Party in sympathy with which I should not, on examination, be found far behind many of your present supporters.'

personal concern, but of great public interest: & such hopes as these are greatly encouraged by your letter.

27. Th.

Wrote to Watson's—Mr Whitbread—Mr Vickers—Mr Balfour—& minutes. H of C. 4–8¾. Spoke on agricult. amendmt.[1] Conclave on honours. Saw Sir A. West—Mr Marj.—Mr Murray. Read Florine—Macbeth—& Tracts.

28. Fr.

Wrote to Ld Rosebery—Mr B. Currie—and minutes. Saw Sir A. West—Mr Marj.—Mr Fowler. Conclave on London Poor Rate. H. of C. 2½–7 and 11–12. Spoke on Ocean Postage.[2] Dined with Lucy: then the Rendel Ball where Katie[3] made her first appearance, so nice in appearance & behaviour. Read Florine finished—Cavour on Ireland[4]—N.C. on do[5]—Various Tracts. Private view R. Academy: with Mr Agnew.

29. Sat. [Hatchlands, Guildford]

Wrote minutes. Arrived at Hatchlands[6] 12¾. Walk in evg with Mr R[endel] & Godley: much conversation. Finished Cavour on I.—Read Girovaghi Italiani[7]—Howell, Island Paradise.[8]

30. 4 S.E.

Parish Ch mg & evg. Wrote to S. Lyttelton. Read Deuteronomy I–X—Addis, Xty & Roman Empire[9]—Woodgate, Layman's Faith[10]—Chernakoff, Versuch der Lehre.[11]

Mond. May One. 1893. [London]

Reached D. Street 1.50. Deputn on Mines 2–3.[12] Five to Dinner. Read Howell, Travels—Addis . . . . .—Adderley's Remarx.[13] Saw Sir A. West—Herbert J.G. (Pistol &c.) H. of C. 3¾–8. Spoke on Egypt: difficult.[14] Backgammon with Mr Rendel.

---

[1] Replying to Chaplin on Dorington's amndt.; 4H 11. 1361.
[2] 4H 11. 1550.
[3] His grand-daughter; see 5 Jan. 82.
[4] See 15 Apr. 93.
[5] Redmond's article, N.C., xxxiii. 559 (April 1893).
[6] Rendel's house.
[7] Untraced.
[8] H. S. Howell, *An island paradise and reminiscences of travel* (1892).
[9] W. E. Addis, *Christianity and the Roman empire* (1893).
[10] W. B. Woodgate, *A modern layman's faith* (1893).
[11] Untraced.
[12] From the Mining Association, opposing the Eight Hours Bill, led by Sir J. Pease, M.P.; T.T., 2 May 1893, 3b.
[13] J. G. Adderley, *Stephen Remarx. The story of adventure in ethics* (1893).
[14] On Dilke's amndt. on British statements on Egypt [i.e. on withdrawal]; 4H 11. 1650. Dilke did not divide the House.

2. Tu.

Wrote to Mr Dobbie—Sir H. Ponsonby—Mr Montagu MP—Abp of Canterb.—
Ld Ripon—Ld Kimberley—Mr Frowde—Mr Chalmers—& minutes. H. of C. 3¾–8
(Tea &c. away).[1] Saw Sir A. West—Mr Morley—Mr Marj.—Mr Asquith. Read
Macbeth (finished)—Addis, Xty & R.E.—E.W.H., Irish Finance.[2]

3. Wed.

Wrote to Mr Mundella—Sir A. Gordon—Ld De Tabley—and minutes. Saw Sir A.
West—Sir H. Vivian—Mr Marj.—Ld Ripon. H. of C. 12½–2½ and 5½–6¾. Spoke on
8 hours Miners Bill.[3] Dined with the Ripons. Read De Tabley's Poems[4]—Argyll,
Unseen Formulations.[5]

Substantive provisions for the Irish liability to Imperial Charges[6]
It would seem that the liabilities of Ireland for Imperial charge may have to be provided
for under three forms.
1. In the existing condition of revenue and expenditure, as known for 1892–3, and
   estimated for 1893–4, the Customs Revenues of Ireland supply a fair acquittance for
   Irish obligations.
2. It may happen that, apart from any great emergency such as that of War, the tendency
   to growth in the public expenditure may require an augmentation of indirect taxation.
   But it may also be assumed that under this head there will be no augmentation of
   Customs' Duties except *in sympathy* with Excise, i.e. on articles which are also excise-
   able.
   Should any augmentation of duties take place, having Excise for its principal object, it
has further to be considered whether the augmentation is to be for Imperial, or only for
British purposes. If for British purposes, I assume that Ireland ought not to contribute:
and that consequently the nett proceeds of the augmentation should be paid over to the
Irish Exchequer.
   There need be no fear of inconvenience in this case from plethora of money, if we are
right in assuming that Ireland like our Municipalities will assuredly wish to borrow for the
supply of her civil and economic wants, so that their receipts would simply cancel so
much debt
   But, if this increase of indirect taxes were for Imperial purposes, could any more equitable mode of proceeding be devised, than that Parliament, where Ireland would be
represented, should *pro re nata*,[7] fix in its Act the proportion of the increased receipt from
indirect taxation, or at any rate from Excise, which should be charged against Ireland, and
made payable from the Exchequer?
   If the augmentation extended to direct taxation also, Parliament would also have to
estimate the amount which ought equitably to be borne by Ireland and to provide for it in
the same manner.

[1] Questioned on the Hull strike; 4*H* 11. 1743.
[2] E. W. Hamilton, writing as 'Nemo', 'The financial scheme of the Home Rule Bill', *C.R.*, lxiii. 609
(May 1893).
[3] Giving qualified support to Wood's bill; 4*H* 11. 1857.
[4] See 2 Apr. 93.
[5] G. D. Campbell, duke of Argyll, *The unseen foundations of society. An examination of the fallacies and
failures of economic science due to neglected elements* (1893).
[6] Initialled and dated 3 May 1893, Add MS 44775, f. 144.
[7] For special business.

The case which remains to be dealt with is the case of great public emergency such as war.

Here we may assume that the additional burdens imposed would certainly extend to Income Tax as well as to indirect taxation and *might* extend to other taxes such as stamps.

It would be for Parliament to estimate the Irish *quota* both of indirect tax and of direct.

In the case of the indirect taxes a distinction might be drawn between Customs and Excise. It may be said that in taking the Customs Revenues we should take them 'for better for worse' and should be entitled to the whole additional yield, as in case of reduction we should bear the whole loss.

But in case of the Excise and of direct taxes I apprehend that Parliament would have to determine. But should it determine the new liability of Ireland in a lump sum? or by way of proportion of the augmented duty about to be imposed? As to Excise, there seems to be no difficulty in stating a proportion. But as to taxes other than the indirect, I presume it would be the best course to constitute a definite charge (of course a preferential charge) upon the Irish Exchequer by authority of Parliament, and to leave to the Irish Parliament the mode of providing the funds to meet it.

Supplemental observations

1. I am afraid it is plain upon consideration of the case, that, as between the 'Fund' plan and the 'Quota' plan, the advantages of the former have reference chiefly to the present, or the first of the cases mentioned above: and that when we come to providing for the future contingencies of altered states, the embarrassments become very considerable: whereas under the quota plan they would hardly arise as to *form* of legislation?
2. Every thing I think tends to recommend some arrangement in the sense of Mr Sexton's suggestion that we should now only fix the figures of any financial arrangement only for a *short* term of years say six or seven—it might be added perhaps 'and until Parliament shall otherwise determine'. (Or as now in Clause 12 sub 3)
3. If the aggregate contribution from Ireland is only to be four or from that to five per Cent of the entire Imperial charges, the effect of any deviation from precision in our arrangements, so far as these charges are concerned, must be small: but I assume that matters of principle shall be clearly laid down, and that the fixed term of years will be short.
4. Every consideration seems to recommend the postponement of the Financial Clauses until after the other Clauses of the Bill shall have been determined.

4. Th.

Wrote to The Queen—Duke of York—Mr Bourne[1]—and minutes. Read Duke of Argyll—De Tabley Poems. Saw Sir A. West—Abp of Canterbury—Mons. de Franqueville—Mr Marj.—Sir W. Harcourt. H. of C. $3\frac{3}{4}$–$7\frac{3}{4}$.[2] Conversation with M. Waddington on Egypt & other matters. Dined with Lord E. Fitzmaurice.

To the DUKE OF YORK,[3] 4 May 1893.   Add MS 44549, f. 85.

I had the honour to receive this morning, the gratifying and most courteous announcement[4] of your Royal Highness's engagement to Princess Mary of Teck, which will encite

[1] Thanking S. Bourne for his assistance to Mrs Cooper; Add MS 44549, f. 85.
[2] Spoke on the strike at Hull; 4*H* 12. 117.
[3] i.e. the future George V. Princess Mary of Teck, 1867–1953, had been engaged to the duke of Clarence who d. 1892; her engagement to the duke of York had been urged by the Queen, but the duke did not propose to her until 3 May.
[4] By telegram; Add MS 44517, f. 143.

the liveliest & most loyal interest throughout the country. On my own part & my wife's I have only to express the fervent hope & prayer that the Almighty may be pleased to crown this union with every blessing.

It is a marked descent from such a subject if I feel myself unable to address a letter to Your Royal Highness without reverting to the virtual promise already given to honour us on some convenient day with Your Royal Highness's company at dinner.

Owing to the state of business in the House of Commons, the only days open for me at present are Wednesdays & Saturdays; and I would venture to suggest Wed. the 31st May if convenient to Your Royal Highness, as the day when we might hope for the honour of receiving you (at 8 o'clock).[1]

I enclose a list of the persons whom if it be approved by Your Royal Highness I should propose to invite.

I do not know whether it would be too extreme a liberty to propose an addition to that list; but if we might presume to invite the Duke & Duchess of Teck with the Princess Mary it would give us much pleasure to see them included in the party.

5. Fr.

Wrote to The Queen—Prince of Wales—M. Drew—and minutes. H. of C. $2\frac{1}{2}$-$5\frac{1}{2}$ and $10\frac{1}{2}$-12.[2] Read D. of Argyll (alas)—Obelisk & Freemasonry[3]—Adderley S. Remarx. Ten to dinner. Backgammon with Mr Rendel. Saw Sir A. West—Mr Morley.

Cabinet. Friday May 5. 93. Noon.[4]
1. Irish Bill. To postpone Financial Clauses.
2. No change as agreed. Clause to be adopted.
3. Second Chamber—to be fought up to division.
4. Solicitor General to attend the Committee so far as needful, Morley writes to Russell.
5. Employers' Liability. To include Govt. servants?[5]
    Principle accepted.

6. Sat.

Wrote to Sir R. Welby—Sir H. Ponsonby—Mr Ridler—E.W. Hamilton—Mr Bolton—and minutes. Dined with the Harrys at Hampstead. Saw Mrs Sands, Lady Stepney, Mrs Matheson, Mr Lyell: and heard the wonderful nine year old Violinist from Tipperary (M'Cartney)[6] a simple & charming child. Worked on books. Read Hist. Cornish Family[7]—Fauriel, Last days of the Consulate.[8]

---

[1] See 7 June 93.
[2] Spoke on Employers' Liability Bill; 4H 12. 221.
[3] Untraced.
[4] Add MS 44648, f. 97.
[5] The Cabinet decided 'it would be right to accept in principle the proposal to place these workmen in the same position as those engaged by private employers'; CAB 41/22/38.
[6] Maud MacCarthy, b. Clonmel 1884; infant prodigy, made her London debut 1893 and retired from concert playing in 1907. See 7 June 93.
[7] Perhaps F. Layland, *Doubts are traitors: the story of a Cornish family* (1889).
[8] C. C. Fauriel, *The last days of the Consulate* (1885).

7. 5 S.E.

Chapel Royal mg (with H.C.) & aft. Wrote to Abp of Canterbury, Queen, D. of York,[1] & Mr Montagu, Telegrams. Saw Ld Breadalbane. Read Life of Keble (Lock)[2]—New England's Memorial[3]—Mad. Novikoff's Article[4]—Theolog. Tracts.

8. M.

Wrote to Ld Ripon—Mr Mundella—Mr Stanford—Wms & Norgate—The Queen l.l.—Ld Chancellor—& minutes. Saw Sir A. West—Mr Marj.—Mr Morley—Mr Murray—Sir H. Ponsonby—HNG (Hn). Audience of H.M. at B. Palace. All well in the manner: substance unaltered. Read Fauriel—New Engl. Memorial. H. of C. $3\frac{3}{4}$–8 and $9\frac{1}{2}$–$12\frac{1}{4}$.[5] I have never known *such* an opposition, one so detached from the merits & from rule. But it is probably suicidal.

9. Tu.

Wrote to The Queen—Ld Tennyson—& minutes. H. of C. $3\frac{3}{4}$–8 and $9\frac{1}{2}$–$11\frac{1}{2}$, working Irish Govt Bill.[6] Katie was presented by C.G. Saw Sir A. West—Ld Houghton—Mr Murray—Sir W. Harcourt. Read Fauriel—Poems by two Brothers.[7]

10. Wed.

Wrote to Mr Mundella—Mr Morley—The Queen l.l.—Ld Rosebery—Ld Chancellor—& minutes. Wrote on Irish Finance. Dined at Sir A. Hayter's. Saw Sir A. West—Ld Vernon—Lady Granville—Mr Knowles—Mr Marj.—Mr Morley. H. of C. $12\frac{1}{4}$–$5\frac{3}{4}$ Irish Govt Bill.[8] Read Fauriel—S. Remarx. Drive with C.

To J. MORLEY, Irish secretary, 10 May 1893.   Add MS 44549, f. 86.

What do you say to the inclosed?[9] It is nearly in words which I used yesterday. I am not unfavourable. In case of accepting perhaps the Preamble might drop.

To LORD ROSEBERY, foreign secretary, 10 May 1893.   N.L.S. 10026, f. 157.

Might not Plunkett (see his No 66) to be [*sic*] informed that when he hears from the Prime Minister of Sweden words distinctly or probably pointing to the military coercion of Norway, he should drop some friendly expression to the effect that he thought his

---

[1] More negotiations about the dinner (see 4 May 93); he accepted for 7 June; Add MS 44517, f. 147.

[2] W. Lock, *John Keble. A biography* (1893).

[3] Probably J. Fiske, *The beginnings of New England, or the Puritan theocracy in its relations to civil and religious liberty* (1889).

[4] O. Novikov, 'Russia, Rome and the Old Catholics', *New Review*, viii. 439 (April 1893).

[5] Spoke on G.I. Bill cttee.; 4*H* 12. 367.

[6] 4*H* 12. 495.

[7] *Poems by two brothers* [in fact three: Alfred, Charles and Frederick Tennyson] (1893).

[8] 4*H* 12. 553.

[9] Untraced; probably a copy of James's amndt. on supremacy (see 16 May 93); this letter crossed with Morley's suggesting 'a little chat'; Add MS 44257, f. 100.

Govt. would earnestly desire that any thing of such a tendency would be very carefully considered beforehand in its 'juridical' as well as its political aspect.
[P.S.] Many thanks for the new Hertslet Memorandum.[1]

11. *Ascension Day.*

Chapel Royal 11–12¾: obliged to leave before H.C. Wrote to Rev. Mr Barker—Mr B. Currie—The Queen. H. of C. 3¾–8½. Spoke at the dinner hour for 30 m after Chamberlain. It is fanatical to say I seemed to be held up by a strength not my own. Much fatigued.[2] Read Fauriel (finished)—Stephen Remarx. Saw Sir W. Harcourt—Sir A. West—Mr Blake—Mr Morley—Mr Asquith.

12. *Frid.* [*Minley Manor, Farnborough*]

Wrote to Avv. Bona[3]—and minutes. Saw Sir A. West—Mr Marj. Read Two Brothers—Froude on the Divorce[4]—Lang, Homer & the Epic.[5] But my reading, always slow, proceeds now at a snail's pace. H. of C. 2¼–3.40.[6] Arr. at Minley, Mr [B. W.] Curries charming place at 5¼. Saw E. Wickham.

13. *Sat.*

Drove to see Bramswell. Saw the beautiful (R.C.) Chapel here. Saw Sir A. Godley—Father Morris. Read Pilgrim Fathers[7]—Froude's Divorce—Lang.

14. *S. aft. Asc.*

Church at 11 and 3. Wrote to J. Morley—Sir W. Harcourt—Mr Fowler—S. Lyttelton. Saw Mr Marj.—Father Morris—Ld Acton. Read Pilgrim Fathers—Milton Samson Ag. &c.[8]—Morris, 'Catholic England'.[9]

To Sir W. V. HARCOURT, chancellor of the exchequer,   MS Harcourt dep. 13, f. 103.
14 May 1893. '*Private.*'

   Except that I do not think that there is any ground of suspicion of the Irish Members, I agree very much with your letter received this morning, and will endeavour to arrange the best I can.[10]

To J. MORLEY, Irish secretary, 14 May 1893. '*Secret*'.   Add MS 44549, f. 87.

   I inclose to you letters which you ought to see from Harcourt & Fowler, *re* supremacy. I do not think there is the smallest ground for any imputation on the Irish Members.

---

[1] Memorandum by Hertslet on Norway incorporating Gladstone's comments; see Add MS 44290, f. 127 ff.
   [2] 4 *H* 12. 689.
   [3] Thanking Signor Bona for his (untraced) work on marriage; Add MS 44549, f. 87.
   [4] J. A. Froude, *The divorce of Catherine of Aragon* (1891).
   [5] A. Lang, *Homer and the Epic* (1893).
   [6] Questions; G.I. Bill cttee.; 4 *H* 12. 792.
   [7] See 7 May 93.
   [8] i.e. Milton's *Samson Agonistes.*
   [9] See 31 Mar. 93.
   [10] Harcourt, Add MS 44203, f. 77, urged the need for decisive and immediate dealing with James's amndt. on supremacy; he criticised the Irish M.P.s for appearing not to accept the principle of Imperial supremacy.

Marjoribanks, who has come down here, tells me it reaches him through the man of the Chronicle that some of our friends are anxious for the adoption of James's amendment. I understand Haldane is opposed to it. Apart from these incidental matters [I am in favour of its adoption on a main ground which I will briefly state. So far as I know we have one & only one great Treaty to uphold & this Treaty has two articles. One is that we are to maintain the Supremacy intact. The other is that we are to give Ireland an effective self government in Irish matters. I think we should not be squeamish in the interpretation of either article. The opposition will press for a rigid, & even a vexatious interpretation of the one, & for a lax & nibbling interpretation of the other. *They* have no claim upon us whatever. We ought to be governed as to both articles by prudence & good faith. As to the first I am disposed to avoid anything meant merely to vex & disparage Ireland: but I think it would be unwise to show any jealousy of declarations which go simply to assert strongly the Supremacy as it is. This is the case with James's amendment: & even if he shall attempt to minimise what he has written to Harcourt I am for taking it. However little he may try to make of it, I think we can make a good deal: it will greatly strengthen our hands in resisting other frivolous & vexatious assertions of it. I would not even spend time on the question of dropping the preamble though I think that if an equitable spirit prevailed it would be dropped. In sum I think it is not wise to fight too heavily upon slippery ground. But as to the second article of the treaty, on every attempt to impair in any way the reality of Irish self-government in Irish affairs, I would fight, a fight *à l'outrance*.

I write all this on principle, not consulting my own taste, but keeping my eye steadily fixed on the main issue. I hope you will be disposed to take the same point of view, & if you do I cannot but think you will agree] Should you think fit, you are free to make known all within my brackets to our three Irish friends.[1]

15. M. [*London*]

Wrote to The Queen l.l.—Abp of Canterbury—Sir W. Harcourt. 12–1¾. To Downing St. Poor C. has had her voice nipped away by a new kind of cold. H. of C. 4–8¼ and 9½–12¼. Spoke on Irish Bill.[2] Saw Sir W. Harcourt—Sir A. West—Mr Marj. Read New England—Morris, Catholic England.

16. Tu.

Saw Mr Marj.—Sir D. Probyn—Sir R. Welby *cum* E. Hamilton—Sir A. West—Sir R.W., E.H., & Mr Milner.[3] Wrote to Mr Morley l.l.—The Queen—Sir W. Harcourt—and minutes. Conclave at 3 on the Supremacy Proviso. H. of C. 4–8¾ and 10–12¼. [Spoke on] Irish Bill.[4] Some conflict on the Bench: difficulty with Morley. Read New England Memorial.

[1] On 16 May, Add MS 44257, f. 105, Morley reported a talk with Redmond ('he had seen in the papers that we were likely to accept it, and was somewhat discomposed by the rumour') and that he had 'represented your views on the same question to Sexton. He replied in the same sense as Redmond ...'. On 17 May, ibid., f. 107, Morley reported an interview with Sexton and Dillon, who argued 'it was hardly fair to accept from the Unionists a proviso tacking Supremacy to the most vital clause in the Bill. I am obliged to say that I entirely concur with them, if my view matters.'
[2] 4*H* 12. 969.
[3] Alfred Milner, 1854–1925; stood unsuccessfully as a liberal 1885; in Egypt 1889–92; chairman, Board of Inland Revenue 1892–7; made large contribution to 1894 budget but blundered over 1893 Irish finances; later a virulent Imperialist.
[4] James's amndt. for explicit recognition of Westminster parliament's supremacy; at the end of the deb. Gladstone accepted the amndt. in principle, reserving the govt.'s right as to where it would appear in the Bill; 4*H* 12. 1086, 1127.

Error[1]

1. Amount [blank] m
2. Not an error introduced into the computations of today but only now discovered & disclosed.
3. A full report is now laid. The source of the error is that there was no practical question involved.
4. Evidence incomplete but what appears probable is that erroneous method crept in many years ago & has been continued without notice.
5. Perhaps ever since the equalization of the duties when the old means became inapplicable.

17. *Wed.*

Wrote to The Queen l.l.—Mrs Sands—and minutes. H. of C. $12\frac{1}{4}$–$5\frac{3}{4}$. Saw Sir A. West—E. Hamilton—Mr Marj.—Sir A. Clark—Ld Cadogan—Sir W. Harcourt. Dined at the Imperial Institute (Ld Herschell). Then walked say $1\frac{1}{2}$ mile at least through a vast party.[2] Saw Ld H—Ld Spencer—Maharajah of . . . . . . Finished New Engl. Memorial: & read the Two Brothers. C. better: may go.

18. *Th.* [*Hawarden*]

Wrote to J. Westell—Mr Channing MP.—J. Morley l.l.—Canons of ChCh[3]—Moderator of Free Ch. Assy—and minutes. Saw Sir A. West—Mr A. Morley—Mr Marj.—Ld Ripon—Mr Morley—Sir John Gladstone. $1\frac{1}{2}$–$6\frac{3}{4}$. To Hawarden Rectory: a fine journey, a dear welcome. Read Froude's Divorce—Duchess of Kingston: Authentic Detail.[4]

To Rev. W. C. SMITH,[5] Moderator of the Free Kirk Assembly,   Add MS 44549, f. 89.
18 May 1893.

I had just been reading in a paper of this morning a friendly notice of your approaching assembly, & was preparing almost at once to quit London, when I learned that a direct notice of the occasion from myself on which I would not have ventured without encouragement, would not be regarded as presumptuous, and wd. even be acceptable.

The original Disruption (for this and not secession is I think the just appellation) in 1843, with the circumstances of the preceding decade, are still fresh in my recollection, and have at all times been regarded by me with lively & sympathetic interest.

---

[1] Undated holograph; Add MS 44775, f. 217. 'Mr G. sent for Welby and me this morning to talk about Irish finance and to hear the worst about the Irish Excise figures. We brought A. Milner with us in order that he might give his own version of the blunder committed by his officers in Belfast. [Gladstone] told me afterwards he was most favourably impressed by Milner whom he had not seen before. The blunder is a serious one. It means that the Excise receipts with which Ireland can properly be credited as her true revenue are less by nearly £200,000 than what we thought we might safely reckon upon. Consequently the bottom has been knocked out of our scheme; and we shall have to start afresh—probably on the lines of crediting Ireland with her Customs as well as other revenue and debiting her with a quota of Imperial expenditure . . .'; E.H.D. 16 May 1893.
[2] 20,000 attended the reception at the Imperial Institute; *T.T.*, 18 May 1893, 5f.
[3] On the regius chair of divinity at Christ Church, Oxford; Add MS 44549, f. 88.
[4] Elizabeth Hervey, Lady Bristol, *An authentic detail of particulars relative to the Duchess of Kingston* (1788).
[5] Walter Chalmers Smith, elected Moderator this day.

I am not personally associated with the Presbyterian Churches, but I conceive it to be historically true that the distinguished leaders of the Free Church movement, some of whom I have had the honour to call my friends, were in the course they followed half a century ago, the genuine representatives of the spirit of the Scottish Reformation.

It is yet more important, and is I think wholly beyond dispute, that the procession of Ap. 19 when it set out from the Assembly Hall, and when its members gave up their temporal goods and expectations for the sake of conscience, exhibited a noble & heart stirring spectacle, of which the glory belongs in the first instance to themselves, & forms a precious inheritance for the Free Church, but which was entitled to excite & did excite, the cordial and even enthusiastic admiration of Christendom. It was indeed justly felt that mankind, and especially Christian mankind, were the better for such an example.

There were other remarkable features of the movement which well deserve commemoration, but which are almost wholly eclipsed by its moral brightness. Truly notable was the statesmanship with which the whole controversy was conducted. And then came the extraordinary financial skill which presided over the new arrangement. I have always understood that this was mainly the skill of Dr. Chalmers. If this be so it is to me a matter of special interest, for about the years 1833–6 I had the honour of some personal intercourse with that remarkable man, which afforded me some particular opportunities of appreciating his absolute indifference, and I think almost contempt, for matters of pecuniary interest in which he was individually concerned.

I trust it may please God that the high qualities which marked the inception of the Free Church may perpetually abound within its borders.

It is highly agreeable to me to address these remarks to one of its most distinguished representatives.

19 Fr.

Ch. 8¼ A.M. Wrote to Ld Kimberley—Ld Rosebery—The Queen—Priv. Sec. Tel.—Mr Grainger—and minutes. Backgammon with S. Visited St John's with him. Read Stevenson's Samoa[1]—Poems by two Brothers—Duchess of Kingston (finished).

To LORD ROSEBERY, foreign secretary, 19 May 1893.   N.L.S. 10026, f. 165.

1. I have written to the Queen about Drumlanrig as you suggested.

2. In naming to you my conversation with Waddington after his abdication I omitted one particular. The Drummond Wolff convention turned up, and I said that I took it for dead in its actual form, but thought the form might be varied so as attain the purpose. He was silent apparently waiting for me to explain *how*. This I did not do.

3. I have thought much upon the question whether, if & when the Egyptian question comes before the Powers it is or is not expedient that we should have secured the support of France. The *condominium* is dead & I am confident Waddington will not be able to make good the high doctrine of duality which he stated to me in conversation. But it remains true that the Govt. of 1880–5 negotiated about Egypt with France after the death of the *condominium*, & would in that way have settled the whole matter but for the unhappy emergence of the question of finance, in which we I fear were more wrong than right. But I have looked at it mainly as a question of policy & easy transaction, &, especially considering the hopeless rascality of the Sultan, I incline to think it would be a real & serious advantage to have secured by prior communication the real support of

---

[1] R. L. Stevenson, *Footnote to history. Eight years of trouble in Samoa* (1892).

France. The compliment to her would be valuable & would not offend. Moreover if she chooses to claim it we are hardly in a position to refuse it.

4. The Muktar telegram of May 17 shows a. how slippery our position is b. What a blunder Salisbury committed by letting in the Turkish Commissioner whom we had always kept out.[1]

20. Sat.

Ch. 8½ A.M. Wrote to Priv. Sec. Tel.—and minutes. Worked much in Saint Deiniol's. But it is rather lame work now with both eyes & hands. Read Two Brothers finished—Veuillot Droit Seigneurial[2]—Froude's Divorce of H VIII. Backgammon with S.E.G. Grave but most satisfactory conversation with Stephen as to the Rectory and St Deiniol's. Also with C.G.

21. Whits.

Ch. 11 A.M. with H.C.—and 6½ P.M. Wrote to Priv. Sec. Tel.—and minutes. Conversation with Mary—with H. Drew—& further with the Rector. Read Fiske, New England[3]—N. Hall on Atonement[4]—Life of Keble.

22 M.

Ch. 8½ AM. Wrote to Priv. Sec. Tel. l.l.l.—The Queen—Mr Marj.—Lady Sherbrooke—Mrs Sands—Sir A. Gordon—Rev. Mr Smithwick—and minutes. Worked at St Deiniol's. Made a short speech on opening the Institute Buildings.[5] Backgammon with S. Read Life of Sherbrooke[6]—Froude, Divorce of H. VIII—[blank] on the Welsh Language.

To E. MARJORIBANKS, chief whip, 22 May 1893.   Add MS 44549, f. 90.

The Queen has consented to the Peers & the Baths, but asks to have the Baronets & Knighthoods reduced, the list being so very large.

Our case of course rests upon our delay (at her desire). But you see from the Birthday lists that, as she chooses to take the point, she has us on the hip to some extent.

I send you a copy of my reply to her, the best I can devise[7]—I think it will be the best course to make a considerable postponement—rather than a reduction which could not be very small—we could then revive the subject I think when our full year is up. The thing is awkward, but we are subject as you know to these interpositions in many forms.

___

[1] Rosebery replied (typed) on 22 May, Add MS 44290, f. 146: 'I think you and I are quite agreed in the denial of the French right of separate treatment. When they declined to join us in 1882 . . . that put an end to our partnership. . . . I am not, however, of opinion that your negociations in 1884 have revived it in the slightest degree. . . . What, however, is clear is this. That there can be no French Government with which we can deal, nor will there be, until after the elections. I think in the mean time therefore we are doing no harm in parleying with the Sultan. . . . I think you will agree that you owe me thanks for sending you this in a type-written form?'

[2] L. F. Veuillot, Le Droit du Seigneur au moyen-âge (1871).

[3] See 7 May 93.

[4] C. Newman Hall, Atonement the fundamental fact of Christianity (1893).

[5] The new Hawarden Institute; T.T., 23 May 1893, 10b.

[6] A. P. Martin, The life and letters of Robert Lowe, Viscount Sherbrooke, 2v. (1893), in whose preparation Gladstone had assisted.

[7] Guedalla, Q, ii. 470, with next day's letter and a table showing liberal abstinence.

Please to address me at Hawarden—I do not know where you are.
[P.S.] I send you the two original lists in case you shd. not have them by you—please return them.

23. Tu.

Ch. 8½ AM and Holy Eucharist. Never I think have my needs been so heavy: but it seems as if God were lovingly minded to supply them only from day to day. 'The fellowship of the Holy Ghost' is the continuing boon which seems the boon for me.
  Wrote to Adm. Egerton—Mr C. Foljambe—Mr White—Sir T. Farrer—Sir H. Vivian—Mr Mowatt—Gen. Donnelly[1]—Mr M. Thompson[2] & 3 more C.B.s—and minutes. Visited our old Lodgekeeper Mrs Jones now dying of Cancer. Drive with C. Worked at St Deiniol's. Read Life of Sherbrooke—Divorce of H. VIII.

To Admiral F. EGERTON, 23 May 1893.   Add MS 44549, f. 91.

  I am sure that you did not arrive at your negative conclusion without good & strong reasons,[3] but I may still be permitted to regret the result alike on personal & on public grounds.
  It was my hearty & warm desire to see you in the H. of Commons, where your utility would have been greatest: but failing this in the H. of Lords.
  I cannot too highly praise the loyalty, self-sacrifice, & legitimate self assertion of our majority in the H. of Commons. It is the most democratic majority I have ever led or known: & it also votes the best, I mean in the sense in which whips & leaders use the phrase.
  It is hard to say how soon the so called Liberal Unionists & the Tories will perceive & will have to own at what rate during these last 7 years they have been propelling democracy, & driving into holes & corners all Liberal ideas that are not democratic.
  If Chamberlain is still at bottom the ultra-radical he used to be, he will be able to boast that he has never served Radicalism half so effectually as he has done by his able though almost rabid opposition to the Conservative measure of Home Rule.
  In every quarter I have desired & striven at least to temper this movement by the introduction into Parliament of such elements as those which you represent: but at almost every point I have altogether failed.
  However all these issues are in better hands than ours & all we can do is to work feebly for the good as we see it.
  Our kindest regards to Lady Louisa.

24. Wed.

Ch. 8¼ A.M. Wrote to Mr Shand Tel. l.—Dr Rainy Tel.—Ld Rosebery—and minutes. Worked on Irish Finance. Went to Chester & had my eyes examined by Mr Grainger. His report was highly favourable: which strange to say I by no means altogether desired. Called on Mr A. Banks. Saw Dr Wilson—S.E.G. ill. He works over hard. Read Henry VIII.—Ships that pass in the Night.[4]

[1] K.C.B. for John Fretcheville Dykes Donnelly, 1834–1902; soldier; secretary to Kensington Science and Art Dept. 1884–99.
[2] C.B. for (Sir) Edward Maunde Thompson, 1840–1929; librarian of the British Museum 1888–1909.   [3] Declined a peerage; no correspondence found.
[4] B. Harraden, *Ships that pass in the night* (1893).

To LORD ROSEBERY, foreign secretary, 24 May 1893.   N.L.S. 10026, f. 172.

I cannot detect any shade of difference in our estimate as to France and Egypt, except this, that I allow something for the historical associations of France with Egypt, especially the great service which she tried to render in 1840.

It may seem odd to you but I like your handwriting better than typewriting,[1] I mean it suits my eyes better.

25 Th.

Ch. 8½ A.M. Wrote to Mr Shand Tel.—Ld Rosebery—Mr Marj. Tel.—Mr Black—Mr Kelly[2]—Mr Morley—& minutes. Worked at St Deiniol's. Tea with Mr Johnson: & agricultural talk. Read By & Bye(!)[3]—'Ships that pass' &c.—Froude's Divorce. Conversation with Sir A. Clark on the 'situation' in the family.

Secret.   *Irish Finances*[4]

1. Shorten term to 7 years.
2. Increase constabulary charge from ⅓ to ½ (if Mr Hamilton is right in thinking this sufficient to square (roughly) the 500m).
3. Retain power to *fix levy* & *manage* Customs, and to *fix* Excise & P.O.
4. For the *present* charge, accept the Customs Revenue as Ireland's Imperial contribution. (*Or* quota of 9/ for each £10 of Imperial expenditure).
5. In the event of an increase of the expenditure under the heads fixed by the Act as Imperial, such that Parliament shall think proper to take notice of it, Parlt. to charge on the Irish Exchequer 9/ for each £10 of it (OR to fix what contribution Ireland shall make).
6. On the basis of these heads, I think the Finance clauses may be materially simplified which has now become an object of importance with a view to progress in the Bill.

To J. MORLEY, Irish secretary, 25 May 1893.   Add MS 44257, f. 109.

My ideas & those of Hamilton & Welby on Irish Finance were given to Harcourt a week ago but I have not had a word from him.

It is clear that when we get back to town action must be prompt & decisive.

In the enclosed Memorandum I have aimed at brevity—completeness in essentials—simplification of the clauses—& option where there was room for it.

If you approve of it I will send it or a copy to Harcourt. Please to return it as I have no copy.

Farmers *here* in high spirits, the country beautiful, & every prospect of an excellent *year*.

[P.S.] Clearly we ought to be prepared to take the Finance Clauses in their present order.[5]

[1] See to Rosebery, 19 May 93n.
[2] Thanking James Kelly for his poem (untraced), the Witanagemote: 'I admire it as a poem; I feel that in assigning to me a part you pay me a compliment; & I seem to find myself in sympathy with its general intention'; Add MS 44549, f. 92.
[3] Untraced.
[4] Initialled and dated 25 May 1893, Add MS 44775, f. 155.
[5] Morley suggested a meeting with Harcourt, Fowler and perhaps Herschell; Add MS 44257, f. 111.

To LORD ROSEBERY, foreign secretary, 25 May 1893.   N.L.S. 10026, f. 175.

I have received this morning M. Deville's interesting and temperate speech.[1]

There is one historical point on which he dwells: which was stated very strongly to me by Waddington in his posthumous conversation: and about which I should much wish to know what is said or thought in the tradition of the Foreign Office.

Waddington I think said that the Article of the Treaty of Paris [1856], which makes every territorial question of the Ottoman Empire a matter of *European* concern, was virtually and really dead since the Congress of Berlin so far as Egypt is concerned.

On my demurring to this statement, he could not quote chapter and verse, and I think admitted it was not in the Treaty or the Protocols. M. Deville seems nearly to revive it. I much wish to know *how far this statement can be sustained*, beyond the fact that Egypt was not dealt with at Berlin.

I do not recollect that Granville's negotiations were ever founded on a definite admission of this kind—I think they proceeded upon policy, with a spice perhaps of sentiment by no means unjust.[2]

26. Fr.

Ch. 8½ A.M. Wrote to Mr Marj. Tel.—Sir A. Gordon—Ld Rosebery—Lady Herbert—Mr Latler[3]—and minutes. Worked at St Deiniol's. Read Ships &c. (finished)—Willink, World of the Unseen.[4]—Froude, Divorce. Conversation with S.: who has been hit but rallies fast.

27. Sat.

Ch. 8½ A.M. Wrote to Mr Morley Tel.—Mr Purcell—Mr Marj.—Mr Hamilton—and minutes. Worked at St Deiniol's. Tea visit to the Hurlburts. Saw Stephy who opened new plans. Read Froude's Divorce—Island Nights[5]—Sherbrooke's Memoirs. Backgammon with A.

28. Trin. S.

Ch 11 A.M. and 7 P.M. Wrote to The Queen (& copy)—Sir W. Harcourt—Mr Marj.—& minutes. Read Life of Keble—Through Conversion to Creed[6]—Comm. on Genesis & Bp King's Preface.[7]—Conversation with S.E.G.

To Sir W. V. HARCOURT, chancellor of the exchequer,   MS Harcourt dep. 13, f. 111.
28 May 1893.

Irish Finance has now become urgent, for communications made by Chamberlain to John Morley seem to indicate that if we ask to postpone the Clauses, the postponement itself will be made the subject of another separate battle. In this view it may seem unwise to propose it.

[1] Untraced speech by Jules Develle.
[2] No comment by Rosebery found.
[3] Librarian at Knowsley; see 10 Oct. 83.
[4] A. Willinck, *The world of the unseen. An essay* (1893).
[5] R. L. Stevenson, *Island nights' entertainments* (1893).
[6] W. H. Carnegie, *Through conversion to the Creed* (1893).
[7] E. King, *Practical reflections upon every verse in the Book of Genesis. With a preface* (1892).

Will you kindly come to me on Tuesday on or after twelve in D. St or to my room in the H. of C. when the Committee begins for I need not be present at the absurd adjourned Debate.

29. M. [London]

Ch. 8½ AM. Wrote to Dr Ginsburg—Pres. of Magdalen—Priv. Sec. Tel. l.l. Read Keble's Life finished—Through Conversion finished—*et alia*. Left at 4.40. D. St. 10.50. Saw H. Drew: he was admirable. Also S. (still in bed). Short speech in Chester to Liberals.[1]

To E. S. PURCELL, 29 May 1893.   Add MS 44549, f. 93.

I am seriously concerned at the loss of Cardinal Manning's Anglican letters to me[2] which in my judgement (resting upon general memory) were most valuable and might even have borne republication in extenso.

They belong to a period between 40 and 60 years ago, and I could give no adequate account of them while even to write generally on him would require time and thought now absolutely beyond my power to give.[3]

30.

Wrote to J. Morley—Ld Rosebery. H. of C. 3¾–8 and 9¾–11½.[4] Saw Sir A. West— Mr Marj.—Mr Morley—Sir W. Harcourt—do cum Mr M.—Mr Sexton—Mr Fowler.

A very anxious & *rather* barren morning on Irish Finance. My present position as a whole certainly seems peculiar: but of this it is unheroic either to speak or think.

Backgammon with Mr A.

To J. MORLEY, Irish secretary, 30 May 1893.   Add MS 44549, f. 92.

To my deep disappointment I understand the plan of a lump payment *to* Ireland is to be revived. Can you come here at the earliest moment?

[1] Presentation of an address arranged at the last minute; *T.T.*, 30 May 1893, 8b.

[2] Purcell reported, 24 May, Add MS 44517, f. 165: 'Manning's Anglican letters to you—unless they were returned to you, are not to be found. I much fear that shortly before his death the Cardinal destroyed them. He told me that you overestimated the value of his letters: that [*sic*] were not worthy of publication.' In 1862 Gladstone and Manning exchanged each other's letters, the Gladstone collection thus containing his own letters, rather than Manning's; Purcell noted in his preface, i. x, that 'all the letters written in his Anglican days to Mr Gladstone were suppressed by Cardinal Manning because . . . their publication would not be expedient. Mr Gladstone . . . was very indignant on hearing from me of their fate.' The letters were not in fact destroyed, being used by Abbé A. Chapeau for his thesis; see P. A. Butler, *Gladstone, church, state and tractarianism* (1982), 5. They have now been transferred from the Westminster Diocesan archives to the U.S.A.

[3] Purcell asked Gladstone, given the absence of the letters, for 'your estimate of these letters and your opinion of Archdeacon Manning's work and influence in the Church of England until he left it'.

[4] G.I. Bill cttee.; 4H 12. 1558.

31. Wed.

Wrote to The Queen l.l.—Ld Rosebery—Miss Hennell[1]—and minutes. H. of C. 12¼–5½; Irish Bill. A heart breaking spectacle for anyone who reveres the historic H. of Commons.[2] Saw Sir A. West—Mr Marj.—Sol. General—Mr Morley. Dined at Sir C. Tennant's. Read Stevenson's Personality[3]—Colclough on Ulster.[4]

To LORD ROSEBERY, foreign secretary, 31 May 1893. *'Private.'*   N.L.S. 10026, f. 187.

I should be very glad if with reference to Plunkett's dispatch of 21st current you included in my reply an expression in the strongest terms of our desire for the maintenance of the Union between Sweden & Norway and of our belief that the only safe course for the attainment of that object lies in the strict observance of the law by the Sovereign.

(Different parts of the King's conversation as reported seem to me not to hang consistently together).[5]

Thurs. June 1. 1893.

Wrote to Mr Rathbone MP—The Queen—and minutes. Saw Mr Marj.—Sir A. West—Mr Hamilton—Mr Morley—Sir H. Jenkyns: held conclave on Irish Finance. Saw Maharajah of [blank.] Read N. Cent. on "Ulster"[6]—Stevenson's 'Personality'. H. of C. 4–8¼ and 9¼–12½. Irish Bill—mournful.[7]

2. Fr.

Wrote to Ld Kimberley—Mr Asquith—Mr Rathbone MP—The Queen—Ld Tweedmouth—and minutes. H. of C. 2½–6¼ [spoke on] I.G. Bill.[8] Read Stevenson (finished)—et alia. Dined with the Harry's at Hampstead. Saw Mr Rendel.

To LORD KIMBERLEY, lord president and Indian secretary,   Kimberley MSS.
2 June 1893.

Taking your point of view as to best mode of dealing with Paul's motion, we—Marjoribanks, Harcourt and I[—]consider that a whip would have been a decided tactical mistake: but we will tell against the motion.[9]

[1] Thanking Sara Sophia Hennell for a copy of her 'Essay on the sceptical tendency in Butler's "Analogy"' (1859) which he had read earlier 'with the utmost interest'; Add MS 44549, f. 93; see 23 Dec. 60.

[2] Series of amndts. to clause 3 (exception from powers of Irish legislature) of G.I. Bill; 4 *H* 12. 1669.

[3] F. S. Stevenson, *Historic personality* (1893).

[4] J. G. Colclough, 'Ulster. Facts and figures', *C.R.*, lxiii. 761 (June 1893).

[5] Rosebery replied, 9 June, Add MS 44290, f. 142: 'I took an opportunity of urging on Plunkett, should an occasion present itself, the necessity of pointing out how suicidal would be a civil war between Sweden and Norway. But I think that the language he used to the King at their interview will have met with your approval.' (Sir) Francis Richard Plunkett, 1835–1907; minister in Stockholm 1888–93.

[6] *N.C.*, xxxiii. 927 (June 1893).   [7] 4 *H* 12. 1812.   [8] 4 *H* 13. 68.

[9] Kimberley replied this day, Add MS 44229, f. 85: 'You are the best judge as to the whip. I have told Russell to speak with the greatest sympathy as to the employment of natives. The objection is not to their employment (subject of course to our retaining the indispensable European element), but to the particular mode of recruitment by open competition in India, which would be a fatal mistake.' Paul's amndt. easing Indian entry to I.C.S. passed in 84:76; 4 *H* 13. 141.

I hope, however, that Russell will speak sympathetically as to the employment of natives *apart from* the intervention of the House of Commons.

To W. RATHBONE, M.P., 2 June 1893.   Add MS 44549, f. 93.

I cannot make any promise, with respect to the amendment you have kindly sent me,[1] on the matter of acceptance, but I will take care to consult with colleagues upon it. At the rate of five days a week in Committee the pressure upon me is such as, I regret to say, to make it impossible to hold a second conversation on the subject of your plan, which I should be most happy to do were it within the limits of my strength.

3. Sat.

Wrote to Ld Kimberley & minutes. Read Howorth[2]—Tebb on Leprosy[3]—et alia. Sir Sir A. West—Mr Marj.—Mr Murray. Missed D. of Argyll at A. Lodge. Tea at Lady Farnboroughs. Gave my birthday Dinner. Arranged with the Prince for communications on the 'situation' of which I stated the elements briefly: also matters about Parnell. Altogether a very free & pleasant conversation. Also conversation with the Speaker—Ld Kelvin[4]—Sir F. Leighton—The Viceroy of I.—Aberdeen.

To LORD KIMBERLEY, lord president and Indian secretary,   Kimberley MSS.
3 June 1893.

I have summoned a Cabinet for Tuesday at twelve.[5] The significant features of last night's miscarriage are these:
1. Defeat by our own friends, of whom hardly *any* voted with us.
2. Defeat which would have been more marked but for the energy in inducing men to go away.
I hope you may not think it necessary to meet it with a simple *non possumus* if any milder method can be found.
The following suggestions occur to me.
1. You cannot be expected to send out this Resolution as a simple *order* to the Indian Government for execution forthwith.
2. I suppose there are many points which they may fairly raise for consideration, such as
   a. is there to be only one examination centre in India?
   b. if several are requisite, what are they to be?
   c. *Supposing* that the Indian Candidates were on the average equal in merit and tenfold in number, are we prepared at once to establish a civil service with native and English divided in that proportion?
   d. are the subjects of the native Princes to be excluded?
3. Would it be unfair to request the Indian Government to report to you, monishing them at the same time against exhibiting a hostile spirit.
Take this only for what it is worth.[6]

[1] Not found.
[2] Sir H. H. Howarth, *Glacial nightmare and the flood*, 2v. (1893).
[3] W. Tebb, *Recrudescence of leprosy and its causation by vaccination* (1893).
[4] William Thomson, 1824–1907; professor of natural philosophy, Glasgow, 1846–99; President, Royal Society 1890–4; Baron Kelvin 1892; a strong Unionist (b. in Belfast).
[5] Kimberley wrote this day, Add MS 44229, f. 87, 'I greatly regret that Paul should have carried his motion yesterday. I need hardly say that I am not prepared to give effect to it.'
[6] Kimberley replied next day, ibid., f. 88: '... I am by no means disposed to a simple "non

4. *1 S. Trin.*

Chapel Royal (Lutheran) mg & evg. Saw the Breadalbanes. Wrote to Ld Duf-ferin—Ld Rosebery. Read Paton, Papal Claims[1]—Watts on Eternal Punt[2]—I Tre Papi.[3]

5. *M.*

Wrote to Sir W.H.—The Queen—Cawthorne & Hutt—and minutes. Saw Sir A. West—HNG—Mr Marj.—Ld Kimberley—E. Hamilton—Mr Morley. Irish con-clave (on finance) at H. of C. $3\frac{3}{4}$–$8\frac{1}{4}$ and $9\frac{1}{2}$–$12\frac{1}{4}$. [Spoke on] Irish Bill &c.[4] Read King Lear—Marvellous!—Sir H. Howorth.

To Sir W. V. HARCOURT, chancellor of the exchequer,   MS Harcourt dep. 13, f. 113.
5 June 1893.

1. I had a few words with the Speaker—quite satisfactory—on Judges.
2. Will you kindly look at Logan's motion on Agriculture and consider how it should be dealt with. It is stiff.
3. I hope to see your suggestions on Irish Finance today. It would be very good if we could dispose of the subject in Cabinet tomorrow. I might be able, if the case arise to communicate with the Irish tonight or Monday night.
4. Remember also the Indian Currency Committee for the Cabinet tomorrow.

6. *Tu.*

Wrote to The Queen l.l.—Mr Asquith—& minutes. Cabinet 12–$1\frac{3}{4}$. Saw the Irish three. Saw Sir A.W.—Mr Marj.—Mr Hamilton. H. of C. $3\frac{1}{2}$–8 and $9\frac{3}{4}$–12.[5] Read Cymbeline.

Cabinet. Tues. June 6. 93. Noon.[6]
1. Lord Mayoralities. Tender [?] to Lpool & Manchester.[7]
2. India Civil Service Examinations. My draft, as amended.[8]
3. India. Mint & Currency.[9] a. To consult Indian Govt. b. No decision as to production of Report until we hear from them. c. Ch[ancellor] to draw a draft & consult upon it. To bear in mind that the *cabinet* ought not to be kitched into a corner.
4. Irish Finance. W.E.G. authorised to induce the Irish MPs if possible to accept paper A as the basis of the Financial proposals.

possumus", if any other way can be found: but the questions at issue go to the very root of our supremacy in India, and a false step may be irretrievable. The points are simple enough. 1. We *must* have a certain minimum of European officers. 2. We cannot employ more than a certain number of Bengalis, since they are by nature altogether unfitted to control the stronger races.' He concluded: 'I like your idea of consulting the Govt. of India. It will give time and opportunity for more mature dis-cussion & consideration.' For Gladstone's public comment, see 8 June 93.

[1] J. Paton, *British history and papal claims from the Norman Conquest to the present day*, 2v. (1893).
[2] R. Watts, *The doctrine of eternal punishment vindicated against recent attacks* (1873).
[3] Untraced.
[4] *4H* 13. 265.
[5] Spoke on G. I. Bill cttee.; *4H* 13. 343.
[6] Add MS 44648, f. 100.
[7] Note on size of Liverpool, ibid., f. 103.
[8] See 8 June 93n.
[9] Various notes by Welby and B. Currie on Indian bimetallism at Add 44648, f. 101.

7. *Wed.*

Wrote to Sir W. Phillimore—Sir W. Harcourt—..... H. of C. $12\frac{1}{4}$–$5\frac{3}{4}$.[1] We entertained the Duke of York & the Teck party to dinner. The little Irish Violinist played afterwards.[2] Saw Sir A.W.—Mr Marj.—Messrs Welby & Hamilton—Mr Morley—Messrs Woods & Pickard—The Irish leaders *cum* Sir R. Welby. Drive with C. Dead tired.

To Sir W. V. HARCOURT, chancellor of the exchequer,   MS Harcourt dep. 13, f. 114.
7 June 1893.

Am I right in supposing you would reserve the rights of Parliament entire as to war taxation without specifying beyond this that it is not included in the one third plan?[3] Of course this must be mentioned to the Irish?

Perhaps you will tell me at the House.

8. *Th.*

(after 8? hours of sleep, six of them *solid*). Wrote to Mr Matthews[4]—Mr F. Shurn[5]—Scotts—The Prince of Wales—The Queen l.l.—A. Att. General Tel.—Sir W. Wedderburn—and minutes. Saw Princess Mary (Duchess of Teck)—Sir A. West—Mr Marj.—Mr Sexton—Sir W. Harcourt. Read Cymbeline—Rogers on Bibliography.[6] Drive with C. H. of C. 4–$8\frac{1}{4}$ and $9\frac{3}{4}$–$11\frac{3}{4}$. Irish Bill.[7]

To Sir W. WEDDERBURN, M.P., 8 June 1893.   Add MS 44549, f. 94.

I have received a Memorial from you & many other members which expresses the desire that more time may be given than heretofore for considering the Finances of India during the present Session.[8] I cannot but admit in addition to the general importance of the subject, the weight belonging to the signatures, & the special interest now attaching to the condition of Indian Finance.

Aware as we all are of these facts, we have also before us the question of the Irish Govt. Bill, & the opposition offered to it in various forms before & now in Committee. Under these circumstances I am not as yet able to give any pledge bearing on the date of the discussion but I feel with you that, even if it be to impose a further sacrifice adequate time ought to be found for it.

[1] Spoke on G.I. Bill cttee.; 4*H* 13. 424.

[2] See 6 May 93.

[3] Harcourt this day, Add MS 44203, f. 79, argued that in a war emergency 'the Imperial Parliament should have the right to impose a special tax or taxes upon the whole of the United Kingdom'.

[4] Thanking him (otherwise unidentified) for M.S. of book on Richard I: 'I have read it and do not think it worthy of being published: so that I am obliged to decline your proposal'; Add MS 44549, f. 95.

[5] Thanking for W. S. Landor's *Letters* (see 9 June 93).

[6] W. T. Rogers, *Bibliography* (1890).

[7] And answered question on Paul's Resolution on standardization in U.K. and India of civil service examinations, stating that there should be 'prompt and careful' discussion of the Resolution by the Indian govt.; his answer led to questions in the Lords; 4*H* 13. 660.

[8] Not found.

Catherine Gladstone, 25 October
1892, photographed by Miss Sarah
Acland

Drawing of W.E. Gladstone after
death, by W.B. Richmond

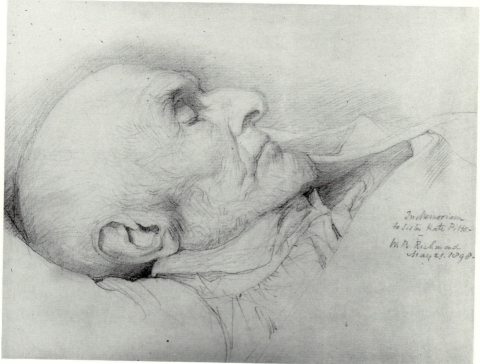

'Enemies on his flank', by F. Carruthers-Gould

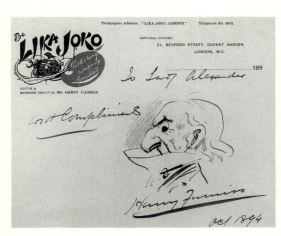

The Gladstone collar, by Harry Furniss

Lord Salisbury: Unionism in action,
by F. Carruthers-Gould

W.E.Gladstone.

'W.E. Gladstone', woodcut by William Nicholson

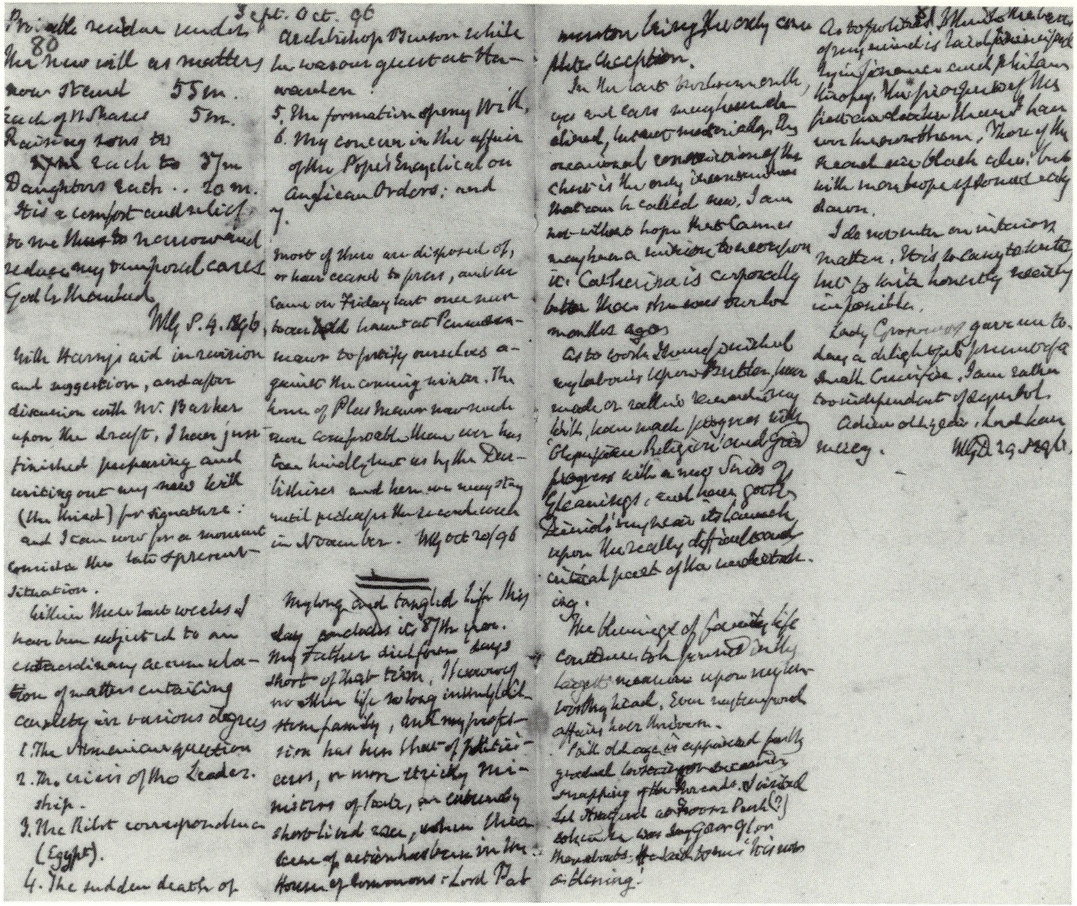

Facsimile of the last two pages of the journal, 4 September - 29 December 1896 *Lambeth 1455, f.81*

9. *Fr.* [*Lion Mansions, Brighton*]

Wrote to Ld Rosebery—Attorney General—The Queen—& minutes. H. of C. 2½-5¼. (The Bill).[1] Then away to Lion Mansions as before.[2] Backgammon with Mr A. Dearest C. made experiments (very favourably) with a speaking trumpet of a clever kind. (Rather a tube). This notes an onward stage. Saw Sir A.W.—Mr Marj.—Sol. General—Sir W.H.—H.J.G. Read Cymbeline (finished)—Landor's Letters.[3]

To J. MORLEY, Irish secretary, 9 June 1893.   Add MS 44549, f. 95.

Please to read this letter which I propose to send to Russell:[4] & to suggest if you see occasion.

8 June.

I wrote a telegram late last night to urge you in the sense of Morley's letter. From my recollection of the devoted & indefatigable service you rendered to Ireland & to the Liberal cause throughout the last Parliament, I can well conceive how you must have felt & suffered under your enforced absence from the great battle, to which everything else was preliminary. But the time has come when an urgent necessity compels us to cooperate in releasing you from the present pressure of our engagement, which has already kept you out of the H. of Commons during a period extraordinarily long, absent from what may fairly be called a life & death struggle.

I may add that those who regulate progress at Paris do not appear much to contemplate or even desire dispatch.

Meantime our position is almost unexampled. Rigby[5] has behaved admirably: but the demands on him to interpret the language of the Bill are incessant, & although everyone respects him as a jurist, yet the strain upon his authority is really too great. We have no Irish Law Officer; Carson[6] is a rather dangerous opponent: he is backed by 4 or 5 Irish Lawyers: Clarke is also there, & at several critical points James's intervention has been brought to bear against him.

We have been for some ten days (I think) in Clause 3 & are not yet out. It requires incessantly legal interpretation. Cl. 4 is of the same character, & still more urgently requires Irish knowledge. When we get into purely political controversies, much as we desire to have you all along, our need now imperative, will I hope be less urgent.

You will I am sure appreciate the necessity which has brought about our rather rude interference.[7]

To LORD ROSEBERY, foreign secretary, 9 June 1893.   N.L.S. 10026, f. 193.

Morley has long been urging Russell to make arrangements for coming to the House of Commons to join in our life and death struggle, where, without an Irish or an English Attorney General to help him, Rigby has to confront a host of lawyers, including

---

[1] Spoke on it; 4*H* 13. 660.

[2] Apartment hired by G. Armitstead; see 30 Mar. 85.

[3] W. S. Landor, *The letters of a conservative: in which are shown the only means of saving what is left of the English church* (1836).

[4] i.e. Sir C. A. Russell, attorney general; involved in the Behring Sea arbitration case for the first part of 1893.

[5] Sir John Rigby, 1834–1903; solicitor general and liberal M.P. Forfarshire 1892–4; judge 1894.

[6] (Sir) Edward Henry Carson, 1854–1935; unionist M.P. 1892–1918; solicitor general (Ireland) June–Aug. 1892; later advocated rebellious opposition to home rule and sat in Cabinet.

[7] Russell returned, speaking in the Commons from 14 June.

especially Sir H. James. We have at length been compelled to send rather peremptorily to Russell to request that he will make arrangements to appear in the beginning of next week and remain till the extreme legal pressure has subsided. It is not only his legal advice that is wanted, but the *authority* of his office: my only wonder is how Rigby (who has behaved admirably) has managed to get on. On the other hand I hope we may be able to release him after a moderate time. According to what I hear, his masters in Paris are in no hurry to get on with their work.

[P.S.] In the race of folly in Scandinavia, Sweden seems at the present moment to get ahead.

10. Sat.

Wrote to S.E.G.—Mr Morley—Ld Rosebery Tel.—Mr Murray Tel.—and minutes. Saw Mayor & Mayoress [of Brighton]. Saw Mr Morley. Read Landor (finished)—Martin Sherbrooke—British in India.[1] Backgammon with Mr A. Drive in aft. Walk with J.M.

To J. MORLEY, Irish secretary, 10 June 1893.   Add MS 44549, f. 96.

Redmond has already, notwithstanding his excellent speeches, ditched his own case & given Chamberlain the whiphand over him. I hope he will refrain from further coups de tête. But after all he may not as to finance comprehend what he has only heard in rough hearsay; and it might be worth while to clear his ideas.

I think the situation is this:
1. Simplification is very vital.
2. It is not compatible with a full financial settlement.
3. Sexton has proposed spontaneously what means a provisional one; with strong reasons to warrant him.
4. We can work this into simplification.
5. It involves postponement of one of the moral claims of Ireland.
6. It is our duty to make it clear that this is postponement *only*.
7. It has other most important practical advantages
8. And it helps in getting very good money terms for the provisional period.

The Irish however are, it seems to me, not indeed quarrelling but considering whether they shall or shall not quarrel with their own bread and butter.

11. 2 S. Trin. St Barnabas

Chapel Royal mg: St Bartholomew's evg. Wrote to Ld Rosebery—Mr Murray tel.—and minutes. Visit to the Pier. Saw Ld Acton—Mr Morley. Read Memoirs of Dr J. Brown[2]—T.A. Kempis—The Priest in Politics.[3]

12. M. [London]

Wrote to Mr Morley—Ld Kimberley—Dr Deed—Sir [blank] Calcraft—The Queen—Mayor of Liverpool—and minutes. Drive & train at 1.20. H. of C. $4\frac{1}{4}$–8 and $9\frac{1}{4}$–$12\frac{1}{4}$. Irish Bill.[4] Saw Sir A. West—Mr Morley—Mr Murray. Read Rogers, Bibliography.

[1] See 8 Apr. 93.
[2] Perhaps John Brown, *The posthumous works of the late Rev. Mr. John Brown* (1797).
[3] P. H. Bagenal, *The priest in politics* (1893).   [4] Spoke on it; 4*H* 13. 802.

Memorandum[1]

The practical reasons against the retention of their present seats by the Irish Nationalists appear to me to be very strong.

1. I take first that it will cause a more unequal distribution of the House numerically on
   the two sides than is necessary. I admit this however to be secondary.
2. They will sit among men with whom they are vitally at variance on the leading
   measure of the Session. This will renew for them the annoyance we suffered throughout the last Parliament. I admit however that they have here[?] the title to judge: but
   we have had an experience which they have not.
3. If they retain their present seats they compell the Dissidents to remain on our side, or
   else to fight with them for seats below the gangway on the Opposition side. Either of
   these alternatives is most objectionable.
4. They wish to show their independence by their position in the House. Now no proposition can be more clearly established than this, that when a party or section as such
   takes its place below the gangway in the House of Commons, the second bench below
   the gangway is the appointed seat of the Leaders. I can I think establish this by *three* if
   not *four* dissident precedents within my memory.
5. Last and perhaps most serious of all. On the Irish Bill, & especially in the Committee
   free & constant communication with the Nationalists will be not only convenient but
   necessary. This will be easy if they sit below the gangway—most difficult, and also
   exposed by any visible signs to ridicule when attempted, if they retain their present
   seats.

13. *Tu.*

Wrote to Ld Rosebery—Rev. A. Hutton—The Queen—Mr Carnegie—&
minutes. Saw Sir A.W.—Mr Marj.—Sir H.J[enkyns], Mr H[amilton], & Sir R.
W[elby] on Finance Clauses 12–2. Read Carnegies Look ahead[2]—Rogers, Bibliography. Backgammon with Mr A. Visited Christies. H. of C. (I.B.) $3\frac{1}{2}$–$8\frac{1}{4}$ and
$9\frac{3}{4}$–$11\frac{3}{4}$.[3]

To A. W. HUTTON, 13 June 1893.   Add MS 44549, f. 97.

I acknowledge with thanks your letter to Lyttelton.[4] I feel more regret than surprise at
the announcement: & of that regret almost the whole is for the disappointment of those
who had embarked so much labour enterprise & intelligence in the undertaking.

14. *Wed.*

Wrote to Rev. Sir G. Philips—Sir J. Lubbock—The Queen—& minutes. H. of C.
$1\frac{1}{4}$–$5\frac{3}{4}$. (I.B.)[5] Dined at Mr Montagu's. The most beautiful old English plate (from
H. VIII) I ever saw. Saw Mr Saunders—Att. General—Sir A.W.—Mr Marj. Read
Bibliography—*et alia*.

---

[1] Initialled and dated 12 June 1893; Add MS 44775, f. 6.
[2] A. Carnegie, 'A look ahead', *N.A.R.*, clvi. 685 (June 1893).
[3] Clause 3 completed; 4*H* 13. 916.
[4] Not found. Presumably termination of the edition by Hutton and Cohen of Gladstone's
Speeches, of which only 2v. were published.
[5] Clause 4; 4*H* 13. 1006.

15. Th.

Wrote to The Queen—Ld Kimberley l.l.—Ld Rosebery—and minutes. H of C. 4–8¼ and 9½–12¼.¹ Saw Sir A.W.—Mr Marj.—Mr B. Currie—Sir H. J[enkyns] & conclave (Irish Finance)—Ld Kimberley—Conclave on I.F. Procedure 1–2. Again: with Harcourt, & then Milman & Jenkins. A very hard day: dead tired. Dined at Mr Armitstead's: met the Carnegies. Read [blank.]

To LORD KIMBERLEY, lord president and Indian secretary,   Kimberley MSS.
15 June 1893. '*Opium*'.

I agree with your late view of the general Commission on Indian Revenue.
And I like your suggestion of a Commission of Inquiry.²
I can conceive two other admirable subjects for Inquiry. 1. on retrenchment. 2. on the equities of the account between Gt. Britain and India, on a view of both sides—probably there is a good deal to say from each point of view. My own conjecture is that India may have grievance in detail, but that we suffer much by the present army arrangements taken at large. Neither of these subjects would cover opium.³

To LORD ROSEBERY, foreign secretary, 15 June 1893.   N.L.S. 10026, f. 208.

Of course we must observe cautious handling on the Arbitration Resolution in the H of C tomorrow night. But viewing the real interest of the matter might I not properly promise to lay the Treaty & papers on the table?

16. Fr. [Dollis Hill]

Wrote to Mr Bryce—Ld Herschell—Mr Balfour—and minutes. H. of C. 2¼–7¼ and 9–10½. Spoke on [international] arbitration.⁴ Dollis at 11.30. Saw Sir A.W.—Mr Marj.—Mr Morley (+)—Mr Balfour. Read [blank]. Much exhausted.

To J. BRYCE, chancellor of the duchy, 16 June 1893. '*Immediate.*'   MS Bryce 10, f. 135.

Upon the basis of this written information and of such conversation as I have had with you, I only see as yet that it should not be *Raleigh* or *Graeber*. Between maybe Carter and Gondig [*sc.* Gondy] I should be thankful for your opinion but of course in confidence the responsibility being wholly mine.⁵

17.

A vegetating life restored me—dozing, reading, meditating. Read Louise de Keroualle.⁶ Saw Sir A. Clark & conversation on S.E.G. and his rectory.

¹ 4H 13. 1079.
² Long letter on the Indian currency, the need for decision urgent; 11 June, Add MS 44229, f. 92.
³ For which see to Kimberley, 22 June 93.
⁴ On arbitration with the U.S.A.; 4H 13. 1249.
⁵ On the Regius Chair of Civil Law at Oxford. Bryce replied marginally supporting Carter; letter undated, MS Bryce 12, f. 127.
⁶ See 14 June 86.

18. 3 S. Trin.

Willesden Ch mg. Prayers on the lawn evg. Saw Ld Tweedmouth—Lady Tw.—
Mr Wyatt—Canon O'Hanlon[1]—Mr Weldon. Read L. de Keroualle—Reynolds on
Immortality[2]—. . . . . . on Nonconformity—Mrs Charles, Early Xtn Missions.[3]

19. M. [London]

Return much refreshed (D.G.) though in great heat: D. St at 11 AM. Wrote to
the Queen l.l.l.—and minutes. Cabinet 12–2. H of C. $3\frac{1}{4}$–$8\frac{1}{4}$ & $9\frac{1}{2}$–$11\frac{1}{4}$.[4] Saw Sir A.
West—Mr Marj.—Sir R. Welby & E. Hamilton—Mr Morley—Sir G. Trevelyan.
Read Early Xtn Missions.

Cabinet. Monday June 19. 93. Noon.[5]
1. Indian Currency. Ld Kimberley: against *doing nothing*. Decide 1. to act now. 2. between
   the Commission & Council[?]: follows Commn. "+ Indian Govt + Council. 3. Act
   without H of C. 4. Make known to H of C on receiving telegraphic reply.
2. Irish Finance. Conversation on the basis of Morley's draft clause. Morley to try to limit
   the final provision[?] to collation and regulation.
   If not then take the Clause bodily.

(During this Cabinet, Harcourt interjected in the oddest way a declaration that six years
hence (as he said) "I shall not be here.")[6]

20. Th.

Wrote to The Queen—Sir H. Ponsonby—& minutes. H. of C. 4–$8\frac{1}{4}$ & $9\frac{1}{2}$–$12\frac{1}{4}$.[7]
Saw Sir A.W.—Mr Marj.—Sir H. Jenkyns—Mr Morley—Att. General. Read Sin of
Janet Aveling.[8]

21. Wed.

Wrote to The Queen—Bull & Auvache—Rev. SEG—and minutes. H of C. $12\frac{1}{4}$–
$6\frac{1}{4}$.[9] Saw Sir A.W.—Mr Marj.—Italian Ambassr—Ld Kimberley (opium)—Ld
Swansea. Read Lyall on India.[10]

22. Th.

Wrote to The Queen—Ottoman Ambr—Rev. SEG—Ld Kimberley—Mr
Gowdy—Sir W. Harcourt—and minutes. H. of C. 3–8 and $9\frac{1}{2}$–$12\frac{1}{4}$.[11] Saw Sir
A.W.—Mr Marj.—Mr Murray—M. Drew—Sir R. Welby & EWH—Conclave at

[1] None of this name found. Perhaps Alexander Patrick Hanlon of Co. Waterford (but not a
canon).
[2] J. W. Reynolds, *The natural history of immortality* (1891).
[3] Mrs. R. Charles, *Early Christian missions* (1893).
[4] Dispute with James on 1881–2; 4*H* 13. 1402.
[5] Add MS 44648, f. 104.   [6] This sentence added later.
[7] Spoke on Irish taxation; 4*H* 13. 1557.
[8] M. Maartens [i.e. J. M. W. van der Poorten-Schwartz], *The sin of Janet Avelingh*, 2v. (1889).
[9] Spoke on Irish higher education; 4*H* 13. 1591.
[10] See 8 Apr. 93.
[11] Spoke on G.I. Bill cttee.; 4*H* 13. 1741.

H. of C. (denominational Colleges)—Mr Morley—Sir T. Acland. Read J. Brown's Memoirs[1]—Ingersoll's 'In Health'.[2] Eight to dinner.

To Sir W. V. HARCOURT, chancellor of the exchequer,   MS Harcourt dep. 13, f. 119.
22 June 1893.

On the procedure in Committee we ought to be as stringent as we can today & tomorrow, and then before resuming on Wednesday make our choice—query on Tuesday afternoon during Supply at a meeting in my room?—between the two methods of closuring each Clause and of reporting on a certain day. There is much to be said for each: I learn that you prefer the first: I am open.

To LORD KIMBERLEY, lord president and Indian secretary,   Kimberley MSS.
22 June 1893.

1. *Qua* Opium Commission (your note[3] calls it Committee—but it seems an error of the pen—) I think the terms of appointment might be amended so as to give the greatest prominence to what seemed last night to be our three most important points
1. Cost, as a thing to be *known*, so far as may be—
2. Disposition of Indian people a. as to bearing cost b. as to use of the drug (under which branch all its merits or demerits might be gone into) c. Native States.
2. [*sc.* 3.] My powers of reading have been of late & must remain most inconveniently contracted; but I shall be glad to see at any time after tomorrow morning any a. *Precis* of what has happened on the Opium question b. Statistics of Opium Revenue c. figures or statements on the three great points.[4]

23. *Fr.* [*Hatchlands, Guildford*]

Wrote to The Queen l.l.—Ld Kimberley—H.J.G.—Sir H. Jenkyns—S. Woods—and minutes. Saw Sir A.W.—Mr Marj.—Mr Sheepshank—Ld Spencer—Ottoman Ambassador—Rev. Mr Legh. To Hatchlands at 5.15. Read Ingersoll on Health—Mrs Grundy's Victims.[5] Ld J. Bowen came: excellent company: much conversation.

24. *Sat.*

Wrote to Priv. Sec. Tel. Drive to Sutton Place, a fine Henry VIII house. Read Lyall's India—Life of J. Martin[6]—Mrs Grundy &c. finished.

25. *4 S. Trin.*

Ch mg and aft.—Drive. Wrote to Mr Wilson MP—Rev. S.E.G.—Ld Spencer—Sir W. Harcourt Tel.—& minutes. Read Saphir on Scripture[7]—Charles Early Missions[8]—Hawker Prose Remains[9]—and [blank.]

    [1] See 11 June 93.   [2] Untraced.
    [3] Of 21 June, Add MS 44229, f. 113; Pease regards a Resolution for a Committee on opium inadequate: 'No proposal that we could make will in any way satisfy Pease and his friends; but it may be possible I suppose to carry an amendment in favour of a Commission.'
    [4] Kimberley replied this day, ibid., f. 115 that 'Committee (opium) was a slip of the pen'; he would send figures and consider enlarged terms of reference.
    [5] Mrs. G. Corbett, *Mrs Grundy's victims* (1893).
    [6] P. A. Sillard, *Life and letters of John Martin . . . and other 'Young Irelanders'* (1893).
    [7] See 16 Apr. 93.   [8] See 18 June 93.
    [9] R. S. Hawker, *Prose works*, ed. J. G. Godwin (1893).

To LORD SPENCER, first lord of the admiralty, 25 June 1893.   Althorp MSS K8.

Here is a stiff question which Mr. Wilson wishes to put to me tomorrow. I have how-ever asked him to postpone it for a day or two that I may communicate with you on the terms which you would suggest for a reply on a subject so grave & requiring such cautious handling.

There is a remarkable warning or caution delivered by Lord Armstrong on the com-pletion of the Victoria.[1]

To C. H. WILSON, M.P., 25 June 1893.   Add MS 44549, f. 99.

The very grave & important character of the question which you propose to put to me tomorrow makes it necessary even at this preliminary stage to be very careful in the answer to be made, & for this purpose to communicate with Ld. Spencer; but I am not sure of being able to do this tomorrow as he may not yet be aware of it, and I shd. be obliged if under the circumstances you would kindly put it off for a day or two.

You will see that I fully appreciate the gravity of the subject.[2]

26. M. [London]

Back to D. Street at 2 P.M. H of C. 4-6½.[3] Read Life of Martin—Heart of Tipper-ary.[4] Dined at Mr Agnews. Saw Sir A.W.—Mr Marj.—Sir W. Harcourt—Mr Goschen.

27. Tu.

Wrote to The Queen—Sir H. Ponsonby—Duke of Devonshire—and minutes. H. of C. 3¾-6¾.[5] Saw Sir A.W.—Mr Marj.—Sir A. Godley—Ld Spencer—Sir W. Harcourt. Conclave 3¾. H. of C. (Mediterranean Command).[6] Conclave (pro-cedure) at do 5 PM-6¾. Dined at Lady Stepney's. Read Brook's Lecture[7]—Heart of Tipperary—Martin's Life.

28. Wed.

Wrote to The Queen l.l.—Mr Morley—Bp of Chichester l. & tel.—Ld Kimber-ley—Mr L. Morris—& minutes. H. of C. 2¼-6¾. The strong measures announced.[8] Saw Sir A.W.—Mr Marj.—H.J.G. Conclave H. of C. on procedure Resolution. Dined at the Russian Ambassador's. Drive with C. (½ h.). Read Life of J. Martin (finished).

[1] Spencer replied next day, Add MS 44314, f. 76: 'I am glad that you have put Mr Wilson off. . . . The Policy as to size etc. of Ships of War, may be affected by this disaster, but it would be premature . . . to declare a New Policy on the spur of the moment.' Sir George Tryon, C. in C. Mediterranean, drowned with 350 officers and men when his instructions caused the *Victoria* to collide with the *Camperdown* in the Mediterranean.

[2] No correspondence found. See this day's letter to Spencer. On 29 June Wilson asked Gladstone about discontinuing battleship construction in favour of a smaller class; Gladstone referred to the Admiralty inquiry into the *Camperdown/Victoria* affair; 4*H* 14. 363.

[3] Spoke on Indian currency; 4*H* 14. 59.

[4] W. P. Ryan, *The heart of Tipperary; a romance* (1893).

[5] Questioned on Indian currency; 4*H* 14. 150.

[6] i.e. the vacancy caused by Tryon's death.

[7] A. Brooke, 'The need and use of getting Irish literature into the English tongue. An address' (1893).

[8] Announcement of next day's Resolution; spoke on G.I. Bill cttee. clause 5; 4*H* 14. 242.

29. Th.

Wrote to Sir A. Gordon—The Queen l.l.—Hitchman—Ld Kimberley—& minutes. H. of C. 4–8¼ & 9½–1¼.[1] Saw Sir A.W.—Mr Marj.—Mr Murray—S. Lyttelton—Ld Spencer. Backgammon with Mr A! Read Mrs Ward & Prof. Harnack in 19th Cent.[2]

30. Fr.

Wrote to The Queen l.l.l.l.—Ld Kimberley l.l.—and minutes. Ten to dinner. Getting up the Opium quest. Examining books. Read Stopf. Brook's Lecture—Heart of Tipperary. H. of C. 2¼–7 and 9–11¾. Between Ireland and Opium, it was stiff work: but thank God went well.[3]

The ebbing tide has been and is for me at present fiercer than the flow. All the circumstances not only invite but force me to the life of faith. And without it I do not feel that I could get through a day. *He* will not break a bruised reed. So be it.

To LORD KIMBERLEY, lord president and Indian secretary,　　　　Kimberley MSS.
30 June 1893.

1. When the [opium] eaters are the dregs, & malaria prevails, is opium deemed medicinal?
2. When the flower of the population consume, they are manful & warlike or sturdy races? (I see this is answered.)
3. Please let me have the figures in *pounds*.
4. Is the whole revenue drawn from duty on export to China?
5. What is the actual present law of prohibition, restraint, or permission,
as to growth
as to export.
6. Can you in any manner put *together* the heads of cost
　　　　　　　　　　　　Revenue
　　　　　　　　　　　　compensation
　　　　　　　　　　　　Native States

however conjecturally.[4]

[The Recto of the back fly leaf contains:—]

Whitmore Station: from Tamworth.
M. Boyer d'Agen 58 Rue de Londres Paris
Mrs Ingram Gardiner Lane King St.
　　　　　　27 U. King St Leicr.
　　　　　9 Grove Terrace
　　　　　　North End Road
　　　　　　　　W

[1] Moved Resolution for guillotining cttee. stage of G.I. Bill, to be completed by 27 July; 4 *H* 14. 373.
[2] Mrs. H. Ward and H. Harnack, both on 'The Apostles' Creed', *N.C.*, xxxiv. 34, 158 (July 1893).
[3] Spoke on the Resolution for closure, and on Webb's motion to abolish Indian Opium revenue (Gladstone supporting inquiry into best means of effecting abolition); 4 *H* 14. 562, 615.
[4] Queries for Gladstone's speech on Webb's motion on opium.

[And in pencil:—]

69 Church St Kensington
Correa Gallowr

Wanborough Main Guildford
        5 Shadcliff   16 Halford st or Rd
                                                Fulham

Marsham

Telegrams

Lough

Beale

Schnadhorst
Chinnery

Black.

[The Verso of the flyleaf contains:—]

H.J. Cohen Esq 5 King's Bench Walk I.T.

[July 1st, 1893 to December 29th., 1896]

[The Verso of the flyleaf contains:—]

9 Grove Terrace N Edn Road
W. Kens. Ln VII.

I every day expect an embassage
From my Redeemer to redeem me hence
Rich. III. II. 1.

Private.

No 41.

July 1. 93–

Texts for the present stress.

O thou of little faith, wherefore didst thou doubt?[1]

My grace is sufficient for thee.[2]

I will lift up mine eyes unto the hills:
from whence cometh my help.[3]

O let it be Thy pleasure to deliver me:
make haste, O Lord, to help me.[4]

Eye hath not seen, nor ear heard.[5]

For we walk by faith, not by sight.[6]

Lead me O Lord in thy righteousness because of mine
enemies: make thy way plain before my face.[7]

If I may but touch his garment, I shall be whole.[8]

[1] Matthew, xiv. 31.
[2] II Corinthians, xii. 9.
[3] Psalm cxxi. 1.
[4] Prayer Book version of Psalm xl. 16.
[5] I Corinthians, ii. 9.
[6] II Corinthians, v. 7.
[7] Psalm v. 8.
[8] Matthew, ix. 21.

[There is also, in pencil at the top of the page, and partly covered by the above:—]

Badge Fund £10
     do   £20.
Treat Hn
   Bolton 3
9 Grove Terrace Kensn

Goodwin £10
Offertories £2

London July 1893.

1. Sat. [Ham House, Petersham]

Wrote to Mme. de Comby—J. Carthy—C.Bannerman—and minutes. 3–5. Went to private performance of scenes by prime members of the Comedie Française. The women *perfect*. Saw Sir A.W.—H.N.G.—Sir A. Lyall—& others. Read Amy Clarefoot[1]—and Two Eternities.[2] To Ham House[3] at 5. Saw C. Acland—Mrs Dixon.

To H. CAMPBELL-BANNERMAN, war secretary, 1 July 1893.   Add MS 41215, f. 48.

I have received your excellent letter,[4] and can only say in reply that I am entirely with you.

2. 5 S. Trin.

I missed a step by defect of sight, and a rather heavy fall led me to lie on my back all day without Church. Saw Lady D. Neville—Lady A. Russell.[5] Arnica,[6] bath and bed early. Read Early Missions[7]—Guettée Eglise Orthodoxe.[8]

[1] *Amy Clarefoot: a romance of the year 1900. By 'Philosophus'* (1893).
[2] Untraced.
[3] To stay with William John Manners Tollemache, 1859–1935; 9th earl of Dysart 1878. On 14 June 1892, Lady Russell wrote to Gladstone that Dysart was 'a recent convert to Home Rule, & very anxious to shew it in every way', and especially keen to have Gladstone to stay; Add MS 44515, f. 45.
[4] Of 29 June, Add MS 44117, f. 119, on Sir F. S. Roberts, returned from India and 'urgent for employment, alleging that . . . he is very poor'; nothing really suitable available, but he can be offered Ireland, or the governorships of Malta and Gibraltar; 'Roberts is a peculiar man. He is a good soldier, a capable administrator, most conciliatory towards the civil population; but he is an arrant jobber, and intriguer, and self-advertiser, and altogether wrong in his political notions, both British and Indian. We may expect that he will make a great noise and complaint: and therefore I thought it right that you should know how the matter stands. His attitude seems to me to be intolerable. . . .'
[5] See 18 Dec. 73.
[6] Medical tincture prepared from the plant.
[7] See 18 June 93.
[8] F. R. Guettée, *Exposition de la doctrine de l'Eglise catholique orthodoxe* (1866).

3. M. [London]

Wrote to Sir A. Clark (Tel.)—The Queen. Saw Sir A. Clark—Mr Marj. Off at 12 to London. Saw Sir A. Clark, but had improved rapidly in the middle of the day. H. of C. 3¾–8¼.[1] Backgammon with Mr A. Bath & bed early. Saw Caxtons, Pictures, & other treasures at Ham House where Ld D[ysart] & all others were most kind. Wrote to Ld Kimberley—Duke of Argyll—The Queen—Miss Marsh— and minutes.

4. Tu.

Only small effects remain. Saw Sir A.W.—Mr Marj.—Sir G. Trevelyan—Mr Knowles. H. of C. 3¾–8¼, 10–12.[2] Wrote on Autobiogr.[3] Wrote to The Queen— Mr Cowan—Mr Caine MP.—Mr Morley—and minutes. Pr. Troubetzkoi[4] came. Read China Inland Mission.[5]

To J. COWAN, chairman of the Midlothian Liberal Association,   Add MS 44549, f. 101.
4 July 1893.

I cannot allow the meeting of our County Association tomorrow to pass without a word of notice & encouragement.

The majority, returned by the electors of the United Kingdom at the General Election, has through courage union & self sacrifice exhibited both a numerical & a moral force abundantly sufficient to carry the Irish Govt. Bill through the H. of Commons.

Its passage into the House of Lords will present to that assembly a great political issue. I will not anticipate the victory of prepossession over foresight. But whatever be the destiny of the Bill in that assembly, its passage through a H. of Commons elected less than a year ago, for the very purpose of trying that issue is a cardinal fact which immensely advances the measure & coming after 7 years of closely sustained conflict, is decisive of its ultimate success.

The self-denial imposed on itself by the majority has been manfully accepted by the constituencies: but I am not less confident than I was 6 months ago that this year will not pass away without leaving recorded on the Statute Book British measures of great value & importance; unless these also should be proscribed by adverse influences after having received the deliberate approval of the H. of Commons.

I make no doubt that the tone of this meeting will be in thorough sympathy with these favourable prospects.[6]

----

[1] Questions; G.I. Bill cttee.; 4*H* 14. 683.

[2] Spoke on privilege; 4*H* 14. 711.

[3] Not found.

[4] Prince Pierre Troubetzkoy; b. Milan 1864; lived in Cobham; portrait painter. A portrait of Gladstone, undated but painted about this time, is in the National Portrait Gallery, Edinburgh, and another, dated 15 July 1893, Downing Street (see 14 July 93) is in the National Portrait Gallery, London.

[5] Untraced.

[6] Cowan replied next day, Add MS 44137, f. 476: 'Your letter was of great value and gave us both much encouragement & joy. Your hopes & resolves incite us to duty. Our meeting was largely attended & was most enthusiastic.'

5. Wed.

Wrote to Mr Lough MP[1]—Mr Stuart Rendel—The Queen l.l.l.—and minutes.
Cabinet 11.30. H. of C. 12¼-4½.[2] Then to Marlborough House party: say 2000!
Conversation with P. of Wales—D. of York—K. of Denmark—saw other
Royalties including the dear Princess who made us have tea in the Royal Tent.
Saw Ottoman Ambassador—Sir H. Ponsonby—Mad. Tolstoi—Mrs Percy Wynd-
ham[3]—Lord R. Cecil—very pleasing. Saw Sir A. West—Mr Marj. Dined at Mr
Stanhope's. Read China Mission.

Cabinet. Tues. Jul. 5. 1893. 11.30 A.M.[4]
1. Question between 80 and 103 [Irish M.P.s].
   (Preamble of the Clause a good relied on.) [*sic*]
2. *Omnes Omnia* &c.
   follow the guidance of Liberal opinion.[5]

To S. RENDEL, M.P., 5 July 1893.   Add MS 44549, f. 102.

I have to acknowledge the receipt of the memorial signed by thirty members, including
yourself, on behalf of Welsh Disestablishment.[6] I think you & they will probably feel that,
in the midst of the present struggle in Committee on the Irish Govt. Bill, the time has
hardly arrived for my making a reply to this memorial. But when that Bill shall have substantially escaped from the battlefield into security I shall be happy to make a further
communication. In the meantime I ought to say a word on the declarations at Newcastle.
I have never heard, & certainly also never considered, that they announced any plan with
regard to the order of business beyond the express declarations which may have been
contained in them. On the other hand I think the Govt. have even in the present over-
crowded Session given some evidence of their desire to go as far as they are able in securing a forward place for Welsh Disestablishment, & I can also assure you that nothing has
been decided or even meditated by us which could tend to deprive the question of the
position which it holds as an essential part of the Liberal policy & plans.

6. Th.

Wrote to The Queen l.l.—Mr Chamberlain—Mr Milman—Mr Provand MP[7]—Sir
W. Harcourt—and minutes. Read Dr J. Brown's Memoirs.[8] Saw Sir A.W.—Mr
Carvell Williams. 12-3½. To the Royal Marriage at St James's:[9] then to Buck-
ingham Palace and the so-called 'Breakfast'. Then H. of C. 3½-8¼ & 9½-11½. A

[1] Thomas Lough, 1850-1922; an Irishman; liberal M.P. W. Islington 1892-1918.
[2] Spoke on G.I. Bill cttee.; 4*H* 14. 924.
[3] Madeleine, wife of Percy Scawen Wyndham, 1835-1911; tory M.P. 1860-85.
[4] Add MS 44648, f. 106.
[5] 'The opinion of the Cabinet was that the Clause [9] should be proposed as it stands, that the
number of 103 should be reduced to 80, and that as to limited or unlimited powers of voting the
Ministers in charge of the Bill should have due regard to the sentiment known or found to be
prevailing in the House'; CAB 41/22/41.
[6] Sent by Rendel on 26 June, after Lloyd George carried a motion for a letter by 30 votes to 1; see
Morgan, *Wales in British politics*, 139.
[7] Andrew Dryburgh Provand, 1838-1915; Manchester merchant; liberal M.P. Blackfriars,
Glasgow, 1886-1900.
[8] See 11 July 93.
[9] Marriage of Duke of York (George V) to Princess Mary of Teck.

scene of fury at the last.[1] The whole debate sad and depressing. But the majority most cordial.

The *service* was very interesting (God bless them) but with room for comment.

7. Fr. [Dollis Hill]

Wrote to The Queen l.l.—Sir H. Ponsonby—Mr Armitstead—and minutes. H. of C. 2½–7.[2] Then drove to Dollis Hill. Great heat. Basked in the night air. Read Les Juifs en Russie[3]—China Mission.

8. Sat.

Wrote to Priv. Sec.—Sir A. West. Read China Mission—Hassencamp's Ireland[4]— *et elia*. Drove to see the Harry's at Hampstead. Saw Mr Matheson. Refreshing storms.

9. 6 S. Trin.

Willesden Ch mg—Neasden evg. Saw Lady Tweedmouth. Wrote to Sir A. West—Mrs Th. Read China Mission—Bompas on Belief[5]—Langen's Innocent III.[6]

10. M. [London]

Wrote to The Queen l—Lady Ribblesdale—Rev. Mr Waterford—Sir H. Ponsonby l.l. & minutes. Read Langen—19th Cent. on Catalogues.[7] Saw Mrs Th.— Sir A. West—Mr Conybeare—Sir A. Gordon. Back to D. St. at 1¼. H. of C. 3¾–8 and 9½–12½. A remarkable evening.[8]

11. Tu.

Wrote to Mr Woods MP[9]—The Queen—and minutes. H of C. 3¾–8 and 10–11¾.[10] Dined at Mr Armitstead's: & played backgammon. Saw Sir A.W.—Mr Marj.—Mr Morley—Mr Sexton—Mr Conybeare. C. went to Windsor, *sola*: a good arrangement. Read N.A. Review, Malta—Irish Idylls.[11]

To S. WOODS, M.P., 11 July 1893.   Add MS 44549, f. 102.
   I am afraid it is not difficult to ⟨those of your c⟩ find the answer to those of your constituents who press for the grant of time with a view to the further discussion of the Eight

[1] Disorder on the opposition benches; 4H 14. 1029.
[2] Series of disputes over privilege and G.I. Bill cttee. clause 9 (Irish representation in the Commons); 4H 14. 1102, 1114.
[3] M. Khmerkin, *Les Juifs en Russie* (1893).
[4] R. Hassencamp, *History of Ireland from the Reformation to the Union* (1888).
[5] M. Bompas, 'The argument for belief', *National Review*, xxi. 632 (July 1893).
[6] J. Langen, *Geschichte der Römischen Kirche von Gregor VII bis Innocenz III* (1893).
[7] *N.C.*, xxxiv. 101 (July 1893).   [8] Chamberlain's speech on Irish M.P.s; 4H 14. 1228.
[9] Samuel Woods, 1846–1915; miners' organiser; liberal/labour M.P. 1892–5, sponsoring Eight Hours Bill.
[10] Spoke on G.I. Bill cttee.; 4H 14. 1307.   [11] J. Barlow, *Irish idylls* (1892).

Hours Miners Bill.[1] In the former joint letter you expressed a desire for a Saturday Sitting, & obviously we cannot cut off the present arrangement for Friday evening.

But even if the House were willing to sit on Sat. it is certain that the proposal would be debated for some hours & would thereby cut into the present scanty time (scanty relative to the tactics of the Opposition) available for making progress with the Irish Bill. It is thus I fear obvious that there is no mode open to us for granting the facilities, which are, very naturally, desired by your constituents.

12. Wed.

Wrote to The Queen—Ld Kimberley—M. Jusserand—The Ld Mayor—& minutes. Saw Sir A. West—Mr Marj.—The Speaker—Mr Brodrick—Ld Dufferin—Sir W. Harcourt—Mr Morley. H. of C. 12¼–5¼. Much speaking.[2] Then followed a visit from the King and Queen of Denmark with Princess of Wales & other royalties. They were beyond anything kind. I was however greatly fatigued. Dined at the Italian Ambassadors.[3] To Her Excellency who spoke only Italian (being Russ) unhappily my deaf ear was turned. Saw also Lady Swansea[4]—Sir Jas Lacaita. Read Westmr Review.[5]

13.

Wrote to Siamese Minr—The Queen—Mr S. Keay MP.—and minutes. Saw Sir A.W.—Sir W.H.—Mr Marj.—Mr Burnes [sc. Burns]. H. of C. 3½–8 and 9¾–1. Voted in the ten Divisions.[6] Read Tuckwell's Winchester.[7]

14. Fr. [Englemere House, Ascot]

Wrote to The Queen—Mr Woods & Mr Pickard[8] MPs—Mr Roundel MP.—Mr Heseltine—& minutes. Prince T. came to paint.[9] Saw Sir A.W.—Mr Marj.—Mr Murray—Mr S.L. H. of C. 2¼–5½.[10] Off to the Ribblesdales (Englemere).[11] Read Irish Idylls.

To LORD ROSEBERY, foreign secretary, 14 July 1893.   N.L.S. 10026, f. 211.

With regard to the enclosed draft I should say that at the time of his conversation I believed M. Waddington to have laid down his office and to be no longer actual Ambassador.[12]

The recital is by no means the same which I should make, especially in this.

[1] Letters from Woods untraced.
[2] On Dublin University representation; 4 H 14. 1390.
[3] Count Tornielli.
[4] Averil, 3rd wife of Sir H. Hussey Vivian, 1st Baron Swansea (cr. June 1893).
[5] W.R., cxl (July 1893).
[6] Carrying clauses 9–26 by the guillotine; 4 H 14. 1545.
[7] W. Tuckwell, The ancient ways. Winchester fifty years ago (1893).
[8] Benjamin Pickard, 1842–1904; miners' organiser; liberal M.P. Normanton 1885–1904. Worked with Woods (see 11 July 93).
[9] Prince Troubetzkoy; see 4 July 93.
[19] Moved address of congratulation on Duke of York's marriage; 4 H 14. 1583.
[11] Ribblesdale was Master of the Buckhounds 1892–5.
[12] See to Rosebery, 19 and 25 May 93.

It is founded largely on the *condominium*. I do not altogether deny to France a special position, but I do not see that she can formally plead the *condominium*. I rather set up against it the article of the Treaty of Paris which brings in all the Powers. He said that article had been virtually repealed at Berlin. I said as it is not repealed in the Treaty can you show that it is virtually repealed by the Protocols. He would not undertake this; and as I thought, so far as the conversation went, he showed nothing. It certainly seems to me that the article of the Treaty of Paris is in full force.

More than two months of very great pressure have elapsed, and I could not undertake to give a trustworthy account; but I certainly adhere to what I have said in the last paragraph. On this head the representation is I think insufficient, and it was the main head. See also my marginal note.

I do not know what is usual in these cases, but I should not like to be bound as to *nuances* by this report. I do not say it has anything untrue, except as to the three words 'au même dégré' which I feel sure are wrong & which he probably would like to remove.

To S. WOODS, M.P., and B. PICKARD, M.P., 14 July 1893.   Add MS 44549, f. 104.

In acknowledging your letter of yesterday[1] I beg to assure you that I share the desire of those who think it unfortunate that the discussion on the 8 Hours Miners Bill should be prevented by the block of business. I should have been glad therefore if your letters had supplied me with evidence of such an amount of desire among the various parties interested for the further discussion on the Bill as would have warranted my asking the House to make an addition by means of sitting on Saturday to its present very severe labours.

At a time when the House has sat for 5½ months with (as is supposed) six or seven weeks before it of work on the Irish Bill and on Supply, I think you will agree with me that I am not in a condition to enter on any particulars as to what might be attempted with respect to important measures now before the House in the event of its determining on Autumnal Sittings.

15. Sat.

Wrote to Ld Rosebery. Saw Mr Asquith—Mr E. Hamilton—Ld Rowton—Sir A. Lyall. Long & beautiful drive. Read . . . .

To LORD ROSEBERY, foreign secretary, 15 July 1893.   N.L.S. 10026, f. 214.

1. I have read with Asquith this morning (or rather he was kind enough to read to me the for me almost invisible grey of the type-writing) the account of your meeting yesterday at the F.O. on the Pamir(?) frontier question.[2] We were both much satisfied with the course taken; among other things with the leaving open the question of an English Envoy and leaving it to the Indian Government to determine what would be the best channel of communication.

We shall no doubt do the best we can for the Ameer, but I think the doctrine that rights have been acquired by occupation of 'no man's land' is hardly tenable in a case where the said land is an *enclave* between rival powers. In such a case it would seem more proper to make it matter of common understanding.

2. I should like to have a few words with you when convenient about the salaries: if anything is to be done it should be rather soon. Undoubtedly there is at this time a disproportion; and our docking the law officers seems rather to specialize the obligation to take note of it.

[1] Untraced. See 11, 18 Aug. 93.
[2] For this, see PRO CP 6281, 6415, 6492.

3. Thursday night was the best we have had: I see nothing now that can touch the vitals of the Bill.

16. 7 S. Trin.

Ch at Welling. Aft. prayers with C. Wrote to Ld Rosebery—Macmillans—Stanford. Went to Wellington 11–4. Tea at Sir A. Gordon's. Read Life of St Margret[1]—Huxley's Romanes Lecture.[2]

17. M. [London]

Wrote to Ld Kimberley—The Queen—Sir H. Ponsonby—Ld Rosebery—& minutes. Read Irish Idylls—Lyall's India[3]—Curzon on Siam.[4] H. of C. $3\frac{1}{2}$–$8\frac{1}{4}$ and 10–$11\frac{3}{4}$.[5] Left our very kind hosts at $11\frac{3}{4}$ for D. St. Backgammon with Mr A. Saw Sir A.W.—Mr Marj.—Sir W. Harcourt.

To LORD ROSEBERY, foreign secretary, 17 July 1893.   N.L.S. 10026, f. 220.

I return the Draft-Egyptian Convention. It seems to me that the Art. IV (augmentation of troops) is utterly bad: and that the substitution of a double term (the second undefined but seemingly meant to be one year) for Salisbury's single term + right of re-entry is a change infelicitous, & inadmissible.

18. Tu.

Wrote to Mr Menzies—The Queen—Ld Rosebery—Ld Acton—Mr Cowan—Chancr of Exr—W. Ridler—and minutes. Saw Sir A.W.—Mr Marj.—Chancr of Exr. Read Tuckwell. H of C. $3\frac{1}{2}$–8 and $9\frac{3}{4}$–$11\frac{1}{4}$. Spoke too long & discursively.[6]

To J. COWAN, chairman of the Midlothian Liberal Association, Add MS 44549, f. 105. 18 July 1893.

I have just received the enclosed from Mr. Hargreaves;[7] of whom I have no present recollection or knowledge. I have two questions to put in relation to his letter:
1. Is he right in supposing that the subject is alive in such a sense as to make it desirable for me to offer explanations, which I think I can do.
2. Should I offer them in a letter to him, or if the matter is seething might I do it to you.
   They would make a longish letter.
Kindly return the enclosed.[8]

To Sir W. V. HARCOURT, chancellor of the exchequer,   MS Harcourt dep. 13, f. 121. 18 July 1893.

1. This is the draft of which I promised you a fair copy this morning. Rosebery saw it & showed no unfavourable sign.[9]

---

[1] Perhaps *The life of St. Margaret* (1886).
[2] T. H. Huxley, *Evolution and ethics* (1893).   [3] See 8 Apr. 93.
[4] G. N. Curzon, 'The Siamese boundary question', *N.C.*, xxxiv. 34 (July 1893).
[5] Questions; G.I. Bill cttee.; 4*H* 14. 1710, 1746.
[6] Replying to Balfour on Irish civil servants; 4*H* 14. 1849.
[7] Letter untraced; secretary's marginal note: 'Scotch Home rule'.
[8] No reply from Cowan found. See 20 July 93.
[9] Harcourt, however, this day replied, Add MS 44203, f. 83, that if the draft was 'to form the basis of a counterproposal . . . it would require very careful consideration and criticism'.

2. I think you would like to notice the current debate of this afternoon on Irish Bill which will deal with terms of retirement for civil servants.
[P.S.] Please return inclosure.

To LORD ROSEBERY, foreign secretary, 18 July 1893.   N.L.S. 10026, ff. 222–3.
[Letter 1:]   Since writing to you yesterday, I have received the printed telegrams from Constantinople, and your Egyptian drafts.

As to *them* I think that as they will constitute a formal commencement of official correspondence on a subject of great moment, and as references to previous correspondence of yours are included, and thus in a manner formulated, these drafts are rather beyond our competency and will need the sanction of the Cabinet.

But I am quite ready if you like to go through them with you in the first instance and could do this
1. at 2¼ today, or
2. In all likelihood, at my room in the H. of Commons, as the discussions on the Irish Bill may today leave me little freedom—
Or, you may like to circulate my drafts.

I would propose Thursday at noon if it suits you?

Meantime I note the following
1. I agree to any amount of discouragement to the Turk's idea of sending a force pleading the occasion
2. or having any thing to do with the amount of our force
3. I am glad of the Sultan's attitude of fear & hope it may continue
4. I think the right of re-entry valuable, if not indispensable.

On the other hand, I doubt, & anticipate doubt in the Cabinet, on the point
1. Whether it would be prudent to treat evacuation as a boon[?] from us requiring 'consideration'. (I am doubtful whether such consideration would not probably be an additional burden.)
2. Q[uer]y whether we should say we require more than the D[rummond] W[olff] convention *gave* us?

I think it would be a great point for us to bring *Europe* into the scheme.

[Letter 2:]   The draft[1] and the despatch were read to me (the writing being so small as to make perusal difficult to me) as *drafts* and I did not detect the error.

"First impressions" and "unofficial" will doubtless do much to prevent misunderstanding.

Turning to the *draft*, I find the last words open to misunderstanding as indicating a purpose. I should think it safer to say (after H.M.G.) "and would not admit of summary treatment".

The idea, I think is quite indisputable. But if you promise 'mature consideration', that without doubt will require the Cabinet. I gather however that you do not think the time for a Cabinet has come. But I think, now that this convention is in your hands, it can hardly be delayed *long*; for, worthless as the draft is in itself, it is a deliberate proposal from the Suzerain to negotiate.
[P.S.] Thanks for the offer to *convert* into a private letter, but I would only ask this if you thought it perfectly convenient, which I rather suppose it could hardly be.

---

[1] Revision of the Drummond-Wolff Convention. Rosebery replied this day, Add MS 44290, f. 153: 'As regards the root of the matter I would say this. Either the convention is illusory—as I regard it: or it contains the basis of a settlement, in which case it should go before the Cabinet.'

19. Wed.

Wrote to Sir J. Lacaita—The Queen—Sir W. Harcourt—and minutes. H. of C. 12½–5½.[1] Dined at the Reform Club with Mr Colman. Saw Sir A.W.—Mr Marj.— Sir W. Harcourt—Ital. Amb. & Marq. Rudini—Mr Justice Wright—Sir [blank]. Cameron. Read Quart. Rev.[2]—Dr John Brown (finished). Garden party at No 10. indoors, for rain.

To Sir W. V. HARCOURT, chancellor of the exchequer,   MS Harcourt dep. 13, f. 127. 19 July 1893.

My paper was written long ago, not as a counterdraft but to get my own ideas into order.[3]

It had reference to Waddington's communication with me in the autumn, and to the general assurances given him.

Turkey is so galled by the occupation, and the Sultan, according to our intimation, so frightened at us, that I think they would accept evacuation on almost any terms, unless adversely swayed by France.

It seems to me that *if* we gave the same sort of priority to France as we gave under the 1880–5 [arrangement] she would not be difficult to manage. We have in this matter something to give, and a vantage ground in giving it.

While giving France some precedence (which I think Rosebery does not much like) we ought certainly—when we propose anything—to bring in *Europe*.

To LORD ROSEBERY, foreign secretary, 19 July 1893.   N.L.S. 10026, f. 232.

After consulting with Marjoribanks and West, I have written the accompanying Draft [on salaries] which I propose subject to your comments to address to you.[4]

When it is settled, I do not know whether you would like on my behalf to make it known to Harcourt: or whether I had better send it to him as from myself & assented to by you.

It was West who suggested re*duc*ing the redu*ction*.

[P.S.] Lord Russell may be taken as an example of a Foreign Secretary on whom the burden of great entertainment[s] (if he gave them) would have been rather severe: or, again, Clarendon.

20. Th.

Wrote to Mr Cowan—The Queen l.l.—Mr Stuart—Ld Kimberley—Ed. Indept Nonconformist—Ld Rosebery—Mr Provand MP.—Sir H. Ponsonby—& minutes. H. of C. 3¾–8¼ and 9¾–12½. Finished 3d batch.[5] Cabinet at noon to 1¼. Saw Sir A.W.—Mr Marj.—Ld Kimberley—Ld Ripon—Mr Hamilton—Mr Havelock Wilson.[6] Backgammon with Mr A. Read Tuckwell.

---

[1] G.I. Bill cttee.; 4*H* 15. 1.

[2] Probably E. Dicey's article on Unionism, *Q.R.*, clxx. 265 (July 1893).

[3] See 18 July 93n.

[4] Not found.

[5] i.e. 3rd batch of clauses (30–40) passed by guillotine; 4*H* 15. 166.

[6] Joseph Havelock Wilson, 1858–1929; trade unionist and labour M.P. Middlesbrough 1892– 1900, elsewhere 1906–10, 1918–22.

Cabinet. Thurs. Jul. 20. 1893. Noon. [1]
Siam
1. Dufferin to go to Paris.
2. a. [he is to] assume that the question of demand 1. concerns Siam only.
   b. to assume—that the demand is in entire consistency with the declaration of French
   Govt. as to the integrity & independence of Siam.
3. Commn. on Agriculture.[2] Reported to be boycotted by the Tories. Try Wantage,
   Belpher. if of our own men Whitbread?
4. Ld. Mayor's Dinner. What happened in 1887?
5. Capt. Macdonald's Report [on Uganda].[3] Rosebery stated the difficulty. Send report of
   Macd. to Lugard for his defence. All to be handed [to a] Committee: Ld. Chancellor,
   Chancellor of the Exchequer, Secretary for War. (Chancellor absent).
   Report very secret.
   Ld R. reported Portal's precipitancy.

To J. COWAN, chairman of the Midlothian Liberal Association,   Add MS 44549, f. 107.
20 July 1893.

I thank you very much for your letter[4] & I concur with all you say. But I am afraid that I
have not brought clearly into your view the point on which I thought the letter of
Hargreaves required consideration. It was the situation created by our ultimate adoption
of the plan which alone we found we could carry through the H. of Commons & under
which the Irish members at Westminster will have the power to vote not only on Imperial
matters but on those which are local, English, Scotch & Welsh.

This arrangement is in the abstract open to the objection that the Irish having an
exclusive power given them over their own local concerns have no claim to interfere with
ours. And the question arises how far a Tory & Unionist agitation band upon this consideration may be likely to disquiet the constituencies generally, or Midlothian in particular.

The arrangement adopted is a consequence flowing from the retention of Irish
members which was demanded (as we consider), by the country—& especially by Scotland & Scottish Liberals.

I think there is a fair case to state which might do much to neutralize any agitation
such as I have indicated. And my last letter really meant this: do you think it would be
expedient to state it, & if so in what form: & may the matter stand over.

To LORD ROSEBERY, foreign secretary, 20 July 1893. '*Secret*'.   N.L.S. 10026, f. 238.

Re Captains Lugard & Macdonald. Salisbury seems to have blundered in appointing a
personal enemy to report on Lugard's acts & has certainly created a difficult situation.

Your suggestion appears to be good: but it would I think be difficult to make the military expert one of the body to examine with authority, if he be not responsible to Parliament. Could C. Bannerman be the Third man? Could they consult a military man as
amicus curiæ?

---

[1] Add MS 44648, f. 107.
[2] Shaw Lefevre's Royal Commission on Agricultural Depression; *PP* 1894 xvi.
[3] Macdonald's Report 'places him in sharp conflict with Captain Lugard with whom it also
appears he has had a previous quarrel. The Report, which is of great length, was referred for
examination to three members of the Cabinet, the Lord Chancellor, the Chancellor of the
Exchequer and the Secretary of State for War'; CAB 41/22/42. See 30 Sept. 92. The Cabinet cttee.
met intermittently for several months; in April 1894 Grey told the Commons that the Report would
not be published. See Perham, *Lugard*, i. 355 ff.
[4] Not found; see 18 July 93.

To J. STUART, M.P., 20 July 1893.   Add MS 44549, f. 106.

I have to acknowledge your letter[1] and to assure you that I feel the importance of the resolutions you inclose. As to the Equalisation of Rates Bill, of course I cannot give a pledge, but I am not without hope. When we see our way about the Irish Bill, we shall have a very important decision to take, involving the consideration & comparison of second subjects. You may rely upon it that this will be among them and will be carefully examined.

21. Fr. [Dollis Hill]

Wrote to The Queen—Lord Mayor—Miss Acland—& minutes. To Dollis Hill 10¾ PM. Saw Sir A.W.—Mr Marj.—Mr Murray. H. of Commons 2¼–7.[2] Morley, & I after him, had a disquieting conversation with Harcourt. I hope good was done. Dined with Mr Knowles: an interesting party. Read [blank.]

22. Sat.

Wrote to S.L. Drive with Helen. Wrote on Theophanies. Read Esmonde[3]—Q.R. on Bookbinding.[4] Much dozing!

23. 8 S. Trin.

Willesden Ch. 11 AM. Afternoon prayers domestic. Wrote to C.G. Saw Charles—Stepneys. Read Early Xtn Missions—China Inland Mission—Saphir on H.S. (a little)[5]—Langen, Römische Kirche.[6]

24. M. [London]

Wrote to The Queen—Ld Kimberley—H.N.G.—Ld Rosebery l.l.—C.G.—and minutes. Back in D. Street 12. Saw Sir A.W.—Mr Marj.—Sir W. Harcourt—Mr Fowler—Mr Asquith—Mr Hamilton l.l. H. of C. 3½–8 and 10–11½.[7] Read Esmonde—Asiatic Quart. on Siam.[8]

To H. N. GLADSTONE, 24 July 1893. 'Secret'.   Hawarden MS 902, f. 206.

Dearest Harry

. Have you any trustworthy information as to Mr Caine M.P.'s reputation in India as a public character? There is a question whether there are insurmountable objections to him as a member of the Opium Commission.[9]

Your affte. Father   WEG

---

[1] Not found.
[2] G.I. Bill cttee.: new clause for financial arrangements; 4H 15. 213.
[3] By Thackeray; see 3 Dec. 52.
[4] Q.R., clxxvii. 178 (July 1893).
[5] See 16 Apr. 93.
[6] See 9 July 93.
[7] G.I. Bill Cttee.; 4H 15. 323.
[8] Asiatic Quarterly Review, vi. 60 (July 1893).
[9] W. S. Caine was controversially appointed; see 25 July, 3 Aug. 93.

To E. W. HAMILTON, 24 July 1893. '*Immediate*'. Add MS 44607B, f. 211.

I am not yet entirely satisfied as to the way out of the collection conundrum.

1. I see plainly that as Ireland pays 3.62 of the Imperial charges, she is entitled to be credited with the whole of her Imperial contributions as nett money—she has already been debited with the cost of collection for it.

But what *else* has she contributed to the cost of collection and why should she not pay on the revenue collected for her as well as on that part of which she pays over to us?

I still hope that the confusion is mine & not yours.[1]

25. *Tu. St James's D.*

Marriage anniv. D.G. Wrote to Ld Kimberley—Rev. Mr Wicksted—Mr Bryce—Sir H. Ponsonby—The Queen—Ld Rosebery—& minutes. Read Esmonde (finished I). Saw Sir A.W.—Mr Marj.—Sir W. Harcourt—Mr Murray—Mr Morley—Mr Murray. H. of C. $3\frac{1}{4}$-$8\frac{1}{4}$ & $9\frac{1}{2}$-$12\frac{1}{4}$. Spoke after Chamberlain, who attacked.[2] This office is odious to me but it comes in the way of painful duty.

To LORD KIMBERLEY, lord president and Indian secretary, Kimberley MSS.
25 July 1893.

I think you are quite right in consulting Pease, and if he will serve it may remove difficulties, but if he will not, and you have no other strong man, or even man reputed strong I think it would be a great pity to shut the door altogether against Caine.[3]

Is it quite clear that these great men in India know more about him than, or even as much as, we do who have been in long contact with him in Parliament? He is by no means an *ultra* in the character of his mind, and he is also a man who would be likely to take a friendly suggestion as to his course in good part.

I have not conclusive information about his repute in India, but what I have is not in concurrence with the official telegram. I am also under the impression that he gave Wenlock an ugly black eye about the famine.

26. *Wed.*

Wrote to Sir G. Trevelyan—The Queen—Ld Kimberley—Ld Cobham—Rev. Dr. Martin[4]—Sir C. Tennant—and minutes. Saw Sir A.W.—Mr Marj.—Ld Kimberley. H. of C. $2\frac{1}{4}$-7.[5] Dinner party at home. Read Esmonde—La Belgique on Dante & Oxford.[6]

---

[1] No reply found.

[2] A violent attack on the new financial clause; in a robust and personal reply, Gladstone compared him to an 'unskilful Devil's Advocate'; 4*H* 15. 583.

[3] See Kimberley's letter of 23 July, Add MS 44229, f. 137: Lansdowne's view is that W. S. Caine's 'appointment to the Opium Commission would give wide offence in India, and would impair the usefulness of the inquiry ... unfortunately Pease is away, and I should not like to select any *anti*-opium member of the Commission without consulting him'; on 24 July, ibid., f. 139, Kimberley reported 'I am afraid I must say that I could not agree to Caine's appointment'. See 3 Aug. 93.

[4] Discouraging Benjamin Martin, convenor of the United Presbyterian Synod, from bringing deputations on Scottish disestablishment; Hawn P and Add MS 44549, f. 109.

[5] Spoke on the financial clause; 4*H* 15. 576.

[6] Untraced.

To Sir E. GREY, foreign undersecretary, 26 July 1893. Add MS 44549, f. 109.

1. I would suggest in the inclosed draft at A "involve matters of British concern"—& at B. "may" so as to avoid prophecy.[1] 2. Admitting that it is better we should continue as we are, I should be glad if the opinion on an Anglo-French frontier in the peninsula were stated less categorically—looking to the North West & Afghan cases, it seems better to keep all the elbow room we can. I think I have heard Ld. Beaconsfield speak rather *for* an Anglo-Russian frontier which is more formidable.

[P.S.] Would it be possible in the interest of infirm eyes to use some ink less pale? Only in the very best light can I read this at all.

To LORD KIMBERLEY, lord president and Indian secretary, Add MS 44549, f. 108. 26 July 1893.

I learn not without surprise that Spencer is commonly named for India[2] & I should be glad to know whether you have ideas on the subject, or whether you can give me a few minutes. I must spend the day at the House but shall be able to see you as soon as you like if you can come. I am here till 12.30. To Spencer's going I am averse if we can keep him.[3]

27. Th.

Wrote to Sir C. Trevelyan—The Queen—Ld Rosebery—Messrs Brown—& minutes. Saw Sir A.W.—Mr Marj.—Mr Murray—Mr S.L.—Ld Kimberley. Worked on draft Letter to Mr Cowan.[4] Read Irish Idylls (finished)—Tuckwell's Winchester. H. of C. 4–8¼ and 9½–1½. Nine divisions: & the sad scene never to be forgotten.[5]

To LORD ROSEBERY, foreign secretary, 27 July 1893. N.L.S. 10026, f. 260.

I have read the Dufferin dispatch which if unsatisfactory in the material points holds out hopes on other points also material.

I fear embarrassment from provisional verbal communications to the House of Commons, which probably cannot now be altogether avoided but might perhaps be narrowed without exciting hostile feeling if you can say any thing favourable about the blockade & give the assurance that there is no unsatisfactory feature thus far in the case as regards the buffer principle.

[1] Grey's draft untraced.

[2] The govt. had considerable difficulty in replacing Lansdowne as Viceroy. Cromer had refused the post; Sir H. Norman accepted but withdrew on medical advice; Elgin was eventually persuaded to go; see Lord Newton, *Lord Lansdowne* (1929), 113–14.

[3] No letter from Kimberley found. On 2 August, Add MS 44229, f. 142, he reported that 'there is no foundation for the supposition that Herschell has any desire to go to India. . . . I had a long conversation with Spencer . . . his bias is rather on the side of remaining at home.' See to Kimberley, 20 Sept. 93.

[4] See next day.

[5] Chamberlain's claim that never since the time of King Herod had there been such slaves to a dictator was met by shouts of 'Judas'; Unionists refused to clear the House for a division; fighting broke out on the floor of the Commons among 'a mass of fully forty members'; eventually the G.I. Bill passed its Committee stage under the guillotine; Gladstone made a report to the Speaker, who was summoned by Mellor, the chairman of the cttee; see Lucy, *Home Rule Parliament*, 197 ff and 4 *H* 15. 727.

[6] On Siam; see PRO CP 6479.

While I trouble you with this suggestion, *valeat quantum*. I beg of you not to take the trouble of writing on it.

[P.S.] The House I think will like assurances as to the presentation of papers at the earliest moment when the communications have reached such a point as to render it advantageous.

28. Fr.

Wrote to Mr Story MP—Mr Channing MP. Finished my draft on omnes omnia, and revised it.[1] Read Esmond. Saw Sir A.W.—Mr Marj.—Mr Murray—Ld Ripon—The Speaker l.l.—Mr Logan—Mr C. Bannerman—Mr Morley. Conclave at 3½ on last night's catastrophe. H. of C. 2¾–5¼ & 10–12¼.[2] Conclave of Irish MPs on the Evicted Tenants. Backgammon with the Rector. Usual drive with C: say 35 min.

29. Sat. [Hatchlands, Guildford]

Wrote to Mr Marj.—Mr Sexton MP.—& minutes. Saw Mr Murray—Ld Spencer (full conversation on the Viceroyalty).[3] Off at 11 to Hatchlands. Much conversation with the Rendel's (on eyesight inter alia). Read Esmond.

30. 9 S. Trin.

Ch mg & evg. Alarm about Siam in evg. Wrote to Mr Foote—Ld Rosebery—S. Lyttelton. Read Langen Römische Kirche—Saphir, Unity of Scripture—The Imitatio.[4]

31. M. [London]

Wrote to Queen l.l.—Priv. Sec. Tel.—The Speaker—Ld Chancellor—and minutes. Read Esmonde. Examined books—Articles in 19th Cent. Dined at Grillion's. Saw Sir A.W.—Mr Marj.—The Speaker—Sir R. Welby—Mr Asquith. H. of C. 3¼–5¼: we got the wretched incident to a close.[5]

To A. W. PEEL, the Speaker, 31 July 1893.   Add MS 44549, f. 110.

I am alike surprised and concerned at the letter which Mr. Fisher has published in the P.M. Gazette.[6]

He boasts of the scandalous disorder which he began; and he makes me the party principally responsible for it.

[1] Published, dated 31 July, in *T.T.*, 2 August 1893, 9a.
[2] Agricultural depression; 4 *H* 15. 813.
[3] Discussion of vacancy in the Viceroyalty of India, which Spencer declined; see 8 Aug. 93 and to Kimberley, 26 July 93.
[4] By Thomas à Kempis.
[5] Gladstone, followed by Balfour, declared the incident closed, Hayes Fisher and Logan having both apologised; 4 *H* 15. 890.
[6] William Hayes Fisher (1853–1920, tory M.P. Fulham from 1885 and later Cabinet minister) wrote that 'the responsibility for the discreditable scene of last night rests even more with Mr. Gladstone than it does with Mr. [J. W.] Logan', the liberal M.P. who contributed to the start of the fighting by crossing the floor and sitting on the Opposition Front Bench; Hayes admitted in his letter that he struck the first blow by seizing Logan 'by the neck' and ejecting him onto the floor of the House; see Lucy, *Home Rule Parliament*, 208 and *P.M.G.*, 28 July 1893, 2a.

The last named circumstance is only so far material that I do not see how after having been made a party and indeed the chief culprit, I am to interfere in the business as Leader of the House.

Further I am bound to say I cannot, if I were to speak on the subject, abide in simple generalities. A member of the House has avowed and boasted of his disorderly conduct. Individually I could not pass by the circumstance in silence. I doubt whether the House can pass it by. But I incline also to think that for the moment I personally am out of it and must refer myself to my colleagues.[1]

Tues. Aug: One 1893.

Wrote to Ld Kimberley—Ld Ripon—Mr Balfour—Lady Ribblesdale—The Queen—and minutes. Saw Sir A. West—Mr Marj. Read Esmond—Seal on State interference.[2]—De Ionio, Spirito &c. Dined with the Courtney Warners. H. of C. $3\frac{1}{2}$–5 & 6–$7\frac{1}{2}$.[3]

To A. J. BALFOUR, M.P., 1 August 1893.   Add MS 44549, f. 110.

Now that our proceedings upon the subject hardly to be named have, as I hope, reached their termination, I cannot refrain from writing to thank you for your not only valuable, but indispensable contribution towards the issue we have arrived at.

I much regretted Mr. Logan's misapprehension as to the order of Explanation (which may be compared perhaps with Mr. Fisher's as to an intention to attack him). It was your intervention which rescued him from an impasse, and saved the laborious efforts from ending in failure.

I might also thank you for your excellent speech, were it not that, from your awarding to me what I did not desire, I should lose any character of impartiality as a witness.

I think that these misapprehensions throw light upon the cardinal fact that a Committee would have had before them a tangled web, and one which they might have found it impossible to unravel.

Pray do not take the trouble to acknowledge this note.[4]

2. Wed.

Wrote to Mr Marj.—Mrs Th—and minutes. C's Garden party 5–7. A long series of truncated conversations. Dined with Mrs Sands. Worked on papers and letters and books. Read Esmond—Memoir of Hosken.[5] Saw Sir A.W.—Mr Marj.—and Mr Murray (on R.B.)

3. Th.

Wrote to Ld Cobham[6]—Ld Kimberley—Mr Gardner—Mr Justice Wright—Mr Rendel MP (draft)—Ld Brassey—Ld Rosebery—Mr Grenfell MP—Ld Kimberley—& minutes. H. of C. 4–$7\frac{1}{2}$ (drive with C. intervening).[7] Six to dinner;

[1] No reply found.
[2] H. S. Seal, *On the nature of state interference* (1893).
[3] Supply; 4H 15. 1011.
[4] Balfour apparently took Gladstone at his word.
[5] J. D. Hosken, *Verses by the way* (1893).
[6] His nephew, C. G. Lyttelton, 8th Viscount Cobham, offering him the chair of the Commission on Agriculture, which he declined; Add MS 44517, f. 215.
[7] Questions; supply; 4H 15. 1208.

backgammon with Mr A. Read Esmond—Tuckwell's Winchester: not an unimportant book.[1] Saw Sir A.W.—Mr Marj.—Sir W. Harcourt—The Speaker—Mr
Hamilton.

To LORD KIMBERLEY, lord president and Indian secretary,   Kimberley MSS.
3 August 1893.

I fear there is a storm brewing in the matter of Caine.[2] It has got out in some way that
his name may be rejected *on the ground of objection from the Viceroy and Indian authorities*.
Such an objection, unless *strongly motivé*, cannot I think be sustained in the House of
Commons. Pray keep the matter open for consideration.

To LORD ROSEBERY, foreign secretary, 3 August 1893.   N.L.S. 10027, f. 1.

Marjoribanks told me of your plan today[3]—I hope & believe nothing need prevent the
fulfilment of your modest hope for a rest of 3 weeks.
Running through subjects as far as I could discern them I took
1. Siam which I trust has set you free. (I am sorry I had not the least inkling of yesterday's
debate or I should have been there. Grey as I learn did admirably well)
2. Viceroyalty of India.[4] Cromer is in the perspective. There seem to be real difficulties
about any body else. They say it ought to be settled within a fortnight.
3. Should not the Sultan's draft treaty receive some formal notice soon?[5] The objections
to particular Clauses are obvious. But besides these, if as I suppose we all think Salisbury's
notion of re-entry was a good one, would it not be well to let him know that we are dis-
satisfied with his dropping it & is there not basis enough for an easy provisional reply.
4. I am under the impression you may have to use some unmusical words about the
Armenian executions. But *I* do not know why any of these subjects should impede you.

4. *Fr.*

Wrote to Mr Caine MP.—Sir W. Phillimore—Ld Bute—Ld Kimberley—Rev. J.
Caswell—and minutes. Dined at Sir G. Trevelyan's. Saw Sir A.W.—Mr Marj.—Ld
Kimberley. H of C. $2\frac{1}{2}$–$6\frac{1}{2}$.[6] Read Esmond—and [blank.] Saw Fr. & Aust: touching.[7]

5. *Sat.*

Wrote to Ld Rosebery l.l.l.—and minutes. Read Esmond (finished): Beatrix is in
act its gem. Also Hops & Hopping.[8] Saw Sir A.W.—Mr Murray. $3\frac{1}{4}$–$6\frac{1}{2}$. To Agric.
Hall: spoke 50 m to a vast audience: *melting*.[9] Worked on my subject.

---

[1] See 13 July 93.
[2] W. S. Caine's membership of the Opium Commission had been discussed since the Commission
was mooted. Despite the objections of the Indian govt., Caine, a well-known critic of the Indian govt.
and supporter of the Congress Party, was appt. to the Commission but illness prevented his serving
on it; Newton, *Lord Lansdowne*, 110. See to Kimberley, 25 July 93.
[3] To go to Holmbury for three weeks on medical advice; Add MS 44290, f. 163.
[4] See 12 Aug. 93n.
[5] Rosebery discouraged this, as likely to cause intrigue at Constantinople and uneasiness in
Britain; ibid., f. 165.
[6] Supply; 4*H* 15. 1349.
[7] Perhaps rescue cases. See 9 Aug. 93.
[8] J. B. Marsh, *Hops and hopping* (1892).
[9] *T.T.*, 7 August 1893, 6e.

6. 10 S. Trin.

Chapel Royal noon with H.C. and Guards Chapel evg. Drove with C. & saw Mrs Th. (*Ten* miles of great thoroughfare gave 6 private vehicles, five of them one— horrid. A real curiosity) [*sic*]. Read Adler's Sermon[1]—Lawrence, Churchman to Churchmen[2]—Blackett Divine Truth[3]—et alia.

7. M.

Wrote to Mr Gardner—Canon M'Coll—Mr Rendel—Ld Spencer—The Queen— and minutes. H. of C. $3\frac{1}{2}$-8, $9\frac{1}{2}$-12.[4] Only half a nights sleep, a thing unusual of late. Saw Sir A.W.—Mr Marj.—Ld Kimberley *cum* Sir W.H. Drive with C. Read British Israel[5]—Hosken's Poems. Examined books.

To LORD SPENCER, first lord of the admiralty, 7 August 1893. Add MS 44549, f. 112.

I thank you very much for your letter.[6] The issue placed before you was undoubtedly a great one & could not with propriety be treated otherwise.

I rejoice in the decision, & it is my firm belief that any other conclusion would have been nothing less than a grave shock to the whole Irish policy.

8. Tu.

Wrote to The Queen l.l.l.—& minutes. Cabinet 12-2. Saw Ld Rosebery l.l.—Sir A. West—Mr Marj.—Read The Red Sultan.[7] H. of C. $3\frac{1}{2}$-$8\frac{1}{4}$, $9\frac{3}{4}$-$11\frac{1}{4}$.[8]

Cabinet. Tues. Aug. 8. 1893. Noon.[9]
   (Marjoribanks attending)
1. Time of House. Dilke's Qu.[10]
   (Marj[oribanks] suggests Frid. 18. 2 PM.)
2. Indian Currency. Chaplin's notice.[11]
3. One-member system. ⟨Harcourt will make a short reply⟩
   Nothing to be done except by general consent.
4. Outlook for Bills. We [   ][12] to Supply as well as H.R. before adjourning. Will have Autumn Sittings.
5. Gov. General India. Kimberley recited names. K. will further consider.
6. Recommend inquiry to House Charges. Suspended as to Friday.
7. Admiralty require money by Aug. 28. To frame a scheme.

[1] H. N. Adler, '*Is it well with thee?' A sermon* (1893).
[2] A. E. Barnes-Lawrence, *Churchmen to churchmen: matters of controversy* (1893).
[3] J. Blackett, *Divine truth in the light of reason and revelation* (1893).
[4] Consideration of amndts. to G.I. Bill; 4*H* 15. 1433.
[5] Perhaps an early copy of C. Lagrange, *The great pyramid . . . an independent witness to the literal chronology of the Hebrew bible, and British-Israel identity* (1894).
[6] Of 6 August, Add MS 44314, f. 81: 'I have come to the decision that I do not desire to go to India, as I think my duty lies more in this country. . . . I wish to remain to support the Liberal party in carrying out the present Irish Policy. . . .'
[7] J. M. Cobban, *The Red Sultan* (1893).
[8] Indian currency; G.I. Bill; 4*H* 15. 1639.   [9] Add MS 44648, f. 110.
[10] Should failure of private Members to use Friday evenings lead to Govt. use of the time; Add MS 44648, f. 111.
[11] Of his movement of the adjournment this day on this question; 4*H* 15. 1558.
[12] Several illegible words here.

India[1]
decl. Spencer
nil Herschell
     Cromer
nil Godley
nil Bradford
     Norman   66? or more
     Loch   66 this year
     Carrington

9. *Wed.*

Wrote to The Queen—and minutes. H. of C. $2\frac{1}{2}$–$5\frac{1}{2}$. 14 to dinner. I had to tell many old stories of politics. Saw A.W.—Mr Marj.—Mr Morley—Naoroji MP[2]—Mr [G. F.] Watts. Garden party between! Saw as on Friday inferior. Read The Red Sultan—Walters on Vases[3]—and divers.

10. *Th.*

Wrote to The Queen l.l.—Mrs Thompson—Mr T. Healy—Ld Kimberley—Mr Watts—Mr Stanford—H.J.G.—and minutes. Read Moore on the Land[4]—The Red Sultan. Saw Sir A.W.—Mr Marj.—Mr Morley. H. of C. $4\frac{1}{2}$–$8\frac{1}{4}$ (on *impasse*: after inquiry, I led the retreat)[5] and $9\frac{3}{4}$–$12\frac{1}{4}$.

11. *Fr.* [*St. George's Hill, Weybridge*]

Wrote to Ld Kimberley—Sir H. Ponsonby l.l.—Mr C. Bannerman—Ld Acton—Sir W. Harcourt—Mr Woods MP[6]—The Queen l.l.l.—Mrs Morton BP—and minutes. Saw Sir A.W.—Mr Marj.—Mr Morley—Mr Balfour. (These *M.*s both special.) (Morley brought me a curious (amiable) message from Balfour to express his delight in my speech of yesterday)—Worked on books. H. of C. $3\frac{1}{2}$–$6\frac{1}{2}$.[7] Then to St George's Hill.[8] Most kind reception. Read The Red Sultan.

To S. WOODS, M.P., 11 August 1893.   Add MS 44549, f. 113.

Eight Hours Miners Bill. The present position as regards the Government is this. We shall propose autumn sittings for business. What business? That must be considered comprehensively. Every important claim and yours among them will be taken into view. But our duty is to the country and we have to choose what will best justify the expenditure of time it may require. It would really be a breach of duty on our part to give away the time piecemeal.

[1] See to Kimberley, 26 July 93.
[2] Dadabhai Naoroji, 1825–1917; Parsee merchant, politician and writer; liberal M.P. Finsbury 1892-5; president of the Indian National Congress 1886, 1893, 1906.
[3] H. B. Walters, *Odysseus and Kirke on a Boeotian vase* (1893).
[4] Perhaps A. L. Moore, *Science and the earth* (1892).
[5] James proposed a new clause, preventing an Irish executive from suspending Habeas Corpus under an Irish Act of 1781; Gladstone accepted the amndt.; 4*H* 15. 1801.
[6] See 1 July 93.
[7] G.I. Bill; 4*H* 16. 35.
[8] Egerton's house; see 6 Aug. 70.

If you say we ought to give the [matter] comprehensive consideration as soon as it is practicable I agree.

In the meantime I commend to you these questions which I think important for your friends to consider:

1. You desire "at least a day". Will 'a day' be of use?

2. or does it mean a day & such other days as may be needed to settle the question at once? This would under the circumstances seem rather a large demand.

3. It appears to me individually that the divided state of opinion among the districts is the greatest among the obstacles in the way. Can you convert the dissentients? If not, can you conciliate them? This is perhaps quite as important a matter as any reply from the Government at this moment.[1]

12. Sat.

Wrote to Ld Rosebery—Mr Murray l.—Mr Marj.—Mr Murray tel.—Mr Gardner —& minutes. Drive in evg: heat great. Read The Red Sultan—and divers. Conversation with Lady L[ouisa] on Ireland: she is intelligent & good: but the mixed opinions of the circle caused reticence.

To Rev. J. B. ARMOUR,[2] 12 August 1893.   Add MS 44549, f. 114.

I have received with pleasure the address from 3500 Presbyterians favourable to Home Rule for Irish purposes in Ireland, which you have been good enough to send me.

I attach to it a great value, and I consider it as indicating a large section of favourable opinion, being well aware of the impediments which might deter many who entertain similar opinions from a gratuitous manifestation of them at the present time. I also observe what you have been good enough to state as to the spontaneous character of the address.

I look forward with confidence to a very large and early return of presbyterians in particular to the sentiments in favour of Union with their fellow countrymen which governed them as a body one century ago. But this will in all likelihood be delayed until the Parliamentary controversy has been closed.

It is certainly assumed by our opponents that what they term the loyal minority is homogeneous on all important matters. The sentiments now placed before me as to the Land Laws reminds me how likely it is that on this subject in particular they will 'ere long be largely undeceived.

To LORD ROSEBERY, foreign secretary, 12 August 1893.   N.L.S. 10027, f. 22.

I acted forthwith on your suggestion about Elgin.[3] Marjoribanks and C. Bannerman back you strongly. Harcourt rather cold, and monitory. Kimberley free and willing. I wrote a recommendation (as I find it is held to lie with me—an aggression, I suspect of Disraeli's), and sent it to Kimberley to forward if he thought fit. He has probably done it. 2. So Cromer is perhaps nearly but not wholly scratched. Elgin has 10 children, and a wife in weak health. In the Cabinet Cromer would have stood No. 1 but for the affair of

---

[1] No reply found. See 18 Aug. 93.

[2] James Brown Armour, 1842–1928; minister of Trinity church, Ballymoney, from 1869; educationalist and Senator of Queen's, Belfast. His memorial, sent with four other principal signatories, and Gladstone's reply are in *Northern Whig*, 15 August 1893, 5c.

[3] Rosebery wrote from Homburg on 10 August to 'earnestly deprecate any idea of appointing Ld. Cromer. If he accepts [the viceroyalty of India], which I doubt, it wd. scarcely be possible to continue any policy in Egypt.... I am inclined to urge you to think seriously of Elgin...'; Add MS 44290, f. 170.

last January which could only have been worse if we had been dealing with Gordon. But there is another buffer. In the Cabinet conversation, Carrington was put back (whom the Q. favours) & Sir H. Norman stood No. 1. although unhappily 67 years of age (this year) which *he* might deem an impediment.

3. *You* know exactly your ground with the Irish [*sic*; *sc.* Sultan] and I do not, so I hope you are right in saying you can without difficulty postpone till your return. His plan is as you have said in itself futile, and if our situation were normal it might fall to the ground. But as matters stand it is a real act of initiative, from the Suzerain who has a case for making it, and who in all likelihood (to say the least) has backers.

4. I am without any present knowledge as to Armenia: Bryce, however, told me that his accounts as to the Sultan's proceedings are deplorable: and I had the idea that he had promised to remit the capital sentence on the five: awkward if true. You call them "astute if pious".[1] I have never heard of their being pious. Astute I suppose they are, & beyond (perhaps) *all* other races, when brought into the outer world & developed there. So the Jews. But how far does this apply to them in their shaded life in Russia or in Armenia.

5. We are well enough satisfied with what we have said & done on the Report stage of Irish Bill, but I fear there is nothing that effectually abridges the calculated time: so, on the other hand, I hope you will get your little holiday in full, to which you were so well entitled. And may it do its full work.

6. I am reading a rather interesting Moorish novel called The Red Sultan—don't read it without some more trustworthy recommendation than mine.

(N.B. you *date* F.O.)

13. 11 S. Trin.

Ch mg. only. Such is the fruit of distance (1¾ m) with old age. Began a *perusal* of Hymns A.M.[2] Read *Paroles d'un croyant*[3]—Théologie internationale.

14. M. [*London*]

Wrote to The Queen—Ld Kimberley—Ld Rosebery—Mr Carvell Williams MP.—and minutes. H. of C. 3¾–8¼ & 9¾–12. Irish Bill: 74th Day.[4] Back to D. St at one. Saw Sir A.W.—S.L.—Mr Marj. Read The Red Sultan.

To LORD ROSEBERY, foreign secretary, 14 August 1893. '*Private.*' N.L.S. 10027, f. 26.

I perfectly appreciated the case as to delay in answering and felt no surprise.

Though I think it just that something should be done in the matter of ministerial salaries there are undoubtedly difficulties in the way: and unless you, or some of the members of the Cabinet who are to be sconced, have a *strong* sentiment in favour of moving I think there would be no use in my stirring the matter: for I feel that on account of my age I ought not to carry any amount of authority on the subject. I do not expect that all the sections would march zealously to the altar.

There is one difficulty probably not known to you, which I can add to your list. The higher political pension can only be taken by men who have had salaries of £2000: these

---

[1] Rosebery added (see previous note): 'I think we have done as much as can be expected about the Armenians. I do not see why we should bear the whole burden of this astute if pious race'; see H. C. G. Matthew, *The Liberal Imperialists* (1973), 198.

[2] *Hymns, ancient and modern* (1861, revised 1875); a tractarian-directed selection.

[3] Perhaps an earlier version of H. F. R. de la Mennais, *Paroles d'un croyant* (1899).

[4] 4*H* 16. 176.

pensions I do not like and would abolish: but it should be done completely and directly if at all.

You have not got hold of the idea which would move me onwards quite as I conceive it. It stands thus.

1. We have been rather vigorous in two points of economy.
(1) Directorships not to be held by members of the Cabinet
(2) Law Officers deprived of private practice.
2. The inequality between the 2m and the 5m Salaries is rather gross
3. It is not however in substance serious except as to two offices which within the last 30 years have made a great spring forwards in both labour and responsibility, and in dignity so far as these carry it. In these two cases, and in these only, the inequality is gross and rather practical.
4. No other office has a case at all. The P[ost] M[aster] G[eneral] has (it happens) £2400. Forgive me for saying the Scotch Secy has no case whatever—and the minister of Education though he has been growing *into* a Minister for same, is not to be compared so far as I know to either of the two.

The question is certainly, as you call it, delicate and irksome; and there would be no use in starting it without a certain amount of propelling power.

P.S. Elgin strongly supported by C. Bannerman & E. Marjoribanks. But H.M. rather kicks.

15. Tu.

Wrote to The Queen—Ld Ribblesdale—Mr T. Healy—Sir H. Acland—Rev. Mr. Webster—& minutes. Saw Sir A.W.—Mr Marj.—Ld Kimberley—H.J.G.—Mr A. Morley—Mr Fowler. Read The Red Sultan—Penins. Balkanique.[1] Drive with C.

To Sir H. W. ACLAND, 15 August 1893.   MS Acland d. 68, f. 93.

With regard to Ruskin, there are indeed already the elements of a strong case.[2] But there are difficulties. I imagine from your letter[3] that he is *unproducible*.

Now
1. How [to] make a man a Peer who never can take his seat? Moreover he is not like Tennyson known to a wide public.
2. Privy Council. Requires attendance & swearing in.
3. Bath. Requires service to State, or Royal Family
4. A Baronetcy—is not open to any of these difficulties.
5. I suppose him to be *well off*. A Pension, if agreeable to him, would be quite warrantable & right.

16. Wed.

Wrote to Ld Justice Bowen—The Queen l.l.—Lord Hannen[4]—and minutes. Saw Sir A. Clark—Sir A. West—Rev. S.E.G.—Mr Marj.—Ld Spencer. H. of C. 12½-5½.[5]

[1] Untraced.
[2] For a peerage, and perhaps a last suggestion for the Poet Laureateship. See 10 Oct. 92.
[3] Not found. In 1897, Acland visited Ruskin at Brantwood and wrote to Gladstone (in fact his last letter to him) that Ruskin's cousin and nurse 'told me, she had heard he was thought of for the great honour—that he was much disappointed that he had had *no* public recognition at the Jubilee'; Acland wondered if a peerage would be appropriate; 13 August 1897, Add MS 44091, f. 278.
[4] James Hannen, 1821-94; lord of appeal 1891; member of Behring Sea fishery commission 1892-3.
[5] Spoke on G.I. Bill; 4H 16. 356.

Dined with E. Hamilton: (Ld W. Neville, and Mrs [blank]). Drive afterwards, & walk: Half Moon St, St James's Squ. Read the Red Sultan—Beresford Correspondence.[1]

17. Th.[2]

Wrote to Ld Acton—The Queen l.l.—Sir C. Cameron—Sir A. Gordon—Mr Macleod—Sir H. Ponsonby—and minutes. Saw Sir A.W.—Mr Marj.[3]—and others. H. of C. 3½-8, 9¾-12. The heat constantly increasing: a speech entirely knocked me up.[4] Finished Red Sultan—Read Beresf. Corr.

Cabinet. Thurs. Aug. 17. 93. 2¼ P.M.[5]
1. Ld. Kimberley explained that the Indian ⟨Govt.⟩ Finance Commee. had sold Telegraphic Transfers at 15⅛ 150 m[ille].
2. Closure. Yes. Mr. Milman's plan. (See Bryce).
   We leaned to announcing tomorrow & moving Thursday.
   Resolutions to be drawn in the Fowler sense & in the general sense. Cabinet to meet on them tomorrow 2.30 at H. of C.

18. Fr. [Holmbury]

Wrote to The Queen l.l.—Mr Asquith—Mr Woods MP—Mr Fowler—Ld Rosebery—Mr Strachey[6]—Mr ....—and minutes. Off at 7 to Holmbury:[7] a closing visit. Saw Sir A.W.—Mr M.—S.L.—Mr Marj.—HNG.—Ossman Bey—Mr Carter. Short Cabinet at H. of C. 2½-3. Read Beresford Corr.

Cabinet. Friday Aug. 19 [sc. 18] 93.[8]
1. Notice of closure.[9] Bill to close Report Stage Friday 25th. Two forms No 1 & No 2.
2. Unemployed. Letter to W.E.G.: Asquith & Fowler to consider terms of reply.[10]

Cabinet. Aug. 18. 93. Cabinet at H. of C. 2½ PM.[11]
Cabinet met for a short time & considered the form of a new Closure Resolution. Also see report to H.M.[12]

To E. STRACHEY, M.P., 18 August 1893.   Add MS 44549, f. 117.
   I very much regret to learn that some difference has arisen between you with others of our friends & my colleague Mr Fowler.[13]

---

[1] J. Beresford, *Correspondence... illustrative of the last thirty years of the Irish parliament*, 2v. (1854).
[2] See 25 Aug. 93.
[3] Entry thus far written on a slip of paper pasted to the page.
[4] Replying to Lord G. Hamilton; 4*H* 16. 493.
[5] Add MS 44648, f. 113.
[6] (Sir) Edward Strachey, 1858–1936; agriculturalist and reformer; liberal M.P. S. Somerset 1892–1911.
[7] Leveson-Gower's house in Surrey; see 19 July 73.
[8] Add MS 44648, f. 117.   [9] See 21 Aug. 93.
[10] i.e. this day's letter to Strachey; the Central Cttee. of the Metropolitan Unemployed demanded immediate expenditure of £1m. on public works.   [11] Add MS 44648, f. 116.
[12] Describing Cabinet consideration of unemployment; *L.Q.V.*, 3rd series, ii. 304.
[13] Gladstone asked Fowler and Asquith, separately, to advise on this reply; Add MS 44549, f. 117. See 26 Aug. 93.

It is however some satisfaction to find that his present difficulty is one of time only, & that he thinks it requisite to wait for the Report of the Commission on the Aged Poor with the evidence & finding.

It seems to me that this argument so far as the Government is concerned can hardly be resisted, & that through this report we shall best approach the consideration of what all must I think feel to be a grave & difficult question. I trust however that care & patience will enable us to find one's [*sic*] way to a happy issue.

To S. WOODS, M.P., 18 August 1893.   Add MS 44549, f. 117.

I am afraid I have entirely failed to convey to your mind the position of the Government and the intention of my letter[1] with reference to your request that I would *now* promise to give a day at least for the Committee Stage of the Miners Bill. If in reply I were to ask you when we could count upon beginning the autumn sittings, and how much time we could have available for them, you would think I was mocking you, and with some justice. And yet it is simple truth that your means of judging on this question, slender as they are, are nevertheless much the same as mine.

Is it a reasonable thing to demand, when I am totally unable to forecast the measure of available time, & when that time ought to be divided and meted out with strict regard to the relative weight of many *great* public claims (a description I freely accede to yours) that I shall not begin to spend the little store on behalf of one of those claims without asking what others are to be?

With all respect I think not. Were a discussion to be specially forced on now I could not move from this ground. It would only encourage other like discussions and merely further abridge the small stock of time at our disposal for practical purposes.

Thinking there must be an interval I also though it worth while, for the sake of your cause, to ask you whether it might not be turned to useful account.[2]

19. Sat.

A day of rest. Conversation with F.L.G. Fine drive by Leith Hill. Read Beresford Corresp.—and [blank.] Yesterday thermom. reached *95 in the shade*.

20. 22 S. Trin.

Ch. mg. Evg prayers with C. Conv. with F.L.G.—G.L.—and others. Read (critically) H[ymns] Ancient & Modern—Apology of Aristides[3]—E. Wickham's Sermon—and [blank.] Wrote to Mr Murray.

21. M. [London]

Wrote to The Queen—and minutes. Saw Mr Murray—Mr Marj. Left kind Holmbury at 12¾. D. St 3¼. H. of C. 3½-8¼ and 10-12¼.[4] Read Beresford—Ulster in 1798.[5]

[1] See 18 Aug. 93.
[2] In *T.T.*, 23 August 1893, 8b.
[3] *The apology of Aristides on behalf of the Christians, from a Syriac MS*, ed. J. R. Harris (1891).
[4] Moved Resolution for closure of consideration of amndts. to G.I. Bill by 25 August; 4 *H* 16. 650.
[5] R. M. Young, *Ulster in '98. Episodes and anecdotes* (1893).

22. Tu.

Wrote to Ld Rosebery—The Queen l.l.l.—Mr Morley—Sir A. Gordon—and minutes. Saw Sir A.W.—Sir W. Harcourt—Mr Marj. H. of C. $3\frac{1}{2}$–$8\frac{1}{4}$ and $9\frac{1}{2}$–12.[1] Read Ulster in 1798—Trotter's Walks through Ireland.[2]

23. Wed.

Wrote to Rev. Wentworth BP.—The Queen—Rev. Carter BP—Mr Bryn Roberts MP[3]—Mr Armitstead—Rev. W. Webster—Mr T.H. Bolton MP[4]—& minutes.— and minutes. Eight to dinner. Conversation with all the guests, including Mr MacColl on Norway and Sweden. Drive with C. H. of C. $12\frac{1}{2}$–$5\frac{1}{2}$.[5]

24. Th.

Wrote to The Queen—Dr Macgregor MP.—Mr Cochrane—Sir H. Jenkyns—Sir C. Cameron—Mr Rathbone—and minutes. Saw Sir A.W.—Mr Marj.—Sir W. Harcourt *cum* Mr A. Morley—Mr Saunders MP. A fatiguing hour!—Att. General—Sir E. Grey. H. of C. $3\frac{3}{4}$–$8\frac{1}{4}$, $9\frac{1}{2}$–$11\frac{1}{2}$.[6] Read Beresford Corr.—Trotter's Walks.

To Sir C. CAMERON, M.P., 24 August 1893.   Add MS 44549, f. 118.

I thank you for informing me[7] some days ago that at a meeting of Liberal Scotch members a desire has been expressed for an inquiry next Session by a Select Committee into the financial relations between Scotland & the Imperial Exchequer. I have also received today indications that such an enquiry would be acceptable to Scotch members of the Opposition. It would I think be the duty of the Government in such a state of things to comply with what appears to be the general wish, and I hope it is unlikely that any Parliamentary difficulty in the way of appointing the Committee should arise.

To W. RATHBONE, M.P., 24 August 1893.   Add MS 44549, f. 118.

It has been reported to me that you think of withdrawing your support of the Irish Government Bill on the important, I might say *all* important, stage of the 3rd Reading by reason of the 9th or retention clause in its present form.

I am very sceptical about this report; for it would surely be a cruel thing to withhold from Ireland the consummation of her own hopes on account of a provision [for] *which she has never asked?*

The responsibility in this matter is that of Great Britain only: and we have expressly & carefully retained for the Imperial Parliament the absolute moral title to deal with the whole subject of retention as it may think fit. If retention is found to be impolitic, we are free to get rid of it. If the present form of retention is faulty or is disapproved we are free to amend it.

If it should be the case that the 9th clause has in any way caused you to doubt as to

---

[1] G.I. Bill; 4 *H* 16. 772.
[2] J. B. Trotter, *Walks through Ireland in 1812, 1814 and 1817* (1819).
[3] John Bryn Roberts, 1843–1931; liberal M.P. Eifion 1885–1906; strong anti-imperialist.
[4] Thomas Henry Bolton, 1841–1916; solicitor; liberal (unionist) M.P., St. Pancras 1885–6, 1890–5.
[5] Spoke ('indistinctly heard') on G.I. Bill; 4 *H* 16. 892.
[6] Spoke on G.I. Bill; 4 *H* 16. 1015.
[7] Letter untraced. A select cttee. was promised but not appt.; 4 *H* 16. 1103, 22. 350, 23. 1683.

your vote on the coming occasion, I hope you will allow me to see you on the subject before the time comes. I regard it as the most important of all occasions, because every vote tells on the grand & supreme question how far it is right that the H. of Lords should in a case like this set aside the judgment of the H. of Commons. But apart from this the occasion as a great stage of the Bill warrants as I hope this intrusion.[1]

25. Fr.

Wrote to The Qu. l.l.—Mr A. Morley—Mr Saunders MP—and minutes. H. of C. 3¾-8 and 9¾-11¾.[2] Read Trotter's Walks.[3] Saw Sir A.W.—Mr Marj.—Sir W. Harcourt—Att. Gen.—Sir E. Grey. Only one stage more.

26. Sat. [Tring Park]

Wrote to Sir G. Trevelyan—Ld Rosebery—Mr Strachey MP.—Mr Rathbone—Hon S.L.—....... & minutes. Off at 11.15 to Tring Park.[4] Large party. Saw Mr Rothschild jun. (& his delightful Museum). Drive to Ashridge Park. Read Jebbs Camb. Address[5]—Trotter's Walks—Beresford Corr.

To W. RATHBONE, M.P., 26 August 1893.   Add MS 44549, f. 119.
    I thank you much for your letter.[6]
    And I wish to add a few words on the particular form of Cl. 9[7] which has troubled you. You will I think consider my propositions undeniable.
1. That form is not due to the Government, who chose the one you prefer.
2. Though we gave way to the feeling of the Liberal majority, yet had the Tories & Dissentients thought fit to support our proposition as it stood, we would have stood by it, & could have carried it. But they carefully avoided saying a word in its favour: they withheld the support which alone would have saved it. *They therefore* are the persons really responsible for its miscarriage.
3. I am sure you will see this being so, how hard it would be upon the Irish members, were any of us to visit upon them by withdrawing force from the majority, a fault of which they are wholly guiltless, the opposition being mainly, & the British Liberals secondarily responsible.
4. Please also to be sure[?] that the right, I mean the moral right, to alter Clause 9 (or even to repeal it) & thus to restore "in & out" to its position of preference, is by special notice in the Bill, i.e. by the prefatory words to Cl. 9, reserved to the Imperial Parliament, independently of Ireland & Irish opinion.
5. Moreover I am strongly of the opinion that if the British Electorate go seriously against the unlimited voting of the Irish, this is the very thing which *will have to be done* & I myself, if still in politics, should be one of the foremost to concur in doing it.

[1] No reply found. See 26 Aug. 93.
[2] Spoke on G.I. Bill, consideration of whose amndts. was then ended by closure; 4H 16. 1179. And received a large dpn. on Scottish disestablishment; T.T., 26 August 1893, 3c.
[3] A section of text about one square inch is here cut out, also affecting 27 Aug. 93, the entry on the versa. The extracted piece of paper is stuck on top of the entry for 17 Aug. 93, with the present text for that day written on it.
[4] The Rothschilds' house in Hertfordshire; see 28 Feb. 91.
[5] R. C. Jebb, *The work of Universities for the nation, past and present* (1893).
[6] Untraced.
[7] Position of Irish M.P.s.

On the whole, then, I feel that you will not think me unreasonable, if while forbearing to take advantage of your kind offer to come up, I ask you to authorise my telling Marjoribanks that he may pair you for the whole coming Parliamentary week.[1]

To E. STRACHEY, M.P., 26 August 1893.   Add MS 44549, f. 119.

With reference to your letter of the 20th,[2] I am glad to find on further inquiry that the Commission on Aged Poor has actually closed its sittings & that the Report is expected to be ready in October giving ample time for consideration before the next Session.

27. 13 S. Trin.

Ch mg & evg. The absentees were many: indeed the country Sundays are unSundaylike. But Lady R. is excellent. Read Hymns A. & M.—Ramsay's New work[3]—All Saints,[4] by the Rector.[5] Long conversation with [Henry] Chaplin—Agriculture & distress. Drive on the high ground.

28. M. [London]

Wrote to The Queen—Sir G. Trevelyan—and minutes. Long conversation with the very intelligent agent. Off at 11½ to London. Saw Sir A.W.—Mr Marj.—Ld Kimberley—Ld Spencer. Ten to dinner. H. of C. 3½–5.[6] Read Trotter—Beresford Corresp. Saw Shane & another [R].

29. Tu.

Wrote to Mr Balfour l.l.—Lady Aberdeen—& minutes. Saw A.W.—Mr M—Mr Marj.—Sir W. Harcourt—The Speaker. Read Trotter's Walks—Beresford Corr. H. of C. 3¾–5.[7] Drive with C. Dined with Welby. Worked on papers for 3 R. Debate.

30. Wed.

Wrote to the Queen—Sir E. Grey—Rev Mr Fenwar—and minutes. Saw Sir A.W.—Mr Marj.—Sir W. Harcourt—Mr Rathbone—on his vote[8]—Mr Balfour cum Sir W. Harcourt (Duke of Edinb.)—Mr Godkin. Dined with Mr Bryce. Read as yesterday. H. of C. 12–2½ and 3–5½. Spoke 1 hour on moving 3 R. Irish Govt Bill.[9]

---

[1] Despite this Rathbone was reported by *T.T.*, 2 September 1893, 10c as having abstained on the 3°R.

[2] Not found. See 18 Aug. 93.

[3] W. M. Ramsay, *The Church in the Roman Empire before A.D. 170* (1893).

[4] William Allen Whitworth, vicar of All Saints', Margaret Street, Marylebone, had sent his *Quam Dilecta: a description of All Saints' Church, Margaret Street, with historical notes of Margaret Chapel* (1891). See 3 Sept. 93.

[5] Text here cut out, see 25 Oct. 93n.

[6] Questions; navy estimates; 4*H* 16. 1219.

[7] Navy estimates; 4*H* 16. 1362.

[8] See 26 Aug. 93.

[9] 4*H* 16. 1457.

31. Th.

Wrote to The Queen l.l.—.............—and minutes. H. of C. 3–8¼.[1] Saw Sir A.W.—Mr Marj.—Ld Chancr—Mr Mather MP. Cabinet 12¼–1¾. Read as yesterday.

Cabinet. Thurs. 31 Aug. 1893. Noon.[2]
1. Resolution on Business of the House. Yes.[3]
2. Employment of the Autumn Sittings
   Plan 1. Parish Councils + Employers Liability (Register 1st. 1894)
   Plan 2. Empl. Liab. + others second—any Bills
   No. 1. adopted.
   Announce today. Meet on the 2d November. Measures on Thursday. (Duke of Edinburgh's Annuity—put off).
Mashona Land. Lobengula very angry. Peace & order lie primary[?] obligations with the Co. It should act defensively if possible.[4] Rhodes wants nothing.
We hold out no expectation of aid. A. Grey & [J. R.] Maguire[5] have asked what we mean to do. Ripon read draft of proposed answer to Bartlett.
Evicted Tenants. Autumn sittings—no: Govt. Bill next year— *Yes*.
Kimberley—Indian Army Bill. Alors comme alors.

Frid. Sept. 1. 1893.

Wrote to Ld Stanmore—The Queen—S. Lyttelton. Saw Sir A.W.—Mr Marj.—Mr Blake MP.—Sir W. Harcourt. Read as yesterday H. of C. 4–7¾ and 10½–1¼. Voted in 301 to 267 for Irish Bill. This is a great step.[6] Thanks be to God. Eight to dinner.

To J. BRYCE, 1 September 1893.   MS Bryce 10, f. 139.
   Many thanks for your letter.[7]
   1. I incline to agree as to Wissant. I had followed what seemed to be a consensus, perhaps a shallow one.
   2. Of the *viridis Ægyptus* I am no judge but I think the Virgil of the Aeneid a great libertine in his dealing with [blank] while Dante is the most rigidly conscientious and consistent of writers.

[1] G.I. Bill 3°R; 4*H* 16. 1587. *T.T.*, 2 September 1893, 10c, reported that of the liberals Saunders and T. H. Bolton voted against 3°R and Rathbone and Wallace abstained.
[2] Add MS 44648, f. 118.
[3] See 4 Sept. 93.
[4] Supported by Rhodes, Jameson was exacerbating the aftermath of the 'Victoria incident' to provoke war with the Matabele led by Lobengula. The Cabinet supported Ripon's dispatch of 26 August prohibiting 'any offensive movement in the interests of the British South Africa Company ...'. But hostilities began in early October, poor African tactics leading to a rapid victory for the Company and imperial troops and the consequent conquest of Matabeleland; see A. Keppel-Jones, *Rhodes and Rhodesia. The white conquest of Rhodesia 1884–1902* (1983), 244 ff. See to Ripon, 4, 10, 14, 28 Oct., 4, 6, 8 Nov. 93 and 4 Nov. 93.
[5] James Rochfort Maguire, 1856–1925; barrister and fellow of All Souls; Home Rule M.P. Donegal 1890–2, Clare 1892–5; Chairman of Rhodesian Railways, later of British South Africa Co.
[6] Government of Ireland Bill 3°R; 4*H* 16. 1836 (also questioned by Vincent and Burns on the unemployed; ibid. 1734).
[7] Of 30 August, MS Bryce 12, f. 141, returning an article on Dante in the *Revue de Belgique*, with various comments by Bryce about Wissant and Flemish dykes, arguing that 'Cadzand seems to answer much better the place mentioned by Dante than Wissant.'

3. I do not think that he supplies any evidence of having cared for industrial towns or pursuits. But my memory may deceive me.

2. Sat.

Wrote to Mr Blake—Lady Drury—and minutes. Saw Sir A. West—Ld Stanmore: an uneasy conversation. I was rather overset by that or some other cause: & spent the day mainly on my back. Worked on Books. Read Trotter finished—Beresford Corresp.

I one day asked Tennyson whether he did not consider Carlyle a Poet. Certainly, he replied. He is a poet to whom nature has denied the faculty of verse.

In perusing 'Richard Coeur de Lion'[1] after this long long interval, I find the case exactly reversed: this is versification without poetry.[2]

To E. BLAKE, M.P., 2 September 1893.   Add MS 44549, f. 121.

I learn with great pleasure that there is to be an Irish day during the Worlds Fair at Chicago; nor am I less satisfied to know that you have undertaken to attend the gathering on behalf of the Irish people, & of their Representatives.

There could not be a more interesting, nor except on the day of the final victory, a more encouraging occasion. After seven years of close & sustained struggle throughout the country, a House of Commons was elected last year, which has passed, after 82 days of debate, a Bill conferring upon Ireland the management, through a freely elected Parliament, of her own domestic affairs. And when at the close of next week the Bill will be rejected by a large minority of the House of Lords, we shall know, the people of Ireland will know, that this rejection will mean no more than a dilatory vote.

You are about to address Americans who, in all ranks & in all parts of their magnificent country, have shown an active & almost an universal sympathy with Ireland, & more especially Irish Americans, through whose energies & inextinguishable affection for Ireland, has been effected the most remarkable oceanic migration ever known in the history of the world.

And you are in a condition to point out to them these two things. First, the distance which has been actually travelled over between the physical misery & political depression that marked the early years of the Century, & the Victory recorded last night, is immeasurable. Secondly, the distance between that recorded Victory & the final investment of Ireland with full self governing control over her domestic affairs is not only measurable but short.

It was unanswerably observed during our debate that the recent success has been brought about by change of opinion where opinion has been most hostile, namely change of opinion in England—Scotch Irish & Welsh Votes were with us in 1886: but we stood in a minority of near one hundred & twenty.

It has been the signal & favourable change in England that has converted this minority into a majority of forty for Home Rule.

Yet England still exhibits her reduced majority, to intercept one of the greatest benefits ever conferred not only upon Ireland but upon her. In this attitude, she is alone among all the peoples of the English speaking race. She has not yet quitted, but she is quitting it. Yet the last struggle still remains, & like the former struggles it will be great. It

[1] A reference to Gladstone's poem in the *Eton Miscellany* (he wrongly recalled it as for the Newdigate Prize at Oxford); he declined a request in 1893 for it to be reprinted; Magnus, 9, Morley, i. 62.
[2] Initialled and dated 2 September 1893; Add MS 44775, f. 236.

will demand the friendly efforts of all those wherever placed, who under God have lifted this great cause out of the abyss & set it on an eminence from which there remains but a single step into the promised land.

I cherish the most sanguine hope that the conduct of the Irish nation, when their great object has been attained, will fulfil every reasonable hope cherished by those who have aided, & will convert its present enemies into friends.[1]

3. 14 S. Trin.

Chapel royal mg: All Saints aft. Saw Mr Rendel—Miss Simmons. Wrote to Mr Whitworth. Wrote theol. Read Hist. All Saints—Sterrett on Hegel.[2]

To Rev. W. A. WHITWORTH, 3 September 1893.[3]   Add MS 44517, f. 232.

I have read with great interest much of your very welcome volume on the history of All Saints' Church:[4] and I am truly glad that the work [which] has been produced for it supplies a needful chapter in the history of the Church of England in the century now expiring.

I was myself little more than an occasional visitant,[5] and external observer; nevertheless the experiences of the old Margaret Chapel are never to be forgotten.

There is one noteworthy point that I do not recollect to have found in the volume: that is to say the close connection of the Chapel with the Evangelical party in the Church.

I think that my first visits to the Chapel were in company with an Oxford friend of the very highest promise, Mr. Anstice, Professor of Classics in King's College, cut off by a very early death. He was a deeply religious man, of Low Church sentiments. He took me there when Mr. Dodsworth was the clergyman, and I remember hearing him preach a most able sermon to shew that the 'total corruption' of human nature was capable of an orthodox sense.

He changed to the Tractarian side: and I had an idea that Mr. Oakeley came there to uphold the old Evangelical character of the congregation: but of this I am not at all certain.

My own visits to Margaret Street were almost wholly on Sunday evenings and occasional week days.

The congregation was of all I have ever seen in any country or communion, the most absorbed in devotion.

It must be admitted that many of the best known went into the Roman Church. Among those who did not were Mr. R. Williams the Banker, Mr. Walker the Engraver, Mr. S. Wood (uncle of Lord Halifax) a man of singularly elevated spirit; and Mr. Geo. Richmond R.A. who I think, of all persons now alive would have most and best to say about it. I am not however quite sure when he began to be connected with it.

The New Version was used, I think exclusively: and the singing was the heartiest and warmest I ever heard. This continued for some time after the settlement in the present noble Church.

I do not recollect ever to have seen in the Church any persons belonging to the

[1] Reads as if for publication, but not found published; for the World's Fair, see *T.T.*, 25 May 1893, 3e.
[2] J. M. Sterrett, *The ethics of Hegel* (1893).
[3] Typed copy.
[4] See 27 Aug. 93.
[5] Hardly an accurate recollection; in 1842–7 Gladstone frequently attended, and it was the meeting place for 'the Engagement' of which he was a member.

'aristocracy' except Lady G. Fullerton (then Leveson Gower) and Mr. Ponsonby after-wards Lord Bessborough. Nor was it visited I think by any politician except myself.[1]

I thought you might like to know these few particulars.

4. M. [On train]

Wrote to Ld Stanmore—Ld Rosebery—Sir W. Lawson—Mr Cobb MP—& minutes. H. of C. $3\frac{1}{4}$–$6\frac{1}{4}$. Moved the astringent, originally too astringent Reso-lution:[2] then away to the North. Saw Sir A. West—Marj.—Mr Morley—Mr Marj.—Ld Rosebery—Mr Evans MP—Ld Kimberley. Off by 8 P.M. Train.

5. Tu. [Black Craig, Perthshire]

At Black Craig[3] (14 m. drive from Cargill) by 8.30 A.M. Much warmth on the road. Wrote to Sir H. Ponsonby—Mr Murray. Drive & walk: 2 miles entirely knocked me up. The Aberdeens came: much conversation. Early bed. Worked on Odes of Horace: pleasant but how difficult.[4] Read Welldon on public schools.[5]

6. Wed.

Wrote to Sir W. Harcourt l.l. & tel.—Mr J. Cowan—& minutes. Morning chiefly with the Abns: conversation respecting H.M. & all matters. Worked on Odes: so slow. Backgammon with Mr A. I have fallen back another step or stride in the power of reading.

To Sir W. V. HARCOURT, chancellor of the exchequer,   MS Harcourt dep. 13, f. 137.
6 September 1893.

The prose of Monday is beaten hollow by the romance of Tuesday.[6] I little thought when roaring down the rail that in a few hours this House of Commons which Harting-ton has so deeply infected with Radicalism was to assail one of the most sacred among our venerable institutions. You may judge the shock to me. The only thing I seem to see clearly (upon the brief notes in Dundee Courier) is that Chamberlain has blundered.

I presume you cannot, if so inclined, *raise* the amount, on report, but only by recommittal.

I presume also that the House of Lords can recoup itself out of the Fees, but I do not know the terms of its arrangement with the Treasury. If the Lords have the power, will not our poor House be rather in a ridiculous position?

In any case the vote seems to be a curious one as a sign of the times.

Tomorrow I shall perhaps hear from you about it.

When we hit the H. of Lords we ought to hit it *clean*.[7]

---

[1] Again, an inaccurate recollection; T. D. Acland, W. Monsell and other political figures attended; see 23 Feb. 45n. and H. C. G. Matthew, 'Gladstone, Evangelicalism and "The Engagement"' in J. Garnett and H. C. G. Matthew, ed., *Religion and revival* (1993).

[2] Resolution for an autumn sitting, with precedence for govt. business and some prevention of 'dilatory motions'; 4*H* 16. 1891.

[3] Armitstead's house, 8 miles N.W. of Blairgowrie.

[4] A return to work on his translation; see 14 July, 27 Dec. 92.

[5] Probably F. C. Searle, *To a boy leaving school for the university. With a preface by J. E. C. Welldon* (1892).

[6] Vote in Commons in 103:95 (agst. the govt.) to reduce salaries of officials in the Lords; Chamberlain voted for the reduction; 4*H* 17. 177.

[7] No reply found.

To E. MARJORIBANKS, chief whip, 6 September 1893.   Add MS 44549, f. 123.

The Midlothian application, you are considerate as ever on my behalf.[1] But I thought it only fair to refer to my excellent Chairman Mr Cowan. Both in *physique* & in morale I am much averse to it: but there is something to be said on the other side, & if he should think it to be a real opportunity I am for going & probably the visit could be limited to a few hours. We bid farewell yesterday to Aberdeen & your sister, both in good heart, though they have had I fear no parting farewell in a high quarter. So far they have been martyrs to the cause. I think their career will be probably a success beyond that of their predecessors, & good for the continuance of the connection. For us it was rather an occasion because they have been so good to us, & because it is unlikely that we, specially that I, should witness their home-coming. I have nothing from the offending uncle—Ponsonby comes here tomorrow. I have been with labour & help spelling out the amazing[?] debate on the Vote for the H. of Lords. So far as I see, all was right on our side. The Blairgowrians turned out for us in great force.

7. *Th.*

Wrote to The Queen—Sir W. Harcourt tel.—Ly Herbert—Mr Marj. Circular drive, & back by Cally Bridge. Saw Mr Shand. Read Portuguese Nun.[2] Worked on Odes. Backgammon with Mr A. Drive.

To Sir W. V. HARCOURT, chancellor of the exchequer,   MS Harcourt dep. 13, f. 141.
7 September 1893.

Re Duke of Edinburgh, I agree with you that the list of English liabilities is a Bogus list.[3]
1. But it shows that he means to keep Clarence House, and his keeping it may be taken to imply visits and expenditure.
2. If from among his items you allow Clarence House, subscriptions &c., and Insurance, these come to £5200. I do not think *much* of the Salaries, for they have been given with knowledge of the Act of Parliament. But throwing them in we get the figure of £6500.
3. However there is a point in the R. information, which also tells on his side. It would seem that of the Income from Coburg of 30m only 15m comes to him personally. In this point of view he would be 10m to the bad by taking Coburg.
4. On the other hand I cannot but believe that having had an income little short of 60m from the time of his marriage, he has not spent anything like it, and there (one might almost say) must be savings; but we can hardly get at them.
5. The figure named by Balfour was 5m. Upon the facts before us I should not be shocked at leaving him ⅓ of the whole = £8333, or even ⅔ = 10m. He ought not to be poorer than heretofore.
6. My impression is that the two Benches can carry anything in reason that leaders agree on: the Irish I apprehend will be conformable.
7. I telegraphed and wrote to Ponsonby yesterday but as yet no reply from him. I am waiting a while before telegraphing to you as to your seeing Balfour. Ponsonby will not be here in any case much before luncheon tomorrow.
8. If Ponsonby comes tomorrow (which you shall know) perhaps you could tell me what you think of my closing figures in No 5.

[1] No letter from Marjoribanks found. See 27 Sept. 93.
[2] M. Alcoforado, *Letters of a Portuguese nun* (1893).
[3] The duke of Edinburgh's accession to the dukedom of Saxe-Coburg and Gotha produced a huge correspondence about his financial settlement in which Gladstone participated voluminously.

9. I think it quite clear that *if* we do not ourselves make a proposal in the House, we must be prepared with a full case to show why we made none.
10. About ⟨i⟩ consent of Parliament; this point strikes me. An Act of Parliament is not consent but *advice and* consent. Therefore the words do not mean an Act. What do you say?[1]

8. *Fr.*

11½–5. Drive to the pass over Pitlochrie. Worked Odes. Sir H. Ponsonby came from the Queen. Long conversation on Duke of Edinburgh's case.[2] He brought a message half inviting me to a limited visit, which I think is well meant. Read Life of Smith.[3]

9. *Sat.*[4]

Wrote to Sir W. Harcourt l.l.—Mr Marjoribanks—Rev W. A. Whitworth—and minutes. Saw Mr Shand—Sir H. Ponsonby. Drove to the Woolfactory and Mr Patullo's. Backgammon with Mr A. Worked on the Odes. Read Life of Smith. Thoughts on Midl. visit.[5] Saw Mr Shand.

To Sir W. V. HARCOURT, chancellor of the exchequer, MS Harcourt dep. 13, ff. 148–9. 9 September 1893.
[Letter 1:]   You have I think done very well to get the Vote for the Lords in Supply out of the way.[6] It is probable however that the circumstances of the moment in the House of Lords itself greatly stimulated the drive to give them a slap in the face. Odd to say I have not yet seen what was the vote actually given though I spelt out the debate, so that I do not know how far there is a difficulty in adjusting the £.s.d.
   I note all your proceedings with much interest: and with much pain so far as the Speaker is concerned. Clearly and at whatever cost he should be encouraged and even stimulated, on public grounds, to do the very best that can be done for himself, and not to hesitate for a moment. I would write to him in that sense if you advise it by telegraph.
   It is not impossible that they may pay to Mellor as Deputy Speaker more respect than he got during his very difficult work as Chairman of Committee.

[Letter 2:]   You will not expect any great results from my conversations with Ponsonby who slept here and has just gone back to Balmoral, but I give you a note; first of what he said or conveyed.
1. As to the general attitude at Balmoral, everything went to confirm the rationality of their attitude.
2. He was quite prepared for difficulties in accepting the (gradually growing) list of the British Charges.
3. He gave a view of Coburg revenues curiously corresponding with the R. information in one point, the division into moiety, but very different as to the amount divisible which according to him is 70m or 75m.

[1] No reply found.
[2] On his controversial succession to the dukedom of Saxe-Coburg and Gotha. See 18 Sept. 93.
[3] H. E. Maxwell, *Life and times of . . . W. H. Smith*, 2v. (1893).
[4] Early this morning, the Lords rejected the Irish Government Bill by 419:41.
[5] See 27 Sept. 93.
[6] No letter from Harcourt found.

4. It was pretty plain that the Duke is not at all disposed to encourage our prying into the *Coburg* reserves which he seems to regard as beyond our cognisance.

5. He shared my impression that there must be savings out of the large income with moderate expenditure, operative for 20 years since the marriage—but I admitted that these can hardly be investigated.

6. The Queen had asked Can he have the 25m for a year or two? This he did not encourage.

7. I understand that Balfour wrote to him in answer to a suggestion of his made at the instance of the Queen. B. wrote in general & rather evasive terms.

On my side

1. I dwelt mainly, following your lead, on the necessity for more *Coburg* information.

2. This to be given not necessarily in much detail, but so as to exhibit clearly the situation with its main bearings.

3. This information to be for those who have to take the decision: should there be any apparent necessity for information of this kind to be given to the House of Commons that could only be by a separate request and permission.

4. I told him of my point about the Act of Parliament, & that you (& as I understand Rigby) attached no value to it.

5. As appearances indicated our having probably to go to Parliament, I thought it likely the matter might have to be considered by the Cabinet.

6. I mentioned your present fear of proposing reduction & said I gathered that Balfour (whose frank & careful mode of proceeding I lauded) agreed in it, and generally took a strict view, while I was less despondent as to carrying a reduction if we could find one thoroughly defensible.

I agree with you that this would never do to hand over to a new Session. Our best chance would be in an 'exhausted receiver'.

10. *S. 15 Trin.*

Wrote to Mr Stuttell Miller—Mr Cowan—Ld Norton. Morning Ch. at Blairgowrie, where some Episcopal ladies looked black at us. C. read prayers for evg. Saw Mr S. Walk to the hill. Tried to read Ramsay first Age,[1] & Budges Thomas of Magra,[2] but made little way.

To LORD NORTON, 10 September 1893.   Add MS 44549, f. 125.

Thank you very much for your letter.[3] It is just like yourself, that is to say kind & generous throughout. Who the assessing peers are I know not, & never shall know, for my eyesight disables me from reading the debate. All the better, I can neither wonder at nor complain of them, when a man like Argyll, my friend for 40 years and my colleague for 20 accuses me (if I understand him aright) of having done what I did in order to get office. In face of the fact that my first act was, shortly after the election,[4] to make known to the [Salisbury] Government that if *they* would settle the Irish question, they should have the

---

[1] Untraced.

[2] E. A. W. Budge, *Book of governors. Historia monastica of Thomas, bishop of Magra* (1893).

[3] Of 9 September, Add MS 44517, f. 240: unable to support home rule, but appalled at the personal attacks on Gladstone in the Lords; 'You know my long established assurance of the high principles, deep religious sense of Duty's call & the sacrifice of self, & noble aim of every action in your great career: which history will certainly maintain against all inferior rivalries.'

[4] i.e. in December 1885; see 15, 20, 23 Dec. 85.

best support I could give them, and that I never said a word against them (though they were a small minority), until they declared in February for coercion. No answer was ever made to my offer,[1] but I know that there are among them men, or a man, who lament that it was not accepted.

Your vote is one of those that it is a special sorrow for me not to have. I was sorry to miss you the last time when I went to Grillion's, especially as I wanted to say with how much pleasure I had read your son's excellent and (at the proper place) entertaining book, which you were good enough to send me.[2] I think of punishing you by sending you a collection which I have made of my papers on the Irish question.

11. M.

Wrote to Ld Rosebery. Saw Mr S. 1–6. Beautiful drive on Glen Islay, & pic-nic. Worked much on Horace's Odes: they are harder & harder to render well & briefly. Backgammon with Mr A. Read Platonia.[3]

To LORD ROSEBERY, foreign secretary, 11 September 1893.   N.L.S. 10027, f. 43.

I have read your draft to Dufferin and with much sympathy, though I have not here the map needed for following the details of the 'zone'.[4] The plan of a joint guarantee seems to me excellent but I am not sure what may be your idea in naming Germany, unless it be to stick a pin into the side of the French by showing this formidable figure on the horizon.

You have made a great impression in the debate, and I think as a whole it has gone well, except that I am disgusted with the vote of the Bishops. I do not understand why for such an occasion the grave should yield up its dead.

Bp. St. Asaph spontaneously said to me in Feb. or March that if the Bill came to the House of Lords he hoped with all his heart that it would pass!

[P.S.] Midlothian invites me on my way back, and I am considering whether or not to take it, with the cost of three or four hours.

12. Tu.

Wrote to Sir W. Harcourt l.l.—The Speaker—Mr Burnand—Adm. Egerton—Sir H. Acland—Mr Prestage—& minutes. Worked on Odes. Picnic at The Patullo farm. Managed to read a little of Shepherd Smith's Life. Much conversation with Ld Acton.

To F. C. BURNAND, editor of *Punch*, 12 September 1893.   Add MS 44549, f. 125.

I thank you very much for the early "Punch" with its capital cartoon.[5]

May the delightful artist long continue to adorn your columns, & may he have better subjects than *me* at least for which he has done so much.

---

[1] Though see 23 Dec. 85n.
[2] *Stephen Remarx*; see 1 May 93.
[3] J. L'Estrange, *Platonia. A tale* (1893).
[4] Proposal for a guarantee for Siam; Rosebery replied that Germany was mentioned as second to Britain in trading with Siam; N.L.S. 10027, f. 45. An Anglo-French protocol established a neutral zone for Siam on 31 July; another, a buffer-state for the Upper Mekong; *PP* 1893–4 cix. 798.
[5] *Punch*, 16 September 1893, 126–7 published Tenniel's cartoon, 'Over the hills and far away', showing Gladstone in tartan trews dozing in the heather, watched by a stag; comic verses on Homer accompanied the cartoon.

To Sir W. V. HARCOURT, chancellor of the exchequer, MS Harcourt dep. 13, f. 151.
12 September 1893.

[Letter 1:] I thank you for your political letter:[1] & as to the Duke of Edinburgh I think that if he does not keep a *habitable* Clarence House that fact will go far to settle the question in favour of root & branch dealing. You hit my point hard about procedure by Joint Resolution: but I do not clearly gather from Herschell's letter whether my argument, such as it is, was before him. The opinion given by Marjoribanks is formidable.

I have written to the Speaker and made use of strong terms. The complaint you name admits of very various forms: let us hope for the best.

I am weighing in the scales a request from Midlothian to speak there. It is a nuisance but there is something to be said for it.

We have here fine days and coldish nights. A good oat harvest, mostly got in.

[Letter 2:] MS Harcourt dep. 13, f. 153.

I have received this morning the news of the vacancy in the Office of Woods, & your letter putting forward your eldest son:[2] and I do not lose a moment in writing to convey my free acknowledgement that the request you make conditionally on his behalf is one which you have a good title to propose, and which it will be to me a pleasure as well as a duty to consider.

I did not like to leave you for a post without a reply and you will understand that a real answer would not be appropriate to the moment of first announcement and its lack of full information.[3]

13. Wed.

Wrote to Mr Marjoribanks l. & tel.—Mr J. Miller—Mr Cowan—Rev. Mr Matheson—Canon M'Coll—& minutes. Drive. Walk with Mr A. Backgammon in evg. Worked on the Odes. Read N.C. on St George Mivart.[4] Conversation with Acton.

14. Th.

Wrote to Mr Marj.—Sir W. Harcourt l.l.—Ld Provost of Edinburgh—Gen. Ponsonby—Mr Stuart—Hon. Mr Rothschild—Sir G. Trevelyan—and minutes. Drive to Erickwood. Conversation with Mr Grinwood(?) Backgammon in evg. Began Dodo.[5] Worked on Odes.

To Sir W. V. HARCOURT, chancellor of the exchequer, MS Harcourt dep. 13, f. 160.
14 September 1893. '*No 1 Secret*'

[Letter 1:] I am not at all surprised at Lulu's answer respecting to the vacant office, and knowing the close & affectionate relations between you it did not seem to me that your letter respecting him was inopportune.[6]

[1] Not found.
[2] Of 11 September; Add MS 44203, f. 96.
[3] Harcourt replied (undated) that Loulou wrote 'absolutely declining any post which would remove him from my side'; he asked Gladstone to not tell Loulou that it was he (Harcourt) who had suggested the appt.; ibid., f. 100; copy dated 13 September in MS Harcourt dep. 13, f. 157.
[4] *N.C.*, xxxiv. 489 (September 1893).
[5] E. F. Benson, *Dodo, a detail*, 2v. (1893).
[6] See 13 Sept. 93n.

I sincerely trust that his services may not go unrewarded nor his capacity and, which are so remarkable, unemployed. I think he is in every way too good to run the risk of being neglected.

If there was reserve in my reply it did not arise from any doubt as to him but 1. because it was right to know who was in the field, 2. because it has always been my rule to give time for an inquiry upon such occasions whether the office need be filled up at all.

I write to you on other matters but will in this note express my regret that you should have been subjected to such very hard work from which I fear that the good long sleep could only afford partial relief. I write with some compunction, feeling that I am in part at least the cause. Nor can I wonder that the pressure should awaken thoughts about the future & a longing for liberty which I feel sure in the public interest that you will not prematurely indulge.

[P.S.] Rely on my silence.

[Letter 2:]   MS Harcourt dep. 13, f. 162.

Many thanks for your full communications:[1] & let me congratulate you on the improving prospects of business.

With reference to the Queen's confident expression about our followers *if* only you and I are what she calls 'firm', I have written a full letter to Ponsonby and have, in a manner the most oblique and delicate, insinuated that she might as well moderate her expectations from a party with whom she has publicly advertised her disgust at having anything to do. (These are not the exact terms.)

Tomorrow I hope to hear from Edinburgh and perhaps be in a condition to fix my movements next week. I am sensible of two lode-stones drawing me to London 1. a possible Chamberlain onslaught in connection with the Appropriation Bill. 2. The Duke of Edinburgh Cabinet *if* one be needed to determine between reduction and extinction.

I do not quite see how you are on any supposition to get over Indian Budget and Appropriation Bill + onslaught next week—Could Chamberlain stoop to make his answer on a Saturday.

The Speaker reports material relief and seems inclined to act with promptitude should the need return.

15. Fr.

Wrote to Ld Rosebery

Mr Miller		Mr Morley
Murray	tel.	Sir H. Jenkins
Marj.		Sir W. Harcourt

.... and minutes. Worked on Odes. Picnic. Walk with Acton. Backgammon in evg. Read Dodo. Much change in my reading power since I read Esmond.

To H. H. ASQUITH, home secretary, 15 September 1893.   Add MS 44549, f. 128.

Once when Palmerston had been put out I commended in speaking to Graham his conduct in opposition as being moderate, when Graham replied to me 'His bones are sore'. My bones are still sore since the Queen laid me on my back for my birthday list of Knights, and made me cut out a fair percentage.[2]

[1] Of 13 September, Add MS 44203, f. 102.
[2] See 22 May 93 f.

I think however, with you that the case is good.[1] But I should wish to reserve it for 3 or perhaps 4 weeks, when there would I think be still time for accomplishing the business before the expiry of this year.

To Sir W. V. HARCOURT, chancellor of the exchequer,   MS Harcourt dep. 13, f. 164.
15 September 1893.
1. Has the statement about Clarence House furniture been verified?[2]
2. If it turns out that the annuity must drop, could we let it remain until the close of the financial year, on the score of the expences of winding up and so forth?
3. I write to Rosebery to find whether & when he will be available after Balmoral where he is to be on 22d.
4. The Dundee paper of today has an interesting & rather favourable account of Portal's proceedings in Uganda. I am not sure whether the case has yet reached such a ripeness as to be fit for Cabinet. I do not think R. is in a hurry.
5. Following the visit of E. M[arjoribanks] I have telegraphed to Edinburgh offering 25th, or 26th (Monday or Tuesday week) for our meeting there.
6. It seems to me that the rapidly approaching close does much credit to your Generalship.

To Sir H. JENKYNS, parliamentary draftsman, 15 September 1893. Add MS 44549, f. 128.
I cannot let the House adjourn without congratulating you on your great share in the labours of the Session.
The change from the old fashioned drafting to the new which has taken place in my time, reminds me of the contemporaneous change in the work of another very important body of men (do not be angry), the dentists. They used simply to crash and smash. Now they wonderfully spare the patient. So you have minimised the pain of getting Bills ready for Parliament, which in my earlier years was most grave.
We had a good opportunity of appreciating our drafted Bill, through the bungling and absurd language of a very large part of the amendments which put themselves into impudent comparison with it.
I only hope your health has not suffered through the long and weary work, while I feel sure that in all other respects even you must be a gainer.[3]

To J. MORLEY, Irish secretary, 15 September 1893.   Add MS 44549, f. 128.
I feel sure you will approve the enclosed note to Sir H. Jenkyns but I do not like to forward it without reference to you, who are by far the first authority on the subject.
I wish you could have come here and you would have found your independence immensely respected by our 'most kindest' host, but I am bound also to respect your monastic leanings.
Almost cut off from reading I have found some employment for my stolen leisure in trying to translate some of the Odes of Horace. This first began at Biarritz. How difficult! But I have the impression that all wrestling with difficulties of language are very useful strains.

[1] Asquith wrote, 14 September, Add MS 44517, f. 246, that Mundella and Herbert [Gladstone] wanted 'knighthoods for their respective Mayors—Sheffield & Leeds'.
[2] No reply found.
[3] Letter of thanks from Jenkyns, 23 September, Add MS 44517, f. 250: 'The improvement in the style of drafting is due to my old chief, Lord Thring; the only credit I can claim is that of following his teaching.'

Acton is here in all his force. I don't think they know at Balmoral or probably the Queen would have hooked him. It is only 40 odd miles.

I cannot but hope that the H.R. Bill of next year will cost its authors very little trouble in correcting the draft.

To LORD ROSEBERY, foreign secretary, 15 September 1893.   N.L.S. 10027, f. 48.

You are I suppose to fulfil the command to Balmoral on the 22d. After that when & where shall you be available? I have been reading an interesting account of Portals report in the Dundee Advertiser. He seems to have done well as far as I can gather, and there is much semblance of a native government in Uganda: Am I right in inferring from what you said of it that you do not think any practical question is yet raised for the Cabinet?[1]

You will have heard, or will hear, sufficiently about the Duke of Edinburghs annuity. I suppose we shall know after hearing what Condy Stephens has to say, whether there will be a question for the Cabinet.[2]

(Lady's P.S.)

Why not take this way to Balmoral and give Mr A. the kindest host in all the world the pleasure of having you? I think you would take 8 PM *admirable* train ⟨from⟩ to Perth and be brought up here for *breakfast, beautiful* drive of 9 miles from Blairgowrie

From here it is a saving of near 120 miles rail, mostly rather flat, and a debit of 30 odd miles posting to Braemar (= Ballater for my equation) with no sort of difficulty over (I believe) the highest pass in Scotland.

16. Sat.

Wrote to Sir H. Ponsonby L. & tel—Sir W. Harcourt l.l.—and minutes. Drive. Backgammon in evg. Worked on Horace's Odes. Read Dodo: a book on which I think that there is much to say and of very mixed character.

To Sir W. V. HARCOURT, chancellor of the exchequer,   MS Harcourt dep. 13, f. 171.
16 September 1893.

I acccept with much content the dissipation of misgivings about a row on the Appropriation Bill. The immediate question now is Condy Stephens who the Queen proposes that I should see. I have telegraphed to propose that he come here on Monday and am awaiting answer.

Meantime Ponsonby writes to me

'He is not fully informed but has explained some of the items'

I gather from this that he has not brought us the information we really want as to the available Coburg income and if so it is useless to think of a formal Cabinet? I ⟨should⟩ shall ⟨be gla⟩ write fully on seeing C. Stephens if he come.

I look for an answer from you about the Clarence House furniture.

He has no rag of a case for any annuity, even under my speech of 1873, unless there is to be permanent expence in England such as would be deemed to be of a reasonable character. ⟨This after all is my speech of 1873⟩

---

[1] Rosebery replied, 17 September, Add MS 44290, f. 181, unable to come to Blackcraig; he would not look at Portal's report until Portal's return to Britain.

[3] Alexander Condie Stephen, secretary of the British legation at Coburg, dealing with the highly contentious matter of the financial settlement to be made for the duke of Edinburgh on his accession to the Saxe-Coburg dukedom.

What he will want is not a mere reimbursement of cash out of pocket here but an available English income *into* pocket.

If the worst comes to the worst for him I incline to think he might have it till the end of the financial year without any resort to Parliament.

Certainly the idea of wasting time under a prolonged opposition is intolerable.[1]

17.

Wrote to Mr Marj.—Mr Cowan—Mr Miller—and minutes. S. gave us the morning prayers, a large family party. Mr A. read what seemed to me a weak Essay Sermon of Bp Westcotts. Worked on A. & M. Hymns. Read Miss Trevelyan[2]—Life of Smith.

18. M.

Wrote to Earl of Mar—Ld Rosebery l. & tel.—and minutes. Mr C. Stephen arrived. Long conversation on the very bad affair of the Duke of Edinburgh's succession. Worked on Hor. Odes. Read Dodo. Drove to Rattray: a lovely place.[3] Backgammon in evg. Began long l. to Harcourt. Saw Mr Shand[4] during all this time.

To LORD ROSEBERY, foreign secretary, 18 September 1893.   N.L.S. 10027, f. 50.

Waiting for an answer, and hoping for a benign answer, to that very attractive Postscript, which I appended to my last letter, I receive today your proposed Draft to Dufferin.

I am really glad you are able to keep your temper in dealing with such propositions as some of those which you inclose.

There are however two impressions in the draft which, while I absolutely agree what is obviously their meaning, seem to me a little entangling.

1. (half way down p. 2)
"on a measure responsible to Siam for"
I am a little afraid of the particular epithet. My alarm would be obviated were you to say any thing like
"bound, by what they think their duty to Siam, to promote to the best of their ability."
2. three quarters down.
"must meet with decided opposition on their part."

It seems to me as if "decided opposition" rather postulated a description of *locus standi* more full and absolute than we possess: more like that of a Parliamentary Opposition. Would not it do to say something of this sort
"are such as it would be unjust on our part to impute to France or to any friendly government"

which in conjunction with the sentence that follows would I think express your idea & reserve your freedom.

I have the less scruple in making these suggestions because I recognise and am in full

[1] Harcourt wrote, 4.30 p.m., this day, that last night he had met the tory whips and agreed a protocol settling final arrangements for the Appropriation Bill; MS Harcourt dep. 13, f. 167.
[2] M. Durand, *Helen Trevelyan; or, the ruling race* (1893).
[3] Jute-spinning town by Blairgowrie.
[4] One of his secretaries; see 23 Dec. 92.

sympathy with the way, excellent as it seems to me, in which you have taken up your position on this Siamese business.

The proceedings of the French, conceived in a spirit of aggressive shabbiness, have given me extreme pain: for I retain from my youth a feeling for the old idea of French alliance, within due limits, which was so cherished by the Grey Government, & that of Peel.

P.S.

3. I am tempted also to suggest a substitution in the closing sentence for the words "we find" Could say (in effect) that if any thing be done which may be construed as showing, & so on.

19. Tu.

Wrote to Mr Coats[1]—Sir W. Harcourt l.l.—Marga [sic] Tennant—Mr Murray—Mr Marj. tel.—and minutes. Further conversation with Mr Condy Stephen: a most painful business.

To C. H. COATS, 19 September 1893.   Add MS 44549, f. 130.

I heartily desire the election of Mr. Asquith to the Lord Rectorship of Glasgow University,[2] & this desire I could not for a moment permit myself to indulge unless I were thoroughly assured from my knowledge of him that he would do honour to the office as well as receive honour from being appointed to it. Beyond this you will excuse my going, for detailed enumeration of qualities as between colleague & colleague are not usual & might not as a rule be efficacious.

To Sir W. V. HARCOURT, chancellor of the exchequer, MS Harcourt dep. 13, ff. 173–9. 19 September 1893.

[Letter 1:] I have seen Condy Stephen this evening & had a conversation with him extremely long and still more unsatisfactory than long. As to the English "liabilities" they are not to be considered as a claim in form, since they were sent for the Queen's information. But there they are. They form a very small part of the case which I think is all black without a redeeming point.

The late Duke appears to have been simply an old rogue and fool. This is a truly shameful & a ruinous Chapter in the case. The present Duke, as I have told Mr C.S., had two admirable opportunities: as Bachelor, chiefly on board ship, with no house, and 15m per ann.; afterwards as married man, with joint income near 60m. He ought with decent prudence to have been a rich man. Instead of that what he has to show is a debt of over 70m (40 of it to his wife).

The account of Coburg income is 15m + x + y, x being half the surplus produced by the public domains after paying costs and his 15m, y being the income of his private domains. No account or estimate of either is forthcoming, while it is quite plain that he has one.

So the information is fatally defective at this point and it is quite plain that nothing can at present be done by the Cabinet as we have not before us the fact which is vital for giving us a view.

He proceeded to state to me the case of the Duke as to liabilities and charges but I told him I did not ask for these. What we wanted was to have before us the Duke's Coburg

---

[1] Of Glasgow university; see this day's letter.

[2] Asquith was defeated by 916:695 votes for the Glasgow Rectorship by Sir J. Gorst. The Coats family of Paisley were Asquithian supporters. Gladstone had declined to stand; see 31 Dec. 92.

income, and I at least was not to be understood as making inquiries in respect to expenditure.

1. The old scamp has left liabilities amounting to 115m which can as I understand only be repudiated, or rather declined, with risk of scandal. On the other hand it seemed open to question whether the assets might not be made to cover this.
2. But he has left in his will a jointure of some 3 or 4m to his wife with no funds whatever to supply it.
3. There are about *twelve* castles (with the domains) several of them in Austria the charge of maintaining which approaches 6m annually.
4. The subventions to the Theatres comes to about the same sum.
5. The Court Officials though low paid are numerous and cannot be retrenched.
6. He gives 1m per ann. to his married daughters (and the Duchess gives another, at least).
7. He has got to pay 3 to 4m for succession duty in Austria.

The sweating down of receipt approaches the sublime,—and the result is that the Coburg revenues *nett*, on which he is to live, amount according to his estimate to 4m annually.

There is a prospective economy in letting or selling castles and shootings, but one which it requires time to bring about.

This Coburg information was allowed to be given under a kind of protest to Mr Condy Stephen by the Private Secretary. It is in a condition to go to the Cabinet, if indeed it be desirable ever to take it there. You will observe that I have made no admission of its relevancy: and I told Mr C.S. that I thought it very likely you would question him *in limine*.

It is important in two points of view at least.

In the first place it illustrates the *meaning* of the Duke's demand. It comes to this: I want the British taxes to supply me with a Coburg livelihood. But when in 1873 I went to the extreme (perhaps) in the sense of royalism, I indicated the likelihood of the Duke's retaining British expenditure, due to partial British residence, and not fairly to be charged upon the people of Coburg.

Of this I heard nothing, and no provision for it, was mentioned. Mr C.S. seems to know nothing as to Clarence House and there was no indication of its being retained.

Secondly. If the facts are truly stated, there is a very awkward situation for the Duke and the question suggests itself whether there is any difficulty to be apprehended in the way of scandal. Of course there is *her* income to ward this off. But I understand from him that this income is not in common stock and the Duke has no power over it.

It is plain that the Duke's difficulties form no reason why the people of England should be taxed, or should remain unrelieved from tax, in order to meet them. If any thing can be done from any other source, well and good: but how?

The inquiry suggested by all this was put by me to Mr Stephen: Had not the Duke before the actual demise, sufficient time and means for ascertaining in substance the financial situation? It is admitted that he had: so next I asked, how came it then that without hesitation or inquiry he accepted the succession. The answer was, there was no time to deliberate or correspond: he had to take the oath the next morning. But this is no answer, for there was plenty of time to feel his ground before the death of the old scamp. And to the answer was appended this explanation: he knew that his Annuity Act said the Queen *may*, he chose to interpret this as meaning that it was a matter for her choice, and he assumed that she would choose in his favour.

The Queen writes to me in terms not I think agreeing with Ponsonby's impressions & report. She is shocked at the idea of cancelling the annuity: and asks me whether it would not be the simplest! way

1. To continue the 25m for a year or two
2. To reduce it after that time to 15m.

There is nothing I think to prevent your making this known to the Chancellor or any colleague with whom you may individually consult. I will show the copy to Rosebery who will come here on Friday for a few hours on his way to Balmoral.

Mr C. Stephen set up two arguments in favour of a liberal course
1. What an anomaly, if the Duchess has a certain 6m in the event of widowhood and he, our British Prince, nothing at all, though he live to ninety.
(I answered "it is not in the bond")
2. The high policy of giving him now a fair start when one may reasonably expect him to hold it, whereas if he is driven to extremities there is no saying what would happen.

I doubt whether these arguments will deeply touch the flinty heart of a Minister of Finance; they do not much impress my own very tender fibre.

[Letter 2:] No 2 'Secret'   Mr Condy Stephen has been with me again this morning and in various respects has from written data modified the figures he gave me last night. In each of the cases (see over) the corrected statement worsens that first given.

He also adds a new item of Pensions to the bad: but on the other hand it appears that before reaching the final 4m stable expenditure had (erroneously I conceive) been put down among the inevitable charges which were beyond his own will.

On the whole he seems to show that he did not speak in a spirit of wilful exaggeration.

He says the Duke is in great depression on this business, and no wonder.

He had been taking for granted that there could be no difficulty in getting the 25m continued. I told him this was impossible.

It seems that the Residences of one kind or another are somewhere about fifteen in number—

A blessed business.

Theatres - - -	£6500
Duchess Dowr. - - -	3750
Palaces maintenance	£8750
Austrian Succession Duty	£7500
also Pensions	3000.

20. Wed

Wrote to Ld Kimberley—The Queen l.l.—Ld Rosebery tel. l.l.—Sir H. Ponsonby —Mr Marj.—Circular to MP.s—and minutes. Showed Acton the very private letters,[1] & conversation. Finished Dodo: a strange mixture. Drive & walk. Backgammon. Read Petersons Tac. de Oratoribus.[2] Saw Mr Shand as usual.

To LORD KIMBERLEY, lord president and Indian secretary,   Add MS 44549, f. 131.
20 September 1893.

The cypher of last night and the letter this morning have taken my breath away.[3] The first sense of necessity which comes upon me is the necessity for a little time to reflect.

[1] Presumably on the negotiation with the Court on the duke of Edinburgh's settlement.
[2] W. Peterson, *Dialogus de Oratoribus* (1893).
[3] Kimberley's letter of 19 September, Add MS 44229, f. 156: Norman's ill-health forced withdrawal of acceptance as Viceroy (see 26 July 93n.); Kimberley suggested 'We might ask Lansdowne to stay another year. . . . If not, I am at a loss for a suggestion. We want a strong man. There are signs of disturbance in India which cause me much anxiety. . . . In these circumstances I cannot help thinking of Spencer. . . .'

I am not surprised that you should be a little at fault for the moment. As Rosebery comes here the day after tomorrow for a few hours I look to conversing a little with him particularly after what you say.

For the proposal to ask Lansdowne to stay on for a year does not greatly smile to me; not only because it is a despairing confession of weakness, but because I do not see in him any such union of force & judgment as would make him specially valuable for various contingencies. I suppose that you may now after Norman's jibbing be compelled by mere time to ask L. to remain for one or two months.

Disagreeable as have been the incidents of the recent disturbances, and aware as I am that you have a nearer & surer view of the subject than I can, I am disinclined at once to entertain the idea of their having any serious aim at British power. Is there not a natural and deep seated antagonism between Mussalman and Hindoo, and is not this rooted in and greatly accounted for by the circumstances of their history? If so are not the disturbances, or may they not be, a mode of venting those sentiments such as in itself is not altogether strange, without the assumption of an ulterior purpose? This however is on the surface, and I wait to hear what is underneath, what evidences are given in support of the apprehensions expressed.

The revival of communication with Spencer, it seems to me at the moment, rather presupposes that the elements of a serious crisis had been proved to exist, & would have a basis quite different from that of proposing another year to the present Viceroy.

It will I think be necessary to go over again the names which have been passed by, or any other names which may be suggested.

I conveyed to you this forenoon a suggestion by cypher telegram which was due entirely to the idea of an approaching dispersion which would tend to limit your available means of consideration, as to this embarrassing and grave matter.

I quite understand the impossibility of pressing Norman. I am not sure whether we ascertained the age of Sir H. Robinson;[1] but I rather think his name was put aside on the ground of time of life.

21. Th.

Wrote to Mr Hargrove—Sir W. Harcourt—Mr Bryce—and minutes. Worked long on Odes. Wrote on the Translator's office.[2] Backgammon with Mr A. Drive. Read De Oratoribus.

To J. BRYCE, 21 September 1893.   MS Bryce 10, f. 141.

I think that the plan of Professor Ramsay[3] is clearly a matter that ought to go to the Chancellor of the Exchequer and that I ought to leave it to him without giving an opinion. He would consult me if he thought fit.

A small sum for a temporary purpose, or to help a subscription, might be given by me from Royal Bounty; but this is a difficult affair.

As far as authority is concerned, I estimate that of Professor Ramsay very highly.

[1] See to Kimberley, 23 Sept. 93n.
[2] Not found.
[3] See Bryce's letter of 20 September, MS Bryce 10, f. 147, on W. M. Ramsay's explorations in Asia Minor and his need for £300 p.a. for 12 years from the Exchequer to fund exploration and publication.

To Sir W. V. HARCOURT, chancellor of the exchequer,   MS Harcourt dep. 13, f. 189.
21 September 1893.

Your letter of yesterday presents the duke of Edinburgh's case in miniature and is so far very acceptable.[1]

I quite agree that Coburg embarrassments constitute no claim upon Britain.

I cannot however help feeling greatly distressed somewhat for him, more for the Queen and others of the Family, with respect to difficulties, which, if they are represented with any sort of truth to us, may issue in something like scandal.

At present she is on her high horse and she will not like dismounting.

I agree with you that among the socalled English claims we cannot recognise the debts: as to the insurance I gathered from Stephen that it was for his children but they can scarcely be regarded as a British brood under the circumstances of his resignation, and in any case it was his duty to provide for them out of his income.

I agree with you also as to the pensions & claims for old servants: but would it not be best *if we can* to get these capitalised and disposed of possibly without an Act, the prospects of which you contemplate with more equanimity than I do.

As to his residing here I probed his Envoy and he told me [he] had heard nothing of any such anticipation. I think the meaning is that he doubts whether any allowance would be made for it which would yield a nett profit. Was it a *canard* about the furniture? N.B. I agree about Spencer.[2]

22. Fr.

Wrote minutes. Drive by Glenfalloch. Backgammon in evg. Rosebery's visit was cut down to 2¼ hours, but they sufficed for adequate conversation on Duke of E. also Viceroyalty—Siam—Egypt—*et alia*. My questions drew out important information upon Egypt, which I think would not otherwise have been noticed. Finished De Oratoribus. Began Soul of the Bishop.[3]

23. Sat.

Wrote to Mr Murray—Ld Kimberley—Mr Mellor—Mr Morton MP—Mr Hitchcock[4]—& minutes. Ld Acton went. He has looked a little at my Horatian work. His visit a daily treat: much today. I told him it seemed likely that eyesight would solve for me the problem of which at present I see no other solution. Read Soul of the Bishop. Worked on Horace's Odes. Received West's reports from London. Backgammon with Mr A.

To LORD KIMBERLEY, lord president and Indian secretary,   Add MS 44549, f. 132.
23 September 1893.

West brings me the last report on the unfortunate affair of the Indian Viceroyalty. But Rosebery had traversed[?] it with an idea which perhaps might not be unacceptable. It is that Elgin might retract. He has something though not much to go upon,—and, with special care to avoid committal he will find out as he expects when passing through Edinburgh southwards next week.

[1] Copy in MS Harcourt dep. 13, f. 182 reporting a talk with Condy Stephen.
[2] A short note of 20 September, Add MS 44203, f. 114, discouraged sending Spencer to India.
[3] J. W. Winter, *Soul of the bishop*, 2v. (1893–5).
[4] Thanking him for a medal; Add MS 44549, f. 133.

With regards to others.[1] I cannot wonder that the name of Marjoribanks should recur, but I feel more strongly the objection to a removal straight.

With regard to Carrington I have no positive knowledge which would warrant me in affirming his claim even to a small extent; and a good judge speaking to me said 'He does not carry guns enough'—I think however he was put aside on the ground of some indiscreet speech; and I should like our having this before us in order to know the exact scope of the offence, in case we have to consider the names again.

West tells me on the other hand that Acland makes a most warm report of his conduct in the Welsh Commn., which gives something of the kind of testimony in his favour which so much accredits Elgin.

I should think it quite worth while to await the issue of Rosebery's design.

[P.S.] When I saw in the papers that Caine was to disappear from the Opium Commn., I treated it as a Canard, but to my bewilderment and regret West tells me it is true.[2]

24. 17 S. Trin.

Mg prayers at home. Drove to Aylth 13 m. No service! But saw Lady Abn. Wrote to Abp of Canterbury—Ld Kimberley—Mr Murray tel. Read Suffield's[3] life: with extreme difficulty—The soul of the Bishop—a *most* inadequate book.

25. M.

Wrote Mr Peterson—Mr Murray tel.—Mr . . . . .—& minutes. Worked much on Odes. I find that I have done 5 to 6 lines an hour while here.

Read Suffield   ⎫
Trevelyan's Works ⎬ little
Drive: walk: backgammon with Mr A.

To F. GOITA, 25 September 1893.   Add MS 44549, f. 133.

I have always regarded with great interest the peculiar position of the Basques with regard to local self-government & that interest has been enhanced of late years by opportunities of receiving some instruction on the subject from the Rev. Mr. Webster now resident at Sare on the Spanish border, who is I believe regarded as one of the highest living authorities on questions concerning the Basques.

I therefore watch with sympathy whatever tends, by giving clearness & additional promise of efficiency & prominence to Basque privileges, also to strengthen the ties which associate them with the rest of Spain.

But I would not presume to address a Spanish Statesman in the sense of offering advice with regard to such a matter. It would be an excess on my part appearing to involve an assumption of competency to which I can make no pretension: and it might be more likely to impede than to advance the cause of Basque people.

[1] Kimberley, 21 September, Add MS 44229, f. 159, reported a talk with J. Morley, discussing Spencer, Houghton, Carrington, Sir Edward Grey ('very young, but his reputation as far as he has gone is excellent'), Marjoribanks, who 'would, as we know, greatly like to go'; his postscript added: 'I forgot to mention Elgin. Rosebery thinks he would go, if pressed. . . . Robinson is too old.'
[2] See 3 Aug. 93n.
[3] M. O. Suffield, *The life of Robert Rodolph Suffield* (1893), the Unitarian with whom Gladstone had had considerable correspondence.

26. Tu.

Wrote to Mr Russell MP.—Princess of Wales—Ld Kimberley—Mrs Bolton—Sir W. Harcourt—Mr Morley—Mr Murray—and minutes. Saw Sir A.W.—Mr A. Cox—Webster boy—H.J.G. (on do. and on Featherstone).[1] Drive. Backgammon with Mr A. Read a little of Miss Trevelyan. Worked on Odes. Tumbled my ideas a little more into order for tomorrow.

27. Wed. [Edinburgh]

Was persuaded by Harry to give £8 to the servants wh I think extravagant. He also gives. Saw Sir A. West. Packed books &c. Worked my subject into order & made rather copious notes which however I found myself rarely able to see the purport of. 12¾-4¼ Journey to Edinburgh. Saw divers friends (Margot [Tennant] included) before & after the meeting. A crowded mass of 1000 in what was the Albert Hall [in Queensferry Lane]. Spoke 1 h. 37 m (so says H.N.G.)[2] Reception excellent: all so kind. Dined & slept at Royal Hotel. Backgammon with Mr A. Unwell in the night, probably from over exertion.

28. Th. [Hawarden]

Wrote to Ld Kimberley—Mr Lewis MP—Mr Budge—and minutes. Saw Mr Conran—Mr Stuttell Miller. 10-4. Rapid & easy journey to Sandycroft. Worked on the Odes. Found all well. Dossy[3] in the utmost force. Began the great work which I call 'Chaos to Kosmos'. I made a confidence to Mr Cowan my Chairman about the condition of my eyes.

29. Fr.

Rose at eleven. Wrote to J. Morley l.l.—Sir W. Harcourt—S.L.—Mr Fowler—The Queen—Ld Spencer—& minutes. Worked on Odes. Family conversations on the state of my sight: I seem to be drowned in kindness on all hands. Made a trial of the good type of my old 8vo Waverley Novels. But with labour & some minutes to each page. Happily my writing work is *much* less affected. Wrote on Horatian Translation which I find almost as fascinating as it is difficult.

To Sir W. V. HARCOURT, chancellor of the exchequer,   MS Harcourt dep. 13, f. 194.
29 September 1893.

1. I never like sending out of my own controul Queen's letters or correspondence. But I rather believe myself to be in the van of objections. Both Acton (a cool head) and my wife insisted on my softening a little what I wrote. I have in black & white told her the 25m is out of the question: have found grave fault with the Duke for his folly and mismanagement: and have been thanked by her in return for my "frankness".

I don't believe he wants to or will keep up Coburg [*sc* Clarence] House, unless he can

---

[1] Use of troops to disperse a crowd at Featherstone colliery, near Wakefield, on 3 September; two men in the crowd were shot by the troops: an important incident in labour history and in Asquith's career. See 7 Oct., 14 Dec. 93.

[2] *T.T.*, 28 September 1893, 4a.

[3] His grand-daughter, Dorothy Drew.

make money from doing it. And I should like to avoid Parliament altogether, for I fear he will be severely and justly censured there.

At the same time I think he is in a fearfully tight place and as an old decrepit servant of the Crown I heartily wish he could be a little relieved by some means not inconsistent with the rights of Parlt. & the people.

I am afraid poor Ponsonby has had a time of it.

2. I write to recommend Stafford Howard.[1]

3. Viceroyalty still unsettled. Rosebery is to pump Elgin anew. Carrington's head just pops above the horizon.

I contemplate with awe the secrecy in which you have shrouded yourself.

To J. MORLEY, Irish secretary, 29 September 1893. '*Private.*'   Add MS 44549, f. 135.

I write separately on Ridgway: and will only add, depend upon my diligence and zeal.

It was a pleasure to me to leave the Liberals of Midlothian in much glee & satisfaction. They said if there were an election now you need not show; the exertion, however, with the air was rather too much: & for a day or two I am a semi-invalid: my general strength thank God is not only good but beyond its ordinary standard. On the other hand the gates of sense of closing in [*sic*].[2] Reading is drawing near its close—writing much more easy & less trying. Hence I have been drawn for all spare hours into the business of the odes. But you will be shocked to hear that, writing as hard as I can, I do not nett more than five to six lines an hour. Nevertheless they take hold upon me, & I know not what they may lead me to. In Scotland I managed to do twelve.

They have also led me to consider much the principles of translation, in which I think the Revisers of the New Testament ought to have undergone a preliminary course of training before they undertook their ill conceived work.

I suppose there is no chance of your coming over at present, but if you come pray remember we are here for the month without any intention to budge.

[P.S.] The pleasure of the Scotch visit was much enhanced by Acton's presence during more than half of it.

30. Sat.

Wrote to Ld Kimberley—S.L.—Sir J. Lacaita—Ld Rosebery l.l.—and minutes. Worked hard upon Books &c. Chaos to Kosmos. Little upon Odes. Saw Mr Toller—Rev. Mr Williams—Rev. Mr Temple. Some small bits of reading.

Oct 1. 1893. 18 S. Trin.

Ch mg with H.C. & evg. Mr Temple preached & came to luncheon & dinner. He has much to say. Wrote to S. Lyttelton—Sir A. West—Lady Stepney—& minutes. Read Bp Harvey on O.T.[3]—Ward, Catholic Revival.[4]

[1] To the Office of Woods.
[2] Probably a mistranscription or omission by the copyist.
[3] A. C. Harvey, *The Book of Chronicles in relation to the Pentateuch* (1892).
[4] W. P. Ward, *William George Ward and the Catholic revival* (1893).

2. M.

Wrote to Rev. S.E.G.—Mr Armitstead—Lady Stepney—& minutes. Ch. 8½ A.M. resumed. Worked on books & papers. Worked hard on Odes with little progress. Read Bp Hervey—Tracts—Freda.[1]

3. Tu.

Ch. 8½ A.M. Wrote to Ld Kimberley—Ld Rosebery—Mr Morley—Ld Elgin—The Queen—Mr Illingworth M.P.—and minutes. Saw Mr Temple. Worked on Book & papers. Worked on Odes. Read Walker's Odes[2]—Sibley on the Lords[3]—Freda. Nine to dinner.

To LORD ELGIN, 3 October 1893.   Add MS 44549, f. 137.

I am happy to learn from Rosebery that you are now prepared to accept the Vice-royalty of India: with a diffidence highly honourable, but one in no way shared by those who know you best.

Accept my hearty congratulations & good wishes.

I shall at once write to the Queen & presume that her former sanction stands.

I trust it may be possible for you to make family arrangements in a satisfactory manner.

4. Wed.

Ch 8½ AM. Wrote to Sir H. Ponsonby—Lord Kimberley—J. Westell—Mr Channing MP.—Mr Fowler MP—& minutes. Saw Roberts on his Farm & the striking result of his experiments on grasses. They ought to be of much importance. Worked on examining & arranging. S.L. who came yesterday now sees me in the forenoon for the dispatch of correspondence. Read Freda—Andrew on Inoculation[4]—Bp of Bangor Charge 1720.[5]

5. Th.

Ch. 8½ AM. Wrote to Mr Blundell—Dowager Ly Ashburnham—Mr Allan—Murrays—and minutes. Saw S.L.—Rev. Mr Wakeford (luncheon)—Lady Grosvenor & her party (walk & tea). Worked on the Odes. Read Freda & scraps.

6. Fr.

Ch. 8½ A.M. Wrote to Ld Rosebery—Mr A. Benson—and minutes. Worked at St Deiniol's with Helen. (In the scarcity of coal, Miss Hughes has had her little store stolen!) Worked on the Odes. Saw S.L. Our family party shifts continually. Read Freda—Admirers on Browning.[6]

[1] [E. A. Hart], *Freda. A novel. By the author of Mrs Jerningham's Journal*, 3v. (1878).
[2] J. Walker, *The academic speaker; or, a selection of parliamentary debates, odes, scenes, and speeches* (1797).
[3] Untraced; perhaps an article.
[4] J. Andrew, *The practice of inoculation impartially considered* (1765).
[5] B. Hoadley, 'An answer to Dr. Hare's sermon, intituled Church authority vindicated' (1720).
[6] Untraced.

7. Sat.

Ch 8½ A.M. Wrote to Dean Liddell—Abp of Canterbury—President of Magdalen—Mr Fowler—Mr Asquith—and minutes. Worked on Odes. Drive: tea with
Gerty. Read Freda.

To LORD RIPON, colonial secretary, 7 October 1893.   Add MS 43515, f. 112.

Thank you for your intimation about Swaziland, & I hope for a favourable course of
affairs in Mashonaland.

You are aware I doubt not that we hope Elgin has retracted his refusal: in case he
should ultimately slip through our fingers, the name of Carrington will come up for consideration, & *if* you are one of those who seemed to incline towards putting a negative on
him I rely on your letting Kimberley or me know.

This month brings to a crisis Morley's difficulty about Ridgway. He has no choice but
to go forward, & we greatly rely upon the joint & several charities of the three Secretaries
of State, to relieve him if possible.

In a list of Peers absent on Sept. 8 I observe a few R.C. names. I should be so glad if you
could confirm my hope that their absence was deliberate. We are thankful for small
mercies from that elevated region.

To H. H. ASQUITH, home secretary, 7 October 1893. '*Private.*'   Add MS 44549, f. 139.

I hear that the minds of some have been exercised by my saying at Edinburgh that the
question of Home Rule will be likely again to emerge next year; & that you are about to
speak & might wish to notice the subject.

I think with others of our colleagues that circumstances *point* to the reintroduction of
the Bill in the House of Lords at the beginning of the Session but that it would be premature to decide this, & improper to indicate it. My intention was to be absolutely general &
I gave hearers & readers credit for knowing & remembering that besides inquiry which is
now hardly in the case there are several modes of proceeding to touch a question, such as
address & Resolution, besides Bill. If however critical suspicion has been awakened it
might be sufficient to say that there are many modes of keeping a subject alive besides
that which was adopted last year & that any reports which may now be put into circulation must from the nature of the case be wholly destitute of foundation.[1]

I congratulate you on your selection of men, as excellent as it was difficult for your
Commission of Inquiry.[2]

8. 19 S. Trin.

Ch. mg & evg. Wrote to . . . . Read Ld A. Hervey on Books of O.T.—Ld Norton, High & Low[3]—Newman on St Paul[4]—Harden on Dogmatic Christianity:[5]
not less pretentious than poor.

---

[1] Asquith replied, 10 October, Add MS 44517, f. 267: 'I am greatly obliged by your letter of the
7th, which quite confirms the impression I had myself of the real meaning of the controverted
passage in your Edinburgh speech. I am glad that you approve of the way in which I have constituted my Commission.'
[2] i.e. the Featherstone inquiry.
[3] C. B. Adderley, Lord Norton, *High and low church* (1892).
[4] F. W. Newman, *James and Paul* (1869).
[5] W. D. Harden, *An inquiry into the truth of dogmatic Christianity* (1893).

9. M.

Ch. 8½ A.M. Wrote Tel. to Ld Elgin—Dr Furnival—Mr Lockwood[1]—Lady Stepney—Mr J.C. Smither—& minutes. Worked on Odes. Tea with the Potters: & agricultural conversation of much interest. Read Freda—Bygone England.[2] Much deliberation on the sad business of Zadok:[3] a stern alternative was set before him by Harry Drew. God help him against his enemy.

10. Tu.

Ch. 8½ A.M. Wrote to Ld Kimberley Tel l.l.—Sir H. Ponsonby l.l.—Ld Ripon—Sig. Ricci—J. Morley—The Queen—and minutes. Changed valet[4]—after what a course of years! Worked on Odes. Read Freda—Lytton on Horace.[5] Orphanage tea *sub Dio*.

To LORD RIPON, colonial secretary, 10 October 1893.   Add MS 43515, f. 114.

Your new war[6] as a war is a calamity but one which I am sure you will do all that can be done to confine within the narrowest limits.

There is another question as to the division of power responsibility & expence.

It happens that in my earliest political life, say about 1835-7 I went much into Cape matters, & took then, against the Antislavery party & (I think) Downing Street, the line of the Colonists, who strove to keep into their own hands the entire business of the frontier wars, whereas the policy adopted was to carry them on by British soldiery, at very heavy British charge, which charge the Colonists had a strong interest in augmenting for their own profit. And a new war came up periodically whenever a sufficient number of young Kafirs had grown up who had not suffered by & knew nothing of the old one.

I am sorry that Harcourt happens to be taking his holiday at the moment of this outbreak: but I hope that as when we once interfere as a Government the responsibility is sure to devolve upon us *in toto*, we shall not have the operations directed by the influence of those who will neither pay nor be called upon to justify. We could have no one better than you to guard against this danger.

I am glad to say that Elgin has today by telegram definitely accepted. Kimberley, very properly as I think, treated Norman's overture as inadmissible.

I am sure you will not forget Morley.

P.S. For reflection, would it be possible for Ashburnham? or for *Bute* whose spirit I always think seems good, or any other R.C. Peer who did not vote on Sept. 8 to bring in the Relieving Bill which the D. of Norfolk laid on the shelf? I could myself undertake writing to either of the two I have named *if you* thought it better for any reason.[7]

---

[1] (Sir) Frank Lockwood, 1846-97; lawyer and wit; liberal M.P. 1885-97; solicitor general 1894-5.
[2] W. Andrews, *Bygone England* (1892).
[3] His valet's alcoholism, which led to his death. He agreed to go to the Keeley Institute, Cromwell Road, London, from which he was released after 3 weeks (P. Gladstone, *Portrait of a family* (1989), 106).   [4] See previous day.
[5] E. G. E. L. Bulwer, Lord Lytton, *Horace, Odes and Epodes* (1893).
[6] Campaign, short and successful, against the Matabele. See 31 Aug. 93.
[7] Ripon replied, 12 October, Add MS 43515, f. 117, that he had nothing to add 'with regard to the unhappy war in S. Africa'; Loch 'has done his best to prevent the outbreak of hostilities'; the forces are mainly 'raised, paid, and supplied' by the Chartered Company; he had told Loch 'the Company must look for no financial assistance'; he had also written privately to Loch today to tell him that 'the policy of the Govt. is to keep the Military operations & their results within the narrowest limits he can'.

11. *Wed.*

Ch. 8½ A.M. Wrote to Ld Elgin Tel. & l.—Ld Kimberley Tel. & l.—Sir J. Mow-bray—Mr Godley—Mr Morley—& minutes. Worked well on Odes. Walk & conversation with Lucy C[avendish]. Also with the nice Wickham girls. Read Freda—Bygone England.

To T. P. O'CONNOR, M.P., 11 October 1893.   · Add MS 44549, f. 141.

The consequences of the Coal Contest[1] have become so grave, I might almost say so cruel, that I can never approach without a certain sympathy any proposal which aims at their removal by a settlement or even simply at their mitigation.

It appears to me however that it would not be expedient for the Government to do anything which could fairly be interpreted as taking sides in the dispute while if the question is one of eleemosynary aid, which would require careful restraint in its administration, I am not prepared to say whether this certainly important question does not rest more safely in the hands of the local public in the several neighbourhoods, than it could do in the hands of the Government whose intervention might be ascribed to all manner of second motives.[2]

12. *Th.*

Ch. 8½ A.M. Wrote to Mr O'Connor MP.—Mr Barry OBrien—Dr Sp. Watson—Rev. Mr Temple—& minutes. Worked on the Odes. Drive with C. Read Freda: finished—Barry OBrien's Introd. to Wolfe Tone's Life.[3] Saw S.L. as usual.

13. *Fr.*

Ch. 8½ A.M. Wrote to J. Morley—A. Godley—D. Pearson—Lord Ripon Tel.—and minutes. Worked on Odes. Read Bygone England—Life of Wolfe Tone—Divers books. Worked at St Deiniol's. Arrivals. *Zadok* deliberations. Worked on Odes. Read Wolfe Tone. Ten to dinner.

14. *Sat.*

Ch. 8½ A.M. Wrote to J. Morley l.l.—Ld Ripon—Mr Blake MP—Ld Bute—and minutes. Worked at St Deiniol's. Worked on Odes. Walk with Miss Wyndham & Mr [Robert] Eyton. Read Wolfe Tone—A Life awry.[4]

To E. BLAKE, M.P., 14 October 1893.   Add MS 44549, f. 143.

I thank you for your interesting communication,[5] and I congratulate you on the result of your labours[6] which it must have required much tact as well as ability to conduct to a successful issue.

It is painful to reflect on the nature of the opposing elements, that such elements

---

[1] General lock-out by the coal-owners began in July; in October Mundella began attempts at conciliation by the government; see H. A. Clegg, A. Fox and A. F. Thompson, *History of British Trade Unions since 1889*, i. 108 ff (1964). See 13 Nov. 93.

[2] No correspondence found.

[3] R. Barry O'Brien, ed., *The autobiography of T. Wolfe Tone* (1893).

[4] P. Pickering, *A life awry*, 3v. (1893).

[5] Not found.

[6] See 2 Sept. 93.

should be engendered from the obstinacy[1] of the controversy. It is like a festering in the natural body and the result is the production of foul matter, likely to propagate itself by contagion, unless wisdom prevail and bring us to a settlement.

To J. MORLEY, Irish secretary, 14 October 1893.   Add MS 44549, f. 143.

I send you a letter from Blake which you should see together with additional matter. I should think he has done well. It is the inveterate character of the Irish question, which causes it to breed such vermin as he has had to deal with. How sad that the opponents do not see that it is a case of Sibyl leaves[2] & that there is immense danger in prolonging the controversy. Disraeli saw this in the case of the Irish Church & carefully abstained from such a policy.

To LORD BUTE, 14 October 1893.   Add MS 44549, f. 142.

Allow me to introduce to your notice a subject which I hope may attract your favourable notice.

It was I think in 1891 that I introduced into the H. of Commons a Bill for removing the unwarrantable & now absurd provisions of our law which prevents Roman Catholics from holding the offices of Lord Chancellor of Great Britain & Viceroy of Ireland.[3]

The Bill it was hoped might receive the acquiescence of the Government who had made Matthews Home Secretary[4]—But they opposed it under strong Orange influence as we understood & it was thrown out.

It was idle to propose it anew in the H. of Commons & pressed as we now are with respect to time, we cannot deal with it there.

But I continue desirous to put it forward in the Lords, and felt that if we could get it proposed there by a Conservative Roman Catholic Peer it would pass easily & would probably then pass the Commons with small expenditure of time. Ripon accordingly applied to the Duke of Norfolk but he declined, why I do not know, although if I remember right he had at a meeting of his coreligionist Peers complained of the conduct of the Government in the matter.

I have communicated further with Ripon & we both desire to prevail upon you to undertake the introduction & conduct of the measure.

I need not argue on its merits. The case is not a very large but it is surely a very strong one: & I cannot believe that you would meet with opposition from any quarter in the H. of Peers.

We should of course be ready to concur in what might appear the best arrangement for the Commons.

Were the Bill in the hands of a friend of our own (and there is small choice of such) its prospects wd. be greatly darkened.

I rely on your courtesy & kindness to take into consideration the case I have laid before you.[5]

To LORD RIPON, colonial secretary, 14 October 1893.   Add MS 43515, f. 124.

1. I sorrowfully admit that your answer about South Australia is conclusive.
2. I have written to Bute about the Disabilities Bill.

[1] Illegible phrase omitted.
[2] In the case of the Cumaean Sibyl, the prophecies were inscribed on palm leaves.
[3] See 2 Feb. 91.
[4] Henry Matthews was a Roman Catholic.
[5] Bute wrote asking for a delay before a full reply (the latter not found); Add MS 44517, f. 279. See 26 Oct. 93.

3. Your account of the South African war[1] exhibits dangerous arrangements but I do not see what more you can do to encounter this contingency.

15. 21 S. Trin.

Parish Ch mg: Sandicroft Evg. Admirable sermon from Mr Eyton. Walk with him. Wrote to J. Morley—Mr Shand—Dr Fairbairn. Read Ld A. Hervey—Life of an Artisan[2]—Dr Fairbairn on Christ in Theology[3]—all with much difficulty.

To Rev. Dr. A. M. FAIRBAIRN, principal of Mansfield College, Add MS 44549, f. 143. Oxford, 15 October 1893.

Your comprehensive & very interesting Volume reached me yesterday. Pray let me offer my best thanks.

My power of reading is now much impaired from a variety of causes: but I have formed some idea of the character of your book by an initial perusal in several places.

The fine passage pp. 7 & 8 on the works of our Lord in the world, pleased me very particularly. And I found the picture of Evangelical & Anglican which follows very perspicacious, just & liberal.

Childhood & boyhood placed me in very close connection with the evangelicalism of those days, & very notable it was.

In one collateral point I think you give it more than it deserves. It had large religious philanthropy e.g. in missions. But little political philanthropy. The great case of Wilberforce was *almost* purely an individual case: nor was he more against slavery than Dr. Johnson.

Speaking generally—I am sorry to say—the Evangelicals of that day were not abolitionists. They left that honour to the nonconformists, most of all to the Quakers. Their Toryism obstructed them; as it does now.

Buxton I admit did a great work but was I think hardly a churchman. Wilberforce on the other hand was a warmly attached one, & of a beautiful & heavenly character.[4]

16. M.

Ch 8½ A.M. Wrote to Sir W. Harcourt—Ld Spencer—Sir R. Welby—Mr Shand Tel.—Rev. S.E.G.—Sir J. Lacaita—and minutes. Conversation with Mr Eyton—who went.[5] Saw HNG—S.L.—Rev. Mr Eyton—Rev. Mr Berry. Worked on Odes. Ten to dinner. Read Wolfe Tone's Life—A Life Awry.

To Sir W. V. HARCOURT, chancellor of the exchequer, MS Harcourt dep. 13, f. 196. 16 October 1893. '*Secret*'

In the West Ridgway matter, 'the fat is in the fire', and the flame such as no one could have anticipated. I have laboured in a long and complex correspondence, but thus so far in vain. I have said that if matters cannot be mended it must go to the Cabinet.[6] But I do not know where the Ministers are and as to those in the Commons it would be cruel to

[1] See 12 Oct. 93n.
[2] J. Gutteridge, *Lights and shadows in the life of an artisan* (1893).
[3] A. M. Fairbairn, *The place of Christ in modern theology* (1893).
[4] No reply found.
[5] But see next day.
[6] Ridgeway, a strong unionist, was moved from Dublin Castle to govern the Isle of Man; see 22, 28 Oct. 93.

call on them *now*. We want therefore fourteen days added to his leave: a matter properly for your consideration had you been here when you could have seen the correspondence and judged the whole matter. In your absence, so well earned, I will try to arrange the matter with Welby. And then I propose to call the Cabinet on Nov. 1. or 2.

To Sir J. P. LACAITA, 16 October 1893.   Add MS 44234, f. 232.

Though sorry you should have been suffering,[1] I am glad that your malady should have turned its back, and should as I gather be running away.

What you say of the state of Italy makes my heart bleed, but I have nothing to add to former utterances.

In making the best answer I can to the interesting inquiry you have sent me, I must premise that there is no well-defined code applicable to political contingencies for constitutional monarchies as a class, although in certain important matters there may be already a considerable uniformity of practice. The contingency you describe is *off* the ordinary lines: and my reply will have reference to this country only.

We have I think two precedents in British History. In 1783 George III dismissed the Coalition Ministry which had a majority of the House of Commons. Pitt (aged 24) acting with infinite insight and tact, held on the Parliament long enough to show that the majority was not solid, and, when he had got numbers to a balance he dissolved and the country largely and decidedly supported him.

But the Throne and the House of Lords were stronger in 1783 than they are now: nor is there always a Pitt at hand.

The second case was in 1834. William IV then availed himself of the removal of Lord Althorp by succession, from the House of Commons, to displace the Melbourne Government. Peel took office and dissolved at once. He largely increased his force but did not obtain a majority, and resigned in April 1835, after fighting for about six weeks. But 1. The King had stood well with the country on account of his supporting the Reform Bill;— he had, so to speak, cash at his Bankers. 2. Melbourne, whom he displaced, was a man whom nothing would have induced to give a shock to the Throne, and who had *also* used language that would to some extent have covered the King. 3. The new House scrubbed the King by an amendment to the Address. 4. It was felt that there would be danger in re*peati*ng the experiment.

And, finally; it cannot be said in this country that the terms of the question excluded altogether the discretion of the Sovereign in the abstract. It is conceivable that a Ministry might misconduct itself, and yet might not be put out by its supporters, while there might also be a palpable and undeniable change of sentiment in the country. But the strain on the Throne would be considerable. To save mischievous consequences, the grounds of action ought to be clear beyond dispute: and the act ought very promptly to be sealed by the voting nation, through the return of a decided majority in the desired sense.

This I think is as much as I dare say. And after all no antecedent description can do much towards laying down with accuracy the conditions of action, great part of which would probably depend upon *l'impréon* [*sic*].

[1] Lacaita's neuralgia prevented a visit to Hawarden. He wrote from Florence that 'the political, financial and social condition of Italy is much worse than I expected', and sent a mem. asking a) whether a constitutional monarch, convinced that Ministers were 'not doing the interest of the country', could dismiss them, b) what were the recent British precedents; Add MS 44234, f. 230.

17. Tu.

Ch 8½ AM. Wrote to Sir G. Trevelyan—The Queen—Mr J. Morley—F. Smith—E. Hamilton—Scotts—J. Westell—Mr Stafford Howard—and minutes. Worked on Odes of Hor. Walk with Harry. Conversation with Mr Eyton. Read Wolfe Tone—A Life Awry.

18. St Luke.

Ch. 8½ A.M. and H.C.—Dear Agnes's birthday: God bless it. Wrote to Mr Holyoake—Sir W. Fraser—Mr Acland—Mr P. Stanhope—and minutes. Worked on Odes. Have found the Carm. Saec.[1] stiff. Drive with C: cottages. Read A Life Awry: sad stuff—Wolfe Tone—Holyoake's Memoirs[2]—Jane Field.[3]

To P. J. STANHOPE, M.P., 18 October 1893.   Add MS 44549, f. 145.

I thank you for your interesting letter[4] & the account of the proceedings of the Peace Conference.

What I always hope is that those members of Legislatures who belong to it will in the several countries direct much of their attention to the *small beginnings* of intervention, which are allowed to pass through supposed insignificance, and which soon grow to unmanageable dimensions. The new chartered Companies & their Charters would have well deserved jealous intervention[:] had any number of persons so minded been hostile critics of the first intervention of the Beaconsfield Government of 1874–80 in Egyptian affairs i.e. the finances of that country, we should not have been in Egypt at this moment for Ld. Salisbury would never have come under his engagement to support a native Government.

[P.S.] I hope you will soon be settled in your new & charming house.

19. Th.

Ch. 8½ A.M. Wrote to A. Morley l. & tel.—E. Hamilton tel.—Watsons—J. Morley Tel.—Mr Illingworth—and minutes. Worked on Odes. Dined at G.G.s. Walk with Mr Armitstead. Read Wolfe Tone—Jane Field.

To A. ILLINGWORTH, M.P., 19 October 1893.   Add MS 44549, f. 145.

The expedient so kindly devised, & brought before me in so flattering a manner, is I am sorry to say not available for the purpose in view.[5] Public banquets were interdicted in my case by Sir Andrew Clark many years ago, not less I think than five or seven since which I have not attended (for example) the Royal Academy dinner or even at Guildhall on Lord Mayor's day.

I have repeatedly expressed my strong sense of the disadvantage at which the Liberal party is placed by my necessarily growing physical disabilities. It is like having a lame man in the ranks of a regiment & it is particularly to be regretted when as you say there are

[1] Horace's *Carmen Saeculare*, included in his Horatian translation.
[2] G. J. Holyoake, *Sixty years of an agitator's life*, 2v. (1892).
[3] M. E. Wilkins, *Jane Field* (1892).
[4] Not found.
[5] Illingworth raised the question of a visit to Bradford on 2 October, Add MS 44517, f. 252; an official invitation apparently followed.

such important & interesting calls on the mind and attention in connection with great public interest & problems.

There are other conspicuous cases where I am in default besides Bradford: but if (which I cannot think probable) I should again undertake a campaign other than in Midlothian, you may be sure that I shall approach the case of Bradford in the spirit to which, I believe, I adverted in my last.

20. Fr.

Ch. 8½ A.M. Wrote to Lady Clark—Mr Shand—Mr Stanford—and minutes. Worked on Odes. Read Wolfe Tone—Jane Field. F. Leveson came. Hawarden Trust Meeting 3½–4½. Saw S.E.G. on St Deiniol's initiatory measures. Backgammon with Mr A: & walk. Dined at Gerty's: an event.

21. Sat.

Ch 8½ A.M. Wrote to Mr Hucks Gibbs[1]—Mr Holyoake—Sir A. Godley—and minutes. Worked on Odes. Walk with F. Leveson. Eleven to dinner.—Backgammon. Finished Jane Field. Read Wolfe Tone.

22. [blank] S. Trin.

Ch. 11 AM and 6½ P.M. Wrote to Ld Advocate—Ld Rosebery. Read Wales under Tudors[2]—Jesuits in Poland[3]—Lpool Ch. Furniture[4] &c.

To LORD ROSEBERY, foreign secretary, 22 October 1893. 'Secret'.   N.L.S. 10027, f. 68.

The death of Vivian may open up expectations in [the] connection with the Ridgway problem as yet unsolved.

In a long correspondence with Morley I have used the *strongest* language I could, but I nevertheless understand him to adhere to his almost incredible resolution to remove *himself* at all hazards unless Ridgway is provided for by the end of this month.[5]

You will see from the inclosed that there is another iron in the fire—the Isle of Man—and perhaps you may like to communicate with A. Morley.[6]

I can sympathise with you in your difficulties as to the diplomatic hierarchy. I am not a competent judge of it: but *so far* as my means of judgment carry me, I think it a most conspicuous failure. I know no class of men so weak & in possession of such dignity & emoluments, as our *bred* diplomatists. I do not know who is responsible for the foundation of the system.

23. M.

Ch. 8½ A.M. Wrote to Ld Kimberley—Mr Morley—Watsons—and minutes. Worked in the Octagon. But my papers overwhelm me. I am like a little mole,

---

[1] Henry Hucks Gibbs (1819–1907, banker and tory M.P. city of London 1891–2) on plans for a dean and chapter at St. Albans; Add MS 44549, f. 145.

[2] Probably J. B. Nevins, *Pictures of Wales during the Tudor period* (1893).

[3] A. F. Pollard, *The Jesuits in Poland* (1892).

[4] Untraced.

[5] Rosebery refused to appoint Ridgway to Rome—or to any Foreign Office posting. Ford should go to Rome; Add MS 44290, ff. 191–3.

[6] See 28 Oct. 93.

who has cast up an enormous hill. Worked on Odes of Horace. I find that last year my progress was *miserable*. This year *measurable*. Read Conington on Horace[1]—Life of Wolfe Tone. Conversations with the Viceroy[2]—and Mr Swetenham.[3]

24. Tu.

Ch. 8½ A.M. Wrote to Bp of Bath & Wells—S. Lyttelton—E. Wickham—A. Morley—J. Morley—and minutes. Worked on Odes—and on *Kosmos*. Began 'To right the Wrong'.[4] I think this has been my best day for Odes: some 59 lines, say 10 per hour: and also I think that for certain light Odes such as II. [blank], I have at last got a metre with the right lilt in it. Ten to dinner. Backgammon with Mr W. Richmond:[5] who is full of light and life.

25. Wed.

Ch. 8½ AM. Wrote to Sir W. Harcourt—Mr Morley—Miss Bayly—and minutes. Odes of Horace. Worked as hard: but with far less result. Walk & drive with W.R. More guests. Backgammon with Mr W.R. Read Edna Lyall: but the eyes, the eyes! (*writing* gives me no difficulty).

To Sir W. V. HARCOURT, chancellor of the exchequer, MS Harcourt dep. 13, f. 200.
25 October 1893.

I hope the prosperous course of your little vacation will have been crowned by a good report in Germany.

Are we to have any further information from Germany? So much time has passed since Condie Stephen's visit that it seems doubtful. You do not seem much inclined to go into the case of the Coburg revenues: and I do not know that it would bear greatly on the judgment we have to form.[6]

I have had a scrap from Ponsonby about Clarence House. The Duke has said that unless he has 15m per ann. he cannot keep it.

Has not the time come when unless more information is coming we should dispose of the business.

I would summon a Cabinet for Friday 3d Nov. and give notice of it at Balmoral in time (if I hear from you by post or wire on Friday).

26. Th.

Ch. 8½ A.M. Wrote to Dr Macgregor MP—Watsons—Mr Purcell—Scotts—Mr Mullick—Ld Bute—& minutes. Worked on Odes. And on arranging papers i.e. *Kosmos*. Drive & walk with W.R. Read Edna Lyall. Long Treasury conversation at night. Guests in full supply.

[1] J. Conington, *Horace. Satires, Epistles and Poetica* (new ed. 1892).
[2] i.e. Houghton, Viceroy of Ireland.
[3] Clement William Swetenham, Cheshire J.P. and landowner.
[4] Edna Lyall, *To right the wrong*, 3v. (1893).
[5] W. B. Richmond, the artist, staying at the Castle; HVB.
[6] Harcourt next day replied, Add MS 44203, f. 120: 'I am all against going into the squalid details of the Coburg *menage*—that is not our affair.'

To LORD BUTE, 26 October 1893.   Add MS 44549, f. 147.

Nothing can be kinder than your note,[1] but I shall be very sorry if you remain of opinion that you cannot undertake the Bill. The time could hardly be before February for *we* are pledged to the overwrought H. of C. not to lay upon it this year any fresh burden of ordinary legislation. I am certain there is no one else who can undertake the duty with anything like your advantages, the Duke of Norfolk having long ago declined. The *one* thing essential (as we cannot give any appreciable *time* to the Bill) is to appease the Tory opposition. This cannot be done except by one not dissociated from them in general politics. I am not sure that Albemarle would have the necessary weight, but however this may be I understand that he is certainly not in a state of health to undertake it. Ripon & I thought Ashburnham but as his party relations are changed he would be at a great disadvantage. The introduction by a Minister would at once cause an opposition in our house that would infallibly defeat the measure by time. You see the complications that surround this apparently simple business, & what a leverage Orangeism has to work with.

Your courtesy does not invest me with any title to press you. But I hope you will consider it open to you, during the time between this date & February to take it in hand. For I am bound to say, looking at the subject with a Parliamentary eye that except in your hands I see little chance for it.[2]

27. Fr.

Ch. 8½ A.M. Wrote to Ld Kimberley—Sir E. Saunders—S.L.—Ly Milbank—Abp Walsh—and minutes. Long (for me) walk with a party: overdone. Worked on Odes. Conversation with Welby on them. Read Little:[3] with growing difficulty. Backgammon with W.R.

28. Sat. SS. S. & J.

Ch 8½ A.M. Took Mr R[ichmond] to St Deiniol's. Wrote to Sir H. Ponsonby—Ld Rosebery—Ld Ripon—and minutes. Saw Sir A. West—Mr Murray. Most of the guests went. Worked on the Odes. Long conversation with Mr Asquith. He will rise. Reading in E. Lyall. But it dwindles!

To LORD RIPON, colonial secretary, 28 October 1893.   Add MS 43515, f. 128.

For once I raise a question on a passage in the letter[4] you have sent me: a question not of commission but of omission. I read it as saying that the Co. will be fully heard on all matters that concern their interests. But ought they not to be fully heard on all matters which concern the pacification? while there can be no doubt that you are right in reserving the decisive power to the Government. Perhaps there is no difference of intention.
2. In a very nice letter, Bute declines. I have asked him—as there is no hurry—to let it stand over: & perhaps between this time and February you will use your influence. He suggests Albemarle: but I am told this is out of the question. I am afraid all Tories would wish to punish Ashburnham, through the Bill, for having shown regard to Irish rights.

[1] Not found; see 14 Oct. 93.
[2] Bute did not introduce a bill in the 1894 session.
[3] Perhaps W. Knox Little, *Sacerdotalism* (1893).
[4] Of 27 October, Add MS 43515, f. 126, reporting a letter written to the British South Africa Company pointing out that the British govt., i.e. Sir H. Loch, retained 'supreme control' of any negotiations at the end of hostilities, though the Co. would play a part, and that in so saying Ripon had 'ventured to assume your approval'. See 4 Nov. 93.

To LORD ROSEBERY, foreign secretary, 28 October 1893.   N.L.S. 10027, f. 74.

1 No doubt Ford at Rome will be an improvement upon Ford at Constantinople. I hope he will be shy of advising the Italian Government: much as I wish they could be effectually advised in the sense of economy and restraint. The last Italian intelligence I received was disagreeable. It is that, under the provocation of the enormous taxes, a party not insignificant has grown up in Rome which favours the restoration of the temporal power. The nationalism of Italy is however immensely strong; it has borne a great strain and perhaps will bear more, but there may be a limit. Had the life of Cavour but been spared!

2. I suppose that G.C.M.G. would be a very proper offer for Russell and Webster. Would Webster accept? I forget whether Northcote did: an analogous case.

3. To my intense relief (in such a case I do not flinch even from a contradiction in terms) the Ridgway affair is I hope closed for us. The Post Office is offered to Walpole: his acceptance is assumed. On that showing, Isle of Man will be offered to Ridgway. This I trust will satisfy the genuinely chevaleresque spirit of John Morley.

29. Oct. 23 S. Trin.

Ch. mg & evg. Wrote minutes—and to Religious Tract Society. Read Sayce's Fresh Light from the Monuments[1]—and scraps in other works. Tea with G.G. conversation on the W. Window.

30. M.

Ch. 8½ A.M. Wrote to Dean Liddell—Mr Bywater—Rev. W. Carter—Ld Rosebery—Z. Outram—and minutes. Worked on Odes. Tea with the Rigbys. Read Bridges Poems[2]—Schreiner's Dream[3]—Mary kindly read aloud to me in evg—but.

To LORD ROSEBERY, foreign secretary, 30 October 1893.   N.L.S. 10027, f. 76.
(An omnibus letter)

1. I think & Murray an able Priv. Sec. who knows many things agrees with me that the Cockpit was West of Whitehall and east of the rambling house I presently inhabit[4]—close to the line of Downing St to the South. I cannot however pretend to certain knowledge. All my books of topography are up at the Iron Library, St Deiniols to be.

2. On your feeling allusion to Clarke I am able to say that our last accounts (by post) there of this afternoon are the best. There is a sort of strength in him. But the case is not wholly free from what are termed complications.

3. On Friday Duke of Coburg may come up, but I expect to hear first from Balmoral.

[1] A. H. Sayce, Fresh light from the ancient monuments (1883).
[2] R. Bridges, Shorter poems (1893).
[3] Olive Schreiner, Dreams (1891).
[4] Rosebery asked, 29 October, Add MS 44290, f. 198: 'Can you say positively where was the Cockpit? There is a strange conflict of testimony.'

4. Also it will then be necessary to condescend upon a quorum for the Guildhall dinner. Let every man prepare to sacrifice himself for his country's good.

4 [*sic*]. I am extremely grieved at what you say of the French, although I fully believe that you will not be wearied in well-doing. It is no less strange than sad. How is it possible that they should wish to estrange us? Even if we were only worth little, we are worth something, and France in the present predicament has nothing to spare.

5. Due on Wendy by Irish Mail

31. Tu.

Ch 8½ A.M. Wrote to Bp of Chichester—Mr Colman MP—Mr H. Hoare—Mr Asquith—Mrs Bolton—Mr Morley—& minutes. Preparations for going. Worked on the Odes. Read the Gledstones & Coklaw[1]—Benson's Poems.[2]

Wed. Nov 1. 93. [London]

Ch. 8½ A.M: and H.C. the best Viaticum for London.

Further preparations. 12½–5¾ to Euston. Worked 'some' on Odes in the train. Saw Gerty—& in town Lady Clark—Sir W. Harcourt—Sir A. West. Dined with Mr A.—Backgammon. Read Gledstones & Coklaw.—Wrote to Sir H. P[onsonby].

2. Th.

Wrote to Sir H. Ponsonby—Ld Spencer—Ld Onslow—& minutes. H. of C. 3½–7¾.[3] Dined at Mr A.s—Backgammon. Saw Sir E. Saunders[4] who set me right. Saw Sir A. West—Mr Morley—Mr A. Morley—Sir G. Trevelyan—Mr Fowler—Mr Marj. Read Lindsay on Progress in Theology.[5] A little work on Odes.

To LORD BESSBOROUGH, 2 November 1893.   Add MS 44549, f. 151.

A Garter has fallen vacant by the lamented death of Ld. Derby.[6] On this occasion I cannot but bear in mind the service which you rendered to the country as Head of the Commission on Irish Land, and its result in the Act of 1881, as also your position in Ireland more generally both as a landlord and with reference to the national movement. For myself I attach a very great value to all which tends to narrow the gap between the people of Ireland & its landed aristocracy particularly in a case where a step in this direction can be taken without risk of misunderstanding.

I therefore have to say that, if you will permit me, I shall have much pleasure in submitting your name to H.M. for the vacant place in the order of the Garter.

[1] Mrs. Florence M. Gladstone, 'The Gledstanes of Gledstanes and Coklaw, 1296–1741', *The Genealogist*, n.s. ix. 153–7 (January 1893).
[2] A. C. Benson, *Poems* (1893); sent by the author, Add MS 44517, f. 254.
[3] Local Govt. Bill 2°R; 4*H* 18. 3.
[4] His dentist.
[5] J. Lindsay, *The progressiveness of modern Christian thought* (1892).
[6] Lansdowne was urged on Gladstone, but he resisted appointing him, instructing Morley and Asquith to seek out a more liberal candidate. Bessborough declined; Gladstone tried again unsuccessfully (Add MS 44549, f. 157): Breadalbane accepted.

3. Fr.

Wrote to The Queen—Ld Bessborough—Ld Ripon—......—& minutes. Read Beattys Poems.[1] H. of C. $3\frac{1}{4}$–$8\frac{1}{4}$.[2] Saw Sir A.W.—Mr Marj.—Sir W.H.—Mr Morley. M. came. Mr A. dined. Conversation on eyes & Pagenstrecher(?)[3] A sad change in Sir A. Clark: imminent danger.[4]

4. Sat.

Wrote to The Queen—Ld Onslow—Ld Ripon—Mr Woods MP—........—and minutes. Cabinet 12–3. Some hard nuts to crack. Dined at Mr Rendel's. Backgammon with Lord R. Read Julius Caesar. A little work on Odes.

Cabinet. Frid. N. 3. [sc. *Sat. N. 4*] *93. Noon.*[5]
1. Ld Mayor's dinner: Ld. Chancellor, Kimberley, Spencer, Mundella, Bryce, C. Bannerman.
2. D. of Coburg. 1. The Naval point. Cabinet have not been able to see how HRH can remain in any other than an Honorary commission with the Navy. 2. The Cabinet have proceeded so far in the examination of the subject as to arrive at the opinion which they deem it their duty to lay before H.M. The only course which would be regarded as really wise and safe would be the retention[?] of the annuity given under the two Acts by the Duke of Edinburgh.[6]
3. Matabele. 1. Form of negotiation.[7] *[?] all of with Co[mpany].* Controul with Govt. 2. Future Govt.[8]
4. Business in H. of C. Independent members a. Contagious Diseases India, b. Miners 8 hours, c. Place of Worship sites, d. Evicted Tenants.

To LORD RIPON, colonial secretary, 4 November 1893.   Add MS 43515, f. 132.

I hope that I am not wrong, but I have written to the Queen that the Cabinet today *reserved* for a future time and riper knowledge the important question as to the mode of future administration for Matabele Land.[9]

To S. WOODS, M.P., 4 November 1893.   Add MS 44549, f. 151.

I have brought fully before the Cabinet the purport of your letter of the 1st[10] which reached me yesterday morning. We are very sensible of the weight of the considerations

[1] P. Beatty, *Spretae carmina Musae. First series. Songs of love and death* (1893).
[2] Answered questions; 4 *H* 18. 109.
[3] Hermann Pagenstecher, German occulist in touch with Lady Harcourt; Add MS 44517, f. 320.
[4] His physician, who died on 6 November.
[5] Add MS 44648, f. 122.
[6] This point added on a separate sheet. See 21 Nov. 93.
[7] Phrase between *...* barely legible.
[8] Conquest of Matabeleland and Mashonaland left an ambiguous authority and title; the Cabinet decided that in practice the whole of Southern Rhodesia should be handed over to the administrative authority of the Company, the position being regularised in British law by an Agreement with the Company on 24 May 1894 and an Order in Council of 18 July 1894; see C. Palley, *The constitutional history and law of Southern Rhodesia* (1966), 110 ff.
[9] Ripon wrote this day, Add MS 43515, f. 133, that the Cabinet's discussion today was 'brief and unsatisfactory considering the importance of the subject.... I regard the system of administration by Chartered Companies as essentially bad. These Companies are really speculative, got up mainly for Stock Exchange purposes ... they are not pleasant instruments of administration....'
[10] Untraced.

which you urge in favour of proceeding immediately with a stage of the 8 Hours Miners Bill. But with very great regret we find ourselves unable to give to those considerations the weight we should desire to secure for them.

The House sat for 8 months before the adjournment at the close of September; and worked harder I believe than any Parliament ever worked before. It consented to meet again at a time of year usually devoted either to comparative repose or to other occupations. This consent was given in order to secure the passing of two important measures which, between them, beneficially affect the interests of nearly the whole labouring population. The House might have preferred your important Bill, or other Bills; but it did not. But it seemed to us to discourage very strongly any additions to the heavy draft we made upon its time & energy. And I am afraid it would be considered a breach of understanding, if not in direct terms a breach of faith, were we to encourage or support the submission to it during the autumn sittings, apart from absolute necessity, of any contentious measure of our own, still more if it were a Bill in the hands of an independent member.

We have therefore thought we should best discharge our duty to the House by declining, so far as we are concerned, to make exceptions to the rule laid down, as we believe, in conformity with its general desire, though doubtless not always in conformity with the desire of each particular member as to the Bill with which he was specially concerned.

With regard to the request for one day I may say I am advised and am convinced that only a series of days could suffice for the purpose you have in view.

The reply which I now most reluctantly send you affords but another illustration of the deplorable arrear of public business and of the necessity of the most determined efforts of Parliament and the country to make effectual provision for meeting the evil.

5. S.

Chapel Royal mg & evg. Read—scarcely. Bp Oxenden Memoir & Sermon[1]— Rainy on Philippians[2]—Bp Sandford Sermons.[3] Wrote to Ld Rosebery. Saw Ld Spencer (Royalty).

To LORD ROSEBERY, foreign secretary, 5 November 1893.   N.L.S. 10027, f. 78.
'*Secret*'.

Jubes renovare dolorem[4]

I might add the epithet. You will recollect from Blackcraig how this business has weighed upon me.[5] What I should really like, especially after your letter, is a conversation with you. Would you dine here tomorrow? at eight? The smallest possible round table. This would be best. *If* you cannot do it, would you come to my room at the H. of C., at your own time (sending me notice) between $3\frac{1}{2}$ and 7 PM.

You speak of the Peers as partially shut out in such a matter: and I am a Peer!!! That is to say, old age, & obstructed sight and hearing have cut down very low my knowledge of the state of opinion in the H. of Commons.

---

[1] A. Oxenden, *Plain sermons... with a memoir* [*by W. Webster*] (1893).
[2] R. Rainy, *The Epistle to the Philippians* (1893).
[3] C. W. Sandford, *Works of counsel to English Churchmen abroad* (1892).
[4] Virgil, *Aeneid*, 2.3: 'Infandum, Regina, iubes renovare dolorem' (O Queen, you bid me renew unspeakable suffering); the epithet is 'infandum', unspeakable.
[5] See Rosebery's letter this day, Add MS 44290, f. 199: 'I must confess that I left the Cabinet yesterday with a bad taste in my mouth (which I suspect you of sharing). I think the proposal as regards the Duke of Coburg as shabby as can well be conceived ... it is deplorable to live under a monarchy and make a football of it, and rejoice in starving it.'

I wish I could with safe conscience appropriate what you charitably suppose to have been the charge of my letter to the Queen. I had the greatest difficulty in writing it. To omit expressing regret in forwarding such an opinion may seem brutal. But on the other hand to have put it forward might have seemed a mockery, and whatever seems a mockery in such circumstances is bitterly resented.

A combination of unhappy circumstances I think all help to darken and perplex this question.

What however are the grounds on which after a succession abroad a continuance of British Income might conceivably be supported.

1. Good faith. That will be observed in the case of the Duchess: but has no application to that of the Duke.

2. The fact of being a British Prince taken in itself, this might have been the basis of the annuity, but was not.

3. Prospective duties in England. Neither he nor the Queen have put forward this ground: and I think some felt yesterday that it might entail differences in Germany. It is not what the Duke means.

4. British outlay or obligations undertaken in the past: *I think* he has a claim in respect of Clarence House: but when I said this yesterday, there was no echo. I hope that in any case there would be acknowledgment under this head: but it is a small matter, say some £50000 [*sic*]. I should incline to taking it by a postponement of the date of renunciation—on our responsibility.—

I feel there is much force in what you say: and wish to look round & round the whole business, & see what can be done. I spoke to Spencer today, and mentioned to him as one of the most hopeful my poor still-born notion. He answered very frankly 'it does not smile to me.'

One of the grave facts of the case is Balfour's attitude.

The appanage business was in my opinion a settlement due mainly to Parnell & his nationalists. The flinching of some on that occasion was rather melancholy. Morley behaved extremely well.

6. *M.*

Wrote to Mr Colman—Bp of Chichester—Ld Ripon. Saw Sir A. West—Mr Marj.—Ld Kimberley—Ld K. & Mr M. cum Ch. of Exr—Ld Spencer—Ld Rosebery—Conclave to meet Mr Stansfeld. H. of C. 3¼–7¾.[1] A little work on Odes. Read Vindication of the Irish 1801.[2]

This afternoon died Sir A. Clark. I must not dwell on the great loss to us; but think thankfully (with all sympathy for his family) on the dear and noble record of his life. It is in full assurance of hope that we may pray for his enjoying the peace of the righteous.

To LORD RIPON, colonial secretary, 6 November 1893.   Add MS 43515, f. 135.

Recollections are divided on the point considered between us on Saturday. But you ought to be made aware that Labouchere will probably move an Adjournment on Thursday or Friday about Matabeleland: will it then be requisite to declare a policy for the future administration of Matabeleland? Must this again be referred to the Cabinet before

[1] Spoke on business of the House; 4*H* 18. 229.
[2] Perhaps *A vindication of the conduct of the Irish Catholics during the late administration. By a Protestant barrister* (1807).

the day comes? Could this, considering how far the matter went on Saturday be determined by a Circulation box putting the query?[1]

7. *Tu.*

Wrote to Sir G. Trevelyan—Sir H. Ponsonby—Sir W. Harcourt—& minutes. H. of C. 3½–8.[2] Mr Thaddeus came for a quasi-sitting.[3] Saw Sir A.W.—Mr Marj.—Deputation on Local Govt Bill at 2.15.[4] Worked on Odes 'some'. Family dinner: much conversation on Sir A. Clark. Read Hogan on Lowe[5]—Musgrave's Inferno +.[6]

To Sir W. V. HARCOURT, chancellor of the exchequer,   MS Harcourt dep. 13, f. 202.
7 November 1893.

I am glad that Sir Hercules [Robinson] has taken the field.[7] There is a strong movement (the same in kind as the Uganda agitation) against your view, which I believe is in substance also mine & that of the Cabinet. Ripon thinks, & it seems to me wisely that we should as much as possible keep the Labouchere discussion within narrow bounds & that a declaration of the future policy would be premature. I even fear it might produce a strong reaction.

To Sir H. F. PONSONBY, the Queen's Secretary,   Add MS 44549, f. 153.
7 November 1893.

I have received your letter. It would I think be difficult to maintain that Disestablishment is a point of religion, and that a Disestablisher is *ipso facto* disabled from performance of a duty as a Divinity Professor. On the other hand I admit that no man has a right to use his office as Divinity Professor in an Established Church for the purpose of teaching Disestablishment. I hope you think this fair. I will send what you have said about Mr. H[erkless] to Trevelyan, and am sure the matter will be thoroughly examined.[8]

8. *Wed.*

Wrote to Mr A. Morley—Sir H. Ponsonby—Sir G. Trevelyan—Mr Ellis MP.— Mrs Bolton—Ld Ripon—and minutes. Mr A. dined. Backgammon. Saw Sir

---

[1] Ripon replied this day, Add MS 43515, f. 140, that in the circumstances it 'would not ... be desirable to declare a policy on Labouchere's motion'; best to say the situation changes daily. On 8 November Ripon sent, after discussion with Buxton, the 'most suitable' statement available; it would be condemned as 'no policy' but it would be unwise 'to commit ourselves further while the position of affairs in Matabeleland is so shifting'. See 4 *H* 18. 586 for Buxton's statement that it was 'premature to attempt' to discuss 'future policy'.

[2] L.G. Bill; 4 *H* 18. 356.

[3] See 27 Jan. 88.

[4] Dpn. of Central Cttee. of Poor Law Conferences; *T.T.*, 8 November 1893, 14a.

[5] J. F. Hogan, *Robert Lowe, Viscount Sherbrooke* (1893).

[6] G. Musgrave, *Dante's Divine Comedy* (1893).

[7] Letter in this day's *T.T.*, recommended by Harcourt, Add MS 44203, f. 126: 'oddly enough he places the extra cost of administering Matabeleland at precisely the sum I fixed of £500,000 per ann. besides having to do all the slaughtering ourselves'.

[8] Proposed appt. to the divinity chair at St. Andrews of Rev. John Herkless, 1855–1920; after further protests from the Queen, A. F. Mitchell, Regius professor of ecclesiastical history, surrendered his chair so that Herkless could be appt. to it, and another candidate was found for the divinity chair. See 13 Nov. 93 and Add MS 44549, f. 158.

A.W.—Mr Marj.—Sir W. Harcourt. H. of C. 3¼–5½.[1] Read Hogan's Lowe—Blunt's Poems.[2] Worked on books.

To LORD RIPON, colonial secretary, 8 November 1893.   Add MS 43515, f. 140.

I think the whole excellent:[3] but should like to see the first part made much more short and general on grounds of policy. My pencil mark[4] shows the limit I assign to the first part[?].

9. Th.

Wrote to Sir R. Welby—Ld Chancellor—..........—Ld Spencer—& minutes. Saw Sir A. West—Mr Marj.—Sir H. Ponsonby—Ld Ripon—Canon McColl. Worked on Odes. H. of C. 3¼–8. (Matabele).[5] Backgammon with S. Read Hogan's Lowe.

10. Fr.

Wrote to Mr Asquith—Lady Aberdeen—A.R. Gladstone—& minutes. Saw Sir A.W.—Mr Marj.—Att. Gen.—E. Hamilton. Quasisitting Mr Thaddeus. Conclave of Commons Ministers 2¾. H. of C. 3¼–8, 10–12¼. *Good* division (19) on contracting out.[6] Read Musgrave's Dante—Hogan's Lowe.

To H. H. ASQUITH, home secretary, 10 November 1893.   Add MS 44549, f. 154.

I am glad to find that the inosculation, or the interosculation, or whatever it may be better called, is of no great extent: & I quite agree as the geographical line.[7] It would be our advantage if in return it could be noted either by an asterisk, or an expansion, which of the Parishes forming part of English Dioceses are (wholly or partially) in Monmouthshire & not in Wales proper. The treatment of Monmouthshire as Wales is I apprehend quite modern though it may be very proper: & if ⟨the⟩ it be the fact that the number of English (Diocesan) Parishes in Wales proper is very small, it may be well that we should be enabled to show this.[8]
[P.S.] I propose to mention your plan of a Committee on the Coal War, provisionally at least, this afternoon. I rather lean to the single committee. Might Stansfeld possibly take the chair?

11. Sat.

Wrote to Sir H. Ponsonby—& minutes. Saw Sir A. West—Sir Jas Paget—Sir H. Acland—Mr Mundella. Drive with C. Dined at Mr Armitstead's. Memorial

[1] Employers' Liability Bill; 4*H* 18. 451.
[2] W. S. Blunt, probably *A new pilgrimage and other poems* (1889).
[3] The draft statement on Matabeleland; see 6 Nov. 93n.
[4] Not found.
[5] Spoke on Labouchere's motion on Matabeleland, accepting govt. responsibility and denying Labouchere's censure of Rhodes; 4*H* 18. 595. See Introduction above, vol. xiii, section vi.
[6] McLaren's motion to permit contracting out by railwaymen was voted down; 4*H* 18. 756.
[7] Question of the treatment of small English diocesan parishes falling within Wales as part of Wales in the Disestablishment Bill Asquith was preparing; Asquith to Gladstone, Add MS 44517, f. 299.
[8] Asquith promised to check the details; ibid., 311.

service in the Abbey for Sir A. Clark. It was well arranged & solemn. I was grieved not to go to the country. Worked on Odes. Read Julius Caesar.

12. 24 S. Trin.

Chapel Royal mg & aft. Wrote to Sir H. Ponsonby—Mr Westell. Read A Layman's Faith[1]—Rainy Philippians—M. Müller Gifford Lectures,[2] and the Psalms: especially 119. Saw Ld Spencer.

13. M.

Wrote to Chr of Exr—Sir H. Ponsonby—The Queen l.l.—& minutes. Signed the letter from Govt to the Coalowners & Miners. Cabinet 12–1¼. H. of C. 3½–8 & 10¼–12¼.[3] Saw Sir A.W.—Mr Marj.—Mr Morley. Read Hogan's Lowe. Worked on Odes.

Cabinet. Monday Nov. 13. 93. Noon.[4]

1. The Miners. Mundella stated communications with Employers & Miners. Rosebery's partial warrant[?], Masters accept conc[iliatio]n[?] of cabinet: Mundella, Harcourt, Acland, Herschell. Pickard a self-seeker in the result.[5]
2. Matabeleland. Kimberley, Bryce, Acland, Ripon. Old Swaziland committee.
3. Duke of Coburg? Recital. Navy matter settled.
4. Cabinet conversed on the proposed appointment of Mr. Herkles[s].[6] Leanings of opinion evident.

To the Miners' and Coalowners' Federations,   *The Times*, 14 November 1893, 10a.
13 November 1893.

The attention of her Majesty's Government has been seriously called to the wide-spread and disastrous effects produced by the long continuance of the unfortunate dispute in the coal trade, which has now entered on its 16th week.

It is clear from information which has reached the Board of Trade that much misery and suffering are caused not only to the families of the men directly involved, but also to many thousands of others not engaged in mining, whose employment has been adversely affected by the stoppage.

The further prolongation of the dispute cannot fail to aggravate this suffering, especially in view of the approach of the winter, when the greatly increased price of fuel is likely to cause distress among the poorer classes throughout the country.

Moreover, the Government have little doubt that the effect of the stoppage of industry is rapidly extending and increasing, and that unless an early settlement is effected, lasting, if not permanent, injury may be done to the trade of the country.

The Government have not up to the present considered that they could advan-

---

[1] See 30 Apr. 93.   [2] F. Max Müller, *Physical religion. The Gifford Lectures 1890* (1891).
[3] Employers' Liability Bill; 4 *H* 18. 777.   [4] Add MS 44648, f. 129.
[5] Gladstone told the Queen: 'It is believed that the Employers might be led to make reasonable concessions. On the side of the men, Mr Pickard M.P., who is believed to exercise a great influence, has shown little disposition to move: others associated with him are more favourable. The Cabinet appointed a few of their number to conduct the further communications. They do not propose to undertake arbitration or mediation, to which they are invited by neither party: but Lord Rosebery has consented to preside at a meeting of the two parties, if it shall appear that the interval to be bridged over is narrow, and that a meeting might fairly be expected to lead to a friendly adjustment'; CAB 41/22/49.   [6] See to Ponsonby, 7 Nov. 93.

tageously intervene in a dispute the settlement of which would far more usefully be brought about by the action of those concerned in it than by the good offices of others. But having regard to the serious state of affairs referred to above, to the national importance of a speedy termination of the dispute, and to the fact that the conference which took place on the 3rd and 4th of November did not result in a settlement, her Majesty's Government have felt it their duty to make an effort to bring about a resumption of negotiations between the employers and employed, under conditions which they hope may lead to a satisfactory result.

It appears to them that an advantage might accrue from a further discussion between the parties of the present position of matters under the chairmanship of a member of the Government, who it is hoped will not be unacceptable to either side.

Lord Rosebery has consented, at the request of his colleagues, to undertake the important duty which such a position involves.

I have therefore to invite the (miners or coalowners') federation to send representatives to a conference to be held forthwith under his chairmanship. In discharging this duty it is not proposed that Lord Rosebery should assume the position of an arbitrator or umpire, or himself vote in the proceedings, but that he should confine his action to offering his good offices in order to assist the parties in arriving between themselves at a friendly settlement of the questions in dispute.

To Sir W. V. HARCOURT, chancellor of the exchequer,   MS Harcourt dep. 13, f. 203.
13 November 1893.

I by no means think that the Coburg case is on all fours; but, if the terms of the D. of E. acts allow of our acting without reference to the H. of C., it helps us up to a certain point.

Parliament appropriated 50m for a given purpose.

Leopold altered that purpose by a Deed of Trust (which was revocable).

The Treasury was formally apprised of the change and formally accepted it.

And the Treasury ordered the Exchequer to recover the back payments.

There is surely *some* help there.

14. Tu.

Wrote to Mrs Th.—Ld Chancellor—and minutes. Worked on Odes. Dined with Lucy. H. of C. $3\frac{1}{4}$–$7\frac{3}{4}$.[1] Saw Cobham—Mr Murray—Sir A.W.—Mr Marj.—Sir H. Jenkyns—S.L.—C. Lyttelton—Chr of Exr.

15. Wed.

Wrote to Sir C. Cameron—Mr . . . .—& minutes. H. of C. $2\frac{1}{2}$–$5\frac{1}{2}$.[2] Worked on Odes. Saw Sir A.W.—Mr Marj.—Mr Murray (Sir A. West)—S. Lyttelton (Ch.) Dined at Lady Cork's. Conversation with Mr Knowles. Read Julius Caesar.

16. Th.

Wrote to Mr Knowles—Mr Paulin[3]—and minutes. Eight to dinner. Saw Sir A.W.—Mr Marj.—Sir W. Phillimore—Mr Allan MP—Ld E. Clinton—Mr

[1] Questions; Employers' Liability Bill; 4*H* 18. 879.
[2] Employers' Liability Bill; 4*H* 18. 970.
[3] Congratulating D. Paulin on his restoration of Sir A. Clark's finances: 'I think that shortly before the commencement of your relations with our common friend he had suffered heavily through Turkish repudiation'; Add MS 44549, f. 156.

Asquith—Chr of Exr. Worked on Odes. H. of C. $3\frac{3}{4}$–$7\frac{1}{2}$ and 10–$11\frac{1}{2}$. Read Louise de Keroualle.[1] We had luncheon with Mrs Th.

17. Fr.

Wrote to S. Woods MP—Ld Chancellor—Storey MP—Mr Leader—& minutes. Saw Sir A.W.—Mr Marj.—Ld Spencer—Mr Murray—Ld Chancellor—Chr of Exr—Mr Asquith—Att. General. Worked on Odes. H. of C. $3\frac{1}{4}$–$6\frac{1}{2}$.[2] Dined at Lincoln's Inn. Saw Pr. of Wales much reduced & seemingly all the better. Also my old signature of 1833, as a L[incoln's] I[nn] Student to a Bond for £100.

18. Sat.

Wrote to E. Wickham—Princess of Wales—Mr Storey MP—Ld Rosebery—Ld Bessborough—& minutes. Worked on Odes. Saw Sir A.W.—Mr M.—Sir H. Ponsonby—Mr B[urne] Jones—Ld Acton—Mr Milner. Nine to dinner. Read L. de Keroualle.

To S. STOREY, M.P., 18 November 1893.   Add MS 44549, f. 157.

I beg to acknowledge the resolutions which you have been good enough to forward to me on behalf of a meeting of Radical & Labour Members of Parliament.

The first resolution expresses the regret of the meeting at the long delay which has occurred in giving effect to the resolution of the H. of Commons on the appointment of Magistrates, and at the deference which has been paid to Lord Lieutenants.

The meeting finds no sufficient explanation of this delay; and further considers that the magisterial bench ought to be fairly representative of all classes & opinions.

This last proposition commands the hearty assent of the Lord Chancellor, as well as my own; and I am sure he is endeavouring to give effect to it. I venture also to speak for him as well as for myself in admitting the fact of long delay, and in regretting it, that is to say in sympathising sincerely with the impatience which has been locally felt in so many cases & which is now so effectively expressed. It plainly follows that every effort will be used to get through that large portion of the rectifying and balancing work which still remains to be done.

I will add some words, as an observer only, in this important matter; void as I am of all claim to the credit which may justly be given to my colleague the Lord Chancellor. I have never known a case in which a Minister of the Crown already charged with heavy responsibilities of his own has freely and voluntarily undertaken as large, I might perhaps say, for the time so vast an addition to his duties.

My own experience, in dealing with recommendations for honours and appointments makes me aware of the difficulties of his task, though I have never had to undertake anything resembling it on so large a scale. Even single appointments become in some cases the subject of many scores of letters. If, as is plain, no absolute deference can properly be paid by the Lord Chancellor to the Lord Lieutenants, there is no other individual in the several places to whom such a deference can be paid, and some of those who have presumably a good title to recommend might perhaps be surprised at the view taken of their recommendations in some instances by others also invested with a presumptive title to speak. The difficulty cannot be met by placing the several recommenders in communication with one another, or, as it might be called, confronting them. I cannot wonder

[1] See 14 June 86.
[2] Answered Lord G. Hamilton on naval policy; 4H 18. 1149.

at the observation that the delay has not been sufficiently explained; for it could only be explained by opening up the whole of the correspondence, when the explanation (if otherwise allowable) would be defeated by its own bulk.

I offer a concluding observation. It is at least possible and it may be the truth that what Lord Herschell has actually done may be small if it be measured by the demands of the entire country, and yet that if it be measured by reference to what one man, already charged with the duties of Lord Chancellor can effect in half a year, it may be considerable and even very remarkable.

I am sure that these observations, which have no claim to authority, will be received with indulgence, and I hope that when the numbers and names of recent appointments are authentically known, it may appear that the reasons for disappointment, all things considered, are less than may have been supposed.

With respect to the second Resolution I need only say that I receive it with unqualified satisfaction, and entertain a sanguine hope that through the determination and the discretion of the H. of C. the Local Govt. Bill will during the present sittings, continued as necessity may require, be passed into law.

19. Preadv. S.

A wild day. Forenoon prayers at home. Chap Royal aft. Wrote on Theol. Read what I could of Dr Biggs remarkable Lectures[1]—Wolfe's Remains.[2] C. read Sermon in evg. LC & Mr A. dined. Ferocious day.

20. M.

Wrote to Mr Morley—The Queen l.l.l.—Sir G. Treveln—Duke of Coburg—Sir H. Ponsonby—Ld Breadalbane—& minutes. Saw Sir A.W.—Mr Marj.—Sir G. Trevelyan—Sir R. Welby—Sol. General. H. of C. $3\frac{1}{2}$-8.[3] Worked on Odes. Read L. de Keroualle. Drive with C.

21. Tu.

Wrote to Mr Spiller—The Queen l.l.l.—Sir H. Ponsonby l.l.—Mr M'Laren MP.—& minutes. Saw Sir A.W.—Mr Marj.—Chief Rabbi[4]—Mr Garten—Mr Davidson QC.[5]—Dean of Westmr—Mr M'Laren. Cabinet 12-1. H. of C. $3\frac{1}{2}$-$7\frac{1}{2}$.[6] Conclave on Duke of Coburg 5-7. Worked on Odes. Dined with Mr Knowles.

Cabinet. Tues. Nov. 21. 93. Noon.[7]
1. Duke of Coburg. Letter read. Not to be communicated.
2. Cabinet prepared to concur with the retention of the sum given by Act of 1873.
3. Fowler. Woman Suffrage.

[1] C. Bigg, *The Christian Platonists of Alexandria* (1886).
[2] See 12 Oct. 93.
[3] L.G. Bill; 4*H* 18. 1285.
[4] Herman Adler, 1839-1911; Chief Rabbi 1891-1911. Gladstone met him at Knowles's dinner party; Adler gave him a paper (not noticed as read) for which Gladstone wrote a note of thanks; Add MS 44549, f. 158.
[5] William Edward Davidson, 1853-1923; Q.C. and counsel to the Foreign Office from 1886.
[6] L.G. Bill; 4*H* 18. 1380.
[7] Add MS 44648, f. 130.

a. as to married women to be put on the ground of equality with single in local
Franchises: Municipal, County, Parish, Poor Law, School Board. Agreed.[1]
b. Separate list to enfranchise locally all women who cd. vote if they were men.
resist.

22. Wed.

Wrote to M. Drew—Lady Carlisle—Sir H. Ponsonby—& minutes. Saw Sir A.W.—
Mr Marj.—Sol. General—Sir E. James—Mr Asquith—Mr Acland—Sir W. Harcourt—Mr Bryce—Ld Spencer—Ld Ripon. Dined at Mr H. Gardner's. Worked
on Odes. Read De Tabley's Orpheus.[2] H. of C. 1–5½.[3]

23. Th.

Wrote to Sir J. Gl.—Mr Carr Gomm—Sir J. Reed—Chief Rabbi[4]—The Queen—
Ld Breadalbane—and minutes. H. of C. 3½–4½.[5] Mr Thaddeus came. Saw Sir
A.W.—Mr Marj.—the E. Talbots—Mr S.L.—Sir H. Ponsonby—Sir J. Cowell—Dr
Reid—The Talbots of Leeds. Odes—a small dose. Dearest Ms birthday.

To E. J. REED, M.P., 23 November 1893.   Add MS 44549, f. 159.

I am in receipt of your letter,[6] and I do not for a moment question your title to regard
the Minute of the Admiralty on the Victoria[7] in the light which you describe. But you will
not fail to observe that the House is completing its ninth month of work with no prospect
of an early termination and that though there are many questions which may be deemed
urgent as well as weighty we have been obliged to enter into engagements to the House
which bind us to confine our action to certain subjects. I am therefore with regret obliged
to decline all requests for the assignment of days with a view to particular discussions.
[P.S.] I need hardly say that I am not able to adopt for myself the opinion which you
express as to the character of the Minute.

24. Fr. [Brighton]

Wrote to Ld Rosebery—Ld Chancellor—and minutes. H. of C. 3¼–4¼.[8] Then
visited Mr Rendel at Brighton, Lion Mansions. Backgammon with Mr R. Went
with Gen. [blank] to the Gardens & splendid floral display. In D. St at 12¼. Saw
Sir A.W.—Sir W. Harcourt—Ld Spencer—Mr Marj.—Mr Rendel. Finished Intro-
ductions Mr L. Gallienne to AHH[9]—Fourchet to Saint Memin.[10]

[1] See Fowler's speech this day; 4H 18. 1384.
[2] Probably an early version of J. B. L. Warren, Lord de Tabley, *Orpheus in Thrace and other poems*
(1901).
[3] L.G. Bill; 4H 18. 1473.
[4] See 21 Nov. 93.
[5] Questions; Employers' Liability Bill; 4H 18. 1555.
[6] Not found.
[7] PP 1893–4 liv. 511; on H.M.S. *Victoria* and the subsequent Court Martial.
[8] Questioned on naval policy; 4H 18. 1705.
[9] R. Le Gallienne, *The poems of A. H. Hallam* (1893); with an introduction; sent by Le Gallienne.
[10] Reading of title and author uncertain.

25. Sat.

Wrote to Priv. Sec. Tel.—Att. General l.l.—Sir H. Ponsonby. Drive with C. Worked on Odes. Wrote on AHH for Autobiogr.[1] Backgammon with Mr R. Read A.H. Hallam—Bryant on Philo.[2] Visited Mrs Sassoon.[3]

26. Preadv. S.

Chapel Royal mg & evg. Wrote to Ld Chancellor—Sir H. Ponsonby—Sir A. West—& minutes. Read Bigg Bampton L.[4]—Bryant on Philo.

27. M. [London]

Wrote to Mr Knowles—Sir H. Ponsonby l.l.—Mr Storey MP—and minutes. Conversation 1½ hour with Mr R. on Welsh Disestabl.[5] Saw Sir A. West—Att. General—Ld Chancellor—Mr Marj.—Chr of Exchr *cum* Mr Mundella. Back to London 2.40. H of C. $3\frac{1}{2}$-$8\frac{1}{4}$.[6] Mr A. Dined. Backgammon. Worked on Odes. Read L. de Keroualle.

28. Tu.

Wrote to Mr S. Rendel—Sir G. Trevelyan—Rev. SEG.—Sir H. Ponsonby l.l.—and minutes. Worked on Odes. Saw Sir A.W.—Mr Marj.—Sir W. Harcourt—Mr Fowler. H. of C. $3\frac{1}{2}$-8.[7] Saw Lady Derby—Long and useful conversation on eyes. Read L. de Keroualle.

29. Wed.

Wrote to C.G.—Sir R. Palgrave—Ld Rosebery—Mr Fordham—& minutes. Dined with Sir W. Phillimore. Large evening party of Church Liberals. C.G. laid up yesterday & today. Calls in Bond for the moment. Saw Sir A.W.—Mr Marj.—M. Whitbread—Mad. Novikoff—Ld Bowen—Lady Clark. H. of C. $2\frac{1}{4}$-$5\frac{1}{4}$.[8] My interview with ladies fatigued me much. Read L. de Keroualle.

30. Th.

Wrote to Mr Morley—Mr Lefevre—The Queen l.l.—& minutes. H. of C. $3\frac{1}{2}$-$7\frac{1}{2}$.[9] Dined at Mr B. Currie's. Saw Sir A.W.—Mr Marj.—Mr S.L.—H.J.G.—Mr B. Currie—Sir A. Godley—Mr Morley. Odes—a 'wee'. Read L. de Keroualle.

---

[1] Prompted by Le Gallienne's edition; in *Autobiographica*, i. 29 and Add MS 44790, f. 84.
[2] J. Bryant, *The sentiments of Philo Judeus* (1797).
[3] Aline C. Sassoon, da. of Baron de Rothschild, wife of Edward Albert Sassoon.
[4] See 19 Nov. 93.
[5] Perhaps the conversation on the Welsh Supremacy Bill recorded by Rendel, dated 26 November; *Rendel*, 101. Gladstone told Rendel on 28 November: 'I mentioned to the Home Secretary [Asquith] [the] main points of our conversation of yesterday'; Add MS 44549, f. 160.
[6] Questions; L.G. Bill; 4*H* 18. 1811.
[7] Questioned on unemployment by Keir Hardie and Burns; 4*H* 18. 1915.
[8] L.G. Bill; 4*H* 19. 1.
[9] Questions; L.G. Bill; 4*H* 19. 105.

Frid. Decr One 1893. [South Park Hill, Bracknell][1]

A trouble came up in the morning: Z[adock] Outram·having mysteriously disappeared.[2] Wrote to Mad. Novikoff—The Queen—Lord Bute—& minutes. Cabinet 12–1½. H of C. 3¼–4½.[3] By 4.45 train to the Hayters. Read L. de Keroualle—Balabari.[4] In vain we made inquiries about Outram in every quarter. No tidings to be had. Only Acton, F. Leveson, & the Wests here.

Cabinet. Friday Dec. 1. 93. Noon.[5]
1. Course of business in H. of C. Mr Fowler's suggestion for tonight adopted.
2. Curtailment or modification of Bill.
   Do not see our way to qualifying elective character of Board. Nor as to compounders.
3. Employment of Poor by Guardians. No authority has asked for the provision of Act of Eliz[abeth][6] to be put in force.
   L[aw] O[fficers] consider the statute still in force.
   Initiative lies with the local authorities.
   Wait until authorities make the demands.
1. Ld Rosebery. Spanish proposal for common action against anarchy. Present laws not inadequate.

2. Sat.

Wrote to C.G.—S. Lyttelton. The suspense about Outram continued, & apprehension increased. Drive to Bagshot and *a giro*. At night the sudden bitter frost broke[?]. Worked pretty well upon the Odes. Read Balabari—so slow!

To Mrs. GLADSTONE, 2 December 1893.   Hawarden MS 780, f. 227.
My own C.
   In one sense no doubt it was a disappointment for I miss you here even more than I should at home. But I cannot do otherwise than in the first place give you credit for an act of great wisdom and also as I well know of sharp selfdenial: and in the second rejoice that you have escaped exposing yourself at so critical a time to great severity of the weather. The rooms provided for us here are delightful and most acceptable but house is by no means warm all over and the thermometer was this morning at 15 degrees of frost, at Bagshot a few miles off at 17. It is now dusk and promising to be colder still, if it does not break as the weatherwise predict on account of the suddeness and as I heartily hope.
   Host and hostess are as kind as they can be and she prays you (us) to come the next week but one. Of this I have not held out much expect.
   They think their place exceedingly healthy on account of the abundance of pine wood,

---

[1] Sir A. Hayter's house.
[2] The valet's body was found in the Thames on 12 December, probably as a result of suicide.
[3] Questions; L.G. Bill; 4H 19. 269.
[4] Untraced, though clearly a work of substance.
[5] Add MS 44648, f. 132.
[6] 43 Eliz. cap. 2, section 1 provided for setting to work persons 'having no means to maintain them', and for raising by taxation materials for them to work on or with; mem. by Fowler summarising the legal position; Add MS 44648, f. 134. Gladstone told the Queen, RA CAB 41/22/51, that the Act was technically still in force, but practically obsolete: 'their revival would be change attended with the gravest social consequences. The Cabinet ... showed a disinclination to favour such a revival' but, there being no application from a local authority, would wait for one and frame their reply accordingly.

and the gravelly and sandy soil. I think it has something of the same effect on me as Brighton and I should not wonder if it drove away the exema, as Brighton did. It came back again in London. Capital for sleeping I think.

It seems that Mr Canning lived here, and invited Pitt to come and visit him at the time when he went to Bath and died in January 1806.

The house has been almost rebuilt since the former Baronet's time and the place as far as I see it is pretty. I have planted a tree by request.

The party consists of the Wests, Acton, and F. Leveson and is light enough in hand[?]. We have had a long drive to Bagshot and Sandhurst, leaving names for the Connaughts. My contemporary E. [W. T.] Hamilton[1] has been over to luncheon, in great form, with a daughter: we had a long crack.

Acton tells me his son stands extremely well for the Foreign Office Examination, and young Granville for the Diplomatic branch, a sadly inferior and much less safe destination in my opinion than the Foreign Office where I suppose there is pretty steady work.

And so I have run on all this way and not said a word yet about the case of poor Zadok which lies so near my heart. It worsens with every hour's delay, and I know we should have heard if there had been anything real to tell. Herbert will probably have told you that he was sure Zadok had been drinking even during the short interval since his leaving the home. This fully coincided—I am sorry to say—with my independent suspicions and yet the fact of his ever increased care and kindness are undeniable, as you too I think have found. After the non-appearance yesterday morning and no intelligence about him to be had, fearful suppositions cropped up one after the other. First Herbert said he might have got far into liquor, lost self mastery and been locked up—but then we should have heard of him from the police early in the forenoon. Then I thought he might have fallen into bad company who occasionally hang about near the [Duke of York's] steps, and if encouraged might have got hold of him and drugged him. I am afraid it is now late even for this: and I suppose there is not the least hope of his being with either of his brothers. Even death is not wholly out of my speculations about him. The case seems in any form of any mild solution [sic]. May God have mercy on him. What poor creatures we are, and how slippery is the ground under our feet.

I am afraid I *must* have seemed to Herbert very hard and unsympathetic about his vexatious business on which I communicate specially with Harry. But this thing cut in upon me in a way I can hardly explain[,] the fact however being that I feel, or ought to feel, very grateful to him for all he has done for me. And now, hoping for a good account early tomorrow, ever your affte   WEG.

3. *Adv. S.*

Parish Ch 11 A.M. and H.C. Health walking with Acton & much conversation. Wrote to Sir T. Acland—Mr Brand MP. Read Le Gallienne, Religion of a Literary man[2]—Bryant on Philo.

Outram's absconding really afflicts & somewhat alarms me. Ever since I began to feel I was growing old I have been his daily care & he has served me with daily intelligence & daily affection. The mystery is stranger. Family, police, fiancée(?)[3] know nothing. But he left his watch behind him, and everything in order.

[1] See 2 June 34.
[2] R. Le Gallienne, *The religion of a literary man. Religio scriptoris* (1893).
[3] Alice Hill, a servant in the Rendel household. At the inquest she stated that she was not engaged to Outram; *T.T.*, 15 December 1893, 12a.

To Sir T. D. ACLAND, M.P., 3 December 1893.   Add MS 44549, f. 162.

I cannot refrain from thanking you for your kind words about my wife,[1] who has repelled her influenza wonderfully, and will I hope be at her usual best in a day or two. Our dear friend & physician Sir A. Clark had a great opinion of her constitution, which on all occasions it seems to justify.

Nor can I view without much interest your renewed excursion in the fields of philosophy. I do not know, we cannot know exactly, the frame of mind in which the jurist would receive the utterances on such subjects of men like you & me who must seem so remote from it. But I think that the interest in its future becomes warmer & livelier every day. The feeling in my mind, great in amount, is very mixed in quality. I recognise with joy much real varied and important progress, especially in the greater justice now done to the mass of God's creatures. And I have rather a sanguine hope that our manual labourers of all descriptions will be enabled to overcome the grave temptations of a social more than a political kind, that lie in their path—It is really for the first time that they are now put upon their trial.

I am rather more painfully impressed with the apprehension that the seen world is gaining upon the unseen. The vast expansion of its apparatus seems to have nothing to balance it. The Church which was the appointed instrument of the world's recovery seems, taking all its branches together, rather unequal to its work. I doubt however, whether any effectual & permanent efforts can be made except within its precincts (largely viewed) and under its laws.

I venture to hope that when you pronounce judgment on the undue predominance of logic in positive dogma & in the negative scepticism, you will not regard these two as standing upon quite the same level in regard to claim upon our respect & deference. It seems to me that the singular mode in which the dogma of the Church was matured in Centuries 3–5, & the obstinate durability it has shown, constitute a great marvel of Providential government. I do not mean that my poor private judgment follows sympathetically *all* the dogmatic procedure of that great period. Were I to take my stand on it, I should say the case of Nestorius was a hard one, & the Nestorianism of today hardly seems to carry all the marks of heresy. But in judging of those conclusions, accepted by the great body of the people of God from that day to this, I feel that I do not approach them upon the level, but have to look a little upwards. As to the present scepticism, I have no such sentiment, & think that the common Christian is entitled to deal with it very freely on its merits. The large family of *isms*, huddled together under its name, present to my view not much either of duty or of strength. They have never had a factitious advantage in this, that the work of clearing orthodoxy of its factitious incumbrances has seemed to be, perhaps has been more or less their work.

I am driven back more & more upon the question "When the son of man cometh, shall he find faith upon the Earth"? which cannot be frivolous or ⟨unnecessary⟩ unmeaning since it was put by our Saviour.

[P.S.] I take the opportunity of sending you two little books, Sayce's Fresh Light from the Monuments & Bp. Ld. A Hervey's Defences, called of the Book of Chronicles, but really embracing or touching the general credit of the older historic books. They are alike, free, or shall I say profuse, in criticising the "higher criticism".[2]

4. M. [London]

Wrote to The Queen l.l.—Mr M'Carthy M.P.—Mr Picton MP. Back to D.S. at 12.15. C. making excellent progress. The Outram matter still a blank. Saw Sir

---

[1] Not found.   [2] No reply found.

A.W.—Mr Marj.—Mr Morley—Mr Bryce—Helen G. H. of C. 3¼-8.[1] Still longing in vain for accounts of poor Outram. Reading a little.

5. Tu.

Wrote to Sir H. Ponsonby—Mr Lefevre—Sir W. Harcourt—& minutes. H. of C. 3¾-8.[2] Worked on Odes. Read L. de Keroualle—and [blank.] Saw Sir A.W.—Mr Marj.—Mr Davison—Sir R. Welby. Drive with C.

To Sir W. V. HARCOURT, chancellor of the exchequer,   MS Harcourt dep. 13, f. 205.
5 December 1893.

I think these papers afford a splendid specimen of muddle.[3]

It is indeed singular if we cannot get an answer to the plain question whether the Duke of Coburg *has or has not acquired a German Nationality*.

Can we not absolve them from all discussions about the German Empire, and about the possibility of a double nationality.

Had we not better ask Rosebery to try to obtain a straight answer to our straight question, throwing overboard all collateral matter?

6. Wed.

Wrote to Mad. Novikoff—V. Chr Oxford—Mr Mundella—Mr [C. Robertson] l. & Tel.—and minutes. H. of C. 1-5½.[4] Saw Sir A.W.—Mr Marj.—Chr of Exr—Mr Asquith—Mr Acland—Mr Lefevre—Mr Mundella—Mr Billson—Mr Haldane[5]—Ld Aberdeen. Worked on Odes. Dined at Sir U. Shuttleworth's & conversation. In anticipation of the newspapers tomorrow I stated to the gentlemen at the party the disappearance of Outram.[6] Finished L. de Keroualle.

To A. J. MUNDELLA, president of the board of trade, 6 December 1893. Mundella MSS.

What information have we on the subject of the Scotch dispute?

What efforts have been made by the two parties between themselves?

These are essential matters. In England we had the case fully before us.[7]

To Chisholm ROBERTSON, 6 December 1893.   Add MS 44549, f. 163.

I received last night the telegram which you had addressed to me during an important discussion in the H. of Commons: & perused it with the utmost interest.

The Government regard with high satisfaction the action of Lord Rosebery in the English Coal dispute, & its result.

But any failure in the proceeding would have had a mischievous effect, & failure was avoided by an exact observation of the circumstances of the case.

Both the parties were then before the Government in one & the same attitude,

[1] L.G. Bill; 4*H* 19. 374.
[2] Questions; L.G. Bill; 4*H* 19. 489.
[3] Sent by Harcourt this day; Add MS 44203, f. 130.
[4] L.G. Bill; 4*H* 19. 573.
[5] R. B. Haldane (see 21 June 86n.) was just completing the report for the inquiry into the deaths at Featherstone colliery. See 26 Sept., 14 Dec. 93.
[6] See para. in *D.N.*, 7 December 1893, 6c: 'Disappearance of Mr. Gladstone's Valet'.
[7] See to Robertson, this day.

whereas the telegram you have sent me is written on behalf of one side only, & I doubt whether you would wish us to proffer any request to the Scottish coal owners concerned.

But the main point of difference is this. We had in the English case full proof of repeated efforts at conciliation by direct communication between the parties themselves, & it was also apparent that their powers of obtaining a settlement by independent efforts were exhausted. On the other hand those efforts had not been futile for they had served to bring about approximations such as to offer a hopeful prospect, if the agency of the Government in a capacity carefully limited was introduced. I have not learned that an equal amount of such independent & local effort at agreement has been used in the Scottish case, & there is no proof before me that the power of such efforts had been exhausted. There is therefore a want of parallelism in the two instances at the present moment.

I must remind you that the moral influence of an administration or of a single Minister in such a matter is not an instrument to which it would be prudent to resort habitually, or upon the occurrence of difficulties which might be otherwise surmountable. We should pause before assenting to use it, unless satisfied that a state of facts existed analogous to that which made the action of Lord Rosebery practicable & expedient.

I have however in consequence of your telegram communicated with the President of the Board of Trade.[1] He will also send down to the North a competent officer of his Department to observe & report upon the state of things. In the meantime I hope that what I have written may assist you & those with whom you act to judge whether the controversy now unhappily subsisting in Scotland is likely to assume such a character as would warrant the consideration of the subject with a practical view by the Government.

7. *Th.*

Wrote to Rev. S.E.G.—Duke of Coburg—Ld Kimberley—Ld Prov. Edinb. Tel.—S.L.—and minutes. Wrote on Horatian Transl. Saw Sir A.W.—Mr Marj.—Mr Lockwood—Chr of Exr. H. of C. 3–8 and 10–12.[2] Eight to dinner. Bilious attack came out at night.

8. *Fr.*

A blank day in bed. Great improvement at night. Saw Sir A.W. who read to me from Balabari. Good time for meditation. C. such a nurse! May she not break down. A good turn at night.

9. *Sat.* [*Lion Mansions, Brighton*]

Wrote to Ld Spencer—Chr of Exr—Mr Knowles—and minutes. Saw Sir A. West—Mr Marj. Down to Brighton with daylight train & drive there. Mr A[rmitstead] our host, at the L.M. Worked on Odes. Backgammon with Mr A. Read a *little* of Ward.[3]

---

[1] See to Mundella, this day.
[2] Questions on Morley's illness; L.G. Bill; 4*H* 19. 652.
[3] See 1 Oct. 93.

To Sir W. V. HARCOURT, chancellor of the exchequer, MS Harcourt dep. 13, f. 207.
9 December 1893.

As far as I understand the betterment affair,[1] it stands thus
1. We adopted a particular proposal with its specified conditions.
But we laid down no rules beyond this, & did not undertake to examine the important question how far a recognition of betterment as a ground of charge could be carried.
2. The House of Lords rejected our proposal.
3. They now propose to us to go backwards—and to go forwards.
Backward⟨s⟩ inasmuch as they have not recognised that in this or in any case betterment is a solid ground to stand upon.
And forwards, inasmuch as they propose, in lieu of dealing with this case, or as a preliminary to dealing with it, to examine into all cases alike & determine the conditions (if they affirm the principle) of acceptance or rejection for them all.
4. My observations are two. First this proposal if made at all ought to have been made before and not after rejecting the legislative provision which we had adopted: Secondly the proposal in its substance I think strictly corresponds with a proposal sometimes made in the House of Commons on a particular Bill, viz. to refer not the Bill but the subject of the Bill to a Select Committee.
It conversely[?] means and covers opposition to the Bill, together with reluctance to declare such Opposition.
And the least it can mean is, the subject is *not ripe* for legislation.
I think that were [we] to accept the proposition, our act could only be justified by our concurring in this opinion, which is in truth an opinion exactly the contrary of the opinion which we do hold, and which we have manifested by our legislation in the Bill.
I write this in compliance with your request. Pray do not let it hamper you or Asquith both of whom probably understand the subject much better than I do.

To LORD SPENCER, first lord of the admiralty, 9 December 1893. Althorp MSS K8.

I inclose a Resolution which seems to be in course of adoption by the "Amalgamated Societies or Society of Engineers"—which seems to demand from me more than a mere acknowledgement.
Perhaps you will communicate with Campbell-Bannerman.
Would it be right for me to acknowledge—to say I have forwarded the Resolution to the heads of the Departments concerned—that so far as I am able to judge that consideration is likely to deal with each case upon its merits & with reference to its particular circumstances rather than by general resolution.[2]

10. *2 S. Adv.*

Chapel Royal mg. Afternoon prayers at home: a congregation of 7. Violent gale. The Cust horror:[3] & that from Paris on which much reflection.[4] Wrote on it to Sir W. Harcourt: and Tel. l.l. Read Bryant's Philo. Wrote Eucharistic Devotions out: great part.[5] Also Theol. Note. Wrote to S. Lyttelton.

[1] Harcourt asked Gladstone, 9 December, Add MS 44203, f. 134, 'to send us a few sentences expressing your views as to the ground on which our refusal to join the Lords is to be placed'.
[2] Spencer replied, 11 December, Add MS 44314, f. 97, enclosing a letter from Campbell Bannerman on the 8 hours day: 'we are much disposed to do it', Spencer wrote, 'but whatever is done must be done in concert . . .'. [3] Obscure.
[4] Explosion, with initially over-pessimistic reports of the casualties, of a bomb in the Chamber of Deputies; *D.N.*, 11 December 1893, 5e. [5] In Lathbury, ii. 421.

To Sir W. V. HARCOURT, chancellor of the exchequer,   MS Harcourt dep. 13, f. 210.
10 December 1893.

We must all be deeply impressed with the horror of this outrage in the French Chamber.

And the question arises ought the House of Commons to be moved to express its ⟨sympathy⟩ pain & horror upon the sad proof that there are persons so deluded as to consider both that indiscriminate destruction is among the legitimate instruments of political warfare and that this frightful example should have been given in the free and august assembly of the representatives of a great nation whose peace as well as prosperity we earnestly desire.

Now as to *pros* and *cons*.

For *pros* we have that our expression of sympathy on a great national insult and an attempt only in part abortive at frightful massacre is reasonable, and that such expressions have a great and good effect especially upon a demonstrative people like the French.

We should of course add our grief for the sufferers and our admiration of the dignity and selfcommand of the Chamber.

Now as to the *cons*. First there is the danger of suggesting imitation by giving celebrity to the perpetration of an outrage. When we show how it has moved us, we shall be understood by Anarchism to shew how terrible, therefore how valuable, is the engine put into action by the enemies of Society. On the force & value of this objection, Asquith & the head of the Police would be able to pronounce with much authority.

There is however another objection short of this which weighs more with me as I prolong reflection on the subject. This form of Anarchy is the Russian Nihilism imparted by way of contagion to a few hopeless subjects in other countries. In Russia the Nihilists have much to say, if not for themselves, yet against their opponents. In other countries, it is in the main a causeless, and therefore a degenerate, Nihilism. Of this vicious fanatical vanity, a very wicked vanity, is apt to become the moving principle. Such vanity feeds most of all upon recognition: and recognition is a prize for it, in proportion as the body which gives it is powerful and august.

I lean to thinking on the whole that the direct action of the House of Commons might do more harm than good by ministering to the blind interests of these unreasoning incorrigible men.

I am reluctant however to remain wholly passive. Would a middle turn be inadmissible?

Might our F.O. write a dispatch to Dufferin (which might perhaps include the Queen) saying how anxious we had been to avoid the evil described above, & on the other hand how Britain could not remain entirely silent: that the Executive Govt. had taken it upon themselves to communicate with the Speaker as the authorised representative of the House and with the leaders of the several parties within it (Balfour, Chamberlain, MacCarthy—as I suppose) and that they felt themselves after such communication authorised to state that they were conveying the unanimous sentiment & judgment of the House when they stated on the one hand the horror and indignation, on the other the sympathy with the sufferers, and profound respect for the dignified conduct of the Chamber which possesses every mind on this painful occasion & of which we desire to convey the assurance to (the President on behalf of?) the French Assembly & the people.

These are on the whole my views: but I shall cheerfully concur in what may be thought & concluded on the spot; and I could easily come up if (contrary to my conclusion on considering all the facts) my presence & action is desired at the meeting of the House.

I send by telegraph the upshot of this letter.[1]

---

[1] Draft at Add MS 44203, f. 136, asking Harcourt to consult the Speaker on a formal Commons response, with a later telegram retreating from 'formal action'; 'explain fully by post'. Harcourt replied, 12 December, MS Harcourt dep. 13, f. 215: the Speaker to write to the President of the French Chamber, the letter being entered in the Journals of the House and debate thus avoided.

11. *M.*

Worked on Odes. Made Computation of work. Saw Holyoake—Ripon—Acton (much & long). Backgammon with R[endel]. Read F. Newman on Hymns.[1]

12. *Tu.*

Wrote to The Queen—Sir W. Harcourt—Sir A. West—Canon McColl—Ld Spencer—Mr Diamond M.P.[2] Tremendous house-shaking storm all day. Worked on Odes. I have now done all but half. Saw Acton: he left. Backgammon with Mr A.

To Sir W. V. HARCOURT, chancellor of the exchequer,   MS Harcourt dep. 13, f. 217.
12 December 1893.

In the matter of the French Chamber I think you on the spot have judged rightly that promptitude was essential and so likewise the exclusion of irresponsible outsiders, and I think the matter is well disposed of.[3] Nothing I suppose now remains except a gracious transmission to the President of the Republic through Dufferin. I am under the impression that the Speaker can and ought to do nothing except with reference to the formal acts of the House: we have more elbow room. Even had there been a formal Act I do not think the Speaker would go beyond the precedents whatever they may be.

As to the compliment I admit that though deserved it might have been thought to be on our part an assumption of *title* to pronounce: so that probably we are as well without it.

I did not happen to know if you were going to Sandringham or I would have written to some one else.

Another violent storm here but the wind not straight on shore.

I am greatly shocked at the popular manifestations in Italy, but not at all surprised. Their *megalomania* has been the root of it all.

We propose to come up tomorrow afternoon

[P.S.] Fowler was not in the least bound by usage to go to Windsor; but he was well entitled to take the relaxation, if it was one.

To LORD SPENCER, first lord of the Admiralty, 12 December 1893.   Althorp Mss K8.

I was not aware that the Eight Hours question had made such large advances.[4] In the actual state of the case I think a letter should be written not from me but on my behalf, simply stating that on communication with the Departments I learn that the matter will be deliberated and carefully examined. If you disapprove or wish to add please send a line to West, & he will suspend action.

[P.S.] It seems that this body does not act from a Centre but through a multitude of Branches, one of which is as good as another & in answering one all are answered.

13. *Wed.* [*London*]

Wrote to Chr of Exr Tel.—Sir H. James—Mr S.L. Tel.—Mr Holyoake—Mr S. Lyttelton. Back by the 2.20. H. of C. 3.50–5.30.[5] Saw Sir W. Harcourt. l.l. Dined

---

[1] F. W. Newman, *Secret hymns* (1892); see 31 Dec. 92.

[2] To Charles Diamond (1858–1934, journalist and home rule M.P. 1892–5) on Irish education; see Add MS 44549, f. 165.

[3] See 10 Dec. 93. Harcourt drew up 'a brief form of words' and released it to the Press; Add MS 44203, f. 139.

[4] See to Spencer, 9 Dec. 93n.

[5] East Indian loan; 4*H* 19. 1269.

with Mr Marjoribanks. Had the news of Zadok's sad end.[1] Much consideration
& conversation. Wished to attend the Inquest, but at any rate I give partial testimony by a letter.[2] Worked on Odes. Read a little in Conington's Preface.[3]

14. Th.

Wrote to The Queen—Mr Morley—Scotts—and minutes.

Excellent letter from S.E.G. on the sad case of Z. Outram. Verdict "Found
drowned".[4] Beaten in Life's battle. God rest his wearied soul. O come quickly is
the upshot.

Cabinet 11–12¾. Rough prospects for Navy charge. H. of C. 3¾–8.[5] Saw Sir
A.W.—Mr Marj.—Mr Bryce. Worked on Odes. Candlelight reading now verges
on the impossible.

Cabinet. Thurs. Dec. 14. 93. 11 AM.[6]
1. Queen's Letters Read.[7] Sense of responsibility.
2. G. Hamilton's motion. Give Tuesday. Mr. G. to move amndt.
3. Christmas Holidays. Resist the Lords Amts. *simpliciter*. (What can the Lords do?)
4. Fowler's proposal. Xmas holidays. Wednesday only.
5. Drage's Report.[8] Asquith—will communicate with Chairman of Commission.
6. Asquith's Inquiry.[9]

To J. MORLEY, Irish secretary, 14 December 1893.   Add MS 44549, f. 166.

We have had a Cabinet today which grew up from circumstances unforeseen.[10] On the
7th the Queen wrote me an alarmist letter about Army & Navy & desired me to read it to
the Cabinet.

[1] Found drowned in the Thames.
[2] Gladstone's communication, in the name of Spencer Lyttelton, was read out at the inquest on
14 December; it offered 'to give evidence as to the high esteem in which he held the deceased, his
gratitude for the admirable and unremitting services rendered by him, and his very high opinion of
his intelligence'; *D.N.*, 15 December 1893, 7e.
[3] See 12 Dec. 93.
[4] The verdict was 'found drowned ... but how he got into the water there was no evidence to
show'; *T.T.*, 15 December 1893, 12a.
[5] Spoke on the state of public business; 4*H* 19. 1399.
[6] Add MS 44648, f. 138.
[7] On 7 December the Queen asked Gladstone to consult his colleagues on the adequacy of the
army and navy, stating her view that an increase in the navy and a strengthening of the army were
essential; she subsequently repeated her request that her letter be discussed in Cabinet; Gladstone
reported that the letter had been read to the Cabinet, which took the view that Hamilton's motion
was a vote of no confidence and that a govt. amndt. would accordingly be moved; Guedalla, *Q*, ii.
478.
[8] i.e. as part of the Royal Commission on the Aged Poor, of which Geoffrey Drage was secretary.
[9] Illegible phrase follows: may read 'No Union but intended'. Inquiry into the Featherstone affair
(use of troops by the magistrates against strikers); Bowen, Rollit and Haldane were appt. to a Special
Commission; see H. H. Asquith, *Memories and reflections* (1928), i. 129ff.
[10] Morley, convalescing in Monte Carlo, replied on 17 December, Add MS 44257, f. 137, that
'there may be a case for a large increase in naval strength' but that he knew no details; he was given
'lively concern that the accident of his office should make Spencer the organ of the alarmists. . . . It is
a serious misfortune that Spencer, whose future position is likely to be so important, should be compelled to take a line in which he may not be followed by some of those who most value him.'

From accidental causes we could not meet until today. Meantime Lord G. Hamilton gave notice of a motion for a Navy scare & Balfour asks me today what course I propose to take with regard to it. It is a Vote of want of confidence & a good deal more, the most factious & dangerous motion I have ever known announced from the opposition Bench. We accept the challenge & I meet it with a traversing amendment: on Tuesday next the Debate is to come. It is regarded as good for us in a party view.

But over & above this there was a disclosure of view & tendencies prevailing at the Admiralty, which Spencer is anxious to bring before us on some early day. In my view they seem to indicate another of these irrational and discreditable panics which generate one another & to which Spencer will probably feel himself obliged to bow; or will think himself so. They seem to indicate a large increase of the Navy estimates probably with most unsatisfactory financial consequences. Many of the Cabinet remained silent. But on the whole & excepting the protests of Harcourt, economy appeared to be not dying but dead. With these indications upon me I felt myself bound in honour to say that I could in no way pledge myself to take part in proposals of such a colour & must reserve active liberty of action which as S. fairly enough said was "very serious". I greatly wished you had been present: for it was one of the conversations that throw light upon the future; unless my estimate of it is too darkly coloured. Nothing more is likely to happen for at any rate the remainder of this present month. By that time you will probably have returned. But I hope you will on no account hurry—make a clean job of it.

Xmas holidays are from 22nd Friday—to meet again Wednesday 27th! No confident estimate can be formed of the time the County Government Bill may still require.

Do not attach too much consequence to this letter: but I did not like to leave you wholly uninformed.

The sad death of Zadok Outram has been a great sorrow to us. There is an inquest on him today.

15. Fr.

Wrote to Scotts—Sir J. Paget Tel.—Ld Spencer—Ld Rosebery—Westell l.l.—and minutes. H. of C. 3½–8¼.[1] Sir J. Paget kindly gave me the benefit of a long conversation on my situation medically, and in respect to the eyes. Decided on examination by Nettleship.[2] Worked on Odes. Drive with C.—my treasure. Arranged my little money presents for the 13 grandchildren. Reading in evg— rather a failure. Saw Mr Rathbone—Mr Everett.

To LORD SPENCER, first lord of the Admiralty, 15 December 1893. Althorp MSS K8.

Will you be kind enough to send me a copy of the paper which the Admiralty has supplied to Harcourt, & which sets forth the condition of the Navy with regard to battle-ships.[3]

Also any similar paper with regard to Cruisers—(I am not certain as to the form in which this information has been given.)

I was glad to find that you had wisely turned your attention to the important question whether & how far it is practicable to shorten the time required for ship-building &

[1] Questioned on the Featherstone inquiry; 4H 19. 1503.
[2] Edward Nettleship, 1845–1913; ophthalmic surgeon at St. Thomas's; operated on Gladstone's cataract 1894.
[3] Memoranda of 1, 5 and 8 December on naval construction 1894–9, the first, on comparative strength of capital ships marked 'Prepared for the Chancellor of the Exchequer'; Althorp MSS K466.

especially (as I presume) for battleships. This seems especially important at a time when, so far as I yet see, the question of ship-building touches mainly the condition of the Navy not in the present but in early future years.

16. Sat.

Wrote to Sir H. James—Helen G.—G.S. Herbert—J.G. Scott—Sir W. Harcourt— Mr Asquith—Mr Mundella—and minutes. Saw Sir A.W.—Mr S.L.—Ld Spencer. Drove to Mrs T.s for tea. She had influenza. Dined at Mr A.s. Backgammon in evg. Spent time in arranging papers. Worked on Odes. Stopped in IV.1. by sheer disgust.[1] C. went to Hawarden—What a spirit! By the same train, the remains of Z. Outram.

To Sir W. V. HARCOURT, chancellor of the exchequer,   MS Harcourt dep. 13, f. 222. 16 December 1893.

You are named prominently in a portion of what I inclose and I fear I must ask you to look at the two letters ⟨inclosed⟩ of Rathbone & Fowler.

I do not think that the Cabinet understood that they were deciding in *Opposition* to Fowler: he evidently thinks the contrary and the point is of some importance. For my own part I accepted the decision without (I think) taking part in the conversation.[2]

To G. S. HERBERT,[3] 16 December 1893. 'Private'.   Add MS 44517, f. 339. My dear Boy,

It is very sad. I feel for you. And I feel with you. As you cannot get to Ireland, so I cannot get home, to my only home, at Christmas. And you I hope will have many, very many, very happy Christmases: but I having had eighty three already, feel I am taking one of my last chances.

Can anything be done? Not by me. But I think your Father could do something, if he thought it right to ask some ten or a dozen of his friends whether they could possibly abate a little the number and length of their speeches? For they are so fond of him that I believe they would then do it. But I could not expect them to do it for my asking. If they did it for him, there is no saying whether it might enable you to go to Ireland.

With best wishes for Christmas, Easter, and all other times.

---

[1] Horace's Ode to Venus; Gladstone's footnote to his translation records: 'The concluding lines of the Ode are purposely omitted.' He omitted the final eight lines:

      ... In dreams at night
      I hold you in my arms, or toil behind your flight
      Across the Martian Field,
      Or chase through yielding waves the boy who will not yield.

(*The Odes of Horace*, translated by James Michie (1964), 223.)

[2] Harcourt replied on 18 December, Add MS 44203, f. 154: 'I had thought that the proposal that the Local County Councillor should be *virtute officii* on the Board of Guardians had been mentioned and disapproved in the Cabinet. It is I think a weak suggestion....'

[3] George Sidney Herbert (Sidney Herbert's grandson), then aged 16, at Eton; he had written to complain of a shortening of the Christmas holidays. His father, Lord Pembroke, was a tory whip in the Lords. The letter was sent to Herbert Gladstone in 1930, who docketed it on 31 August 1931.

17. *3 S. Adv.*

Ch. Royal mg & aft. Wrote to C.G.—Mr Westell. Wrote Autob. MS.[1] And Euch. Devotions. Read the remainder of Newman's Hymns—and Bryant on Philo. Saw Sir A. West.

18. *M.*

Wrote to Ld Rosebery—Sir H. Ponsonby—Mr Fowler—Mr Rathbone—Att. Gen.—Sir A. Godley—Ld Spencer—The Speaker—M. Drew—C.G.—& minutes. H. of C. $3\frac{3}{4}$–$8\frac{1}{4}$ (Drive).[2] Saw Sir A.W.—Mr Marj.—Mr S. Rendel—Ld Rosebery—Sir W.H. *cum* Mr Marj. Worked on Navy Facts. Worked on Odes. A troubled night physically, in brain only. This is certainly the weakness of old age unfitting me for Parliamentary effort. I was however able to hold to my rule. Read Pericles.[3] Mr Ponsonby brought me a troubled & troubling letter from the Speaker.[4]

To Mrs. GLADSTONE, 18 December 1893.   Hawarden MS 780, f. 232.
My beloved C.

Greatly pleased with your satisfactory accounts. We shall look with much interest for the Outram funeral. Much & long will he be missed.

We have a day which yields no news for you but that the Duke of Coburg has signed his renunciation so that business ought to be disposed of before Christmas.

And that there is much more folly in the world than I had supposed: so that it will be no easy matter tomorrow to state the truth and hardly possible to get fair play for it. Some steering will be required.

Helen is beyond anything active, quiet, and valuable. Sir Wilfred Lawson has been with her about sending a daughter to Nuneham [*sc.* Newnham College].

Did you observe in a Lesson yesterday from Isaiah that both the priests & other prophets were he says taken with & overthrown by strong drink

Love to G. & the three
Your ever affte. WEG

To LORD ROSEBERY, foreign secretary, 18 December 1893.   N.L.S. 10027, f. 97.

1. I am bound in fairness to admit that though I said truly in the Cabinet that I had not seen signs of alarm, I have since become aware that there is more folly in the world *re* Naval scares than I had given it credit for. Of course in this I make no reference to the question of our strength or weakness in the Mediterranean which is a question of distribution.[5]

2. Will you send me (what I think you described to me *vivâ voce*) copy of your record of the position in which you left the Egyptian question in Conference with the Ottoman Ambassador. Is there not something curious in the long silence of the Turk, and the still longer silence since Waddington gave tongue.

[1] On auricular confession and the 1840s; *Autobiographica*, i. 158.
[2] Questions; L.G. Bill; 4*H* 19. 1616.
[3] i.e. Shakespeare's play.
[4] Intending resignation; see next day's letter.
[5] Rosebery replied, 18 December, N.L.S. 10027, f. 99, that 'if as I think it possible from your letter today, you are prepared to fall in with the general anxiety for the increase of our fleet, I would most earnestly urge you to let this be plainly evident in your speech tomorrow'.

19 Tu.

Wrote to Sir A. West—Sir H. Ponsonby—C.G.—and minutes. Much bothered with altered figures from the Admiralty. Saw Sir A.W.—Mr M.—Lord Spencer. Put together Notes for speech. Drive with H.—H. of C. $3\frac{1}{2}$-$8\frac{1}{4}$ and 10-$12\frac{3}{4}$. Moved my amendment. Majority 36.[1] The situation almost hopeless when a large minority allows itself in panic and joining hands with the professional elements works on the susceptibilities of a portion of the people to alarm.

To Mrs. GLADSTONE, 19 December 1893.   Hawarden MS 780, f. 234.

My own C.

Today I have a *job* to do in the House of Commons. Whether I shall do it tolerably or not, I can not tell. In this matter as in all others I am in the hands of God and am content so to be.

The account of poor dear Christian's operation from Florence is very touching; & it seems uncertain whether the results if good will be confined to the stopping further mischief and she had no chloroform.

The Speaker sent me a letter last night offering resignation, & desiring 6 weeks absence. My answer was to put resignation aside & to say whatever rest he wanted he must have. He goes away on Friday. They say he is a good deal *hypped*.

I inclose a note from Mrs. T. She has cooked up a habit of much fuss about small things.

I *hope* your return will be Thursday: but of course you must be governed by the reason of the case. My Friday prospects not good at present. Ever your afft. WEG

I write at 1.30. Boys not here yet.

20. Wed.

Wrote to Mr Balfour—The Queen—and minutes. H. of C. $1\frac{1}{4}$-$5\frac{1}{2}$.[2] Cabinet *conclave* $11\frac{1}{2}$-$12\frac{1}{2}$. Saw Sir A.W.—Mr Marj.—Mr Balfour—Ld Spencer—Sir W. Harcourt—Mr Walpole. Dined at A. Morley's. Worked on Odes. Read Life of Khama.[3] C. returned from Hn has developed *erythema*—has I fear worked too hard.

21. Th.

Wrote to Ld Rosebery—The Queen l.l.—Sir R. Welby—Dep. Speaker—and minutes. Drive with Helen. Read Pericles: finished. Saw Sir A.W.—Mr Marj.— Archd. Sinclair—Mr Asquith—Sir W.H. Dined with Mrs Sands. H. of C. $3\frac{3}{4}$-$7\frac{1}{2}$. Narrow escape on the Duke of Coburg's case from a 'tight place'.[4] C. has still her Erythema. Saw Deputation on the Clark Memorial.[5]

[1] Moved amndt. to Lord G. Hamilton's motion on the navy; 4*H* 19. 1771.
[2] Lords amndts. to Employers' Liability Bill; 4*H* 20. 3.
[3] W. Knight-Bruce, *The story of an African chief: Khama* (1893).
[4] His statement on Saxe-Coburg's annuities challenged by Labouchere and Dàlziel; 4*H* 20. 105.
[5] See 3 Apr. 94.

To LORD ROSEBERY, foreign secretary, 21 December 1893.   N.L.S. 10027, f. 102.

I construed or misconstrued your letter of the 18th[1] as a consigning to paper of what you had *said* when you were here last, but for fear I should have been wrong I write this line to say that my declaration at this moment would (& I have consulted Spencer on this) roll down again the storm which on Tuesday night we rolled up with great labour but there is a further difficulty, it would at once lead to a demand for *action*, i.e. Lord G. Hamilton over again. But, aware of the desire to get matters forward I have recommended Spencer at once to hold communication with Harcourt, and this I believe will be the quickest way of putting matters in train for an early decision by the Cabinet.

22. *Fr.* [*Lion Mansions, Brighton*]

Wrote to S.L.–.......–and minutes. Saw Sir A.W.–Mr Marj.–Sir Jas Paget *cum* Mr Bond (consultation on C.G. good)–Sir P. Currie (H. of C. 2–3¼.)[2] Ld Spencer. To Brighton by 4.20. Backgammon with Mr A. Worked a little on Odes. Read 'Two Noble Lives'.[3]

23. *Sat.*

Wrote to C.G.–Duke of Coburg. Worked on Odes. Read Newmans Preface–Two Noble Lives. Walk with Mr A. Also drive. Also backgammon. Saw Mrs Oppenheim.[4]

To Mrs. GLADSTONE, 23 December 1893.   Hawarden MS 780, f. 236.
Beloved C.

Though the indefatigable kindness of Mr A. has already 'wired you' I know you will like such detail as the case admits of. Our little affairs are all prosperous but as we are only two and the accommodation better if possible than ever the luxury seems ⟨good⟩ to have increased and I to be more drowned in it: the only thing wanted is a good odoscope to see continually how you are getting on. My faith in your rallying power after you have once taken the turn is great & I am come greatly sanguine as to your rate of progress. We had good nights' sleep in the bedroom some frost and a little fog but the sun is now breaking through (in the room Mr Rendel took) and shining on my back but Mr A. will not consent to dine behind the curtain for fear of dinner smell.

Helen's appearance here today will be a good sign of you but I hope she will not come on my account because I am already so well looked after that I have not a rag of a pretext for even wishing it. We were nearly ½ hour late yesterday and I fear she will have a great crowd and exercise of patience today. If we know the time we will send Richmond to meet her.

I was struck by the facility with which Paget entered into medical particulars & seemed thoroughly *up* in them. Query it strikes me whether after all he might not at any rate as referee be the best available substitute for Clark?

We are looking forward to walk & drive but the trip is & now must remain short & imperfect without you. Am also missing Zadok at every turn: in all these years he had fitted into the nooks & crannies of one's life.

[1] See 18 Dec. 93n.
[2] Questioned on navy; 4*H* 20. 213.
[3] A. J. C. Hare, *The story of two noble lives* [Lady Canning, Lady Waterford], 3v. (1893).
[4] Isabel, *née* Butler, wife of H. W. M. Oppenheim.

I say nothing to hasten you for I fear I did mischief by stimulating your return from Hawarden, in making you do too much.

I inclose the first Xmas telegrams from the ever faithful Hall. Ever your afft. WEG

24. 4 S. Adv.

Chapel Royal mg & evg. Read Bryant on Philo—Two Noble Lives—Hills Ed. Tatians Diatessaron.[1] Wrote to C.G.—H.N.G. Wrote on Theol. Walk with H. & Mr A. Wild day.

25. Xm D. M.

Chapel Royal mg with H.C. and evg. Lord & Lady Cork dined: much friendly conversation. Read the Two Noble Lives. Finished Bryant on Philo. Read also . . . .

26. Tu.

Wrote to Prof. Murray—The Queen. Drive to Devil's Dyke. Worked on Odes. Read Two Noble Lives.

27. Wed. [London]

Wrote to The Queen. Off at 9.30. D. St 11.45: much fog. H. of C. $12\frac{1}{4}-5\frac{1}{2}$.[2] Eight to dinner. Saw Harcourt: on the great admiralty scare. Also H. with Sol. General—Mr Murray. Read Durgesa.[3]

28. Th.

Wrote to Chancr of Exr—Ld Rosebery l.l.—Ld C. Russell—J. Morley—Mr Westell—Ld Chancr—and minutes. Honours conclave. 12-1 Unemployed Deput.[4] Saw Mr Murray—Mr Mundella cum Mr Fowler—Deputation on the unemployed—Ld Acton—Mr Marj. Worked on Odes! H. of C. $3\frac{1}{2}-8$.[5] Read Two Noble Lives.

To Sir W. V. HARCOURT, chancellor of the exchequer,   MS Harcourt dep. 13, f. 232.
28 December 1893.

(Question V. Gibbs)

Can you send me the terms of your recent reply about the Naval Lords? I would found upon it, & know nothing beyond?[6]

[P.S.] Subject of last night *stiffen* in my mind more & more.

---

[1] J. H. Hill, *The earliest life of Christ: Diatessaron of Tatian* (1893).
[2] Questions; L.G. Bill; 4 *H* 20. 269.
[3] *Durgesa Nandini, or the Chieftain's daughter. A Bengali romance . . . tr. C. C. Mookerjee* (1880).
[4] Dpn. from various London local authorities on public works; Gladstone had several sharp exchanges with members of the depn.; *T.T.*, 29 December 1893, 5f.
[5] L.G. Bill; 4 *H* 20. 348.
[6] Harcourt replied next day that he had been through the figures with Shuttleworth, that they were very different from those related by Spencer ('not an adept at figures') and that the average expenditure p.a. for the last 5 years on new construction had been £4.5 million (including £2 million p.a. out of the Consolidated Fund); Add MS 44203, f. 156.

To J. MORLEY, Irish secretary, 28 December 1893.   Add MS 44549, f. 170.

In our Naval debate I personally laid it down in strong terms that there existed no condition of Naval danger *or* I think emergency. I am at present puzzled to find an answer to
the question how, as matter of honour, such a declaration would stand in the light thrown
upon it by the adoption a month afterwards of the stronger scheme which was in our
mouths last night.[1]

29.

I record my 84th birthday with thanks and humiliation. My strength has been
wonderfully maintained but digestive organs are I think beginning to fail: deafness is (at present) a greater difficulty, and sight the greatest.

I sometimes hope it has been a year of some improvement: certainly of more
vivid sense of need. But oh how far am I at all times & in all things from the true
Christian pattern.

I have had a heavy loss in Sir A. Clark: & a touching one in Zadok Outram.
The love & service of C[atherine] remains wonderful: that of all my children
hardly less so.

Wrote to Ly Aberdeen—Ld R. Gower—Mr R. Meade—Lord Kelvin—The
Queen—Arthur Lyttelton—Honours Circulars. Cabinet 12–1¾. H of C. 3½–7¾.[2]
Eight to dinner. Worked on Odes. Read Othello. Saw Mr Murray—Mr Marj.—
Do cum Sir W. Harcourt—Mr Morley. Drive with H.

Cabinet. Frid. D. 29. 93. Noon.[3]
Local Govt. Bill. Harcourt recited particulars of a conference with Balfour, A. Douglas, &
Long on 1. Time, 2. Amendments. Require—Whole Bill by 19th.
Amendments.
1. Beach 2 coopted[?] Grant.
2. Hiring of land. Extend term to 21 [years] if necessary.
3. Four acres. Adhere—especially as to grass. (It was felt that one acre was the proper
   ordinary limit[)]
4. Buildings on lived land—agree.
5. Good land not to be broken up—agree.
6. Hobhouse's amendment. Discretionary loan to L.G. Board or arbitrator.
7. Land under contract of sale—exclude bogus contracts. May deal.
8. Parish rooms raised by one denomination—accept definition read by Bryce.
If all is broken off, resolution for closure by compartments from day to day.

30. Sat.

Wrote to S.E.G.—Sir W. Harcourt—Mr Gardner—Duke of Rutland—Mr Morley
—Col. Larkins[4]—& minutes. Drive with H. & calls. Worked on Odes. Read Dur-
gesa: what a ruffian! Dined at Mr A.s: backgammon. Saw Mr Murray—Mr
Marj.—Ld Acton.

[1] Morley reported, 30 December, Add MS 44257, f. 139, that Harcourt informed him of 'a complete misunderstanding as to the comparative magnitude of Spencer's demand'.
[2] Questioned on Egypt, on the Speaker; L.G. Bill; 4 *H* 20. 442.   [3] Add MS 44648, f. 140.
[4] Thanking his cousin (see 29 May 57) for 'the Memorial of my boyhood which you have been so
good as to send me'; Add MS 44549, f. 171.

To Sir W. V. HARCOURT, chancellor of the exchequer,   MS Harcourt dep. 13, f. 233.
30 December 1893.

Does not the amended view of the proposal[1] come to this:

An *exceptional* expenditure having been proposed by the late Govt. to make up arrears
& lay in a stop for the future—and having been a good deal objected to for excess (as well
as on financial grounds) by the Liberal party—it is proposed to adopt a rate equal to the
whole of that exceptional expenditure, and to add to it a million & a half?

There ought really to be clear & intelligible figures from the Admiralty as a *preliminary*
to any discussion on this subject.

Lastly are you quite sure about the *average* of the last five years taken as the standard.

31. S. aft. Xm.

Ch. Royal mg and evg. Wrote to K. of Belgians Tel.—M. Drew—H. Drew. Saw
Mr Murray. C.G. at afternoon Ch. Read Law's 1st Letter—Gore's Introduction[2]—Luccock on Scotch Ch.[3]

Farewell, old year. Will there be another?

Th[eology][4]

The Thirty Nine Articles walk (as it seems to me) at times along the edge of a precipice,
yet without actually tumbling down.

I have signed and could sign them. The *imponens* is the English Church. If the framers
were the original *imponentes*, I should not like to be bound to all their opinions.

The titles of the Articles are not I believe part of the Articles. Had they been imposed I
think I must have kicked scores of years ago at the Thirteenth, which according to the
title[5] would affirm that all works done 'before justification' have the nature of sin. In the
body of the Article this is predicated not of works before justification, but of 'works done
before the grace of Christ and the inspiration of his Spirit'. That is a different matter. For
the grace of Christ and the inspiration of His Spirit may reach infinitely farther than what
we 'forensically' term justification: whether this was or was not present to the minds of
men under the many narrowing influences of the Reformation controversy. Is there then
no good among Heathens and non-Christians? Take the self-sacrifice of Regulus, an
imperfect but true martyrdom. Take the deaths of the two brothers ([blank]) in Herodotus,[6] after drawing the car of the god. Take the hymns recently published by Professor
Newman.[7] Our Blessed Lord is alas studiously expunged from them; but it would (so far
as I see) be absolutely profane to deny that they contain some piety.

We are not however wholly extricated from difficulty. The Article is not content with
its dogmatic assertion: it adds the reasons why works done before an access of grace have
the nature of sin. It is because they 'spring not from faith in Jesus Christ'. No: and as I
would not venture to make any assertion about any works done before the 'grace of
Christ' has had some access to the soul in its now faulty and degenerated condition. No
direct difficulty then arises upon the words of the Article. But they throw a curious light

[1] See 28 Dec. 93n.
[2] J. O. Nash and C. Gore, *William Law's defence of Church principles. Three letters to the Bishop of Bangor 1717-1719* (1893).
[3] See 9 Apr. 93.
[4] Holograph dated 31 December 1893; Add MS 44775, f. 258.
[5] 'Of Works before Justification'.
[6] See 16 Dec. 92.
[7] F. W. Newman, *Secret hymns* (1892); see 11 Dec. 93.

upon the ideas of the framers. Let us consider the matter logically. Certain works have the nature of sin. Why? because they are not founded upon faith in Christ. Therefore in the minds of the framers all works have the nature of sin, which are not founded on faith in Jesus Christ. That means a faith consciously founded upon him. Therefore it would seem they thought all works sinful, except such as were performed (of course I do not refer to those of the elder covenant) out of a faith consciously resting on this everblessed nature. This has an aspect somewhat horrible.

These works, says the Article have the nature of sin. What then is sin? Is it not voluntary conflict with the will of God? But in the Litany we speak, and I suppose correctly, of our 'sins negligences and ignorances.' The last term denotes what we absolutely did not know. Our negligences are ignorances in thought, or omissions in action, of what we ought to have known and might have known. For both of them we ask pardon from God. Yet would it not be over stern to say that all our ignorances, for example, 'have the nature of sin?' Is it intended to lay down the doctrine that everything that falls short of perfection, and so far as it falls short of perfection, being undoubtedly imperfection, is therefore also sin? Sin is indeed a terrible and an awful thing. Especially in an age which seems so largely to have blunted the edge of the old conceptions about it, and which seldom I fear hears it denounced as it deserves. But may it not be very seriously questioned whether to stretch the notion of it beyond its true and exact conception, while it seems to aim at loftiness and dignity of tone, is the true way for those who desire to see the hatred of it made vigorous and intense. The result may be not so much stringency of dealing with elements comparatively innocent, as confusion and laxity in our mental apprehension of the monster-mischief, and a consequent coolness and slackness as to the remedial means necessary for putting it down.

London Jany 1894.

Mond. Jan One. Circumcision.

Wrote to the Queen—J. Morley—& minutes. Worked on the Navy figures: they seem but too conclusive. Worked on Odes. Drive $\frac{1}{2}$ h. with H. Six to dinner: backgammon. Saw Mr M.—Ld Acton—Mr Marj.—Sir W. Harcourt. H. of C. $3\frac{1}{4}$–$7\frac{1}{2}$.[1] Read Two Noble Lives: Dove Andiamo.

Separating the charge under the Naval Defence Act from the forces as an ordinary charge, we find that
1. In 1888–9, the year before the N.D. Act, the Estimates were 13 ₥
2. For the first year *under* the N.D. Act the Naval Expenditure was 15,271m showing an increase of 2,271m within a year: all paid out of the *revenues* of the year.
3. The average expenditure for these five years was 16,190m.
4. The charge for 1888–9 may be considered as representing the normal charge. The average for the five preceding years had been 13,235m including the expenditure of 3,500m from the vote of credit: or something over $12\frac{1}{2}$ ₥ without that expenditure.
5. My point of departure is the 13 ₥ of 1888–9.
6. In addition to this Parliament has already imposed by the Naval Defence Act on the finance of the year 1894–5 the sum of £1429m in respect of money previously laid out but by law then to be repaid. This makes the charge £14,429m. Possibly something more making about 1500m.
7. To this as I understand it is proposed by the Admiralty to add 4 ₥ making 18,429m.
8. Thus the charge, under the law as it stands, would be 2,239m above the average of the five years of the Naval Defence Act.
9. If by a change in the law the sum of 1429m already spent were thrown upon the future, the charge would then be 810m *above* the average of these five years of extraordinary expenditure.
10. The highest expenditure heretofore provided for the revenue of the year was (1892–3) 15,731m. The scheme now in contemplation would entail a charge of 17 ₥, or an increase of £1,689m.

WEG Jan 1. 94[2]

2. Tu.

Wrote to Mr Leake—Ld Kimberley—Ld Spencer—& minutes. Managed some work on O[des]. H. of C. $3\frac{1}{2}$–$7\frac{3}{4}$.[3] Saw Sir A.W.—Mr Marj.—Mr Haynes. Backgammon with H. Sir W. Harcourt came to me on the Navy imbroglio: rather severe. Worked further on Navy question. Read & C.G. read to me, The Two Noble Lives.

---

[1] Questions; L.G. Bill; 4*H* 21. 552.
[2] Holograph; Add MS 44776, f. 1. Details of naval expenditure since 1835, in a secretary's hand, follow, ibid., ff. 3–9.
[3] Questions; L.G. Bill; 4*H* 21. 655.

To LORD SPENCER, first lord of the Admiralty, 2 January 1894.[1]   Althorp MSS K8.

I thank you very much for letting me see your memorandum[2] at once.

I append certain remarks on it, *apart* from what is to me the main question.

1. I think some correction of the press is needed as to the present comparison of strength in first class battleships.

2. I presume that in European waters you include the Black Sea. I do not know whether this is a recognised use: There is also an important question as to reckoning the Black Sea Fleet as if it were *free*.

3. Your plan is a five year plan. Such a plan according to the Tories requires an Act; & you may find this argument hard to get rid of. You cannot altogether bind the estimates of the future.

4. The promise, not the mere hope, under the N.D. Act was double: it was 1. to make up arrears, 2. *to lay in a stock*.

With regard to what I have termed the main matter, I am entirely at your command at any hour tomorrow. If later than 12 it should be in my room at the H. of Commons.

[P.S.] I send you a paper in which I have attempted to embody the facts so far as I had heard them. Your paper adds about $\frac{1}{4}$ million to the charge as taken by me. Please return it.

3. *Wed.*

Wrote to The Queen—Mr Adams Acton—and minutes. Murray read me the Spencer Memm.[3] H. of C. 1-3$\frac{1}{2}$, 4$\frac{1}{2}$-9$\frac{1}{2}$.[4]

I have felt myself rather hard hit from a combination of circumstances: I seem to stand alone though Morley is sympathetic: my sleep is a good deal disturbed: but 'it is the Lord: let him do what seemeth him good['].

The perpetual more or less dark fog[5] odd to say contributes: I have always been open in a degree to this influence.

Today I saw Spencer 1-2 and explained everything. In tone and temper, there was nothing to be desired. Of substantial progress hardly any.

We agreed that in any case I ought to wind up the present Session.

Eight to dinner. Read Othello. Helen read to me Two Noble Lives. Wrote also to Ld Spencer—J. Morley—Mary Drew.

To LORD SPENCER, first lord of the admiralty, 3 January 1894.   Althorp MSS K8.

On a point secondary but not unimportant I send a word. Your figures you said were approximate figures. A Cabinet never (so far as my knowledge goes) definitively adopts Estimates except upon exact figures, or what may be called such.[6]

---

[1] Misdated '1893' by Gladstone.

[2] In Althorp MSS K466; see also *Spencer*, ii. 233.

[3] See to Spencer, the previous day.

[4] L.G. Bill; 4*H* 21. 753.

[5] London was enveloped in a pea-soup fog.

[6] Spencer replied next day, Add MS 44314, f. 101, explaining that the nature of shipbuilding meant that figures could prospectively only be 'approximate', and apologised for his inexperience in preparing Estimates; 'if the Cabinet approved of the general propositions, I should of course expect that they should be reviewed & gone over in detail . . .'.

4. *Th.*

Wrote to Ld Kimberley—Ld Spencer—Lady Cork—Sig. Villari—Rev. S.E.G.—and minutes. H. of C. 3½–8.[1] Saw Sir A.W.—Mr Marj.—Mr Carvell Williams—Mr Morley 12 to 1: on the Navy question—most sympathetic. Savage weather. Worked on Odes. Helen read to me Two Noble Lives. Could hardly get on at all by candlelight in my large type Othello.

The "approximate figure" of charge involved in the new plan of the Admiralty is £4,240,000 say 4¼ millions. Being an increase (subject probably to some further increase in becoming exact)
1. on the normal Navy Estimate (i.e. before the Naval Defence Act) of in round numbers (1888–9) 4¼ millions.
2. On the first year's total charge under the Naval Defence Act of 2 millions (1,979,000).
3. On the *Estimates* of last year
   1893–4 of . . . . 3 millions
4. On the total charge of 93–4 of 1½ million (1571m)
5. On the highest amount ever defrayed from the year's revenue (1892–3) 1½ million
6. On the highest *Expenditure* of any year under the ND Act which included 1150m. of Gov. vowed money . . . . 359 m.

[The increase made in 89–90, under the N.D. Act, on the expenditure of 88–9 was 2¼ ⋔
a. to reduce the great danger to Liberal party and policy.
b. to alter the character of the proceeding as a stimulus to militarism][2]

WEG Jan 4. 94
Copy to Mr Morley[3]

With J. Morley[4]
1. Personal position
2. European effect. Militarism.
3. Graduation.[5]

To LORD SPENCER, first lord of the admiralty, 4 January 1894.   Althorp MSS K8.

I admit at once all the difficulties you have stated;[6] but the practice I apprehend is to cover them by a fairly liberal allowance against yourself. I consider it to be an admitted as well as a politic rule that every estimate should in its total be an outside estimate; so that the *main* danger may be avoided, that of understating cost to the House of Commons.

And there has been no such thing, within my recollection, as binding assent of a Cabinet to the 'general principles' of an annual estimate for defence.

The difficulty if there be one from your point of view may readily be surmounted by observance of the rule I have mentioned, that is to say allowing a margin.

[1] Questions; L.G. Bill; 4*H* 21. 830.
[2] This section lightly deleted.
[3] Holograph; Add MS 44776, f. 12.
[4] Holograph; dated 4 January 1894; Add MS 44776, f. 11.
[5] Of death duties, introduced in Harcourt's 1894 budget to pay for the navy programme.
[6] See 3 Jan. 94n.

5. Fr. [Brighton]

Wrote to S.E.G.—Mr Carvell Williams MP—Sir E. Saunders—Rev. Mr Under-
hill—Mr Morley l.l.—and minutes. H. of C. 3¼-4¼.[1] Saw Sir A.W.—Mr Marj.—Sir
J. Kennaway. Arr. Brighton 6½ PM. Worked on Odes. Read Othello. Backgammon with Mr A[rmitstead].

To J. MORLEY, Irish secretary, 5 January 1894.   Add MS 44549, f. 174.

[Letter 1:] I inclose an instruction to summon Cabinet, which you have only to send
on.[2]

To do this is only the fulfilment of an engagement to you & Spencer. But before sending the instruction forward please to consider (Query advise on it with one or two
selected) well (what I believe West apprehends) whether it will give an increased chance
of leakage; (2) whether it will tend to sharpen the edges of the situation.

A very great difficulty in this matter for me is that circumstances have imposed on me
an *absolute* isolation. It was in process of time determined for, not by, me that a large portion of my political character & action should be lodged outside this country. I feel keenly
for my colleagues that this is hard upon them, that they should have to act under or with
a man who has been moulded, and that by pretty strong hands, under influences to which
they are wholly strangers.

Sympathies like yours, and you are not alone, can bridge the gap which really severs
me from (especially) my Commons colleagues. But this cannot be expected from them in
general. A man like Stansfeld, odd to say, would have greater advantages in some
respects.

During the Peel Government the Duke of Wellington was regarded by that Cabinet as
an ultra alarmist and habitually over-ridden. But oh that he were alive now.

[Letter 2:]   Add MS 44257, f. 173.

As you are my depositary, I request you to take particular note that my concession (so
to speak, and it is only one from my point of view) would admit in round numbers
1. of an increase of 2¼ millions on the normal Naval Estimate (of 1888-9) being equal to
the augmentation actually made upon it under the Naval Defence Act in the *first year*
1889-90;
2. of an increase of a million on the estimates or voted monies of the preceding, i.e. the
present year—not upon its total expenditure.

This is so large a proceeding that it requires effort to justify it to myself. But j'y suis et
j'y reste (Forbid the omen)[3]

6. Sat.

Drive in cold and fog. Worked fairly on Odes though much haunted by the
Spectre in front. Read Othello. Backgammon with Mr A. In the Odes I am now
well over half. But my quality? Dearest C.s birthday. We missed the hour of
celebration:[4] but had Matins at St P. Saw The Speaker.

[1] L.G. Bill; 4H 21. 926.
[2] Morley replied next day, Add MS 44257, f. 146, that he, Campbell-Bannerman, Asquith and
Acland had met and agreed 'it will be best to have the Cabinet'.
[3] The remark of MacMahon as he (successfully) held the Malakoff tower at Sebastopol.
[4] Of holy communion.

7. 1 S. Epiph.

Ch. Royal 11 A.M. H.C: also an admirable Sermon. H. Drew gave us the prayers in the evening. All was most appropriate: not indeed for laying the spectre, but for facing it. Wrote to Bp of Chichester—Bp of St Andrew's—J. Morley—& minutes. A little conversation with C. & Mary on the sore subject. Read Pusey's Life.[1] The services were *so* appropriate: a great blessing to me.

Church music[2]

The change in our Church music commensurate with my life time, has been radical in character, and extraordinary in amount.

During my youth the Cathedrals and they only (to speak generally) kept the torch burning. At Eton we had a choir with anthems and chanting: but the general effort was not in the least devotional and the reading was of a character such as effectually to neutralize any tendency in that direction: The first time of my hearing the Cathedral Service in its ordinary way was at Gloucester:[3] and it made a deep impression upon me, which I was too young to analyse or fully comprehend.

The Evangelical congregations had the enormous advantage of congregational singing for the Psalms or Hymns: in this respect not unnaturally and laudably following the example of the Nonconformists.

In the bulk of our parish Churches, the music (so-called) was alike contemptible from a musical point of view and utterly inefficient for the purposes of divine worship. By the recitation of Psalms, which did not discourage in any way the repetition several times of some fraction of a word, opportunity was given for displaying the vulgarity, ignorance and incompetence of singers. For a long period, when the desire of reform in our public worship was in a state of youthful and genuine yet timid vigour, a Choir was regarded as on the lines of flat Popery. The Choirs of the country must now be counted by thousands, the men and boys employed in them almost by hundreds of thousands. Of these in my belief the enormous majority have been founded within the last thirty years. What I for one now fear is lest we should travel not too slow but too fast. Are the congregations really in a state of preparation for choral service? Does the inward spirit seek more onwards and upwards with it? Is it in the majority of cases more likely so to move, than it would have been if the services had been made careful and reverent by the clergyman as to all that he has to do, with a steady prosecution of the great business of responding and of congregational singing. I cannot answer this question. But my apprehension is that in very many cases the music is ahead of the worshipper, and in leaving him behind increases his distance, alack always too great, from the Eternal Throne and from Him that sits thereon. Music in Church should never cease to be simple except in the rear of the real demands of the devotional spirit.

When we consider miscellaneous character of the body, the intoning of the Clergy is far better than could have been expected, and far better than much of their articulation, in reading for example the Sermons. But my first wide and general proposition would be that the officiating clergyman, in dealing with the offices of the Church should do nothing except what he can do without visible strain, and perfectly well.

My second proposition is alike broad and unhesitating. I can hope that on paper it will

[1] First volume of H. P. Liddon, *Life of Edward Bouverie Pusey, D.D.*, 4v. (1893–7).
[2] Holograph, possibly incomplete, dated 7 January 1894; Add MS 44776, f. 16.
[3] The Gladstones were living in Gloucester when William Gladstone began to keep this diary; see 31 July, 21 Aug. 25.

command general assent: but I do not think it has been yet imparted into our established sentiment and practice. It is this. There should be no music permitted in the services of the Church except such as can (1) be devoutly shared by the congregation at large, or also (2) devoutly listened to by them.

If I am told that the serious adoption of this rule would greatly abridge the enormous volume of our Anthems and our Hymns, I for one should hail that result, the entire Psalter (and there are many parts of it never sung) is not in bulk one tenth part of the Anthem Book most commonly in my hands in London.

The third proposition I have to submit relates to Choirs in particular but extends also to the whole of our congregations, who have a bad example set them by the choirs. It connects itself with the general and often gross defect of the English nation in respect to articulation. It relates to vocalising in music. My proposition is broad and may seem to some to be paradoxical. It is this: that every single syllable sung ought to be as plainly audible as if it were a syllable spoken.

I do not believe that there is here any real difficulty. It is a case of carelessness, exalted into slovenliness. As a rule, the being articulately audible (except in the solos) of an anthem is never thought about. It is not in Churches only, but the fault is characteristic of English singers generally.

I will mention one or two circumstances that give room for a remote hope. Italian singers in general vocalise, or used to vocalise, to perfection. Mrs. Weldon,[1] a really great singer, was keen on this subject, and my impression is she went the whole length of my daring proposition. I have heard the service vocalised in Wells Cathedral, under Mr Richardson?, in a measure coming very near perfection, if not absolutely reaching it.

There remains the consideration of the general rules of congregational hymn-singing.
1. The tunes and words should be thoroughly familiar to the ordinary habitual attendant.
2. Being moderate in number they should also be easy. The Church is not a music school where the master is ever straining to carry his pupils onward, for he is justly relentless in his *Da capos*. In church there is no such resource: a difficult operation without guidance becomes full of errors: errors uncorrected harden and vitiate the whole method.

The tunes should in pitch be accommodated to the ordinary registers, avoiding its extremes.

To J. MORLEY, Irish secretary, 7 January 1894.   Add MS 44549, f. 174.

I thank you for your letter.[2] As to Tuesday I have to go to the stake (so to speak) & perhaps the sooner the better. Probably on general grounds you are right. I once made a speech of 3 hours in Cabinet. This will not be so long.

There is one point on which I am at once desirous not to be misunderstood. Clipping & paring the estimates is good in itself and may have an immediate utility for others; but it has none for me. The dominant consideration with me has been European militarism. In the face of that monster, I have asked myself for a multitude of reasons how far I could go. The result is given in the two figures of accession which I mentioned in my letter of Friday. (By the bye I remember writing stupidly j'-y suis instead of j'y-suis)[3] namely a +2¼ 𝕞 on the last normal estimate, and +1 𝕞 on the last N.D. Estimate. This is for me a great & startling strain. It carries me *up to* breaking point. Any addition breaks me.

I do not commonly proceed, and least of all did I in this occasion proceed, among friends, to ask (in round numbers) a half, meaning to take a quarter.

---

[1] See 13 July 63.
[2] See 5 Jan. 94n.
[3] See 5 Jan. 94—evidently the copyist corrected Gladstone's French.

Quite apart from myself, I think the proposal a most alarming one. It will not be the last. It is not the largest piece of militarism in Europe, but it is one of the most virulent.
    All good attend you—Any hope of Biarritz?

8. M. [London]

Wrote to The Queen—Ld Kimberley l.l.—and minutes. Drive before starting. D. St at 3.50. Saw Mr Murray. Long conversation with Morley. Saw Herbert. H. of C. $3\frac{1}{2}$–$7\frac{3}{4}$.[1] Drew out heads of statement. Worked on Odes! Helen read to me Two Noble Lives.

To LORD KIMBERLEY, Indian secretary, 8 January 1894.   Kimberley MSS.
    I have every desire to devise something for Lansdowne, mainly, I own, in deference to you. But notwithstanding the easy levity with which the Queen treats the matter I own that the Extra Garter appears to me by far the worst suggestion that has been made. It has never been given you will see, according to the list of precedents, except to persons in the first rank or on the greatest occasions. To give it to Lansdowne would be to alter fundamentally the conditions, and in no small degree to lower the order. I cannot but think you will be pretty much of this opinion if you consider the cases. For my own part I should have considered a promise of the first vacant Garter quite enough. But the offer of Dukedom better than the Extra Garter.[2]

9. Tu.

Wrote to The Queen l.l.l.—Ld Rosebery—& minutes. H. of C. $3\frac{1}{2}$–8.[3] Seven to dinner. Backgammon with Mr A.
    Cabinet 12–$2\frac{1}{4}$ on Navy Estimates. H, and in some degree R, pursued a remarkable course: different however. In the end the matter stood over but without a ray of hope against this mad & mischievous scheme.
    Saw J. Morley—Sir A.W.—Mr Marj. Visited Sir E. Saunders 11 A.M.
    Conversation with Herbert. This is sad for him & hard on him. My family, within *vivâ voce*, are made aware. The special responsibility is on Spencer and Harcourt.

Cabinet. Jan. 9. 94. Noon.[4]
Navy Estimates. WEG made his statement (50 m[inutes]). See Notes.
    And Note within of what occurred afterwards.
Cabinet broke up 2.15.[5]
    Heads of statement.[6]
1. Personal preface.
2. Figures of the plan.
2a. Points advisedly omitted.

    [1] L.G. Bill; 4 *H* 21. 1035.
    [2] Kimberley wrote next day, Kimberley MSS, quite satisfied with a Dukedom for Lansdowne, and finding an extra Garter objectionable. Gladstone in a second letter this day suggested an extra G.C.B. rather than the next Garter; Kimberley MSS.
    [3] L.G. Bill; 4 *H* 21. 1155.   [4] Add MS 44648, f. 142.
    [5] Gladstone told the Queen: 'the Cabinet reserve for further examination the question what advice they shall tender to Your Majesty as to amounts and particulars'; CAB 41/23/1.
    [6] Add MS 44648, f. 143.

3. Relations the old plan.
4. The Two-Navy Rule.
5. Effect on Party.
6. Effect abroad.
7. My plan.
8. For gradual ascent.
9. Lastly the time. When the Session ends.

For
Cabinet preliminary Jan. 9. 94[1]

1. Personal preface.
2. Figures of the plan.
　　2.a Points advisedly omitted.
3. Relation the old plan.
4. The Two-Navy Rule.
5. Effect on Party.
6. Effect abroad.
7. My plan.
8. For gradual ascent.
9. Lastly the time
　　　When this Session ends.

A
1. W.E.G.　　{ Could not say a word in defence
　 The time.　{ Survival. (Pitt to Peel)
　　　　　　 { Eyes & ears.
2. As to the Party　{ Tradition P.R.R.
　　　　　　　　　 { Future
3. As to the nation　{ excessive
　　　　　　　　　　{ and unworkable.
4. As to finance. questionable.
5. As to the basis of computation. (Russian Black Sea Fleet)
　 The demand is unreasonable.
6. As to Europe
　 a. alarm: a belief that we look to encouraging F. &c.
　 b. stimulate them to larger operations
　 c. may produce a disposition to draw others into a (defensive?) contribution.
　　　The "Armed Neutrality."
7. If there is to be such an ascent it ought to be *gradual*: as it was in and after the N[aval] D[efence] Act.

I. PERSONAL PREFACE.[2]
　 a. Silent—and disgraced.
　 b. a survival.
　　 $\frac{3}{4}$ of my life, a continuous effort for economy.
　　 Who *could* thus break himself in pieces?

[1] Add MS 44648, f. 143. Overwritten on second page is 'For interview with Spencer. Jan 3. 94.' A draft perhaps used on that day.
[2] Add MS 44648, f. 145; undated holograph.

c. Eyes and ears
   Warrant ample for going
            scanty for staying.
   These wd. furnish ground.

2A. POINTS DESIGNEDLY OMITTED.
1. Taxation—excessive
2. Finance—equivocal.
3. The changed relations with the professional element.

3. RELATION TO PLAN OF 1888-9.
1. It was exceptional
2. Object twofold
   a. efface arrears
   b. lay in a stock.
3. *Accepted on these assurances.*
4. A new plan—before the old is paid for by 3 ₥.
5. Shall we postpone the 3 ₥.
6. If we do, we add, in peace, *Defence Charges to Debt.*

4. THE *TWO NAVY* RULE.
1. Not cast-iron
   but supple.
2. Why not to be applied if timely[?] to *Russia*—Black Sea.
3. Why not *now*
   Is it short of absurd to shut out from view the *three fleets* probably adverse

A[ustria]	1 ₥	France	9 ₥
I[taly]	4,100 m	Russia	4,547 m
G[ermany]	4,275 m		13,547 m
	9,375 m		

5. EFFECT ON PARTY
1. Plan is *beyond expectation*
2. Admit[?] my retirement an evil. *Cobdenite saying.*
3. The mere proposal a grave calamity. Tories talking.
4. Immediate issue quite uncertain.
   With me or without.
   Tories have double chance
   1. Plan
   2. Finance of plan

6. EFFECT ABROAD.
1. Tension of relations.
   A movement towards the *Triple Alliance.*
2. Further increase of construction in *France* and *Russia.*
3. Enhanced jealousy of England.
   Possible *defensive* league. material outside the three great lumps. 9¾ ₥. *available for this*
4. *Far above all*
   Stimulus & provocation to the accursed militarism.

7. MY PLAN.
1. Bisection—
2. *Of total*: not of each item

3. With *a margin*.
4. Means postponement
   not necess[ari]ly abandonment.
5. Advantages
   a. to be minus somebody
   b. to have probably gone through a testing Dissolution.
6. Its chief numerical factors.
   a. On normal Estimate + $2\frac{1}{2}$ ⋔.
   b. On *Estimate* 93–4, N[*aval*] D[*efence*] *Act*, + 1 m
   c. On expenditure 93–4, 400 to 500m.

8. THE ASCENT
   if right, should be *gradual*
1. for adjustment in Cabinet
2. For Parliamentary prudence.
   The *financial dangers*
3. *The* Precedent.
   from 1888–9 *incr. 1y*. . . $2\frac{1}{4}$ m
              2y. . .
4. WOULD the 3 Admirals resign?

Jan. 9.[1] Harcourt considers the plan noneconomy and uncalled for. Agrees generally with me respecting it. The Admirals would resign.
We desire &c.
Postponement strikes at the essence[?]
Thinks nothing could induce him as a Minister to enter into a war for any purpose what ever.
   The N.D. Act was foolish. But is a thing done.
Rosebery urged immediate decision.
Trev[elyan] for securing the fruits.
Sp[encer] Estimates can be provisionally prepared. His plan agreed with the Admirals' minimum.

Secret.   *J. M[orley] saw Ja. 9, 10.*[2]
✔Mundella
✔Lefevre
✔Bryce
✔Fowler

✔C. Bannerman—already known
✔Acland—seen today
✔Asquith—virtually known
   (Harcourt—known from yesterday's speech)

✔Morley
✔Rosebery
✔Spencer
✔Trevelyan

All these like Trevelyan think we should first wind up the Session, or agree to doing so.[3]

---

[1] Undated holograph: Add MS 44648, f. 154.   [2] Holograph; Add MS 44776, f. 21.
[3] This sentence written at right angles, down the right-hand side of the page.

To Rev. E. C. WICKHAM, 9 January 1894.   Add MS 44549, f. 175.

I regret, so far as you are concerned that circumstances have occurred which make my continuance in office extremely uncertain.[1]

I do not think the prospects of a suitable offer to you are in any way limited to the period of my official tenure.

But I wish to know whether if at the last moment a Canonry of Canterbury should chance to be vacant & at my disposal you would like to have it?

My stay in town is not certain beyond Friday night. An aye or No by telegraph might be desirable.

William wrote me an excellent and a scholarlike letter.

10. Wed.

Wrote to Sir W. Harcourt—Bp of Norwich—Queen l. & tel.—Ld Kimberley—and minutes. Fuller conversation with my children. It is hard for them to understand. The Odes—a feeble attempt!—Read R. Lowe.[2]

We dined with Spencer.

The scheme is in my opinion mad.

Rosebery paid me a very kind call.

J. Morley with much activity, last night, & today after a long conversation with me prosecuted & brought into action the plan for time. I am to go to Biarritz on Saturday. The Estimates will be prepared departmentally as usual. The Session will be wound up shortly after Feb. 12. No Cabinet at present.

1848[3]

Defence Estimates when presented?

Were they withdrawn and reduced estimates presented? When?

Amounts

Army

Navy

Ordnance

To Sir W. V. HARCOURT, chancellor of the exchequer,   MS Harcourt dep. 14, f. 3.
10 January 1894.

I am sorry to say that I entirely or in the main differ as to your statement[4] about 1860 for which and the following years I was as you say justly responsible. At the same time I admit that it was a year of alarmism: and to that sentiment stimulated from many high quarters the fortifications were due.

As far as Estimates were concerned they were

1859–60 .... 25.8

1860–61 .... 28.2

Increase .. 2.4

Of which was due to hostilities in China in my statement

July 16. 1860 1.7

Increase apart from China ...... £ 700.000.

---

[1] Wickham was Gladstone's son-in-law. He became dean of Lincoln on the unexpected death of the dean later this month. See to Wickham, 23 Jan. 94.

[2] See 7 Nov. 93.   [3] Holograph; Add MS 44776, f. 22.

[4] Letter of this day, with 1853–69 statistics; Add MS 44203, f. 161.

The total charge of the China war is beyond that given in the Abstract which compiled at the B. of Trade takes no note of the facts mentioned by me on July 16.

The total charge of the China war was, according to me, £7,700.

The China war was followed by the Trent affair.

And in the main the heavy military charges of 1860-3 were due to *cause* and not to scare, though scare had something to do with them.

But in 63-4 we had got down the charge again to 25.5, rather *less* than it had been in 59-60, after deducting from that year the Chinese Expenditure.

To LORD KIMBERLEY, Indian secretary, 10 January 1894.　　　Kimberley MSS.

I am afraid your letter[1] does not enable me to act about Lansdowne, but we may have another *prog* [*sic*] from the Queen.

You properly disapprove of the Extra Garter.

I find the idea of the Dukedom very repulsive to many colleagues: I believe all who have given an opinion.

Advancement from Marquis to Duke is in fact a different thing from and a higher thing than advancement from any of the other orders of the Peerage to the one next above it.

I adhere to the readiness I formerly expressed but I am bound to confess that even a contingent Garter does not seem to 'smile' to our colleagues.

[P.S.] Ripon kindly undertook to convey to you the effect of the significant though indeterminate Cabinet of yesterday.

11. Th.

Wrote to Bp of N. Tel.—Abp of Canterbury—E. Wickham Tel.—Ld Rosebery l.l.—Atty General—Ld Spencer—The Queen—Rev. S.E.G.—Mr Morley—Hawarden Postmistress. Saw Sir A.W.—Mr Marj.—Mr Murray—S.L.—Ld Spencer—Conclave on D. of Coburg—J. Morley—Ld Acton. Seven to dinner. Drive with H. I am now like the sea in swell after a storm, bodily affected, but mentally pretty well anchored. It is bad: but oh how infinitely better than to be implicated in that plan! Read R. Lowe—Madden's Reflections.[2]

To J. MORLEY, Irish secretary, 11 January 1894.　　　Add MS 44549, f. 176.

Can you not get a short postponement of the Sexton question, say 24 hours, in order to enable you to communicate with Childers?[3] This I throw out. I frankly own the answer does not altogether smile to me.

Rather too much or perhaps too little.

I think you can hardly hand over to a Commission a point so specific definite & important in the Bill as the percentage to be paid by Ireland. On the other hand they ought by a full enquiry to be in a condition to point by implication if not to an exact figure to something very near it.

Certainly before such an entire delegation of such a matter is made the Cabinet would expect to be consulted.

On the other hand I think the historical field ought to be opened not as here in a corner of a head, but broadly and distinctly, & it ought to include the nature & character

---

[1] Not found; see 8 Jan. 94n.

[2] Probably R. R. Madden, *Reminiscences from 1798 to 1886* (1891).

[3] Childers' Royal Commission on the financial relations between Great Britain and Ireland; first report *P.P.* xxxvi. 1 (1895).

of the Irish debt at the date of the Union, though perhaps this should be rather implied than expressed.

To LORD ROSEBERY, foreign secretary, 11 January 1894. '*Secret*'. N.L.S. 10027, f. 127.

Upon reflection I find that there was one observation lacking to the completeness of my long *rigmarole*, or statement, whichever it may be, on Tuesday. It was this, that my sense of the enormous mischief of the pending proposal (with its sequels in the future) would have been partially, perhaps sensibly, abated, though I cannot say essentially altered, had we been so happy as to have arrived by this time at the conclusion of some plan for the evacuation of Egypt.

I need not trouble the Cabinet with this postscript. If I inflict it upon you I hope you will not think I am carrying my sting in my tail.

The other purpose of this note is to ask you to be so kind as to send me a copy of the written record of your conversation with the Ottoman Ambassador, in which you conveyed a reply to the Draft Convention proposed by his Government. You will recollect describing it to me in conversation and telling me that it was on paper in the (I believe) usual course.

Your dirge on the nullity of honours for the Foreign Office on Tuesday, between the P. C.ship of Monday, and the Knighthood of yesterday, exhibits a briskness which reminds me of the rapid precocity of Hermes in the quasi-Homeric Hymn; at sunrise he was born; at noon he played the lyre; at sunset he stole the oxen of Apollo. The climax I admit lies the other way.

[P.S.] I ask no reply except the paper named.

To LORD SPENCER, first lord of the admiralty, 11 January 1894.   Althorp MSS K8. '*Secret*'.

In the present very grave state of affairs you will agree with me that all the facts ought to be clearly before us; and in consequence I trouble you with two questions, on which I had no information, or no distinct information, before the statement I made on Tuesday.
1. While you have made large exceptions and deductions from the schemes of the three Admirals for years after 94–5, I understand that the scheme for 94–5 which is now before the Cabinet corresponds as to amount with their scheme. Is this so? If not so, what is the difference expressed in money?
2. As to the question how much of the scheme under the Naval Defence Act remains unliquidated. We have from the figures of former years under this head £3,146,000. But is there an addition to be made to this for parts of the Naval Defence Act plan undertaken but not yet paid for, & to be paid for in the coming Estimates? And if so how much.
3. I should like to add a third single question to which I hope it would give no trouble to reply. It is this: how much is included in the proposed Estimates for the construction of first Class Battle Ships (giving also the number): *and* how much for Torpedo (including anti-Torpedo[ )] Expenditure?

If, without troubling to write, Shuttleworth could give me the figures, will you kindly ask him to do it?[1]

---

[1] No reply with the details requested found. Spencer this day wrote wishing Gladstone rest in Biarritz and regretting he had had to bring to Cabinet 'proposals to which I quite understand you objected strongly'; Add MS 44314, f. 105. Various mem. by Sir Ughtred James Kay-Shuttleworth (1844–1939, liberal M.P. Clitheroe 1885–1902; Secretary to the Admiralty 1892–5) in Althorp MSS K466 ff., but unclear whether any sent to Gladstone.

12. Fr.

Wrote to The Queen l.l.l.—Ld Spencer—Mr G. Russell—Sir H. Ponsonby—and minutes. H. of C. 3¾–7½.[1] Spent most of the morning with Mr Granger in a very full and many testing examination of the eyes. The result is alas that my cataract is of the kind most obstinately slow. Saw Sir A.W.—Mr M.—S.L.—Mr Marj.—Mr Lefevre—Ld Spencer—Mr Mundella—Mr J. Morley—Ld R. Churchill—Sir M.H. Beach. Dined with Lady F. Marj. Worked on Odes. Read Lowe—Rosebery's gift.[2]

To LORD SPENCER, first lord of the admiralty, 12 January 1894.   Althorp MSS K8.
'*Secret*'.

You were justly cautious & reserved when I raised the question yesterday whether I might not without inconsistency be a party at any rate to asking tenders for *one* Battleship. But (writing with imperfect information) I am under the impression that if the number of battleships to be laid down were largely reduced *all* would be executed in the Dockyards. I fear therefore that the 'one' would involve me in difficulty which it [*sic*] would not answer your purpose & *might* cause a misinterpretation of your intentions.[3]

13. Sat. [On train]

Left London by 10 A.M. train. Saw on the platform J. Morley—S. Lyttelton—G.H. Murray. A prosperous and luxurious journey: but some mouth-trouble. Finished Rosebery's Pitt & Wilberforce collection. Began Massons extraordinary Introduction.[4]

14. 2 S. Epiph. [Grand Hotel, Biarritz]

Ch. 5.30 P.M. Arrived Biarritz 7¾. Bed. Mouth better. Read Pusey's Life—Religion & Myth[5]—Addis—Xty & Empire (not much of any).[6] Conversation with Acton.

The Cabinet.[7]

	No.	W.E.G.
Aye	No	Sir W. Harcourt
	Aye	Rosebery
		The Lord Chancellor
	Aye.	Kimberley
	Aye	Ripon
		Asquith
	Aye	C. Bannerman.
	No.	Morley J. (on the merits)
		Morley A.

[1] Questions; L.G. Bill; 4*H* 21. 1468.
[2] Materials concerning Pitt and Wilberforce collected by Rosebery and later privately published by him as *Pitt and Wilberforce* (1899).
[3] In *Spencer*, ii. 236.
[4] F. Masson, *Napoleon at home*, 2v. (1894), with an Introduction; or see 8 Feb. 94.
[5] J. Macdonald, *Religion and myth* (1893).
[6] See 30 Apr. 93.
[7] Holograph; Add MS 44776, f. 39.

     No. Lefevre
          Trevelyan
          Fowler
          Bryce
          Mundella
     Aye. Spencer.
          Acland Asquith.

                                                               WEG Jan 14. 94
     West's report Jan 20. 94.

15. M.

Wrote to Mr Chignell[1]—Rev. Mr Knowles—Mr Murray Tel.—Lady Mount-
temple—& min. Worked on Odes. Read Masson—Othello. Drive. Backgammon in
evg.

To R. CHIGNELL, 15 January 1894.   Add MS 44549, f. 177.

    With reference to your letter of the 9th inst.[2] I regret to say that I fear there is an error
in the principal recital; for I have unfortunately for myself never been at the Hague. You
do me much more than justice in attaching any weight to my estimate of Mr Cole's
powers & performances. It is therefore as a rather selfish act of pure pleasure to myself
that I record the feeling with which I was inspired by his picture of the Thames below
London Bridge. I do not remember whether it was called the Pool or not, but the identification is easy. What I do recollect is the seizure, I cannot use any other word, which the
picture made upon me as I first came up to it in the Exhibition. I was walking with Mr
Agnew and he gave his really valuable warrant to my rather hot eulogy.
    I cannot now recollect details. But the dominant idea was that of admiration for the
genius of a man who had been able not only to produce a very large & effective combination effective alike for the eye and the mind, but had been able so to represent a scene of
commercial activity as to impress upon it, so I thought, the idea and character of gran-
deur. The picture seemed to speak and to say "you see here the summit of all the commerce of the world".

16. Tu.

Wrote to E. Wickham Tel.—Ld Dufferin—Rev. Webster—Canon Venables.[3]
Drive. Backgammon with Mr A. Saw the Consul.[4] Worked on Odes. Read
Othello.

17. Wed.

Wrote S. Lyttelton—Canon Venables—Ld Kimberley—The Queen l.l.l.l.:
unpleasant mostly. Worked on Odes. Walk with Mr A[rmitstead]. Read
Troublesome World.[5]

---

[1] Robert Chignell, barrister, had doubtless written for information about Gladstone's view of
George Vicat Cole, 1833–93, painter, whose life he wrote in 3v. (1896); 'The pool of London' was
one of Cole's most popular paintings.   [2] Not found. See this day's note.
    [3] Edmund Venables, historian, precentor and canon of Lincoln cathedral; on the death of the
dean; Add MS 44549, f. 178. Gladstone appointed his son-in-law, E. C. Wickham. See 23 Jan. 94.
    [4] Edmund Hooke Wilson Bellairs, consul in Biarritz from 1879.
    [5] *This troublesome world. By the authors of 'The medicine lady'* (1893).

18. *Th.*

Wrote to Ld Dufferin—Abp Kirby[1]—Ld Kimberley—Lady Harcourt. Worked on Odes. Read Othello: a wonderful play: Iago perhaps unmatched: but the most faulty of the four supreme?[2] Backgammon with Mr A. Weather wild but soft: less powerful than Brighton air. Second conversation with Acton: Navy matters. Not a ray.

To LORD KIMBERLEY, Indian secretary, 18 January 1894.   Kimberley MSS.

I am truly sorry that during your sharp attack (which I trust has now substantially passed off) you should so often have had to hear of the Lansdowne affair much accentuated by the Queen's anxiety and (to use a mild word) keenness.

I do not wonder that under the circumstances there should have been (if I am right in thinking there was) a little deviation from the usual freedom of your correspondence. Contrary to your intention, yet not unnaturally, your telegram was understood to mean that I had been the opposing force in the matter of honours to Lord Lansdowne—and to this was added that *my* party spirit seemed to be the cause.

You will recollect that my proposal was to combine as an alternative with the Grand Cross the contingency of a Garter vacancy (which would not have been popular with our colleagues) and that the single offer was founded on a message from you.

You speak with far greater authority than any of us on the Viceroy's performances as a whole: but the general view of Ministers as far as I know is that his career has been a very chequered one. This view I share but my desire has been to go as far as possible in the way of honours though the special duty of my office is to be on the stingy side, in order to keep value.

I send you herewith copy of a letter written last night to the Queen on precedents in regard to the Grand Cross of the Bath:[3] which I rather think was a little damaged by Salisbury through lax preferments.

Do not take the trouble to answer unless you see cause.[4]

19. *Fr.*

Wrote to The Queen—. . . . . . .—& minutes. Worked on Odes. 7 to dinner. Backgammon. Saw Baron von R. Read Troublesome W.

20. *Sat.*

I had with W[est][5] my tenth(?) long conversation on the coming events. Wrote to Ld Dillon. Worked on Odes. D. and backgammon as yesterday. Read Troublesome W.—Antony & Cleopatra. Long conversation with West on the situation. He is most kind & loyal: but weary talks cast no light whatever on the matter.

[1] Tobias Kirby, archbishop of Ephesus and rector of the Irish college in Rome, sent a volume and 'the thanks of Irishmen throughout the world'; Add MS 44518, f. 3.

[2] Gladstone probably regarded Hamlet, Othello, King Lear and Macbeth (which he read quite frequently) as Shakespeare's foremost plays.

[3] In Kimberley MSS.

[4] Kimberley wrote on 20 January, Add MS 44229, f. 203: 'Promising the next K.G. seems to me the only fitting offer now possible.'

[5] West was sent by various Cabinet members (especially Harcourt) to try to arrange an accommodation over the navy estimates; he returned feeling he had wholly failed; see West, *P.D.*, 247 ff.

The plan.[1]

I deem it to be in excess of public expectation.
I know it to be in excess of all precedent.
It entails unjust taxation
It endangers sound finance
I shall not minister to the alarming aggression of the professional elements[?]
to the weakness of alarmism
to the unexampled manoeuvres of party
not lend a hand to dress Liberalism in Tory clothes.
I shall not break to pieces the continuous action of my political life, nor trample on the tradition received from every colleague who has ever been my teacher
Above all I cannot & will not add to the perils & the coming calamities of Europe by an act of militarism which will be found to involve a policy, and which excuses thus the militarism of Germany, France or Russia. England's providential part is to help peace, and liberty of which peace is the nurse; this policy is the foe of both. I am ready to see England dare[?] the world in arms: but not to see England help to set the world in arms.

My full intention is that of silence till the matter is settled in the regular course of sessional proceedings; when they are at an end, in the event of new circumstances and prolonged controversy, I may consider my duty afresh, upon the principle which guides me throughout, namely that of choosing the ultimate good and the smallest present evil. The smallest of all the present evils is the probable disparagement of myself (for surmise will arise, and probably will not be put down): great and certain evils are the danger to the party, and new uncertainties for Ireland. But these in my opinion are inherent in the plan itself, and would not be averted were it possible for me to say aye to it.

21. Sept S.

Ch 11 A.M. & H.C.: (seeking strength for the day of need)—also 5.30. Sea magnificent at the Rocher. Saw Ld Acton again on the dilemma (not mine). Also West. Read Life of Pusey—Intr. & Mem. of Dean Stanley.[2] Such a book is useful. It makes me feel my inferiority.

22. M.

Wrote to Mr Stubbs[3]—E. Wickham Tel.—Bp of Lincoln. Backgammon in evening. From 8¾-6¾ Trip to San Sebastian; very interesting: with more to say than I can here put down. The rock & views, The Cathedral: the Council Hall: the Bullring: the authorities: who were most courteous. Worked well on Odes: & some doggrel. Backgammon. Read Troublesome W.

Tu. 23.

Wrote to The Gobernador Civil—Rev. E. Wickham—Ld Kimberley. Polemical talk with Herbert. He argued as well as any. I hope I have now nearly done.

[1] Holograph dated 20 January 1894; Add MS 44648, f. 145.
[2] R. E. Prothero, *The life and correspondence of A. P. Stanley*, 2v. (1893).
[3] Offering the deanery of Ely to Charles William Stubbs, 1845-1912; Christian socialist; later bp. of Truro.

They have been
Harcourt 1 (interview)
Spencer 2.
J. Morley 3. agreed
Lefevre 1   do
Acton 3.
West 2
Herbert 2: besides *short*.
Worked on Odes. Read Taine[1]—Troublesome World.

To Rev. E. C. WICKHAM, 23 January 1894.   Add MS 44549, f. 179.

We spent yesterday in a visit to San Sebastian, a trip of great interest & getting back
between 6 & 7 I learned the Queen's approval & at once sent you a telegraphic message.
The Deanery of Ely is offered to Mr [C. W.] Stubbs a good & able man, rather strong I am
told in the Wellhausen[2] sense but within allowable lines, but known perhaps for his early
& meritorious association with the movements for allotments. I wrote at once to the
Bishop [King] on your appointment to pave your way so far as I could. Canon Venables
an old member of the Chapter was a particular friend of Sir S. Glynne, & so far as I know a
very good & an accomplished a judicious man. The letters which I have received respecting the late Dean & his wish are by my direction sent on to you & had best I think remain
with you. That noble Cathedral especially with its commanding site are of themselves a
great inspiration. God bless & prosper [you] in the new office. You are the third Dean of
Lincoln recommended by me.[3] I was disappointed in Blakesley. He was appointed
because he had been awake: having got into that haven he (so far as I know) slept for the
rest of his life—a not uncommon case: which will not be yours.
[P.S.] I am afraid you will have a heavy tailor's bill for the provision of the requisite
costume.

24. Wed.

Wrote to Ld Rosebery—Ld Kimberley. Worked on Odes: not very effectively.
Dined with the Tollemaches.[4] He in particular is a very interesting person.
Drive to St Jean de Luz (NB Church) and walk.

25. Th.

Wrote minutes: and to M. Drew. Wrote on Horace's Odes. Worked a little on
Translating. Drive to Bayonne &c. Backgammon with Mr A. Finished this
Troublesome World. Nagging conversation on the 'situation'.

[1] *Le Régime moderne*, the last volumes of Taine's *Origines* (see 10 Apr. 84).
[2] i.e. as a follower of Julius Wellhausen, 1844–1918, German exponent of biblical higher criticism.
[3] Gladstone's previous appointments were J. W. Blakesley (1872) and W. J. Butler (1885). Wickham's promotion to a deanery had been strongly urged by Benson as abp. of Canterbury on 31
October 1892, Add MS 44109, f. 223.
[4] See account in Tollemache, *Talks*, 97.

26. Fr.

Wrote to The Queen—Mr B. Jones—Mr Watts—Ld Kimberley. Read Verrall on Odes[1]—Col. [*sic*] Tempest[2]—MS on Mosaic Sanitary laws (past).[3] Worked *some* on Odes. Nagging conversation. Backgammon with Mr A.

To E. C. BURNE-JONES, 26 January 1894.   Add MS 44549, f. 180.

With the sanction of Her Majesty, I have to propose to you that you should accept the honour of a Baronetcy, in recognition of the high position which you have obtained by your achievements in your noble art. Perhaps I give more pleasure to myself in writing this letter, than I shall give to you in receiving it. But I hope that it may be agreeable to you to fall in with my views; for, setting aside private satisfaction, their aim is to promote a due distribution of public honour, in a great profession, which has not always received in this respect anything approaching to liberal treatment.[4]

To G. F. WATTS, 26 January 1894.   Add MS 44549, f. 180.

I indulge today in what is to me a very great pleasure. It is the pleasure of writing (with Her Majesty's sanction) to say that the offer of a Baronetcy, which you long ago declined,[5] is now renewed through the medium of this note. You had then even ample title to this honour. That title has since been amplified, & further elevated, by well known causes.

I earnestly hope that you may be inclined to accept it & I hold this hope in the interest of British art, which must always receive some healthful impulse when public honour is awarded in quarters the best entitled to it.[6] Pray make my best compliments to Mrs. Watts.

27. Sat.

Wrote to Ld Rosebery l.l. (serious)—Canon Furze.[7] Worked on Odes. Drive—& backgammon. Saw Ld Acton, general—Mary: again. The beautifully printed Cambridge Shakespeare, by the best candlelight, took me more than five minutes of most laborious reading per page of say twenty lines. Read Verrieur [*sc.* Verrall] on Horace—Di Tempest.

28. Sexa S.

Ch 11 AM 5.30 P.M. Wrote to Mr Montagu MP—S. Lyttelton Tel. l.l. Finished the MS on Mosaic Sanitary Laws. Read, or rather read in the Pusey & Stanley Lives & Taine's First Chapter. With C. to the Rocher.

---

[1] A. W. Verrall, *Studies literary and historical in the Odes of Horace* (1884).

[2] M. Cholmondeley, *Diana Tempest*, 3v. (1893-4); see Tollemache, *Talks*, 121–2.

[3] S. Montagu had sent the MS of a lecture 'Sanitation as taught by the Mosaic Law', by the Chief Rabbi, H. Adler, which Gladstone suggested be printed; Add MS 44549, f. 181 and Tollemache, *Talks*, 108.

[4] No reply found. Burne-Jones accepted.

[5] In 1885; see above, x. clxviii and to Ponsonby, 3 Feb. 94.

[6] Watts again gratefully but definitely declined; see to Ponsonby, 3 Feb. 94 and Watts to Gladstone 30 January, Add MS 44518, f. 24: 'I value social distinctions more I think than most people . . . therefore I think they should be justified if bestowed, & their duties comprehended if inherited'.

[7] Charles Wellington Furse, 1821–1900; canon of Christ Church, Oxford 1873–94; archdeacon of Westminster from 1894.

29. M.

Wrote to J. Morley—E. Marjoribanks—Rev. SEG.—Ld Rosebery—Ld Leigh.
Worked on Odes. Read Di Tempest—Antony & Cleopatra. Mr Tollemache and
Miss C. dined.[1]

To E. MARJORIBANKS, chief whip, 29 January 1894.   Add MS 44549, f. 181.

I have no great desire to recall your mind prematurely to the habitual cares & worries;
but if you have any particular ideas about me & my case which you think I ought to know,
you will I hope make them known without fear or favour. Of the reality & sufficiency of
these impediments (except to writing) which are connected with the senses I have daily
& increasing evidence—and this I think will be the proper basis for a communication in
time to my excellent Chairman. You may have further ideas about Midlothian. If not I am
disposed to reserve the subject either till we meet or at any rate for the present. Nothing
has yet been settled or even said here as to the [date;] to be in London on the 10th Sat.
evening, is what I have thought of—but here again anything you may write will be closely
weighed. I assume that on Monday 12th there will be no real business except the Scotch
Fisheries. We have had here a curious succession not of cold but of broken uneasy & wet
weather.[2]

To J. MORLEY, Irish secretary, 29 January 1894. '*Secret*'.   Add MS 44549, f. 182.

1. Your letter arrived on Saturday, your figures today.[3] They are most interesting. I should
like the addition of 1891, as '92 was a mixed[?] year & the dangerous month of it was ours.
2. I agree that it is time for you to be about making a list for the Financial Commission.
Clearly there should be a Liberal Irish infusion. Should it not include one or two Irish
Tories? Would that [*sic*] Plunkett be fit? Is Carson possible? Don't have the ex-Rev. M.P.
As to the infusion generally you might obtain some guidance perhaps (not materials)
from the composition of the latest Committee, of which Northcote I rather think was
Chairman. 3. Like you, I reckon on no 'swing round'.

The waters may even be smooth at first: so much the worse for this will delude. In my
opinion the proposal will be a calamity to the party as well as to the Country & to Europe.
I even think it will exceed expectation, but most opinions are against me, & mine is a
mere opinion. Nothing has happened since I came here to cast one ray of new light on
the matter so far as I am concerned. Those who object to me, quickly pass by my conten-
tions i.e. motives which operate upon me, & give me speculations of their own which I
find not new & not strongest. The fact is I am, speaking roughly, married to the present
Cabinet like Lady B. Coutts to Bartlett.[4] If this be not a complimentary or savory comparison, it is at least impartial, & *I* do not get the best of it! My daughter tells me you told
her my decision was wrong. I told her you had not told me so. I did not ask & do not: for
good reasons.

[1] Account in Tollemache, *Talks*, 108.
[2] Marjoribanks replied, 2 February, Add MS 44332, f. 251, regretting that he gathered from 'the
tone of your letter that nothing has occurred to change your mind' about retiring, and that this
grieved him. He mentioned Thomas Gibson Carmichael, 'though he has not quite all the go I should
wish', as the probable successor in Midlothian (he so became).
[3] Irish crime figures, sent on 25 January, Add MS 44257, f. 148.
[4] Baroness Burdett-Coutts was 37 years older than her husband, W. L. Ashmead Bartlett.

To LORD ROSEBERY, foreign secretary, 29 January 1894.   N.L.S. 10027, f. 132.
'*Secret*'.

I rather suppose it to be according to your intention that Spencer Lyttelton ⟨has⟩ has made mention to me of a conversation between the Queen and you about Lansdowne.[1]

Certainly the Queen did not know any thing about an offer of the Garter, for it had never been named to her. Some confusion arose evidently owing to Kimberley's illness & consequently imperfect command of papers. I wrote to him saying I was willing to recommend the G.C.B. with some opening of a Garter in perspective. He made no reply. When I recalled his attention to the subject, he answered concurring in the offer *of the Bath*. Knowing time to be important, I wrote accordingly. All this is in black and white.

But there is another matter which I had better name. It is of infinitely small moment to me: *morituri te salutant*. But it may be otherwise to my colleagues and juniors. Having broached the subject of Lansdowne's honours, and having received from me an instant promise of careful attention, and then not hearing directly, she asks nothing from me, but first 'appeals' to the Indian Secretary, and then converses with the Foreign secretary: no communication coming to me except a letter, which for her sake I do not wish to describe and do not mean to show[?].

This is an inconvenient and so far as I know a novel, manner of conducting the business of the country.

Communications with Minister B on the recommendations of Minister A, especially perhaps if he be the Prime Minister, are a slippery affair: The subject however can hardly be disposed of by any general *dictum*: and in three former Governments I never recollect any case like this, or any error or inconvenience arising. In this case, the main consequence has been that the Queen has been misled, and is in confusion.

Of course the Minister B is placed in difficulty when his Mistress (with an experience of 56 years) opens these subjects: and he can only make the best of it.

Former governments: 57 years: but *quantum mutata ab illa*.

30. Tu.

Wrote to Mr J. Morley—and minutes. Read Di Tempest. Saw Mr Webster in afternoon. 12¾–5. To St Jean de Luz for luncheon. Saw Le Maire: & the fine Louis XIV vestments.[2] Worked on Odes. This has prospered: if the work done be decent.

Wed. 31.

Wrote to Mrs Bolton—Lady Finley—Sol. Gen for Scotland—Mr Marjoribanks.

At 5/30 I came in from a visit to the Tollemaches & found West in a great state with a telegram from London (P.M.G.) announcing that I had determined on resigning almost immediately. I framed a contradiction, rather a tough business, in terms carefully weighed: read it again & again to West & Herbert: we got it shortened & then dispatched in West's name, on my behalf.

---

[1] Rosebery wrote on 26 January, Add MS 44290, f. 226 (apparently not received when Gladstone's letter was written) that, on the Queen raising the question of an honour for Lansdowne, 'I said that I did not see how the Cabinet could do more—an extra G.C.B.: or, if that were unwelcome, the next K.G. She then said that she had never heard of the K.G. I said that no doubt you would communicate this to her, when you found that the G.C.B. was unwelcome. I was dragged into this discussion most unwillingly....'

[2] Louis XIV was married in St. Jean-de-Luz to the Infanta Marie Theresa.

It may eventually turn to good.[1]

Eight to dinner. Backgammon. Saw the Tollemache party. Had a fair day on Odes. Read Di Tempest: I part company in Ch. X.

To H. N. GLADSTONE, 31 January 1894. '*Private.*' Hawarden MS 902, f. 210.

My dearest Harry,

Thinking over the future I would suggest to you whether you might do well one of these days to open indifferently with Mr Rendel the subject of my eyes and ears, and convey to him that the case of sight has now for some time become greater *with reference to the* performance of my official duties. As to ears I daresay he knows that much over half of what is said in the House of Commons is inaudible to me. This is a statement really within the truth. It is also true however that as regards writing I suffer comparatively little of obstruction or inconvenience in any shape.

I may say something of the same sort to our most kind host here.

We think of ourselves as due in London on Saturday the 10th *inst* and I am glad for our own sakes to hear that you are likely to be there not long after. Serious business in the House of Commons will have to be done on and probably after the 13th.

Our weather here has been not cold but wild and wet. The place has not lost ground in our estimations but the climate, if free from some of the critical changes of the Riviera, appears to be of a climate decidedly less southern.

I am delighted with your account of the Rendels' new purchase and hope he may with his family long enjoy it.

Herbert has been busy with incessant goffing (or golfing).

Ever your affte. Father W. E. Gladstone.

Thurs. Feb. One/94.

Wrote to J. Morley Tel.—The Queen—Rev. S.E.G.—Dalzell Agency Tel. Phare:[2] & then the Benedictine convent (bad) and the Bernardines, interesting. Worked on Odes. Read Di Tempest. Backgammon in evening.

2. Fr.

Ch 11 A.M. & H.C.: with, especial reference to the dedication of St Deiniol's today. Wrote to Ld Ripon. Read Di Tempest—Budget Speech Jul. 59.[3] Back-gammon in evg. Presented books to Dossie[4] with an inscription as good as my old hand could make it.

Two more conversations on the situation: with H. & M. who read me Acton's letter.[5]

[1] The statement, issued in West's name, is in *T.T.*, 1 February 1894, 3e: 'The statement that Mr. Gladstone has definitely decided, or has decided at all, on resigning office is untrue. It is true that for many months past his age, and the condition of his sight and hearing have, in his judgment, made relief from public cares desirable....'

[2] Lighthouse on Cap St. Martin, north of the town.

[3] See 18 July 59; it put 4d. on income tax; dispute over the reasons for this increase played a part in the arguments about naval expenditure; see West, *P.D.*, 243, 251-2, 266.

[4] His grand-daughter.

[5] Long refutation by Acton of Gladstone's arguments against naval expenditure; memorandum, dated London, 31 January 1894, sent with a note to Mary Drew ('what interests me more is that all the colleagues are unanimous in hoping that he will repudiate them'); Add MS 44094, f. 248. Printed in Figgis and Laurence, 246 ff.

To LORD RIPON, colonial secretary, 2 February 1894.   Add MS 44549, f. 182.

The suggestion of proceeding by Act in lieu of estimate, as a possible means of forcing me about, springs from a kind motive, & is appreciated by me according to its source. In any other point of view, I do not quite understand it: but it helps to show more & more how the reasons that command my mind are hardly even present to the minds of others. It was from *their* point of view that the subject appeared to me one that might grow into inconvenience: from mine, it is rather like the choice between the dagger & the book, a choice the offer of which is undoubtedly prompted by humanity. Let me here repeat, by way of adhesion, what I believe West said to you by message. I will add that there are three conceivable motives for a judgment opposite to mine: the party; Ireland; the merits. The two last, or one of them, I conceive to be yours: & these are they which command from me an entire respect.[1]

[P.S.] I earnestly hope that Lady Ripon holds all her ground.

3. Sat.

Wrote to Sir R. Welby—Mr S. Lyttelton Worked on Odes. Drive. Backgammon. Read Di Tempest. Bad in religion, bad in art. So it seems to me.

To Sir R. E. WELBY, 3 February 1894.   Add MS 44338, f. 331.

Kindly let me know by telegraph at the earliest moment you can (I write to Spencer Lyttelton to put him at your disposal by way of aid)

a. What is the necessary number of days *now* between dissolution & assembling of a new Parliament.

b. What is the minimum number of days after reassembling & before new votes can be proposed for Army, Navy, & Civil Services irrespective of any prolongation of debate on the Address?—i.e. assuming that this need not by law interfere with business deemed necessary.

I hope it may be possible to reply to this by *a* & a numeral following; b. & a numeral, or if necessary to from X to Y. (like L. or M. in the Catechism).

We have probably an expedition on Monday but get back well before post.[2]

4. Quinqua S.

Ch 11 AM—5½ PM. Wrote to E. Marjoribanks—Sir H. Ponsonby—Sir A. West. Ploughed (I refer to the physical operation alone) through Apocal. XXI, XXII, wonderful & noble Chapters. *Dipped* in Addis, Lady Canning et alibi. Walk to Phare & back: rather much. Under 3 m.

To Sir H. F. PONSONBY, the Queen's secretary, 4 February 1894. Add MS 44549, f. 183.

Mr Watts again declines gratefully the honour designed for him by the Queen. Burne Jones as gratefully accepts. Both announcements will be made public. You would understand the reason of our telegraphing directly to you on Wednesday.[3] The cart came before the horse, but the horse without the cart would have been a greater disturbance. You would observe the frank admission about the eyes & ears for which there is reason.

[1] Ripon replied, 5 February, Add MS 43515, f. 143, and Wolf, *Ripon*, ii. 205, urging Gladstone to find means, if unable to continue, of keeping Ireland to the fore for the next election.
[2] Welby felt a reply by telegram likely to confuse, and wrote at length on 5 February, Add MS 44338, f. 333; a) the 1852 Act fixed not less than 35 days between dissolution and assembling; b) votes might be taken on the 5th day if the deb. on the Address concluded on the same day as the Speech.   [3] 'Resignation rumour' (secretary's marginalia).

5. M.

Wrote to Mr Morley—Sir W. Harcourt. Worked on Odes. Finished Di Tempest: *bad*. Read some Ant. & Cleop. Backgammon with Mr A. Saw West, finally. 8.30–6.30. To Bayonne, Cambo, Pied de Fort, St Jean.[1] The officer on duty took us up to the citadel, a work of interest, he intelligent, the drive from Cambo lovely. The Bishop with us.

To Sir W. V. HARCOURT, chancellor of the exchequer,   MS Harcourt dep. 14, f. 9.
5 February 1894.

I have been out all day and send a late and hurried line.

I am looking with deep interest & anxiety at the proceedings in the Lords. Until Friday or Saturday's news came here they had not assumed the character which it now seems possible they may bear—that of a virtual destruction of the entire year's work of the Commons. If they do this it seems to raise a hard & very large question indeed: possible [*sic*] one large enough to carry us for the *moment* into some new current.

On the year of 1859 I will only say that I never regarded it as a scare but justified ⟨it⟩ warmly in the House of Commons the very large augmentations of charge there proposed. I thought it an expenditure truly exceptional, necessary in order to enable us at the Italian crisis to bear our proper part, and also as bound to be followed by reductions which the China War & the Trent affair delayed, but which after this delay actually arrived.

6. Tu.

Wrote to Mr Marj.—Mr Mundella—Sir A. West—Ld Acton—Rev. Mr M'Coll. Bp [G. H.] Wilkinson dined: a privilege to see him. Ten to dinner. Saw the Maire—Mr J. Murray—Mrs Williamson. Drive. Worked on Odes. Finished Antony & Cleopatra. That fifth Act is indeed most wonderful.

To LORD ACTON, lord-in-waiting, 6 February 1894.   Cambridge University Library.
'*Secret*'.

When Mary read me your last letter, I had not received the materials necessary to refresh my memory on the proceedings of 1859: and while many deemed that it laid the ground fairly for an augumentum *ad hominem*, no one had thought it relevant or material to look back to my own contemporary exposition of my proceedings at that date which were in my view as compared with the present proposal chalk & cheese.

I have not been able to complete an account, which I wished to make full, of the rather complex & much varying situation of 1859–60; but I send herewith an extract from a letter[2] that I have been writing to a colleague, which contains the *essential* as to my own views & proceedings. There is no other man alive (unless C. Villiers!) who had lot or part in the transactions of that period.

---

[1] i.e. up the valley of the Nive, into the foothills of the Pyrennees.
[2] Copy in Mrs. Gladstone's hand of a letter this day to E. W. Hamilton.

To A. J. MUNDELLA, president of the board of trade,   Add MS 44258, f. 328.
6 February 1894. '*Secret*'.

Nothing can be kinder than your letter.[1] I thank you for it heartily, & I trust you will believe in the heartiness of my thanks, although the plainness with which it may be necessary for me to speak may seem to approach to roughness, or even rudeness. After all the main point in such a case is that, with a view to the public interest, ideas should be stated in their full breadth.

I agree with you that a grave calamity overhangs the Liberal party in connection with the plan which I described to you in two familiar monosyllabic epithets. But it is not in my power to avert that calamity by becoming a partner in the scheme which is its cause. Liberalism cannot put on the garb of Jingoism without suffering for it, & suffering for it justly, whether soon or late.

You request me not to eschew this partnership: but you will be the first to acknowledge that this matter cannot be settled by requests: &, were I to request Spencer to withdraw his proposal, he would not, & ought not to comply.

I am told that the Government cannot go on without me. I have not adopted that opinion. But if others adopt it, I will, for argument's sake, suppose it to be true. The meaning is that the country has a confidence in the party with me at the head, which it will not have if I am not at the head. *If* this be so, some essential part of that confidence is confidence in me. If it is confidence in me, it is founded on my life & my actions. Now in them has been embedded for sixty years a constant effort to do all I could for economy & for peace: not the peace of this country only but of the world. I do not put the two (peace & economy) *quite* on the same footing; & it is not now economy but peace which supplies the key note of the situation; & which together with honour also supplies the highest standard of duty for a public man. Because then, I have (so it is supposed) acquired confidence by my life & acts, I am now asked to depart from their essential law, & to use all such authority as they have acquired for me, in order to become (as I should be) the main recommender of a policy which in my view directly contradicts them. I ask you how can I do this?

If the thing is to be done at all let it be done by those who think it *right*.

But then it is felt, & even said, you have done it before. No, I have not. (Even if I have, that fact would not of itself acquit me).

Two things I have done, which, if in kindred subject matter, are totally different from what is now proposed.

I have made limited concessions to 'Scares': in 1860 & again in the Northbrook & Brassey case, of which I forget the exact year [1884]. But never any such concession as large as that which I tendered in the Cabinet of January 8, & which was dismissed (quite consistently & properly I admit) without a single word.

Besides this, I have repeatedly been responsible for extraordinary financial provisions, having reference to some crisis of the day.

I did this 1. By a preliminary Budget in 1854: 2. By the final Budget of July 1859: by the Vote of Credit in July 1870: & again by the Vote of Credit in 1884. Every one of these was special, & was shown in each case respectively to be special by the sequel: no one of them had reference to the notion of establishing dominant military or even naval power in

---

[1] Of 3 February, Add MS 44258, f. 325, written from Valescure, hoping the govt. 'will continue during the term of its natural life to enjoy the inestimable advantage of your leadership. This I believe is indispensable not only to its existence, but also to the existence of a United Liberal Party'; Gladstone should not underestimate the consequences of his retiral; 'if you leave us now, disintegration and discomfiture will inevitably follow . . .'.

Europe. Their amounts were various, but were adapted to the view taken, at least by me, of the exigency actually present.

This might be taken for granted as to 1854, 1870 & 1884. That it was equally true in my mind of 1859 may be seen by anyone who read my Budget Speech of July 18. 1859. I defended the provision as required by & for the time, & for the time only. The occasion in that year was the state of the Continent. It was followed by the China War (No. 3) & by the Trent affair (1861-2) but when these had been disposed of economy began; and, by 1863-4, the bulk of the new charge had been got rid of.

There is also the case of the Fortifications in 1860 which would take me too long to state fully. But I will state briefly (1) My conduct in that matter was mainly or wholly governed by regard to peace, for I believed & believe now that, in 1860, there were only two alternatives; one of them the French Treaty, & the other war with France. And I also believed in July 1860 that the French Treaty must break down, unless I held my office. 2. The demand was reduced from 9 millions to about five (Has this been done now?) 3. I acted in concert with my old friend & colleague Sir J. Graham. We were entirely agreed.

In this matter, besides speaking for near an hour to the Cabinet, I have held seventeen confidential conversations, had some writing, & incessant thought. The upshot is, that I am (as I said on January 8) a survival. But a survival, if honour is to be kept, must have some regard to the ideas, & to the histories of which he or it was once a living part. [P.S.] Due in London not *later* than 10th. You are quite welcome to show this to any colleagues.

The Lords *may* raise for us another not less urgent question crossing the scent. The unforeseen sometimes does much in politics.[1]

7. *Ash Wed.*

Ch 11 A.M. (evg missed by accident). Wrote to S. Lyttelton Tel.—Ld Kimberley Tel.—Sir W. Harcourt—Sir H. Ponsonby. Worked on Odes. And on statement of July 18. 1859: for extracts.[2] Read Mrs Besant's Autobiography[3]—Stanley's Life. Dippings! Drive, & backgammon.

To Sir W. V. HARCOURT, chancellor of the exchequer,   MS Harcourt dep. 14, f. 11. 7 February 1894.

Many thanks for the citations you have sent me.[4] Those for which I am responsible quite agree with what I *expected* or supposed that I should have said at the respective dates. Speaking from memory I think that the great Italian occasion of 1859-60 had then passed away, and a new state of relations with France had sprung up.

I think that *a* question of naval reconstruction was involved in the Budget of 1859, even as prepared by the Derby Govt: but I have not *found* any references to it in the Financial Statement.

The words cited from Lord Granville are unknown to me and unless modified by the content are by no means in touch with the statements in my Financial exposition.

[1] Mundella replied, 15 February, Add MS 44258, f. 331, from London, thanking Gladstone for his 'explanatory letter', hoping that if the charges of 1859-60 were 'got rid of later' the same might happen in this case, and reiterating his grief at Gladstone's retiral.
[2] See 2 Feb. 94n.
[3] A. Besant, *Annie Besant. An autobiography* (1893).
[4] Not found.

8. *Th.*

Wrote to Mr J. Cowan—S.L. Tel.—Ld Acton—Mr Westell. Drive, walk, back-gammon. Waves wonderful at the Phare. Worked on Odes. Read Mrs Besant. In four of this good type I have got through say 60 pages: this is my *best*. Read Webster on Petite Eglise[1]—Masson on the Josephine Marriage.[2]

To LORD ACTON, lord-in-waiting, 8 February 1894.   Add MS 44549, f. 185.

With reference to the 'West' telegram, without doubt it constitutes a new difficulty at first sight; but one which I think on examining its terms diminishes or disappears.

On your three 'certains' (1) I agree that a mistake is irreparable; either way. (2) The 'action' which has brought about the difficulty is no action of mine. It is the action of others to which I am asked to conform. (3) Whether it be true that every one of my best friends is against me I do not know. I admit that I am without support. But the world of today is not the world in which I was bred and trained and have principally lived. It is a world which I have had much difficulty in keeping on terms with and these difficulties increase and are not wholly confined to this matter. I will not draw comparisons.

I take the *worst* at the worst and say that if the whole generation be against me, even that is far better than that I should with my eyes open (to say nothing of this country) do anything (according to my measure) to accelerate, exasperate, widen, or prematurely take or verge towards taking a part in, the controversies of blood which we all fear and seem to see are hanging over Europe.

To J. COWAN, chairman of the Midlothian Liberal Association,   Add MS 44137, f. 486. 8 February 1894. '*Private & Confidential.*'

You have I doubt not noticed the recent false statement in the "Pall Mall Gazette" and the contradiction given by Sir A. West, the terms of which of course were mine.

The falseness of the statement in the P.M.G. lay in this, that it stated a decision had been taken, which had not & has not; namely a decision irrespective of circumstances & fixing a time. But in the contradiction I have been obliged to embody distinct notice of a fact which is for me a grave one, and which for a long time past, and increasingly during the last six or eight months, has kept the likelihood of that decision impending over me. The truth is that I am considerably disabled in hearing & largely in sight, for the discharge with any efficiency of duties which are vital to my office. Writing is little affected but reading very formidably. I am almost absolutely, for example, cut off from the newspaper press! There has been inconvenience in regard to both senses for a consider-able time: but the obstruction of sight has only become grave within six or eight months past. It has therefore been true for some time that my tenure of office might at any moment cease. The time should of course be chosen carefully, with regard to circum-stances & opportunity. The choice is not made: but the time *may* be very near.

Of course I shall bear particularly in mind as duty & feeling alike require, my relation to my kind & excellent constituents; among whom to their Chairman especially.

This is really a letter hardly admitting an answer, one of premonition only, not infor-mation.

I have much to be thankful for in my old age as throughout my life: but the movement of the hands upon the old clock of time is an inexorable movement.

We are due in London on Saturday evening.[3]

---

[1] Untraced.
[2] F. Masson, *Napoleon: lover and husband* (1894).
[3] Cowan replied, 12 February, Add MS 44137, f. 490, hoping Gladstone's strength would con-

9. Fr. [On train]

Tel. to S.L. Drive: Phare, Bois de B. Farewells. Worked pretty well on Odes. Packing. At 9 A.M. the Bp of St A[ndrews][1] gave us a private Celebration: very timely as I hope. Off at 5.30.

10. Sat. [London]

Paris 7.30. Downing St 6.30 P.M. Luxurious journey: but bad passage. Saw the Chairman of RR—(a Dutch gentleman)—Mr Marj.—Sir A. West—Mr Mundella. —Mr A. Dined. Backgammon. Read 'Strange Sins' (2).[2] Dossie has in travelling undergone a marked development.

11. 1. S.L.

Chapel Royal morn and evg. Wrote to Warden of Keble (cancelled)—J. Morley —Mr Marj.—The Queen l.l.—.......—& minutes. Saw S.L.—Mr Murray—Lucy Cavendish. Long & interesting conversation with J. Morley. He says he has sold his soul for Ireland & does not know whether he will get money for it. Also if I *went* on the Naval plan he must do the same.[3]

12. M.

Family conversation on the situation.

Wrote to The Queen—Mr Channing. Saw Sir A.W.—Mr Marj.—Mr Morley— Lucy C.—Ld Kimberley. Cabinet 12–1. H. of C. $3\frac{1}{4}$–$7\frac{1}{2}$.[4] Drive with C. She read me 'Two Noble Lives'.[5] Read a little Cymbeline.

Found I could not read even the better print of a newspaper. *This is a step downwards*.

Worked on Odes.

Cabinet. Monday Feb. 12. 94. Noon.[6]
1. Ld Ripon mentioned the N.S. Wales Act which in error has been passed without being reserved & is consequently invalid. Confirming is requested[?] at once.[7] Agreed.
2. Lords Amendments on Employers Liab. Bill. Dudley's amt. substantially brought back. Asquith proposes a time limit of permission (to 3 years) to existing societies.[8] *Yes*.
3. Scotch Sea Fisheries. reject the vital change. amnd in details.
4. Local Govt. Bill. Report[9] of the Committee of Cabinet is that when the Bill reaches H. of C. we should simply '*reject all or nearly all*' (Harcourt's words, accepted by all).
   1. Population condition. 200 raised to 500.
   2. Allotments clause destroyed.
   3. Charities Claim virtually destroyed.

tinue, and reporting he had 'asked four of our leading friends to meet on Wednesday that we may carefully consider our duty to our great and much honoured representative and also to our constituency'. See to Cowan, 13 Feb. 94.

[1] G. H. Wilkinson.   [2] J. C. Kernahan, *A book of strange sins* (1893).
[3] The pages of Morley's diary on this conversation have been mutilated.
[4] Scottish Fisheries Bill; 4*H* 21. 287.   [5] See 22 Dec. 93.
[6] Add MS 44648, f. 157. See also below, Appendix I.
[7] The Cabinet agreed at once to introduce a bill validating the Colonial Act; CAB 41/23/2.
[8] Proposed next day; 4*H* 21. 400.   [9] Word scrawled.

4. *Elected* persons to be actually payers of rates.
5. Use of parish schools for Council.
6. Exclusion of London Vestries.
7. Abolition of compulsory compounding for the future.

13. Tu.

Wrote to Mr Cowan—Ld Kimberley—Ld Spencer—E.W. Hamilton. Worked on Odes. H. of C. 3½–7¾.[1] Read Earles' Psalter[2]—Cymbeline. Seven to dinner. Drive with C. Saw Sir A.W.—Mr Marj.—Mr M.

To J. COWAN, chairman of the Midlothian Liberal Association,   Add MS 44549, f. 186.
13 February 1894.

I thank you for your very kind letter;[3] & I add a word on the subject of secrecy, which might perhaps, & naturally enough, not occur to you.

We have important & complex matters still pending between the two Houses. They may be (*possibly*, I do not say more) accommodated, or they may grow into a serious crisis. In this state of matters, it is of great consequence that not even a whisper should go forth with any semblance of authority of the Government in dispensing of the very important residue of business belonging to the present Session. It seems pretty certain that this will be disposed of next week, but possibly well on in next week. If you can trust the four to whom you refer absolutely as yourself I see no difficulty in the conversation you propose, & certainly some convenience. But if there be any doubt even as to any *one* among them I would ask you to postpone the meeting or the confidential part of the subject for a week.[4]

To E. W. HAMILTON, 13 February 1894. '*Private.*'   Add MS 48607B, f. 214.

My wife tells me you have spoken to her of the figures of 1859. They have very naturally been referred to by various persons, but most of those who have so quoted them have not even read my contemporary official exposition of them.

I stated that they were due to a present emergency, the state of affairs abroad, which in my view absolutely required them. I called them temporary, provisional, ambiguous (meaning that they were neither of peace or war, rather hanging between the two, like the Belgian vote of credit in 1870 or the Russian in 1884): & even that within the six months of the year then remaining we should probably have passed into a new state & should be either better or worse. Such was, as I stated on behalf of the Government, their distinction and leading character. And in proof that this was mainly just, look to the sequel. The bulk of the charge imposed was subsequently removed; although that removal was delayed by several grave causes; the Savoy & Nice annexation, the China War, and the Trent affair.

There were also naval reconstructions going on at that period, but these were a secondary element.

There is a resemblance of *amount*, and there resemblance begins & ends.[5]

---

[1] Questions; Employers' Liability Bill; 4 *H* 21. 394.
[2] J. Earle, *Psalter of the Great Bible of 1539* (1894).
[3] See 8 Feb. 94n.   [4] No reply found.
[5] Hamilton replied this day, Add MS 48697B, f. 216, that he and Welby had read Gladstone's 1859 speech, and his other contemporary remarks ('the speech of 1859 must not, I venture to think, be read alone'), and that he drew from these 'somewhat different conclusions' from those of Gladstone.

To LORD SPENCER, first lord of the admiralty, 13 February 1894.   Althorp MSS K8.
'*Private.*'

Although the state of my sight prevents my reading the speech of your Naval Lord on Defence,[1] I am given to understand that it implies that the Departmental Estimates have been actually adopted by the Government, and you will have seen the manner in which it is turned to account by the Times.

It seems to me that he must have been somewhat imprudent, and I am absolutely certain that if he has been so he has spoken without any authority other than his own.

But it is not a case where something may require to be done. I should be very sorry to have that something made disagreeable to him. And I am perfectly contented to leave the matter in your hands.

Probably the needful would be sufficiently done if it were pointed out to him or otherwise that according to the established practice of our Government for long, if not at all times past, Estimates in preparation rest upon Departmental authority, and undergo the consideration of the Cabinet, and are finally fixed by it, shortly before the time when they are presented to Parliament.[2]

14. Wed.

Wrote to Ld Strathmore l. & tel.—Sir H. Ponsonby—Sir R. Cameron. Saw A.E.W.—Mr Marj.—Mr Morley—Sir R. Welby cum E. Hamilton on the figures— S.L. on his case. Drive with C. Dined at Ld Reays—conversation with French Ambr & Ambassadress—Lady E. Fitzmaurice—Mr Gilbert—M. (Dutch). St James's $5\frac{3}{4}$ PM (part). Worked on Odes.

15. Th.

Wrote to Mr Mundella—Ld Kimby—Rev. B. Wilberforce—Sir H. Ponsonby—Ld Lansdowne Tel.—Conversation with Harry respecting Mr Rendel.—Drs. Rainy & Mitchell. Saw Sir A.W.—Mr Marj.—Mr Lefevre—S.L.—H.J.G. re Armitstead &c. H. of C. $3\frac{1}{2}$–8 & 10–$12\frac{1}{4}$.[3] Read Cymbeline. Worked on Odes.

16. Fr.

Wrote to Sir H. Ponsonby Tel.—Sir J. Pease—Sir E. Saunders. Saw Sir A.W.—Mr Marj.—Welsh Deputation. Conclave on final honours. H. of C. $3\frac{1}{2}$–$7\frac{3}{4}$, 10–11.[4] Worked on Odes. Read Cymbeline. We now dabble in arrangements with an ultimate view to house-clearing.

To Sir J. W. PEASE, M.P., 16 February 1894.   Add MS 44549, f. 188.

I have received your letter & inclosure;[5] & by the same post a memorial from the Leith Chamber of Commerce praying for more naval armaments.

You see which way the tide runs, but the Cabinet never decide these matters till rather close upon the time for producing Estimates for the coming year.

---

[1] Speech on the navy plan in *T.T.*, 9 February 1894, 12b (with leader on 12 February 1894, 9b) by Edmund Robertson, 1845–1911, liberal M.P. Dundee 1885–1908; Civil Lord of the Admiralty 1892-5.

[2] Spencer replied that Robertson in his opinion had not announced 'definite proposals to which serious exception could be taken'; 13 February, Add MS 44314, f. 107.

[3] Questions; L.G. Bill; $4H$ 21. 460.   [4] Questions; L.G. Bill; $4H$ 21. 608.

[5] Not found; on naval expenditure.

I suppose it will be best to meet the communication of this morning with simple acknowledgement.

Perhaps when we meet we may exchange more words upon·the subject.

17. Sat.

Wrote to Mr Mundella. Worked on Odes. Saw Sir A.W.—Mr Murray—Ld Ripon—Ld Rosebery—Ld Herschell—Chr of Exr (on eyes). Cabinet dinner. All. I believe it was expected I should say something. But from my point of view there is nothing to be said.[1] Read Cymbeline—Lefevre on Commons.[2]

To A. J. MUNDELLA, president of the board of trade,   Add MS 44549, f. 188.
17 February 1894.

The question whether it is possible to regard the plan described by my two epithets[3] (which I am quite sensible might be retorted) can be regarded as analagous in that respect to 1859 may be brought to an easy and conclusive issue:—will it be described in the [Queen's] Speech submitting it to Parliament.

Reflection day by day continually blackens my opinion of it. But perhaps I am like the recalcitrant juryman who complained that he was associated with eleven of the most obstinate, impractical, incomprehensible fellows on the face of the earth.

18. 2 S.L.

Chapel Royal mg. Trinity Evg. Strong Sermon from Mr Eyton. Fine choir. Bad hearing for me. *Dabbled* in reading: read A. Besant. Wrote to S.E.G. Wrote on The Atonement.[4]

19. M.

Wrote to Sir H. Ponsonby—Mr Cowan—Margot Tennant.[5] Read Cymbeline (*poco*). Saw Sir A.W.—Mr M.—Mr Marj.—Mr Asquith—Alfred L.—Ld Acton. Ten to dinner. H. of C. $3\frac{3}{4}$–8. I was led by temptation, and Sir R. Webster into a little speech: a rarity now for me: not far from a funeral oration.[6]

To J. COWAN, chairman of the Midlothian Liberal Association,   Add MS 44549, f. 188.
19 February 1894. '*Secret*'.

I have nothing new to say at the moment about eyes & ears. But the Session may come to an end rather promptly. And, viewing the likelihood that then may be the moment for

[1] 'Asked Mr. Gladstone whether he was going to make any announcement to the Cabinet at the [eve of Session] dinner tonight. "What announcement have I to make?" he said. "Well, about your intentions." "Oh no, they know everything."

I then suggested getting Ponsonby up, but he thought Thursday or Friday time enough. "For, before that," he said, "we shall know what the Lords will do, and they may alter things, for in the case of a dissolution I should go to the country with them."' (West, *P.D.*, 278). See also Appendix I.

[2] G. L. Shaw Lefevre, *English commons and forests* (1894).

[3] 'Mad and drunk', the adjectives Gladstone was reported as using frequently to describe the navy plan.

[4] Start of work on 'True and false conceptions of the Atonement', *N.C.*, xxxvi. 317 (September 1894). On Annie Besant (see 7 Feb. 94).

[5] Her engagement to H. H. Asquith was announced this day.

[6] A defence of the autonomy of charities and trusts; 4*H* 21. 763.

claiming my liberty on the ground that I have already mentioned to you, & the latest opportunity I may have for tendering any recommendation to the Queen, I write briefly to say that if it would be agreeable to you that your name should be laid before Her Majesty for a Baronetcy, I should be most ready to submit that recommendation. And I believe that not only your friends & your country, but the public of Scotland in general would hail such an acknowledgement of your character & services.[1]

To H. F. PONSONBY, the Queen's secretary, 19 February 1894. Add MS 44549, f. 188.

If as I understand the Queen's coming up is fixed for Thursday, you I conclude *will* move from Osborne on that day & perhaps you would make that the day for calling on me, at *any* hour you like to name as it will probably be a blank day in the House of Commons.

To Miss E. A. M. ('Margot') TENNANT, 19 February 1894.   Add MS 44549, f. 188.

I need not say that I receive your letter with warm interest.[2] In no case ought marriage to be lightly spoken of least of all in yours, for you are about to unite your lot with a man of such power, character, & prospects, that you are undertaking a very solemn charge which requires a not less solemn self-devotion. I earnestly hope & pray that the Almighty may adorn & enrich the union with every blessing, most of all with the blessings which are his best.

20.

Wrote to Sir R. Palgrave—Rev. B. Wilberforce—The Queen—Ld Kimberley—Mr Granger Ln (tel.)—Ld Strathmore. Finished Cymbeline—at last. Saw Sir A.W.— Mr Marj.—Mr Murray—Mr . . . . . H. of C. $3\frac{1}{2}$–$7\frac{3}{4}$. Short speech on Empl. Liaby Bill.[3] Dined with Lucy C.

To F. M. GRANGER, physician, 20 February 1894. Telegram.   Add MS 44518, f. 37. '*Strictly confidential*'.

I am highly sceptical about the singular report in the Westminster Gazette where you are introduced especially about the part relating to my continuance in office which cannot be reconciled with Sir A. West's authoritative telegram[4] from Biarritz.[5]

---

[1] Cowan replied, with thanks, accepting the baronetcy, Add MS 44137, f. 491; on 7 March he sent a Resolution of the Midlothian Liberal Association deeply regretting Gladstone's retiral, especially recalling the 1885 Representation of the People Act, and requesting him to continue as M.P.; ibid., f. 492.

[2] Of 17 February, Add MS 44518, f. 26: 'I am engaged to be married to Mr Asquith & I am very happy'; see 10 May 94. Gladstone wrote to Spencer, 27 March 1894, Althorp MSS K444: '. . . The Asquith-Tennant marriage is of extreme interest. She has very fine qualities & capabilities. I should be glad were she to add to them more of humility and dependence. He has a great future.'

[3] Opposing the Lords' amndts. to the Employers' Liability Bill; 4*H* 21. 851.

[4] See 31 Jan. 94.

[5] Granger replied this day that he had not seen the paper; Gladstone sent him the clipping; Granger wrote on 22 February that a clerk on the *Chester Chronicle*, to whom he had spoken about a story in the *New York Tribune*, must have somewhat exaggerated the remarks he made to him; Add MS 44518, f. 33 ff. See 23 Feb. 94.

To LORD KIMBERLEY, Indian secretary, 20 February 1894.   Kimberley MSS.

We will have a Cabinet on Friday at noon, on what I understand to be your request, in order that you may obtain full authority as to the course you have to take that evening in the Lords.

I also gather from West that you are in some doubt as to my intentions that is I presume as to some particulars of time and circumstances.

You will remember that on Tuesday Jan 9 the Cabinet tacitly agreed to take time for considering the case before it, including and perhaps principally meaning the question whether we were to 'gather in our harvest' (to use Trevelyan's words). I afterwards understood that this was the general view, and I suppose there is no doubt of it.

Having had not the smallest title to doubt the persistence of the Cabinet I have had nothing to consider except the time of communication to the Queen. However desirable it might be from some points of view for me to have *notice* as soon as may be I have thought it my absolute duty to my colleagues to say and do nothing which might by possibility tend to impair the solidarity of the Government until the questions between the two Houses are settled. In this I hope you will think I was right.

On Friday matters may have sufficiently advanced to enable me to mention the limited though important question which yet remains as to *time*. We might perhaps then consider the question of the Speech which must I presume be of the briefest.[1]

21. Wed

Wrote to Ld Kimberley—Mr Watts. A day of conversation. Sir W.H. 1½ hour.—Lady Lothian 1¼ hour.—Lady S. Spencer—Mr Knox—Sir E. Watkin—Mr Roundell—Mr Marj.—Ly F. Balfour. Worked on papers connected with the coming events. Drive with C. Six to dinner. Read Bp Dowden, Letters to Sharp.[2]

1. It is probable that when the remaining business of the Session and any matter immediately connected with it have been disposed of I may have a communication to make to Her Majesty, which it might be for H.M.s convenience that she should have the opportunity of reflecting on before it actually reaches Her.
2. I am strictly bound in honour to say nothing which if it went beyond H.M. could have the effect of creating doubt or speculation as to the complete responsibility and solidarity of the whole Government as it stands for the purpose above mentioned, if it were to go beyond Her Majesty.
3. On the other hand I have no title in making a communication to Her Majesty to impose any condition of secrecy even if only for a time.
4. The sole motive of the following inquiry is the convenience of Her Majesty.
5. In these circumstances I ask Sir H. Ponsonby whether it would be agreeable to his duty and his judgment to receive from me an indication of the communication I refer to,

[1] Kimberley replied this day, Add MS 44229, f. 216, that a Cabinet was necessary for instructions on the Local Govt. Bill in the Lords; 'The rest of your communication, if I rightly understand it, is a matter of great grief to me, and this feeling will I know be shared by all our colleagues'; he agreed 'nothing should be done which would tend to impair the solidarity of the Govt., until the questions between the two Houses are settled. I think however it would be desirable that *some* indication as to time should be given, if possible, to the Cabinet on Friday'. He wrote next day, Kimberley MSS, sending a memorandum on proposal of the Indian government to re-impose cotton duties and asked for its urgent discussion by the Cabinet.

[2] J. Dowden, ed., *Thirty-four letters written to James Sharp... by the Duke and Duchess of Lauderdale* (1893).

and to give me the assurance that I should not in any way depart by making it from that obligation of honour which I have described.

WEG F. 21. 9.[1]

To LORD KIMBERLEY, Indian secretary, 21 February 1894.   Add MS 44549, f. 189.

You will find me here till 3.30. The question I should like to put for the chance of an answer is whether there is anything that can be called a native public opinion in India on the question of the Cotton duties and if so what it is.[2]

Are there any other protective duties involved in the question besides cotton?

22. Th.

Wrote to Ld Chanc.—Mr Conybeare—Sir J. Pease—Sir H. Ponsonby (Tel.)—Ld Stalbridge. Worked further on papers. Worked on Odes. Saw Sir A.W.—Mr Marj.—Sir W. Harcourt—J. Morley—Mr Murray. Read Richard III. Dined with the Campbell Bannermans.

Conversation with Sir H. Ponsonby[3]

I have a question to put, the inclusive object of which is Her Majesty's convenience.

It requires a Preamble which is this;

1. I should be glad to convey an intimation to the Queen which I think it would be for H.M.s convenience to receive.
2. But I am bound in honour to others not to make it unless it were to be absolutely confined for the present to herself.
3. While on the other hand I am not entitled to make any condition of that nature with Her Majesty.

I am willing to convey the intimation to you, if you are willing to receive it and able to give me the assurance that it will be so used as strictly to conform to the obligation of honour (2) by which I am bound.

Are you willing and able as above stated?

[I must also add that this obligation of mine would be infringed if the purport of the present conversation were made known beyond the limit proposed for the ulterior one.][4]

23. Fr.

Wrote to the Queen—Mr Grainger—Ld Spencer—The Speaker. Cabinet 12–1¾. Work on honour cases. Saw Sir A.W.—Mr Marj.—Sir W. Harcourt. Visit to Marlborough House at 3. We were most kindly received. Dossie *un*impressed. Made my explanation to Mr Armitstead: all well. Inspected Mr Wood's[5] bust of Sir A. Clark. Five to dinner. Backgammon. Read Rich. III.

---

[1] Holograph; Add MS 44776, f. 61. For the meeting with Ponsonby, for which this is the first of several preparatory notes, see 24 Feb. 94.

[2] See 20 Feb. 94n. and 23 Feb. 94.

[3] Holograph dated 22 February 1894; Add MS 44776, f. 53. See 24 Feb. 94.

[4] Gladstone's brackets.

[5] Probably Francis Derwent Wood, 1871–1926; sculptor and painter.

Cabinet. Frid. Feb. 23. 94.[1]
2. Course to be taken in the Lords on Local Govt. Bill.
3. Speech before Prorogation.
4. WEG informs.[2]

Indian Cotton Duties[3]

1. Indian Budget—Taxation—Cotton Duties.
No. 1. [India] Adopt plan of a possible deficit und[er?] the circs.—& recommend more military & other reduction.[4]
No. 2. [Local Government and the Lords] Hiring—no change—of substance.
Purchase—not ours. The District Council.
resist Abp. of York
resist Amt. in Clause 6 to power of Churchwardens.
Salisbury option—resist.

To F. M. GRANGER, physician, 23 February 1894. '*Private.*'   Add MS 44518, f. 46.

I received your letter[5] with regret. In it you say that 'the report is fairly reasonable', and you take no exception to the following words contained in it: 'There is no necessity for him to resign the premiership so far as his eyesight is concerned'.

I have previously through Sir A. West telegraphed to the Press from Biarritz on the 31st. of Jan. In this message after referring to my age and the state of my sight and hearing I said (I change to the first person) 'my tenure of office has been at any moment liable to interruption from these causes in their nature permanent'.

It appears to me that it is difficult to reconcile these statements.

If you can do it I shall be glad. If not it appears that you virtually contradicted a published statement of mine, and did not restrain your interviewer from publishing the contradiction.

In no case shall I refer to the statement in the Westminster Gazette, unless I am compelled to do so, but if compelled I may have to state not what science can discern in my eyes, but what are the experimental facts of my actual vision.

I shall do this, if at all, with the desire to soften rather than exaggerate.[6]

To LORD SPENCER, first lord of the Admiralty, 23 February 1894.   Althorp MSS K8.

While I gladly and thankfully receive your letter,[7] let me assure you without reserve that I have all along felt assured that you entertained every kind warm and manly sentiment it expresses, though I am indeed aware that some of them are much beyond my due. I beg you to believe that nothing which has happened, and nothing which can

---

[1] Add MS 44648, f. 161.
[2] Gladstone's announcement to the Cabinet that he would retire at the Prorogation.
[3] Introduction of a cotton duty for India; see P. Harnetty, 'The Indian cotton duties controversy, 1894-96', *E.H.R.*, lxxvii. 684 (1962).
[4] Gladstone told the Queen: 'The Cabinet however are of opinion that, in the present state of Indian finance, and with the powerful operation on it of causes which fluctuate almost from day to day, this important subject should not be taken up, that the prospect of a deficit, both problematical and small, may be faced; and that efforts should be made to provide against it by greater effort in the reduction of military and other expenditure'; CAB 41/23/3.
[5] See 20 Feb. 94n.
[6] Granger replied, 24 February, Add MS 44518, f. 51, regretting his letter had upset Gladstone, but effectively holding to his position that Gladstone's sight was, when he saw him six weeks previously, not in itself a reason for resignation; he noted that the statement of 31 Jan. 94 mentioned hearing as well as sight, the combination meaning 'the question is a very different thing'.
[7] Letter from Spencer this day, Add MS 44314, f. 109 and *Spencer*, ii. 239.

happen, will alter my estimate of your character, or reduce it by one jot or tittle from the high place which all who know you assign to it.

My convictions indeed on the policy which the Cabinet have adopted are very strong, so strong that no words can go beyond them. And so strong that it is to me a great solace, in such circumstances to reflect, that I do not deem it my duty to express them: on the contrary I deem it a very distinct duty to refrain from expressing them both at the present moment and in any circumstances I can now foresee as probable, though of course no one can in public affairs account for the unforeseen.

And I am most glad to believe that as between us personally everything will continue as before; and I wish you from the bottom of my heart a long happy and distinguished life in the service of your country, which has no son more worthy to serve it.

24. Sat.

Write to Archdeacon Watkins—.......... Saw Sir A.W.—Mr Marj.—Mr Murray—Sir W. Harcourt. Worked much on books: in preparation: & arranged for a supply to Harry. Dined with Mr Marj[oribanks]. At five, interview with Sir H.P. excellent; but at night a letter from Windsor announced impediments.[1] Saw one [R]. Read Richard III.

Feb. 24. 94. For interview with Sir H. Ponsonby[2]
1. Object—H.M.s convenience.
2. Have an intimation to make
3. Cannot honourably make it unless certain it will not go beyond.
4. Cannot impose condition.
5. Can he give the assurance
6. My *bond* includes present interview.

25. 3 S. Lent.

Chapel Royal mg & evg. Wrote to Sir H. Ponsonby—Sir W. Harcourt—Central News Tel.—Ld Rosebery—& minutes. Read Barclay[3]—A Modern Heretic[4]—Sketch of Bp Lightfoot—how noble.[5] Saw Mr Murray—Lady S. Spencer walked me home—& spoke so admirably.

To Sir W. V. HARCOURT, chancellor of the exchequer,   MS Harcourt dep. 14, f. 15. 25 February 1894. '*Secret*'.

The trying occasion which has overtaken us, unexpectedly I presume to most or even all until within the last few months, has given a vent to all the generous forces of your nature, which are so many and so strong.[6] And you have covered me with ascriptions to

---

[1] Ponsonby to Gladstone, 24 February 1894 (Guedalla, *Q*, ii. 489): 'I repeated to The Queen the substance of my conversation with you. Her Majesty asked what was the message you desired to give her. I of course said I knew nothing but The Queen replied that she could not bind herself to preserve secrecy on a matter of which she knew nothing and asked for some hint. . . .'

[2] Holograph; Add MS 44776, f. 50.

[3] Perhaps H. Barclay, *The justice's digest of the law of Scotland* (1894).

[4] *A modern heretic . . . a novel with a purpose* (1894).

[5] *Bishop Lightfoot. A sketch of his life and works* (1894); reprinted from *Q.R.*, with a note by B. F. Westcott.

[6] Letter of 24 February, Add MS 44203, f. 172: 'With your departure the great luminary of the Liberal Party will be quenched. . . .' Harcourt read this letter to the 'blubbering cabinet' on 1 March.

which I could, in the eyes of an impartial judge, lay no just claim. This, however, I feel in common with you: that while the combination of forces against us is one at all times formidable, the case has now a real aggravation: the loss of an old man, especially on the ground laid down by Cobden (which has a real solidity of its own), is in this country a grave loss. I think indeed that the Cabinet has in it plenty of strength: but then I think also, indeed it is plain from my point of view, that it is about to subject that strength to a sharp and somewhat abnormal trial.

I have done what for me was the outside of possibility, in order to avert evils and dangers, on the existence of which there can be little difference among us. But the failure of the effort proves that the discordant tendencies were, at least in the majority, profound, and when such tendencies exist it is perhaps best, or least bad, that they should take their course.

There is an assurance which I could have given you yesterday, and which, after your letter of such overflowing warmth and kindness, it is even easier to give. It is both my hope and my expectation that, in the matter of personal relations, not only with you but with all my colleagues, there will not be a particle of change. It is, indeed, hard to speak of the future in the whirlpool of political contingencies: but such is the forecast which the present suggests to me.

It is also a solace that the struggle which I have been carrying on against the defects of sense, though it is hard to say in what week or even month it would have ended, could not have lasted for any valuable length of time.

I am going to ask Rosebery, from whom I have had a letter of extreme kindness, to look in tomorrow at 10 minutes before 12, when I should like to let you & him learn from me the upshot of my interviews with Ponsonby.

To LORD ROSEBERY, foreign secretary, 25 February 1894.   N.L.S. 10027, f. 151.
'*Secret*'.

I am very grateful for your letter,[1] which I accept, as I hope, in the spirit which has prompted it.

But for the kindly spirit which repelled a painful construction, I am afraid it was too plain that when I said my final letter to the Queen ought to be delayed until the Prorogation Speech had been sanctioned, and asked the assent of my colleagues to that proposition, the only question open was not whether there should be a final letter but what should be its precise day or hour.

It is indeed a real solace, and a much needed one, that the case of my defective and declining senses is such a solid case. Apart from our most painful differences, and assuming, as I must assume, that visual disalibity [*sc.* disability] continued to grow as it has grown for the last six or seven months, I think that continuance through the Session would have been impossible; and resignation in the middle of it would [have] been as a practical matter, of intolerable inconvenience.

The revelation of differences between colleagues, among whom close cooperation, and what is more a certain community of mind are indispensable, is something like analogous revelations after marriage. But where they lie deep, as is I fear the case in the present instance, it is probably to be desired, as a choice of evils, that they should take their course. We have still the recollection of battles fought, possibly even of victories won, side by side in a good cause; and we also have still the hope, and as far as depends upon our poor human wills the determination, that personal relations shall remain absolutely unchanged.

---

[1] Rosebery's valedictory letter, 24 February, in Crewe, *Rosebery*, ii. 438 and Add MS 44290, f. 227.

I am so glad that I leave you, in your department, with the settlement about the Pamirs about to become an accomplished fact: and I hope this may be followed, whenever it is needful, by other similar achievements.

If you could look in here ten minutes before Cabinet tomorrow I should like to tell you the upshot of an interview I have had with Ponsonby. Harcourt will also be here.

26. M.

Wrote to The Queen—Sir E. Saunders—Ld Strathmore. H. of C. $3\frac{3}{4}$-$8\frac{1}{4}$.[1] Dined at Ld Northbourne's. Cabinet 12-$1\frac{3}{4}$. Saw Sir A.W.—Mr Marj.—Mr Murray—Ld Ripon + Sir W. Harcourt: *cum* Ld Rosebery—Mr & Mrs Corbet (Italy). Read K. Richard III.

Cabinet. Mond. Feb. 26. 94. Noon.[2]
1. Lords Amts. [to] Local Govt. Bill considered. Resist them.
2. See Paper of Amts.[3]
3. [Queen's] Speech further but not final.[4]

27. Tu.

Wrote to Sir A. Godley—Ld Kimberley—Mr Fowler—The Queen[5]—J. Morley—Mr Conybeare. Worked on Odes. Saw Sir A.W. l.l.—Mr Marj. l.l.—J. Morley (on the situation). Dined at A. Lyttelton's. Read K. Richard III.—Drive with Mary. Family conversation on the situation.

28. Wed.

Wrote to Arcicons[olo] Acc[ademia] La Crusca[6]—Ld Coleridge—Sir H. Ponsonby—The Prince of Wales. Worked on Odes. 15 to dinner: heavy in one quarter. Saw Sir A.W.—Mr Marj.—Lady Londonderry—The other Secretaries—Mr Morley—Sir H. Ponsonby—Italian cum Ambassador +. Audience of H.M. at 3 P.M. Wrote Mem. *q.v.* Finished Richard III.

I had an audience of the Queen, for 30 or 35 minutes today: doubtless my last in an official capacity. She had much difficulty in finding topics for an adequate prolongation:

[1] Questions; L.G. Bill; 4*H* 21. 1042.

[2] Add MS 44648, f. 164.

[3] Printed paper of amndts. with Gladstone's marginalia; Add MS 44648, f. 165.

[4] Deleted draft of notice that the Cabinet advised the Queen of need to refer in the Speech to divisions between the Houses on the local govt. bill amndts.; Add MS 44648, f. 169.

[5] 'Mr Gladstone presents his humble duty to Your Majesty, and believes himself now authorised to convey to Your Majesty the preliminary intimation which he has thought it would be for the convenience of Your Majesty to receive.

It is to the effect that, when the business of the present Session, and any matter immediately connected therewith, shall have been disposed of, he believes it will be his duty to tender to Your Majesty, on physical grounds, his resignation of office.

As his present object is simply to inform Your Majesty, without asking or desiring even a formal acknowledgment of this letter, he reserves all explanation of particulars until the day, perhaps a very early one, when he humbly proposes to carry his intention into effect' (Guedalla, *Q*, ii. 491 and *L.Q.V.*, 3rd series, ii. 364).

[6] G. Milanesi of the Academy of Florence, thanking him for an honour; Add MS 44549, f. 191.

but fog and rain and the coming journey to Italy all did their duty and helped. I thought I never saw her looking better. She was at the highest point of her cheerfulness. Her manner was personally kind throughout. She asked about my wife, and about the Rector; also on an occasion which arose about Harry. To me she said she was sorry *for the cause* which brought about my resignation. She did not however show any curiosity for particulars as to eyes and ears.

I asked whether the day for the journey to Italy was yet fixed. Yes the Queen said she was going *on the 13th*, and it could not be later as if it were delayed she would get into Passion Week and seemed to anticipate impediments not very intelligible to me. I had told her that according to present appearances the Speech Council might be on Saturday and the prorogation Monday. For how long she asked? Not longer than a week I apprehended. That however would be till the 12th. From hence I derived the impression, an impression only, and drawn from this part of the conversation, that she has at present no idea of any thing but a simple & limited reconstruction such as is necessarily consequent upon the retirement of a Prime Minister, and has no idea of resorting to the Tories or Opposition: further that she will not ask any advice from me as to the head, and further still that she will send for Rosebery. All this grew out of the almost casual reference by me to the day of departure for Italy. It was the only part of the conversation that had any importance.

She spoke however of Italy and deplored its condition: did not dissent when I ascribed it mainly to ambition. She spoke of Crispi and did not like him: of course in horror at his marital proceedings. She seemed rather surprised when I said that Cavour was older than I was. She thought the Italians very friendly to us which is true. They have however expectations from us, with our [*sc.* which are] without foundation. She returns to London on Monday next.

I said that, if we had the Speech Council on Saturday my definitive letter might go to her on that day.

Any fear that the intelligence I had to give would be a shock to her, has been entirely dispelled. Certainly the impression on my mind is that she does not even consider it a trouble, but regards it as the immediate precursor of an arrangement more agreeable.

All this is subject to illustration and modification from the immediate future. Of modification however I do not expect much. WEG Feb. 28. 94.[1]

Thurs. March 1. 1894.

Wrote to Sir C. Dilke—Author Life of Abp Laud[2]—Sir Horace Farquhar[3]—The Queen l.l. Saw Sir A.W.—Mr Marj.—Sir W. Harcourt—Mr Morley.
    Dined at Ld Rosebery's.
    Final Cabinet 12–1¾. A really moving scene.
    H. of C. 3¼–5. 'His last speech['']. I tried to follow the wish of the Cabinet: with

[1] Add MS 44776, f. 57. For Victoria's record of the occasion, see *L.Q.V.*, 3rd series, ii. 365: 'Saw Sir Henry Ponsonby, and then Mr. Gladstone, who was looking very old and deaf. I made him sit down, and said I had received his letter, and was sorry for the cause of his resignation. He said very little about it, only that he found his blindness had greatly increased since he had been at Biarritz. Then he talked of some honours for his friends, but not many. Then discussed various other topics.' See also *Autobiographica*, iv. 93.
    [2] Thomas Longueville, anon. author of *A life of Archbishop Laud. By 'a Romish recusant'* (1894), of which he had doubtless sent a copy.
    [3] Sir Horace Brand Townsend Farquhar, 1844–1923; London County Councillor and director of British South Africa Co.; liberal unionist M.P. 1895–8.

a good conscience. The House showed feeling: but of course I made no outward sign.[1]

Worked on Odes.

Cabinet. Thurs. Mch. 1. 94. Noon.[2]

1. How shall we deal with the Lords Amts. [to the Local Government Bill]?
   1. Refuse?
   2. *Accept & protest? We adopt this.*[3]
2. Speech agreed on to be forwarded to H.M.[4]
3. Mr. Gladstone's words in the House of Commons today—(much importance assigned to).[5]
4. Words of Farewell.
   Ld Kimberley
   Sir W. Harcourt
   W.E.G.[6]

To Sir C. W. DILKE, M.P., 1 March 1894.   Add MS 43875, f. 297.

You will forgive my pleading eyesight, which demanded the help of others and thereby retarded operations, as an excuse for my having failed to acknowledge the paper on Naval Defence which you were so good as to send me.[7]

---

[1] He took part in his last question-time (speaking on the procedures for private members' bills) and spoke on the Lords' amendments to the Local Government Bill, withdrawing opposition to them 'under protest': '. . . The issue which is raised between a deliberative Assembly occupied by many men of virtue, by many men of talent, of course with considerable diversities and varieties, is a controversy which, when once raised, must go forward to an issue'; the 'reserve and circumspection of the Lords', hitherto their safeguard, 'may have gone by'; 'Having said this, and thanking the House for the attention they have given me, I have only to signify that it is the intention of the Government to acquiesce in the Amendments which have been made by the House of Lords.' Such were Gladstone's final words (on his final appearance) to the House of Commons; 4*H* 21. 1152.

[2] Add MS 44648, f. 170.

[3] i.e. the amndts. not to be opposed, so as to keep the bill alive; it received Royal Assent on 5 March.

[4] Speech read and Parliament prorogued on 5 March; 4*H* 21. 1166.

[5] 'Everybody was urgent that in accepting Lords' amendments Mr. G. shd. make a strong appeal against the Lords generally . . . I sd., "What they want, Mr. Gladstone, is a dose of very bad language against the H. of L." And so, without enthusiasm, he agreed'; Morley's diary, 1 March 1894.

[6] 'Kimberley and Harcourt settled to say farewell on behalf of the members generally; both looked rather oppressed. Kimberley came to my room afterwards with tears rolling down his cheeks. He said it was most touching, and that Harcourt had broken down. Mr. Gladstone had been quite calm; said he was sorry for the difference of opinion that had arisen, but that in any case the time had come when his eyesight must force him to retire'; West, *PD*, 286.

Gladstone's last cabinet letter to the Queen concluded: 'Looking forward to the likelihood that this might be the last occasion, on which Mr Gladstone and his colleagues might meet in Cabinet, Lord Kimberley and Sir William Harcourt, on their own part and on that of the Ministers generally, used words, undeservedly kind, of acknowledgement and farewell.

Lord Kimberley will pray Your Majesty to appoint a Council for Saturday at as early an hour as may be convenient'; CAB 41/23/5.

See also Appendix at end of this volume and Introduction, section VI.

[7] Dilke, G. Chesney, H. O. Arnold-Forster and Spenser Wilkinson sent a letter proposing improvements in the representation of the defence depts. in the Cabinet; it was discussed with Balfour in December 1893 and circulated in final form to him, Salisbury, Devonshire and Chamberlain on 12 February, appearing in the press with their replies on 28 February; see Gwynn, ii. 417, 451–7 (with Gladstone's letter).

You will I fear find me a less interesting correspondent, than some who have replied to you at a certain length, for I fear I ought to confine myself to assuring you that I have taken care it shall come to the notice of my colleagues.

2. Frid. [*Windsor Castle*]

Wrote to The Speaker—Mr Budge—Mr A.J. Balfour—Mr Cowan—Ld Kimberley—Mr Rendel—Sir H. Ponsonby—Mrs Th.—Mr Armitstead. A busy morning. But worked *some* on Odes. Saw Sir A.W.—Mr Marj.—Priv. Secretaries—Ld Spencer—J. Morley.

Off by 5.5. All the time to 9 P.M. dinner passed in conversations. Sir H. Ponsonby—Ld Acton. The Queen, long & courteous, but of little meaning on "fundamentals". She was also careful rather to put me forward in the after dinner circle. Two interesting conversations with Empress Frederick, & Duchess of Albany: both *low*, one in European matters, the other domestic. Household circle & Acton afterwards. Read I Hen. VI. Completed the materials of my letter for tomorrow.

To A. J. BALFOUR, M.P., 2 March 1894.   Add MS 44549, f. 191.

You will probably have divined with others that the current of speculation & announcements about me, though unauthorised and for the moment untrue are not without meaning. That I should give them such a meaning until after tomorrow when I expect to bring my responsible action to a virtual close would be improper, and I must ask you kindly to bear this in mind. But I am anxious that you should know from myself that it is my intention after a Council which will be held tomorrow to tender my formal resignation to Her Majesty. And I hope you will accept this letter as a personal acknowledgement from me—the only one in my power to offer, for the marked courtesy & kindness towards me individually which has marked your conduct in Parliament as Leader of the Opposition. Believe me with many pleasant recollections and with every good wish.
[P.S.] Forgive me if this note bears tokens anywhere of visual powers not so good as they once were; and pray do not consider this letter as one leading to an answer.[1]

To Sir W. V. HARCOURT, chancellor of the exchequer,   MS Harcourt dep. 14, f. 17.
2 March 1894.

Please to read Ponsonby and me, and then to turn to the Draft. It has Kimberley's approval and I think is in the manifest sense of the Cabinet. If you agree I will re-send the Draft accordingly, and soon, to Windsor.

To A. W. PEEL, the Speaker, 2 March 1894.   Add MS 44549, f. 191.
'*Private & confidential*'.

The footing on which you have kindly always allowed me to stand with you has been such as to make me most unwilling that you should learn otherwise than from myself the immediately approaching termination of my official life. Disabilities of sense have reached with me a point at which they grievously impair my discharge of public duty, specially in connection with the operation of reading. Your Parliamentary print is large & good but I do not think that during the last 6 months I have read in the House six lines of it. I am tomorrow to tender to the Queen my formal resignation of office on the ground of

[1] Balfour replied this day, Add MS 44518, f. 65 with an effusive note and referring to himself as 'a private friend'. He did not preserve Gladstone's letter in his papers.

these disabilities. When that has been done all need for secrecy will have disappeared; but there cannot I think be any further announcement before Monday.

I earnestly hope that the present remission of duties in the Chair, though short, may be found greatly available for the re-establishment of your full strength, a matter which as I believe is regarded by the entire House as one of great public importance.[1]

To S. RENDEL, M.P., 2 March 1894.   Add MS 44549, f. 192.

The announcements of all kinds made about me in the public journals are wholly without authority & are in the letter without foundation. But a foundation will as I expect, after tomorrow be supplied for them. The Queen has already had in confidence a preliminary intimation. I am a party in advising the (brief & meagre) speech which will be delivered before the prorogation. I expect that speech to receive final sanction at a Council tomorrow, & it is my intention then to place in Her Majesty's hands the formal tender of my resignation. It will perhaps be announced in the newspapers of Monday.

The occasion is one on which dispatch is desirable. The new session ought not to begin later than Monday 12th & the time for reconstruction is not [un]limited. Your own personal share in these proceedings will of course be looked after in good time.

It is always serious to do anything for the last time: & the closing of so long a career is for me a solemn event, & may be collaterally more or less grave. We shall I hope have before very long opportunities for conversing on it. At present I will only say how sensible I am of the infinite personal kindness, I might indeed say tenderness which you have shown me since the first opportunity for it was afforded in these last years: & which has had a real warming & cheering influence on my public as well as private life.

Pray remember me most kindly in your circle: accept my congratulations on your beautiful house according to all I hear of it.[2]

3. Sat. [London]

Chapel Prayers, a Vale. The whole congregation was 21. Not one Lady. It is a new form of paying tithe: the inmates exceed 200. St George's at 10.30 A.M. The verger kindly showed me the Mitchell plate & read to me the inscription. Also I had a conversation with Sir [blank] Parrot especially about dearest Willy.[3] Wrote to The Queen l.l.[4]—Ld Vernon—Ld Carington—Mr Cowan—Sir H. Ponsonby—Lady Alice Portal. See Mems. for today. To London with the Council train. Saw West—Mr Marj.—S.L.—Mr Bryce—Ld Kimberley—Sir W. Harcourt. Interesting interview with the Albany children & their notable governess. Also

[1] Peel replied this day, Add MS 44270, f. 358, appreciative of Gladstone's letter to him: 'Your retirement is a fact of such great public import & significance that it seems out of place to allude to anything private & personal. But it is just these occasions which give one an opportunity of saying what otherwise might never have been said—and it is impossible for me to forget the many instances of consideration which I have experienced at your hands: and the many occasions on which regard for the Father has been shown in acts of favour to his Son. You gave me a start in public life—you nominated me for the chair of the House of Commons. . . .'
[2] No reply found.
[3] Sir Walter Parratt (see 12 Dec. 62), organist at Windsor. W. H. Gladstone had composed and published hymns.
[4] Letter of resignation as First Lord of the Treasury and Lord Privy Seal with the Queen's brief reply this day, which greatly pained Gladstone (see 10 Mar. 94); *L.Q.V.*, 3rd series, ii. 371, Guedalla, *Q*, ii. 492 and Morley, iii. 514. Ponsonby this day informed Gladstone that the Queen had sent for Rosebery.

saw the Moonshee.[1] Dined at Ld Kimberley's to make the list for Sheriffs. Read I. Hen. VI. And *finished* my version of the Odes of Horace. But *what* is it worth?

Saturday, March 3. 1894.
As I crossed the quadrangle at 10.20 on my way to St. George's Chapel, I met Sir H. Ponsonby who said he was anxious to speak to me about the future. He was much impressed with the movement among a body of Members of Parliament against having any peer for Prime Minister. I signified briefly that I did not think there should be too ready a submission to such a movement. There was not time to say a great deal and I had something serious to say, so we adjourned the conversation till half past eleven, when I should return from St. George's.

He came at that time and opened on the same lines desiring to obtain from me whatever I thought proper to say as to persons in the arrangements for the future. I replied to him that this was in my view a most serious matter. All my thoughts on it were absolutely at the command of the Queen. And I should be equally at his command, if he inquired of me from her and in her name: but that otherwise my lips must be sealed. I knew from him that he was in search of information to report to the Queen, but this was a totally different matter.

I entered however freely on the general question of the movement among a section of the House of Commons. I thought it impossible to say at the moment but I should not take for granted that it would be formidable, or regard it as *in limine* disposing of the question. Up to a certain point, I thought it a duty to strengthen the hands of our small minority and little knot of ministers in the Lords by providing these ministers with such weight as attaches to high office. I related to him, but without mentioning any names, the strong resistance which I was obliged to overcome (without any assistance, I might have added) to my giving Ripon the Colonial Office, the Chancellorship of the Duchy being proposed for him instead, to which I would not consent to bring him down. All this, or rather all that touched the main point namely the point of a peer Prime Minister he without doubt reported.

The Council train came down and I joined the ministers in the Drawing room. I received various messages as to the time when I was to see the Queen, and when it would be most convenient to me. I interpret this variety as showing that she was nervous. It ended in fixing the time after the Council and before luncheon. I carried in with me a box containing my letter of resignation, and, the Council being over handed it to her immediately. She asked whether she ought then to read it. I said there was nothing in the letter to require it. It repeated my former letter of notice, with the requisite additions.

I must notice what though slight supplied the only incident of any interest in this, perhaps rather memorable audience, which closed a service that would reach to 53 years on September 1[2] when I was sworn Privy Councillor before the Queen with her swollen face and eyes *laudably* red. When I came into the room and came near to take the seat she has now for some time courteously commanded, I did think she was going to 'break down'. I do not know how I could be mistaken, it being a matter within my poor powers of vision. But perhaps I was in error. If I was not, at any rate she rallied herself, as I thought, by a prompt effort, and remained collected and at her ease. Then came the conversation which may be called neither here nor there. Its only material feature was negative. There was not one syllable on the past: except a repetition, an emphatic repetition, of the thanks she had long ago amply rendered for what I had done, a service

[1] The Queen's Indian servant.
[2] In fact 3 September; see 3 Sept. 41.

of no great merit, in the matter of the Duke of Coburg; which I assured her would not now escape my notice if occasion should arise.[1] There was the question of eyes and ears, of German *versus* English oculists, she believing in the German as decidedly superior. Some reference to my wife, with whom she had had an interview, and had ended it affectionately. And various nothings. No touch on the subject of the last Ponsonby conversation. Was I wrong in not tendering orally my best wishes? I was afraid that any thing said by me should have the appearance of *touting*. A departing servant has some title to offer his hopes and prayers for the future: but a servant is one who has done, or tried to do service in the past. There is in all this a great sincerity. There also seems to be some little mystery as to my own case with her. I saw no sign of embarrassment or preoccupation. The language of Wednesday's Mem. may stand.

The Empress Frederick was outside in the corridor. She bade me a most kind and warm farewell, which I had done nothing to deserve.

WEG Mch. 5. 94[2]

4. 4 S.L.

Chapel Royal at noon with H.C. and at 5½ P.M. Wrote to The Queen l.l.—Sir H. Ponsonby—Sir W. Harcourt—Ld Rosebery l.l.[3]—Ld Chesterfield. Saw Sir A. West. Luncheon with Harry. Read 10 pages Butler:[4] Gray's Elegy,[5] wonderful: dipped into new Life of Archbishop Laud.

To Sir W. V. HARCOURT, chancellor of the exchequer, MS Harcourt dep. 14, ff. 18–21. 4 March 1894. '*Private.*'

[Letter 1:] When you asked me last night what were my recollections of the special relations between the Prime Minister and the Foreign Office, I felt that, in so far as those recollections were special and involved my own experience, my best plan would be to refer to an account of them which in the autumn of 1892 I embodied in a letter.[6] Unfortunately as far as present researches go I believe that letter is at Hawarden. If I find it here I will refer you to it as preferable in authority and accuracy to anything I could now hastily speak or write after a longer interval.

The general upshot is that I was made habitually privy, in the time of Clarendon & Granville to the ideas as well as the business of the Foreign Ministers, and in consequence the business of that Department, if and when introduced to the Cabinet, came before it with a joint support as a general rule.

My own recollections of the short term of 1866 are less distinct but in no way inconsistent. They also go back in a less defined form to several other ministries.

[Letter 2:] In the letter I wrote two hours ago[7] my reference to Lord Russell was too curt. I did not mean that the case was parallel with [that] of Clarendon 1868–70, or of Granville after him, but that I never remember feeling any deficiency in such knowledge of ⟨such⟩ F.O. business as was wanted in the H. of C.

---

[1] Arrangements for his annuity; see Guedalla, ii. 481.
[2] Holograph; Add MS 44776, f. 59 and *Autobiographica*, iv. 94.
[3] Copy of this day's letter to Rosebery is the last in the final Letter Book (Add MS 44549, f. 192). Subsequently, Gladstone had no regular secretarial support and there was no systematic copying of letters, though Shand seems to have continued to assist.
[4] Resumption of work on his edition of Joseph Butler's *Works*; see 23 Dec. 95.
[5] T. Gray, *Elegy in a country churchyard* (1750).
[6] See 25, 27 Sept. 92.
[7] This second letter headed '7 PM'.

To Sir H. F. PONSONBY, the Queen's secretary, 4 March 1894. Add MS 44549, f. 192.

I really was ashamed last night at your kindness in writing to me when you are under such pressure, locomotive and other, and when it is I who have been the means of bringing it upon you.

Pray take no more trouble, and let me take my chance as one of the public. Interesting as all intelligence is under the circumstances it is probably better that for the time at any rate, I should remain an extraneous person. And with many thanks for all your goodness & kindness. . . .

To LORD ROSEBERY, first lord of the treasury, 4 March 1894. Add MS 44290, f. 231. ['Cancelled']¹

[Letter 1:] I thank you for your note which at such a time I grudge your having had the trouble of writing it [*sic*].

Ponsonby kindly wrote to me yesterday evening to apprise me of what was going on.

I think that, speaking generally, in the peculiar circumstances of the case, and with the feelings I am both bound to entertain, and happily in entertaining, towards all parties concerned, it may be as well for me to avoid the formation, unless of special cause, of opinions upon facts current variable, & more or less fugitive [*sic*].

But I think you would not have met the expressed desire of the Queen in any way other way [*sic*] than that you have adopted, as I also think it was the duty of her ministers generally to desire that arrangements should be made for the continuance of the liberal Government in power. And, wishing this, though I cannot wish well to something that you wot of,² I must and do specially wish well to you, as the warrior placed in the front of the battle, chief in responsibility and effort. Further, speaking most frankly[,] I do not think the nation either ought to perceive, or will perceive, the incongruity of which you speak³ in your assumption of the place I have been holding.

'*Private.*'   N.L.S. 10027, f. 153.

[Letter 2:] Thanks for your note, multiplied & enhanced by the recollection when, & in what circumstances it was written.⁴ The fewer words I give you to read in return the better: and I will only say, apart from every other matter, that I think you acted rightly in not declining the overture of the Queen, and that I hope God may bless your efforts and conduct them to happy issues.

[P.S.] No fear of the idea of incongruity which you anticipated.

5. M.

Wrote to Ld Bute—Sir H. Ponsonby l.l.—Mr Lucy—Lady F. Marjoribanks—Ld Swansea—Mr Rathbone—Hon. E. Blake—Mr Rendel—Sir R. Welby—Mr Atkins—Sir A. Hayter—Mr C. Bannerman—Mr J. Cowan l. & tel. Saw Attorney General—Sir W. Harcourt—Mr Morley—Mr M'Carthy—Sir A. West—Sir F. Knollys—Sir H. Jenkyns—E. Hamilton—Sir A. West—Private Secretaries—Sir H. Farquhar—E. Hamilton—Earl of Rosebery: who told me of the arrangements. Nine to dinner: rather interesting. Read I Hen. VI.

---

¹ Rosebery's note, to which this is a draft reply, is untraced. Gladstone did not send this letter, but sent the shorter note which follows.

² i.e. the navy estimates.

³ Rosebery's membership of the House of Lords.

⁴ Not found; Gladstone's holograph copy of this letter is marked 'Cancelled', but as the original is in the Rosebery MSS it presumably was sent.

To A. H. D. ACLAND, vice-president of the education   Add MS 44549, f. 201.
committee, 5 March 1894.

It is now so uncertain when or even whether I may fall in with you that I must write a line to thank you heartily for your letter,[1] & to express to you very heartily the pleasure which I have derived from political relations & intercourse with you. Your name would of itself have given me a lively interest in your welfare, but your personality is not less operative in inspiring it & I trust that the great capacity you have shown in thought & expression, & the qualities of character with which I believe it to be combined, may secure for you a distinguished & lasting place of honour in the annals of your country.

To H. H. ASQUITH, home secretary, 5 March 1894.[2]   MS Asquith 9, f. 85.

I cannot sufficiently thank you for the letter[3] which you have added to the other touching utterances I have received from my colleagues, whom I cannot yet quite bring myself (as I must soon) to call my late colleagues.

It is in one sense a satisfaction to me to feel daily the solidity of the ground on which my resignation has been based: because it prevents all necessity from moving onwards in mind to that other ground which by the calendar and the clock we are fast approaching.

The future is in my mind a clouded picture: but I am glad that the prolongation of my political life has given me an opportunity of helping the arrangements under which you have taken your stand in political life. I well remember the impression made on me by your speech at the Eighty Club, the first time I ever saw or heard you. It has since been, of course, deepened and confirmed. Great problems are before us: and I know no one more likely to face them, as I hope and believe, not only with a manly strength, but with a determined integrity of mind.

I most earnestly hope that you may be enabled to fulfil your part, which will certainly be an arduous one.

[1] Acland wrote on 2 March, Add MS 44518, f. 63: 'Though I am one of the youngest of your colleagues in the Cabinet, I do not wish to remain quite silent. The simple words that Kimberley used yesterday best express what I should wish to say. The heavy loss which we now sustain we shall realize even more fully as time goes on.
I shall always feel that the honour of having served under you is and will remain the highest honour of my life. Please do not answer this.'
[2] Typed copy (wrongly dated 1897).
[3] Of 4 March, Add MS 44518, f. 75: 'Kimberley expressed in simple & moving language on Thursday what everyone of us felt & will continue to feel. But I cannot forbear asking you to allow me to say for myself how deeply sensible I am of the personal & political ⟨bereavement⟩ loss which we are now sustaining. It will always be the happiest & most inspiring memory of my public life that I was permitted for a year and a half to sit in your last Cabinet as its youngest member, and that I owed that privilege to your favourable judgment. As I look back upon the time—short as it is—I am conscious in how many ways I have fallen below the high standard of public duty which for fifty years you have done more than any English statesman to maintain. But I shall always recall your unvarying courtesy, your encouraging kindness & patience, & the "little nameless unremembered acts" which make you dear to all whose honour it is to serve under you. These things are graven upon my heart & beyond the touch of time & change. What you have been to England, to your party, and to a hundred great causes, the world knows & history will tell.
But no one who has not been near you in the close & daily intimacy of a colleague can know the secret springs of your power, or the abiding & inspiring influence of your character and example.
It is with a profound gratitude that will always endure, and a sense of personal loss which no words can express that I remain your loyal and devoted follower.'

To H. CAMPBELL-BANNERMAN, war secretary, 5 March 1894. Add MS 41215, f. 55.

The pain of simple severance, and the further pain of a profound disagreement approaching have received every mitigation that was possible from the extreme kindness of colleagues, among the indications of which kindness your most friendly letter is conspicuous.[1]

Pray accept my thanks for it and with them the expression of my fervent hope that in whatever department you may be called upon to serve the Crown and country you may be enabled to preserve and consolidate its best traditions and to repress those which are of an opposite or inferior order.

To H. W. LUCY, 5 March 1894.   Add MS 44549, f. 201.

Though under very great pressure I must thank you for your kind letter.[2]

I must add a word to your statement of the solitude in which the Daily News[3] took & gallantly ⟨held⟩ maintained its post. I remember a day on which the Pall Mall Gazette under its clear but queer erratic Editor [W. T. Stead] published an object lesson of the field of battle on the Irish question. On one side were Daily News & Pall Mall Gazette—on the other the rest. I took my Pall Mall Gazette, drew a noose round the fighting figure & with a long line with a ∧ at the end of it, carried it over to the other side, & by this verifying process placed the support of the Pall Mall Gazette at its then value, & left Daily News occupying absolutely alone its place of honour.

I hope my account is intelligible.

To Sir H. F. PONSONBY, the Queen's secretary, 5 March 1894. Add MS 44549, f. 197.

[Letter 1:]   The first entrance of a man to Windsor Castle, in a responsible character is a great event in his life: and his last departure from it is not less moving.

But in & during the process which led up to this termination on Saturday, my action has been in the strictest sense sole, & it has required me in circumstances partly known to harden my heart into a flint.

However it is not even now so hard but that I can feel what you have most kindly written: nor do I fail to observe with pleasure that you do not speak absolutely in the singular. If there were feelings ⟨which⟩ that made the occasion sad, such feelings do not die with the occasion.

But this letter must not be wholly one of egotism. I have known, & have liked & have admired all the men who have served the Queen in your delicate & responsible office: & have liked most probably because I knew him most, the last of them, that most true-hearted man General Grey. But forgive me for saying you are 'to the manner born' & such a combination of tact & temper with loyalty intelligence & truth I cannot expect to see again—Pray remember these are words which can only pass from an old one to one much younger though trained in a long experience.

---

[1] Of 1 March, Add MS 44117, f. 127.

[2] Lucy wrote on 4 March, Add MS 44518, f. 77: 'I send herewith a copy of this morning's *Observer* containing a 'Cross Bench' article probably, I am sad to think, the last I shall have the opportunity to devote to the most striking personality in the House of Commons. I suppose of all the journalists I have had the closest and the widest touch with the English-speaking race all over the world. I can truly say that there is nothing I have written during the last twenty years about yourself that I would withhold from your view'; he recalled his satisfaction on becoming editor of the *Daily News* in January 1886 in maintaining 'it alone amongst the London morning papers, loyal to the Chief, & to the cause he with rare selfsacrifice had espoused'.

[3] Lucy edited the *Daily News* 1886–7, then returning to the Press Gallery.

[Letter 2:] It must not be forgotten in this *Whimwan* that I hold a second office of which I shall have to be discharged by the delivery or transmission of the Privy Seal. All in due time.

6. Tu.

Wrote to Sir A. West—Mr Asquith—Mr G. Russell—Mr Murray—Mr Cowan—Mr E.R. Jones MP.[1]—Ld Coleridge—minutes. My Private Secretaries gave me a most interesting *Vale* dinner.[2] Mary gave me a very interesting account of Mrs Bishop. It is also puzzling, as to my own duty.[3] Saw Mr S.L.—Mr Murray—Mr Mellor—Mr Knowles—Mr Hibbert—Lord R. Churchill—Lady Harcourt. Drive with Mary. Dinner given by my Private Secretaries at Brooks's. Worked on arranging books.

To E. R. JONES, M.P., 6 March 1894.   Add MS 44549, f. 204.

I return my best thanks for the intimation which you & Mr [E. J. C.] Morton have kindly sent me.[4]

Apart from every political question & looking at sight & hearing only, I think that the choice before me has lain between the resignation now effected on the break in public affairs supplied by the close of the Session & the short continuance of a struggle against difficulties best known to myself, with the certainty that it must in any ⟨sense⟩ case terminate in the midst of the business of the session & with much greater inconvenience to the party, the Ministry, & all who might have reason to feel an interest in the subject.

But I am most sensible of the honour done me by the gentlemen who have taken part in the movement you describe, & I hope never to say or do anything which should belie my past life or forfeit any title which I may be thought to possess to their indulgence.

To G. W. E. RUSSELL, Indian undersecretary, 6 March 1894.   Add MS 44549, f. 202.

I did not find time last night as I had hoped to do for the purpose of thanking you for your most kind letter.[5] Your regard and your sympathy personal as well as political will always be most highly valued by me. I cannot but be very glad that you are replaced in the political career. At the same time my speculative view into the future shows me a very mixed spectacle and a doubtful atmosphere. I am thankful to have borne a part in the emancipating labours of the last 60 years; but entirely uncertain how, had I now to begin my life, I could face the very different problems of the next 60 years. Of one thing I am & always have been convinced. It is not by the State that man can be regenerated and the terrible woes of this darkened world effectually dealt with. In some & some very important respects I yearn for the impossible revival of the men and the ideas of my first 20 years which immediately followed the first Reform Act. But I am stepping out upon a

[1] Evan Rowland Jones, 1840–1920; journalist, educationalist and liberal M.P. Carmarthen 1892–5.
[2] Present were: Welby, Godley, West, Meade, Carmichael, Hamilton, Primrose, Leveson-Gower, Seymour, Lyttelton, Murray and Shand (West, *P.D.*, 291). W. B. Gurdon and C. L. Ryan were still alive, but not present.
[3] Her life of Mrs Craven; see 17 Dec. 94.
[4] Not found.
[5] Of 3 March, Add MS 44295, f. 92: 'I was brought up by my parents to admire and revere you. As soon as I was old enough to think about politics, your name became my watchword. It was the fascination of your leadership which, in the heart-searching days of the Eastern Question, drew me into active politics; and the example which you have set of a devoted Christian life lived in the tumult of public business has been to me in literal truth a "Means of Grace"....'

boundless plain. May God give you strength of all kinds to perform your appointed work in the world.

7.

Nature gave way having gone through the struggle gallantly. A stiff bronchial cough. I wrote letters: but it was quite wrong. Wrote to [blank.] Saw S. Lyttelton—Dr Bond mg & evg. Conversation in hurry.

To Sir T. D. ACLAND, M.P., 7 March 1894.   Add MS 44549, f. 204.

I thank you for reviving at this moment the memories of an old & never broken friendship.[1]

The physical machine which has (Biarritz notwithstanding) been under much pressure for the last two months has now that active duties are nearly accomplished a little given way, & I am today in bed under treatment for hoarseness today. I have every hope that a day or two of close care will see me set right again.

The opinion or misgiving of mine which you quote is certainly one of long standing & it is a matter of interest to me to know from you that I held it fifty years back in the heyday of youth, and in the season of sanguine anticipations.

Yet I am certain & cannot be too thankful that we have been appointed to work with our generation in a good & even a great time[,] the half century which will be known as the half century of Emancipation.

The work is not quite complete but I hope it is near completion.

I trust that in the Providence of God your old age is to be long prosperous & happy. . . .

To H. H. FOWLER, Indian secretary, 7 March 1894.[2]   Add MS 44549, f. 205.

I thank you for your very kind letter.[3] Fresh in my memory is the recollection of having for the first time heard you speak at Birmingham where I was the guest of Chamberlain & we had among other occurrences a colossal meeting in the rink.

I remember the impression made upon my mind by your speech & by either one or two others was to the following effect: if one of the provinces is so rich in speaking power what ought not the centre to be. The centre has since made good its claims to you & with that excellent effect which we have last witnessed in your general conduct of the debate on the Local Government Bill.

I am glad that my retirement has made room for your receiving a distinguished recognition.[4]

There is much that I should like to say about India: but I write from my bed & this spares you the infliction.

The sum of the matter would come to this. The transfer to Parliament was probably inevitable;[5] & has been in certain respects most beneficial: but it has not in my view been successful all round & I am by no means sure that all those who work the Government in India (I do not mean the Viceroy) are under as effective a controul as formerly.

[1] Acland's letter untraced.
[2] Version printed in *Fowler*, 284.
[3] Of 6 March, Add MS 44518, f. 86, on his retirement; *Fowler*, 285.
[4] Fowler had become Secretary of State for India under Rosebery.
[5] i.e. following the Indian Mutiny.

8. *Th.*

Worst day. The throat too irritable for any speaking. Dr B. mg & evg. Much dosing & perspirations. So I was cut off instantly from hearing, seeing, speaking, writing. Seemingly a blank existence. The outer world props were cut away. This is that the inner world props may be felt: the god-companionship of the Brighton preacher.

9. *Fr.*

Decided improvement; no relaxation except that speaking had become possible. Good news for Herbert at Leeds[1] pleased us all. Saw S.L.

10. *Sat.*

Rose at noon. Wrote to Rosebery.—Saw S.L.—Herbert—Murray—Sir J. Cowan— Mr Marj. (now Ld Tweedmouth). Bed at 10 P.M. Further improvement. Got to my sitting room. Made a selection of Odes: what I think the lightest & as a whole.[2] Herbert sworn in, at Windsor.[3] Bond mg & evg.

The Queen's note addressed to me on Saturday March 3[4] is the only *piéce* [*sic*] proceeding from Her Majesty in the process which has wound up an account reaching over 52½ years from September 1. 1841 [*sc.* September 3] when I was sworn of the Privy Council.
   There were also three interviews; one on Wednesday February 28: one on Friday March 2: and a very short one on Saturday March 3. They add nothing material to the contents of the brief note. On the Wednesday she expressed her regret for the '*cause*' somewhat emphasised which had brought about the intimation of a probable event then conveyed to her, and at the last on Saturday she had expressed anew, orally, thanks for my efforts in the case of the Duke of Coburg, which had already been given in writing at the time of the little debate in the House of Commons.
   Substantially then the proceeding was brief though the interviews were greatly eked out with secondary matter.
   The same brevity perhaps prevails in settling a tradesman's bill, when it reaches over many years.
   The note says it is not written for the purpose of accepting my resignation as this had been previously done.
   But the facts stand thus. There was no tender of resignation made by me until I wrote out at Windsor on Saturday forenoon the letter in which it was contained. It appeared to me to require some moderate length and particularity of statement. I put it into a box and carried this box, after the Council, into the small room where the Council meets. I gave it to the Queen and told her it contained my tender of resignation.
   [It was at this point that there occurred, if at all, what would have been indeed a circumstance in my rather dry record.][5]

---

[1] His re-election on his appt. as First Commissioner for Works was unopposed.
[2] See 14 July 92.   [3] As Privy Councillor.
[4] '. . . She therefore writes these few Lines to say that she thinks, that after so many years of arduous labour & responsibility he is right in wishing to be relieved at his age of these arduous duties. And she trusts he will be able to enjoy peace & quiet with his excellent & devoted wife in health & happiness & that his eyesight may improve. The Queen would gladly have conferred a Peerage on Mr. Gladstone but she knows he wld. not accept it'; Guedalla, ii. 493.
[5] Gladstone's brackets.

She asked me if she need read it before conversing with me. I said that rested wholly with Her Majesty. Then followed the short conversation: and on retirement I kissed hands. Not one word was said of the resignation: and it seems that if it was accepted it was in some way accepted *before* it was tendered.

I did not on retiring, proffer service as I did in writing to the Prince of Wales: for what was my service worth? Not one syllable proceeded from Her Majesty either as to the future or the past. I could not go *touting*.

Mch. 10. 94.[1]

At the Duke of York's Dinner on Wednesday the 7th, Rosebery sat by my wife and talked freely with her. Among other things he said 'he hates the Queen, doesn't he?' She defended me. But the proper defence would have to say that any one giving countenance to this cruel imputation, ought at least to be supplied with the evidence of some act done, or some word written or spoken, which would give countenance of some kind to it.

There is and can be no such act, no such word. In writing to Rosebery on the matter of Lansdowne's honour[2] I certainly spoke (as a milder thing than sending him the document) in censure of a letter she had sent to me. But this, if he had no other foundation to build on, was ludicrous.

Let me now make in a few words a clean breast of it.

I am as I hope loyal to the Throne.

I admire in the Queen many fine qualities which she possesses.

I certainly used [to] admire still more: and frankly I do not see that the Queen has improved in the last twenty years. (Dean Wellesley spoke to me of a change in her before I perceived it myself.) But there is plenty of room remaining for the admiration of which I speak. Further I am grateful to the Queen as I have expressed it in my letter for many kindnesses received at various periods of my service under her.

Every one knows her attitude towards Liberalism. But taking relations to me since 1844, as a whole, there is in them something of mystery, which I have not been able to fathom, and probably never shall.

I hope my duty to Her and her family has never in fact, as it has never in intention, fallen short.

And I have a new cause of gratitude to H.M. in her having on this last occasion admitted my wife anew to a footing of confidence and freedom. She had too long, I think, been suffering on my behalf. I am delighted that this chapter is well closed.

God save the Queen.

WEG. Mch. 10 and 11. 94.[3]

11. *6 S.E.*

Church alack strictly forbidden. I fight for Brighton. (London is bad to recover in) i.e. tomorrow. Bond mg. Helens done very well. Saw Mr Armitstead—Ld Leigh—Mr Rendel—Mr Murray. Afternoon prayers at home. Wrote to Sir A. Godley—Ld Northbourne—Ld Acton. Dipped in Bp Butler on Necessity[4]—& in Sermons for Youth.[5]

---

[1] Holograph; Add MS 44776, f. 61; *Autobiographica*, iv. 96.
[2] See 29 Jan. 94.
[3] Holograph; Add MS 44776, f. 98; *Autobiographica*, iv. 98.
[4] Ch. vi of Part I of Butler's *Analogy*.
[5] Perhaps R. G. Soans, *Sermons for the young* (1891).

12 M. [Lion Mansions, Brighton]

Wrote to Mr Knowles—S. Lyttelton. Backgammon with Mr A. Saw Sir W. Harcourt. Saw Mr Shand: *eager*. Saw Dr Bond: & off to Brighton at 11.40. The air put new life into me. But the weather ungenial, rooms cold. Read II Henry VI. Mr A. kind as ever.

13. Tu.

Some progress. Not equal to correspondence, or much conversation: but advancing. Wrote on Butler. Classified more Odes. Backgammon in evg. Read Mrs Tweedie on Norway[1]—II Henry VI. Mary read me some of the Argyll poetry.[2]

14. Wed.

Rose at nine. Startling news of last night in H. of C.[3] Wrote to Sir W. Harcourt L. and tel.—S. Lyttelton—G.H. Murray—Mr Crockett—Mr Roundell—Duke of Argyll—Ld Chancellor. Saw Dr Bond: he was satisfied. Drive: successful. Backgammon with Mr A. Read II H. VI—Also Butler before S.P.G.[4] Worked on Classification of the Odes. C. much tried with diarrhoea at night. What a couple! But she *will* work as nurse.

To LADY HAMPDEN, 14 March 1894.   Add MS 44518, f. 106.

Though your request is not pressing in point of time, yet, having received it, I feel myself pressed in spirit until I have complied with it.

It is a request of great interest to me. Your husband was one of whom knowing much simply stimulated the desire to know more: & I have always greatly regretted that, while his kindness again & again invited me to know you all in your domestic circle at Glynde, the incessant hurry of my life, and the deceitfulness of delays, prevented our ever finding the desired opportunity.

The relation between us was only fully developed in 1865-6, when I became leader of the Liberal party in the H. of Commons. It was a year, however, rich in experience, & I had seen a good deal in the six preceding years of the Palmerston Government, with the most difficult and anxious work of which I was closely associated.

I regarded him as one thoroughly imbued with the spirit of the old and great Parliamentary tradition. I thought very highly of his judgment: and, knowing as I did his thoroughly moderate and constitutional frame of mind, I derived the utmost comfort & satisfaction from his support in the final Irish crisis of 1886.

But the quality of his intellect was inseparably united with the qualities of his character. Every one is aware of the perfection to which sweetness of temper had attained in him. But this delightful gift is in some persons allied more or less with shallowness of feeling, & with an escape in this way from some sharp sufferings of life. In him there was no trace of such an alliance. On the contrary, I thought him as sensitive on all questions of

---

[1] E. B. Tweedie, *A writer's jaunt to Norway* (1894).
[2] G. D. Campbell, duke of Argyll, *The burdens of belief, and other poems* (1894).
[3] Labouchere's amendment to the Queen's Speech—effectively a censure on Rosebery—was carried by 2 votes.
[4] Joseph Butler's sermon preached before the S.P.G.; in *Works*, ii. 277.

honour & principle, as he was inaccessible to any even the smallest movement of resent-
ment & to that spirit of wrath which finds entry into us by ways so subtle & so hard to
trace.

It always seemed to me that a righteous indignation, in that equivocal period, broke
down his health for the time, & I regarded this union of patriotic sensibility with utter
insensibility to selfish annoyances, as the most remarkable among the winning qualities
redundant[?] in his character.

He was, I cannot but think eminently entitled to the blessing of the peacemaker.

There is an undeniable mask of lapse[?] attaching in different methods & degrees to
mankind in general: but I used to think how little does he carry of this sad note of kindred
with his race.

These of mine are but a few haphazard touches which can contribute little indeed
towards a portrait.

But they are not infected with any conscious exaggeration which I should regard as a
very grave offence in a very sacred class of subject.

Alike in retrospect & in prospect, it is pleasant to me to contemplate his image: & I
cannot but regard your lot as his wife, though now severed for a moment, as one of great
blessing.

To LORD HERSCHELL, lord chancellor, 14 March 1894.   Add MS 44518, f. 108.

The smart attack which I was suffering last week obliged me reluctantly to postpone
answering your letter, & now obliges me to answer it most unworthily, for I am still rather
weak from a flood of lowering medicine necessary to expel the vicious cough. I am sorry
first because it must appear ungrateful; & secondly there is so much to say on the position
in which I have not very spontaneously left you. However one word I must say—you owed
your appointment in 1880 to merit & distinction such as it was impossible (even perhaps
for a man with cataract) to overlook. One discovery remained for me to make; & that was
made when you freely but with the greatest public advantage took your place on the
Bench beside Law (that admirable man) & me on what was *then* considered the very
prolonged proceedings in Committee on the Irish Land Bill. You have supplied a parallel
to that truly generous devotion in your recent dealings with the Magistracy. Your reward
has not fully come: but come it must.

It is indeed delightful to me to think that affection enters into our farewells & I heartily
reciprocate the feeling you express with the sanguine hope that in two respects only you
may resemble your well known precedessor Eldon, the weight of your judicial authority,
& the length of your reign at the head of your great profession.

To C. S. ROUNDELL, M.P., 14 March 1894.   Add MS 44518, f. 10.

After the heavy illness of last year, I am sorry, but not surprised, & yet very sorry
indeed, that the House is about to be deprived of the advantages your presence confers
upon it alike in point of character & capacity. The future is not so clear of clouds as to
make it a light matter when any one disappears whose presence helps to maintain a pure
atmosphere. What a state of things have we reached when I was obliged to escape! 1. A
great arrear of public work undone. 2. On the back of all this, the Irish question. 3. On the
back of both hereditary wisdom has rashly clapped a second previous question, that
whether election is in a reasonable sense to govern, or to be bullied *ad libitum* by descent
nominative & honorary. Remember me very kindly to Mr K. I advance; but have still
ground [to] make.

15. *Thurs.*

Wrote to Dowager Lady Hampden—S. Lyttelton—Scott & Co.—Mr Channing MP. Ld Acton came. Much conversation. Unbosomed myself on R.s very imprudent declaration.[1] Backgammon with Mr A. Finished II Hen. VI. Read Mrs Tweedie. Drive: & walk 1%. Wrote on Horace. C. rallied.

16. *Fr.*

Wrote to Mr Murray—Miss Swanwick—Scotts—Mr Nettleship—Ld Bowen—Mr Westell. Saw Ld Acton. Saw Mr Wilfrid Ward. Drive: walk: backgammon with Mr A. Read III H. VI—Mrs Tweedie—Helen also read Mrs T. to me.

17. *Sat.*

Wrote to Dowager Dss of Marlborough—Lady Aberdeen—Sir J. Cowan l.l. (The reply to my constituents was as much as I could manage)[2]—and minutes. Saw Ld Tweedmouth—Ld Acton—Gertrude G.—Bp of Chichester: a marvel. Backgammon with Mr A.

18. *Palm S.*

Chap. Royal mg: prayers at home evg. Saw Dr Bond—Ld Tweedmouth—A. Morley. Wrote on Atonement (Pardon).[3] Helen read to me A.L. on Sacrifice. Read Butler's Charge[4]—& Bp Halifax on do.[5]

19. *M.*

Wrote to H.N.G.—G.H. Murray—Mr Miles. Wrote Pol. Mema. Saw Ld Tweedmouth. Read III. Hen. VI—Mrs Tweedie's Norway—Epodes of Horace. Backgammon with Mr A. Nights good: but cough not conquered. Drive.

Secret. Pol[itics].

With reference to the foregoing memorandum[6] on the attitude of the Queen in reference to my resignation and retirement I do think there has been some mystery about the extreme dryness of the relations which she has maintained with me now through a considerable tract of years: in contrast with those which subsisted when (in and after) in 1868 I had come in to disestablish the Irish Church.

But I think the facts of the recent juncture have been perfectly plain. On Tuesday the 28th [*sc.* 27] I heard that the Queen after the drawing room was overdone, rheumatic, and out of sorts. I was quite sorry to think on Wednesday of burdening her with an interview and before it I said to Ponsonby with some feeling 'how is the Queen today?' He answered briskly, 'quite well'. It seems that she had conceived no idea of my resignation

[1] Rosebery's statement in the Lords on 12 March, agreeing with Salisbury that before Parliament could concede home rule, England, as the 'predominant partner' would have to be convinced of 'its justice and equity'; 4*H* 22. 32.
[2] *T.T.*, 22 March 1894, 8d.
[3] See 18 Feb. 94.
[4] Butler's 'Charge to the clergy of . . . Durham', in *Works*, ii. 397.
[5] Samuel Halifax, bishop of Gloucester, *The works of Joseph Butler*, 2v. (1804).
[6] See 10 Mar. 94.

and personal retirement. When she found this distinctly stated to her as an immediate likelihood, the intimation acted as a sovereign remedy. She was free, cheerful, and disengaged, during the interview of that day, in an unusual degree. And so she continued to be at Windsor during the remaining interviews of the 2nd and 3rd of March. There was an evident sense of liberation, of a weight taken off her mind. Of course I do not include the moment when I seemed, rightly or wrongly, to observe a passing sign of emotion. Upon the whole it is painful to be troublesome to any one, especially to a woman, especially among women to a Queen, and to an old and much respected Queen. I am very sorry for it: and I should be much more sorry still, had I cause to suspect that I had either by wilfulness or by neglect myself caused aggravations of the mischief.   (Mch. 19. 94)[1]

Autobiog. [19] *Mch. 94.*[2]
Secret.

I seem to have awakened, with a slowness which argues a want of quick and lively gratitude, to the fact that a great blessing, which I had for years, almost for scores of years, desired, but had almost ceased to hope, has after all been wrought out for me by ways not of my own seeking or devising, with a completeness which leaves nothing to be desired, and with accompaniments an hundred fold more gratifying than I had either claim or reason to expect.

Politics are like a labyrinth, from the inner intricacies of which it is even more difficult to find the way of escape, than it was to find the way into them. My age did something but not enough. The deterioration of my hearing helped, but insufficiently. It is the state of my sight which has supplied me with effectual aid in exchanging my imperious public obligations for what seems to be a free place on [']the breezy common of humanity'. And it has only been within the last eight months or thereabouts that the decay of working sight has advanced at such a pace as to present the likelihood of its becoming stringently operative at an early date. It would have been very difficult to fix that date at this or that precise point without the appearance of making an arbitrary choice: but here the closing of the parliamentary session (1893–4) offered a natural break between cessation and renewal of engagements which was admirably suited to the design. And yet I think it if not certain yet very highly probable at the least [that] any disposition of mine to profit from this break would, but for what *I* call the 'mad and drunk' scheme of my Colleagues on the Naval Estimates have been frustrated by their desire to avoid the inconveniences of a change and by the pressure which they would have brought to bear upon me in consequence. The effect of that scheme (the most wanton contribution in my view to accursed militarism that has yet been made in any quarter, unless possibly by the Crispian Italy) was not to bring about the construction of an artificial cause or pretext rather of resignation, but to compel me to act on one which was rational, sufficient, and ready to hand.

This operation of retirement, long ago attempted, now at length effected, must I think be considered to be among the chief *momenta* of my life. And like those other chief *momenta* which have been numerous they have been set in motion by no agency of mine, and have all along borne upon them the marks of Providential ordination.

At the General Election of 1892 I had no adverse knowledge except that the sight of my right eye was bad. When soon after Mr. Grainger [*sc.* Granger] of Chester announced cataract in both eyes he also said that the sight of the better eye would probably continue for a long time, I think a time measured by years without material change. And it seems to have been in September of 1893 that I told Lord Acton of my desire to escape, of my

[1] Add MS 44776, f. 65; *Autobiographica*, iv. 98.
[2] Add MS 44790, f. 101; *Autobiographica*, i. 121.

total inability to draw a *political* map that would supply for me a way, and of my hope and even expectation that the 'eye and ear' question, especially the conditions of the eyes, might provide what was requisite.

If anyone had then predicted to me the 'mad and drunk' scheme of the present Estimates I should have treated the prophecy as that of a pure visionary. But am I *Athanasius contra mundum?* or am I Thersites, alone in the Achaian Assembly? Three only of the sixteen were in sympathy with me on the *merits* of the scheme. Thirteen against me! But this I must say, I have upon me the responsibilities of the training I have received and the experiences of crises remembered and confronted, under or in concert with such men as Peel, Aberdeen, Graham, Lord Russell, Clarendon, and Granville: and thus I have had more & better teaching & experience in international & European questions than all the thirteen put together.

The withdrawal of the demands, excitements and appliances of responsible office may leave behind at the moment the sense of a blank. But in this matter I cannot plead that I am taken by surprise. It is my deliberate conviction that the political life of the present and the future, so far as I can estimate it is not to be preferred to the life outside of politics. It is not from inside but from outside the political circle that man if at all is to be redeemed. This is a new and great subject, not now to be opened with any good effect.

20. *Tu.*

Wrote to Mr Shand—Wright. Wrote Secret Mema. Read [Horace's] Epodes— III. Henry VI (finished)—Tweedie's Norway. Backgammon with Mr A. Walk: but the cold continues.

Secret. Pol[itics].

The force of a resemblance really compels me to put a word on paper which I had not intended, which will stand alone, and which will never pass the door of my lips on its passage to the ear of any human being.

In the autumn of 1838 I made the *giro* of Sicily from Palermo by Girgenti and Syracuse to Messina, in two or three weeks riding, on the back of a mule. The beast was wholly inaccessible to notes of kindness by voice or hand, and was disposed to lag, so that our muleteer, Michele, used to call out, '*Pugna, signor, pugna*': an uncertain[?] process of only momentary effect.[1] But we rode usually with little interval from 6 a.m. to 4 p.m. and its undemonstrative, unsympathetic service was not inefficiently performed. In due time we arrived at Messina to take our departure from the Island. There my mule and I of necessity parted company.

But I well remember having at the time a mental experience, which was not wholly unlike a sense of indigestion. I had been on [the] back of the beast for many scores of hours; it had done me no wrong; it had rendered me much valuable service. Yet it was in vain to argue. There was the fact staring me in the face, I could not get up the smallest shred of feeling for the brute, I could neither love nor like it.

A rule of three sum is all that is necessary to conclude with. What that Sicilian mule was to me, I have been to the Queen; and the fortnight or three weeks are represented by 52 or 53 years. A friend, now a peer, told me he knew shameful things had been reported of me to her:[2] and from one point of view I have been pleased. I recollect that in consequence of *less* grave rumours which had reached her in 1868 about Clarendon she sent me a message before the Ministerial crisis to express her desire that he should not be

[1] For Michele and his mules, see 24-25 Oct. 38.　　　[2] Reports of his rescue work.

Foreign Secretary in the forthcoming administration; a dictum of much rashness from
which she ingenuously receded.[1]   Mch. 20. 94[2]

21. Wed. [London][3]

Wrote to Mr Nettleship—Scotts—Ld Brassey—C.G.—...... Off at 9.45. Long
and satisfactory interview with Mr Nettleship. Made Mem. of it. Saw Mr
Shand—Mr Murray—Sir W. Harcourt—Mr Lefevre—Ld Tweedmouth—H.N.G.
Worked hard & long on books papers &c. Read [blank.]

I spent nearly an hour today with Mr. Nettleship[4] who spoke with great clearness and
frankness and like a man who knew what he was about. He examined my eyes by strong
lights very minutely, and we conversed on a number of points relating to them.

The upshot was simple and in some respects went beyond my expectation. Especially
in this, that it is not now thought necessary to wait for maturity of cataract in a second
eye before operating on the first. He considers, as I understand him that the cataract in
my right eye is ripe and that an operation might at once or almost at once take place; but
he recommended for the greatest advantage that it should be postponed until the longer
days. He would like a time not earlier than May nor later than October. I told him that for
my general purposes the sooner it could be the better.[5]

There is hardly any pain; not always though usually consciousness that the operation is
going on. I asked what precautions were usually taken against motion of the head or face
which might disturb the process. He said this was mainly confined to excitable cases and
appeared to think there was no danger in a case like mine. I had told him I could formerly
resist pain but that I did not now feel very certain of myself as against some twitch, or
sudden movement, without the power of bringing forethought to bear upon it. I asked if
the head were held by others to prevent movement. Not commonly I understood: but
there is no difficulty whatever in having it done.

I forgot to ask about the method to be pursued, and the probable time of confinement,
after the operation.

Cocaine is used to make the eyeball insensible.

He does not object to the use of *bella donna* during the intermediate period to improve
vision temporarily.

He attaches great importance to good general health: and he also desires the absence
of all marked gouty tendency. I showed him my chief gouty indications on the middle
finger of the left hand. He seemed to attach no sort of importance to them.

Almost before I was out of the house, the Press Association was down on him for a
report but he declined to give any without my permission. *I* advised in reply saying no
more than that there was no circumstance of complication.

On the whole the result of the interview was every way satisfactory to me and a cause
for thankfulness.[6]

---

[1] See 6 Dec. 68.   [2] Holograph; Add MS 44776, f. 67 and *Autobiographica*, iv. 99.
[3] Rosebery did not move into 10 Downing Street until 1895; Gladstone was consequently able to
live there for a little time after his resignation.
[4] See 15 Dec. 93.   [5] See 24 May 94.
[6] Holograph dated 21 March 1894, 10 Downing Street; Add MS 44790, f. 105; *Autobiographica*, iv.
100. Nettleship reported to Mrs Gladstone this day, Add MS 44518, f. 126: 'Mr. Gladstone has
cataract in both eyes & the failure of sight is fully accounted for by this condition. The eyes are
otherwise sound & good . . . there is therefore no reason why at the proper time an operation should
not be performed with good results'; operation of the right eye delayed by Gladstone's cough, that
on the left for the future.

To Mrs. GLADSTONE, 21 March 1894.[1]   Hawarden MS 780, f. 240.
My own C.

My day's hard labour began with my visit to Nettleship. I inclose a memorandum of it from which you will see that it has been more satisfactory than I could have expected. It will require much consideration. It seemed better to make a Memm. I have put the material into a letter, in order that it might be shown as far as needful.

2. I have been working hard all day and it will be difficult for me to manage by tomorrow the clearing out from these rooms. Harry has not been able to be here for work today.

Marjoribanks has been here and has inquired on Rosebery's behalf whether it would be agreeable to us that *you* should receive a Peerage. It is thought there has been some suggestion from the Queen. I said that the subject must go to you for cons[ideratio]n & that I would write it today. For my part I look upon it with no favour, but should not in any way press this. I should on all grounds very greatly prefer what would *cost* more, viz. the recovery of the old title to which you are supposed to have a good claim.[2]

He thinks of letting Brook House, possibly of selling it. Says Guisachan is most expensive: cost 12 to 14,000 a year!

Hope to return by the 4.40 tomorrow and to find you *well* and Dossie in a state of prosperous advance. Ever your afft. WEG.

22. Th. [*Lion Mansions, Brighton*]

Wrote to Ld Thring—Margot Tennant (Inscr)[3]—Dr Spencer [*sc.* Spence] Watson—M. Léon Say. Saw Westell—Miles—H.N.G.—H.J.—H.J.G.—E. Hamilton—Ld Ripon—Ld Rosebery—Mr Knowles—J. Morley—and shopping. Off by 4.30 PM. L.M. at 6¾. C. on the sofa. Backgammon with Mr A. Began Richard II.

23. G. Friday.

Ch. Royal at 11 AM., then St P. 1¼–3¼. Wrote to Ld Tweedmouth—Helen G. Read L. Tolstoi on the K. of God.[4]—Bp Butler—Farewell Love.[5] In this my most unlenten Lent, I found my cough today at once aggravated by underfeeding: which I must not repeat.

24. E. Eve.

Efforts for Church—failed by unhappy error. Wrote to J. Morley Tel.—Mr Nettleship—H. Shand—Sir J. Lubbock—Mr Murray—Ld E. Clinton. Drive. Backgammon with Mr A. Conversation with Mr A.—MD—H.N.G.—Dr Sanderson.[6] Read Tolstoi K. of God—Farewell Love—Richard II.

[1] Part in Bassett, 259; thought by him to be Gladstone's last extant letter to his wife; in fact that of 14 October 1894 survives.
[2] Some years previously Mrs. Gladstone had been urged by the Heralds' College to claim the baronies of Percy and Poynings, to which, by virtue of her Glynne ancestry, they held that she was entitled; Bassett, 259. She appears to have taken no action in the matter.
[3] To a set of *Gleanings*; facsimile of inscription in Countess of Oxford and Asquith, *Off the record* (1943), 94; see also Add MS 44518, f. 135.
[4] L. N. Tolstoi, '*The Kingdom of God is within you*', tr. A. Delano (1894).
[5] M. Serao, *Farewell, Love! A novel* (1894).
[6] Robert Sanderson, physician in Brighton.

25. E. Day.

Ch Royal (and H.C.) mg. Aft. prayers in C.s room. The extreme heat of the Church irritated my cough. Wrote to Rev. Symonds—G.H. Murray—Rev. Barker—Mr Paine. Read Tolstoi—strangest of books—Bp Butler.

26. E. Mond.

Kept the house: it answered I think. Wrote on Butler. Read Butler—Richard II— Farewell Love. Backgammon with Mr A. Dr Habershon[1] came & examined me fully. 'The cough will go.' I think he will thrive.

27. Tues.

Wrote to Ld Spencer—Mr Morley. Worked on Horace's Odes: correction. Lucy came—Jacob Bright[2] dined. Backgammon with Mr A. Drive with the party. Read Rich II—Farewell Love—Hor. Odes.

28. Wed.

Wrote to Rev. J. Owen—Rev. Roberts—Sir G. Trevelyan—Archdn Farrar—Mr Armitstead—Mr M'Coll. Morning conversation on our funeral arrangements.[3] Wrote on Horace. Backgammon with Mr A. Read Rich. II. finished—Farewell Love—Butler.

29. Th.

Wrote to Mr Murray—Mr Fare—H.N.G. Walk: suffered: hot sun, cold wind. Saw Dr Nicholson[4]—Mr Sanderson. Read Henry IV. I.—Farewell Love—Butler. Back-gammon with Mr A. Saw Mr J. Bright. He is pacific.

30. Fr.

Wrote to The Queen—Mr Murray—Ld Tweedmouth—Watsons. Cough rather bad. But C. better. Read H. IV—Farewell Love (finished)—Butler—Taine Régime Moderne Vol. I.[5] Backgammon with Mr A.

31. Sat.

Wrote to J. Westell—Mr Hislop. Drive. Backgammon with Mr A. Worked on Horace. Saw Mr Morley & had much talk. Saw Dr Nicholson: much pleased. Saw Mr S. Read Henry IV—Taine.

[1] See 25 June 91.
[2] The liberal M.P. (see 22 Jan. 69); Gladstone had made him P.C. in the resignation honours.
[3] Apparently a discussion on prospective arrangements. Gladstone was buried in Westminster Abbey after a funeral notable for the absence of military trappings; Catherine Gladstone's body was laid next her husband's two years later.
[4] Arthur Nicholson, Sanderson's partner in their Brighton practice.
[5] See 23 Jan. 94.

Low S. Ap. One. 94.

Morning prayers in C.s room. Afternoon St Paul's. Wrote on The Succession.[1]
Read Holland, Serm.[2]—The B.V.M.s Tumbler[3]—Hyacinthe Letters[4] &c. Dr
Nicholson gave me *terebine*[5] which works very well. Saw Herbert G.—A. Morley.

2. M.

Wrote to HJG—D. of Argyll—Rev. Nicholson—Messrs Hubbard. Saw Herbert.
The terebine answers. Worked on letters & papers. Read H. IV. P. II.—Social
Evolution.[6] Worked on Butler.

3. Tu.

Wrote to Mr Murray—Ld F. Hamilton—and . . . . . The turpentine played me a
trick in the stomach. Sir A. Godley & Dr N. dined. Saw Godley on Horace &c.
Backgammon with Mr A. Saw Dr N.[:] C. prospers. Read Kidd—2 H. IV.

4. Wed.

Wrote to HNG—Mr Murray—Mr Vaughan—Miss Burney. Saw Godley. Worked
on Butler. Read Kidd—II. H. IV. Drive. We all mend.

5. Th.

Disturbed night & had to keep my bed. Saw the Dr—Mr A. Read Social Evolution—2 Hen. IV. (finished).

6. Fr.

Bed all day. C. & I in neighbour [rooms] but cannot communicate. Our doctors
are skilful. Read Social Evolution (many pros & more *cons*)—Henry V. (not
great).

7. Sat.

Wrote to Mr Murray—Mr Tomkinson Griffin—Sec. Trin. House—Rev. Padre
Giani—Canon M'Coll. Saw Dr Sanderson—Mr Laing—The Wickham party—
The Tweedmouths. Drive. Backgammon with Mr A. Almost recovered: C.
much better. Read Henry V. Much conversation with Ld T. & with E.W.

8. 2 S.E.

Chapel Royal mg: prayers at home evg. Wrote on Butler. Read Behrend on
Future Life[7]—Butler, Sermons—Hymns A & M. I hope they will some day be
thoroughly recast. Well yesterday but got wrong tonight. Wrote to Ld Rendel.

---

[1] Perhaps on Rosebery's succession as Prime Minister; but not found.
[2] H. Scott Holland, *God's city and the coming of the kingdom* (1894).
[3] *Our Lady's Tumbler. A twelfth century legend* (1894).
[4] C. J. M. Loyson, Père Hyacinthe, *Catholic reform. Letters, fragments, discourses by Father Hyacinthe*
(1874).
[5] Medicine extracted from the turpentine tree.
[6] B. Kidd, *Social evolution* (1894).   [7] Untraced.

9. M.

Wrote to Cawthorn & Hutt. Long conversation with E.W. on Horatian matters. Saw Dr Sanderson: partially lay up. Read King John—Taine Regime Moderne— Odes of Horace. Backgammon with Mr A. Ill again at night. Ld Bowen dead. A heavy loss.

10. Tu.

Spent in bed: but mending. Dr twice. Backgammon with Mr A. Read King John—Ly Granville's Letters[1]—Taine, Régime Moderne.

11. Wed.

Wrote on Bp Butler (H.S.) Read K. John (finished)—Granville Letters—Bp Butler. Rose at 4 PM. Backgammon with Mr A.

12. Th.

Misbehaviour in the night. Saw Dr Sanderson. Rose at 2.30. Arrowroot breakfast. Saw Dr Nicholson. Drive. Wrote to the Queen—E.W. Hamilton—G.H. Murray—Rev. J.H. Cooke—A. Ireland—Th. Watson—D. Robertson. Read Granville Letters. Last backgammon with Mr A.

13. Fr. [Dollis Hill]

Wrote to Lady Holker—Mr Condenriotes.[2] Read Granville Letters—Mrs Green's History.[3] Saw Dr Nicholson. $1\frac{1}{2}$–$4\frac{3}{4}$. We both made out the journey to Victoria and Dollis wonderfully well and indeed enjoyed the drive with the lovely bursting spring. Went to bed 7.30. Harry came.

14. Sat.

Uneasy night. Ailment unsubdued. Dr Habershon came. I like much his care & apparent skill. He gave bismuth which was very effective. Read in my way some of Mrs Green—Granville Letters—Tomkinson Diary.[4] Saw Canon M[acColl] & Rev. Mr G. [blank] on Palmer. O that 23d Psalm. What an opportunity this gives me of seeing that God's ways are not as our ways and of learning simple conformity. A quiet day, in bed.

3 S.E.—Ap 15.

Mg prayers alone. Evg with family. Saw Dr. H—Mrs Sands—Ld Tweedmouth— Herbert J G. Read Butler—Worked on Psalms Days 1–6.

---

[1] H. E. Leveson Gower, Lady Granville, *Letters*, ed. F. Leveson Gower, 2v. (1894).
[2] *Sic?*; untraced.
[3] Alice Stopford Green, *Town life in the fifteenth century*, 2v. (1894), sent by the author, Add MS 44518, f. 176. Gladstone suggested further examples; see ibid., f. 208. See 9 May 94n.
[4] W. Tomkinson, *The diary of a cavalry officer* (1894).

16. M.

Wrote to J. Morley. All very quiet now for nursing. Kept bed until 4 PM. Back-gammon with H. Read Granja[1]—Granville Letters—Green's History. My best reading day for a long time—with the aid of atropine (bella-donna).[2] Dr H. came: pleased, rather surprised at speed of progress. Backgammon with H: (who is invaluable).

17. Tu.

Disturbed in the night: return to bismuth & the discipline of an earlier stage. Tel. to Dr H. who was not surprised. Good later night under bismuth. Thank God C. advances steadily. Read Granja—Granville Letters (much to say on them).

18. Wed.

A day of recovery: still in bed. Read Lady Granville—Granja—Mrs Greens 'Town Life'. Helen read me Kenilworth.[3] Saw Dr H.—N. Lyttelton—Ld Rose-bery[4]—his boy Neil—& others. Wrote to Mr Knowles—H.J.G.

19. Th.

Wrote to Mr Knowles—H.J.G.—Mr Nettleship. Went down stairs in afternoon & made a beginning to arrange. Saw Dr H. Read Grania—Mrs Green. Worked on Select Odes.

20. Fr.

A day of relapse, especially late at night. Read Mrs Green—Grania (finished)—J. Morley[5]—Tomkinson Diary. Saw Sir A. West—Walter James: most pleasing—Herbert G.

21. Sat.

A good night from 2 AM after Chlorodyne. Read Tomkinson Diary—Mrs Green Hist. and [blank.] Reviewed proofs for N.C.[6] Saw Dr H. who inclines to propose consultations with Sir W. Broadbent.[7] He returned in the afternoon with Sir W.B. whom I liked much. All is confirmed and approved. J. Morley came down, long & interesting talk with him. He carried off my Five Odes for the N.C.[8]

[1] E. Lawless, *Grania: the story of an island*, 2v. (1892–4).
[2] Deadly nightshade.
[3] Scott; see 31 Aug. 52.
[4] See Crewe, *Rosebery*, ii. 473.
[5] J. Morley, probably *Aspects of modern study* (1894).
[6] Article on Horace; see the end of this entry.
[7] Sir William Henry Broadbent, 1835–1907; physician to royal family; cr. bart. 1893.
[8] W. E. Gladstone, 'Love Odes of Horace. Five specimens', *N.C.*, xxxv. 701 (May 1894); extracted from his larger selection (see 14 July 92).

22. 4 S.E.

Mg prayers alone. Evg with C., Mary reading. Downstairs but strictly on my back 12–5. Wrote to Mr Knowles. Wrote on Heresy & Schism.[1] Saw Sir C. Tennant—Ld & Lady Spencer. Read Scott Holland—C. Rossetti (delightful)[2]—G. Smith.[3] Saw Dr H.—early.

23. M.

Wrote to Lady Holker. Read Mrs Green—Tomkinson Diary—Progress.[4] Saw Constance G.—Katey & Mr Wickham—Lady Harcourt—and gave Harry at night a financial retrospect & prospect of my life & affairs.

24. Tu.

Saw Dr H.—Mr Childers. Read as yesterday: and began Athenais.[5] By permission, sat for some time: it gave me a less easy night. Wrote to Dr [H. S.] Lunn[6]—Mr Houston.

25 Wed.

Wrote to Mr Childers. In bed all day, C. much the same as I. It is now thought we have *both* had influenza. Read Tomkinson (finished)—Mrs Green (began II)—Daughter of Leontius (Athenais)—Investor's Manual. I have much restoration of reading power through using the 'atropine of bella donna'. Saw Dr H.

26. Th.

Rose at one but kept on my back. Wrote to [blank.] Read Marcella (began)[7]—Jusserand's Piers Ploughman[8]—Mrs Green—A. Forster, Citizen Reader.[9] Saw Dr Habershon.

27. Fr.

Saw Dr H. Wrote to Sir W. Harcourt—Rev. S.E.G.—......—Mr Fisher Unwin. Read Piers Plowman—Mrs Green—Marcella. Kept to first floor. Conversation with M. about S. Macneill's reports to Lady Ribblesdale.[10]

---

[1] W. E. Gladstone, 'The place of heresy and schism in the modern Christian Church', *N.C.*, xxxvi. 157 (August 1894).   [2] C. G. Rosetti, *Verses* (1893).

[3] Goldwin Smith, *Essays on questions of the day. Political and social* (1894?).

[4] Possibly A. J. Balfour, *A fragment on progress* (1892). Or, simply, progress in reading (see 25 Apr. 94).

[5] J. D. C. Houston had sent his *Daughter of Leontius [Athenais]: Byzantine life* (1894).

[6] On Christian reunion, supporting the reunion movement but judging that 'the time has not come for alterations in organic laws'; *Review of the Churches*, vi. 67 (May 1894). Henry Simpson Lunn, 1859–1939; travel agent and ecumenist.

[7] Mrs. Humphry Ward, *Marcella*, 3v. (1894).

[8] J. A. A. J. Jusserand, *Piers Plowman [by W. Langland]. A contribution to the history of English mysticism* (1894).

[9] H. O. Arnold Forster, *The citizen reader* (1886).

[10] Obscure.

28. Sat.

Wrote to Sir W. Harcourt—Mr Acland—Miss Loveless[?]—Mr Everett. Read Marcella—Mrs Green's Hist.—Piers Plowman. Saw Dr Habershon.

29. 5 S.E.

Much progress. Able to attend the celebration (choral & very devout) Willesden Ch 12¼-1¼. Mg prayers alone. Evg with family. Saw Ld Tweedmouth—A. Lyttelton (Arthur)—Alfred Lyttelton—Sir W. Phillimore. Read Athenais (finished) —Cobbold's Religion in Japan.[1]

30. M.

Rose at noon. Wrote to Hubbard Peck. Co.—Miss Marsh—Mr Flower—Mr J. Gould—Miss Holyoake.[2] Began faintly struggle with my Chaos. Cuckoo on Saturday: the first Rose today. Read as on Saturday. Saw Dr Habershon.

Dollis Tues. May 1. 94.

A good day; followed by a bad night. Drive with C. Saw Dr. Habershon—Dr Mackenzie[3]—Sir J. Paget—Mr A. Hutton. Wrote to Ld Aberdeen. Read as yesterday.

2. Wed.

Saw Dr H. Kept my bed the whole day for the chance of being able to appear tomorrow. Saw Mr Balfour who most kindly came down. Read Marcella—Mrs Green—& began Hutton Essays Vol. I.[4]

3. Th.

A holy Thursday without public offices. Coaxing myself for the afternoon. Saw Dr Habershon. Off at 3.15. Spoke at the Clark meeting from my seat for 15 or 20 min.[5] Back at 5.40 none the worse. Read Mrs Green—Marcella—Church's Memoir of Clark.[6] Worked on Odes.

4. Fr.

A good day. Wrote to Mrs Green. Read Hutton's Essays—Marcella. Worked on Odes. We drove to Mrs Th.'s. Saw Miss Ponsonby. Gerty came. Worked on my Chaos: a bold venture. I was very ill satisfied with Huxley's excuse yesterday.[7]

[1] G. A. Cobbold, *Religion in Japan* (1894).
[2] Emily A. Holyoake, daughter of G.J.; in correspondence with Mary Drew, see Add MS 44518, f. 200.
[3] Probably Stephen MacKenzie, physician in Cavendish Square.
[4] R. H. Hutton, *Criticisms of contemporary thought and thinkers*, 2v. (1894).
[5] Proposing a memorial to Sir Andrew Clark, seconded by Cardinal Vaughan; *T.T.*, 4 May 1894, 11a.
[6] Memoir of Sir A. Clark by W. S. Church in *Transactions of Medico-Chirurgical Society*, lxxvii (1894).
[7] Huxley sent apologies to the Clark memorial meeting; *T.T.*, 4 May 1894, 11a.

5. Sat.

Wrote to Mrs Huxley—Mr Craig—Mr G.H. Nye—Mr Wilson—Miss Phillimore—Rev. S.E.G. Saw Dr Habershon. Drive with C. Asquith & Margo dined. Much conversation. Worked on Odes. Read Marcella—Hutton's Essays.

6. S. aft. Asc.

Mg prayers alone. Aftn in family. Holy Commn at Willesden midday. Read Butler—Hutton's Essays—Religion in Japan. Saw G. Russell—Mr Wyatt—Mr [blank.]

7. M.

Wrote to D. of Argyll. Worked on Odes. Read Marcella (finished)—C. Naden[1]—and [blank.] Saw Dr H. Drive with Mary. Saw Sir A. West and Constance—Mrs F. Neville—Countess Tolstoi—Headmaster of Harrow. Lavinia Talbot came.

8. Tu.

A slight throwback. Worked on Odes. Saw Ld Rendel. Read Divine Worship—Poesie di D.F. de' Medici[2]—in varying moods.

9. Wed.

A good day. Wrote to Rev. D. Farabulini[3]—Miss Phillimore—Mr Colman—Ld Kimberley—Mrs Green[4]—Mr Murray—Mr Vickers. Saw Dr Habershon—Duke of Argyll—Mr G. Russell—Mr Bryce. Worked on Odes.

10. Th.

We attended with impunity the Margot and Asquith marriage;[5] Dossie faultless. Saw Mr A. Balfour—Mr Morley—Rev. Cooke. Worked on Odes. Read Hutton & began with the 'All long [illegible]'.

11. Frid.

Ld Acton dined: also E. Hamilton. Worked on Odes. Wrote to Murray with a *batch* of Twenty. Wrote to Mr Armitstead—Mr Jackson—Mr Caine—Ld Stawson [*sic*]—Licencees—Mr M.—Ld Kimberley. Read Horace. Drive.

12. Sat.

Saw Dr H. Tea with Mrs Turner. Worked on Odes. Drive with C. Read Horace.

[1] C. C. W. Naden, *Complete poetical works* (1894).

[2] Perhaps L. de Medici, *Poesi*, ed. W. Roscoe (1791).

[3] David Farabulini, priest and professor in Rome.

[4] Alice Sophia Amelia Stopford Green 1847–1929; historian and widow of J. R. Green. See 13 Apr. 94. Gladstone invited her to visit Dollis Hill on 29 May; Add MS 44518, f. 237.

[5] Gladstone was one of the four past, present and future prime ministers who acted as witness to the marriage of H. H. Asquith to Margot Tennant.

13. Whits.

Services and celebration as last Sunday. Drive with C. Saw Mrs Sands. Read Murray on Scripture.[1]—Barrett on the Pulpit[2]—Dallaway on Churches[3]—and Butler.

14. M.

Wrote to Mr J. Murray. Drive with C. Saw Dr Habershon. Worked on Odes: long fruitless search for three missing ones. Read Horace. Worked on Odes.

15. Tu.

Wrote to Mrs Asquith—J. Murray—..........Worked on Odes. Read Horace. Drive. Saw divers.

16. Wed.

Wrote to [blank.] Worked on Odes. Vicar, Mr Agnew & Mr [W. B.] Richmond dined. Read Horace. Wrote on the Hymn, 'Jesu Lover of my Soul'.[4]

17. Th.

A day of reaction: cause obscure. Drove to Mrs T.s to inquire.[5] Bad account. Saw Mr Nettleship.

18. Fr.

Wrote to Princess Bonaparte—Messrs Novello[6]—J. Murray—W.G. Miller—C. Lamb—Mr Mundella—Dowager Ly Tweedmouth. Saw Dr Habershon—Lady Penrhyn—Mr Murray. Drive with C. Read Horace—Waif from the Waves.[7]

19. Sat.

Wrote to Mr Knowles. Wrote Preface for my Odes. Read Waif from the Waves—Hor. Sat. (finished). Saw Ld Cork—Dr Habershon.

20. Trin S.

Services as on Sunday last. Wrote on the Butler-Clarke Correspondence.[8] Read Butler—Knox Little (finished). The Turner party came to tea.

[1] Probably A. Murray, *Love made perfect* (1894).
[2] Probably G. S. Barrett, *Religion in daily life* (1893).
[3] J. Dallaway, *Observations on English architecture* (1806).
[4] Not found.
[5] She was in ill-health and died in her cottage in Hampstead on 30 May 1894; since Gladstone's regular diary entries stop on 23 May, there is no note of her death in the diaries.
[6] The music publishers.
[7] W. J. Knox Little, *The waif from the waves, a story of three lives* (1894).
[8] Published as an appendix in his ed. of Butler's *Works*, i. 413.

Th[*eology*][1]

In order to realise fully the idea of a Church, in its interior, two things seem to [be] specially necessary: the first that it should convey at once the sense of the supernatural: and the second that it should in like manner promptly show that it is in familiar and incessant use, as the idea of the Gospel is Pray always, not intermittent but perpetual worship, and as the memorial of the Sacrifice on Calvary is a perpetual memorial.

Th[eology][2]

I here air various modes under which in a book of devotion the sentiment of the human soul towards God may be manifested: Dread of God, fear that is to say reverence of God, trust in God, dependence upon God, love of God. All these are in the Book of Psalms. But there is another sentiment found largely there and hardly found in antiquity outside it, namely the desire of God, which possessed the soul of the Psalmist even as the hart pressed in the chase is tortured and consumed by thirst. This wonderful and beautiful speciality speaks trumpet tongued of its own special cause, the light from above diffused in the breast of the chosen people of God.

21. M.

Wrote to J. Murray—G.H. Murray. Dr H. came: & delivered his best report; so he declared it. A bad night followed. Charged upon a small bit of roast beef! Read Butler—Merry Wives of Windsor. Drive with C. HNG. came. Worked on 'Heresy & Schism'.[3]

22. Tu.

Work & reading as yesterday (Read Tempest). Saw C. & Mary Cobham. A good day.

23. [May] Wed.

Wrote to Dean of St Paul's: & fair copy. Read the Tempest—Butler. Worked on Heresy and Schism &c.

[22 June 1894] Theology[4]

The most terrible and also the most conspicuous fact of human observation and experience is one on which at the present day even the messager of the Gospel sometimes, in a manner or for a moment, fears to dwell. It is the wide and universal prevalence of sin. Yes sin is more conspicuous than virtue: evil than good. Creation is like a fair writing over the whole of which there has run a foul disfiguring blot, darkening it at every point and at many making it illegible. Like the Noachian deluge this dishonouring flood has covered the valleys and the plains and has gone wellnigh to the hilltops. O for the voice of a Baptist in this wilderness to cry and to warn us that we must repent for the kingdom of heaven is at hand.

[1] Holograph dated 20 May 1894; Add MS 44776, f. 70.
[2] Holograph dated 20 May 1894; Add MS 44776, f. 69.
[3] See 22 Apr. 94.
[4] Holograph dated 22 June 1894; Add MS 44776, f. 78.

[*13 July 1894*]   *In the thought of Death*[1]

He that hath been so long within me
Will yet a little longer be
He that in daytime gave His light
Will not withdraw His torch at night
He that my body made and soul
Will render the parts again a whole

O Thou that in the waters' face
Didst all the arching world embrace
Brood upon this dark world again
And free inaction from its pain.
Cow the rebel powers of ill[2]
And all the realm of grace fulfil.

Thursday July 19 1894.

The journal which I had kept for 70 years was interrupted at this date[3] [23 May]
by the disabling effect of the operation on my eye for cataract.

Today after eight weeks Mr Nettleship came to examine my eye, and as he
hoped to equip me with spectacles for practical vision but he was obliged to
report the condition not wholly satisfactory. Firstly the sac or capsule of the
lens is not transparent and must be removed by 'needling', a common and easy
operation. Secondly the *fluid behind* is in some degree opaque. He hopes but
cannot be certain that this is due to the little blow inflicted by me soon after the
operation: and if so that it may be only temporary. I am sorry for his disappointment. Good hope still remains.

[*25 July 1894*] For the first time in my life there has been awarded to me by the
Providence of God a period of compulsory leisure, reaching at the present date
to four and a half months. Such a period drives the mind in upon itself, and
invites, almost constrains, to recollection, and the rendering at least internally
an account of life: further, it lays the basis of a habit of meditation, to the formation of which the course of my existence, packed and crammed with occupation
outwards, never stagnant and ofttimes overdriven, has been extremely hostile.
As there is no life, which in its detail does not seem to afford intervals of brief
leisure, or what is termed 'waiting' for others, engaged with us in some common
action, these are commonly spent in murmurs, and in petulant desires for their
termination. But in reality they supply excellent opportunities for brief or
ejaculatory prayers.

As this new period of my life has brought with it my retirement from active
business in the world, it affords a good opportunity for breaking off the

[1] Holograph dated 13 July 1894; Add MS 44776, f. 93.
[2] The transcription of this line is uncertain.
[3] On 24 May Nettleship operated on the cataract in Gladstone's right eye. 'Mr. Nettleship came
at 9 with Dr. H[abershon] and without any delay drew out the cataract. Father had cocain drops in
his eye and was totally unagitated; it only lasted a moment and was perfectly done. Mama and I in
the next room with the door open, I watching Nurse Pitts who had front place for watching him'
(Mary Gladstone, *Diaries and letters*, 425).

commonly dry daily Journal, or ledger as it might almost be called, in which for seventy years I have recorded the chief details of my outward life. If life be continued, I propose to note in it henceforward only principal events or occupations. This first breach since the latter part of May in this year has been involuntary: when the operation on my eye for cataract came, it was necessary for a time to suspend all exercise of vision. Before that, from the beginning of March, it was only my out-of-door activity or intercourse which had been paralysed. In looking back over the period I think it may warrant a summary review inasmuch as it has constituted a new chapter of my life, in which my dealings with my fellow men have been contracted, and those with my great Judge somewhat enlarged: at least I have seemed more nearly to have assigned to me the attitude of one who stands before the final bar.

There has been a certain amount of kindly personal intercourse with several among my colleagues. With two of them, Rosebery and Harcourt, it has not been properly speaking confidential. Rosebery has been under no obligation to give me his confidence, and he has entirely withheld it as to inner matters, while retaining unimpaired all his personal friendliness. He does not owe his present position in any way to me, and has had no sort of debt to pay. My bringing him to the Foreign Office was indeed an immense advancement, but was done with a belief, not sustained by subsequent experience, in his competency and wisdom.[1] Harcourt only held to me the language he held universally when he announced to me, without any invitation or suggestion, some two months ago, his fixed intention to resign his office after he should have passed his Budget of this year. It is now apparent from the tone of his conversation that he has entirely abandoned this intention: but, in more recent conversation with me, he has not breathed a syllable upon the subject. He will without doubt fret and wince in the future, as in the past, under the premiership of one who is his junior by a score of years in age, and by nearly half that term in official life: who was moreover at no very recent date his own Under-Secretary. Whether he or whether Rosebery ought either of them to have come to the top, are different questions. My choice upon the whole would have ⟨been⟩ fallen upon Spencer. Less brilliant than either he has far more experience, having entered the Queen's service over thirty years ago: he has also decidedly more of the very important quality termed weight, and his cast of character I think affords more guarantees of the moderation he would combine with zeal, and more possibility of forecasting the course he would pursue. He is not I think well placed at present, being more of a statesman than an administrator. But the opportunity has gone by: and gone by in all likelihood once for all.

When the occasional impediment offered by the state of my vision led me to resign, I had in view though not in actual touch the outrageous mischief as I estimated it of the Navy Estimates for the year, to which it was absolutely impossible for me to be a party on any terms. Since they were produced the financial proposals of the year have been introduced and carried. They constitute by far the most Radical measure of my lifetime. I do not object to the principle of graduated taxation: for the just principle of ability to pay is not

---

[1] This sentence, dated February 1897, was added later in the margin.

determined simply by the amount of income: and further, the reduction and abolition of taxes on the ground of their falling largely on the less wealthy classes really involves the same principle as the graduated tax. But, so far as I understand the present measure of finance from the partial reports I have received, I find it too violent. It involves a great departure from the methods of political action established in this country, where reforms, and especially fiscal reforms, have always been considerate and even tender. In striking so heavily at the owners of realty, it rules very summarily a question which seems to me to involve much doubt, namely whether realty is absolutely devoid of claim on the ground that this description of property bears exclusively the heavy charge of the rates: a subject on which I for one could not decide without much more thorough investigation than I have ever had occasion to give it. I do not yet see the ground on which it can be justly held that any one description of *property* should be more heavily burdened than others, unless moral and social grounds can be shown first: but in this case the reasons drawn from those sources seem rather to verge in the opposite direction, for real property has more of presumptive connection with the discharge of duty than that which is ranked as personal. No doubt the ownership of land carries with it social and political advantages, for which men may be willing to pay: but there remains behind the question of amount, and amount may appertain to essential justice.[1]

Besides this large matter for inquiry, the aspect of the measure is not satisfactory to a man of my traditions (and these traditions lie near the roots of my being) in several respects.

A land or house owner having £100,000 a year, and now paying say £3000 a year for Income Tax, will have his estate valued at 2½ millions, and will on succession to the fee simple be called upon to pay £200,000: a similar payment again becoming exigible from the next successor say thirty years hence. Even if we consider the 200 m[ille] as spread over the thirty years (whereas it is all payable at the outset) it amounts to nearly three times the income tax, and is of course in reality much more. For the sudden introduction of such a change there is I think no precedent in the history of this country. And the severity of the blow is greatly aggravated in moral effect by the fact that it is dealt only to a handful of individuals. I do not think there can be two hundred persons in the country owning land or land and houses to the value of a million sterling.

Further, as I understand the owner of land in settlement (and such are the great bulk of landowners) will have the power of attaching the tax to the *corpus* of the estate and charging himself only with the annual interest of the sum. This I am afraid many successors will do: their successors in turn following their example. Thus the incumbrances on the land will be progressively and heavily increased. But that the land of a country should be heavily incumbered is known to be a great public evil. This great public evil will be put under a process of involving its rapid increase. The ultimate result will be the forcing out of the old possessors and the introduction of new [perhaps after long struggles to retain a crippled and impotent ownership].[2] Some will reply; no:

---

[1] This sentence added in the margin.
[2] The words in brackets added later.

the result will be the breaking up of the estates. I am not sure that the substitution of smaller non-occupying landowners is necessarily or usually a good. But as it seems certain that the creation of new fortunes in personalty to a vast amount will continue, will not this class supply buyers for the estates in block? In this multiplication of the *neo-ploutoi* I can find nothing to give me satisfaction.

And I fear that the operation of the Act may be to drive more and more land into settlement with a view to the mitigation of the present and immediate burdens. I am not certain, however, that in this point I understand the probable operation of the measure.

Another most grave objection remains. The great evil of the death duties is the enormous amount of incidental expenditure which they entail, in association with long delays and great uncertainties. It ought, in my judgment, to have been a primary object in any great change of those duties to operate a fundamental reform by sweeping away as much as possible of the necessity for this expenditure. And my opinion is that this advantage might have been gained. If so we might have had a large increase of revenue without any proportional increase of burden to the tax payer, perhaps, in numerous cases without any increase at all. But the present plan entirely passes by this great and primary object of policy: nay, tends if I understand it right in certain ways to create an enhanced necessity for the intervention of the lawyer.

All this is drawn from me by the importance of the case: but is no better than a digression with reference to the immediate object of this paper, which is to review briefly a morsel of my life not to arraign the politics or politicians of the day.

I have had very free communications with Tweedmouth and with J. Morley. From them I gather that we have a prospect of an anarchical Cabinet, abundant pledges, obstructive opposition, compulsory acquiescence in small achievement, and an apathy and languor in the general mind curiously combined with a decided appetite for novelties and for promises apart from the prospect of performance.

For my own part, the *suave mari magno*[1] steals upon me: or, at any rate, an inexpressible sense of relief from an exhausting life of incessant contention. This is an immense blessing.

A great revolution has been operated in my correspondence, which had been for many years a serious burden, and at times one almost intolerable. During the last months of partial incapacity I have not written with my own hands probably as much as one letter *per day*. I have had most efficient aid in my family, especially from my daughter Helen: but I do not think the demand on her in connection with this matter has been very large. Few people have a smaller number of *otiose* conversations, probably, than I in the last fifty years; but I have of late seen more friends, and more freely though without practical objects in view. Many kind friends have read books to me; I must place Lady Sarah Spencer at the head of the proficients in that difficult art: in distinctness of finished articulation, with low clear voice, she is supreme. Dearest C[atherine] has been my chaplain from morning to morning, my churchgoing has been

[1] Lucretian tag: the pleasant sense of repose while others struggle.

almost confined to mid-day communions, which have not required my abandonment of the reclining posture for long periods of time. Authorship has not
been quite in abeyance: I have been able to write what [*sic*; *sc.* when?] I was not
allowed to read, and have composed two theological articles for the *Nineteenth
Century* of August and September respectively. Independently of the days of
blindness after the operation, the visits of doctors have become a noticeable
item of demand upon time. Of physic I incline to believe that I have had as
much in 1894 as in my whole previous life. I have learned for the first time the
extraordinary comfort of the aid which the attendance of a nurse can give. The
influenza which seized me early in March has not yet wholly withdrawn its
hold: it began with the chest and then descended to the lower bowels. The eye
process has been curiously intermixed with the controversy in a lower region.
My wife has suffered from an attack of influenza for the most part curiously
similar: but she thank God is well and this is the main matter. My health will
now be matter of little interest except to myself. But I have not yet abandoned
the hope that I may be permitted to grapple with that considerable armful of
work, which has been long marked out for my old age; the question of my
recovering sight being for the present in abeyance.[1]

Frid. Jul 25 [sc. 27] 94.

Mr N. today made another and closer examination in his own house. The report
thank God was rather more favourable. It is even *hoped* that there may have
been some small improvement in the eye since the 19th.

It was settled that he should come to Hawarden for the needling in the latter
half of September.

Tu. Jul 31. 94.

My old & kind friend Lacaita[2] came to tea. He described to me without any
murmuring *his* ailments. With bronchitis he coughed incessantly for five hours
from each midnight. He has now certified *angina pectoris*. He suffers also from
rheumatism and has not a complaint of the kidneys, but difficulty in the
operations of that department. Such is his case. How gently am I touched!

Saturday Sept. 1 1894. [Hawarden Castle]

After breaking up the practice of seventy years, I now mean to proceed by leaps
and bounds, making an occasional note.

We have spent a month here since leaving Dollis, and it has been thank God
a month of progress both as to my eyes & as to the attack of influenza on the
bowels. I am still however under bismuth and my range of physical exertion is
not greatly extended. Nights good. C. holds her ground.

I have not been able to resume morning Church: but go sometimes in the
evening and find a nice little congregation of from 20 to 30.

[1] Holograph dated 25 July 1894; Add MS 44790, f. 142; *Autobiographica*, i. 163; Morley, iii. 517.
The final phrase was added later.
[2] Sir J. P. Lacaita; see 13 Nov. 50. He d. 1895.

We breakfast in bed and rise mostly about ten. I write the Atonement article:[1] & have done a good deal upon the Odes. My correspondence growing again but is not yet exorbitant and Helen gives me very efficient help.

I have worked pretty steadily on arranging books & papers. Little heavy reading. A good deal of Walter Scott (7 novels in all). The fête was a disturbance. Numbers are put at 54000: it strained me a little.

My supplemental operation stands for the 20th.

Harry Drew has returned & I have proposed to him a temporary charge at St Deiniol's.[2]

We drive daily: have some visitors: & sometimes a game at backgammon in evg.

[13 Sept. 94] The appearance of cataract in my eyes, announced to me in the middle of 1892, by the Chester oculist [Granger], bore witness to the progressive exhaustion of Nature in one great organ, after hard labour had been faithfully performed by it during more than fourscore years. It furnished a premonition that the like exhaustion must arrive in other organs, and preparation so be made for the fatal change.

The untouched eye served me with its expiring force to the best of its ability, through the time when it appeared doubtful whether the operated eye would be able through proper spectacles to supply me with such vision as science can provide in substitution for Nature. The last book I read with the natural eye was Sir W. Scott's *Pirate*: and I got through with difficulty. The first reading with the operated eye was Wilkinson's Tract on Disestablishment,[3] and then *the Vicar of Langthwaite*,[4] Grote on Socrates,[5] and Hoffmann (U.S.) on the office of the State.[6]

By the resignation of office, which the superintendence of the Almighty so notably and quietly enabled me to bring about, I have passed into a new state of existence. I am not yet thoroughly accustomed to it, in part because the remains of my influenza have not yet allowed me wholly to resume the habits of health. But I am thoroughly content with my retirement: and I cast no longing lingering look behind. I pass onward from it *oculo irretorto*.

There is plenty of work before me, peaceful work, and work directed to the supreme, i.e. the spiritual, cultivation of mankind, if it please God to give me time and vision to perform it.[7]

(Oct. 1)[8]	As far as I can at present judge, all the signs of the eye being favourable, the new form of vision will enable me to get through in a given time about half the amount of work which would have been practicable under the old. I speak of reading and writing work, which have been principal with me when I had the option. In conversation there is no difference, although there are various drawbacks in what we call society.

[1] See 18 Feb. 94. The article must have been finished by 1 September, as it appeared in that month's *N.C.*
[2] Harry Drew was curate of St. Saviour, Claremont, Cape Colony 1893–4, partly for reasons of health. From September 1894 he lived at Hawarden Castle.
[3] Untraced, probably by G. H. Wilkinson.
[4] By Lily Watson (1894).
[5] See 8 Feb. 68.
[6] F. S. Hoffman, *The sphere of the state; or, the people as a body politic* (1894).
[7] Holograph dated 13 September 1894, Add MS 44790, f. 166.
[8] i.e. continued on 1 October 1894, Add MS 44790, f. 167.

On the 20th ult, when I had gone through my series of trials, Mr. Nettleship at once declared that any further operation would be superfluous.

I am unable to continue attendance at the daily morning service, not [on] account of eyesight but because the condition of the bowel department does not allow me to rise before ten at the earliest. And so a Hawarden practice of over 50 years is interrupted: not without *some* degree of hope that it may be resumed. Two evening services are at 5 p.m. (the other at 7) and these afford me a limited consolation.

I drive almost every day: and thus grow to my dissatisfaction more burdensome. My walking powers are limited: once I have exceeded two miles by a little, but there is fear of disturbance. A large part of the day remains available at my table: daylight is especially precious: my correspondence is still a weary weight though I have admirable help from children.

Upon the whole the change is considerable. In early and mature life, a man walks to his daily work with a sense of the duty and capacity of self provision, a certain αὐτάρκεια[1] (which the Greeks carried into the moral world). Now, that sense is reversed: it seems as if I must, God knows how reluctantly, lay burdens upon others: and as if capacity were, so to speak, dealt out to me, mercifully, oh how mercifully, but yet by armfuls.

Monday Dec. 17. 94

While I enjoy the relief from the small grind of the Daily Journal, I think it may be well still to note certain dates: and also books read. For a main difficulty with me now is to know *where* I have read this and that: and a list will be a help. Tracts I shall rarely mention. I begin with three Biographies: strange in succession, still more in their mixture.
Life of Dean Church[2]
    C. Bradlaugh[3]
    Mrs Craven[4]
Do of Robert 'Duca di Northumbria'[5]—Ross on Future Retribution[6]—Anderson's curious Communion Office for the Presbyterians[7]—Memoir of Ld Seton[8]—Rev. [blank.] Poems.

We came from Dollis on Aug 2. & remained without any serious break until

Dec 24 (St Th.) 1894.

I find that I began public political life with my canvass at Newark on Tues. Sept. 25. 1832.
Was *returned* to Parlt Dec. 24. 1832.
First accepted office (at the Treasury Sat. Dec. 20. 1834.

[1] 'Self-sufficiency'.
[2] *Life and letters of R. W. Church*, ed. M. C. Church (1894).
[3] H. Bradlaugh, *Charles Bradlaugh. A record of his life and work* (1894).
[4] M. C. Bishop, *A Memoir of Mrs. Augustus Craven* (1894), with much Gladstoniana.
[5] J. T. Leader had sent his *Life of Sir Robert Dudley, Earl of Warwick and Duke of Northumberland* (1895), also published as *Vita di Roberto Dudley, Duca di Northumberland* (1895); Leader's letter refers to the English version, but Gladstone's entry appears to refer to the Italian; Add MS 44519, f. 278.
[6] W. S. Ross, *The bottomless pit* (1894).
[7] *The order of the administration of the Lord's Supper . . . for the use of the Church of Scotland* (1881); published by Robert Anderson of Glasgow.
[8] G. Seton, *Memoir of Alexander Seton, Earl of Dunfermline* (1882).

Monday D. 24. 94.

At the close of last week A[lfred] Lyttelton came to tell me he had become an opponent of the Government.[1]

At the same time came a furious gale which overthrew three of our great beeches near the house including one the most perfect in development I ever saw which I used to say was worth £500. On the lawn.

Finally I had a fall over one of the drawers of my writing table, on my forehead, with the whole weight of my body: it impaired my vision but with rest this has thank God returned nearly to what it was.

(Much worse: at the same time Sat. evg an accident on LNWR killed 14 persons).

Books.

Life of Mrs Craven.[2]
Le Bon Sens du Curé de Meslin[3]
Il Male Occhio[4]

    No: I *cannot* do it.

We left home, and enjoyed Harry and Maud's hospitality in London, on Monday the 7th January. I had had a succession of incidents on some preceding days.

Thurs. 3d. [January 1895] I had to write a Latin inscription for plate to be presented to Mr Skrine the Warden of Glenalmond College.[5]
On Friday, to address a letter in French to the (schismatical) Bishop of Tenos who had addressed to me a most fervent and urgent demand for my reconciliation with the Chair of Peter: it was indeed pious & kind but hyper-ultramontane.[6]
On Sat the 5th a long and very strong representation to poor B. Potter[7] on the threatening hold which alcohol has lately taken on him: God grant he may recover.
On the 8th we started for our journey without a break to Cannes. It took $34\frac{3}{4}$ hours: but caused me no inconvenience in the peccant department. It was admirably engineered by Harry: and we were warmly received by Lord Rendel in his beautiful Château de Thorenc, which he has made no less than a little palace.

(Jan. 23).

[1] His wife's nephew (see 7 Feb. 57); he was elected in 1895 as a liberal unionist.
[2] See 17 Dec. 94.
[3] J. Meslier, *Le bon sens du curé J. Meslier* (1822).
[4] Literally, 'the bad eye'.
[5] Lord Lothian, chairman of the Glenalmond governors, requested the inscription for the presentation plate to John Huntley Skrine, the retiring Warden; Add MS 44520, f. 8. The inscription is printed in the *Glenalmond Chronicle* (January 1896), 3.
[6] Michael, Roman catholic bishop of Tenos; copy of diarist's letter in Add MS 44520, f. 11.
[7] A servant.
[8] For Rendel's notes of conversations with Gladstone, see *Rendel*, 107 ff.

On Jan 27 while at Ld Rendel's I found that the action of my influenza on the bowel department appeared at length to have ceased. So that now again as in 1882 the climate of Cannes had acted so as to impart a beneficial stimulus to my constitution. It is now a month since this experience: which has been sustained at Capmartin and has never wavered. It is no small comfort & blessing.
F. 28. 95.

March 22. [1895] Left Capmartin.

Sat 23. arr. London.
Fr. 29 arr. Lincoln.[1]
Ap. 2. arrived Hawarden. After two months of complete recovery, the enemy showed signs but slight ones.
Easter Day: They have I hope disappeared.
In June we had a fortnight on board the Tantallon Castle. It set me up entirely: and seemed to agree with C.
Except a visit of ten days to Hams and Hagley, we have not since left home. (N. 6)
These dinner *parties* at Hams I think threw me out and I took to medicine again in Octr.

Cruise to the Baltic in the Tantallon Castle. We did not see the places we mainly wished: but the weather was very good, the hotel incomparable & the sanatory effect admirable! It was from June 12 to 24. And we remained in London till Sat. 29. I spent much time on Butler books in the B. Museum.
Jul. 13. After a fortnight, I am now, beyond expectation, at the level reached at Cannes. D.G.

On Sept. 30 ended our wonderful summer of six months.
On Oct 12 Sir W. Phillimore came here and on Monday Oct 14 met the intending Trustees and we discussed largely the particulars. Six present + WEG.[2]
On Sat Nov. 2 I made over to Harry for the Financial Trustees all the Bonds at my Bankers (say 21 m[ille]) also the Library and Furniture: and ordered the transfer of 8 m[ille] Highland RR Stock say £9000. Nothing now remains but the Land and Buildings perhaps about 1/20 part.
I am now nearly 40 m[ille] poorer than this day week. All right: & may God prosper the work.
WEG N 6. 95.

I have this day constituted my Trust at St Deiniol's.
The cost of the work has been I think £41 to £42000. including some charges of maintenance to Dec. 31. 95. May God of His mercy prosper it.
C. was taken ill nearly two months ago, and suffered a good deal. Excellently tended by Dr Dobie[3] she has in great measure recovered. She had also an

---

[1] To stay with his daughter Agnes and her husband, now dean of Lincoln.
[2] Establishment of the Deed of Trust for St. Deiniol's library.
[3] See 1 Apr. 82.

admirable friend nurse in Lucy Phillimore. She still has very uncertain nights. But we hope to reach Biarritz [*sc.* Cannes] early on Dec. 29 and trust this may set her sleep right.

I finished my work on the two Vols of Butler[1] on Saturday the 21st. And about 200 pages of the Third[2] have been printed, or dispatched for printing, in preliminary forms.

WEG D. 23. 95.

Jan. 2. 1896. [*Cannes*][3]

We arrived here before 8 AM on Sunday my birthday D. 29: none the worse for our journey, made rather luxurious as it was by kindness. We had left Hawarden on Friday forenoon, and slept at the Pavilion Folkestone; then straight through.

I think my dearest wife has nearly though not quite recovered from her tedious and at first painful though not dangerous illness. My own case is this. Of the obstinate influenza hardly a trace. Hearing goes downward. Sight is on the whole wonderfully effective for reading & writing, more than for any other purpose: and these purposes are to me most essential. My walking power is *very* much gone down: and is my weakest point. I am wonderfully blessed in the love and care around me: am out of the wild: my temptations are more inward, but are I hope losing somewhat of their force. At the same time my knowledge of my utter unworthiness (a knowledge more of common sense than spiritual insight) is so profound and unmoved that the richness of God's present bounties seems to supply my best founded hope for those of the future.

I anxiously try, while faculty remains, to get on with my work.

Butler (the Works) is I hope on the very eve of issuing.

While it is on my mind, I place on record here awaiting some more formal method, my strong desire that after my decease my family shall be most careful to keep in the background all information respecting the personal relations of the Queen and myself during these later years, down to 1894 when they died a kind of natural death: relations rather sad in themselves though absolutely unattended with the smallest ruffle on their surface.

It was the kind and generous farewell from Ponsonby which had to fill for me the place of a farewell from my Sovereign.

Incidental to Resignation.[4]

We may sometimes, even if it be rarely, obtain a morsel of self knowledge through the medium of a dream.

Aware by signs perfectly unequivocal if partly negative, [of] the state of the Queen's feelings towards me, I have regretted to be in such ill odour with one in whom there is so much to admire and respect; but, as I seem to myself conscious without mistrust of

---

[1] *The works of Joseph Butler, D.C.L. . . . edited by . . . W. E. Gladstone*, 2v. (1896).
[2] W. E. Gladstone, *Studies subsidiary to the works of Bishop Butler* (1896).
[3] Again staying with Rendel; see *Rendel*, 128 ff.
[4] Holograph dated 2 January 1896; Add MS 44791, f. 22; rendering in *Autobiographica*, i. 168.

having invariably rendered to her the best service that I could, I have striven to keep down that regret, and set it, as it were, behind me, and to attain as nearly as I could to indifference in the matter.

Since my retirement I have dreamt sometimes of Parliament and sometimes (both of them very rarely) of the Court, but without much meaning. Last night I dreamed that I was at Windsor. There had been a sort of breakfast, fugitive and early, at which several attended, and the Queen appeared, but without incident. However it was conveyed to me through one of the 'pages' (servants out of livery?) that *I* of all people in the world was to breakfast alone with the Queen at ten o'clock: a circumstance which I never remember to have heard of in regard to any one, and which was not accordant with what is known as to H.M.'s (very judicious) habits with reference to the early part of the day. Well, the time slid on, and the hour approached, and I was getting duly into what I may call a small perturbation as to the how and where of access. But the dream had lost its tail. The hour never came. And the sole force and effect of the incident is to show that the subject of my personal relation to the Queen, and all the unsatisfactory ending of my over half a century of service, had more hold upon me, down at the root, than I was aware.

I take the opportunity of recording another point. Grant that the absence of every act and word of regard, regret, and interest is absolutely deserved. But then I have a wife. Of her, H.M. in her concluding letter, wrote in terms (which conveyed some implication of reproach to me) of the warm[est] interest and praise. What a fine opportunity of conveying by language and by token to this wife herself some voluntary offering, which would have been so well merited and appropriate, and would have furnished a conclusive answer to any criticism which might have been suggested by the cold negations of her conduct to me. But there was nothing of the kind. For I cannot reckon as any thing what appeared to be a twopenny-halfpenny scrap, photographic or other, sent during the forenoon of our departure, by the hand of a footman.

[*25 March 1896. Hawarden*]

We left Cannes March 9 and after three nights in London under Harry's hospitable roof, and with the days almost choked by interviews, we came here on Friday the 13th. By resolute work I have since then got off to press over my half my Supplemental volume (for which I have not yet got a tolerable title): another quarter I hope to dispatch in the course of next week. The remainder will require more actual work but not of a different kind: I hope to finish with the Clarendon [Press] in April.[1]

My limitations necessarily continue with a tendency to grow slowly: but my general health, the health of my trunk, is excellent. Dearest Catherine's is also according to the doctors obstinately good although she continues to have her sleep very uncertain and much interrupted.

I have also sent to the Guardian a fishing Circular for a Warden of St Deiniol's.[2]

Mch 25.

[1] Gladstone's edition of Butler and his subsidiary studies were published by the Clarendon Press, the academic branch of Oxford University Press.

[2] Harry Drew acted as Warden and Chief Librarian of St. Deiniol's during the planning stage; after the Library was formally constituted by the Deed of Trust on 1 January 1896, the first Warden under the deed was the Revd. G. C. Joyce, who held the position from 1897 until 1916.

[*3 May 1896*]

Yesterday I dispatched to Oxford the final revises (as I believe) of my 'Studies, Subsidiary &c.['] May the Almighty accept and bless this poor offering. It may prove barren from the unworthiness of treatment but not from want of weight in the subjects.

WEG May 3. 96.

[*27 July 1896*]

After our outing of one night on loyal service to Aberystwyth, where Will acquitted himself *ad unguem*[1] and all went well, we had another call, which C. even liked and I with all my immobility thought it a duty to obey. We made a journey to London for $3\frac{1}{2}$ days, to attend the Royal Marriage.[2] So, after nearly $2\frac{1}{2}$ years we saw the Queen once more. It was well ordered. From want of information, we did not stay for the Luncheon. The Prince of Wales as we heard expressed regret and we were invited to Marlborough House at $1\frac{1}{2}$ on.

They were both extraordinarily kind. The Prince kissed C.s hand. I cannot avoid thinking that they do so much towards us from a sense of the Queen's deficiencies. For it was surely strange that H.M. should have taken *no* notice even by a messenger of a lady of 84 who had come near 200 miles to attend the service, whom she must have seen in the Chapel, and on whom even in her notable farewell letter she bestowed the highest praise.

God bless them all. They are much to be felt for.

My time mainly filled up with conversations: interesting though to a deaf man fatiguing.

Harry, as ever, an excellent host.

WEG Jul 27. 96.

[*4 September 1896*]

I have now completed the arrangement for a third and probably last partition of property among my children: the execution of it is committed to Harry.

Each of the three surviving sons has now had from me 20 m[ille] + 2 m + 5 m = 27 m[ille]

Each of the three daughters
10 m + 2 m + 3 m = 15 m[ille]
making in all 60 m + 45 m = 105 m[ille]

The arrangement for an extra 5 m[ille] to Herbert is now cancelled, upon a view of the entire position.

I have also drawn out my new will which awaits copying, revising (probably)

---

[1] To a nicety.

[2] Wedding of Princess Maud, daughter of the Prince and Princess of Wales, to Prince Charles of Denmark; they became King and Queen of Norway 1905.

and signatures. My remaining property (besides copyrights if they are worth anything) consists of

1. Elswick shares, estimated value . . . . . . 35 m
2. Darjeeling do   20 m
3. Govt Braz, Loan £2900.
          say in all 58 m[ille]

Probable residue under the new will as matters now stand 55 m. Each of VI shares 5 m. Raising sons to each to 37 m. Daughters each . . . 20 m.

It is a comfort and relief to me thus to narrow and reduce my temporal cares. God be thanked.

WEG S. 4. 1896.

[20 October 1896]

With Harry's aid in revision and suggestion, and after discussion with Mr Barker upon the draft, I have just finished preparing and writing out my new Will (the third) for signature: and I can now for a moment consider the late & present situation.

Within these last weeks I have been subjected to an extraordinary accumulation of matters entailing anxiety in various degrees

1. The Armenian question[1]
2. The crisis of the Leadership.[2]
3. The Ribot correspondence (Egypt).[3]
4. The sudden death of Archbishop Benson while he was our guest at Hawarden.[4]
5. The formation of my Will.
6. My concern in the affair of the Pope's Encyclical on Anglican Orders:[5] and
7. [blank]

Most of these are disposed of, or have ceased to press, and we came on Friday last once more to our old haunt at Penmaenmawr to fortify ourselves against the coming winter. The house of Plas Mawr now much more comfortable than ever has been kindly lent us by the Darbishires and here we may stay until perhaps the second week in November.

WEG Oct 20/96.

[1] His last great public speech, at Hengler's Circus, Liverpool, on the Armenian question; *T.T.*, 25 September 1896, 5a; the speech precipitated Rosebery's resignation as party leader.
[2] Rosebery resigned as leader of the liberal party on 6 October 1896, being succeeded by Harcourt. His resignation letter mentioned 'some conflict of opinion with Mr. Gladstone' on the Eastern question; *T.T.*, 8 October 1896, 7f.
[3] In Add MS 44524, ff. 85–178.
[4] Benson's death in Hawarden Church during a service; see *Life of E. W. Benson*, ii. 773–8.
[5] When Leo XIII commanded an investigation of the validity of Anglican orders, Gladstone encouraged it in his 'Soliloquium' (May 1896, *Later Gleanings*, 384); however the Pope's Bull, 'Apostolicae Curae' of 13 September 1896 condemned Anglican orders as invalid through defect of both form and intent. Gladstone responded in his 'Postscript', 26 March 1897 (*Later Gleanings*, 394).

[The 'Declaration', *7 December 1896*]

With reference to rumours which I believe were at one time afloat, though I
know not with what degree; [*sic*] of currency: and also with reference to the
times when I shall not be here to answer for myself; I desire to record my
solemn declaration and assurance, as in the sight of God and before His judgment seat, that at no period of my life have I been guilty of the act which is
known as that of infidelity to the marriage bed.

I limit myself to this negation, and I record it with my dear Son Stephen, both
as the eldest surviving of our sons, and as my pastor. It will be for him to retain
or use it, confidentially unless necessity should require more, which is unlikely:
and in any case making it known to his brothers.

                                                        WEG Dec. 7. 1896.[1]

[*29 December 1896*]

My long and tangled life this day concludes its 87th year. My Father died four
days short of that term. I know of no other life so long in the Gladstone family,
and my profession has been that of politicians, or more strictly Ministers of
State, an extremely shortlived race, when their scene of action has been in the
House of Commons: Lord Palmerston being the only complete exception.

In the last twelvemonth, eyes and ears may have declined, but not materially.
The occasional constriction of the chest is the only inconvenience that can be
called new. I am not without hope that Cannes may have a mission to act upon
it. Catherine is corporally better than she was twelve months ago.

As to work I have finished my labours upon Butler, have made or rather
remade my Will, have made progress with 'Olympian Religion'[2] and good
progress with a new Series of Gleanings,[3] and have got St. Deiniol's very near its
launch upon the really difficult and critical part of the undertaking.

The blessings of family life continue to be poured in the largest measure
upon my unworthy head. Even my temporal affairs have thriven.

Still old age is appointed for the gradual loosening or successive snapping of
the threads. I visited Ld Stratford at Froom Park(?) when he was 90 or 91 or
thereabouts.[4] He said to me 'It is not a blessing'.

---

[1] Lambeth 2760, f. 204. This 'Declaration', as it came to be known by Gladstone's children, was
placed in a sealed envelope. On the outside of it Gladstone wrote: 'Rev. S. E. Gladstone. *Only to be
opened after my death*'; he initialled the envelope in the bottom left-hand corner. It was opened on 19
September 1900 for the use of John Morley (though he does not refer to it in his biography). Correspondence about its possible use as evidence in the Wright case in 1927 is in Lambeth 2759. Against
the inclinations of H. N. and H. J. Gladstone, Sir Charles Russell advised against reference to it, and
the document was not referred to in court. See also above, iii. xlvi–xlvii.

[2] Never completed.

[3] *Later Gleanings. A new series of Gleanings of Past Years* (1897); the title page was given the subtitle
'Vol. VIII. Theological and Ecclesiastical' so that the volume could be bound in with the 7 volumes of
Gleanings. The first edition included 'General Introduction to Sheppard's Pictorial Bible' and was
withdrawn for copyright reasons; the second edition substituted 'Ancient beliefs in a future state'
(see 12 Sept. 91) for the offending piece.

[4] Stratford de Redcliffe lived at Frant Court, Tunbridge Wells; for the visit, see 7 June 79;
Gladstone then recorded that his host's 'freshness at his great age is truly wonderful'.

As to politics I think the basis of my mind is laid principally in finance and philanthropy. The prospects of the first are darker than I have ever known them. Those of the second are black also: but with more hope of some early dawn.

I do not enter on interior matters. It is so easy to write, but to write honestly nearly impossible.

Lady Grosvenor[1] gave me today a delightful present of a small Crucifix. I am rather too independent of symbol.

Adieu old year. Lord have mercy.

WEG D. 29. 1896.

[The rest of the book is blank, except that on the Verso of the leaf before the flyleaf, in pencil:]

Bryn 105/-	Arm. £50 + 50
	HD 100
	Offy 2
	St D. 37
	Do Bailey 3.9.4.
	1896 to F.3. 242.9.4
	Cannes
	Repairs St P. 2.0.0.

[And on the Recto of the flyleaf:—]

[In pencil:] 9 Grove Terrace North End Road W

[In ink on a piece of paper pasted to the flyleaf:]
K. Lear V.2.   Men must endure
Their going hence, even as their coming hither:
Ripeness is all.
Ibid. .V.3. Edgar loq.
        'Let's exchange charities'.

[In pencil:] Drew Test. £5 Ja 16

[In ink:] Where I may think the remnant of my thoughts
        In peace, and part this body and my soul
        With contemplation and devout desires.
                    K. John. V. iv.

---

[1] Sibell Mary, Lady Grosvenor (see 9 Oct. 82); she was a well-known religious figure and was President of the League of Mercy.

[In pencil:] 95. Feb.
Rckt £100
Cannes gifts 10£
Aspm. £2
Lawlor F.25–£25.

Mch 25 C.G. owes £1 + 5/6
Also bound Gleanings?

APPENDIX I

EXTRACTS FROM THE DIARIES OF JOHN MORLEY, 1892–1894[1]

Dalmeny, July 12–14 [*1892*]

Got to the house about 7.45. My host [Rosebery] met me in the hall, and carried me to his sitting room. Could not contain his weariness ⟨and almost loathing⟩ of the interior situation. They had passed a horrid week of dejection and dismay, the telegrams of the polls coming to the house all day long, and smashing to atoms the illusions of many months. Then dreadful news of Mr. G.'s sight. It was really tragic as he [Rosebery] cried out in ⟨his intense⟩ the bitter intensity of repugnance to it all, "Oh, my dear M., as I sit with him half-deaf & three parts blind, and ⟨how⟩ see him feverishly clutching at straws here and straws there, a downright horror comes over me." He then told me that Armitstead had been actually summoned by telegraph to conduct the G. party to Braemar for change of air, ⟨bu⟩ & that A. was at that moment in the house. Was there ever anythg. so ⟨abominable, so revolting⟩ desperate?

The dinner bell sounded before he wd. let me go, so full ⟨& uncontrollable⟩ was the pent up ⟨bitterness⟩ severity of a fortnight's endurance.

Dressed in a mighty hurry, and found them all half thro' the soup. A place next to Mr. G. left for me. With his dark goggle-glasses on, he looked like another man. ⟨After⟩ He was evidently not in a confused mind. After a few common remarks on this & that, he put his hand before his mouth ⟨⟨a gesture of his family that does not please me⟩⟩ & ⟨said⟩ in a deep hoarse whisper made me ⟨the⟩ a confidential comment, "I don't wish it mentioned; I should like to submit it to you; I wonder what you will think of it." I was all ears, and as he was on my deaf side I needed all my ears—and then came the immense & commanding climax—"I think I ⟨have a⟩ see my way to disestablishing the Scotch church in three clauses!!!" Then the Old Man turned the monstrous glasses full upon me, as if to pierce my very soul at this earth-shaking announcement. I laugh at it to-day, but at the moment, like Rosebery, I felt something ⟨like⟩ horrible & gruesome about it. I don't know, but it recalled Miss Ferrier's painful semi-squalid picture of a meal at Abbotsfort in Scott's last days. When the time came for leaving the drawing-room, Mr. G. begged me to follow him; and I went up with him to his dressing-room. This time, alas, not to compose a triumphant cabinet with a three figure majority, but to adjust a H.R. policy to a parlt.

[1] Morley kept two diaries during these years, a Letts's office diary with entries written on most days, sometimes very brief, but sometimes extensive, and a series of 'Red Books' (red exercise books) used as a supplement to the office diaries. Both sets of diaries have been seriously mutilated, with pages and parts of pages cut out. The remaining text of both sets of diaries contains substantial alterations in red ink, of a sort that suggests that Morley later amended his text with a view of publication (he appears to quote from them in his *Recollections*, 2v. (1917) but those extracts, for 1894 at least, seem to be rewritten passages presented as quotation). The extracts in this Appendix contain the amended MS text, with the deletions shown in ⟨ ⟩. They are all from the 'Red Books'. I am most grateful to A. F. Thompson for making Morley's diaries available to me.

situation with hardly a trustworthy majority at all. ⟨Poor Old Man—it made one's heart ache.⟩ He first recited his famous 3 clauses for the speedy and effectual dispatch of the Scottish establishment. Somehow, tho' I'm a sworn admirer of the Scotch, they dress up their political dishes with such a sauce of thistles, that they have no savour to my palate. So I listened to all this, rather with seemly resignation than with any vivid enthusiasm.

Then he came to H.R. and I pricked up my ears. The centre of gravity, he sd., had shifted to English questions. We were much in the position of ⟨Mebb⟩ Melbourne in 1835. He lived by the leave of the Irish, ⟨and⟩ gave them good administration, and dealt with English legislation. But there are two ways of carrying on such a policy, a brisk method and a slack method. Melbourne took the slack method. We ought to follow the brisk method. ⟨We su⟩ He produced a bit of paper, containing a list of bills wh. we might bring forwd. at once, and then present them like pistols at the head of the Lords. They must by the necessity of things be short bills—and bills that the Opposition in the Commons wd. find it embarrassing to obstruct or oppose.

And Ireld., I modestly interjected.

The Irish must see that the composition of the majority was such, and its dimensions such, as to make it obvious that we must first strengthen our position by English legislat[io]n. What we might do wd. be to frame a Cabinet minute about H.R.; embody that in a resolution; and submit the resolution to the Ho. of C. and also to the H. of L. This wd. be the basis of future legislat[io]n. It wd. be impossible for us to take in our first session ⟨the⟩ three or four months of parliament. time, with the certainty that by the subsequent action of the Lords, the time wd. prove to have been time wasted. Meanwhile, we must Drummondize the administration in Ireld.

On this, I took up my candle and went off to bed, ⟨but not to sleep.⟩

July 13. [*1892*]
The Mid Lothian poll to be declared to-day. Mr. G.'s agent on leaving sd. he thought he cd. ⟨produce⟩ promise him a majority of 2000. "Well," sd. Mr. G., with a groan, "I confess I shd. have liked 3000 a deal better." We all pottered about rather wearily all the morning. Armitstead, good fellow as he is, lumbered with much serving, in the shape of all means of preparations, trains, saloon carriages, rooms at Aberdeen, and all the rest of it. He took me by the arm, & walked me into the garden. "Now, look here. You must come with us. Don't say no. It is your duty to come. Yes, your duty. The Old Man leans upon you. You can see it for yourself. He leans more & more on you." ⟨To⟩ These kind importunities I find it downright hard to resist. Rosebery, too, was equally importunate that I shd. go a yachting with him at the end of the week. But the truth is that I am completely done up with all the distractions, anxieties, and chagrins, of the last few days—and I cannot breathe in this fevered atmosphere, in wh. small things, & great, mighty things & paltry, are all ⟨jostling⟩ mercilessly jostling one another, and with a horrid ⟨black⟩ pall of physical decline hanging over all, slowly immersing the scene and its great actor in ⟨dismal⟩ dreary night. When the time comes for the pall to descend on me, may it not find me struggling, striving, wrestling, clutching.

Yes—but who can help wondering & admiring ⟨at⟩ the energetic fortitude, the indefatigable resource, the unresting[?] fertility. Just before luncheon, the wire brought us half a dozen brilliant victories; then came Midlothian—not 4000, not 3, not 2, but 690!! His chagrin was undoubtedly intense, for he put forth all his strength, every atom of it, in this campaign. But with that splendid suppression of vexation wh. is one of the good lessons that one learns in public life, he put a brave face on it, and was ⟨pro⟩ perfectly cheery all thro' the luncheon.

⟨After lunch,⟩ Then, he took me into the music room, and with much eagerness told me of two new points that had suggested themselves in connection with a H.R. Bill. One was draw [sic] from some provision in Kimberley's plan of govt. for Cyprus—the other a provision, I think in the Bank Charter Act that such and such an arrangement shd. go on until partlt. shd. otherwise determine. I felt a little impatient with details of this kind, when I thought of the doubtful aspects ⟨of a⟩ and prospects of any H.R. bill whatever. Yet ⟨one cannot but admire⟩ think of the boundless agility and indomitable tenacity of such a man, worrying out all these details half an hour after receiving such a facer as the Midlothian poll.

Then he returned to his point of the night before, but still more bluntly put, that the Irish "must be told" that (in short) they wd. have to wait. I said, once more, that the Irish must be very delicately handled. "They must be told," he reiterated, "that their quarrelling has lost us many a vote in Engld; that they are now little more than $\frac{3}{5}$ instead of $\frac{4}{5}$" &c. &c. I rejoined that if we used too blunt language, they wd. put us out. He only shrugged his shoulders. It was left that I was to place myself as soon as I could in communicatn. with our western friends.

He then talked of himself, and what talk it was. With the most complete tranquility he informed me that cataract had formed over one eye, that its sight was gone, and that ⟨with⟩ in the other eye he was infected with a white speck. "One white speck," he said, almost laughing, "I can do with, but if the one becomes many, it will be a bad business. They tell me that perhaps the fresh air of Braemar will do me good." All this with a quiet gravity of tone that brought the catastrophe home to my very heart. Then ⟨the old man rise⟩ he rose up, and said as if almost he were speaking to himself, "I cannot tell you what a comfort it has been to me to see you here." Not often, not often, have I felt the lacrymose return[?], the tears that lie in mortal things, so poignantly. One duty is[1]

Monday, Jan. 8. [*1894*]
Letter from Mr G. very ominous. One from Spencer, not at all encouraging. Wrote to Asquith, suggesting that he shd. press upon Rosebery as an argument against precipitating a crisis, that any reconstruction wd. have to be accompanied by a declaration of Irish policy as a condition of ⟨the⟩ Irish support, or else by such a distribution of posts on the Treasury Bench as wd. not be easy. I heard afterwards that this proved to be very weighty in R.'s mind. . . .[2]

To I.O. Worked at questions for an hour. Then to lunch at the Admiralty, Asquith with me. Agreed to go down to Osborne for a council on Thursday, but

[1] Rest missing, cut out.   [2] Paragraph omitted.

⟨when I found that Harct. is going⟩, I drew off. A. and I had long talk with the First Lord [Spencer] ⟨He did not shew any grasp, and had even less than usual any power of exposition. Rather painful, and⟩ horribly discouraging to my notion of him as possible head of a govmt. ⟨He agreed that Shuttleworth might explain the figures to us, if we cared for it. Asquith and I settled that it shd. be so.⟩

⟨After⟩ Asquith reported to me that he had found R. in a very rational frame of mind; but not believing that any crisis was possible: was sure that domestic influence wd. be too strong.

After questions, I asked Mr. G. to see me in his room. He had just come up from Brighton. Was at his lowest, looking old and worn and anxious and a little ⟨angry⟩ ready for anger. I told him that Spencer held out no hope—that he cd. not come below 3 millions increase—that I was going to examine the figures with Shuttleworth. "Do, if you like; but that will do no good: departments always best you at that; ⟨the⟩ you only run your head against a rock; nothing moves a great spending department except the discovery that either the Cabinet or the H. of C. positively won't stand it."

Thus cheered on my way, I went into my room with Shuttleworth. Present, Asquith, C.B., and Acland. S. not over handy, but then as C.B. said, you must not be too exacting. Figures prepared from one point of view cannot be in an instant adjusted to some other quite different view. The upshot of it was that what we may call the scare[?] item of increase hardly went beyond a million.

At a few minutes before 7 went into Mr G.'s room, and was detained there for nearly an hour. One of the most uncomfortable & painful hours of my life. I had roused him from a doze, but he insisted on getting into conversation. It was not exactly an incoherent conversation, but there was no *suite* or continuity to it. He brushed aside my proceedings with Shuttleworth, as absolutely unimportant. Departments can always show any sheet they please. Mere waste of time. Would not listen to one single word. Tried again to press the effect of his retirement upon the party ⟨it⟩ and upon the Irish question. Utterly futile. Showed me the notes for his allocution ⟨the⟩ to the Cabt. next day. I shd. say it will take an hour. "It is necessary", he sd. "I cannot trust in a matter of this magnitude to the give and take of ordinary cabinet conversation. I must state my views in continuous outline. This is no ordinary occasion for me. It is not a question of a million here or a million there. It is a question of a man resisting something wh. is a total denegation [*sic*] of his whole past self. More than that," he sd. with suppressed passion, "I seem to hear, if I may so say, I seem to hear voices from the dead encouraging me." ⟨Gesture⟩ With a gesture pointing to a distant corner of the darkened room. He soon turned to what was, I verily believe, the real root of his vehemence, anger, and exaltation. "The fact is," he sd. "I'm rapidly travelling down the road that leads to total blindness. You are all complaining of fog. I live in fog that never lifts. I see books, the sea, the sky, you, all through fog. You'll find a Horace in the drawer before you. Not so long ago I got on very well with the text, and cd. just manage the notes. Now the notes have gone, and I can hardly manage the text." ⟨I told him⟩ I opened the book; the notes were in nonpareil or pearl or some such inhuman type: "I can make nothing of this myself", sd. I. But he wd. not be consoled. They sd. in 1886, I remember, ⟨that⟩

after he had broken his party by H.R., that he wd. one day feel like Ajax, when he awoke to find the havoc he had made with the sheep-flock. To-night, if I remember my Sophocles aright, he was in the mood of Philoctetes. This was perhaps the most painful thing about it[1]—no piety, no noble resignation, but the resistance of a child or an animal to an incomprehensible & ⟨incredible⟩ torment. I never was more distressed. The scene was pure pain, neither redeemed nor elevated by any sense of majestic ⟨meeken⟩ meekness before decrees that must be to him divine. Not the right end of a life of such power & ⟨such⟩ long and sweeping triumph. Let us pray with all our hearts that this may not be the end, and that when he knows the inevitable word has bn. spoken, he will be as great, ⟨as high⟩ as magnanimous, and as high at the close, as he has been in a long & transcendent prime.

At a quarter to 8, he ⟨got up⟩ rose ⟨we⟩ with an air of Saturnian weariness from his chair; said "Good night, and thanks to you—many thanks—many thanks—" with all his charm of courtesy come back to him for the instant.

Went downstairs to dinner with Asquith and Acland. Told them of the prospect for the morrow. Much talk—⟨with one or two points on my part that the talk might not much concern me personally.⟩

In the course of a division, I sd. to Balfour:—"It is very unfair to ask an oracle to be his own interpreter, I know. At Ld. Ribblesdale's you told me that ⟨you⟩ we shd. find you and your friends perfectly malleable on naval expenditure. I have looked out malleable in every dictionary that I cd. lay my hands upon, but I cannot for the life of me make sure what you meant." He laughed: "Oh, I'll tell you at once. I ⟨me⟩ meant that we ⟨go⟩ go to any length you liked in strengthening the navy."

Tuesday, Jan. 9. [*1894*]
The first thing I did was to write a note to Mr. G. with Balfour's explanation of his own oracle. For Mr. G. somehow always attaches what I think absurdly exaggerated importance to casual words lightly spoken by politicians great & small. He *distinguishes* ⟨speakers & word⟩ either speaker or word less than anybody—when it happens to chime in with his object at the time. I saw that he had my note before him on the table at the Cabinet, and he referred to it, without names.

Watson of N'cstle[2] came for an hour. Without disclosing it as *actual*, I put the point of my possible retirement from the administration. "If you and Mr. G. both go," he cried, "it is all over." W. quite amazed that I shd. expect to lose the election in the country when the time comes.

At noon to the Cabinet, and a memorable cabinet it was. Mr. G. was already there. Quite light and cheerful shook hands with us as we entered. By a quarter after nine we were all assembled, save Kimberley who is ill. Mr. G. opened with a few words about the Q.'s demand for Ld. L[ansdowne], that if he refused dukedom, he shd. be made an extra K.G. This last honour had bn. conferred on Castlereagh after Vienna, on Ld. Grey after Reform Bill, on Ld. Derby after being three times Prime Minister. What has L. done? (Later in the day, I sd.

[1] Rest of paragraph much altered, and deleted in red ink.
[2] Robert Spence Watson, president of the National Liberal Federation.

something about ⟨my⟩ the Ld. Lt. becoming an Earl, and then being of rank for
the garter. Mr. G. quite reproved me for any such thought. There are different
species of the genus Earl, it seems, and only those who are of the most highly
developed order were held worthy of this high decoration. ⟨Wh. rubbish!⟩
"Besides," sd. Mr. G., "the Q. ⟨hates him, as she⟩ hates everybody who is associated with the Irish policy. Well, perhaps not you. I don't know about you." I do
though. Then Mr. G. got to work. He had the shaded brass reading lamp at his
left hand, and a red box with his papers at his elbow. He sat in his usual place
between me and Harcourt, the latter sitting a little behind, I quite close. His
voice was clear, grave and steady, and he spoke slowly, without anything like
heavy solemnity or anything of the sepulchral, but with a sort of composed
authority, that was in the highest degree impressive. His opening was admirable in simplicity, sincerity, and the pathos of a tragical reality. It was not overdone by a single stroke; nothing cd. have struck more absolutely true. Perhaps
the most telling sentence was when he sd., "I cd. not help you. I cd. be of no use
to you. I cd. not speak for the plan. *I shd. sit by, a silent and a dishonoured man.*"
There was a thrill, as he uttered these words in deep and concentrated tones.
He wound up at the end of fifty minutes with only one or two tame & casual
sentences, of a merely business character.

Spencer followed—evidently controlling nervousness, but saying very shortly
and quietly that he felt sincere pain, but that he cd. not accept Mr. G.'s plan, or
go back from his own. Then[1] the irresponsible broke forth, and the C. of E.
treated us to a mess of bad taste, bad logic, and bad feeling of wh. nobody but
himself wd. have been guilty. He began by pronouncing the plan unnecessary
and uncalled for, and wound up by a declaration that naval supremacy was the
guarantee for our neutrality, and by the implication that what he had just
denounced was both necessary & called for. The ⟨violent⟩ most obnoxious
passage, was one ⟨however was a spiteful attack⟩ deliberate reference to Mr.
G.'s conduct in 1860, in providing funds for the scare of that time. Nothing cd.
have been more forced, irrelevant, or ill-natured, ⟨superfluous, ungracious, or
profoundly detestable.⟩ This malicious outburst provoked Mr. G. very considerably, and he ⟨trounced H⟩ charged H. with gross error &c. Finally, he delivered
a thundering sentence about some men "without either understanding or conscience or principle." This satisfactorily quelled our behemoth.

Rosebery pressed for prompt decision; the govmt. wd. be broken up either
way; either Spencer & others wd. be obliged to go, or Mr. G. and those who
thought with him wd. go; it was not a situation that permitted suspension until
Feb. 15. For this was the question—was Mr. G. to leave now, or at the end of the
session.

The only man who spoke for delay was G.O.T.,[2] who feared for the Bills. He
was direct & to the point. Mr. G. sd. afterwards to me that it was about the only
contribution that he had ever heard G.O.T. make to Cabinet discussion.

After some talk, I made the suggestion that we should now adjourn, and then
informally among ourselves consider whether there ought to be a cabinet for
definitive decision this week or whether the ⟨ful⟩ retirement shd. be postponed

---

[1] Rest of paragraph deleted with red ink.   [2] G. O. Trevelyan.

⟨for⟩ until February. The wearied, dejected, and perplexed men flew to this solution, and off we went.

Harct. then ⟨in his best hustling bustling way⟩ dragged Rosebery, C.B., and me into the Exchequer House, wanted us to discuss, to lunch, and—to listen to prolonged repetition of the ⟨choice⟩ discourse ⟨to⟩ on wh. he had just regaled us. With one accord we refused, did not even take off our hats, and after standing vaguely about for a single minute ⟨we⟩ disappeared. Harct. crying out that men were always postponing ⟨small⟩ great things to small, & we all with a laugh protesting that lunch is not a small thing but a great. So have I seen undertakers come laughing away from a funeral, with their legs pleasantly dangling from the hearse.

Rosebery took me up to B.S. in his brougham & Asquith followed. We talked away about what we had just gone through, but talked without saying anything, as men are able to do. The view undoubtedly[1]

Monday. Feb. 12. [*1894*]

All the forenoon full of the idea that we had at last got to the day big with the fate of Cato and of Rome. No such thing. Cabinet met at noon. Everybody there, full of expectation. Mr. G. easy and cheerful. In the most matter of fact way he opened the fateful sitting. Ripon, he sd., had something to say about N.S. Wales. ⟨Before⟩ What Ripon had to say was that the Govt. had assented to a bill belonging to a class which ought by the Statute to have been reserved: ⟨a great⟩ it was a redistribution bill; an election was about to take place under its provisions; the body so elected & all its acts wd. be without legal validity: only remedy to pass a legalising act in hot haste thro' Parlt. Of course, it was agreed to in a minute, but I wonder to how many of us it occurred that this was not a striking illustration of the *finality* of great organic statutes, fixing the relations between imperial parlt. & autonomous ditto. Next, we passed to Employers' Liability. Asquith stated his point: with admirable clearness. Then to Parish Councils. About twenty minutes on this. That brought us to the end of the agenda. Now the moment had come. The declaration of his final purpose must now be made. ⟨The cruel suspense of all these weeks was now at an end.⟩ We drew in our breath⟨s⟩. Mr. G. moved in his seat—gathered up his notes—and in dry voice with a touch of a sigh of relief in it sd., "I suppose that brings us to an end for to-day." Out we trouped, like schoolboys ⟨when⟩ dismissed from their hour of class. Never was dramatic surprise more perfect. Harct. went down to the Secretaries' room. They were all anxious, eager, expectant; had the Rubicon at last been crossed? ⟨Harct.⟩ They ⟨glanced at⟩ were amazed that it shd. have been crossed so quickly. We had only been forty minutes in council. ⟨The Chancellor of the⟩ They looked up nervously to read the countenance of the Chancellor of the Exchr. Lo, he was in fits of laughter. It had indeed been an hour of dupery, and the Old Man left alone in the Cabinet room, as he surveyed the confusion of the 16 ⟨17⟩ empty chairs might have been forgiven if he chuckled over the thought of the worse confusion of the 16 equally empty gentlemen who had just left them.

[1] Next three pages excised.

The Cabinet of Jan. 9 had broken up with the understanding that we were to re-assemble, after we had all had time to make up our minds as to the naval policy. Here was the re-assembling, but where was the ⟨decision as to⟩ naval policy?[1] It was never mentioned. Mr. G. may ⟨think⟩ be thinking that he will be able to give out that when he left the govmt., no decision had been taken, and therefore anybody who charges him with leaving no naval policy, will be ⟨by⟩ palpably lying!!! This wd. be a very characteristic bit of Gladstonian subtlety as it is called—childish duplicity is what it ought to be called. What shall we have to say? That we came to no decision on naval policy until within a week of the new session? ⟨and aft⟩ We cannot say that, because Robertson's speech will give us the lie. Robertson of course with Spencer's authority, stated that we were going to do this and that. I cannot conceive a position more tortuous for us, nor one more scandalously humiliating.[2]

Three hours later, sitting on the bench between Mr. G. and Asquith I recd. a card for a cabinet dinner on Saturday. The others got theirs by & bye. Nobody had heard a word of this. What a curious ⟨silent⟩ move. Doubtless ⟨we shall be taken⟩ he means to make this an occasion for telling us that he is off, and being a dinner, he will not have to report to the Queen. The delay for a week makes our position in respect of reconstruction, budget, and other business almost impracticable. Query, supposing the definite announcement to be made to us on Saty., what will be the next step? Will any of us have a right, or feel it decent, to promote or take a part, in active ⟨effecr⟩ effective and definite pourparlers, as to ⟨we⟩ the new govmt.? It must be done. Somebody, ⟨part or not⟩ in a non-combatant position, must make it his business to ⟨con⟩ carry on ⟨so⟩ informal, provisional, and non-committed negotiations. Perhaps Asquith or Marjoribanks. Harcourt, be it observed is the only man of us who had never yet sd. one single word. We are wholly in the dark about him, ⟨seen as to⟩ unless the talk of Loulou is to be taken as inspired and authorised.

In one of the divisions this afternoon, Mr. G. ⟨who is visibly aging,⟩ touched me on the arm in the lobby and we sat down. "Perhaps you will think me impertinent," he began, "but I shd. like to ask one question. I am like adamant. But is it not odd that no attempt shd. have been seriously made to meet me, and to halve Spencer's plan. The Chancellor of the Exchequer is of ⟨to⟩ course the man who wd. usually[?] work in this direction. ⟨His⟩ But Harcourt is incomprehensible. He has surrendered without a struggle. I don't understand him. I cannot talk to him about it. I am willing to go as far as three new battleships. Seven are monstrous." I defended myself by saying that he had brushed aside figures on Jan. 8. He retorted that these were figures for justification, the very opposite of reduction. I intimated that I shd. see Spencer that night, and wd. see what cd. be done. This might look like a desire, such as that of Jan. 11, to have a bridge built. Only there is the ⟨declaration⟩ preliminary declaration ⟨as to⟩ about adamant. A rumour got about among us that he is preparing a memorandum.

After the Cabinet, I ought to say, Asquith, Acland, and I lunched at the Athm., declining both Spencer & Rosebery. I stuck to my text, that all was over

---

[1] Next two sentences deleted in red ink.
[2] This sentence deleted in red ink.

in Mr. G.'s mind. Profoundly significant support for that in the fact mentioned to me by West, that ⟨he⟩ poor Mrs. G. had it in her head that the devoted Armitstead shd. take them right away to Italy, the moment after the blow was struck. There he wd. see no English newspapers, & cd. fling himself into books, etc. Somebody had sd. something to him as to ⟨the diff⟩ time hanging heavy on his hands, if he was out of public life. He was very wroth at this—as if politics, forsooth, were the only interest he had. Wd. it not have been better if they had been his only interest.

⟨Asquith W⟩ We all agreed at lunch, that the re-formed govmt. wd. not have been long at work before malign hints, of the Friederichrühe[1] sort, wd. begin to figure in the newspapers. ⟨The body of this party wd. not let us escape scot free.⟩ The story of the ships will come out. It will come out that he was for dissolution, and that it was the Cabinet who ⟨funked⟩ dreaded dissolution. It will be more or less plainly indicated that he was edged out by the ambitions and the restlessness of his[2]

Thursday. Mar. 1. [*1894*]
The day of Mr. G.'s last cabinet; a painful day it has been. At the opening we were all as cheerful as usual, chatting and laughing at our very best. Discussion on the Parish C. Bill; settled on a conciliatory line, saving the Bill. Any other course wd. have been sheer insanity. Then the Q.'s speech. Mr. G. much in love with a paragraph regretting that legislation had bn. abridged by divergence between sentiments of H. of L. and those entertained by H. of C., and hoping that some solution for such difficulty wd. be found. We debated the word "sentiments" for quarter of an hour. I forget what was substituted for it. After that, arose the quest. whether the Q. wd. resist, & if so, whether we shd. insist. Much disputation. At last, they came to my mind, that we shd. get the para if we could, and not fight if we cd. not get it. Everybody was urgent that in accepting Lords' amendmts. Mr. G. shd. make a strong speech against the Lords generally. The case did not particularly invite any such declaration, for what was called the mutilation and ruination of our bill, was in fact to restore the bill to the condition in wh. we had introduced it, only rather better. But "our people" and "our fellows", so there! ⟨with that sham theatric accent of his⟩ assured us, demanded a declaration. I sd., "What they want, Mr. Gladstone, is a dose of very bad language against the H. of L." And so, without enthusiasm, he agreed. The business was over. Then began the short, but truly painful, ⟨& in part the nauseous⟩, scene. Kimberley cleared his throat, amid profound stillness, and began his words of farewell. But almost in an instant the ⟨brave⟩ honest fellow's voice gave way, and he cd. not get on. However, he bravely forced out a few broken sentences—⟨and⟩ with many tears—& good honest sentences they were. ⟨The sight of⟩ Such simple & unaffected emotion was as manly as cd. be, & touched everyone of us to the core. We cd. see that a good many of us were as near breaking down as Kimberley, and as for me, I sat there next to the Old Man, choking. ⟨Now followed a horrid performance, grotesque, nauseous, almost obscene. No less than this.⟩ Harct. had three or four days ⟨go⟩ ago,

[1] Friedrichsruh was Bismarck's country house.
[2] Rest of this page and next excised.

written Mr. G. an elaborate letter of farewell, ⟨full of Rhodian rhetoric, and fine phrases about the penumbra of the coming eclipse, and other wonderful things. This letter had bn. received and ⟨ful⟩ duly & fully answered.⟩ So, Harct.[1] with tears in his eyes & sobs in his voice, lugs this composition out of his breast pocket, and struggles thro' every sentence & every word of it, mouthing his penumbras as well as his broken voice and streaming eyes wd. allow, at times hardly able to go on; then once more tackling the dolorous job, and keeping us all on tenter-hooks ⟨of shame and anguish for⟩ until he had got his four quarto pages fairly out. Never, never, was such an exhibition of bad taste and want of tact & decency & sense of the fitness of things. Mr. G. sat quite composed & still. The emotion of the cabinet did not gain him for an instant. At length Harct. came to his closing sentence,—a true masterpiece:—how it had been his inestimable privilege for so many years to *lighten Mr. G.'s toils*, and with what bitter and lasting grief he shd. realise that "*the congenial task*" was henceforth for ever at an end. Why, he has been the bane and torment of Mr. G.'s life on every occasion of stress & difficulty in the last eight years, as many a page of this poor diurnal most faithfully records.[2]

[Gladstone] went slowly out of one door; while we with downcast looks and depressed hearts filed out by the other; much as men walk away from the grave-side.

[1] Rest of entry almost all deleted in red ink.
[2] Rest of page, except last three lines, excised.

APPENDIX II

Gladstone's pamphlets, articles and books written in 1887–1896

This list, which does not include political speeches reprinted as pamphlets or letters published in daily newspapers, is in the order of appearance in the diary. The date gives the reference to the footnote describing the work in full; the note is usually placed at the day on which the start of planning or writing is noticed by Gladstone.

'Notes and queries on the Irish demand', *N.C.*, xxi. 165 (February 1887) ...... 6 Jan. 87
'The great Olympian sedition', *C.R.*, li. 757 (June 1887) ...... 20 Jan. 87
'The history of 1852–1860, and Greville's latest Journals', *E.H.R.*, ii. 281 (April 1887) ...... 20 Jan. 87
'The Greater Gods of Olympos. I. Poseidon', *N.C.*, xxi. 460 (March 1887) ...... 22 Feb. 87
'The greater gods: part II: Apollo', *N.C.*, xxi. 748 (May 1887) ...... 6 Mar. 87
'The greater gods: part III: Athenê', *N.C.*, xxii. 79 (July 1887) ...... 7 Apr. 87
'The Homeric Herê', *C.R.*, liii. 181 (February 1888) ...... 25 Apr. 87
Review of vols. v and vi of Lecky's *History of England in the eighteenth century*, *N.C.*, xxi. 919 (June 1887) ...... 16 May 87
'Universitas Hominum; or, the Unity of History', *North American Review*, cxlv. 589 (December 1887) ...... 11 June 87
'Mr. Lecky and political morality', *N.C.*, xxii. 279 (August 1887) ...... 8 July 87
'Letter to Pearsall Smith on International Copyright', *N.C.*, xxii. 602 (November 1887) ...... 15 Aug. 87
'Electoral facts of 1887', *N.C.*, xxii. 435 (September 1887) ...... 16 Aug. 87
'The future of the English-speaking races', *Youth's Companion* (November 1888) ...... 22 Aug. 87
'Ingram's History of the Irish Union', *N.C.*, xxii. 445 (October 1887) ...... 2 Sept. 87
'Lessons of Irish History in the eighteenth century', in J. Bryce, ed., *A handbook of home rule* (1887) ...... 24 Sept. 87
'An olive branch from America', *N.C.*, xxii. 611 (November 1887) ...... 31 Oct. 87
'A reply to Dr. Ingram', *Westminster Review* (January 1888) ...... 8 Dec. 87
'Colonel Ingersoll on Christianity', *N.A.R.*, cxlvi. 481 (May 1888) ...... 31 Dec. 87
'Further Notes and Queries on the Irish Demand', *C.R.*, liii. 321 (March 1888) ...... 30 Jan. 88
'Robert Elsmere and the Battle of Belief', *N.C.*, xxiii. 766 (May 1888) ...... 6 Apr. 88
'The Elizabethan settlement of religion', *F.R.*, xxiv. 1 (July 1888) ...... 1 June 88
'Mr. Forster and Ireland', *N.C.*, xxiv. 451 (September 1888) ...... 6 Aug. 88
'Queen Elizabeth and the Church of England', *N.C.*, xxiv. 764 (November 1888) ...... 18 Sept. 88
'Phoenician affinities of Ithaca', *N.C.*, xxvi. 280 (August 1889) ...... 15 Oct. 88
'Daniel O'Connell', *N.C.*, xxv. 148 (January 1889) ...... 26 Nov. 88
'Free Trade', *N.A.R.*, cl. 1 (January 1890) ...... 10 Dec. 88
'For the Right', by C. E. Franzos, *N.C.*, xxv. 615 (April 1889) ...... 27 Feb. 89
'Italy in 1888–89', *N.C.*, xxv. 763 (May 1889) ...... 18 Apr. 89
'Plain speaking on the Irish Union', *N.C.*, xxvi. 1 (July 1889) ...... 23 May 89

'True and false conceptions of the Atonement', *N.C.*, xxxvi. 317 (September 1894)   18 Feb. 94
'Love Odes of Horace. Five specimens', *N.C.*, xxxv. 701 (May 1894)   21 Apr. 94
'The place of heresy and schism in the modern church', *N.C.*, xxxvi. 157 (August 1894)   22 Apr. 94
The works of Joseph Butler, 2v. (1896)   12 June 95
Studies subsidiary to the works of Bishop Butler (1896)   23 Dec. 95
Later Gleanings. A new series of Gleanings of Past Years (1897) 29 Dec. 96

APPENDIX III

ADDENDA AND CORRIGENDA

The compilation of the Index (Volume XIV) has provided further information on a number of people, authors and titles. This has been incorporated in the '*Dramatis Personae*' and '*Gladstone's Reading*' sections of the Index and for the most part is not included in this Appendix, which is chiefly confined to the correction of error.

Further 'Addenda and Corrigenda' to Volumes I and II will be found above, ii. 649 ff.

Vol. I

p. 19	19 Nov. 27	For 'fomer', read 'former'
p. 105 n. 7	11 Mar. 27	For '1845', read '1854'
p. 123 n. 6	26 June 27	Tristram Merton is pseud. for T. B. Macaulay
p. 255 n. 5	21 Aug. 29	Possibly Mrs. Magdalen Dixon, wife of Lt. Gen. Alexander Dixon of Mount Annan, Dumfriesshire

Vol. II

p. 99 n. 11	1 Apr. 34	For 'Chantry', read 'Chantrey'
p. 120 n. 9	30 July 34	Perhaps James Spedding 'Substance of a speech against political unions delivered in a debating society in the University of Cambridge' (1832)
p. 257 n. 10	9 Sept. 36	For '4796', read '4296'
p. 285 n. 10	18 Mar. 37	Probably in fact Sismondi's *Italian Republics*, for which see 6 Apr. 33 and 15 July 34

Vol. III

p. 30 n. 4	22 May 40	The note should describe H. W. Bellairs (details at 9 Sept. 73 n.)
p. 44 n. 9	9 July 40	Possibly 'The Courts and the Kirk' in *British Critic*, xxviii. 1–87 (July 1840), attributed to Wilberforce
p. 58 n. 4	8 Sept. 40	For 'I doubt either has ever wanted to', read 'we must always wish for'
p. 67 n. 3	10 Nov. 40	For '2–3 Sept. 31', read '2–16 Sept. 31'
p. 167 n. 1	26 Dec. 41	For 'Gifford', read 'Giffard'
p. 236 n. 11	7 Nov. 42	Palmer's dates are 1803–85, not 1811–79
p. 449 n. 17	23 Apr. 45	For 'fratte', read 'tratte'
p. 464 n. 3	26 June 45	For 'March', read 'May'
p. 485 n. 14	1 Oct. 45	Perhaps Carl Adolf Constantin von Hoefler, author of *Concordat und Constitutionseid der Katholiken in Bayern* (1847)
p. 486 n. 4	3 Oct. 45	For 'Protestanismus', read 'Protestantismus'

Vol. IV

p. 31 n. 3	(flyleaf)	For 'on', read 'quoted in'
p. 167 n. 3	21 Nov. 49	For 'xxii', read 'xii'
p. 190 n. 12	6 Mar. 50	For 'James', read 'John'
p. 193 n. 4	15 Mar. 50	Granville was lord president 1852–4, 1855–8, 1859–66; and Chancellor of the Duchy 1854–5
p. 255 n. 1	31 Oct. 50	For 'Guisto', read 'Giusto'
p. 269 n. 1	11 Nov. 50	For 'looked at', read 'kept'
p. 492 n. 1	26 Jan. 53	Mrs. Fanny Boulting, of 60 George Street, Euston Square, sister of Caroline Uppington (see 26 Feb. 46). She had written on 25 Jan. about some money belonging to her late sister.
p. 535 n. 9	16 June 53	For 'Communi', read 'Comuni'
p. 575 n. 8	10 Dec. 53	For '4 Jan. 53', read '7 Jan. 53'
p. 577 n. 8	21 Dec. 53	Should read: James G. Marshall, *Minorities and majorities: their relative rights* (1853)

Vol. V

p. lxvi, line 11		For 'twenty-eight', read 'twenty-six'
p. 1	1 Jan. 55	(line 7) for 'manner", read 'mammon'
p. 38 n. 2	18 Mar. 55	Note should read: 'Untraced MS on reunion between the Catholic churches; see 27 Mar. 55'
p. 70 n. 7	16 Aug. 55	For '*Gatylus*', read '*Catylus*'
p. 115 n. 11	17 Mar. 56	Read note 12
p. 115 n. 12	18 Mar. 56	Read note 11
p. 155 n. 13	19 Aug. 56	More probably, James Darlington of Wigan, mining engineer, who was boring for coal for the estate.
p. 196	11 Feb. 57	This day's undated mem. should be printed at 25 February 1857
p. 227 n. 14	31 May 57	For '26 Mar. 56', read '25 Mar. 56'
p. 231 n. 15	17 June 57	For '17 June 52', read '21 June 52'
p. 236 n. 7	10 July 57	For 'Tottenham', read 'Dyers Hill, Sheffield'
p. 319 n. 9	20 Aug. 58	Or, possibly, Mary Russell Mitford, *Our Village: sketches of rural character and scenery* (1824–32)
p. 370 n. 7	17 Feb. 59	For 'Guildford', read 'Guilford'
p. 388 n. 11	21 Apr. 59	For 'Guiseppi', read 'Giuseppe'
p. 527 n. 8	23 Oct. 60	For 'G. Goldoni', read 'C. Goldoni'

Vol. VI

p. 5 n. 13	23 Jan. 61	For '18 Feb. 1858', read '17 Feb. 1858'
p. 37 n. 1	3 June 61	For 'lxii', read 'lxvii'
p. 50	29 July 61	Not Sybella, but Marianne Mildmay, *née* Vernon (see 14 Nov. 44, 12 Dec. 61).
p. 97 n. 6	13 Feb. 62	For '26 Nov. 59', read '28 Nov. 59'
p. 104	19 Mar. 62	Bottom line should read: 'they had none of the same assumption to direct the conscience, none'
p. 154	15 Oct. 62	Mr Sutherland is Edwin Sutherland of Great Mancott Main Colliery, Queensferry
p. 183 n. 2	18 Feb. 63	For '1862', read '1863'
p. 279 n. 9	31 May 64	Note should read: 'See 5 Feb. 64'

p. 290 n. 13	20 July 64	For '1865', read '1864'
p. 311	4 Nov. 64	For the visit to Chester Infirmary, see J. G. McKendrick, *The Story of My Life*, p. 58
p. 380 n. 1	25 Aug. 65	For 'Morley 343', read 'Morley i. 343'
p. 387 n. 1	28 Sept. 65	For '4 June 65', read '3 June 65'
p. 474	22 Oct. 66	Line 9: for 'sotterrandi', read 'sotterranei'
p. 475	22 Oct. 66	Line 3: for 'forse', read 'fosse'; for 'nazion', read 'nazione'
p. 545 n. 7	3 Sept. 67	Note should refer to Reginald Yonge (see 22 Dec. 72), br. of Richard Yonge
p. 546 n. 3	6 Sept. 67	For '1 Nov.', read '11 Nov.'
p. 565 n. 8	28 Dec. 67	For 'Dana', read 'Darrah'; correspondence with Gladstone published in *Bee-Hive*, January 4, 1868, p. 2

Vol. VII

p. 39 n. 1	11 Mar. 69	For 'Gerald', read 'Gerard'
p. 495 n. 9	13 May 71	For 'Grinqualand', read 'Griqualand'

Vol. VIII

p. 22	16 Aug. 71	For 'Eilsen', read 'Eileen'
p. 30 n. 5	3 Sept. 71	[on Tennyson's 'Arthurian poem'] in *The Spectator*, xliii. 15–17 (January 1870)
p. 240 n. 5	22 Nov. 72	For 'Grinqualand', read 'Griqualand'
p. 385 n. 1	7 Sept. 73	Philojudaeus, Jewish Platonist, ca. 100 A.D., author of 'Of the Contemplative Life', ed. W. Bowyer (n.d.)
p. 509	9 July 74	For 'Wilmarleigh', read 'Winmarleigh'
p. 524 n. 6	10 Sept. 74	For 'Freiberg' read 'Freiburg'

Vol. IX

p. liv, lines 11–12		The passage in [ ] should read: '[the Tory M.P. and Tory candidate in 1874 for the two-member constituency]'
p. lxxvi, note 10		See 19, 26 June 80. Bessborough was made chairman after Devonshire's refusal was assumed.
p. lxxvii, note 10		See 23 Oct. 80; first printed in Hammond, 198
p. xcv, line 23	For '1845', read '1842'	
p. 398 n. 4	18 Mar. 79	Letter of apology for absence from the Royal Colonial Institute; printed in *The Times*, 19 March 1879

Vol. X

Vol. XI

p. 339 n. 4	13 May 85	*For the term of his natural life*, is the 1885 London edn of Marcus Andrew Hislop Clarke, *His Natural Life* (Melbourne 1870–2)
p. 387	29 Aug. 85	Charles Lindley Wood, 2nd Viscount Halifax

APPENDIX IV

RESEARCH AND *THE GLADSTONE DIARIES*: A ROLL CALL

The number of those upon whose advice the Editors have drawn is legion; the names of the chief of them are recorded in various Prefaces. The following have, at one time or other, either full-time or part-time, been directly involved in the research and textual preparation of the edition:

Editors: M. R. D. Foot (to 1972)
          H. C. G. Matthew (since 1972)

Butler, Dr. Perry
Cassidy, Miss Irene
Clarke, Dr. M. A.
Condon, Mrs. Susan
Crutch, Ms. Beth
Gieve, Mrs. Katherine
Gilliland, Mrs. Jean
Griffith, Mrs. Fiona
Heimann, Dr. Mary
Holding, Mr. John R.
Hugh, Ms. Katharine
Keep, Mrs. Vera
Lawton, Professor H. W.
McCreery, Ms. Cindy

Manville, Mrs. Katherine
Marsland, Ms. Laura
Mitchell, Ms. Elizabeth
Morshead, Ms. Catherine
Mott, Mrs. Nicole
Phillips, Mrs. Francis
Puddephatt, Ms. Karen
Russell, Lady Sarah
Stoecklin, Ms. Tina
Sullivan, Miss Mary
Sweeney, Dr. J. Morgan
Webber, Dr. Theresa
Winter, Mrs. Helen

WHERE WAS HE?
1892–1896

The following list shows where the diarist was each night; he continued at each place named until he moved to the next one. Names of the owners or occupiers of great houses have been given in brackets on the first mention of the house.

9 January 1892	Pau	22 October	The Deanery, Christ Church, Oxford
12 January	Toulouse		
15 January	Valescure, St. Raphael	25 October	London
9 February	Nice	12 November	Hotel Metropole, Brighton
25 February	On train		
26 February	Paris	14 November	London
29 February	London	25 November	Windsor Castle
12 April	Hawarden	26 November	Hawarden
27 April	London	16 December	London
29 April	Dollis Hill (Aberdeen)	20 December	Folkestone
2 May	London	22 December	Biarritz
3 May	Dollis Hill	9 January 1893	On train
23 May	London	10 January	London
28 May	Hatchlands, Guildford (Rendel)	21 February	Windsor Castle
		22 February	London
30 May	London	3 March	Lion Mansions, Brighton (Armitstead)
2 June	Hawarden		
13 June	London	8 March	London
25 June	Hawarden	10 March	The Durdans, Epsom (Rosebery)
29 June	Dalmeny House (Rosebery)		
		20 March	London
13 July	Aberdeen	30 March	Brighton
14 July	Fife Arms Hotel, Braemar	6 April	London
		7 April	Brighton
20 July	Pitlochry	10 April	London
21 July	Hawarden	29 April	Hatchlands, Guildford
27 July	London	1 May	London
4 August	Hatchlands	12 May	Minley Manor, Farnborough (B. W. Currie)
8 August	London		
9 August	Hatchlands	15 May	London
11 August	London	18 May	Hawarden
15 August	Osborne House	29 May	London
16 August	London	9 June	Brighton
20 August	Hawarden	12 June	London
12 September	Beddgelert, Snowdon (Watkin)	16 June	Dollis Hill
		19 June	London
15 September	Barmouth	23 June	Hatchlands, Guildford
22 September	Hawarden	26 June	London
28 September	London	1 July	Ham House, Petersham (Dysart)
30 September	Hawarden		

3 July	London	1 November	London
7 July	Dollis Hill	1 December	South Park Hill, Bracknell (Hayter)
10 July	London		
14 July	Englemere House, Ascot (Ribblesdale)	4 December	London
		9 December	Brighton
17 July	London	13 December	London
21 July	Dollis Hill	22 December	Brighton
24 July	London	27 December	London
29 July	Hatchlands, Guildford		
31 July	London	5 January 1894	Brighton
11 August	St. George's Hill, Weybridge (Egerton)	8 January	London
		13 January	On train
14 August	London	14 January	Grand Hotel, Biarritz
18 August	Holmbury	9 February	On train
21 August	London	10 February	London
26 August	Tring Park	2 March	Windsor Castle
28 August	London	3 March	London
4 September	On train	12 March	Brighton
5 September	Black Craig, Perthshire (Armitstead)	21 March	London
		22 March	Brighton
27 September	Edinburgh	13 April	Dollis Hill
28 September	Hawarden		

The following dates are those recorded spasmodically in the diary

7 January 1895	London	25 June	London
8 January	en route for Cannes	30 September	Hawarden
9 January	Cannes	27 December	Folkestone
27 February?	Cap Martin	29 December	Cannes
23 March	London		
29 March	Lincoln		
2 April	Hawarden	10 March 1896	London
12–24 June	On board the 'Tantallon Castle' in the Baltic	13 March	Hawarden

LIST OF LETTERS BY CORRESPONDENT
PUBLISHED IN VOLUME XIII

A note on the editing of these letters will be found with the equivalent list in
Volume VII

Acland, A. H. D., *M.P.*
  23 October 1892
  5 March 1894
Acland, Sir H. W.
  10 October 1892
  17 October 1892
  15 August 1893
Acland, Sir T. D., *M.P.*
  3 December 1893
  7 March 1894
Acton, J. E. E. D., 1st Baron Acton
  24 August 1892
  19 September 1892
  26 September 1892
  5 October 1892
  7 October 1892
  10 October 1892
  17 October 1892
  6 February 1894
  8 February 1894
Adderley, C. B., 1st Baron Norton
  10 September 1893
Armour, Rev. J. B.
  12 August 1893
Asquith, H. H., *M.P.*
  18 September 1892
  23 September 1892
  7 October 1892
  14 October 1892
  1 December 1892
  23 February 1893
  26 February 1893
  15 September 1893
  7 October 1893
  10 November 1893
  5 March 1894

Balfour, A. J., *M.P.*
  1 August 1893
  2 March 1894
Balfour, J. B., *M.P.*
  18 July 1892

Bannerman, H. Campbell-, *M.P.*
  1 October 1892
  2 November 1892
  23 January 1893
  1 July 1893
  5 March 1894
Benson, E. W., Archbishop of Canterbury
  8 December 1892
  9 December 1892
  25 April 1893
Bessborough, Earl of, see Ponsonby
Blake, E., *M.P.*
  2 September 1893
  14 October 1893
Brand, E., Lady Hampden
  14 March 1894
Brassey, T., 1st Earl Brassey
  3 September 1892
Bruce, J., 8th Earl of Elgin
  3 October 1893
Bryce, J., *M.P.*
  15 August 1892
  1 October 1892
  19 October 1892
  6 December 1892
  27 February 1893
  16 June 1893
  1 September 1893
  21 September 1893
Buchanan, R. W.
  12 January 1893
Burne-Jones, see Jones
Burnand, F. C., Editor of *Punch*
  12 September 1893
Bute, Marquis of, see Stuart

Cameron, Sir C., *M.P.*
  24 August 1893
Campbell, D., American historian
  17 October 1892
Carnegie, A.
  19 September 1892

Jenkyns, Sir H., parliamentary draftsman
  15 September 1893
Jones, E. C. Burne-
  26 January 1894
Jones, E. R., *M.P.*
  6 March 1894
Jones, Rev. J. M.
  17 September 1892

Kimberley, Earl of, see Wodehouse
Kinnaird, Mrs.
  2 December 1892
Knowles, J. T., Editor of the *Nineteenth Century*
  9 October 1892

Labouchere, H., *M.P.*
  22 August 1892
  25 August 1892
Lacaita, Sir J. P.
  28 March 1892
  2 September 1892
  16 October 1893
Lefevre, G. J. Shaw-, *M.P.*
  9 December 1892
Leighton, Sir F., President of the Royal
    Academy
  20 April 1893
Leopold II, King of Belgium
  30 September 1892
Lucy, H. W.
  5 March 1894

Marjoribanks, E., *M.P.*
  6 September 1892
  18 September 1892
  1 February 1893
  4 March 1893
  5 March 1893
  22 May 1893
  6 September 1893
  29 January 1894
Mather, W., *M.P.*
  25 February 1893
Morley, A., *M.P.*
  12 April 1893
Morley, John, *M.P.*
  26 August 1892
  16 September 1892
  26 September 1892
  10 October 1892

15 October 1892
17 October 1892
9 November 1892
11 November 1892
12 November 1892
15 November 1892
16 November 1892
26 November 1892
13 December 1892
28 December 1892
2 January 1893
12 January 1893
17 January 1893
22 January 1893
15 February 1893
16 March 1893
10 May 1893
14 May 1893
25 May 1893
30 May 1893
9 June 1893
10 June 1893
15 September 1893
29 September 1893
14 October 1893
14 December 1893
28 December 1893
5 January 1894
7 January 1894
11 January 1894
29 January 1894
Mundella, A. J., *M.P.*
  5 December 1893
  5 February 1894
  17 February 1894

Northbourne, Baron, see James
Norton, Baron, see Adderley

O'Connor, T. P., *M.P.*
  11 October 1893

Pease, Sir J. W., *M.P.*
  16 February 1894
Peel, A. W., *M.P.*, The Speaker
  31 July 1893
  2 March 1894
Pickard, B., *M.P.*
  14 July 1893

Ponsonby, Sir H. F., the Queen's Secretary
23 August 1892
1 September 1892
18 October 1892
7 November 1892
4 February 1894
19 February 1894
4 March 1894
5 March 1894
Ponsonby, F. G. B., 6th Earl of Bessborough
2 November 1893
Poulis, H.
15 December 1892
Primrose, A. P., 5th Earl of Rosebery
19 July 1892
4 August 1892
15 August 1892
18 August 1892
23 August 1892
24 August 1892
26 August 1892
30 August 1892
3 September 1892
7 September 1892
11 September 1892
13 September 1892
17 September 1892
20 September 1892
21 September 1892
22 September 1892
23 September 1892
24 September 1892
25 September 1892
26 September 1892
27 September 1892
3 October 1892
6 October 1892
7 October 1892
13 October 1892
15 October 1892
21 October 1892
28 October 1892
1 November 1892
2 November 1892
3 November 1892
4 November 1892
6 November 1892
12 November 1892
14 November 1892

21 November 1892
25 November 1892
9 December 1892
11 December 1892
13 December 1892
16 January 1893
17 January 1893
20 January 1893
21 January 1893
22 January 1893
26 January 1893
30 January 1893
1 February 1893
4 February 1893
5 February 1893
6 February 1893
30 March 1893
5 April 1893
6 April 1893
15 April 1893
17 April 1893
24 April 1893
10 May 1893
19 May 1893
24 May 1893
25 May 1893
31 May 1893
9 June 1893
15 June 1893
14 July 1893
15 July 1893
17 July 1893
18 July 1893
19 July 1893
20 July 1893
27 July 1893
3 August 1893
12 August 1893
14 August 1893
11 September 1893
15 September 1893
18 September 1893
22 October 1893
28 October 1893
30 October 1893
5 November 1893
18 December 1893
21 December 1893
11 January 1894
29 January 1894
25 February 1894
4 March 1894

Purcell, E. S., biographer of Manning
29 May 1893

Rathbone, W., *M.P.*
2 June 1893
24 August 1893
26 August 1893
Reed, Sir E. J., *M.P.*
4 October 1892
23 November 1893
Reid, R. T., *M.P.*
16 February 1893
Rendel, S., *M.P.*
3 September 1892
13 October 1892
12 November 1892
5 July 1893
2 March 1894
Ripon, Marquis of, see Robinson
Robertson, Chisholm
6 December 1893
Robinson, G. F. S., 2nd Earl de Grey, 1st
Marquis of Ripon
14 August 1892
21 August 1892
13 September 1892
30 September 1892
12 October 1892
15 November 1892
12 December 1892
5 April 1893
7 October 1893
10 October 1893
14 October 1893
28 October 1893
4 November 1893
6 November 1893
8 November 1893
2 February 1894
Romanes, G. J.
9 September 1892
18 October 1892
Rosebery, Earl of, see Primrose
Roundell, C. S., *M.P.*
14 March 1894
Russell, Sir C., *M.P.*
14 September 1892
Russell, G. E. W., *M.P.*
6 March 1894

Schnadhorst, F.
6 October 1892

Smith, Goldwin
27 October 1892
Smith, Rev. W. C.
18 May 1893
Spencer, J. P., 5th Earl Spencer
13 July 1892
23 July 1892.
26 September 1892
11 December 1892
25 June 1893
7 August 1893
9 December 1893
12 December 1893
15 December 1893
2 January 1894
3 January 1894
4 January 1894
11 January 1894
12 January 1894
13 February 1894
23 February 1894
Stanhope, P. J., *M.P.*
18 October 1893
Stanley, Mrs. H. M.
7 October 1892
Stansfeld, J., *M.P.*
25 March 1893
Stepney, Lady
3 October 1892
18 October 1892
Storey, S., *M.P.*
18 November 1893
Strachey, E., *M.P.*
18 August 1893
26 August 1893
Stradbroke, Lady
9 December 1892
Stuart, J., *M.P.*
20 July 1893
Stuart, J. P. C.-, 3rd Marquis of Bute
14 October 1893
26 October 1893
Sutherland, Duke of, see Gower

Tennant, Miss E. A. M. (later Asquith)
19 February 1894
Tennyson, Hallam, 2nd Baron Tennyson
8 October 1892
27 October 1892
7 December 1892

Trevelyan, Sir G. O. *M.P.*
  6 October 1892

Vincent, C. E. H. *M.P.*
  17 February 1893

Watkin, Sir E. W., *M.P.*
  26 September 1892
  1 October 1892
  26 October 1892
Watts, G. F.
  26 January 1894
Wedderburn, Sir W., *M.P.*
  8 June 1893
Welby, Sir R. E.
  3 February 1894
Whitworth, Rev. W. A.
  3 September 1893
Wickham, Rev. E. C., son-in-law
  9 January 1894
  23 January 1894
Wilson, C. H. *M.P.*
  25 June 1893
Wilson, Sir C. Rivers
  20 September 1892
Wodehouse, J., 1st Earl of Kimberley
  24 August 1892
2 September 1892

  8 September 1892
  12 September 1892
  12 November 1892
  5 January 1893
  4 March 1893
  2 June 1893
  3 June 1893
  15 June 1893
  22 June 1893
  30 June 1893
  25 July 1893
  26 July 1893
  3 August 1893
  20 September 1893
  23 September 1893
  8 January 1894
  10 January 1894
  18 January 1894
  20 February 1894
  21 February 1894
Woods, S., *M.P.*
  10 July 1893
  14 July 1893
  11 August 1893
  18 August 1893
  4 November 1893

York, Duke of, see George

DRAMATIS PERSONAE, 1887–1896

An index to the whole work, including a complete 'Dramatis Personae' (with more details than this one) will be found in Volume XIV. Readers of Volumes XII and XIII may be helped by this list of persons first mentioned in them; most of the date references are to the date of first mention. A plain date indicates a first mention in the diary or letter text, usually with a footnote at that date if the person has been identified; a date with 'n' (e.g. 27 Oct. 93n) indicates a mention in a footnote to a person or event noticed by the diarist that day.

Readers who wish to identify a person mentioned in the diary, but who is not in this list below, should refer to the lists at the backs of previous volumes or to the complete list in Volume XIV. To increase the list's usefulness as a guide to identification, priests have their initials prefixed by *Rev.*, *Bp.* etc., and some other occupations have been briefly indicated.

People with double-barrelled, or particuled, surnames appear under the last part of the name, except that Irish names in O' are under O and some names with 'de' are under D.

Rulers and royal dukes are given under their regal or Christian names. Other peers are listed under their surnames and married women are listed under the name of their last husband.

Benison, H. W., 24 May 88
Benjamin, E., 2 May 87
Bennett, J., 10 Feb. 90
Bennett, T. J. W., 4 Feb. 90
Benson, E. F., 31 Oct. 91
Benson, *Mrs.* M. E., 29 Nov. 91
Bent, J. T., 6 Dec. 89
Bentley, *Miss*, 19 Feb. 89
Bentley, 9 Feb. 91
Benucci, *Sig.*, 6 Jan. 88
Ber, *Mr.*, 30 Jan. 87
Bere, *Mr.*, 24 Aug. 88
Beredin, A., 11 Dec. 88
Beresford, *Lord*, C. W. De La P., 21 May 88
Bergendahl, *Miss*, 15 Mar. 87
Bernard, 6 Feb. 91
Bernhard, *Duke of Saxe-Meiningen*, 3 Feb. 93
Bernt, *Rev. Mr.*, 4 Jan. 90
Berraios, A., 3 Oct. 88
Berry, *Rev.* C. A., 8 Nov. 88
Berti, D., 6 July 88
Bertie, H., 7 Feb. 90
Bertram, *Rev.* R. A., 27 May 88
Bewes, W. A., 17 Aug. 89
Bhumgara, P., 31 Aug. 89
Bierle, L., 22 Aug. 87
Biese, *Dr.* A., 25 Mar. 87
Biese, M. E., *née* Gladstone, 25 Mar. 87
Bigland, E., 15 July 90
Bilia, *Sig.*, 14 Jan. 89
Bilkeley, O. T., 20 Jan. 91
Billard, *M.*, 28 Mar. 89
Binks, L. J., 21 Aug. 91
Birch, T., 13 Jan. 89
Birchell, C., 28 Oct. 87
Birinna, *Sig.*, 3 Jan. 88
Birkbeck, H., 16 May 90
Birkbeck, R., 30 Nov. 88
Birkett, *Capt.*, 17 July 88
Birks, *Rev.* E. B., 5 Sept. 87
Birkwyn, *Mr.*, 18 Oct. 90
Birrell, A., 10 Apr. 90
Bisgood, J. J., 11 June 92
Black, *Rev.* R. C., 4 Apr. 90
Blackburn, *Messrs.*, 5 Feb. 87
Blackledge, *Rev.* J. E., 6 Oct. 88
Blackwood, *Capt.* P. F., 27 July 89
Blagg, J. W., 13 Nov. 88

Blair, J., 23 May 90
Blair, L. S., 7 Aug. 91
Blair, O. P., 20 May 89
Blaisdell, *Rev.* J., 23 Sept. 89
Blake, E., 21 Jan. 93
Blathwayt, *Rev.*, 16 Nov. 91
Blind, *Miss* M., 16 Oct. 89
Blissard, *Rev.* W., 11 Oct. 91
Blogg, *Rev.* H. B., 9 June 92
Blundell, C. J. Weld-, 22 Oct. 89
Blunson, *Messrs.*, 30 Apr. 91
Blunt, *Lady* A., 13 Feb. 88
Blunt, W., 1 Oct. 87
Blyth, *Bp.* G. F. P., 26 Nov. 88
Boddy, J. H., 26 Nov. 87
Bodkin, M. M., 26 Jan. 90
Bodley, J. E. C., 17 Oct. 90
Bogle, W. R., 15 Aug. 91
Boguschevsky, *Baron* N. De, 28 Sept. 88
Boissevain, G. M., 11 Feb. 91
Bojanowski, P. S. A. von, 13 Sept. 89
Bokkell, *Mr.*, 30 Aug. 88
Boles, *Rev.* R. H., 8 Aug. 90
Bolitho, T. B., 9 July 89
Boller & Stewart, 1 Jan. 87
Bolton, T. H., 23 Aug. 93
Bona, *Sig.*, 12 May 93
Boning and Small, *Messrs.*, 30 Mar. 91
Bonnor, C. M., 28 Dec. 89
Bonwell, *Dr.*, 28 Aug. 89
Boot, W. O., 16 Aug. 90
Booth, C., 15 Sept. 91
Booth, *Gen.* W., 11 Nov. 90
Booth, *Gen.* W. Bramwell, 19 Oct. 91
Borley, M. W., 7 Jan. 87
Boryll, *Mrs.*, 11 July 88
Bosanquet, R. C., 5 Dec. 89
Boscawen, *Col.* E. E. T., 30 July 88
Botha, C. De, 11 Jan. 90
Bourdache, M., 5 Jan. 91
Bourne, S., 4 May 93
Bourne, *Miss*, 2 Feb. 87
Bow, H., 24 Aug. 90
Bowen, *Judge* C. S. C., *1st Baron Bowen*, 13 Feb. 88
Bowen, E. F., *née* Rendel; Lady Bowen, 14 Nov. 88
Bowen, H., 4 Jan. 92
Bowes, J. L., 10 Oct. 90
Bowie, *Rev.* W. C., 12 Oct. 90
Boyer d'Agen, *Mons.*, 30 June 93

Canard, L., 18 Oct. 90
Canny, *Mr.*, 25 Feb. 87
Canton, W., 4 Apr. 92
Capebianco, *Cav.*, 18 Jan. 89
Capellini, *Prof.* G., 25 Sept. 88
Caprano, *Sig.*, 26 Jan. 88
Capston, *Mr.*, 4 Nov. 87
Carbutt, E. H., 27 July 83
Carley, G. C., 3 Oct. 90
Carlyle, *Rev.* G., 11 July 91
Carnegie, L., *née* Whitfield, 13 June 87
Carnot, *President*, 29 Dec. 87
Carr, J. R., 3 Feb. 90
Carretto, *Countess*, 31 Jan. 89
Carrick, *Rev.* J. P., 16 July 92
Carrick, *Rev.* R. M., 7 Sept. 90
Carrington & Barker, 11 Apr. 91
Carroll, A., 17 Nov. 87
Carson, *Sir* E. H., 9 June 93
Carter, *Rev.* S. M., 10 Aug. 88
Carton, H. A., 27 Jan. 90
Casenove, *Dr.* 7 July 92
Cassano, *Princess* De, 24 Aug. 92
Casson, R. J., 14 Apr. 89
Castelar, *Sig.*, 2 June 92
Castell, A., 21 May 90
Castellaneta, *Duca di*, 1 Feb. 88
Catchpool, W., 7 May 89
Causton, R. K., 27 July 87
Cavendish, *Lord* V. C. W., *9th Duke of Devonshire*, 24 May 92
Caverns, *Rev.* C., 6 Nov. 89
Cawthorn & Hutt, *Messrs.*, 22 Nov. 87
Cecil, A., 16 Mar. 92
Cecil, *Lady* F. M., 4 Aug. 87
Cecil, *Rev. Lord* R. W. E. Gascoyne-, 4 Aug. 87
Cerreti, *Sig.*, 21 Jan. 88
Cesaresco, *Countess* E. Martinengo-, 18 Apr. 90
Chadwick, W. H., 22 Sept. 88
Chalmers, J. K., 14 July 88
Chambers, *Sir* E. K., 28 Feb. 88
Chambers, *Miss* V., 21 Aug. 87
Chapman, *Miss* E. R., 8 Jan. 90
Charles of Denmark, *Prince, King Haakon of Norway*, 27 July 96
Charley, H. B. K., 24 Dec. 89
Charrington, F. N., 2 June 90
Charteris, *Rev. Prof.* A. H., 9 Jan. 87
Chase, *Mrs.* K., 29 Oct. 87

Chaster, A. W., 16 Nov. 87
Chaver, S., 14 June 88
Cheeseman, *Rev.* H. J., 20 May 89
Cherriton, E. A., 28 Sept. 88
Cherry, J. R., 22 May 90
Cheston, C., 31 Jan. 91
Chignell, R., 15 Jan. 94
Childs, G. W., 15 Aug. 90
Chisholm, H. W., 17 Dec. 87
Chondry, P. M., 12 Oct. 91
Chopin, A., 15 July 90
Christodoulaki, N., 17 Dec. 89
Chrystal, R. L., 1 Nov. 91
Church, *Rev.* C. M., 1 Apr. 89
Church Pastoral Aid Society, 21 Dec. 89
Church and People, editor of, 21 Dec. 89
Churchill, *Lady* J. Spencer-, *née* Jerome, 12 Mar. 90
Cichelli, *Sig.*, 6 Feb. 89
Cipriani, F., 20 June 87
Clancy, J. J., 19 Oct. 88
Clark, *Rev.* H. W., 14 Oct. 88
Clark, *Mrs.* J. A., 11 Apr. 92
Clark, *Mr.*, 8 July 90
Clarke, *Rev.* C. C., 12 Jan. 87
Clarke, J. L., 3 June 92
Clarke, W. R., 5 Sept. 87
Claveley, T. V., 21 Apr. 92
Cleghorn, *Mr.*, 25 Feb. 87
Clews, H., 26 May 89
Cloak, J., 27 Apr. 88
Clyne, *Mr.*, 21 Oct. 87
Coate, C. H., 30 Dec. 92
Coates, *Rev.* J. I., 1 Dec. 89
Coats, C. H., 19 Sept. 93
Cochrane, R., 18 Jan. 87
Cochrane, *Mr.*, 27 May 90
Codronchi, *Count*, 3 May 89
Cody, W. ('Buffalo Bill'), 28 Apr. 87
Coffey, G., 22 May 88
Coghill, *Mrs.*, 13 Aug. 91
Cohen, H. J., 26 Apr. 90
Coit, S., 3 June 91
Colburn, G., 28 Sept. 91
Coldstream, J. P., 30 Sept. 90
Cole, G. V., 15 Jan. 94
Colenso, *Miss*, 19 July 90
Collalto, M., 19 July 88
Collinet, P., 3 Dec. 87
Collins, C., 3 Oct. 87
Collins, J. C., 15 Jan. 91

Dampier, *Rev.* A., 28 Feb. 93
Damrong, *Prince*, 25 Sept. 91
Daniel, C. H. O., 8 Nov. 91
Daniell, *Mrs.*, 27 Mar. 90
Darby, E. W., 21 Feb. 89
Darke, C., 30 Sept. 87
Darlington, R., 10 July 88
Darton, F. R. 18 Sept. 89
Dashwood, L., 24 May 89
Dashwood, *Mr.*, 4 Mar. 91
Davidson, E. M., *née* Tait, 14 Mar. 91
Davidson, J. M., 28 Nov. 88
Davidson, W. E., *Q.C.*, 21 Nov. 93
Davies, F., 15 Sept. 91
Davison, *Miss*, 26 Apr. 89
Dawson, *Rev.* J. M., 13 Feb. 90
Dawson, W. H., 31 Oct. 89
Day, S. H., 3 Jan. 91
Deakin, *Messrs.*, 3 Jan. 87
Deal, *Rev.* J. G., 30 Apr. 87
Debidor, A., 15 Nov. 90
De Caux, J. W., 16 Aug. 90
De Coverley, R., 6 Sept. 90
Dee Embankment Trust, 29 May 90
Deed, *Rev. Dr.* J. G., 14 Apr. 92
Deevey, W. F., 17 Oct. 1890
De Fontaine, F. G., 5 June 89
De Hagen, *Miss*, M., 21 Oct. 87
D'Eichthal, A., 14 Jan. 91
Delabruère, P. B., 1 June 87
Delbert, P., 10 May 91
De Leon, T. C., 16 Sept. 90
De Lille, J. D., 21 Mar. 87
Dellow, H., 30 May 92
Dempsey, J., 7 Nov. 88
De Nino, *Sig.*, 9 Jan. 88
Denelly, W. A., 1 Nov. 90
Denny, W. H., 16 Apr. 92
Denora, *Col.*, 31 Dec. 87
D'Eremas, *Dr.* J. P. Val, 18 May 88
De Reszke, J., 23 June 88
Dermott, *Miss*, 25 Apr. 88
De Roque, *Baron*, 10 May 90
De Roque, *Baroness*, 10 May 90
De Simone, *Cav.*, 3 Jan. 89
De Steding, *Mons.*, 17 Nov. 92
Des Voeux, *Sir* G. W., 6 Jan. 93
Deverell, J. C., 4 Aug. 91
De Vita, *Signora*, 19 Jan. 88
De Winter, *Mr.*, 21 Oct. 87
Dexter, *Messrs.*, 1 Sept. 87

Deym, *Count*, 18 Mar. 91
Deym, *Countess*, 18 Mar. 91
Dick, G. H., 22 Nov. 87
Dickinson, G. Lowes, 17 June 91
Dickson, *Miss*, 31 Dec. 87
Diestelkampf, *Rev.* L., 8 Mar. 90
Digby & Long, *Messrs.*, 28 Aug. 90
Dight, M. L., 25 May 89
Dike, *Rev. Dr.*, 6 Sept. 88
Dillon, L., 28 Nov. 88
Dinard, *Mr.*, 22 Jan. 87
Dixie, *Lady* F., *née* Douglas, 15 Mar. 90
Döllinger, *Miss* J., 5 Nov. 92
Dobbie, *Rev.* R. W., 24 Feb. 90
Dobbyn, *Mr.*, 22 Jan. 87
Dobell, B., 8 Aug. 89
Dodd, Mead & Co., 20 Dec. 89
Dodds, *Rev. Prof.* M., 24 Oct. 90
Dodshon, A., 16 May 88
Doig, D. C., 22 Oct. 91
Donegan, W., 24 Dec. 87
Donisthorpe, W., 31 July 88
Donnelly, *Gen. Sir* J. F. D., 23 May 93
Dopping, *Lieut. Col.* James Henry, 27 Oct. 87
Dornbusch, K., 13 July 87
D'Orsay, A. J., 6 Oct. 91
Dotti, *Sig.*, 13 Jan. 88
Dougherty, *Prof.*, 28 May 92
Doughty, H. M., 19 Nov. 90
Douglas, D., 11 Nov. 90
Douglas, J., 10 June 92
Douglas, *Rev.* R. L., 18 Oct. 91
Douglas & Fordham, *Messrs.*, 30 Oct. 88
Doveton, F. B., 27 Apr. 88
Dowden, B., 18 May 89
Dowden, *Prof.* E., 22 Dec. 87
Downe, H., 18 June 90
Downing, S., 11 Dec. 88
Dowson, T. D., 21 Oct. 89
Drage, G., 14 Dec. 93
Draper, *Rev.* G., 14 May 87
Drennan, *Mr.*, 27 Apr. 88
Drohan, M., 13 Nov. 90
Drummond, T., 13 July 94
Du Chaillu, P. B., 5 Feb. 90
Dudderidge, G., 22 Nov. 87
Dugdale, A. F., *née* Trevelyan, 15 Apr. 87
Dugdale, W. S., 15 Apr. 87
Du Lac, *Rev.* S., 22 May 88
Du Maurier, G. L. P. B., 7 May 89

Fiore, *Prof.* P., 8 Feb. 89
Fioretto, *Prof.* G., 2 May 89
Fisher, W. H., 31 July 93
Fitzgerald, *Miss* G. P., 20 Jan. 91
Fitzgerald, J. G., 29 Jan. 91
Fitzhenry, *Mr.*, 6 Jan. 87
Fitzroy, *Miss* A. I., 20 Nov. 91
Flemyng, *Rev.* W. W., 5 June 90
Fletcher, A. E., 20 Sept. 89
Fletcher, C. R. L., 31 Jan. 90
Flood, L., 20 Dec. 89
Flood, W. H. Gratton, 6 June 92
Florador Food Co., 26 May 88
Floyer, E. A. 12 Oct. 92
Fluegel, *Rabbi* M., 2 Dec. 88
Flynn, *Dr.*, 10 Sept. 88
Fogge, *Mr.*, 15 July 92
Foggo, A., 22 Nov. 87
Folkard, *Mr.*, 4 Mar. 90
Forbes, J. C., 5 May 91
Ford, *Sir* F. C., 30 Jan. 93
Fore, J. A., 10 Aug. 87
Forster, *Rev.* C. T., 15 Sept. 87
Forth Bridge Co., *secretary of*, 24 Feb. 90
Forwood, *Sir* W. B., 9 Dec. 92
Fotheringham, L. M., 12 Sept. 91
Fournet, R., 27 Nov. 89
Fowler, J. C., 13 Sept. 88
Fox, H. F., 22 Nov. 90
Fox, T. H., 14 July 88
Fox, *Father*, 4 Aug. 87
Fox, *Mrs.*, 15 July 87
Franceschini, P., 9 Jan. 88
Franchi, *Messrs.*, 24 Jan. 88
Francis, S. T., 5 Oct. 91
Francoudi, D., 9 Dec. 90
Frank, J. H., 23 Dec. 90
Freeman, G., 15 May 89
Freeman & Marriot, 25 July 89
French, H., 25 Nov. 89
French, *Mme.*, 16 Jan. 88
French, *Mr.*, 4 July 88
Frethey, *Mrs.*, 20 June 92
Freunkel, *Dr.*, 7 Aug. 88
Friedlander, S., 7 Dec. 92
Friend, M. K., 12 Feb. 90
Friesenhaben, M., 13 June 92
Frölich, R., 7 Oct. 91
Fullarton, R. W. M., 29 Dec. 92
Fullerton, W. M., 13 Feb. 90
Funk & Wagnall, *Messrs.*, 29 Sept. 88

Furlong, M., 5 Jan. 87
Furlsham, T. H., 19 Apr. 92
Furness, C., 5 Jan. 91
Furniss, H., 7 May 89

Gabbitas, P., 16 Feb. 87
Gadesden, V., 1 Oct. 90
Gaekwar of Baroda, 21 June 92
Gaffney, J. P., 18 Oct. 88
Galiero, *Sig.*, 13 Feb. 90
Galletti, *Sig.*, 4 Jan. 89
Galton, A., 27 June 87
Gambart, *Mr.*, 15 Feb. 92
Gamlin, E., 5 Apr. 87
Gamlin, *Mrs.* H., 23 Dec. 89
Gammoll, G. B., 28 Jan. 90
Garaghty, *Mr.*, 20 May 87
Garbett, E. R., 29 Dec. 89
Garcia, J. & Co., 18 Oct. 90
Gardiner, *Mrs.* I., 30 June 93
Gardiner, W., 11 June 92
Gardner, *Lady* W., *née* Herbert, 6 May 90
Gardson, S., 18 Aug. 89
Garment, W. H., 24 Nov. 88
Garnett, F. E., 23 Nov. 91
Garrick Theatre, 18 Mar. 90
Garrivon, *Mrs.*, 20 June 92
Garwood, W. W., 14 Nov. 88
Gascoigne, *Col.* W. J., 15 June 91
Gasquet, *Cardinal* F. A., 10 Oct. 89
Gasterstein, *Mr.*, 31 July 1888
Gaulin, *M.*, 7 Jan. 88
Gavarre, *Sig.*, 9 June 87
Geary, *Miss*, 3 July 88
Gee, *Rev.* T., 20 June 92
Gehlsen, H. J., 14 Mar. 87
Gell, P. L., 26 Nov. 91
Gemmall, J. A., 19 Apr. 89
Geohegan, *Mr.*, 25 Dec. 87
George, D. Lloyd-, 29 May 90
George, J. B., 9 May 89
George, W. H., 3 Mar. 88
George, *Messrs.*, 16 Oct. 88
Gerahty, *Mr.*, 13 Mar. 88
Gerdi, E., 31 Dec. 88
Gerhardi, L. L., 11 Apr. 87
Ghosa, M., 1 Dec. 91
Giani, *Padre*, 7 Apr. 94
Gibb, T. E., 24 Sept. 87
Gibb & Bruce, *Messrs.*, 5 Jan. 87
Gibson, H. C. W., 4 Aug. 88

Gibson, *Mr.*, 28 Feb. 87
Gifford, *Ven.* E. H., 9 Apr. 88
Gilbert & Fowler, *Messrs.*, 8 Oct. 91
Gilderson, T., 1 Apr. 91
Gilkes, *Rev.* A. H., 12 July 87
Gill, J., 21 Apr. 89
Gillies, D., 3 Apr. 91
Gillies, *Dr.* H. C., 15 Nov. 91
Gillig, *Mr.*, 3 July 88
Gilliland, M., 11 Feb. 91
Gillow, J., 22 Oct. 88
Giltspur, C., 14 Oct. 87
Girardot, C. E., 14 Jan. 90
Gisdale, G. G., 24 May 90
Giudice, *Sig.*, 4 Feb. 89
Gladstone, Catherine, 26 May 87
Gladstone, Charles Andrew, *6th Baronet*, 28 Oct. 88
Gladstone, George Herbert, 10 Sept. 88
Gladstone, *Miss* I. N., 16 Jan. 89
Gladstone, Maud Ernestine, *née* Rendel; *Lady Gladstone*, 18 Sept. 89
Gladstone, Robert Steuart, 20 June 92
Glaiser, J. W., 30 Nov. 88
Glendinning, *Mrs.*, 25 Oct. 88
Glenn, *Messrs.*, 17 Mar. 90
Glennon, J., 14 Nov. 89
Gloag, *Gen.* A. R., 16 Sept. 87
Goadby, E., 13 Dec. 89
Goadby, M., 6 Mar. 90
Godbolt, A., 19 Sept. 88
Goddard, D. F., 15 Nov. 89
Gofton, S., 1 July 87
Goita, F., 29 Dec. 91
Gomm, C., 23 Nov. 93
Gomm, F. C. Carr-, 17 Jan. 87
Gonsalez, *Miss* V. E., 12 Aug. 89
Goodhart, *Prof.*, H. C., 15 Dec. 91
Goodhart, R., *née* Rendel, 15 Dec. 91
Goodkind, E., 21 Aug. 89
Gordon, *Maj. Gen.* C. G., 22 Jan. 84
Gordon, D., 12 Oct. 87
Gorsham, J., 31 Jan. 91
Gort, A., 25 Apr. 87
Gosse, *Sir* E. W., 5 Nov. 89
Gostwick, *Mrs.*, 1 Aug. 90
Gotley, *Rev.* G. H., 29 Oct. 87
Gouraud, *Lieut. Col.* G. E., 25 May 90
Govoni, *Marchese*, 2 Feb. 88
Gowdy, *Mr.*, 22 June 93
Gowe, H. T., 9 May 90

Gower, C. S. Leveson-, *4th Duke of Suther-land*, 7 Oct. 92
Graden, J. G., 16 Jan 91
Grandt, *Mrs.*, 16 Apr. 91
Granger, *Dr.* F. M., 25 June 92
Granini, *M.*, 4 Feb. 89
Grant, *Mr.*, 22 Apr. 91
Grassi, *Mr.*, 14 May 90
Gray, *Rev. Dr.* H.B., 11 July 90
Gray, J. M., 19 Dec. 89
Gray, J. T., 16 Feb. 89
Gray, T., 16 July 88
Grayson, *Mrs.*, 4 Oct. 90
Greavy, E. T., 30 Dec. 89
Grece, Clair James, 8 July 87
Green, *Mrs.* A. S. A., 13 Apr. 94
Green, C., *née* Symonds, 5 Feb. 90
Green, *Rev.* G. R., 2 Jan. 87
Green, J., 26 Dec. 89
Greene, E. P. S., 21 Oct. 89
Greene, W. A., 27 May 87
Greenhill, W. A., 2 Sept. 90
Greenhill, *Rev.* W. R., 28 Mar. 91
Greenlees, G., 22 Apr. 89
Greensmith, *Mr.*, 11 Nov. 90
Greenway, S., 8 Jan. 87
Greenwood, J., 1 Jan. 87
Greenwood, T., 19 Oct. 91
Greg, R. P., 7 Aug. 89
Gregorio, *Marchese* A. di, 9 Jan. 88
Greig, J. S., 26 Sept. 90
Grenfell, W., 21 Mar. 90
Grevel, *Messrs.*, 2 Mar. 92
Grey, *Lady* E. A., *née* Howard, 11 Nov. 89
Grey, *Rev.* F. R., 11 Nov. 89
Griffin, T., 7 Apr. 94
Griffith, E., 14 Aug. 90
Griffiths, T., 3 Sept. 90
Grifoni, Alisse, 2 Jan. 88
Groom, *Miss*, 24 Sept. 87
Groome, F. H., 1 Dec. 91
Grosvenor, *Prof.* E. A., 1 Aug. 89
Grousset, P., 12 Dec. 87
Grove, T. N. A., 23 Mar. 88
Grubb, *Sheriff*, 11 Aug. 90
Grueber, E., 4 Feb. 90
Gruenbaum, *Mr.*, 8 Nov. 87
Gubernatis, *Sig.* de, 22 Mar. 92
Guccia, *Sig.*, 25 Aug. 91
Guest, *Rev.* T. H., 19 Oct. 91

Guild, *Mrs.* E. M. C., 4 Mar. 92
Gullick, T. J., 23 Mar. 92
Gullifer, *Mrs.*, 2 June 90
Gunn, A. H., 16 Jan. 89
Gunn, *Mrs.*, 30 July 91
Gunnill, J. A., 22 Feb. 89
Guppa, *Prof.*, 11 Nov. 90
Gutekunst, F., 12 Mar. 90
Guthrie, J. R., 15 Sept. 91
Gutteridge, *Mr.*, 11 Jan. 89
Guttery, T., 7 Apr. 89
Gwilt, C., 16 Mar. 87
Gye, *Capt.*, 29 Dec. 87

Habershon, *Dr.* S. H., 25 June 91
Hadfield, S., 12 Aug. 87
Haed, E. A., 3 Jan. 87
Hagen, *Messrs.*, 13 Aug. 89
Haldane, J. W. C., 20 Sept. 90
Hales, *Prof.* J. W., 2 Apr. 89
Hales & Freeman, *Messrs.*, 15 Mar. 87
Hall, *Rev.* H. A., 10 Nov. 88
Hallifax, S., 28 Aug. 89
Hamer, *Mrs.*, 12 Mar. 88
Hamilton, C. E., 19 Apr. 90
Hamilton, *Miss* C. Nisbet-, 3 July 88
Hamilton, G. G., 17 Dec. 88
Hamilton, J. B., 31 July 90
Hamilton, J. M., 6 Dec. 89
Hamilton, S., 30 July 89
Hammond, *Rev.* J., 25 May 89
Hancock, T. H., 8 Aug. 88
Hancock, U. M., *née* Dunstan, 8 Aug. 88
Hand, *Miss* S. C., 30 Nov. 87
Handlon, H. V., 4 Aug. 90
Hangham, *Mrs.*, 7 Jan. 87
Hanlon, *Rev.* A. P., 18 June 93
Hannen, *Judge* J., *1st Baron Hannen*, 16 Aug. 93
Hanwell, A. W., 20 Nov. 91
Harcourt, *Lady* E., *née* Motley; formerly Mrs. Ives, 14 Mar. 88
Hard, *Rev.* C. P., 2 July 90
Hardie, J. K., 8 Dec. 89
Harding, C. S., 18 Nov. 91
Harding, G., 16 Nov. 90
Harding & Willby, *Messrs.*, 25 June 88
Hare, A. W., 25 Sept. 91
Hare, *Sir* John, 18 Mar. 90
Harington, *Rev.* J. R. S., 6 Jan. 90

Harriman, *Miss*, 14 Oct. 90
Harris, *Rev.* C., 20 Nov. 90
Harrison, P., 23 Sept. 90
Harrower, *Rev.* G., 8 Sept. 90
Harshaw, *Rev.* R. H., 29 May 88
Harte, F. Bret, 21 Nov. 88
Hartley, J. P., 4 Jan. 87
Hartley, *Miss*, 7 Nov. 87
Hartwell, E. H. B., 3 Jan. 89
Harvey, Annie, 30 July 87
Harvey, *Miss* D., 23 Dec. 87
Harvey Beales & Co., *Messrs.*, 21 July 91
Haskell, B. D., 15 Jan. 90
Hassard, A., 14 July 1891
Hattori, Ayawo, 6 Feb. 91
Haverty, *Mrs.*, 20 Aug. 88
Hawkins, *Judge Sir* H., *1st Baron Brampton*, 23 Dec. 91
Hawkins, S., 23 June 88
Hawkins, W. T., 25 Sept. 88
Hawthorn, W., 4 Apr. 91
Hay, *Rev.* J., 26 Nov. 89
Hayes, *Mr.*, 2 Jan. 94
Hayne, C. H. Seale, 9 June 89
Haynes, W. H., 24 Sept. 87
Hayward, *Mr.*, 12 June 88
Hazell, Watson & Viney, *Messrs.*, 17 Apr. 90
Hazlehurst, G. S., 7 Oct. 92
Headlam, A. C., 7 Feb. 90
Healy, J. J., 22 Nov. 87
Heaps, J. L., 7 Jan. 87
Heathfield, W. E., 31 May 89
Heinemann, W., 24 Feb. 90
Hel, *Mr.*, 9 July 90
Helmore, R. H., 2 June 87
Hemingway, F. P., 4 Apr. 89
Henniker, *Mrs.* F., 10 May 91
Henry, W. W., 10 June 92
Henslow, *Mr.*, 14 Oct. 89
Heppell, W. J., 8 Aug. 91
Herbert, G. S., 16 Dec. 93
Herbert, G. E. S. M., *5th Earl of Carnarvon*, 5 July 90
Herkless, *Rev. Prof.* J., 7 Nov. 93
Hernbrook, *Mr.*, 14 Aug. 90
Hertyka, *Dr.*, 8 Jan. 92
Hervey, *Lord* J. W. N., 19 May 90
Hewett, *Rev.* E. B., 2 Nov. 91
Hibbert, H., 20 Sept. 87
Hibjame, F. J., 8 Apr. 90

Jacobs, M., 4 Feb. 90
James, E., 8 Apr. 93
James, I., 5 Oct. 87
James, W. H., 30 Sept. 92
Jameson, *Dr.* L. Starr, 31 Aug. 93
Janni, *Rev.* U., 31 Mar. 90
Janotti, Natalie, 28 Oct. 89
Janssen, M., 21 Nov. 89
Jaques, J. W., 26 Feb. 91
Jarrold, J. & Sons., 20 Jan. 87
Jaunnes, *Comtesse*, 4 Feb. 87
Jay, *Rev.* A. O., 19 Nov. 87
Jeaffreson, *Mr.*, 6 Feb. 88
Jeans, J. S., 27 Sept. 88
Jehanger, S., 8 Feb. 90
Jehangier, C., 14 June 90
Jehangier, *Mrs.* C., 14 June 90
Jenkins, *Sir* J. J., 14 Jan. 93
Jennings, *Sir* P. A., 11 July 87
Jennyr, A., 13 Oct. 88
Jephson, A. W., 27 June 90
Jephson, H., 16 Feb. 92
Jerries, *Mr.*, 5 Nov. 87
Jesty, H. J., 29 Apr. 91
Jewett, H. M., 18 Apr. 90
Jockinson, J. W. H., 11 Dec. 89
Joel, G., 29 Mar. 90
John, *Rev.* G., 5 Apr. 92
Johns, W. S., 14 Oct. 87
Johns, W. T., 29 July 91
Johnson, A. H., 7 May 90
Johnson, *Prof.* J. J., 2 Jan. 91
Johnson, J. R., 14 Nov. 87
Johnston, *Rev.* J. C., 1 Jan. 87
Johnston, *Rev.* J. O., 16, Mar. 91
Johnston(e), G., 27 Aug. 87
Joissant, J., 8 Nov. 89
Jones, *Miss* A., 30 Sept. 90
Jones, A. C., 24 Aug. 91
Jones, *Rev.* E. R., 24 Aug. 88
Jones, E. R., 6 Mar. 94
Jones, F. M. H., 5 Mar. 87
Jones, H., 17 Apr. 88
Jones, H. Lloyd, 4 Dec. 89
Jones, *Rev.* J. S., 3 Oct. 87
Jones, L. A. Atherley-, 5 Mar. 92
Jones, M., 24 Sept. 87
Jones, R. A., 29 Oct. 87
Jones, T. H., 10 June 87
Jones, *Rev.* T. W. S., 30 Jan. 89
Jones, *Rev.* W. M., 17 Sept. 92

Jones, *Mrs.*, 23 May 93
Jopher, *Rev.* H., 2 May 88
Jopson, S. P., 30 Sept. 91
Joseph, F., 22 Feb. 89
Joseph, N. S., 18 July 91
Journot, M., 23 Jan. 92
Judd, *Prof.* J. W., 8 Oct. 88
Jung, *Sir* S., 2 Nov. 87
Jusserand, J. A. A. J., 19 June 89

Kane, *Rev.* R. R., 20 Aug. 87
Kavanagh, *Rev.* J. D., 27 Dec. 90
Kay, E., and son, 17 Dec. 89
Keane, W., 5 Mar. 89
Keay, J. S., 29 May 88
Keenan, E., 24 Aug. 91
Keene, *Rev.* R. R., 26 Aug. 87
Keighley, T. D., 25 July 91
Keith, J. M. N., 7 Jan. 90
Keith, J., 27 Dec. 89
Kelher, W. A., 11 May 89
Kelland, S., 6 Jan. 87
Kellie, *Messrs.*, 31 July 88
Kellie, *Miss*, 19 Feb. 91
Kelly, J., 25 May 93
Keltie, *Sir* J. S., 12 Dec. 90
Kempster, J., 22 May 90
Kendall, *Miss*, 19 June 90
Kendrick, J., 17 July 88
Kennedy, A. C., 6 Dec. 87
Kenny, *Miss*, 27 Sept. 88
Kent, C. B. R., 8 May 91
Kent, E. A., 12 Nov. 89
Keppel, G. T., *6th Earl of Albemarle*, 26 July 90
Kerr, J., 19 Jan. 87
Keyworth, W. W., 7 Jan. 90
Khalil Khaggatt, 27 Oct. 87
Khambata, *Mr.*, 31 July 88
Kidson, *Rev.* J., 18 Feb. 87
Kilkenny, *Mayor of*, 7 Jan., 87
Kinnaird, *Mrs.*, 2 Dec. 93
Kinsman, W., 16 Dec. 89
Kirk, H. C., 2 Jan. 90
Kirk, R. S., 10 Nov. 88
Kirkby, *Abp.* T., 18 Jan. 94
Kirkpatrick, *Rev.* A. F., 3 May 91
Kitchin, D. B., 22 Mar. 90
Knau, C. T., 17 Dec. 89
Knight, F. A., 7 Dec. 89
Knowles, *Sir* L., *1st Baronet*, 6 Aug. 89

Long, W. H., *1st Viscount Long*, 13 Aug. 90
Lord, *Dr.* J., 16 Oct. 87
Lorimer, *Miss*, 10 Nov. 88
Lorimer, *Rev. Mr.*, 6 Jan. 87
Louisville, *Mayor of*, 28 Dec. 89
Lovett, H. W., 7 Sept. 90
Low, *Rev.* J. G., 31 Aug. 91
Lowe, R. W., 13 Nov. 90
Loysdael, *Mr.*, 4 Jan. 87
Lozzo, *Count* C., 18 Mar. 89
Luard, *Col.*, 10 Nov. 91
Lucas, W. W., 11 July 90
Luckock, *Canon* H. M., 15 Oct. 88
Luenze, *Sig.* D., 24 Jan. 88
Lugard, *Sir* F. D., 23 Sept. 92
Lumley, W., 19 Nov. 89
Lunn, *Mrs.* G., 21 Dec. 89
Lunn, *Sir* H. S., 24 Apr. 94
Lunn, *Rev. Dr.* J. R., 16 Jan. 92
Lusted, C. T., 2 Mar. 89
Lyall, *Sir* A. C., 16 June 90
Lynch, F. C., 25 Nov. 89
Lynn, *Miss* D., 21 July 87
Lyons, *Mons.* A., 21 May 90
Lyons, L., 6 Oct. 87
Lyttelton, A. C., 26 Feb. 87
Lyttelton, E., *née* Balfour, 2 Mar. 92
Lyttle, W. G., 4 July 89

MacAnally, *Rev.* D. L., 30 Mar. 87
Macaulay, *Rev.* M., 24 Sept. 88
MacBride, J. J., 12 Apr. 89
MacCarthy, J. G., 16 July 88
MacCarthy, Maud, 6 May 93
MacCurran, *Mr.*, 5 Apr. 93
MacDevitt, *Rev.* J., 24 Apr. 89
MacDonald, *Gen. Sir* J. R. L., 30 Sept. 92
MacDowall, A. B., 5 Mar. 88
MacGange, W., 25 June 88
Macgeagh, R., 19 Apr. 93
MacGillivray, *Rev.* A., 16 Nov. 88
MacGillivray, *Messrs.*, 7 Nov. 87
MacGlashan, *Mr.*, 14 Sept. 89
MacGregor, J. S., 26 Sept. 90
Machan, J. D., 10 Sept. 91
Machin, *Messrs.*, 8 Sept. 91
Macintosh, *Miss*, 12 Jan. 87
Mackarness, *Rev.* C. C., 26 July 92
Mackay, *Rev. Dr.* A., 2 Sept. 87
Mackay, J. S., 19 May 88

Mackay, M., *known as* 'Marie Corelli', 3 June 89
Mackay, T., 24 Jan. 91
Mackenzie, *Sir* M., 2 Feb. 91
Mackenzie, *Dr.* S., 1 May 94
MacKew, *Dr.* S., 28 Dec. 91
MacKey, *Rev.* G., 10 Mar. 87
Mackirmal, *Dr.*, 9 June 87
MacLagan, *Bp.* W. D., 20 July 90
Macleod, G. G., 13 Oct. 90
Macleod of Macleod, N., 19 Nov. 90
Maclunivan, *Mr.*, 25 Nov. 87
MacMeach, G., 27 Oct. 88
Macphail, A., 5 Dec. 89
Macphail, *Messrs.*, 12 Sept. 91
MacQuoil, *Mr.*, 22 Dec. 87
Maddocks, J., 1 May 89
Maden, *Sir* J. H., 16 Jan. 92
Madhuvdas, R., 25 Sept. 90
Maggs, U., 16 July 87
Maghen, J., 24 Nov. 88
Magniac, H., 25 Nov. 91
Maguire, J. Rochfort, 31 Aug. 93
Maguire, *Miss* M., 12 Nov. 87
Maguire, T. M., 15 June 87
Mahony, P. C. de Lacy, 7 Nov. 88
Mainwaring, J., 5 Aug. 91
Mairr, *Dr.* J., 20 Nov. 89
Malabari, Bahramji Mehrbanji, 14 July 89
Malatesta, *Sig.* B., 24 Jan. 88
Maldarelli, *Prof.*, 8 Feb. 89
Maldock, A. H., 13 Mar. 91
Malhet, M., 18 Jan. 92
Malinverni, *Sig.*, 9 Jan. 88
Malone, T. S., 11 Jan. 90
Malpas, *Rev. Mr.*, 5 Nov. 87
Malvezin, M., 29 Jan. 92
Mamoli, *Sig.*, 29 Sept. 88
Mancioni, *Sig.*, 8 Feb. 89
Mandeville, *Mr.*, 20 Aug. 88
Manfroni, *Dr.* Mario, 14 Aug. 88
Mann, *Rev.* G. H., 9 May 90
Mann, S., 12 Aug. 90
Mansfeld, *Mr.*, 29 Mar. 89
Mappin, *Sir* F. T., *1st Baronet*, 12 Nov. 90
Marchese, *Rev.* V., 1 Feb. 89
Marchmont, A. W., 4 Aug. 91
Marcotti, G., 9 Jan. 88
Marcus, A., 23 May 89
Marens, A. A., 17 Jan. 90
Marghen, J., 24 Nov. 88

Margoliouth, *Prof.* D. S., 4 Feb. 90

Marino, *Prof.*, 23 July 88

Marjoribanks, E., *2nd Baron Tweedmouth*, 25 Apr. 87

Marjoribanks, *Lady* F. O. L., *née* Churchill; *Lady Tweedmouth*, 1 Aug. 90

Markham, J. S., 11 Aug. 90

Marlet, *Mad.*, 10 Mar. 87

Marriott, J. R. C., 7 Jan. 90

Marshall, A. G., 17 Jan. 89

Marshall, *Rev.* D., 2 June 88

Marshall, *Rev.* V., 7 Jan. 88

Marsham, R., 24 June 92

Martelli, C. F., 13 July 87

Martin, E. R., 8 Sept. 87

Martin, L. C., 4 June 87

Martinelli, G., 16 Apr. 91

Martyn, *Miss*, 12 Feb. 90

Mary of Teck, *Princess*; *Duchess of York*; *Princess of Wales*; *Queen*; 4 May 93

Mason, E. A., 10 Nov. 88

Mason, E., 8 Oct. 91

Massey, G., 2 Jan. 91

Massey, J. B., 8 Oct. 91

Massingham, H. W., 5 Oct. 91

Mather, *Sir* W., 18 Mar. 89

Matheson, *Mrs.*, 6 May 93

Mathesons, the young, 3 July 88

Mathew, *Judge* J. C., 30 June 90

Matthews, *Count* A. J. P., 2 Aug. 89

Matthews, D. W., 13 Dec. 88

Matthews, *Messrs.*, G., 18 Dec. 88

Matthews, T., 2 Aug. 88

Matthews, *Mr.*, 8 June 93

Matthews & Brookes, *Messrs.*, 27 Sept. 88

Matthews & Co., 30 Dec. 89

Mattos, E. De, 26 Sept. 89

Maturin, *Rev.* B., 5 Sept. 87

Maxted, R. G., 15 Mar. 87

Maxwell, A., 17 Oct. 90

Maxwell, *Lady* M., 4 June 89

May, G. H., 8 Apr. 87

May, K., 3 Feb. 91

May, S., 14 Sept. 89

May, C. & Co., 28 May 89

Mayhew, M. E., *née* Joyce, 27 Feb. 89

Mayow, S. S. W., 31 Aug. 90

Mazzini, *Dottore*, 21 Jan. 88

McCalmont, J. M., 17 Sept. 87

McCarrell, R., 13 May 90

McCaw, *Messrs.*, 29 July 91

McCleary, J. T., 19 Nov. 90

McClennan, *Rev.* J. B., 6 Jan. 91

McClinchy, U., 6 Sept. 88

McCrewe, G., 14 Oct. 90

McFadden, *Father*, 15 Apr. 89

McGregor, *Mr.*, 28 Jan. 87

McHardy, *Lieut. Col.* A. B., 19 Nov. 89

McKay, N., 10 Dec. 88

McKechnie, A., 12 Dec. 89

McKenzie, *Miss* H., 15 Apr. 91

McKinnon, *Sir* W., 23 June 90

McKinnon, *Mr.*, 18 Nov. 89

McLaren, W. S., 18 Jan. 90

McNiven, *Mr.*, 18 Oct. 90

McSweeney, J. G., 25 Jan. 90

McSweeney, *Mr.*, 16 July 88

Mearns, *Miss*, 13 Aug. 90

Medge, *Mrs.* E., *née* Cole, 26 Jan. 90

Medge, *Mr.*, 27 Jan. 90

Mee, A., 2 Feb. 89

Meehan, *Messrs.*, 5 Mar. 89

Melba, *Dame* N., 15 July 89

Meleagros, P., 24 May 90

Meletapoulas, C., 14 May 89

Mellor, J. W., 11 Jan. 87

Menken, E., 14 July 91

Menpes, M., 2 June 92

Merryweather, *Messrs.*, 29 Oct. 91

Messina, *Prefect of*, 26 Jan. 88

Methuen, *Messrs.*, 18 Oct. 89

Meupes, M., 5 Sept. 90

Meuricoffre, T., 27 Dec. 88

Meux, *Mr.*, 22 Mar. 93

Meyer, A., 13 Aug. 90

Michael, *Bp.*, 24 Dec. 94

Michil, W., 9 Oct. 89

Mickiewicz, L., 28 Aug. 88

Migliorini, R., 31 Dec. 88

Mijatovich, C., 17 Apr. 92

Milanesi, G., 28 Feb. 94

Milbanke, M., *née* Stuart Wortley; *Lady Wentowrth*, 20 Oct. 88

Milbanke, R. G. N., *13th Baron Wentworth*, 20 Oct. 88

Mild, A., 19 Mar. 90

Miles, W. T., 8 Sept. 91

Mill, *Miss* H. T., 20 Sept. 89

Millan, R. M., 13 Feb. 90

Millard, *Miss* C., 26 Apr. 92

Miller, *Miss* F. F., 30 May 90

Millet, P., 5 Mar. 92
Milligan, S. F., 30 July 88
Mills, A., 5 May 90
Mills, C. W., 2 May 87
Mills, *Rev.* J. R., 24 Aug. 88
Mills, L. H., 6 Oct. 91
Mills, *Mrs.* R., 23 July 90
Mills, *Rev.* T., 27 Sept. 90
Millwaters, H., 18 Mar. 87
Milne, G., 12 Nov. 89
Milnes, M., *née* Primrose; *Lady Crewe*, 22 Jan. 87
Milnes, R. O. A. Crewe-, *2nd Baron Houghton*; *Earl of Crewe*, 22 Jan. 87
Milnes, S., *née* Graham; *Lady Houghton*, 22 Jan. 87
Mingley, G. W., 11 July 90
Minissy, M., 3 Aug. 91
Mirafiore, *Countess* R., 1 Feb. 88
Mitchell, *Rev. Prof.* A. F., 7 Nov. 93
Mitchell, C. A., 9 Nov. 91
Mitchell, *Rev.* D., 14 May 89
Mochizuki, K., 21 Apr. 91
Modena, *Sig.* C., 24 June 87
Moderna, C., 18 Feb. 90
Mogford, J., 7 May 89
Mohammed Hassan, 20 Aug. 91
Momerie, *Rev. Prof.* A. W., 31 Mar. 89
Monaco, D., 7 Feb. 89
Monceau, P., 8 Dec. 91
Monckton, *Rev.* J., 20 July 91
Montefiore, C. G., 28 Mar. 90
Montessori, *Sig.*, 8 Feb. 89
Monti, *Prof.* G., 26 Jan. 87
Moore, R., 23 Aug. 90
More, C., 26 Mar. 87
Morgan, H., 11 July 92
Morghen, R., 5 Jan. 88
Morifalcone, M., 18 Nov. 90
Morlati, *Sig.*, 12 Jan. 89
Moro, *Prof.*, 2 Feb. 89
Morrah, *Rev.* H., 30 Jan. 90
Morris, *Judge* W. O'C., 7 Dec. 87
Morris, *Father*, 13 May 93
Morris & Jones, *Messrs.*, 18 May 89
Morrison, H., 16 Aug. 92
Morrison, *Lady* S., *née* Leveson-Gower, 16 Aug. 92
Morton, E. J. C., 13 Sept. 88
Morton, *Rev.* G. V., 19 May 88
Morton, *Mrs.*, 11 Aug. 93

Moscheles, F., 22 Dec. 87
Moschini, *Sig.*, 12 July 88
Moscow, *Mr.*, 25 Apr. 92
Moss, A. B., 9 Apr. 90
Moss, E. H., 6 Aug. 89
Motte, R., 23 Sept. 87
Mowat, R. A., 23 Feb. 91
Mozley, *Miss* A., 24 Jan. 91
Mugford, *Mr.*, 23 Apr. 91
Muir, *Rev.* G. S., 28 Oct. 90
Mulholland, *Miss*, 12 Jan. 89
Mull, W., 13 Sept. 88
Mullderson, *Mr.*, 20 Aug. 87
Munich, C. J., 1 Apr. 90
Munro, G. F., 5 May 91
Murchison, *Mrs.*, 20 Feb. 90
Murphy, C. J., 4 Apr. 91
Murphy, J., 26 May 87
Murphy, *Father*, 30 July 87
Murray, A. E., 18 Mar. 90
Murray, H. B., 16 Mar. 87
Murray, R. J., 26 Mar. 90
Murray, *Mrs.*, 14 Mar. 88
Murtagh, J., 24 May 89
Mwanga, *Kabaka of Buganda*, 23 Sept. 92
Myer, I., 14 Sept. 88
Myers, E., *née* Tennant, 25 Apr. 90
Myers, T. F., 16 Oct. 90

Nachez, *Mr.*, 5 Mar. 90
Naden, C., 29 Dec. 89
Naganowski, E. S., 7 Sept. 88
Naismith, W., 6 Oct. 91
Naoroji, D., 9 Aug. 93
Napier, G. G., 8 Aug. 89
Napier, J., 28 May 89
Napier, *Major* J. S., 8 Feb. 88
Nash, T. A., 1 Apr. 87
Negroponte, *Miss*, 11 Aug. 91
Nesbit, Edith, 28 Aug. 91
Nettleship, E., 15 Dec. 93
Neuwille, O. der, 3 Feb. 90
Nevill, *Lady* D. F., *née* Walpole, 12 Feb. 90
Nevill, *Rev.* J. H. N., 22 Jan. 91
Neville, *Bp.* S. T., 12 Nov. 91
Neville, *Rev.* W., 7 Nov. 88
Newbigging, T., 22 June 87
Newman, H. S., 12 June 92
Newman, W. F., 27 Jan. 92

Patti, *Miss* A., 21 Oct. 90
Patullo, *Mr.*, 9 Sept. 93
Paul, H. W., 4 Mar. 93
Paul, *Sir* J. Balfour, 5 June 91
Paulin, D., 16 Nov. 93
Paull, H. J., 12 Apr. 90
Paull, *Mrs.*, 12 Apr. 90
Payne, E. S., 14 Oct. 90
Peabody, G. F., 18 Apr. 89
Peacock, *Rev.* M. H., 17 May 89
Pearce, *Miss* K., 13 Nov. 88
Pearson, E., 4 July 92
Pearson, Karl, 24 Mar. 90
Pease, A. E., 4 Apr. 89
Peckover, E. J., 15 Mar. 89
Peddie, R., 13 Sept. 89
Peel, A. G. V., 1 Feb. 90
Pelham, *Prof.* H. F., 31 Jan. 90
Pellet, *Mons.* G., 4 June 90
Pelliccioni, *Prof.* G., 13 Aug. 88
Pells, S. F., 10 Sept. 91
Penel, J. B., 9 June 90
Penny, *Mrs.*, 26 July 92
Penruddocke, *Rev.* J., 24 Apr. 89
Perigal, F., 13 Aug. 89
Perkins, C. H., 8 Jan. 87
Perks, *Sir* R. W., *1st Baronet*, 30 July 90
Perrott, *Rev.* F. D., 21 Sept. 91
Perry, E. C., 10 Apr. 88
Perry, *Rev.* J. J. M., 7 Dec. 89
Persia, *Grand Vizir of*, 9 Sept. 92
Peters, S., 8 June 87
Petrocchi, P., 30 Jan. 87
Petroni, *Sig.*, 20 Feb. 91
Phear, *Sir* J. B., 18 June 89
Philipp, *Messrs.*, 11 Aug. 87
Phillimore, Lucy, 6 Nov. 95
Phillips, *Mr.*, 20 July 88
Phipson, E. A., 27 Aug. 90
Phythian, A. T., 10 Nov. 91
Piché, *Rev.* E., 26 Aug. 87
Pichler, Louisa, 19 Aug. 91
Pickering, *Messrs.*, 24 Sept. 88
Pickles, J., 29 Aug. 89
Pigott, *Miss* E., 31 July 91
Pigott, R., 28 Apr. 87
Pike, *Mrs.* E. M., 9 Feb. 87
Pink, H., 17 Aug. 89
Pinto, D., 26 Nov. 88
Pironneau, A., 8 Jan. 92

Pirouti, *Count*, 4 Feb. 89
Piry, *Capt.*, 31 May 89
Pitkethlie, *Mr.*, 15 Nov. 87
Pixell, *Rev.* C. H. V., 31 Aug. 91
Plat, A. du, 6 Aug. 91
Playfair, *Gen.* E. M., 10 Dec. 88
Plini, G. B., 11 Nov. 89
Plunkett, *Sir* F. R., 31 May 93
Podasta, *Baron*, 23 Jan. 88
Poerio, *Baron*, 11 Jan. 89
Pohlmann, *Mrs.*, 13 Oct. 88
Pollard, A. W., 10 Jan. 87
Pollard, J., 16 Oct. 87
Pollitt, *Mr.*, 20 Nov. 91
Pomeroy, *Dr.* H. S., 23 Oct. 88
Pommaris, *Mr.*, 2 Dec. 90
Poole, R. L., 21 July 87
Poole, *Messrs.*, 8 Sept. 88
Portal, *Sir* G. H., 17 Sept. 92
Portelas, Amelia, 30 Aug. 88
Porter, *Rev.* J., 28 Feb. 89
Poste, *Mr.*, 14 Mar. 88
Potter, B., 24 Dec. 94
Potter, *Dr.* J. W., 21 Sept. 87
Poulis, H., 15 Dec. 92
Powell, W. R. H., 17 Apr. 89
Power, P. J., 29 Aug. 89
Power, R., 29 Aug. 89
Powis, J., 7 Feb. 91
Pozzi, G. E., 28 Oct. 89
Preggin, *Mrs.*, 17 Mar. 88
Premi, *Sig.*, 19 Sept. 89
Presland, *Rev.* J., 7 Feb. 87
Preston, D. U., 21 May 90
Preston, J. W. J., *14th Viscount Gormanston*,
  17 Dec. 92
Preston, *Rev. Dr.* W., 31 July 89
Price, *Capt.* G. E., 12 Jan. 91
Prideaux, *Miss*, 6 Jan. 87
Primrose, *Rev.* C., 25 Aug. 91
Primrose, N. J. A., 29 Oct. 91
Prout, *Rev.* E. S., 24 Jan. 87
Provand, A. D., 6 July 93
Pulitzer, J., 9 July 87
Pullan, H. T., 28 Dec. 89
Pulling, *Mrs.* C. M., 15 Nov. 88
Puttick & Simpson, *Messrs.*, 28 Apr. 90
Pwlheli, Secretary to Library of, 9 Nov. 87
Pye, C. G., 15 Jan. 90

Quantin, *Maison*, 3 Feb. 87

Quartier, W., 21 Aug. 90
Quinn, *Miss* C., 6 May 87

Rafereddin Ahmed, 24 Nov. 91
Raffalovitch, *Mlle.*, 31 July 88
Ragouet, *Mons.*, 12 June 88
Ralph, *Mr.*, 30 Jan. 87
Ram, S., 13 Dec. 88
Ramke, J., 9 July 88
Ramsden, *Miss* E., 30 May 88
Raposardi, *Sig.*, 21 Jan. 89
Rashdall, *Rev.* H., 6 Oct. 92
Rasponi, *Countess* A., 23 Jan. 88
Rasponi, *Madame*, 31 Jan. 88
Rasponi, *Mons.*, 31 Jan. 88
Rauch, T. J., 13 Jan. 87
Read, G. R., 24 Dec. 90
Reade, A. A., 6 Jan. 87
Readwin, T., 14 July 87
Realf, *Mr.*, 13 Apr. 92
Rebrey, *Madame*, 27 June 90
Red Shirt, *Chief*, 28 Apr. 87
Redmond, *Miss*, 17 July 89
Reeves, J. S., 17 Mar. 88
Reich, *Dr.* E., 26 Oct. 92
Reid, F. N., 12 Feb. 89
Reid, H., 19 Feb. 90
Reid, R. T., *1st Baron Loreburn*, 9 June 92
Reid, W. H. B., 9 June 90
Reitzenstein, *Baroness* F., 17 Jan. 92
Remington, *Messrs.*, 18 Oct. 88
Renald, *Mr.*, 30 Jan. 93
Rendel, E. S., *née* Hubbard; *Lady Rendel*, 28 Jan. 87
Rendel, G., 22 Dec. 88
Renier, *Dr.* A. D., 26 Aug. 87
Renouf, *Sir* P. Le Page, 5 June 90
Rhode, R., 23 Sept. 91
Rhodes, C. J., 14 Mar. 87n
Rhodes, F., 23 Nov. 92
Rhodes, *Mr.*, 14 Mar. 87
Rhomaides, *Dr.* C. B., 17 Oct. 90
Rhys, E., 26 June 91
Rhys, *Prof.* J., 7 Sept. 88
Riaz Pasha, 17 Jan. 93
Ribetti, *Sig.*, 27 Sept. 87
Ricasoli, *Baron* V., 25 Jan. 88
Ricci, *Marchese*, 16 Jan. 88
Riccio, V., 5 Nov. 89
Riccioni, *Sig.*, 5 Jan. 91
Rice, R., 26 Oct. 87

Richards, *Capt.*, 19 July 87
Richter, M. H. Ohnefalsch-, 3 Feb. 93
Riddell, *Sir* J. W. B., *11th Baronet*, 6 Apr. 89
Rideing, W. H., 22 July 87
Ridelle, H., 9 Aug. 90
Ridgeway, *Sir* J. W., 23 Nov. 91
Ridgway, *Miss*, 20 Feb. 87
Ridley, *Sir* M. W., *5th Baronet*, 22 Nov. 88
Rigby, *Sir* J., 9 June 93
Riley, A., 19 Nov. 90
Riley, *Mrs.*, 20 Nov. 89
Rimmel, E., 17 Mar. 88
Rines, W., 20 Sept. 87
Riso, I. De, 15 Nov. 88
Ritso, *Miss*, 10 Apr. 92
Ritso, *Mr.*, 10 Apr. 88
Ritter, *Miss*, 24 Dec. 87
Rix, H., 18 Sept. 88
Robartes, M. Agar-, *née* Dickinson; *Lady Robartes*, 12 June 89
Robb, W., 8 May 91
Robbins, H., 26 Nov. 87
Roberts, C. W., 30 Sept. 91
Roberts, *Rev.* G. B., 16 Apr. 92
Roberts, *Dr.* J. V., 3 Feb. 90
Roberts, J. B., 23 Aug. 93
Roberts, L. D., 27 Mar. 90
Roberts, M. H., 14 Aug. 90
Roberts, O. E., 20 Sept. 87
Roberts, *Messrs.*, 12 Dec. 89
Robertson, C., 6 Dec. 93
Robertson, J. Forbes-, 13 Jan. 93
Robertson, *Miss* S., 29 Sept. 91
Robertson, W., 4 June 88
Robins, Cameron and Kemm, *Messrs.*, 20 Nov. 87
Robinson, E. A., 22 June 88
Robinson, *Dr.* F., 13 Apr. 89
Robinson, *Sir* T., 25 Mar. 92
Robinson, *Mr.*, 6 Apr. 89
Robson, *Mr.*, 16 May 87
Roby, H. J., 22 Oct. 90
Rodd, J. Rennell, 12 Dec. 91
Rodriguez, J. C., 11 May 89
Rogers, *Rev.* R. R., 12 Nov. 90
Rolandi, *Sig.*, 26 Jan. 88
Rolfe, E. N., 7 Feb. 89
Rolffs, *Mrs.*, 20 July 88
Rollins, *Miss* K., *also known as 'Mrs. Scarsdale'*, 22 Aug. 89

Romanes, G. J., 4 May 88
Ronel, *Miss* M., 22 July 87
Roose, *Dr.*, 18 Dec. 89
Rootem, *M.*, 18 Feb. 89
Roper, *Rev.* J. C., 7 Feb. 90
Roper and Drowley, *Messrs.*, 8 Jan. 90
Rosina, *Countess of Mirafiore*, 1 Feb. 88
Rosinsky, *Miss*, 7 Dec. 88
Ross, A., 8 May 91
Ross, E., 4 Jan. 87
Ross, H. J., 3 Jan. 88
Ross, *Mrs.* J. A., 3 Jan. 88
Roth family, 4 Apr. 93
Rothschild, *Lady* L., 31 Mar. 88
Rous, A., *Lady Stradbroke*, 9 Dec. 92
Routledge, E., 10 July 87
Rowden, *Rev.* F., 19 Nov. 87
Rowlands, F., 16 Feb. 87
Rowlands, J. E., 16 Feb. 87
Rowlands, W. B., 20 Nov. 89
Rowley, *Rev.* C. C., 6 Oct. 91
Rowley, *Misses*, 3 Sept. 90
Roy, H. E., 22 May 90
Royan, *Baroness*, 24 Oct. 90
Royle, T. R. P., 25 May 90
Rubinstein, *Mr.*, 22 Dec. 87
Rudini, *Marquis*, 19 July 93
Rummals, *Mr.*, 22 May 89
Rumney, P. J., 7 May 89
Russell, F. A. Rollo, 28 Apr. 87
Russell, J. M., 23 Feb. 87
Ruth, H. M. B., 5 Mar. 92
Ryan, *Father*, 3 Aug. 91
Rylands, J. P., 7 Dec. 89
Ryley, *Mrs.*, 21 May 89

Sabuco, *Gen.*, 18 June 87
Sadler, *Rev.* W. E., 15 Feb. 87
Saint Clair, G., 13 June 88
Salazari, *Mons.*, 4 Feb. 89
Salmond, D. S., 1 June 91
Salmonè, *Mrs.*, 21 Nov. 91
Saluse, R., 6 Aug. 89
Salvani, N., 31 Dec. 88
Salvo, R., 15 Jan. 89
Sambourne, E. L., 7 May 89
Sampson, *Rev.* E. F., 3 Feb. 90
Samuelson, G. B., 24 Mar. 92
San Donato, *Duca di*, 13 Sept. 92
Sanders, H., 1 Sept. 87

Sanderson, *Prof. Sir* J. S. Burdon-, 12 Nov. 88
Sanderson, *Dr.* R., 24 Mar. 94
Sandys, *Mrs.*, 27 July 87
Sanfelice, *Cardinal* G., 5 Feb. 89
Sannervanni, *Dr.*, 9 Aug. 89
Sargent, *Gen.* J. N., 12 Mar. 90
Sasse, M., 19 July 92
Sassoon, A. C., *née* Rothschild, 25 Nov. 93
Sassoon, E. A., 25 Nov. 93
Satouroff, M., 20 Feb. 90
Säuger, *Madame*, 2 Aug. 90
Saumarez, A., 8 Feb. 87
Saunders, H., 1 Sept. 87
Savellarides, J., 21 Jan. 90
Sawyer, F. J., 30 Mar. 91
Scalera, *Sig.* F., 1 Feb. 88
Scarlet, H., 19 Nov. 89
Schayer, *Mlle.*, 11 Feb. 92
Schenkhauser, *Mr.*, 6 May 91
Schilizzi, *Baron*, 16 Jan. 89
Schlüter, *Miss* A., 17 Oct. 90
Schofield, *Rev.* J. W., 30 Apr. 89
Schofield, S., 15 Jan. 91
Schreiner, *Miss* Olive E. A., 1 June 89
Schumbacher, *Dr.*, 29 Nov. 87
Schwande, *Mons.*, 8 Nov. 90
Schwann, *Sir* C. E., *1st Baronet*, 19 July 90
Schwann, E., *née* Duncan; *Lady Schwann*, 19 July 90
Scotcher, R. G., 1 Dec. 87
Scott, C. P., 3 Oct. 91
Scott, J. W. R., 28 Aug. 88
Scott, L., 26 Nov. 88
Scott, *Miss*, 26 Apr. 89
Script Phonography Co., 11 Jan. 90
Scrope, S. T., 1 June 87
Scrumola, *Senator*, 31 Jan. 89
Scunn, *Miss* O., 14 Aug. 91
Seaman & Smith, *Messrs.*, 23 Aug. 90
Seath, W., 16 Nov. 89
Seaton, *Miss* R., 28 Sept. 91
Seidenbusch, *Bp.* R., 17 Nov. 88
Seligman, De W. J., 18 Nov. 90
Sembrey, *Mr.*, 17 Nov. 88
Serarty, *Mons.*, 29 Nov. 88
Serristori, *Conte* U., 7 Oct. 87
Seward, F. W., 15 Apr. 91
Seymour, M., 1 May 88
Shakespeare, *Mr.*, 18 July 91
Shalcross, J. H., 5 Apr. 87
Shamling, *Rev. Mr.*, 10 May 90

Stern, S. J., *1st Baron Wandsworth*, 22 Sept. 91

Steuart, J. A., 9 Oct. 90

Stevens, *Miss* A. de Grasse, 8 Dec. 88

Stewart, A., 13 Dec. 87

Stewart, *Rev.* A., 20 Mar. 93

Stewart, A., 19 Aug. 89

Stewart, H., 4 Dec. 91

Stewart & Douglas, *Messrs.*, 8 Jan. 87

Stibbs, E. C. O., 27 Dec. 89

Stock, *Lady* G. G., *née* Douglas, 5 Jan. 92

Stockwell, T. H., 23 Apr. 92

Stoker, Bram, 18 Nov. 90

Stokes, *Rev. Prof.* G. T., 7 Dec. 87

Stokes, *Sir* W., 18 Dec. 88

Stone, F. F., 28 Nov. 90

Stone, F. J., 7 Feb. 91

Stone, *Rev.* H. E., 7 Aug. 89

Stoneham, *Messrs.*, 14 Jan. 87

Storey, A. T., 11 Sept. 90

Stout, E. H., 14 June 90

Stow, A. H., 1 Apr. 91

Strachey, *Sir* E., 18 Aug. 93

Strahan, *Dr.* S. A. K., 15 Apr. 92

Strange, E. F., 30 Sept. 91

Streatfield, *Miss*, 25 Mar. 90

Street, C. J., 20 Sept. 90

Stringfellow, *Mr.*, 27 Nov. 89

Strutt, C. H., 6 Jan. 87

Stubbs, *Dean* C. W., 22 Jan. 94

Stucarini, L., 31 Dec. 88

Stuckey, S. W., 21 Feb. 89

Studart, *Sig.*, 9 June 91

Sturge, E., 7 May 89

Sturrah, T., 24 Feb. 90

Sutton, R. H., 20 Aug. 91

Swamy, *Lady* C., *née* Beeby, 25 Apr. 92

Swan, Sonnenschein, *Messrs.*, 9 May 88

Swann, *Messrs.*, 24 Nov. 87

Swetenham, C. W., 23 Oct. 93

Swift, M. D., 16 June 87

Swinburn, *Mrs.* C. M., 5 July 87

Swinburne, *Lieut. Col.* M., 5 July 87

Sykes, *Mr. & Mrs.* J. T., 4 Dec. 91

Synge, W. W. F., 19 Dec. 89

Syon, C., 20 Dec. 87

Szyrma, *Rev.* W. S. Lach-, 23 Dec. 87

Tait, J., 27 May 90

Tallack, T. A., 8 May 91

Talmage, *Rev.* T. de Witt, 23 Feb. 90

Talookdar of Majeddinpur, 1 Dec. 91

Tangye, A., 8 Dec. 88

Tanner, *Dr.* C. K. D., 21 July 87

Tansley, *Mr.*, 26 Nov. 89

Tarrine, *Rev.* W., 5 May 88

Tasker, *Miss*, 8 Apr. 88

Tattersall, J. F., 23 Sept. 91

Tattersall, W., 15 Aug. 87

Tattersall, *Mr.*, 8 Jan. 87

Taylor, J. P., 10 Apr. 88

Taylor, *Rev.* S. B., 15 Feb. 87

Taylor, W., 20 June 92

Taylor, *Messrs.*, 19 Sept. 87

Tcheharcheff, *Mme.*, 19 Jan. 88

Tchirny, *Mons.*, 30 May 92

Teale, G., 3 Sept. 91

Teape, *Rev. Dr.* C. R., 14 Aug. 88

Tebb, W., 2 May 87

Teller, J., 6 Jan. 90

Tennant, C. C., 6 Jan. 90

Tennant, H. J., 5 Nov. 90

Tennant, H., *née* Duff, 5 Nov. 90

Tensenberg, J. H., 5 Jan. 87

Thackeray, *Rev.* F. St. John, 3 Jan. 90

Thaddeus, H. J., 24 Jan. 88

Thafer, W. R., 25 Sept. 89

Thatcher, T., 23 Feb. 87

Thayer, Eli, 13 Apr. 87

Theodoli, *Marchesa* L., 17 Oct. 92

Theresa, *Empress of Brazil*, 6 Feb. 88

Thiedemann, H., 18 June 90

Thomas, *Rev.* D. R., 17 Nov. 90

Thomas, *Rev.* H. E., 24 Apr. 89

Thomas, *Mrs.* J., 9 Aug. 88

Thomas, *Miss* L. H., 3 Oct. 87

Thomas, N. W., 2 May 87

Thomas, *Mrs.* S. G., 19 Apr. 91

Thomas, *Rev.* U. K., 7 Dec. 87

Thomas, *Rev.* W., 2 Jan. 87

Thompson, F. E., 29 Mar. 90

Thompson, S. E., 8 June 88

Thompson, S., 30 Nov. 88

Thompson, T. J., 3 Apr. 91

Thomson, D. C., 14 Sept. 89

Thomson, *Prof.* W., *1st Baron Kelvin*, 3 June 93

Thorn, J. L., 12 Jan. 87

Thornely, R., 6 Sept. 87

Thornitz, Laura, 26 Sept. 87

Thorpe, G., 8 Jan. 87

Thursfield, *Sir* J. R., 8 Mar. 88

Wakeman, H. O., 1 Nov. 87
Waldstein, *Sir* C., 14 July 91
Walford, E. L., 23 Sept. 90
Wall, G., 12 Aug. 87
Wall, R., 1 Dec. 87
Wall, T. S., 4 Nov. 87
Wallace, *Miss*, 23 Dec. 91
Wallenstein, H. L., 23 Aug. 89
Wallentine, *Mr.*, 16 July 88
Waller, G. E., 18 Nov. 91
Wallis, H. M., 20 Nov. 90
Wallis, *Miss*, 8 Dec. 90
Ward, W. P., 21 Nov. 90
Wardleworth, *Mr.*, 16 Apr. 89
Warmisham, *Mrs.* E., 24 Mar. 88
Warne, F., 11 Aug. 91
Warring, *Principal* C. B., 24 June 88
Wartegg, *Mr.* De, 17 July 88
Wastall, E., 15 June 88
Watkin, H. G. B., 8 Jan. 90
Watson, *Rev.* A. G., 7 Aug. 89
Watson, H. B. M., 13 May 90
Watson, *Dr.* R. Spence, 2 Oct. 91
Watson, W., 28 Oct. 92
Watts, C. A., 14 Aug. 88
Weale, *Rev.* R. M., 23 Dec. 89
Weaver, A. E., 4 Apr. 88
Webb, A. J., 6 May 91
Webb, C. J., 2 Mar. 88
Webb, Sidney, 14 Dec. 87
Webb, T. H., 16 Feb. 87
Weber, F., 4 Nov. 91
Webster, *Rev.* W., 5 Jan. 92
Wedderburn, *Sir* W., *4th Baronet*, 8 June 93
Weigall, H., 27 July 88
Weil, S., 30 Apr. 87
Weir, J. G., 2 Aug. 88
Weldon, *Rev.* G. W., 4 Feb. 87
Welldon, *Rev.* J. E. C., 3 Apr. 87
Wellhausen, *Prof.* J., 23 Jan. 94
Wellman, W. G., 29 May 88
Wells, M., 23 Dec. 89
Wendt, *Dr.*, 27 Jan. 92
Werner, *Miss* H., 1 Dec. 87
Wertheimer, J., 20 June 87
West, A. W., 31 July 90
West, E. M., *née* Trevor, 31 July 90
West, H. W., 3 June 92
Westgarth, W., 28 May 89
Wharlow, J. R., 11 Mar. 87

Wheatley, L. A., 20 Aug. 91
Wheatley, *Messrs.*, 11 Dec. 89
Whipple, *Bp.* H. B., 22 July 88
Whitburn, T., 26 Mar. 90
White, C., 21 Apr. 87
White, F. A., 11 Sept. 91
White, *Rev.* H. V., 24 May 90
White, *Rev.* J. S., 9 May 92
White, *Rev.* J. N., 20 July 91
Whiteway, *Sir* W. V., 26 Apr. 93
Whitfield, E. E., 9 Dec. 89
Whittingham, *Messrs.* W. B., 3 Sept. 87
Whitworth, *Rev.* W. A., 27 Aug. 93
Whyte, R. D., 3 Apr. 91
Wichart, *Messrs.*, 25 Apr. 87
Wicker, H. B., 9 Aug. 90
Wiel, A. J., *née* Lawley, 23 Jan. 88
Wild, *Miss*, 3 Feb. 90
Wildridge, T., 17 Apr. 89
Wilkins, L. H., 15 July 90
Wilkins, W. H., *wrote as* W. H. De Winton, 1 Mar. 91
Wilkinson, E. H., 13 Mar. 90
Wilkinson, H. S., 1 Mar. 94
Willdridge, T. T., 31 May 88
Williams, H. R., 8 Aug. 91
Williams, M. R., 10 May 88
Williams, O. O., 4 Apr. 91
Williams, *Rev.* R., 11 Nov. 92
Williams, S. N., 15 Apr. 89
Williams, *Rev.* T., 1 Apr. 88
Williamson, *Rev.* D. R., 13 Nov. 90
Williamson, J., *1st Baron Ashton*, 16 July 90
Willis, W., 12 Nov. 89
Wills, *Sir* F., *1st Baronet*, 23 Dec. 90
Willyams, *Mrs.* S. Brydges, 17 Mar. 88
Wilson, C. H., 24 May 89
Wilson, *Rev.* H. W., 24 May 90
Wilson, *Rev.* J. M., 10 July 87
Wilson, J. H., 20 July 93
Wilson, T., 22 Oct. 88
Wilson, *Dr.*, 29 Oct. 87
Wimbush, *Miss*, 8 Jan. 88
Winks, A. F., 8 Jan. 90
Winslow, *Mrs.* I., 19 June 90
Winter, A., 23 Feb. 88
Winter, D. L., 21 Oct. 87
Wintle, *Rev.* W. J., 16 Apr. 91
Wise, C., 15 Nov. 90
Witburn, P., 15 Jan. 91
Witham, P., 26 June 90